THE MAUDSLEY

The Maudsley Series

The Maudsley Series

HENRY MAUDSLEY, from whom the series of monographs takes its name, was the founder of The Maudsley Hospital and the most prominent English psychiatrist of his generation. The Maudsley Hospital was united with the Bethlem Royal Hospital in 1948 and its medical school, renamed the Institute of Psychiatry at the same time, became a constituent part of the British Postgraduate Medical Federation. It is now a school of King's College, London, and entrusted with the duty of advancing psychiatry by teaching and research. The South London & Maudsley NHS Trust, together with the Institute of Psychiatry, are jointly known as The Maudsley.

The monograph series reports high quality empirical work on a single topic of relevance to mental health, carried out at the Maudsley. This can be by single or multiple authors. Some of the monographs are directly concerned with clinical problems; others, are in scientific fields of direct or indirect relevance to mental health and that are cultivated for the furtherance of psychiatry.

The Maudsley Series

Schizophrenia

The Final Frontier — A Festschrift for Robin M. Murray

Edited by Anthony S. David, Shitij Kapur and Peter McGuffin

HOVE AND NEW YORK

First published 2011
by Psychology Press
27 Church Road, Hove, East Sussex BN3 2FA

Simultaneously published in the USA and Canada
by Routledge
711 Third Avenue, New York, NY 10017

Psychology Press is an imprint of the Taylor & Francis Group, an Informa Business

British Library Cataloguing in Publication Data
A catalogue record for this book is available from the British Library

Library of Congress Cataloguing-in-Publication Data

Schizophrenia : the final frontier : a festschrift for
Robin M. Murray / edited by Anthony S. David,
Shitij Kapur, and Peter McGuffin.
p. ; cm. -- (Maudsley series)
Includes bibliographical references and index.
ISBN 978-1-84872-077-0 (hbk)
1. Schizophrenia. I. David, Anthony S., editor. II. Kapur, Shitij, editor.
III. McGuffin, Peter, editor. IV. Murray, Robin M., 1944- , honoree.
V. Series: Maudsley series.
[DNLM: 1. Murray, Robin M., 1944- 2. Schizophrenia—Festschrift. WM 203]
RC514.S336445 2011
616.89'8–dc22 2010044157

ISBN: 978-1-84872-077-0 (hbk)
ISBN: 978-0-203-80877-1 (ebk)

Typeset in Times New Roman by RefineCatch Limited, Bungay, Suffolk

Printed and bound in Great Britain by TJ International Ltd, Padstow, Cornwall

Contents

Plates

Colour section between pages 32 and 38

Figures

Tables

Contributors

Judith Allardyce, Department of Psychosis Studies, Institute of Psychiatry, King's College London, London, UK

Matt Allin, Institute of Psychiatry, King's College London, London, UK

Paul Bebbington, Department of Mental Health Sciences, University College London, London, UK

Tejas Bhojraj, Harvard Medical School, Boston, MA, USA

Jane Boydell, Department of Psychosis Studies, Institute of Psychiatry, King's College London, London, UK

Elvira Bramon, Department of Psychosis Studies, Institute of Psychiatry, King's College London, London, UK

Ed Bullmore, Department of Psychiatry, University of Cambridge, Cambridge, UK

Tyrone D. Cannon, Departments of Psychology & Psychiatry & Behavioural Sciences, University of California, Los Angeles, CA, USA

Paola Casadio, Department of Psychosis Studies, Institute of Psychiatry, King's College London, London, UK

David J. Castle, University of Melbourne, Melbourne, Australia

Kodavali V. Chowdari, Department of Psychiatry, University of Pittsburgh School of Medicine, Pittsburgh, PA, USA

Tim J. Crow, SANE Prince of Wales International Centre, Warneford Hospital, Oxford, UK

Anthony S. David, Section of Cognitive Neuropsychiatry, Institute of Psychiatry, King's College London, London, UK

Paola Dazzan, NIH Biomedical Research Centre, Institute of Psychiatry, King's College London, London, UK

Marta Di Forti, Department of Psychosis Studies, Institute of Psychiatry, King's College London, London, UK

Graham Dunn, Community Based Medicine, Manchester University, Manchester, UK

Lauren M. Ellman, Departments of Psychology & Psychiatry & Behavioural Sciences, University of California, Los Angeles, CA, USA

Paul Fearon, St Patrick's University Hospital and Trinity College Dublin, Dublin, Ireland

Daniel Freeman, Department of Psychology, Institute of Psychiatry, King's College London, London, UK

Philippa Garety, Department of Psychosis Studies, Institute of Psychiatry, King's College London, London, UK

Paul J. Harrison, Department of Psychiatry, University of Oxford, Oxford, UK

Jari Haukka, Department of Mental Health and Substance Abuse Services, National Institute for Health and Welfare, Helsinki, Finland

Sheilagh Hodgins, Department of Forensic Mental Health Science, Institute of Psychiatry, King's College London, London, UK

Oliver D. Howes, Department of Psychosis Studies, Institute of Psychiatry, King's College London, London, UK

Gerard Hutchinson, Psychiatry Unit, University of the West Indies, Trinidad

Matti Isohanni, Department of Psychiatry, University of Oulu, Oulu, Finland

Suzanne Jolley, Department of Psychology, Institute of Psychiatry, King's College London, London, UK

Peter B. Jones, Department of Psychological Medicine, University of Cambridge, Cambridge, UK

Shitij Kapur, Department of Psychological Medicine & Psychiatry, Institute of Psychiatry, King's College, London, UK

Katherine H. Karlsgodt, Departments of Psychology & Psychiatry & Behavioural Sciences, University of California, Los Angeles, CA, USA

Matcheri S. Keshavan, Harvard Medical School Department of Psychiatry, Boston, MA, USA

Julia Lappin, Department of Psychosis Studies, Institute of Psychiatry, King's College London, London, UK

Kristin R. Laurens, Department of Forensic Mental Health Science, Institute of Psychiatry, King's College London, London, UK

Shôn Lewis, Department of Adult Psychiatry, University of Manchester, Manchester, UK

A. Javier Lopez, Department of Biological Sciences, Carnegie Mellon University, Pittsburgh, PA, USA

James H. MacCabe, Department of Psychosis Studies, Institute of Psychiatry, King's College London, London, UK

Hader Mansour, Department of Psychiatry, University of Pittsburgh School of Medicine, Pittsburgh, PA, USA

Peter McGuffin, MRC Social, Genetic & Developmental Psychiatry Centre, Institute of Psychiatry, King's College London, London, UK

Philip McGuire, Department of Psychosis Studies, Institute of Psychiatry, King's College London, London, UK

Jouko Miettunen, Department of Psychiatry, University of Oulu, Oulu, Finland

Vijay Mittal, Departments of Psychology & Psychiatry & Behavioural Sciences, University of California, Los Angeles, CA, USA

Valeria Mondelli, Section of Perinatal Psychiatry & Stress, Psychiatry and Immunology, Institute of Psychiatry, King's College London, London, UK

Craig Morgan, NIH Biomedical Research Centre, Institute of Psychiatry, King's College London, London, UK

Kevin Morgan, Department of Psychology, Westminster University, London, UK

Paul D. Morrison, Department of Psychosis Studies, Institute of Psychiatry, King's College London, London, UK

Robin M. Murray, Department of Psychosis Studies, Institute of Psychiatry, King's College London, London, UK

Sridhar Natesan, Department of Psychological Medicine & Psychiatry, Institute of Psychiatry, King's College, London, UK

Emma Nicholson, University of Melbourne, Melbourne, Australia

Vishwajit L. Nimgaonkar, Department of Psychiatry, University of Pittsburg School of Medicine, Pittsburg, PA, USA

Chiara Nosarti, Department of Psychosis Studies, Institute of Psychiatry, King's College London, London, UK

Alessandra Paparelli, Department of Psychosis Studies, Institute of Psychiatry, King's College London, London, UK

Carmine M. Pariante, Section of Perinatal Psychiatry & Stress, Psychiatry and Immunology, Institute of Psychiatry, King's College London, London, UK

David Porteous, Molecular Genetics Section, University of Edinburgh Centre for Molecular Medicine, Western General Hospital, Edinburgh, UK

Konasale M. Prasad, Department of Psychiatry, University of Pittsburgh School of Medicine, Pittsburgh, PA, USA

Trevor W. Robbins, Department of Experimental Psychology and Behavioural and Clinical Neurosciences Institute, University of Cambridge, Cambridge, UK

Kerry Ross, Department of Psychosis Studies, Institute of Psychiatry, King's College London, London, UK

Bart P. F. Rutten, Department of Psychiatry & Neuropsychology, Maastricht University Medical Centre, Maastricht, The Netherlands

Madiha Shaikh, Institute of Psychiatry, King's College London, London, UK

Daqiang Sun, Departments of Psychology & Psychiatry & Behavioural Sciences, University of California, Los Angeles, CA, USA

Jaana Suvisaari, Department of Mental Health and Substance Abuse Services, National Institute for Health and Welfare, Helsinki, Finland

Eric A. Taylor, Department of Child and Adolescent Psychiatry, Institute of Psychiatry, King's College London, London, UK

Jim van Os, Department of Psychiatry & Neuropsychology, Maastricht University Medical Centre, Maastricht, The Netherlands

Ruud van Winkel, Department of Psychiatry & Neuropsychology, Maastricht University Medical Centre, Maastricht, The Netherlands

Helen Waller, Department of Psychosis Studies, Institute of Psychiatry, King's College London, London, UK

Annie M. Watson, Department of Psychiatry, University of Pittsburgh School of Medicine, Pittsburgh, PA, USA

Daniel R. Weinberger, Genes, Cognition and Psychosis Program IRP, Bethesda, MD, USA

Marieke Wichers, Department of Psychiatry & Neuropsychology, Maastricht University Medical Centre, Maastricht, The Netherlands

Joel A. Wood, Department of Psychiatry, University of Pittsburgh School of Medicine, Pittsburgh, PA, USA

Foreword

I am honored and delighted to write this foreword to *Schizophrenia: The Final Frontier* a Festschrift for Robin M. Murray. Professor Murray's contributions to our understanding of schizophrenia and to shaping the research horizon of the last quarter of the twentieth century and well into this one have been seminal and deeply heuristic. He is singularly responsible for spawning and nurturing a new generation of leaders of psychiatry in the UK and for opening avenues of research that have changed the landscape of this discipline. He has been at the leading edge of several very important thematic changes in schizophrenia research over the past thirty years, including a renaissance in understanding of environmental factors in the pathogenesis of schizophrenia, the importance of early brain development, the role of genes as developmental risk factors, and ultimately the critical interactions of genes and environment.

I first met Robin in 1985 when he was particularly interested in viruses and obstetrical complications as environmental causes of schizophrenia. At that time I was early in my career at the National Institutes of Mental Health in Washington, DC, and I was primarily involved in applying neuroimaging strategies and studies of post-mortem schizophrenia brain tissue to understanding the phenomenology and potentially the mechanisms of schizophrenia-related changes in the brain. Robin was already an established investigator and leader at the Institute of Psychiatry. Though from very different backgrounds, it was obvious to me at that time that there would be a close affinity between us, since we were both determined to try to understand that most enigmatic condition, schizophrenia, and help relieve the suffering that patients and their families endure. Robin's commitment to helping solve this puzzle, his deeply felt sensitivity to the suffering of affected individuals and of their families was clear from my first encounter with him. I thought this quality was especially unusual and inspiring and particularly rare among the leading-edge researchers of that time.

I had a hard time endorsing the viral hypothesis in those days, largely because I thought there were too many holes in the data and our own studies of viral-related measures consistently came up negative. Robin soon drifted away from viruses as a centerpiece of his work, a shift which put him at odds with another major force in British Psychiatry at the time, Tim Crow. The Murray–Crow debate became a regular event at international schizophrenia meetings in the 1990s, and while always entertaining, it was educational for the field and fostered a rigorous and critical evaluation of emerging epidemiologic data. I found myself more often than not tending to weigh in on Robin's view of that debate. We had not yet explored the association of illness with obstetrical complications, but I had published several years earlier a study showing an association of early childhood social adjustment to ventricular enlargement during adulthood. This finding prompted me to reconsider Kraepelin's suggestion that early childhood social difficulties often observed in the history of adults with the diagnosis of schizophrenia might be early life manifestations of what he called the same "morbid pathology". This observation, along with Robin's work on obstetrical complications and our failure and the prior failures of many other investigators to find evidence of degeneration of brain tissue at post-mortem examination, led to speculation that the origins of schizophrenia were related to early brain development. Robin's thinking was moving in the same direction. Our paths crossed irrevocably around this idea and what soon emerged was a heuristically meaningful formulation of important pathogenic events related to early brain development, the so-called "neurodevelopmental hypothesis". While there is no formal "neurodevelopmental hypothesis" per se, the neurodevelopmental model, which has preoccupied both of our careers, has joined us at the hip and guided much of what we have subsequently done, including direct collaboration on projects such as the relationship of cognitive development with genetic risk for schizophrenia.

It is no surprise to me that Professor Murray is Britain's most highly cited psychiatry researcher and that he built up and led the one of the largest and most productive research groups in major mental illness in the world. I remember my first visit to the Maudsley Hospital in the 1990s and my first lecture there. Robin, who was dean at that time, was of course a gracious and generous host, but, more importantly, he was eager to engage in an honest and open discussion about emerging research that might be seen differently on opposite sides of the Atlantic. What I remember most vividly in my discussions with staff was how supportive he was of dissenting opinions and views. In fact, there were a number of his colleagues in his own institution who disagreed with his interpretation of data and his research, but this was actively encouraged. Robin created an academic environment that fostered creativity, originality, and individual growth and curiosity.

The impact of Robin's work and his legacy stands on the shoulders of a rich tradition in British psychiatry during the second half of the twentieth century. In the 1960s and 1970s, British psychiatry had a solid reputation for its work derived from the social sciences and for careful diagnosis and descriptive psychopathology. This changed to include neuroscience after his first major publications based on the famous "Maudsley Twin Series" of monozygotic and dizygotic discordant twins with schizophrenia, in which Murray and colleagues showed that the affected co-twin had more apparent cerebral atrophy evident on CT scanning. I had published a paper around the same time showing that patients with schizophrenia had larger ventricles than their unaffected siblings, though the sib ventricles were slightly larger than those of healthy comparison controls. Both studies suggested that there were illness-related effects on brain morphology, but potentially some changes also related to increased genetic risk. At that time, the late 1970s early 1980s, we shared more than just some overlapping research findings: we were both, perhaps, trying to "catch-up" with Tim Crow and his uniquely productive unit at Northwick Park.

Robin's work on the computerized tomography scans of the Maudsley twin series combined with other work led him to suggest that there might be two routes to schizophrenia—one predominantly genetic and the other acquired. This proposal, a new variation on an old theme, stimulated much research world wide although it is only now that we have research tools up to the task: molecular genetics, cell and molecular biology on the one hand and neuroimaging—functional, structural and molecular—on the other. Robin later began to reason that these two routes might be more accurately conceived of in different terms, with the major one leading to schizophrenia, being traceable to the earliest origins of the individual and to neurodevelopment. Again this was a convergent line of thinking that we shared, though with different emphases.

It is perhaps ironic that some of Robin's distinctive contributions to schizophrenia research could be described broadly as belonging to the nurture side of the nature–nurture equation, or at least the non-genetic, environmental domain. He has been a leading voice for establishing the influences of obstetric complications, early infections, social milieu and ethnicity, cannabis use, and so on, in increasing risk for schizophrenia. However, viewing Robin as an "environmentalist" is an overly restrictive view of his work and certainly of his thinking. He has consistently explored the role of genetic risk in sensitivity to environmental factors. Indeed, this work is becoming even more informative recently with his observations of the impact of specific genes on the psychotogenic properties of cannabis and with work from my lab on the impact of obstetrical complications in the context of specific risk-associated genes. This broad range of influences that he and his team have studied over the years attests to Robin's unique bandwidth, his open mindedness, his intellectual reach and his continued energy and determination to challenge accepted dogmas. Indeed, he and I are often asked to share a podium and debate controversial scientific issues, which we may not always see in the same light. I find these encounters immensely rewarding and enjoyable, as Robin is a formidable opponent in such settings, not only for his grasp of the literature, understanding of the issues and foresight, but quick wittedness, eloquence and charm. No matter how much we may occasionally disagree on issues of science, I have never found a mean bone in his body.

All of these qualities were evident during the Festschrift conference held in Robin's honor at the Institute of Psychiatry, November 2009 and are captured in this book. This was a truly wonderful event and was I honored and very moved to be a participant. I also got to see for myself Robin's secret weapon. One of Professor Murray's greatest talents is his ability to spot young researchers, to nurture them, and to bring out their own creativity yet steer them in the most fruitful direction. He is clearly a gifted teacher who inspires admiration and loyalty. Many of his former students contributed to the conference and have set down succinct and up-to-date accounts of their work in this volume. As a result, Tony David and the other editors have produced a particularly readable yet authoritative account of the state of the art of our field.

In closing, I wish to offer my deep-felt congratulations and gratitude to Robin Murray for being such an important factor in the enlightened renaissance in schizophrenia research that has emerged over the past thirty years. We have learned more about schizophrenia during this period than in all of past history. We have the first objective clues to etiology (i.e., genes), and the first objective clues to pathogenic mechanisms. We are on the threshold of dramatic new approaches to therapeutic advancement, based on this enlightened understanding. We would not be here without the work of Professor Murray and we would not be heading towards an optimistic future of important breakthroughs in schizophrenia research were it not for his influence on the next generation of scientists and clinicians. I feel privileged and honored to be his colleague and to be part of this celebration of his career.

Daniel R. Weinberger
IRP, NIMH, NIH, Bethesda, MD, USA

Preface

After 35 years at the Maudsley-Institute of Psychiatry, around 25 of which were spent combining clinical work and research with a leading administrative role of one form or another, Professor Robin Murray decided to step down as head of the Department of Psychiatry. During his 35 years there have been huge advances (and some retreats) in the understanding of schizophrenia and its treatment. Robin Murray is arguably the most productive and influential British psychiatrist of his generation. His work has mostly concerned schizophrenia and has touched on almost all aspects of this perplexing condition. For example: genetics—from early twin studies to later family and molecular studies; neuropathology from CT to MRI and chemical imaging; epidemiology, which showed different incidence rates in different ethnic groups, changes in incidence over time, to the relationship to prenatal insults, developmental deviance and cannabis. He has also overseen some landmark work in therapeutics such as large UK trials of typical and atypical antipsychotic drugs. In 2010 he was made a fellow of the Royal Society and in 2011, a Knights Bachelor for services to medicine in the new year's honours list.

To honour his contribution the then Dean of the Institute, Peter McGuffin, his appointed successor, Shitij Kapur and myself decided to hold an international conference that would reflect this body of work in a densely packed two-day programme to take place, fittingly, at the Institute of Psychiatry, London. It was only possible to invite a fraction of the friends and colleagues who had a connection with Robin Murray to speak at the meeting and I am grateful to those not able to be given such a platform, for their gracious acceptance of the situation. Some of the most eminent and productive researchers in the field agreed to give lectures and present their latest findings, many of whom had collaborated, sparred and disagreed with Professor Murray. A large number of the speakers trained under his stewardship as clinicians or researchers and so were encouraged to put their work within a personal perspective. This festschrift represents a distilled collection of the papers given.

Robin's natural modesty may have made him somewhat reluctant to discuss the meeting plan in the earlier stages. However, after going through phases of denial and ambivalence, he finally achieved acceptance. During preliminary planning meetings Robin made it clear that he wanted the conference to be forward looking and when brainstorming for a suitable title, someone mentioned the phrase "the

Next Generation". From this innocent remark, a whole train of Star Trek associations was triggered including the famous phrase: the Final Frontier. None of the editors nor Robin himself is a particularly avid follower of the 1970s science fiction TV series or its subsequent reincarnations, movies and spin offs, but somehow the label stuck. In fact, the choice of theme turned out to be fortuitous, stimulating organizers, presenters and attendees alike to creative flights of fancy—in their dress, orations and scientific vision. Any danger that this festschrift conference would be a solemn or pompous occasion was emphatically dispelled.

The event took place on the 5th and 6th of November 2009. There were many, many highlights and I will only mention two which stand out in my mind: first, the moving tribute by Graham Murray for his father and, second, since it conveys the flavour of the entire enterprise (sic), Tim Crow's panoramic critique of schizophrenia research delivered with characteristic and indeed flagrant disregard to cosmic literary convention, in a Darth Vader costume.

Much about the meeting was truly unforgettable. The atmosphere was intense and productive yet joyous and relaxed; respectful of the past but ambitious for the future; intellectually demanding yet unashamedly emotional. By some magical alchemy a festschrift was produced which perfectly reflected the person who inspired it. Thank you Robin, this is for you.

Tony David
January 2011

Acknowledgements

The conference organizers are grateful to Janssen Cilag, Eli Lilly, Lundbeck and Schering Plough and King's College London for financial support and to Averil Baxter and Caroline Zanelli for their practical assistance.

The editors are especially grateful to Sandra Randell for her considerable secretarial support.

Part I

Development

1 The neurodevelopmental hypothesis of schizophrenia

Katherine H. Karlsgodt, Lauren M. Ellman, Daqiang Sun, Vijay Mittal and Tyrone D. Cannon

Schizophrenia has an insidious onset, with full manifestation of the disorder occurring in late adolescence and early adulthood. Onset is complex and includes cognitive and social changes in early childhood as well as a more proximal prodromal phase in which functioning undergoes a pronounced deterioration and subpsychotic symptoms emerge. Based on this trend of slow change, it was initially thought that schizophrenia might be degenerative, similar to other gradually emerging disorders such as Alzheimer's disease. However, with an increased understanding of the associated neural changes, a neurodegenerative process appeared less likely. For instance, despite early findings (Weinberger, Wagner, & Wyatt, 1983), it became evident that any gliosis present in schizophrenia could not explain the degree of neuroanatomical changes observed (Harrison, 1999). Further, findings that ventricular enlargement (originally presumed to be evidence of neural degeneration) positively correlated with a history of obstetric complications (OCs; Reveley, Reveley, & Murray, 1984) supported the importance of environmental influences on early development. Simultaneously, a deeper understanding of later neurodevelopmental processes began to emerge, notably that normal development includes a natural pruning process that can in itself cause a decrease in cortical thickness or brain volume (Huttenlocher, 1979) and that in areas critical for schizophrenia, such as the prefrontal cortex, these processes reach completion around the age of disease onset (Huttenlocher, 1990; Pfefferbaum et al., 1994). The confluence of these findings, with work by Robin Murray at the forefront, lead to the emergence of the widely influential neurodevelopmental hypothesis of schizophrenia, in which a subtle, static brain lesion (caused by a combination of genetic and environmental factors) later interacts with normal maturational processes in the brain to result in schizophrenia (Murray & Lewis, 1987).

Ongoing work unraveling the neurodevelopmental hypothesis indicates that there are three key periods across the lifespan that may influence risk for and development of schizophrenia: (1) conception; (2) early developmental; and (3) later developmental periods (see Figure 1.1). First, at conception, the genetic make-up is determined, and genetic liability for the disorder, in the form of risk genes, is conferred. While genetic liability is instantiated at conception, the degree of risk is not fixed; rather, there can be interactive effects leading to changes in

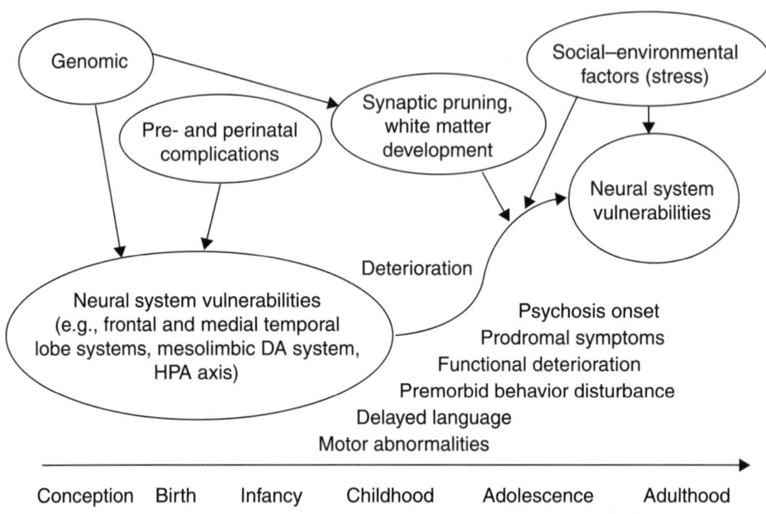

Figure 1.1 Developmental model of schizophrenia.

risk across the lifespan even against the same genetic background. For instance, predisposing genotypes may interact with both normal and disrupted developmental processes and environmental events that occur during specific phases of development. Two primary periods are likely to have significant influence. The "early" period includes pre- and perinatal brain development and may be impacted by factors such as OCs (Lewis, Owen, & Murray, 1989) and prenatal maternal infection (Buka, Cannon, Torrey, & Yolken, 2008). Further, these factors may interact with genetic liability for the disorder to result in neuroanatomical changes seen in the disorder (T. Cannon, van Erp et al., 2002; van Erp et al., 2002). These pre- and perinatal disturbances may interfere with some fundamental process during the development of neural circuitry, thereby leaving the organism more vulnerable to potential insults later in development. The presence of a very early developmental change is consistent with the view that the neural changes associated with the development of schizophrenia are partly present from birth and may therefore explain early neurocognitive and social deficits in many of the children who later develop schizophrenia (Bearden et al., 2000; Cannon, Huttunen et al., 2002; T. Cannon et al., 2000; Jones, Rodgers, Murray, & Marmot, 1994; Rosso et al., 2000; St Clair et al., 1990).

However, despite these early influences, and the presence of observable differences in childhood, formal diagnostic symptoms and signs of schizophrenia still do not fully emerge until late adolescence or early adulthood. Thus, risk factors occurring during this "later" developmental period may also play an important role in disease onset. Late adolescence and early adulthood represents a period of continuing developmental brain change and refinement, as well as a period of substantial neuroendocrine influence. Importantly, a normal pruning process takes place (Feinberg, 1982; McGlashan & Hoffman, 2000) reducing extraneous excitatory synapses and honing more mature circuitry. Findings of progressive anatomical deterioration in schizophrenia (Gur et al., 1998; Thompson et al., 2001) suggest that additional factors active during the late developmental period and more proximal to the onset of schizophrenia, in addition to early acting genetic and perinatal risk factors, may play a role in the etiology and pathophysiology of schizophrenia. Here we discuss the relationship of recent findings in these early and late periods, including those from our own research group, as related to the neurodevelopmental model and to Dr Murray's work.

Early developmental changes

Support for the involvement of early stage developmental factors comes from repeated associations between OCs and risk for schizophrenia (Cannon, Jones, & Murray, 2002) and findings that schizophrenia patients are more likely to have OCs than other psychiatric patients (Lewis & Murray, 1987). OCs encompass any aberration in normal development occurring in the prenatal, perinatal, and early neonatal periods (McNeil, 1988). A number of OCs have been found in the histories of patients with schizophrenia, including low birth weight, exposure to maternal infections during pregnancy, fetal hypoxia (lack of oxygen to the fetus), malnutrition during pregnancy, and maternal diabetes during pregnancy (Brown, 2006; Cannon, Jones et al., 2002; T. Cannon, 1997; Dalman et al., 2001; Ichiki et al., 2000; Susser, St Clair, & He, 2008). One type of OC, fetal hypoxia, has been found in 20–30% of patients with schizophrenia, a rate substantially higher than that in the general population, 5–10% (Buka, Tsuang, & Lipsitt, 1993).

These studies support the notion that exposure to certain environmental conditions could alter the course of early development resulting in schizophrenia. Nevertheless, the question remains whether OCs cause schizophrenia on their own (phenocopy model), depend on genetic influences (interaction model), aggregate with genetic influences (additive influences), are correlated with genetic influences (gene–environment covariation), and/or change the function and structure of genes (epigenetic influences). Our research group, and others, have addressed these questions in order to determine the relative contributions of genetic and obstetric factors to the neurodevelopmental course of schizophrenia (Mittal, Ellman, & Cannon, 2008).

Determining the correct model is critical for understanding whether OCs contribute to the developmental course of schizophrenia and has implications for primary prevention and early intervention strategies. If the gene–environment covariation model is correct, OCs may be correlated with the genes for schizophrenia and obstetric events would be confounded with genetic factors. Studies finding an increased prevalence of OCs in the pregnancies and deliveries of mothers diagnosed with schizophrenia support this model (Bennedsen, 1998). Although mothers with schizophrenia clearly carry risk-genes, they also show increased health-risk behaviors during pregnancy that are themselves associated with OCs (Delpisheh, Kelly, Rizwan, & Brabin, 2006; Raatikainen, Huurinainen, & Heinonen, 2007; Smith et al., 2006), such as lack of prenatal care, polydrug use, alcohol consumption, use of psychiatric medications, and smoking (Bennedsen, 1998). Moreover, discontinuation of antipsychotic medication during pregnancy has been associated with worsened symptoms, which impact prenatal health via factors such as increased stress, poor nutrition, poor self-care, suicide attempts, attempts at premature delivery, and other deleterious behaviors (McNeil, Kaij, & Malmquist-Larsson, 1984; Miller, 1997).

To test whether increases in OCs are associated with risk-genes and/or increased health-risk behaviors, our group has conducted population-based studies in Finland. First, we found that mothers with a genetic liability for schizophrenia (a first-degree relative with schizophrenia) exhibit no increased risk of OCs compared to control mothers (Ellman, Huttunen, Lonnqvist, & Cannon, 2007). This finding substantially weakens the gene–environment covariation model, which would predict increased OCs among women with genetic risk. Second, we found that smoking mediated the relationship between maternal schizophrenia status and decreased birth weight, suggesting that health-risk behaviors may, in part, account for the increased prevalence of OCs in offspring of mothers with schizophrenia (Ellman et al., 2007). Although we observed a higher rate of OCs in the pregnancies and deliveries of mothers diagnosed with schizophrenia, we only examined one health-risk behavior in this study, therefore a number of other experiential factors associated with schizophrenia could potentially account for this observed result.

OCs may also result in a more severe form of schizophrenia characterized by an earlier age of onset, more severe premorbid difficulties, and more pronounced alterations in brain structure. Associations have been found with OCs and earlier onset (Verdoux et al., 1997). Accordingly, we have found that hypoxia-associated OCs were significantly related to increased risk of schizophrenia, which appeared to be restricted to cases with an earlier age of onset (T. Cannon, van Erp et al., 2002; Rosso et al., 2000). In addition, a prospective study following high-risk (i.e., prodromal) adolescents found that a history of OCs (including hypoxia-associated events) significantly increased the odds of conversion to an Axis-I psychotic disorder in a two-year period and was strongly associated with both positive and negative symptomatology (Mittal et al., 2009). This is consistent with the idea that early insults may interact with processes that occur throughout development to influence timing of disease onset. Further, our data indicate that increases in hypoxia-associated OCs were not observed in the histories of unaffected siblings of schizophrenia cases, diminishing the possibility of gene–environment covariation with respect to this class of OCs.

Exposure to OCs also results in childhood motor and cognitive problems that appear to be restricted to children who later develop schizophrenia. Specifically, hypoxia-associated OCs predicted unusual movements at age 4, but not age 7, among children who developed schizophrenia but not in unaffected siblings or controls (Rosso et al., 2000). Similarly, we have found that serologically documented maternal influenza infection during pregnancy was related to decreases in verbal IQ scores among 7-year-old offspring who developed schizophrenia in adulthood (Ellman, Yolken, Buka, Torrey, & Cannon, 2009) and not among control children with similar exposure. These findings suggest that a genetic and/or environmental factor associated with schizophrenia likely rendered the fetal brain vulnerable to the effects of fetal hypoxia and infection, resulting in childhood difficulties occurring far before the onset of psychotic symptoms.

In addition, it has been found that a history of hypoxia-associated OCs is associated with more pronounced brain abnormalities in patients. While seminal work by Robin Murray's group first indicated that in patients with schizophrenia, OCs such as intraventricular hemorrhage were correlated with ventricular enlargement in adulthood (Murray, Lewis, & Reveley, 1985; Reveley et al., 1984), our group has extended this to find that hypoxia-associated OCs predicted ventricular enlargement in patients, but not their unaffected siblings or controls (T. Cannon, van Erp et al., 2002). Similarly, hippocampal volume decreases with genetic liability for schizophrenia, with the smallest volumes among patients, followed by their unaffected siblings, and then control participants. Among the cases with schizophrenia, a history of hypoxia-associated OCs was associated with further reductions in hippocampal volumes, suggesting that genetic contributions to hippocampal volume reductions in patients were worsened by a history of fetal hypoxia (van Erp et al., 2002). These data suggest that brain anomalies commonly found among patients with schizophrenia (Wright et al., 2000) may have some neurodevelopmental origins. Moreover, our findings further support the possibility that there is some existing vulnerability for schizophrenia that renders the fetus susceptible to the damaging influences of OCs, such as fetal hypoxia and maternal infection.

Further support for this possibility comes from recent work examining brain derived neurotrophic factor (BDNF) levels in umbilical cord sera from those who developed schizophrenia in adulthood compared to non-psychiatric controls (T. Cannon, Yolken, Buka, & Torrey, 2008). BDNF in cord sera is entirely from fetal origins and plays a critical role in neuronal development, as well as the survival of neurons under stressful conditions (T. Cannon et al., 2008; Lee et al., 2004; Meng et al., 2005). Among control sera, hypoxia-associated OCs were associated with an increase in BDNF levels; this was expected given that fetal hypoxia should evoke a neuroprotective BDNF response by the fetus. In contrast, among cases, hypoxia was associated with decreased BDNF that was not explained by other OCs or by the BDNF Val66Met polymorphism. These findings suggest that there is disrupted neurotrophic signaling in response to hypoxia-associated pre- and perinatal complications among those who ultimately develop schizophrenia.

Cumulatively, the evidence on pre- and perinatal complications supports the neurodevelopmental hypothesis and suggests that these factors may lead to a more severe form of schizophrenia. Further, there is preliminary evidence for the possibility that genetic susceptibility to schizophrenia renders the fetus vulnerable to the influences of specific OCs. However, it remains unclear whether obstetric events lead to a cascade of neurodevelopmental sequelae culminating in risk for schizophrenia or whether OCs create a brain "lesion", the effects of which emerge during adolescence when they are unveiled by normal developmental processes. Therefore, a complementary body of work explores the changes that occur in the later developmental period, more proximal to onset, to help understand how the changes and symptoms observed in adult patients with schizophrenia ultimately emerge.

Later developmental changes

Investigations of later stage (adolescence to early adulthood) developmental changes can inform our understanding of how the observed early changes ultimately affect neuroanatomy, cognition, and symptomatology. In particular, understanding the trajectory of change over time will help differentiate whether early insults or genetic risk factors lead to a static deficit that ultimately causes schizophrenia, whether the deficit interacts with a normal pattern of change during adolescence, or if it is a combination of the two in which an initial insult is compounded by disrupted development. For example, a recent 30-year follow-up investigation of cognitive factors indicates that while verbal and visual learning and reasoning show a chronic deficit from early childhood, more complex factors relying on later developing brain regions such as the frontal lobe (processing speed, attention, working memory, problem solving) show an additional lag that becomes apparent later, indicating a different late trajectory (Reichenberg et al., 2010). This indicates that deficits based on both early and later developmental factors are relevant for schizophrenia. Exploring the neural basis of cognitive deficits and symptoms in patients is most powerfully accomplished using imaging techniques, such as structural MRI, functional MRI, and diffusion tensor imaging (DTI). Our group, and others, have worked to explore the neural basis of the developmental hypothesis of schizophrenia by examining trajectories of change across development in both grey and white matter.

Grey matter

Generally, two types of neurodevelopmental events affect postnatal brain volume changes: progressive phenomena, such as cell proliferation, dendritic arborization, and myelination; and regressive phenomena, such as apoptosis, synaptic pruning, and atrophic processes (Pfefferbaum et al., 1994). Synaptogenesis begins mid-gestation (Monk, Webb, & Nelson, 2001) with synaptic density peaking in visual cortex at 3 months of age, and a delayed peak in frontal cortex around 3.5 years (Huttenlocher & Dabholkar, 1997). Initially, synapses are over produced (Webb, Monk, & Nelson, 2001), and structural refinement continues until adulthood (Blows, 2003; Giedd et al., 1996; Huttenlocher, 1979). Namely, a normal reduction of grey matter (GM) volume, largely attributed to synaptic pruning (Thompson et al., 2000), results in the elimination of about 40% of cortical synapses (Huttenlocher, 1979) and is thought to increase the overall efficiency of the brain (Feinberg, 1982). In humans, different cortical regions undergo pruning at different rates with the prefrontal cortex maturing last (Pfefferbaum et al., 1994), reaching an adult level of synaptic density by age 16 (Huttenlocher, 1990).

The pruning hypothesis of schizophrenia proposes that pruning is disrupted in patients, leaving them below a "psychotic threshold" (Hoffman & McGlashan,

1997). This may occur in a variety of ways, for example, genetic anomalies or pre- or perinatal insult could result in a paucity of synapses so that even a normal pruning process would result in low numbers of functional synapses. Alternatively, synaptogenesis may be intact, but pruning is either prolonged or excessive, again resulting in too few functional synapses. Finally, it is possible that there is a combination of early and late factors at play, such as an early deficit and a disrupted pruning trajectory. By using imaging techniques to assess cortical thickness across this critical age range and across disease stages, we can begin to elucidate this issue.

Volumetric deficits have been observed in the prodromal and early stages of schizophrenia (Pantelis et al., 2005; Shenton, Dickey, Frumin, & McCarley, 2001), suggesting that abnormalities may exist before illness onset. Findings of abnormal brain asymmetry and cortical folding, signs of relatively early developmental deviations, in patients (Nakamura, Nestor et al., 2007; Yucel et al., 2001) further support the early neurodevelopmental model of schizophrenia (Murray & Lewis, 1987, 1988; Weinberger, 1987). Such findings do not exclude the possibility of further changes occurring more proximally to onset. Indeed, accumulating evidence from longitudinal neuroimaging studies have shown excessive progressive brain volume loss beginning around the onset of psychosis and across at least the early stages of the disease. These findings of progression support the late developmental hypothesis of schizophrenia, which posits the involvement of later neurodevelopmental events including synaptic pruning or axonal myelination during adolescence and early adulthood.

Recent studies have demonstrated progressive volume loss in various brain regions such as accelerated ventricular expansion (DeLisi, Sakuma, Maurizio, Relja, & Hoff, 2004) and progressive frontal volume loss (Gur et al., 1998) initially reported in first-episode/chronic patients and subsequently replicated (Ho et al., 2003; Koo et al., 2008; Mathalon, Sullivan, Lim, & Pfefferbaum, 2001; Nakamura, Salisbury et al., 2007; Rapoport et al., 1999; Sun, Stuart, Jenkinson et al., 2009). Excessive temporal lobe volume loss has been reported (Nakamura, Salisbury et al., 2007; Rapoport et al., 1999) and seems mainly attributable to changes in the superior temporal gyrus (Kasai et al., 2003; Mané et al., 2009; Takahashi et al., 2009; Thompson et al., 2001).

Progressive brain volume loss around psychosis onset has also been reported. Initially, progressive GM loss was detected in individuals at high-risk (UHR) for psychosis at intake who then had a psychotic onset during follow-up, but the changes were non-significant (Job, Whalley, Johnstone, & Lawrie, 2005; Pantelis et al., 2003). However, with technical advances, two recent longitudinal MRI studies convincingly showed that UHR individuals who later converted did experience significantly greater regional volume loss in areas including the prefrontal regions and the superior temporal gyrus than UHR individuals who did not become psychotic (Sun, Stuart, Phillips et al., 2009; Takahashi et al., 2009).

The profile of progressive brain volume loss in schizophrenia was examined in a recent longitudinal study using cortical pattern matching methods (Thompson et al., 2004) in combination with Structural Image Evaluation using Normalization of Atrophy (SIENA; S. Smith et al., 2002) in first-episode schizophrenia patients and controls, by mapping local brain surface contractions away from the skull throughout the lateral cortical surface (Sun, Stuart, Jenkinson et al., 2009). Both patients and controls demonstrated similar anatomical patterns of surface contractions, showing prominent prefrontal contraction, but with that of patients exaggerated in magnitude. Interestingly, this pattern was prominent in UHR individuals with later psychotic onset (Sun, Stuart, Phillips et al., 2009). The high anatomical correlation between differential rates of surface contraction in homologous brain regions between healthy individuals, UHR individuals who became psychotic, and schizophrenia patients is in line with the hypothesis of synaptic over pruning in schizophrenia (Feinberg, 1982; McGlashan & Hoffman, 2000; Woods, 1998), and the pattern of greater prefrontal involvement is also in line with pathological findings of reduced neuronal connectivity (Glantz & Lewis, 2000; Selemon, Rajkowska, & Goldman-Rakic, 1995, 1998). Taken together, these findings indicate the involvement of late developmental deviations in the neuropathophysiology of schizophrenia.

White matter

In addition to GM, white matter (WM) microstructure continues to mature later in life as well. Basic axonal connections are laid down early in the prenatal period (Krasnegor, Lyon, & Goldman-Rakic, 1997); once connections have formed, the axons begin to myelinate. While myelination begins around ten weeks, and much of the brain is myelinated by a year after birth (Paus et al., 2001), the hippocampus and frontal lobes undergo the majority of their myelination during adolescence up into early adulthood (Arnold & Rioux, 2001). In fact, normally during early adolescence, GM volume decreases due to synaptic pruning, but WM volume undergoes a simultaneous increase due to myelination (Paus et al., 2001).

WM microstructure was difficult to measure in vivo until the advent of DTI, a powerful MRI-based tool. Fractional anisotropy (FA), the primary DTI measure, serves as an index of neuronal integrity, potentially reflecting both myelination and organization of the tracts. DTI studies in schizophrenia have shown decreased FA in many major tracts (Kyriakopoulos, Vyas, Barker, Chitnis, & Frangou, 2008). These tracts represent long fibers facilitating inter-regional communication, and their disruption could potentially impact a wide range of cognitive abilities. DTI changes have been observed in tracts associated with both working memory (Karlsgodt et al., 2008) and long-term memory (Karlsgodt, Niendam, Bearden, & Cannon, 2009), and FA changes have been correlated with cognitive changes and symptoms (Karlsgodt et al., 2008; Szeszko et al., 2008) indicating that structural connectivity deficits have behavioral implications.

A number of DTI studies have examined developmental changes in WM. Studies in older samples suggest that changes in diffusion (Paus et al., 1999; Schmithorst, Wilke, Dardzinski, & Holland, 2002) and FA (Klingberg, Vaidya, Gabrieli, Moseley, & Hedehus, 1999; Mukherjee et al., 2002; Schmithorst et al., 2002) are likely to persist into late adolescence or early adulthood (Ashtari et al., 2007; Giorgio et al., 2008, 2010; Snook, Paulson, Roy, Phillips, & Beaulieu, 2005). That this aspect of neural structure is still ongoing so proximal to disease onset makes differences in the pattern of WM maturation of particular interest for understanding the emergence of schizophrenia.

One way to assess the trajectory of WM development in schizophrenia is to look at changes across age. While few longitudinal studies exist, deficits have been found even in adolescence (Schneiderman et al., 2009). Interestingly, the pattern of changes appears to be linked to the overall pattern of WM development, in which more posterior regions develop first, with the regions such as the frontal and temporal lobes reaching maturity later. Specifically, when comparing adolescent-onset subjects, primarily parietal deficits were found, while in those with adult onsets additional frontal temporal deficits were observed (Kyriakopoulos et al., 2008). This is consistent with the idea that there may be a different trajectory of WM development in patients with schizophrenia, such that regions that should come online later in development fail to reach the same level of maturity as those in controls.

Another approach to assessing developmental trajectories is to look across disease states, at patients at high-risk for developing schizophrenia and at chronic patients. WM changes have been shown to be present even in the first episode (Begre et al., 2003; Federspiel et al., 2006; Hao et al., 2006; Price, Bagary, Cercignani, Altmann, & Ron, 2005; Szeszko et al., 2005), suggesting that they occur during development and are not secondary to the disease or its treatment. Recently, our group has begun to assess changes in DTI measures prior to the onset of schizophrenia, in an UHR population. In a cross-sectional investigation, temporal lobe tracts have shown a pattern across adolescence and young adulthood in which controls increase FA with age, while high-risk subjects fail to show the same increase. This pattern may indicate that the differences in some WM tracts observed in adult patients arise gradually via an abnormal developmental process in adolescence (Karlsgodt et al., 2009). Furthermore, FA in these regions was predictive of later functional outcome. In support of these findings, other groups have noted changes in clinically defined high-risk subjects (Jacobson et al., 2010) as well as those at genetic high-risk for the disorder (Hao et al., 2009; Hoptman et al., 2008; Munoz Maniega et al., 2008).

Conclusions

The neurodevelopmental hypothesis continues to play a key role in our understanding of schizophrenia. With the inclusion of both early and late developmental periods, the framework it provides can accommodate a substantial range of evidence, including epidemiological findings of early pre- and perinatal risk factors, early childhood and premorbid findings, work in the prodrome and early onset patients, and cognitive and imaging studies in adolescent and adult patients. As research progresses and new discoveries are made, Robin Murray's work will undoubtedly continue to provide substantial contributions to revising and conceptualizing this model.

References

Arnold, S. E., & Rioux, L. (2001). Challenges, status, and opportunities for studying developmental neuropathology in adult schizophrenia. *Schizophrenia Bulletin*, *27*(3), 395–416.

Ashtari, M., Cervellione, K. L., Hasan, K. M., Wu, J., McIlree, C., Kester, H., et al. (2007). White matter development during late adolescence in healthy males: A cross-sectional diffusion tensor imaging study. *NeuroImage*, *35*(2), 501–510.

Bearden, C. E., Rosso, I. M., Hollister, J. M., Sanchez, L. E., Hadley, T., & Cannon, T. D. (2000). A prospective cohort study of childhood behavioral deviance and language abnormalities as predictors of adult schizophrenia. *Schizophrenia Bulletin*, *26*(2), 395–410.

Begre, S., Federspiel, A., Kiefer, C., Schroth, G., Dierks, T., & Strik, W. K. (2003). Reduced hippocampal anisotropy related to anteriorization of alpha EEG in schizophrenia. *NeuroReport*, *14*(5), 739–742.

Bennedsen, B. E. (1998). Adverse pregnancy outcome in schizophrenic women: Occurrence and risk factors. *Schizophrenia Research*, *33*(1–2), 1–26.

Blows, W. T. (2003). Child brain development. *Nursing Times*, *99*(17), 28–31.

Brown, A. S. (2006). Prenatal infection as a risk factor for schizophrenia. *Schizophrenia Bulletin*, *32*(2), 200–202.

Buka, S. L., Cannon, T. D., Torrey, E. F., & Yolken, R. H. (2008). Maternal exposure to herpes simplex virus and risk of psychosis among adult offspring. *Biological Psychiatry*, *63*(8), 809–815.

Buka, S. L., Tsuang, M. T., & Lipsitt, L. P. (1993). Pregnancy/delivery complications and psychiatric diagnosis. A prospective study. *Archives of General Psychiatry*, *50*(2), 151–156.

Cannon, M., Huttunen, M. O., Tanskanen, A. J., Arseneault, L., Jones, P. B., & Murray, R. M. (2002). Perinatal and childhood risk factors for later criminality and violence in schizophrenia. Longitudinal, population-based study. *British Journal of Psychiatry*, *180*, 496–501.

Cannon, M., Jones, P. B., & Murray, R. M. (2002). Obstetric complications and schizophrenia: Historical and meta-analytic review. *American Journal of Psychiatry*, *159*(7), 1080–1092.

Cannon, T. (1997). On the nature and mechanisms of obstetric influences in schizophrenia: A review and synthesis of epidemiologic studies. *International Review of Psychiatry*, *9*, 387–397.

Cannon, T. D., Rosso, I. M., Hollister, J. M., Bearden, C. E., Sanchez, L. E., & Hadley, T. (2000). A prospective cohort study of genetic and perinatal influences in the etiology of schizophrenia. *Schizophrenia Bulletin*, *26*(2), 351–366.

Cannon, T. D., van Erp, T. G., Rosso, I. M., Huttunen, M., Lonnqvist, J., Pirkola, T., et al. (2002). Fetal hypoxia and structural brain abnormalities in schizophrenic patients, their siblings, and controls. *Archives of General Psychiatry*, *59*(1), 35–41.

Cannon, T. D., Yolken, R., Buka, S., & Torrey, E. F. (2008). Decreased neurotrophic response to birth hypoxia in the etiology of schizophrenia. *Biological Psychiatry*, *64*(9), 797–802.

Dalman, C., Thomas, H. V., David, A. S., Gentz, J., Lewis, G., & Allebeck, P. (2001). Signs of asphyxia at birth and risk of schizophrenia. Population-based case-control study. *British Journal of Psychiatry*, *179*, 403–408.

DeLisi, L. E., Sakuma, M., Maurizio, A. M., Relja, M., & Hoff, A. L. (2004). Cerebral ventricular change over the first 10 years after the onset of schizophrenia. *Psychiatry Research*, *130*(1), 57–70.

Delpisheh, A., Kelly, Y., Rizwan, S., & Brabin, B. J. (2006). Socio-economic status, smoking during pregnancy and birth outcomes: An analysis of cross-sectional community studies in Liverpool (1993–2001). *Journal of Child Health Care*, *10*(2), 140–148.

Ellman, L. M., Huttunen, M., Lonnqvist, J., & Cannon, T. D. (2007). The effects of genetic liability for schizophrenia and maternal smoking during pregnancy on obstetric complications. *Schizophrenia Research*, *93*(1–3), 229–236.

Ellman, L. M., Yolken, R. H., Buka, S. L., Torrey, E. F., & Cannon, T. D. (2009). Cognitive functioning prior to the onset of psychosis: The role of fetal exposure to serologically determined influenza infection. *Biological Psychiatry*, *65*(12), 1040–1047.

Federspiel, A., Begre, S., Kiefer, C., Schroth, G., Strik, W. K., & Dierks, T. (2006). Alterations of white matter connectivity in first episode schizophrenia. *Neurobiology of Disease*, *22*(3), 702–709.

Feinberg, I. (1982). Schizophrenia: Caused by a fault in programmed synaptic elimination during adolescence? *Journal of Psychiatric Research*, *17*(4), 319–334.

Giedd, J. N., Snell, J. W., Lange, N., Rajapakse, J. C., Casey, B. J., Kozuch, P. L., et al. (1996). Quantitative magnetic resonance imaging of human brain development: Ages 4–18. *Cerebral Cortex*, *6*(4), 551–560.

Giorgio, A., Watkins, K. E., Chadwick, M., James, S., Winmill, L., Douaud, G., et al. (2010). Longitudinal changes in grey and white matter during adolescence. *NeuroImage*, *49*(1), 94–103.

Giorgio, A., Watkins, K. E., Douaud, G., James, A. C., James, S., De Stefano, N., et al. (2008). Changes in white matter microstructure during adolescence. *NeuroImage*, *39*(1), 52–61.

Glantz, L. A., & Lewis, D. A. (2000). Decreased dendritic spine density on prefrontal cortical pyramidal neurons in schizophrenia. *Archives of General Psychiatry*, *57*(1), 65–73.

Gur, R. E., Cowell, P., Turetsky, B. I., Gallacher, F., Cannon, T., Bilker, W., et al. (1998). A follow-up magnetic resonance imaging study of schizophrenia. Relationship of neuroanatomical changes to clinical and neurobehavioral measures. *Archives of General Psychiatry*, *55*(2), 145–152.

Hao, Y., Liu, Z., Jiang, T., Gong, G., Liu, H., Tan, L., et al. (2006). White matter integrity of the whole brain is disrupted in first-episode schizophrenia. *NeuroReport*, *17*(1), 23–26.

Hao, Y., Yan, Q., Liu, H., Xu, L., Xue, Z., Song, X., et al. (2009). Schizophrenia patients and their healthy siblings share disruption of white matter integrity in the left prefrontal cortex and the hippocampus but not the anterior cingulate cortex. *Schizophrenia Research*, *114*(1–3), 128–135.

Harrison, P. J. (1999). The neuropathology of schizophrenia. A critical review of the data and their interpretation. *Brain*, *122*(4), 593–624.

Ho, B. C., Andreasen, N. C., Nopoulos, P., Arndt, S., Magnotta, V., & Flaum, M. (2003). Progressive structural brain abnormalities and their relationship to clinical outcome: A longitudinal magnetic resonance imaging study early in schizophrenia. *Archives of General Psychiatry*, *60*(6), 585–594.

Hoffman, R. E., & McGlashan, T. H. (1997). Synaptic elimination, neurodevelopment, and the mechanism of hallucinated "voices" in schizophrenia. *American Journal of Psychiatry*, *154*(12), 1683–1689.

Hoptman, M. J., Nierenberg, J., Bertisch, H. C., Catalano, D., Ardekani, B. A., Branch, C. A., et al. (2008). A DTI study of white matter microstructure in individuals at high genetic risk for schizophrenia. *Schizophrenia Research*, *106*(2–3), 115–124.

Huttenlocher, P. R. (1979). Synaptic density in human frontal cortex—Developmental changes and effects of aging. *Brain Research*, *163*(2), 195–205.

Huttenlocher, P. R. (1990). Morphometric study of human cerebral cortex development. *Neuropsychologia*, *28*(6), 517–527.

Huttenlocher, P. R., & Dabholkar, A. S. (1997). Regional differences in synaptogenesis in human cerebral cortex. *Journal of Comparative Neurology*, *387*(2), 167–178.

Ichiki, M., Kunugi, H., Takei, N., Murray, R. M., Baba, H., Arai, H., et al. (2000). Intrauterine physical growth in schizophrenia: Evidence confirming excess of premature birth. *Psychological Medicine*, *30*(3), 597–604.

Jacobson, S., Kelleher, I., Harley, M., Murtagh, A., Clarke, M., Blanchard, M., et al. (2010). Structural and functional brain correlates of subclinical psychotic symptoms in 11–13 year old schoolchildren. *NeuroImage*, *49*(2), 1875–1885.

Job, D. E., Whalley, H. C., Johnstone, E. C., & Lawrie, S. M. (2005). Grey matter changes over time in high risk subjects developing schizophrenia. *NeuroImage*, *25*(4), 1023–1030.

Jones, P., Rodgers, B., Murray, R., & Marmot, M. (1994). Child development risk factors for adult schizophrenia in the British 1946 birth cohort. *Lancet*, *344*(8934), 1398–1402.

Karlsgodt, K. H., Niendam, T. A., Bearden, C. E., & Cannon, T. D. (2009). White matter integrity and prediction of social and role functioning in subjects at ultra-high risk for psychosis. *Biological Psychiatry*, *66*(6), 562–569.

Karlsgodt, K. H., van Erp, T. G., Poldrack, R. A., Bearden, C. E., Nuechterlein, K. H., & Cannon, T. D. (2008). Diffusion tensor imaging of the superior longitudinal fasciculus and working memory in recent-onset schizophrenia. *Biological Psychiatry*, *63*(5), 512–518.

Kasai, K., Shenton, M. E., Salisbury, D. F., Hirayasu, Y., Lee, C. U., Ciszewski, A. A., et al. (2003). Progressive decrease of left superior temporal gyrus gray matter volume in patients with first-episode schizophrenia. *American Journal of Psychiatry*, *160*(1), 156–164.

Klingberg, T., Vaidya, C. J., Gabrieli, J. D., Moseley, M. E., & Hedehus, M. (1999). Myelination and organization of the frontal white matter in children: A diffusion tensor MRI study. *NeuroReport*, *10*(13), 2817–2821.

Koo, M. S., Levitt, J. J., Salisbury, D. F., Nakamura, M., Shenton, M. E., & McCarley, R. W. (2008). A cross-sectional and longitudinal magnetic resonance imaging study of cingulate gyrus gray matter volume abnormalities in first-episode schizophrenia and first-episode affective psychosis. *Archives of General Psychiatry*, *65*(7), 746–760.

Krasnegor, N. A., Lyon, G. R., & Goldman-Rakic, P. S. (1997). *Development of the prefrontal cortex: Evolution, neurobiology, and behavior*. Baltimore, MD: Paul H. Brookes Publishing Co.

Kyriakopoulos, M., Vyas, N. S., Barker, G. J., Chitnis, X. A., & Frangou, S. (2008). A diffusion tensor imaging study of white matter in early onset schizophrenia. *Biological Psychiatry*, *63*(5), 519–523.

Lee, H. T., Chang, Y. C., Wang, L. Y., Wang, S. T., Huang, C. C., & Ho, C. J. (2004). cAMP response element-binding protein activation in ligation preconditioning in neonatal brain. *Annals of Neurology*, *56*(5), 611–623.

Lewis, S., Owen, M., & Murray, R. (1989). Obstetric complications and schizophrenia: Methodology and mechanisms. In S. Schulz & C. Tamminga (Eds.), *Scientific progress* (pp. 56–68). New York, NY: Oxford University Press.

Lewis, S. W., & Murray, R. M. (1987). Obstetric complications, neurodevelopmental deviance, and risk of schizophrenia. *Journal of Psychiatric Research*, *21*(4), 413–421.

Mané, A., Falcon, C., Mateos, J. J., Fernandez-Egea, E., Horga, G., Lomeña, F., et al. (2009). Progressive gray matter changes in first episode schizophrenia: A 4-year longitudinal magnetic resonance study using VBM. *Schizophrenia Research*, *114*(1–3), 136–143.

Mathalon, D. H., Sullivan, E. V., Lim, K. O., & Pfefferbaum, A. (2001). Progressive brain volume changes and the clinical course of schizophrenia in men: A longitudinal magnetic resonance imaging study. *Archives of General Psychiatry*, *58*(2), 148–157.

McGlashan, T. H., & Hoffman, R. E. (2000). Schizophrenia as a disorder of developmentally reduced synaptic connectivity. *Archives of General Psychiatry*, *57*(7), 637–648.

McNeil, T. (1988). Obstetric factors and perinatal injuries. In M. Tsaung & J. Simpson (Eds.), *Handbook of schizophrenia. Vol. 3: Nosology, epidemiology, and genetics* (pp. 319–343). New York, NY: Elsevier Science Publishing Company.

McNeil, T. F., Kaij, L., & Malmquist-Larsson, A. (1984). Women with nonorganic psychosis: Mental disturbance during pregnancy. *Acta Psychiatrica Scandinavica*, *70*(2), 127–139.

Meng, M., Zhiling, W., Hui, Z., Shengfu, L., Dan, Y., & Jiping, H. (2005). Cellular levels of TrkB and MAPK in the neuroprotective role of BDNF for embryonic rat cortical neurons against hypoxia in vitro. *International Journal of Developmental Neuroscience*, *23*(6), 515–521.

Miller, L. J. (1997). Sexuality, reproduction, and family planning in women with schizophrenia. *Schizophrenia Bulletin*, *23*(4), 623–635.

Mittal, V., Willhite, R., Niendam, T., Daley, M., Bearden, C., Ellman, L., et al. (2009). Obstetric complications and risk for conversion to psychosis among individuals at high clinical risk. *Early Intervention in Psychiatry*, *3*, 226–230.

Mittal, V. A., Ellman, L. M., & Cannon, T. D. (2008). Gene–environment interaction and covariation in schizophrenia: The role of obstetric complications. *Schizophrenia Bulletin*, *34*(6), 1083–1094.

Monk, C. S., Webb, S. J., & Nelson, C. A. (2001). Prenatal neurobiological development: Molecular mechanisms and anatomical change. *Developmental Neuropsychology*, *19*(2), 211–236.

Mukherjee, P., Miller, J. H., Shimony, J. S., Philip, J. V., Nehra, D., Snyder, A. Z., et al. (2002). Diffusion-tensor MR imaging of gray and white matter development during normal human brain maturation. *American Journal of Neuroradiology*, *23*(9), 1445–1456.

Munoz Maniega, S., Lymer, G. K., Bastin, M. E., Marjoram, D., Job, D. E., Moorhead, T. W., et al. (2008). A diffusion tensor MRI study of white matter integrity in subjects at high genetic risk of schizophrenia. *Schizophrenia Research*, *106*(2–3), 132–139.

Murray, R. M., & Lewis, S. W. (1987). Is schizophrenia a neurodevelopmental disorder? *British Medical Journal (Clinical Research Edition)*, *295*(6600), 681–682.

Murray, R. M., & Lewis, S. W. (1988). Is schizophrenia a neurodevelopmental disorder? *British Medical Journal (Clinical Research Edition)*, *296*(6614), 63.

Murray, R. M., Lewis, S. W., & Reveley, A. M. (1985). Towards an aetiological classification of schizophrenia. *Lancet*, *1*(8436), 1023–1026.

Nakamura, M., Nestor, P. G., McCarley, R. W., Levitt, J. J., Hsu, L., Kawashima, T., et al. (2007). Altered orbitofrontal sulcogyral pattern in schizophrenia. *Brain*, *130*(3), 693–707.

Nakamura, M., Salisbury, D. F., Hirayasu, Y., Bouix, S., Pohl, K. M., Yoshida, T., et al. (2007). Neocortical gray matter volume in first-episode schizophrenia and first-episode affective psychosis: A cross-sectional and longitudinal MRI study. *Biological Psychiatry*, *62*(7), 773–783.

Pantelis, C., Velakoulis, D., McGorry, P. D., Wood, S. J., Suckling, J., Phillips, L. J., et al. (2003). Neuroanatomical abnormalities before and after onset of psychosis: A cross-sectional and longitudinal MRI comparison. *Lancet*, *361*(9354), 281–288.

Pantelis, C., Yücel, M., Wood, S. J., Velakoulis, D., Sun, D., Berger, G., et al. (2005). Structural brain imaging evidence for multiple pathological processes at different stages of brain development in schizophrenia. *Schizophrenia Bulletin*, *31*(3), 672–696.

Paus, T., Collins, D. L., Evans, A. C., Leonard, G., Pike, B., & Zijdenbos, A. (2001). Maturation of white matter in the human brain: A review of magnetic resonance studies. *Brain Research Bulletin*, *54*(3), 255–266.

Paus, T., Zijdenbos, A., Worsley, K., Collins, D. L., Blumenthal, J., Giedd, J. N., et al. (1999). Structural maturation of neural pathways in children and adolescents: In vivo study. *Science*, *283*(5409), 1908–1911.

Pfefferbaum, A., Mathalon, D. H., Sullivan, E. V., Rawles, J. M., Zipursky, R. B., & Lim, K. O. (1994). A quantitative magnetic resonance imaging study of changes in brain morphology from infancy to late adulthood. *Archives of Neurology*, *51*(9), 874–887.

Price, G., Bagary, M. S., Cercignani, M., Altmann, D. R., & Ron, M. A. (2005). The corpus callosum in first episode schizophrenia: A diffusion tensor imaging study. *Journal of Neurology, Neurosurgery and Psychiatry*, *76*(4), 585–587.

Raatikainen, K., Huurinainen, P., & Heinonen, S. (2007). Smoking in early gestation or through pregnancy: A decision crucial to pregnancy outcome. *Preventive Medicine*, *44*(1), 59–63.

Rapoport, J. L., Giedd, J. N., Blumenthal, J., Hamburger, S., Jeffries, N., Fernandez, T., et al. (1999). Progressive cortical change during adolescence in childhood-onset schizophrenia. A longitudinal magnetic resonance imaging study. *Archives of General Psychiatry*, *56*(7), 649–654.

Reichenberg, A., Caspi, A., Harrington, H., Houts, R., Keefe, R. S., Murray, R. M., et al. (2010). Static and dynamic cognitive deficits in childhood preceding adult schizophrenia: A 30-year study. *American Journal of Psychiatry*, *167*(2), 160–169.

Reveley, A. M., Reveley, M. A., & Murray, R. M. (1984). Cerebral ventricular enlargement in non-genetic schizophrenia: A controlled twin study. *British Journal of Psychiatry*, *144*, 89–93.

Rosso, I. M., Cannon, T. D., Huttunen, T., Huttunen, M. O., Lonnqvist, J., & Gasperoni, T. L. (2000). Obstetric risk factors for early onset schizophrenia in a Finnish birth cohort. *American Journal of Psychiatry*, *157*(5), 801–807.

Schmithorst, V. J., Wilke, M., Dardzinski, B. J., & Holland, S. K. (2002). Correlation of white matter diffusivity and anisotropy with age during childhood and adolescence: A cross-sectional diffusion-tensor MR imaging study. *Radiology*, *222*(1), 212–218.

Schneiderman, J. S., Buchsbaum, M. S., Haznedar, M. M., Hazlett, E. A., Brickman, A. M., Shihabuddin, L., et al. (2009). Age and diffusion tensor anisotropy in adolescent and adult patients with schizophrenia. *NeuroImage*, *45*(3), 662–671.

Selemon, L. D., Rajkowska, G., & Goldman-Rakic, P. S. (1995). Abnormally high neuronal density in the schizophrenic cortex. A morphometric analysis of prefrontal area 9 and occipital area 17. *Archives of General Psychiatry*, *52*(10), 805–818; discussion 819–820.

Selemon, L. D., Rajkowska, G., & Goldman-Rakic, P. S. (1998). Elevated neuronal density in prefrontal area 46 in brains from schizophrenic patients: Application of a three-dimensional, stereologic counting method. *Journal of Comparative Neurology*, *392*(3), 402–412.

Shenton, M. E., Dickey, C. C., Frumin, M., & McCarley, R. W. (2001). A review of MRI findings in schizophrenia. *Schizophrenia Research*, *49*(1–2), 1–52.

Smith, G. C., Shah, I., White, I. R., Pell, J. P., Crossley, J. A., & Dobbie, R. (2006). Maternal and biochemical predictors of spontaneous preterm birth among nulliparous women: A systematic analysis in relation to the degree of prematurity. *International Journal of Epidemiology*, *35*(5), 1169–1177.

Smith, S. M., Zhang, Y. Y., Jenkinson, M., Chen, J., Matthews, P. M., Federico, A., et al. (2002). Accurate, robust, and automated longitudinal and cross-sectional brain change analysis. *NeuroImage*, *17*(1), 479–489.

Snook, L., Paulson, L. A., Roy, D., Phillips, L., & Beaulieu, C. (2005). Diffusion tensor imaging of neurodevelopment in children and young adults. *NeuroImage*, *26*(4), 1164–1173.

St Clair, D., Blackwood, D., Muir, W., Carothers, A., Walker, M., Spowart, G., et al. (1990). Association within a family of a balanced autosomal translocation with major mental illness. *Lancet*, *336*(8706), 13–16.

Sun, D., Stuart, G. W., Jenkinson, M., Wood, S. J., McGorry, P. D., Velakoulis, D., et al. (2009). Brain surface contraction mapped in first-episode schizophrenia—A longitudinal magnetic resonance imaging study. *Molecular Psychiatry*, *14*(10), 976–986.

Sun, D., Stuart, G. W., Phillips, L., Velakoulis, D., Jenkinson, M., Yung, A., et al. (2009). Progressive brain structural changes mapped as psychosis develops in "at risk" individuals. *Schizophrenia Research*, *108*(1–3), 85–92.

Susser, E., St Clair, D., & He, L. (2008). Latent effects of prenatal malnutrition on adult health: The example of schizophrenia. *Annals of the New York Academy of Sciences*, *1136*, 185–192.

Szeszko, P. R., Ardekani, B. A., Ashtari, M., Kumra, S., Robinson, D. G., Sevy, S., et al. (2005). White matter abnormalities in first-episode schizophrenia or schizoaffective disorder: A diffusion tensor imaging study. *American Journal of Psychiatry*, *162*(3), 602–605.

Szeszko, P. R., Robinson, D. G., Ashtari, M., Vogel, J., Betensky, J., Sevy, S., et al. (2008). Clinical and neuropsychological correlates of white matter abnormalities in recent onset schizophrenia. *Neuropsychopharmacology*, *33*(5), 976–984.

Takahashi, T., Wood, S. J., Yung, A. R., Soulsby, B., McGorry, P. D., Suzuki, M., et al. (2009). Progressive gray matter reduction of the superior temporal gyrus during transition to psychosis. *Archives of General Psychiatry*, *66*(4), 366–376.

Thompson, P. M., Giedd, J. N., Woods, R. P., MacDonald, D., Evans, A. C., & Toga, A. W. (2000). Growth patterns in the developing brain detected by using continuum mechanical tensor maps. *Nature*, *404*(6774), 190–193.

Thompson, P. M., Hayashi, K. M., Sowell, E. R., Gogtay, N., Giedd, J. N., Rapoport, J. L., et al. (2004). Mapping cortical change in Alzheimer's disease, brain development, and schizophrenia. *NeuroImage*, *23*(Suppl. 1), S2–18.

Thompson, P. M., Vidal, C., Giedd, J. N., Gochman, P., Blumenthal, J., Nicolson, R., et al. (2001). Mapping adolescent brain change reveals dynamic wave of accelerated gray matter loss in very early onset schizophrenia. *Proceedings of the National Academy of Sciences of the United States of America*, *98*(20), 11650–11655.

van Erp, T. G. M., Saleh, P. A., Rosso, I. M., Huttunen, M., Lonnqvist, J., Pirkola, T., et al. (2002). Contributions of genetic risk and fetal hypoxia to hippocampal volume in patients with schizophrenia or schizoaffective disorder, their unaffected siblings, and healthy unrelated volunteers. *American Journal of Psychiatry*, *159*(9), 1514–1520.

Verdoux, H., Geddes, J. R., Takei, N., Lawrie, S. M., Bovet, P., Eagles, J. M., et al. (1997). Obstetric complications and age at onset in schizophrenia: An international collaborative meta-analysis of individual patient data. *American Journal of Psychiatry*, *154*(9), 1220–1227.

Webb, S. J., Monk, C. S., & Nelson, C. A. (2001). Mechanisms of postnatal neurobiological development: Implications for human development. *Developmental Neuropsychology*, *19*(2), 147–171.

Weinberger, D. R. (1987). Implications of normal brain development for the pathogenesis of schizophrenia. *Archives of General Psychiatry*, *44*(7), 660–669.

Weinberger, D. R., Wagner, R. L., & Wyatt, R. J. (1983). Neuropathological studies of schizophrenia: A selective review. *Schizophrenia Bulletin*, *9*(2), 193–212.

Woods, B. T. (1998). Is schizophrenia a progressive neurodevelopmental disorder? Toward a unitary pathogenetic mechanism. *American Journal of Psychiatry*, *155*(12), 1661–1670.

Wright, I. C., Rabe-Hesketh, S., Woodruff, P. W., David, A. S., Murray, R. M., & Bullmore, E. T. (2000). Meta-analysis of regional brain volumes in schizophrenia. *American Journal of Psychiatry*, *157*(1), 16–25.

Yucel, M., Stuart, G. W., Maruff, P., Velakoulis, D., Crowe, S. F., Savage, G., et al. (2001). Hemispheric and gender-related differences in the gross morphology of the anterior cingulate/paracingulate cortex in normal volunteers: An MRI morphometric study. *Cerebral Cortex*, *11*(1), 17–25.

2 Is earlier intervention for schizophrenia possible?

Identifying antecedents of schizophrenia in children aged 9–12 years

Kristin R. Laurens, Sheilagh Hodgins, Eric A. Taylor and Robin M. Murray

The outcome of schizophrenia worsens as treatment is delayed. Individuals experiencing a longer duration of untreated psychosis present greater severity of global psychopathology and positive and negative symptomatology, poorer functional outcomes, and more marked structural brain abnormalities (Keshavan & Amirsadri, 2007; Marshall et al., 2005). This association between delayed treatment and poor outcome has spurred intensive international efforts to develop early intervention services for individuals experiencing their first episode of psychosis.

More recently, clinicians have recognized that attenuated symptoms and significant disability precede the onset of frank psychosis in the majority of patients. This awareness has led to even earlier intervention strategies, targeting help-seeking individuals in the prodromal phase of schizophrenia. These individuals have been identified clinically, using a combination of attenuated psychotic symptoms (Yung et al., 2003) or subtle self-experienced basic symptoms in a range of domains (Klosterkotter, Hellmich, Steinmeyer, & Schultze-Lutter, 2001) and a positive family history of schizophrenia. Results obtained to date suggest that these innovative services have successfully delayed, but not averted, transition to psychosis (Yung et al., 2007).

Prevention of schizophrenia might be more successful if we could recognize and help at-risk individuals even earlier, prior to the typical onset of the prodrome during adolescence. In doing so, we might be able to reduce the underlying deviant development and resulting disability. Such a strategy, however, presents the significant challenge of prospectively identifying children who are at elevated risk for the development of schizophrenia and the spectrum disorders. A positive family history confers increased risk of schizophrenia (with degree of risk associated directly with the degree of biological relatedness to an afflicted individual), but it is an inherently limited identification strategy: less than 40% of adults with schizophrenia have an affected relative (Gottesman & Erlenmeyer-Kimling, 2001). Our group has therefore sought to develop a new, cost-effective, and feasible method for identifying children from the general community who are at elevated risk for developing schizophrenia and the spectrum disorders. This chapter presents the rationale underlying our method and summarizes recent findings indicating that children identified by this method present biological and sociodemographic features that are characteristic of patients with schizophrenia. In the longer term, these features may represent markers of evolving disease that could be targeted with prevention programmes.

A novel method for identifying at-risk children

The neurodevelopmental hypothesis attributes schizophrenia to abnormal brain development beginning in the pre- or perinatal period (Murray & Lewis, 1987; Weinberger, 1987). Accordingly, although the diagnostic signs and symptoms of schizophrenia do not emerge typically until early adulthood, subtle markers of illness present earlier in development. From prospective longitudinal investigations of child relatives of patients with schizophrenia and of population cohorts, there is robust evidence of multiple putative antecedents of schizophrenia that are present before age 12 years. These childhood antecedents, which distinguish individuals who later develop schizophrenia from those who do not, include: motor and language delays and abnormalities; intellectual and cognitive impairments; psychotic symptoms; social, emotional, and behavioural disturbances; adolescent cannabis use; obstetric complications and pre-/perinatal factors such as virus exposure, maternal stress, restricted physical growth, and older paternal age; and sociodemographic factors such as migration, urbanicity, and socioeconomic status (see Niemi, Suvisaari, Tuulio-Henriksson, & Lonnqvist, 2003; Welham, Isohanni, Jones, & McGrath, 2009, for reviews).

These antecedents offer a potential means of identifying children who may present elevated risk for schizophrenia. However, childhood antecedents of schizophrenia spectrum illnesses are typically non-specific. For example, anxiety, depression, attention-deficit/hyperactivity disorder, and conduct/oppositional defiant disorder show homotypic continuity through adulthood as well as heterotypic continuity to a range of adult psychiatric disorders including schizophreniform disorder (Kim-Cohen et al., 2003). Psychotic symptoms at age 11 years precede both schizophreniform and anxiety disorders assessed at age 26 years, though not mania and depression (Poulton et al., 2000). Other childhood antecedents, such as impairments in intelligence and in motor and language development (Cannon et al., 2002), have low positive predictive value and do not lead to schizophrenia for the majority of affected individuals. We reasoned, therefore, that a combination of the replicated antecedents would identify children at risk for the illness with greater sensitivity and specificity than any single factor.

Given the rarity of schizophrenia, we anticipated needing to screen large numbers of children aged 9–12 years in order to assess the presence of antecedents. This limited our selection of antecedents to those that could be assessed using questionnaires. We designed questionnaires for children and their primary caregivers requesting information on a triad of putative antecedents: (i) caregiver-reported delays or abnormalities in speech and/or motor development; (ii) child-reported internalizing problems, and/or caregiver-reported externalizing problems and/or peer relationship problems in the clinical range; and (iii) child-reported psychotic-like experiences. We previously published findings describing the prevalence of the triad of antecedents, and each individual antecedent domain within the triad, in a pilot sample comprising questionnaires from 264 child and caregiver dyads (Laurens et al., 2007). We further examined the associations of ethnicity and migrant status with the antecedent triad in a sample of 595 children and caregivers (Laurens, West, Murray, & Hodgins, 2008). In this manuscript, we re-examine these measures in an expanded sample of 1,347 children and caregivers with complete antecedent triad data.[1]

Prevalence and impact of the antecedents of schizophrenia in a deprived community sample

Children aged 9–12 years and their primary caregiver were recruited from 56 primary schools located in the Greater London area, within the London Boroughs of Southwark, Lambeth, Lewisham, Tower Hamlets, Brent, Bromley, and Harrow. Ninety percent of the sample were recruited from the first five of those boroughs, which rank within the most deprived 15% of all English local authorities according to the *Index of Multiple Deprivation* 2007 (Noble et al., 2008), and fall within the lowest scoring 10% of English local authorities on the *Local Index of Child Well-Being* (Bradshaw et al., 2009).

Children completed questionnaires in class, with questions read aloud by a researcher who ensured that children responded independently. Children were subsequently issued with a caregiver questionnaire to be completed at home and returned via reply-paid mail. In total, 7,579 children and caregivers were eligible to participate. Completed questionnaires were obtained from 7,168 children (94.6% of eligible children) and 1,366 caregivers (19.1% of eligible caregivers). The analyses reported in this manuscript are based on the 1,347 child and caregiver dyads for whom full questionnaire data were available (702 female; mean age 10 years, 4 months, *SD* 8 months). Children's self-reported data did not vary as a function of the availability of data from caregivers on 12 of 14 indices compared, suggesting that the caregiver questionnaire data returned was generally representative of the eligible population of caregivers.[2]

Child and caregiver questionnaires

Questionnaire items were described previously in Laurens et al. (2007). In brief, the child questionnaire comprised: (i) the self-report version of the Strengths and Difficulties Questionnaire (SDQ; Goodman, 2001), which incorporates four psychopathology scales assessing emotional symptoms, conduct problems, hyperactivity–inattention, and peer-relationship problems, and a scale indexing prosocial behaviour, and (ii) nine items assessing psychotic-like experiences (PLEs), including five items adapted from the Diagnostic Interview Schedule for Children (Costello, Edelbrock, Kalas, Kessler, & Klaric, 1982). All SDQ and PLE items were rated "*not true*", "*somewhat true*", or "*certainly true*".

In 865 (64%) of the 1,347 children with complete triad data, two additional ratings were obtained concerning the impact (distress and functional impairment) associated with PLEs. Any child indicating a "*somewhat true*" or "*certainly true*" response to any of the nine PLE items was asked to further indicate (via a dichotomous "*yes*" or "*no*" response) whether the experience(s) upset them and/or whether the experience(s) caused difficulties for them at home or at school.

The caregiver questionnaires comprised four sections: (i) sociodemographic information on the family; (ii) quantitative (3 items) and qualitative (6 items) measures of developmental delays or abnormalities in speech and motor function; (iii) the parent-report version of the SDQ; and (iv) a parent-report version of the PLEs.

Children experiencing the triad of putative antecedents of schizophrenia (ASz) were those who presented: (i) at least one caregiver-reported delay or abnormality in speech and/or motor development; (ii) an "*abnormal*" rating (i.e., top tenth percentile on UK population norms) on at least one SDQ psychopathology scale (i.e., child-reported emotional symptoms, or caregiver-reported conduct problems, hyperactivity–inattention, or peer-relationship problems); and (iii) child-reported "*certain experience*" of at least one PLE.

Antecedent prevalences

Table 2.1 indicates the percentages of children who present each of the putative antecedents of schizophrenia, who present none of the antecedents, and ASz children presenting antecedents in all three domains. Almost one third of the children obtained SDQ scores within the clinical range in at least one domain, and just over one quarter of children experienced a delay or abnormality in speech/motor development. Strikingly, almost two thirds of children reported at least one "*certainly true*" PLE. Of these children, most (72.1%, 72.9% boys, 71.3% girls) reported multiple "*certainly true*" PLE ratings. The three most frequently endorsed experiences—auditory hallucinations, paranoid thoughts, and visual hallucinations—have been shown to accurately predict psychotic symptoms elicited during diagnostic interview with a clinician (Kelleher, Harley, Murtagh, & Cannon, 2011). Comparatively, caregivers reported any "*certainly true*" PLE rating for only 10.0% of children (10.3% boys, 9.8% girls; with rates for individual items ranging from 0.9 to 3.1%). This discrepancy between child- and caregiver-reported PLEs is consistent with previous reports (Kelleher et al., 2011; Wellham, Scott et al., 2009), and implies that children do not necessarily report these phenomena to adults or that they interpret these experiences differently than do their caregivers. Overall, nearly 10% of children presented the triad of putative antecedents of schizophrenia, while almost one quarter of children presented none of the antecedents. The prevalence of the antecedent triad exceeds the prevalence of adult psychotic disorders, and may index a vulnerability to schizophrenia that evolves according to the action of a variety of risk and protective exposures.

Logistic regression analyses were conducted to examine whether the presence/absence of each antecedent varied by sex and by age (grouped as < 10.5 years

Table 2.1 The percentages of children (total sample, boys, and girls) who present each putative antecedent of schizophrenia (antecedent domains indicated in *italics*), none of the antecedents, or the triad of antecedents; and the association of each antecedent with sex (expressed relative to a female reference group, and adjusted for the effect of age-group and sex-by-age-group interaction)

Antecedent	*Total (%)*	*Boys (%)*	*Girls (%)*	*OR*	*95% CI*	*p*
Emotional symptoms (child reported)	12.1	8.4	15.5	0.5	0.4–0.7	<.0001
Conduct problems (caregiver reported)	10.8	12.9	8.8	1.5	1.1–2.2	.02
Hyperactivity–inattention (caregiver reported)	9.6	12.4	6.1	2.4	1.6–3.5	< .0001
Peer problems (caregiver reported)	13.9	15.3	12.7	1.2	0.9–1.7	.2
Any SDQ psychopathology ("abnormal" range)	*32.4*	*35.0*	*30.1*	*1.3*	*1.0–1.6*	*.05*
Delay or abnormality in speech development	21.5	29.1	14.7	2.4	1.9–3.2	< .0001
Delay or abnormality in motor development or motor coordination problem	9.4	10.9	8.1	1.4	0.9–2.0	.09
Any speech and/or motor problem	*26.1*	*33.0*	*19.8*	*2.0*	*1.6–2.6*	*< .0001*
Have you ever heard voices that other people could not hear?	34.0	37.2	31.1	1.3	1.1–1.7	.01
Have you ever thought that you were being followed or spied upon?	30.3	29.9	30.6	1.0	0.8–1.2	.8
Have you ever seen something or someone that other people could not see?	27.3	28.5	26.1	1.1	0.9–1.5	.3
Have you ever known what another person was thinking even though that person wasn't speaking?	22.7	25.5	20.1	1.4	1.1–1.8	.02
Have you ever felt as though your body had been changed in some way that you could not understand?	20.4	20.6	20.2	1.0	0.8–1.4	.8
Do you have any special powers that other people don't have?	19.4	22.0	16.9	1.4	1.1–1.9	.01
Have you ever felt that you were under the control of some special power?	13.1	13.9	12.3	1.2	0.8–1.6	.3
Have you ever believed that you were being sent special messages through the television?	9.4	10.0	8.8	1.2	0.8–1.7	.4
Some people believe that their thoughts can be read. Have other people ever read your thoughts?	9.0	9.5	8.5	1.2	0.8–1.7	.4
Any "certainly-true" psychotic-like experience rating	*63.0*	*66.7*	*59.5*	*1.4*	*1.1–1.7*	*.006*
No antecedent reported	23.6	18.8	27.9	1.7	1.3–2.2	<.0001
All three domains of the antecedent triad reported	*9.5*	*13.2*	*6.1*	*2.3*	*1.6–3.4*	*<.0001*

Note: OR = odds ratio; CI = Confidence Interval.

and ≥ 10.5 years), with associations expressed as odds ratios (OR). Each model was adjusted for the potential effects of the other variable and their interaction (i.e., analyses of the association of the antecedents with sex were adjusted for the potential effects of age and a sex-by-age interaction, and vice versa). As presented in Table 2.1, boys were at higher risk of experiencing conduct problems, hyperactivity–inattention, and speech delays, and of hearing voices, reading minds, and having special powers than girls, but were half as likely as girls to present emotional symptoms. Boys were more likely to present the antecedent triad, and each of the three domains comprising the triad, and less likely to present none of the antecedents, than girls.

Self-reported emotional symptoms were less likely among older than younger children (OR = 0.5, 95% CI: 0.4–0.8, $p = .004$), as were five of the nine self-reported PLEs, including hearing voices, feeling followed/spied upon, experiencing unexplained body changes, having special powers, and having one's thoughts read (each OR in the range 0.5–0.7, all $ps \leq .01$). Older children presented significantly lesser odds than younger children for presenting a "*certainly true*" response on at least one of the nine PLE items (0.8, 95% CI: 0.6–0.9, $p = .005$), but age did not relate to the odds of obtaining any SDQ score in the clinical range or to a speech/motor delay or abnormality. Nor did the age groups differ in their likelihood of presenting the triad, though older children were significantly more likely to present none of the antecedents than younger children (OR = 1.5, 95% CI: 1.2–2.0, $p = .001$). These results imply that children either experience less internalizing symptomology and PLEs as they age, or that they become less inclined to report such symptoms on questionnaires.

Impact of psychotic-like experiences

Table 2.2 presents the percentages of children who experienced none, one, two, or all three of the antecedent domains, and the type of antecedent. The table additionally indicates the percentages of children reporting: (i) distress; (ii) functional impairment; (iii) either distress or impairment; and (iv) both distress and impairment relating to their experience of any PLE. ASz children experienced the greatest impact associated with PLEs, with over one third reporting both distress and functional impairment relative to less than 4% among children who presented no antecedent domain. Comparing ASz children ($n = 83$) with all other children ($n = 782$) in whom impact data were obtained, a significantly higher percentage of ASz children reported either distress or impairment (68.7%) than did the other children (37.2%): $\chi^2(1) = 30.9, p < .0001$; and reported both distress and impairment (36.1% ASz children vs. 12.0% other children): $\chi^2(1) = 35.5$, $p < .0001$. Longitudinal follow-up of the children will permit an examination of whether distress and/or functional impairment relate to the persistence of PLEs as children develop into adolescence and adulthood. The persistence of subclinical PLEs has been posited as a key factor underlying transition to psychosis for a significant proportion of individuals (van Os, Linscott, Myin-Germeys, Delespaul, & Krabbendam, 2009).

Table 2.2 The percentages of children displaying antecedents within each domain of the antecedent triad and the percentages of children with each antecedent who reported impact from psychotic-like experiences, that is, distress only, functional impairment (FI) only, either distress or FI, or both distress and FI; impact data available in $n = 865$[a]

Antecedent domains presented	*Prevalence (%)*	*Distress (%)*	*FI (%)*	*Either (%)*	*Both (%)*
Antecedent triad	9.5	50.6	54.2	68.7	36.1
Two antecedents	26.0				
PLE + SDQ	14.8	41.5	48.7	67.2	22.7
PLE + Speech/Motor	7.9	30.8	30.8	47.0	13.6
SDQ + Speech/Motor	3.3	11.1	18.5	25.9	3.7
One antecedent	40.9				
PLE	30.8	29.3	26.4	40.7	15.0
SDQ	4.8	25.0	17.5	32.5	10.0
Speech/Motor	5.3	14.3	18.6	23.3	9.5
No antecedents	23.6	10.3	11.7	18.2	3.7

Note: PLE = at least one "certainly-true" rating on a psychotic-like experience item; SDQ = an "abnormal" (top 10% on UK norms) rating on at least one of the four Strengths and Difficulties Questionnaire psychopathology subscales (i.e., child-reported emotional symptoms, and/or caregiver-reported conduct problems, hyperactivity–inattention, and/or peer-relationship problems); Speech/Motor = at least one caregiver-reported delay/abnormality in speech or motor function; [a] PLE Impact was calculated for any child reporting a "*somewhat-true*" or "*certainly-true*" rating on any of the nine PLE items (i.e., for 94.2% of children; 93.5% males; 94.9% females)

Demographic correlates of the antecedents

The incidence of schizophrenia and non-affective psychoses are elevated among various ethnic minority groups in the UK relative to the white British population, with particularly elevated rates apparent among African-Caribbean and black African groups (Coid et al., 2008; Fearon et al., 2006). In a preliminary sample of 595 children and caregivers, we previously examined the associations of ethnicity and migrant status with the antecedent triad (Laurens et al., 2008). Migrant status was not associated with the antecedent triad, whereas ethnic group was. Children of African-Caribbean ethnicity presented increased prevalence of the antecedent triad relative to white British children. Conversely, children of South Asian and Oriental ethnicity (grouped together due to small participant numbers) were less likely to present the triad of antecedents, but this difference was not statistically significant.

In the larger sample examined here (and with the South Asian and Oriental children grouped separately), migrant status again showed no relationship with the antecedents, while ethnicity showed a strong association. Ethnicity was examined within seven categories: white British, white other (predominantly European), African-Caribbean (including mixed-white children), black African (including mixed-white children), South Asian (predominantly Indian, Pakistani, and Bangladeshi), Oriental (predominantly Chinese), and other ethnicity (predominantly

Latin American and mixed ethnicities). Table 2.3 presents the percentages of children within each ethnicity. The white British reference population comprised slightly over one third of the total sample. The table summarizes, within each ethnic group, the percentage of children who present the triad of antecedents, as well as each individual antecedent. Logistic regression analyses (adjusted for age, sex, and the interaction of these variables with ethnicity) were used to determine whether the presence/absence of the antecedent triad and each antecedent domain within the triad varied by ethnic group. Relative to white British children, children of African-Caribbean, black African, and "other" ethnicity were significantly more likely to present the triad of putative antecedents of schizophrenia, whereas children of South Asian ethnicity were significantly less likely to do so. Children of African-Caribbean and black African ethnicity also presented significantly increased odds for each of the antecedents comprising the triad. By contrast, the lower prevalence of the antecedent triad among children of South Asian ethnicity was observed in spite of these children being significantly more likely than the white British children to obtain scores in the clinical range on at least one SDQ psychopathology scale. Relative to white British children, Oriental children were significantly less likely, and White-other children significantly more likely, to report at least one "*certainly true*" rating on a PLE item. The elevated prevalence of the triad of antecedents of schizophrenia among children of African-Caribbean and black African ethnicity, and ethnicities classified as "other", is consistent with the increased incidence of schizophrenia among these groups in the UK (Fearon et al., 2006). Equivalent incidence rates of schizophrenia in South Asian and white British populations have been reported previously (Fearon et al., 2006), although others have distinguished modest elevation in non-affective psychoses specifically among female South Asian adults (Coid et al., 2008). The differential incidence of psychotic illness in different ethnic groups has been suggested to result from differences in levels of social isolation, social support, and family structure (Cantor-Graae & Selten, 2005; Coid et al., 2008; Kirkbride et al., 2008). The variance in the prevalence of children presenting the triad of antecedents of schizophrenia in different ethnic groups presents an important opportunity to identify risk and protective factors for psychosis that operate prior to illness onset.

Children presenting the antecedent triad also present functional abnormalities characteristic of schizophrenia

Longitudinal follow-up of ASz children is necessary to determine the specificity and sensitivity with which the triad of antecedents identifies individuals who subsequently develop schizophrenia. Presently, we are undertaking a series of studies with ASz children to determine the extent to which they present abnormalities associated with schizophrenia. These studies compare ASz children with typically developing (TD) children who present none of the antecedents and no family history of schizophrenia or schizoaffective disorder. No child completing assessments had taken psychotropic medication or received a diagnosis in the schizophrenia spectrum. Preliminary investigations completed to date in relatively

Table 2.3 The prevalence of the antecedent triad and each antecedent domain comprising the triad within each ethnic group; and the association of ethnicity with the antecedent triad and with each antecedent domain

Ethnicity	*Prevalence (%)*	*Antecedent triad*				*Psychotic-like experiences*				*SDQ psychopathology*				*Speech/Motor problem*			
		(%)	*OR*	*95% CI*	*p*	*(%)*	*OR*	*95% CI*	*p*	*(%)*	*OR*	*95% CI*	*p*	*(%)*	*OR*	*95% CI*	*p*
White British [a]	38.1	7.0	1.0			58.4	1.0			26.2	1.0			21.4	1.0		
White other	11.7	10.2	1.5	0.8–2.8	.2	67.9	1.6	1.1–2.3	.02	32.5	1.4	0.9–2.0	.1	25.8	1.3	0.9–2.0	.2
African-Caribbean	18.9	12.9	2.0	1.2–3.3	.006	70.7	1.7	1.3–2.4	.001	40.0	1.9	1.4–2.7	.00006	30.0	1.7	1.2–2.3	.004
Black African	17.6	12.7	2.0	1.2–3.3	.01	71.5	1.9	1.3–2.7	.0002	36.6	1.7	1.2–2.3	.003	32.0	1.7	1.2–2.4	.005
South Asian	7.1	1.0	0.1	0.02–1.0	.05	49.0	0.7	0.5–1.1	.1	35.4	1.6	1.0–2.5	.05	23.5	1.2	0.7–2.0	.5
Oriental	3.0	7.5	1.0	0.3–3.3	1.0	37.5	0.4	0.2–0.8	.008	27.5	1.0	0.5–2.1	.9	32.5	1.7	0.8–3.4	.1
Other	3.6	18.8	3.3	1.5–7.5	.004	60.4	1.2	0.6–2.2	.6	35.4	1.7	0.9–3.1	.1	31.3	1.7	0.8–3.2	.1

Note: OR = odds ratio; CI = Confidence Interval; SDQ = Strengths and Difficulties Questionnaire; [a] ORs are expressed relative to the white British reference group, with each model adjusted for sex, age-group (< 10.5 years; ≥ 10.5 years), and the interaction of these variables with ethnicity (see text for detail).

small samples suggest that ASz children present: (i) brain function abnormalities on event-related potential (ERP) recordings, even in the context of preserved task performance (Laurens et al., 2010); (ii) intellectual and cognitive deficits on standardized neuropsychological tests (Cullen et al., 2010) that are of comparable magnitude to those indicated by meta-analysis of prospective and follow-back investigations of children who later develop schizophrenia (Dickson, Laurens, Cullen, & Hodgins, 2011); (iii) and involuntary dyskinetic movement abnormalities of the face and upper body (MacManus et al., 2011).

Using ERP techniques, Laurens et al. (2010) compared 22 ASz and 26 TD children during performance of a Go/No-Go paradigm to index the brain response elicited during processing of errors (i.e., false alarm responses on No-Go trials). The functional abnormality observed in ASz children during error processing is suggestive of dysfunction in the anterior cingulate cortex (ACC), a region characterized by functional and structural abnormalities in clinically or genetically defined high-risk youth in the years immediately preceding transition to psychosis (Fornito et al., 2008; Whalley et al., 2006).

Early dysfunction of the ACC, as well as the dorsolateral prefrontal cortex, was also implied by the prominence of deficits in performance on tests of executive function-inhibition and working memory presented by 28 ASz children relative to 28 matched TD children (Cullen et al., 2010). Additional deficits were observed among the ASz children in intelligence and verbal memory. The deficits in intelligence, mathematics performance, and motor function presented by the ASz children are as great as those shown by children of similar age who subsequently developed schizophrenia (Dickson et al., 2011).

Further evidence of motor dysfunction in ASz children has been indicated using blind-rater codings of muted video-taped recordings of child interviews in a small sample of 21 ASz and 31 TD children (MacManus et al., 2011). Using a method applied previously to rate involuntary dyskinetic movements in adolescents at high-risk for schizophrenia (Mittal, Neumann, Saczawa, & Walker, 2008), ASz children were found to present significantly more facial (e.g., tics, grimacing, blinking, chewing/lip smacking, puckering/sucking/thrusting lower lip, tongue thrusts, tonic tongue, tongue tremor, athetoid/myokymic/lateral tongue) and upper body (e.g., shoulder/hip torsion, writhing extensions of fingers or wrist) dyskinetic movements than TD children. It has been proposed that dyskinesias, as well as PLEs, result from dysregulation of striatal dopamine (Mittal et al., 2008).

Implications for research and clinical practice

Preliminary evidence indicates that children presenting a triad of antecedents of schizophrenia also present functional abnormalities characteristic of patients with schizophrenia. Assessment of other biological and psychosocial measures in the children is underway in order to provide a more comprehensive characterization of the abnormalities they present. Follow-up of the ASz children will allow us to examine the stability of the deficits, to determine the extent to which these deficits represent a general vulnerability to psychopathology or confer specific risk for schizophrenia, and to identify the emergence of other abnormalities prior to illness onset. Given that functional and structural brain maturation, particularly in prefrontal cortices, continues into young adulthood (Casey, Giedd, & Thomas, 2000; Lenroot & Giedd, 2006), there is an exciting prospect of remediating function with early intervention in childhood, and potentially preventing the development of psychosis in children who present the triad of putative antecedents plus the specific abnormalities described here.

Acknowledgements

The authors thank the children and caregivers who participated in the study, and the researchers and students who contributed to data collection. The research was supported by funding awarded to KRL from a National Institute for Health Research (NIHR) Career Development Fellowship, a Bial Foundation Research Grant, a NARSAD Young Investigator Award, and the British Medical Association Margaret Temple Award for schizophrenia research. All authors are affiliated with the NIHR Specialist Biomedical Research Centre (BRC) for Mental Health at the South London and Maudsley NHS Foundation Trust and Institute of Psychiatry, King's College London, UK.

Notes

1. Data available from an additional 127 child and caregiver dyads recruited via general practitioners' surgeries, which were incorporated in previous manuscripts, are excluded from the present manuscript.
2. Self-reported data from children whose caregivers did versus did not supply accompanying questionnaires were compared for the prevalence of a rating in the "abnormal" range (i.e., scores in the top 10th percentile of UK population norms) on any of the four SDQ psychopathology subscales, for the prevalence of a "*certainly-true*" response on a PLE item, and for prevalence of a "*certainly-true*" rating on at least one of the nine PLE items assessed. Prevalence did not vary for child-reported SDQ emotional symptoms, SDQ hyperactivity–inattention, SDQ peer-relationship problems, or on any of the nine individual PLE items. Prevalence rates of self-reported SDQ conduct problems and of a "*certainly-true*" response to at least one of the nine PLE items were significantly more prevalent in children whose caregivers did not supply questionnaire data: Conduct problems = 19.5% vs. 14.7%, OR = 1.4 (95% CI: 1.2–1.7), $p < .0001$; any PLE = 66.8% vs. 63.0%, OR = 1.2 (95% CI: 1.1–1.3), $p = .007$, but this latter effect was due to a significant difference amongst girls only, i.e., 64.9% vs. 59.5%, OR = 1.3 (95% CI: 1.1–1.5), $p = .008$. On these two indices of child difficulties, the present data set may thus underestimate the population prevalence.

References

Bradshaw, J., Bloor, K., Huby, M., Rhodes, D., Sinclair, I., & Gibbs, I. (2009). *Local index of child well-being: Summary report*. London, UK: Department for Communities and Local Government.

Cannon, M., Caspi, A., Moffitt, T. E., Harrington, H., Taylor, A., Murray, R. M., et al. (2002). Evidence for early childhood, pan-developmental impairment specific to schizophreniform disorder: Results from a longitudinal birth cohort. *Archives of General Psychiatry*, *59*(5), 449–456.

Cantor-Graae, E., & Selten, J. P. (2005). Schizophrenia and migration: A meta-analysis and review. *American Journal of Psychiatry*, *162*(1), 12–24.

Casey, B. J., Giedd, J. N., & Thomas, K. M. (2000). Structural and functional brain development and its relation to cognitive development. *Biological Psychology*, *54*(1–3), 241–257.

Coid, J. W., Kirkbride, J. B., Barker, D., Cowden, F., Stamps, R., Yang, M., et al. (2008). Raised incidence rates of all psychoses among migrant groups: Findings from the East London first episode psychosis study. *Archives of General Psychiatry*, *65*(11), 1250–1258.

Costello, A., Edelbrock, C., Kalas, R., Kessler, M., & Klaric, S. (1982). *NIMH Diagnostic Interview Schedule for Children: Child version*. Rockville, MD: National Institute of Mental Health.

Cullen, A. E., Dickson, H., West, S. A., Morris, R. G., Mould, G. L., Hodgins, S., et al. (2010). Neurocognitive performance in children aged 9–12 years who present putative antecedents of schizophrenia. *Schizophrenia Research*, *121*(1–3), 15–23.

Dickson, H., Laurens, K. R., Cullen, A. E., & Hodgins, S. (2011). *Meta-analyses of cognitive and motor function in youth aged 16 years and younger who subsequently develop schizophrenia*. Manuscript submitted for publication.

Fearon, P., Kirkbride, J. B., Morgan, C., Dazzan, P., Morgan, K., Lloyd, T., et al. (2006). Incidence of schizophrenia and other psychoses in ethnic minority groups: Results from the MRC AESOP Study. *Psychological Medicine*, *36*(11), 1541–1550.

Fornito, A., Yung, A. R., Wood, S. J., Phillips, L. J., Nelson, B., Cotton, S., et al. (2008). Anatomic abnormalities of the anterior cingulate cortex before psychosis onset: An MRI study of ultra-high-risk individuals. *Biological Psychiatry*, *64*(9), 758–765.

Goodman, R. (2001). Psychometric properties of the strengths and difficulties questionnaire. *Journal of the American Academy of Child and Adolescent Psychiatry*, *40*(11), 1337–1345.

Gottesman, I. I., & Erlenmeyer-Kimling, L. (2001). Family and twin strategies as a head start in defining prodromes and endophenotypes for hypothetical early interventions in schizophrenia. *Schizophrenia Research*, *51*(1), 93–102.

Kelleher, I., Harley, M., Murtagh, A., & Cannon, M. (2011). Are screening instruments valid for psychotic-like experiences? A validation study of screening questions for psychotic-like experiences using in-depth clinical interview. *Schizophrenia Bulletin*, *37*(2), 362–369.

Keshavan, M. S., & Amirsadri, A. (2007). Early intervention in schizophrenia: Current and future perspectives. *Current Psychiatry Reports*, *9*(4), 325–328.

Kim-Cohen, J., Caspi, A., Moffitt, T. E., Harrington, H., Milne, B. J., & Poulton, R. (2003). Prior juvenile diagnoses in adults with mental disorder: Developmental follow-back of a prospective-longitudinal cohort. *Archives of General Psychiatry*, *60*(7), 709–717.

Kirkbride, J. B., Boydell, J., Ploubidis, G. B., Morgan, C., Dazzan, P., McKenzie, K., et al. (2008). Testing the association between the incidence of schizophrenia and social capital in an urban area. *Psychological Medicine*, *38*(8), 1083–1094.

Klosterkotter, J., Hellmich, M., Steinmeyer, E. M., & Schultze-Lutter, F. (2001). Diagnosing schizophrenia in the initial prodromal phase. *Archives of General Psychiatry*, *58*(2), 158–164.

Laurens, K. R., Hodgins, S., Maughan, B., Murray, R. M., Rutter, M. L., & Taylor, E. A. (2007). Community screening for psychotic-like experiences and other putative antecedents of schizophrenia in children aged 9–12 years. *Schizophrenia Research*, *90*(1–3), 130–146.

Laurens, K. R., Hodgins, S., Mould, G. L., West, S. A., Schoenberg, P. L., Murray, R. M., et al. (2010). Error-related processing dysfunction in children aged 9 to 12 years presenting putative antecedents of schizophrenia. *Biological Psychiatry*, *67*(3), 238–245.

Laurens, K. R., West, S. A., Murray, R. M., & Hodgins, S. (2008). Psychotic-like experiences and other antecedents of schizophrenia in children aged 9–12 years: A comparison of ethnic and migrant groups in the United Kingdom. *Psychological Medicine*, *38*(8), 1103–1111.

Lenroot, R. K., & Giedd, J. N. (2006). Brain development in children and adolescents: Insights from anatomical magnetic resonance imaging. *Neuroscience and Biobehavioral Reviews*, *30*(6), 718–729.

MacManus, D., Hodgins, S., Walker, E. F., Brasfield, J., Riaz, M., & Laurens, K. R. (2011). *Movement abnormalities and psychotic-like experiences in childhood: Markers of developing schizophrenia?* Manuscript submitted for publication.

Marshall, M., Lewis, S., Lockwood, A., Drake, R., Jones, P., & Croudace, T. (2005). Association between duration of untreated psychosis and outcome in cohorts of first-episode patients: A systematic review. *Archives of General Psychiatry*, *62*(9), 975–983.

Mittal, V. A., Neumann, C., Saczawa, M., & Walker, E. F. (2008). Longitudinal progression of movement abnormalities in relation to psychotic symptoms in adolescents at high risk of schizophrenia. *Archives of General Psychiatry*, *65*(2), 165–171.

Murray, R. M., & Lewis, S. W. (1987). Is schizophrenia a neurodevelopmental disorder? *British Medical Journal (Clinical Research Edition)*, *295*(6600), 681–682.

Niemi, L. T., Suvisaari, J. M., Tuulio-Henriksson, A., & Lonnqvist, J. K. (2003). Childhood developmental abnormalities in schizophrenia: Evidence from high-risk studies. *Schizophrenia Research*, *60*(2–3), 239–258.

Noble, M., McLennan, D., Wilkinson, K., Whitworth, A., Barnes, H., & Dibben, C. (2008). *The English indices of deprivation*. London, UK: Department for Communities and Local Government.

Poulton, R., Caspi, A., Moffitt, T. E., Cannon, M., Murray, R., & Harrington, H. (2000). Children's self-reported psychotic symptoms and adult schizophreniform disorder: A 15-year longitudinal study. *Archives of General Psychiatry*, *57*(11), 1053–1058.

van Os, J., Linscott, R. J., Myin-Germeys, I., Delespaul, P., & Krabbendam, L. (2009). A systematic review and meta-analysis of the psychosis continuum: Evidence for a psychosis proneness-persistence-impairment model of psychotic disorder. *Psychological Medicine*, *39*(2), 179–195.

Weinberger, D. R. (1987). Implications of normal brain development for the pathogenesis of schizophrenia. *Archives of General Psychiatry*, *44*(7), 660–669.

Welham, J., Isohanni, M., Jones, P., & McGrath, J. (2009). The antecedents of schizophrenia: A review of birth cohort studies. *Schizophrenia Bulletin*, *35*(3), 603–623.

Welham, J., Scott, J., Williams, G., Najman, J., Bor, W., O'Callaghan, M., et al. (2009). Emotional and behavioural antecedents of young adults who screen positive for non-affective psychosis: A 21-year birth cohort study. *Psychological Medicine*, *39*(4), 625–634.

Whalley, H. C., Simonotto, E., Moorhead, W., McIntosh, A., Marshall, I., Ebmeier, K. P., et al. (2006). Functional imaging as a predictor of schizophrenia. *Biological Psychiatry*, *60*(5), 454–462.

Yung, A. R., McGorry, P. D., Francey, S. M., Nelson, B., Baker, K., Phillips, L. J., et al. (2007). PACE: A specialised service for young people at risk of psychotic disorders. *Medical Journal of Australia*, *187*(7 Suppl.), S43–46.

Yung, A. R., Phillips, L. J., Yuen, H. P., Francey, S. M., McFarlane, C. A., Hallgren, M., et al. (2003). Psychosis prediction: 12-month follow up of a high-risk ("prodromal") group. *Schizophrenia Research*, *60*(1), 21–32.

3 The black hole of the adolescent brain

Matt Allin and Chiara Nosarti

Introduction

Why does schizophrenia happen when it does? The neurodevelopmental hypothesis championed by Robin Murray provides a powerful explanatory framework for addressing this question (Murray, Lappin, & Di Forti, 2008). The hypothesis is that psychosis arises from the interaction of a very early brain lesion (which could be genetic, environmental or a combination of the two) with adolescent neurodevelopment. The perturbation of neurodevelopment during the critical period of adolescence then gives rise to the syndrome that we call psychosis. This compelling model contains two "Black Holes", which are not straightforward to investigate. First, what is the nature of the early lesion(s)? Second, what is going wrong with brain development during the transition from adolescence to adulthood? In this chapter we will explore the second Black Hole in a group of people who were at high risk of early brain injury by virtue of being born prematurely. By considering how their brains grow and develop between adolescence and adulthood we hope to give some insights into adolescent neurodevelopment. But first, some more background information is in order.

Adolescence and the brain

What is adolescence? A short answer would be that there is no single universally accepted definition. A pragmatic, but imprecise, approach is to define it simply as the period of physical, psychological and social transition from childhood to adulthood (Blakemore, 2008), and we will avoid getting into this further here. To answer the question about what might be going wrong with brain development in psychosis, it will be useful to review what happens when development is going right. With magnetic resonance imaging (MRI) it is possible to see the structure and function of the living brain in more and more sophisticated ways. And, crucially, because MRI can be performed non-invasively in the living brain, it can be done more than once, allowing us to follow brain development longitudinally. Giedd et al. (1999) performed one of the first such developmental MRI studies, subsequently refined and extended by other researchers from the same group. For instance, cortical changes across the lifespan have been documented, including non-linear age effects in large areas of the frontal and parietal regions until approximately 30 years of age (Sowell et al., 2003; Toga, Thompson, & Sowell, 2006). It has been suggested that such lifetime dynamic brain changes may serve to optimally adapt our lives to our environments and experiences (Peper, Brouwer, Boomsma, Kahn, & Hulshoff Pol, 2007).

The general pattern is for grey matter to increase during the transition from childhood into adolescence, peaking in motor and sensory cortex first and later in "association" areas thought to underlie cognition and complex adaptive behaviour (Gogtay et al., 2004). This pattern is subsequently followed by grey matter reduction during adolescence and the transition into adulthood. The heterogeneous pattern of development was recently further refined by Shaw et al. (2008), who suggested that late-maturing brain regions are phylogenetically more recent, and associated with "higher" cognitive function. The maturational decrease in grey matter is often taken to reflect synaptic pruning, associated with "tuning" of the cortex and increasing its efficiency, in line with the idea that developmental changes that occur in adolescence may involve improvements in processing capacity, rather than the development of new skills (Luna & Sweeny, 2004). An alternative explanation is that the apparent reduction of grey matter actually reflects myelination of axons that penetrate the cortex (Toga et al., 2006). These explanations are, of course, not mutually exclusive.

A different developmental trajectory applies to white matter, which appears to increase in volume and in organization in a more-or-less linear fashion from childhood through to adulthood (Ashtari et al., 2007). The most plausible candidate process here is myelination, but other possibilities—increase in axon diameter, for example, or even growth of new axons (Chklovskii, Mel, & Svoboda, 2004)—remain possible.

Premature birth—a neurodevelopmental model

In 1979, the department of Neonatal Paediatrics at University College Hospital, London, began enrolling infants born before 33 gestational weeks ("very preterm" or "VPT") into a follow-up programme, initially to determine the utility of neonatal ultrasound in predicting later neurological disability (Stewart et al., 1983). Fifteen years later, Robin Murray hit on the idea of following up this group as they made the transition from adolescence to adulthood.

Psychiatric and behavioural consequences of very preterm birth

While neuronal proliferation is predominantly complete by the end of the second trimester of gestation, the vast majority of brain development occurs in the third trimester, with the volume of the whole brain more than doubling and the volume of cortical grey matter increasing approximately four-fold (Huppi et al., 1998). Being born at an immature developmental stage can compromise brain development because many fundamental processes—such as neurogenesis, neural migration and gyrification—are occurring between 24 and 32 gestational weeks. Due to their rapidly developing and complex characteristics, these neurodevelopmental processes are likely to be vulnerable to exogenous and endogenous insults (Volpe, 2009). Not surprisingly, therefore, children born at or before 32 weeks are more likely to experience sensorimotor and/or cognitive impairments than children born at term (Foulder-Hughes & Cooke, 2003), although the majority are not disabled by them (Powls, Botting, Cooke, & Marlow, 1995). As a group, very preterm children do not perform as well at school as term-born children (Saigal & Doyle, 2008) and there seems to exist a "gradient" relation between gestational age and educational outcomes (Taylor, Klein, Minich, & Hack, 2000). Furthermore, children who need to repeat grades or require special education assistance in primary school are at greater risk than other children for long-term learning and behaviour problems (Aylward, 2005).

Preterm birth is an "obstetric complication" of the kind that is associated with psychosis in adult life (Cannon, Jones, & Murray, 2002; Walshe et al., 2005), although the exact aetiological mechanism is not yet known. Lindström, Lindblad, and Hjern (2009) investigated the psychiatric outcome of premature birth using Swedish birth and hospitalization records, and showed convincingly that preterm birth is associated with an increased risk of being admitted to a psychiatric hospital as an adult. There was a "dose–response" relationship between the risk of hospitalization as an adult and the degree of immaturity at birth, although most of those who were subsequently hospitalized had what was categorized as "moderate" degrees of prematurity (29–32 gestational weeks). We are also currently studying preterm birth as an independent risk factor for psychiatric disorders in adulthood using Swedish birth and hospitalization records. Preliminary results suggest that very preterm birth is significantly associated with increased risk for psychiatric hospitalization in a dose-dependent manner across a range of psychiatric disorders, including psychosis, bipolar affective disorder and severe depression, after controlling for indicators of intrauterine growth restriction and delivery-related asphyxia, maternal characteristics and sociodemographic variables (Nosarti, Hultman et al., 2008).

Other evidence suggests that adults born very preterm have different personality styles, including reduced risk taking (Hack, Carter, Schluchter, Klein, & Forrest, 2007), lower extraversion (Allin et al., 2006) and increased behavioural inhibition (Pyhälä et al., 2009). Whether such differences arise from early brain lesions, early life experiences (such as neonatal intensive care), parenting style, interactions with peers or constitutional (genetic) factors—or more likely a combination of all of them—is not known at present. We have recently shown higher rates of anxiety and depression in very preterm compared to term-born 19-year-olds, with an interaction with family history that further increased this risk (Walshe et al., 2008). Whether such mood disorders are primary, or prodromal to later psychotic illness can only be answered by further follow-up of such cohorts. However, this does suggest that there is an interaction between genotype and birth injury that influences psychiatric outcome in this group.

MRI studies of adolescents born preterm

Being born very preterm is associated with changes in the brain that can be seen on structural MRI scans in childhood and adolescence. These changes include smaller cortical volumes and larger lateral ventricles (Nosarti et al., 2002) and reduced size of the hippocampus (Nosarti et al., 2002), cerebellum (Allin et al., 2001, 2005), caudate nucleus (Abernethy, Palaniappan, & Cooke, 2002), thalamus (Giménez et al., 2006) and corpus callosum (Nosarti et al., 2004). In mid-adolescence, cortical grey matter is reduced in volume (Nosarti et al., 2002), specifically in temporal, frontal and occipital cortex, and white matter distribution is altered in frontal, parietal, temporal and occipital lobes (Nosarti, Giouroukou et al., 2008; see Plate 3.1). Using diffusion tensor MRI (DT-MRI), which tells us about the microstructure of white matter, including its coherence, its organization, and the density and degree of myelination, Skranes et al. (2007), Vangberg et al. (2006) and Kontis et al. (2009) have demonstrated white matter disturbances in the internal capsule and corpus callosum in premature adolescents and young adults. Some of these cortical and subcortical abnormalities are associated with cognitive impairment and executive function (Nosarti, Giouroukou et al., 2008), and in the domains of memory (Giménez et al., 2004) and language (Allin et al., 2001, Giménez et al., 2006, Nosarti et al., 2004). Others, such as the caudate nucleus, have been associated with behavioural problems—such as attention deficit–hyperactivity symptoms (Nosarti, Allin, Frangou, Rifkin, & Murray, 2005).

But damage to the brain may well be only part of the story. We have also to consider the effects of early brain lesions on overall later neurodevelopment. Alterations in key structural brain regions after VPT birth are likely to cause changes in the structure and function of widespread brain systems. For example, development of alternative neural pathways could enable the compromised brain to maintain its cognitive performance. Functional MRI (fMRI) techniques can provide a window into this restructuring in a way that is not shown on structural MRI. For example, there may be residual responsiveness within regions of partial brain damage, or abnormal responses distant to the brain-damaged area. Thus, fMRI studies have shown that VPT adolescents have differential neural activation patterns relative to controls in a variety of cognitive tasks including spatial memory (Curtis, Zhuang, Townsend, Hu, & Nelson, 2006) and response inhibition and selective attention allocation processing (Nosarti et al., 2006). A few fMRI studies have selected preterm participants on the basis of known structural brain alterations. Thus adolescent VPT boys with thinning or atrophy of the corpus callosum have altered patterns of neural activation to auditory and visual tasks (Santhouse et al., 2002) and phonological and orthographic processing (Rushe et al., 2004). Recently, we reported altered patterns of activation in a fronto-parietal-cerebellar network during tests of attention allocation and inhibitory control in VPT young adults (mean age 20 years; Lawrence et al., 2009). During paired associate learning, which is an essential, everyday cognitive operation, VPT participants compared to controls showed differential activation in the hippocampus (Giménez et al., 2004) and in fronto-parieto-occipital networks and the caudate nucleus (Narberhaus et al., 2009; see Plate 3.2). Similar abnormalities of activation have been found in individuals with schizophrenia using similar fMRI tasks (Hall et al., 2009; Koch et al., 2008).

Adolescent brain development after preterm birth

Since adolescence is a crucial developmental period, with obvious relevance to the neurodevelopmental hypothesis of psychosis, we have endeavoured to carry out a truly longitudinal study of brain development during this time. The experimental design was a longitudinal case-control study, with 72 VPT and 34 term-born controls scanned twice—first in adolescence (14–15 years) and again in young adulthood (19 years) using a standard structural MRI sequence. The change in size of various brain regions over this time was assessed, along with young adult mental health, using the General Health Questionnaire (GHQ-12; Werneke, Goldberg, Yalcin, & Ustun, 2000) and cognitive function, using the Wechlser Abbreviated Scale of Intelligence (Wechsler, 1999).

The trajectories of total grey matter and white matter change were similar in VPT and term control groups. That is, grey matter was decreasing and white matter increasing, as would be predicted from the normative studies discussed above. At this relatively crude level of analysis, brain development thus appeared normal in preterm born adolescents. However, on looking more closely, we found unexpected deviations in the adolescent development of two brain structures in the preterm group—the corpus callosum and the cerebellum. Furthermore, these deviations had functional consequences. They are discussed below.

The incredible shrinking cerebellum

The first unexpected finding was that the cerebellum, which we had previously found to be reduced in size in VPT individuals, got smaller in this group between 14 and 19 years. The decrement was about 3% in the VPT group, compared to no apparent change in the control group (Parker et al., 2008). What is more, this shrinking of the cerebellum had functional consequences—it was associated with worse self-reported mental health (in the GHQ domains of: concentration; feeling useful; confidence; decision-making capacity; and feelings of worthlessness).

The amazing expanding corpus callosum

In both VPT and control groups, the corpus callosum was expanding between 14 and 19 years—in the term control group it grew by around 3% (consistent with the growth of white matter overall, and with what was already known about the developmental course of the corpus callosum; Giedd et al., 1996; Pujol, Vendrell, Junqué, Martí-Vilata, & Capdevila, 1993). In the VPT group, the corpus callosum grew by a much larger amount—approximately 13%—and again this had functional consequences. The more the corpus callosum expanded, the higher was the IQ score at age 19 (Allin et al., 2007).

Making sense of adolescent brain development

One possibility is that these alterations of developmental trajectory represent developmental delays. For example, it is possible that the great expansion of the corpus callosum and the shrinking of the cerebellum are normal developmental events, but ones that usually happen earlier in life—and that have presumably already happened in our control group in childhood or earlier in adolescence. However, there is little evidence to support this. In the case of the cerebellum, there is unfortunately little normative data to draw on. The corpus callosum has been better studied, but here the data do not support a developmental spurt occurring before 14 years. Giedd et al. (1996) reported a linear association between age and corpus callosum size, and Pujol et al. (1993) put the timing of peak growth between 15 and 20 years.

If developmental delay is not the mechanism, could this be a developmental process that is specific to VPT adolescents in some way? There are good reasons for suspecting that the cerebellum is developmentally vulnerable. Cerebellar granule cells are actively differentiating and migrating around the time of VPT birth (Rakic, 2002), and it has been suggested that they are therefore especially vulnerable to the consequences of VPT birth, like hypoxia/ischaemia, infections and deficits in nutrition (Johnston, 1998; Sohma, Mito, Mizuguchi, & Takashima, 1995). This would result in a deficit of granule cell numbers, or in their dendritic connections, which would in turn lead to a reduction in the cerebellum's processing power (Leiner, Leiner, & Dow, 1993), or a loss of cerebellar "reserve". This could impair cerebellar function in many neural networks of which it is a part, including those underlying cognitive function and affect regulation (Makris et al., 2003; Schmahmann & Sherman, 1998). Speculatively, a cerebellum that has a reduced computational "reserve" might struggle to cope with the increased social, cognitive and behavioural demands imposed on it, as the individual makes the transition from adolescence to adulthood. Cerebellar deficits associated with cognitive function have been reported by our group in VPT 14-year-olds (Allin et al., 2001, 2005).

Young adults born very preterm have withdrawn and less exploratory personality styles (Allin et al., 2006; Hack et al., 2007; Pyhälä et al., 2009). Could cerebellar changes therefore simply be the physiological consequence of living a relatively "quiet life"? However, it is hard to see how a relatively restricted environment would cause the cerebellum to decrease while the corpus callosum simultaneously grows, especially since white matter is known to change in response to behavioural demands (Bengtsson et al., 2005; Schmithorst & Wilke, 2002). This underlines how much we have yet to discover about how the brain changes during development and in response to environmental changes.

Environmental influences are present right from the beginning, of course. For example, the physical environment of the neonatal intensive care unit can have a long-lasting impact on nociceptive circuits, leading to alterations in behavioural responses to pain (Fitzgerald, 2005). Clinical trials have been conducted into the effects of reducing the potential harshness of the early ICU environment, such as the Neonatal Individualized Developmental Care and Assessment Program

(NIDCAP). This programme has been shown to influence clinical developmental outcome and also brain development itself. Infants who received NIDCAP demonstrated increased brain "connectivity"—shown by increased electroencephalogram (EEG) coherence in frontal and occipital cortices and higher relative anisotropy (measured by DT-MRI) in the internal capsule (Als et al., 2004). Although at a preliminary stage, such research demonstrates the potential for using neuroimaging measures as biomarkers to evaluate the impact of neurological interventions.

A model of adolescent plasticity after preterm birth

We have used the above observations to develop a rudimentary model of adolescent neurodevelopment after preterm birth. We propose that cerebellar changes are a primary deficit, and corpus callosum growth a compensatory response. A cerebellum that has been impaired by birth injury may fail to cope adequately with the behavioural and social challenges of adolescence. Enhancement of inter-hemispheric connections through the corpus callosum may represent a plastic response through which the brain partially compensates for this deficit. Interestingly, both parts of this simplistic model, the deficit (the cerebellum) and the plastic response (the white matter growth) might be expected to cause alterations of functional and structural connectivity that have been postulated to underlie psychosis. Such functional dysconnectivity has been recently documented in VPT adolescents (Schafer et al., 2009). We are currently focusing on longitudinal changes in other brain regions, which will help to refine this model.

Summary

Very preterm birth is an "obstetric complication", implicated in the aetiology of psychosis. Individuals born VPT are at risk of early neurodevelopmental lesions, and the work that we report here suggests that their neurodevelopment during adolescence is altered as a result. Clearly a lot of work needs to be done on this model, and clarifying the role of genes, upbringing and environmental exposures such as cannabis use will also be important. We can't fully understand our brains without considering the developmental processes that modelled them, and continue to re-model them to adapt to changing circumstances throughout our lives.

References

Abernethy, L. J., Palaniappan, M., & Cooke, R. W. (2002). Quantitative magnetic resonance imaging of the brain in survivors of very low birth weight. *Archives of Disease in Childhood*, *87*, 279–283.

Allin, M. P. G., Matsumoto, H., Santhouse, A. M., Nosarti, C., Al-Asady, M. H. S., Stewart, A. L., et al. (2001). Cognitive and motor function and the size of the cerebellum in adolescents born very preterm. *Brain*, *124*, 60–66.

Allin, M. P. G., Nosarti, C., Narberhaus, A., Walshe, M., Frearson, S., Wyatt, J., et al. (2007). Growth of the corpus callosum in adolescents born preterm. *Archives of Pediatrics and Adolescent Medicine*, *161*, 1183–1189.

Allin, M. P. G., Rooney, M., Cuddy, M., Wyatt, J., Walshe, M., Rifkin, L., et al. (2006). Personality in young adults who are born preterm. *Pediatrics*, *117*, 309–316.

Allin, M. P. G., Salaria, S., Nosarti, C., Wyatt, J., Rifkin, L., & Murray, R. M. (2005). Vermis and lateral lobes of the cerebellum in adolescents born very preterm. *NeuroReport*, *16*, 1821–1824.

Als, H., Duffy, F. H., McAnulty, G. B., Rivkin, M. J., Vajapeyam, S., Mulkern, R. V., et al. (2004). Early experience alters brain function and structure. *Pediatrics*, *113*, 846–857.

Ashtari, M., Cervellione, K. L., Hasan, K. M., Wu, J., McIlree, C., Kester, H., et al. (2007). White matter development during late adolescence in healthy males: A cross-sectional diffusion tensor imaging study. *NeuroImage*, *35*, 501–510.

Aylward, G. P. (2005). Neurodevelopmental outcomes of infants born prematurely. *Journal of Developmental and Behavioural Pediatrics*, *26*, 427–440.

Bengtsson, S. L., Nagy, Z., Skare, S., Forsman, L., Forssberg, H., & Ullen, F. (2005). Extensive piano practice has regionally specific effects on white matter development. *Nature Neuroscience*, *8*, 1148–1150.

Blakemore, S.-J. (2008). The social brain in adolescence. *Nature Reviews Neuroscience*, *9*, 267–277.

Cannon, M., Jones, P. B., & Murray, R. M. (2002). Obstetric complications and schizophrenia: Historical and meta-analytic review. *American Journal of Psychiatry*, *159*, 1080–1092.

Chklovskii, D. B., Mel, B. W., & Svoboda, K. (2004). Cortical rewiring and information storage. *Nature*, *431*, 782–788.

Curtis, W. J., Zhuang, J., Townsend, E. L., Hu, X., & Nelson, C. A. (2006). Memory in early adolescents born prematurely: A functional magnetic resonance imaging investigation. *Developmental Neuropsychology*, *29*, 341–377.

Fitzgerald, M. (2005). The development of nociceptive circuits. *Nature Reviews Neuroscience*, *6*, 507–520.

Foulder-Hughes, L. A., & Cooke, R. W. I. (2003). Motor, cognitive and behavioural disorders in children born very preterm. *Developmental Medicine and Child Neurology*, *45*, 97–103.

Giedd, J. N., Blumenthal, J., Jeffries, N. O., Castellanos, F. X., Liu, H., Zijdenbos, A., et al. (1999). Brain development during childhood and adolescence: A longitudinal MRI study. *Nature Neuroscience*, *2*, 861–863.

Giedd, J. N., Rumsey, J. M., Castellanos, F. X., Rajapakse, J. C., Kaysen, D., Vaituzis, A. C., et al. (1996). A quantitative MRI study of the corpus callosum in children and adolescents. *Developmental Brain Research*, *91*, 274–280.

Giménez, M., Junqué, C., Narberhaus, A., Botet, F., Bargallo, N., & Mercader, J. M. (2006). Correlations of thalamic reductions with verbal fluency impairment in those born prematurely. *NeuroReport*, *17*, 463–466.

Giménez, M., Junqué, C., Narberhaus, A., Caldu, X., Salgado-Pineda, P., Bargallo, N., et al. (2004). Hippocampal gray matter reduction associates with memory deficits in adolescents with history of prematurity. *NeuroImage*, *23*, 869–877.

Gogtay, N., Giedd, J. N., Lusk, L., Hayashi, K. M., Greenstein, D., Vaituzis, A. C., et al. (2004). Dynamic mapping of human cortical development during childhood through early adulthood. *Proceedings of the National Academy of Sciences*, *101*, 8174–8179.

Hack, M., Cartar, L., Schluchter, M., Klein, N., & Forrest, C. B. (2007). Self-perceived health, functioning and well-being of very low birth weight infants at age 20 years. *Journal of Pediatrics*, *151*, 635–641.e2.

Hall, J., Whalley, H. C., Marwick, K., McKirdy, J., Sussmann, J., Romaniuk, L., et al. (2009). Hippocampal function in schizophrenia and bipolar disorder. *Psychological Medicine*, *7*, 1–10.

Huppi, P. S., Warfield, S., Kikinis, R., Barnes, P. D., Zientara, G. P., Jolesz, F. A., et al. (1998). Quantitative magnetic resonance imaging of brain development in premature and mature newborns. *Annals of Neurology*, *43*, 224–235.

Johnston, M. V. (1998). Selective vulnerability in the neonatal brain. *Annals of Neurology*, *44*, 155–156.

Koch, K., Wagner, G., Nenadic, I., Schachtzabel, C., Schultz, C., Roebel, M., et al. (2008). Fronto-striatal hypoactivation during correct information retrieval in patients with schizophrenia: An fMRI study. *Neuroscience*, *153*, 54–62.

Kontis, D., Catani, M., Cuddy, M., Walshe, M., Nosarti, C., Jones, D., et al. (2009). Diffusion tensor MRI of the corpus callosum and cognitive function in adults born preterm. *NeuroReport*, *20*, 424–428.

Lawrence, E. J., Rubia, K., Murray, R. M., McGuire, P. K., Walshe, M., Allin, M. P. G., et al. (2009). The neural basis of response inhibition and attention allocation as mediated by gestational age. *Human Brain Mapping*, *30*, 1038–1050.

Leiner, H. C., Leiner, A. L., & Dow, R. S. (1993). Cognitive and language functions of the human cerebellum. *Trends in Neurosciences*, *16*, 444–447.

Lindström, K., Lindblad, F., & Hjern, A. (2009). Psychiatric morbidity in adolescents and young adults born preterm: A Swedish national cohort study. *Pediatrics*, *123*, e47–e53. (doi:10.1542/peds.2008–1654)

Luna, B., & Sweeney, J. (2004). The emergence of collaborative brain function: fMRI studies of development of response inhibition. *Annals of New York Academy of Sciences*, *1021*, 296–309.

Makris, N., Hodge, S. M., Haselgrove, C., Kennedy, D. N., Dale, A., Fischl, B., et al. (2003). Human cerebellum: Surface-assisted cortical parcellation and volumetry with magnetic resonance imaging. *Journal of Cognitive Neuroscience*, *15*, 584–599.

Murray, R. M., Lappin, J., & Di Forti, M. (2008). Schizophrenia: From developmental deviance to dopamine dysregulation. *European Neuropsychopharmacology*, *18*, S129–S134.

Narberhaus, A., Lawrence, E., Allin, M. P. G., Walshe, M., McGuire, P. K., Rifkin, L., et al. (2009). Neural substrates of letter fluency processing in young adults who were born very preterm: Alterations in frontal and striatal regions. *NeuroImage*, *47*, 1884–1893.

Nosarti, C., Al-Asady, M. H. S., Frangou, S., Stewart, A. L., Rifkin, L., & Murray, R. M. (2002). Adolescents who were born very preterm have decreased brain volumes. *Brain*, *125*, 1616–1623.

Nosarti, C., Allin, M., Frangou, S., Rifkin, L., & Murray, R. M. (2005). Decreased caudate volume is associated with hyperactivity in adolescents born very preterm. *Biological Psychiatry*, *13*, 661–666.

Nosarti, C., Giouroukou, E., Healy, E., Rifkin, L., Walshe, M., Reichenberg, A., et al. (2008). Grey and white matter distribution in very preterm adolescents mediates neurodevelopmental outcome. *Brain*, *131*, 205–217.

Nosarti, C., Hultman, C. M., Cnattingius, S., Lambe, M., Rifkin, L., & Murray, R. M. (2008). Preterm birth and psychiatric outcome in adolescence and early adulthood: A study using the Swedish National Registers. *Schizophrenia Research*, *98*(Suppl. 1), 76.

Nosarti, C., Rubia, K., Smith, A. B., Frearson, S., Williams, S. C. R., Rifkin, L., et al. (2006). Altered functional neuroanatomy of response inhibition in adolescent males who were born very preterm. *Developmental Medicine & Child Neurology*, *4*, 265–271.

Nosarti, C., Rushe, T. M., Woodruff, P. W., Stewart, A. L., Rifkin, L., & Murray, R. M. (2004). Corpus callosum size and very preterm birth: Relationship to neuropsychological outcome. *Brain*, *127*, 2080–2089.

Parker, J., Mitchell, A., Kalpakidou, A., Walshe, M., Yeon-Jung, H., Nosarti, C., et al. (2008). Cerebellar growth and behavioural & neuropsychological outcome in preterm adolescents. *Brain*, *131*, 1344–1351.

Peper, J. S., Brouwer, R. M., Boomsma, D. I., Kahn, R. S., & Hulshoff Pol, H. E. (2007). Genetic influences on human brain structure: A review of brain imaging studies in twins. *Human Brain Mapping*, *28*, 464–473.

Powls, A., Botting, N., Cooke, R. W. I., & Marlow, N. (1995). Motor impairments in children 12 to 13 years old with a birthweight less than 1250 g. *Archives of Disease in Childhood*, *72*, F62–F66.

Pujol, J., Vendrell, P., Junqué, C., Martí-Vilata, J. L., & Capdevila, A. (1993). When does human brain development end? Evidence of corpus callosum growth up to adulthood. *Annals of Neurology*, *34*, 71–75.

Pyhälä, R., Räikkönen, K., Pesonen, A.-K., Heinonen, K., Hovi, P., Eriksson, J. G., et al. (2009). Behavioral inhibition and behavioral approach in young adults with very low birth weight—The Helsinki study of very low birth weight adults. *Personality and Individual Differences*, *46*, 106–110.

Rakic, P. (2002). Pre- and post-developmental neurogenesis in primates. *Clinical Neuroscience Research*, *2*, 29–39.

Rushe, T., Temple, C., Rifkin, L., Woodruff, P., Bullmore, E., Stewart, A., et al. (2004). Lateralisation of language function in young adults born very preterm. *Archives of Disease in Childhood Fetal and Neonatal Edition*, *89*, F112–F118.

Saigal, S., & Doyle, L. W. (2008). An overview of mortality and sequelae of preterm birth from infancy to adulthood. *Lancet 371*(9608), 261–269.

Santhouse, A. M., ffytche, D. H., Howard, R. J., Williams, S. C. R., Stewart, A. L., Rooney, M., et al. (2002). The functional significance of perinatal corpus callosum damage: An fMRI study in young adults. *Brain*, *125*, 1782–1792.

Schafer, R. J., Lacadie, C., Vohr, B., Kesler, S. R., Katz, K. H., Schneider, K. C., et al. (2009). Alterations in functional connectivity for language in prematurely born adolescents. *Brain*, *132*, 661–670.

Schmahmann, J. D., & Sherman, J. C. (1998). The cerebellar cognitive-affective syndrome. *Brain*, *121*, 561–579.

Schmithorst, V. J., & Wilke, M. (2002). Differences in white matter architecture between musicians and non-musicians: A diffusion tensor imaging study. *Neuroscience Letters*, *321*, 57–60.

Shaw, P., Kabani, N. J., Lerch, J. P., Eckstrand, K., Lenroot, R., Gogtay, N., et al. (2008). Neurodevelopmental trajectories of the human cerebral cortex. *The Journal of Neuroscience*, *28*, 3586–3594.

Skranes, J., Vangberg, T. R., Kulseng, S., Indredavik, M. S., Evensen, K. A., Martinussen, M., et al. (2007). Clinical findings and white matter abnormalities seen on diffusion tensor imaging in adolescents with very low birth weight. *Brain*, *130*, 654–666.

Sohma, O., Mito, T., Mizuguchi, M., & Takashima, S. (1995). The prenatal age critical for the development of the pontosubicular necrosis. *Acta Neuropathologica*, *90*, 7–10.

Sowell, E. R., Peterson, B. S., Thompson, P. M., Welcome, S. E., Henkenius, A. L., & Toga, A. W. (2003). Mapping cortical change across the human life span. *Nature Neuroscience*, *6*, 309–315.

Stewart, A. L., Thorburn, R. J., Hope, P. L., Goldsmith, M., Lipscomb, A. P., & Reynolds, E. O. (1983). Ultrasound appearance of the brain in very preterm infants and neurodevelopmental outcome at 18 months of age. *Archives of Disease in Childhood*, *58*, 598–604.

Taylor, H. G., Klein, N., Minich, N. M., & Hack, M. (2000). Middle-school-age outcomes in children with very low birthweight. *Child Development*, *71*, 1495–1511.

Toga, A. W., Thompson, P. M., & Sowell, E. (2006). Mapping brain maturation. *Trends in Neurosciences*, *29*, 148–159.

Vangberg, T. R., Skranes, J., Dale, A. M., Martinussen, M., Brubakk, A. M., & Haraldseth, O. (2006). Changes in white matter diffusion anisotropy in adolescents born prematurely. *NeuroImage*, *32*, 1538–1548.

Volpe, J. J. (2009). Brain injury in premature infants: A complex amalgam of destructive and developmental disturbances. *Lancet Neurology*, *8*, 110–124.

Walshe, M., McDonald, C., Taylor, M., Zhao, J., Sham, P., Grech, A., et al. (2005). Obstetric complications in patients with schizophrenia and their unaffected siblings. *European Psychiatry*, *20*, 28–34.

Walshe, M., Rifkin, L., Rooney, M., Healy, E., Fern, A., Wyatt, J., et al. (2008). Psychiatric disorder in young adults born very preterm: Role of family history. *European Psychiatry*, *25*, 527–531.

Wechsler, D. (1999). *Abbreviated Scale of Intelligence*: New York, NY: The Psychological Corporation.

Werneke, U., Goldberg, D. P., Yalcin, I., & Ustun, B. T. (2000). The stability of the factor structure of the General Health Questionnaire. *Psychological Medicine*, *30*, 823–829.

4 The contribution of Nordic population registers to the search for the causes of schizophrenia and other psychiatric disorders

Peter B. Jones, Matti Isohanni, Jaana Suvisaari, Jari Haukka and Jouko Miettunen

Introduction

Many reviews of Nordic registers and their uses in medical research have focused on specific topics or on only one country (Cappelen & Lyshol, 2004; Gissler & Haukka, 2004; Mortensen, 2004; Munk-Jørgensen, Kastrup, & Mortensen, 1993). We describe a range of Nordic registers that have been used in psychiatric research and discuss a number of general issues related to register-based research. We then review a selection of studies in psychiatric epidemiology arising from Denmark, Finland, Norway and Sweden that have made use of such registers, and highlight some, such as a study of the psychiatric sequelae of viral infections of the nervous system during childhood, that we feel epitomize the scope for opportunistic research in this context.

Of the eight Nordic countries, the four largest, Sweden, Denmark, Finland and Norway, have many interwoven threads in their social and political histories. Their populations (9.3, 5.5, 5.3 and 4.8 million, respectively) have remained remarkably stable in spite of periods of emigration and, more recently, immigration. While the same basic systems of national and local government administration have been in place for centuries, there was early and prescient adoption of relevant computer systems throughout the region. This has set the scene for a range of important epidemiological studies in these countries that have contributed greatly to our understanding of the determinants and outcomes of many diseases. This is particularly the case for psychiatric epidemiology, an area that we recently reviewed (Miettunen et al., 2011). Here, we recast that review to reflect the influence and seminal contributions of Robin Murray.

General points regarding register-based research

The main registers used in psychiatric research are *psychiatric case registers* (Häfner & an der Heiden, 1986) and *administrative health and welfare registers* (Byrne, Regan, & Howard, 2005). Such case registers are usually kept locally and include all referrals to psychiatric services in a particular community; the Stockholm County In-patient Register is a good example (Allebeck & Wistedt, 1986). Truly nation-wide registers, such as the Norwegian Case Register of

Mental Disorders and the Danish Psychiatric Central Register, are found only in the Nordic countries. They are used for health-system planning (Bloor, 1995; Wierdsma, Sytema, van Os, & Mulder, 2008). Administrative registers, such as the Finnish Hospital discharge register, are maintained at the national level for largely administrative and management purposes, although they can be deployed as powerful tools for scientific research as described, below.

National registers have great strengths in terms of statistical power and representativeness; indeed, some approach their analysis by eschewing statistical testing because they *are* the population rather than merely a sample. They have enabled the investigation of associations involving rare exposures and/or disorders and high drop-out rates that would otherwise have been difficult or impossible to study. Many epidemiological studies have high drop-out rates and attrition for other reasons, problems that dog studies of severe mental illnesses such as schizophrenia, biasing results and limiting their interpretation (de Graaf, Bijl, Smit, Ravelli, & Vollebergh, 2000). Unlike the situation in most countries, in the Nordic region it is possible to compare participants and non-participants in clinical epidemiological studies in terms of prior information in the population registers and to model the effects of attrition (Haapea et al., 2007). Importantly, the registers concerned can be used for statistical and scientific purposes without specifically asking the subjects for their consent; obtaining informed consent for large study samples would be impossible for practical reasons and limits ambitious research in other countries with the Nordic approach. Thus, registers of this kind provide an excellent basis for efforts to improve health and welfare (Wierdsma et al., 2008).

Registers for use in psychiatric research

As mentioned above, the Nordic countries have quite similar administrative registers of relevance to health care, although their coverage over time and accessibility vary. Table 4.1 summarizes the coverage of selected health registers in the four countries. Most of the information available is in English as well as the relevant native tongue. Denmark and Finland have additional register centres

Table 4.1 Inception date for various nationwide health-care registers in Nordic countries

Register	*Denmark*	*Finland*	*Norway*	*Sweden*
Hospital discharge register	1969[1]	1967[2]	1990[3]	1965[4]
Causes of death register	1970[5]	1969	1951	1952
Disability pension register	1996	1962	1967	1971
Prescription register	1994	1994	2004	2005
Medical birth register	1973	1987	1967	1973
Cancer register	1987	1953	1953	1958

Notes: [1] Attempted suicide since 1989; [2] Full coverage since 1972; [3] The data are not identifiable to person (personally identifiable data are now being gathered and when finished will be available from 1 March 2007); [4] Full coverage since 1987; [5] Suicides.

where information and links related to register-based research are coordinated. We will briefly describe the various registers and focus on details in those from Finland, the content being generally similar to this in registers from Denmark, Norway and Sweden.

Representative national samples for research can be obtained in Finland from the Central Population Register, known also as the Population Information System, which is maintained by the Population Register Centre and local registry offices throughout the country (Statistics Finland, 2004). Similar systems and agencies exist in the other Nordic countries. The individual-level data include name and personal identity code, address, nationality and native language, marital status, dates of birth and death, and dates of emigration or immigration. The information is updated mainly by the authorities, but changes of address have to be notified by the individuals themselves. Information on the dead and those who have emigrated is also retained in the register, duly marked.

Hospital discharge registers

The most commonly used health-care registers are hospital discharge registers. The Finnish Hospital Discharge Register (FHDR), maintained by the National Institute for Health and Welfare, covers periods of treatment received in all public and private hospitals in Finland since the early 1970s. Data are listed regarding the beginning and end of each in-patient stay, together with the primary diagnosis and up to three subsidiary diagnoses and a hospital identification code. There is a negligible number of erroneous personal IDs in the Finnish administrative registers and the quality of the FHDR data has improved continuously (Pajunen et al., 2005). The FHDR and the Register of Causes of Death both use the ICD classification including complete diagnostic codes. Similar hospital discharge registers exist in all the Nordic countries. Information on out-patient treatments has also been included since the 1990s, first in Denmark and then in Sweden, although the coverage of the out-patient treatment data varies greatly.

The *validity and reliability* of an FHDR diagnosis of schizophrenia or schizophrenia spectrum psychosis (ICD-9 diagnosis code 295; World Health Organization, 2009) have been investigated in several studies, all indicating good concordance between clinical and research diagnoses for any psychosis (Arajärvi et al., 2005; Isohanni et al., 1997; Mäkikyrö et al., 1998; Pihlajamaa et al., 2008). Finnish clinical diagnoses made by practising psychiatrists have been found to be remarkably conservative or specific, with over 40% of cases with a research diagnosis of schizophrenia having a register (i.e., clinical) diagnosis of non-schizophrenic psychosis (Isohanni et al., 1997; Moilanen et al., 2003). It appears that Finnish clinicians use a narrow definition of schizophrenia in clinical practice, a finding not incompatible with that of Taiminen et al. (2001) who found rather poor validity for schizophrenia diagnoses, the kappa value between clinical diagnoses and the best-estimate research diagnoses being only .44 for schizophrenic disorders as subjects not given a clinical schizophrenia diagnoses are recorded as such on the register. The reliability of hospital diagnoses of schizophrenia has also been investigated in the other Nordic countries and has been found acceptable (Dalman, Broms, Cullberg, & Allebeck, 2002; Kristjansson, Allebeck, & Wistedt, 1987; Löffler et al., 1994). A twin study (Kieseppä, Partonen, Kaprio, & Lönnqvist, 2000) validated bipolar-disorder diagnoses in the FHDR, finding 92% accuracy for both bipolar I disorder and the manic type of schizoaffective disorder.

The reliability of other psychiatric diagnoses has not been investigated, although several studies have investigated the reliability of diagnoses of other medical conditions (Elo & Karlberg, 2009; Ingelsson, Arnlöv, Sundström, & Lind, 2005). When investigating less severe disorders it is important to remember that the registers cover only patients treated as in-patients in hospital and will underestimate the true incidence and prevalence figures, with those who appear on the registers having more severe, persistent or otherwise atypical disorder.

Medication data and pharmaco-epidemiology

Antidepressants and antipsychotics are some of the most widely prescribed drugs in the community. Randomized clinical trials (RCTs) provide the gold standard evidence regarding efficacy and effectiveness of drug treatment, but have drawbacks (Flay, 1986). Rigorous inclusion criteria mean that RCTs often include only a subset of people generally treated with a particular drug and, even in large trials, the samples are generally too small to detect rare but potentially dangerous side effects. While randomization underpins inference from clinical trials, selective and often massive drop-out and/or drop-in during a long-term trial, e.g., over 70% discontinuation of allocated treatment in the CATIE schizophrenia trials (Lieberman et al., 2005) and similar findings in the UK CUtLASS study (Jones et al., 2006), can considerably complicate the interpretation of the results and their application to "real-world" situations.

Due to these problems with RCTs, large-scale *observational register linkage studies* can provide invaluable, additional information on drug treatment. Nevertheless, these phase IV or post-marketing surveillance studies require high-quality register data on prescriptions and both community and hospital care. Such studies are particularly required for drugs such as antipsychotics, which are usually taken continuously for very long periods of time. Prescription registers and other sources of administrative data have become an important source of information for carrying out pharmaco-epidemiological studies, yielding data that can be used to study the pattern of medication use in large populations and to estimate individual exposure for assessments of the effectiveness and safety of drug treatment.

Prescription registers and medication reimbursement registers are the two pillars of this endeavour. All Nordic countries have *prescription databases* (Furu, 2008; Gaist, Sørensen, & Hallas, 1997). Similar in content, we present the Finnish prescription register as an exemplar. This contains information on all medications purchased in accordance with a doctor's prescription, provided that their cost exceeds the reimbursement threshold. This limitation restricts the use of the register in studies of very cheap but important drugs such as aspirin.

Furthermore, prescription databases do not cover drugs used in hospitals or routine care by hospitals or nursing homes. Despite these caveats, the prescription data available from the state-controlled Finnish Social Insurance Institution (SII) are rich. The data include the generic name of the drug, its anatomical therapeutic chemical (ATC) classification system code, the brand name (if any), the formulation and packaging, the amount, the date when the drug was purchased, the prescribing practice (primary vs. secondary health care), and the prescribing physician's area of specialization. The validity of the prescription database compared with patient-reported medication data in Nordic countries has been found to be good for antipsychotics and antidepressants though somewhat poorer for sedatives and hypnotics (Glintborg, Hillestrom, Olsen, Dalhoff, & Poulsen, 2007; Haukka, Suvisaari, Tuulio-Henriksson, & Lönnqvist, 2007).

Mortality registers

Mortality or cause of death registers are among the oldest registers in the Nordic region. The Finnish Causes of Death Register (FCDR), maintained by Statistics Finland, provides data on dates and causes of death and also stores death certificates. Statistics Finland has stored death certificates since 1936, with a computerized file beginning more recently in 1969. A large validation study concluded that none of the personal identification codes in the CDR was incomplete (Pajunen et al., 2005). The register includes the personal identification number of each deceased person, sex, age, place of residence and the principal, underlying and contributory causes of death.

The routine validation of death certificates coupled with, in some countries such as Finland, a relatively high proportion of causes of death confirmed by autopsy (Lahti & Penttilä, 2001) means that the Nordic cause of death registers have good validity by international standards (Johansson & Westerling, 2000). Cause of death registers have been used in psychiatric research, for studying such topics as mortality due to various somatic disorders, and especially suicides (Heilä, Haukka, Suvisaari, & Lönnqvist, 2005). When studying suicidal behaviour it is also possible to include data on suicide attempts, which may be included in hospital discharge registers as external causes of hospitalization (Haukka, Suominen, Partonen, & Lönnqvist, 2008).

Other registers

Several additional nationwide registers and biobanks include data collected more for the purposes of research than administration; some examples are given below. The Finnish Maternity Cohort, started in 1983, currently contains approximately 1.5 million serum samples from about 750,000 pregnant women (~ 98% of all pregnancies during that period). These samples can be used for scientific research and linked to data from other sources, including personal identification numbers, numbers of pregnancies and deliveries and places of residence (Holl et al., 2008). Denmark has been storing dried blood spot samples from all newborn infants since

1982 as a part of a neonatal screening programme. This biobank has been regulated by specific legislation since 1993, granting it a unique position among biological specimen banks. Specimens from this source can also be used for research purposes, and have been used to investigate prenatal and neonatal infections and their association with schizophrenia, for example (Mortensen et al., 2007a, 2007b).

In Sweden there are some *specific registers*, such as the Multi-generation Register and Quality Registers. The former provides information on everyone who has been resident in Sweden since 1960, who was born in 1932 or later and on their biological parents. This makes it possible to trace all first-degree relatives and second-degree relatives of these people who were alive in 1947 or later. The Quality Registers (www.kvalitetsregister.se) collect data on particular areas of health care, e.g., costs and outcomes, in order to motivate improvements. Of relevance to psychiatry, data were collected in 2009 regarding the treatment of eating disorders and substance dependence.

There is a strong tradition of twin studies in Nordic countries (Bergem, 2002; Kaprio, 2006) with many relying on registers. In Finland, for instance, multiple births since the 1950s can be identified through the use of family member links added in the early 1970s for all persons in the database of the Population Register Centre (Kaprio, 2006). Specific twin registers also exist (Bergem, 2002; Lichtenstein et al., 2002; Skytthe et al., 2006). Family registers have underpinned adoption studies of schizophrenia genetics in Finland (Tienari et al., 2000) and Denmark (Rosenthal, Wender, Kety, Welner, & Schulsinger, 1971); these studies also rely on other registers to find individuals with schizophrenia who have had a child adopted (e.g., adoption registers) and in following-up the adoptees (e.g., hospital discharge registers).

The Finnish and Swedish *conscript registers* have been also used for research purposes. The prototypic study of the association between cannabis use and later schizophrenia in Swedish conscripts being published more than twenty years ago (Andréasson, Allebeck, Engström, & Rydberg, 1987) and spawning a rash of replications and enhancements in this and other cohorts, worldwide. These findings have been prominent in Robin Murray's writings over the past decade and have supported his influence on government policy and clinical practice in this area (Arseneault, Cannon, Witton, & Murray, 2004); these findings are considered further below. The reasons that conscripts are so informative include the fact that they undergo a statutory medical examination, but men known to have severe handicaps or chronic diseases are generally excluded from the draft. The assessment usually takes place at 17–19 years of age and consists of a health examination and an IQ test. In the latter regard, the Finnish and Swedish *school and education registers* have also been used in psychiatric research (Isohanni et al., 1998).

Register research in Denmark

Denmark has been a pioneer of register-based research, in 1981 becoming the first country to entirely abandon questionnaire-based censuses and base its censuses solely on register data. The use of registers for psychiatric research purposes in Denmark has mainly encompassed epidemiological studies of schizophrenia, mania, depression and suicide. In their milestone work on the effects of family history and place and season of birth on the risk of schizophrenia, Mortensen, Pedersen, and Westergaard (1999) showed that although family history is a strong risk factor, other more common risk factors such as place and season of birth may play a more prominent role at the population level. They estimated that the population-attributable fraction (PAF) of having a parent or sibling with manifest schizophrenia was 5.5%, whereas that of factors summarized by place of birth amounted to a staggering 34.6%. This work required the linkage of the Danish Civil Registration System with the Danish Central Psychiatric Register. Later, the same group showed that the more urban the area of upbringing, the higher the risk of developing schizophrenia in adult life (Pedersen & Mortensen, 2001). Seminal research from Denmark has also included other risk factors for schizophrenia such as advanced paternal age (Byrne, Agerbo, Ewald, Eaton, & Mortensen, 2003), autoimmunity (Eaton et al., 2006), prenatal infections (Mortensen et al., 2007a, 2007b; Westergaard, Mortensen, Pedersen, Wohlfahrt, & Melbye, 1999), and prenatal maternal stress (Khashan et al., 2008).

The Danes have also investigated the outcomes of *children of parents with severe mental disorders*, finding, for example, that their perinatal mortality is elevated, an effect that persists during the first year of life (Bennedsen, Mortensen, Olesen, & Henriksen, 2001; King-Hele et al., 2007) and into adolescence and young adulthood (Webb, Pickles, Appleby, Mortensen, & Abel, 2007). The power of large-scale register linkage was also shown to great effect in a study negating any association between autism and exposure to measles, mumps and rubella (MMR) vaccination (Madsen et al., 2002), the material for which was obtained by linking data from the Danish Civil Registration System, Danish Central Psychiatric Register, vaccination data reported by general practitioners to the National Board of Health, the National Hospital Registry and the Danish Medical Birth Registry. The overall coverage was 537,303 children (82.0% vaccinated) and over two million person-years of follow-up through the period of risk for autism. The outcome was a body of strong evidence against the hypothesis that MMR vaccination causes autism, and an important plank of evidence to stem the tide of harm that had arisen from spurious claims that it did so, research at the very opposite end of the spectrum of quality and probity than that possible using these epidemiological approaches.

One example of a Danish *pharmaco-epidemiological register linkage study* used a population of 2.1 million individuals aged 50 years and over to study the association between increased use of antidepressants and decreasing suicide rates (Erlangsen, Canudas-Romo, & Conwell, 2008). The authors were able to show that only a small proportion of the individuals concerned were receiving treatment with antidepressants at the time of their death, and they concluded that active treatment with antidepressants seems to account for only 10% of the decline in the suicide rate. Another study in which the Danish Civil Registration System was linked with the Danish Central Psychiatric Register found no support for the hypothesis that depression independently increases the risk of cancer (Oksbjerg Dalton, Mellemkjaer, Olsen, Mortensen, & Johansen, 2002).

That many Danish studies have focused on *suicide* is due in large part to the very high suicide rate in Denmark during the 1980s. Nordentoft and colleagues (1993) showed that natural and unnatural mortality remained high 10 years after an attempted suicide. A nationwide study showed that people with mental disorders also run the risk of death by homicide and other unnatural causes (Hiroeh, Appleby, Mortensen, & Dunn, 2001). Risk factors for suicide are different for psychiatric patients, the emphasis being on high incomes and postgraduate employment, which does not appear to be the case in the general population (Agerbo, 2007). Frequent changes of residence in childhood were associated with an increased risk of suicide in a study that used the Danish Civil Registration System combined with the Central Psychiatric Register (Qin, Mortensen, & Pedersen, 2009).

Register research in Finland

The many and versatile registers available in Finland have underpinned many studies, some involving international scientific collaboration, and lead to substantial new findings of major clinical relevance. Several reports in the early 1990s (e.g., Munk-Jorgensen & Mortensen, 1992), including one by Robin Murray and colleagues (Der, Gupta, & Murray, 1990), suggested that the *incidence of schizophrenia* was declining. A Finnish study combined information from the hospital discharge register, pension register and medication reimbursement register and carried out an age-period-cohort analysis of changes in the incidence of schizophrenia among birth cohorts born between 1954 and 1965 (Suvisaari, Haukka, Transkanen, & Lönnqvist, 1999). The incidence had declined, and the effects of period and cohort on the change were both significant. While the effect of period reflects the operation of related confounding factors such as changes in diagnostic criteria, the cohort effect suggests that the intensity or frequency of one or more risk factors for schizophrenia may have decreased in these birth cohorts.

A recent Finnish study found a high *lifetime prevalence* of psychotic disorders (DSM-IV; American Psychiatric Association, 1994) in Finland, 3.1%, which rose to 3.5% when the non-responder group and their register diagnoses were included. Registers were the most important and reliable screening method, the kappa value for psychotic disorders being .80 for the hospital discharge register, while the Composite International Diagnostic Interview (CIDI) section on psychotic symptoms was able to identify only 27% of the persons with psychotic disorders, due to considerable underreporting of psychotic episodes and symptoms (Perälä et al., 2007). Researchers in Finland have found marked regional variation in the incidence and prevalence of schizophrenia, but negligible urban–rural variation (Haukka, Suvisaari, Varilo, & Lönnqvist, 2001; Perälä et al., 2008). The Finnish Adoptive Family Study of Schizophrenia used registers to follow up adoptees. The main finding of the study was that adoptees at high genetic risk are significantly more sensitive to adverse versus "healthy" rearing patterns in adoptive families than are adoptees at low genetic risk (Tienari et al., 2004). Studies of Finnish twin cohorts have also utilized registers in studies of various psychiatric disorders (Kaprio, 2006). Finnish twin studies based on national registers have found over

80% heritability for schizophrenia (T. Cannon, Kaprio, Lönnqvist, Huttunen, & Koskenvuo, 1998) and bipolar disorder (Kieseppä, Partonen, Haukka, Kaprio, & Lönnqvist, 2004).

The relationship between *antidepressant treatment and the risk of suicide and overall mortality* has been examined through a nationwide computerized database. Tiihonen and colleagues (2006) observed a substantially lower mortality in those when receiving a selective serotonin reuptake inhibitor. Current use of medication among the subjects who had used an antidepressant at some time was associated with a markedly decreased risk of completed suicide and mortality as compared with no current use of medication. The lower mortality was attributable to a decrease in cardiovascular and cerebrovascular deaths during selective serotonin reuptake inhibitor use. Later, these researchers also studied the association between *prescribed antipsychotic drugs and outcome* in cases of schizophrenia or schizoaffective disorders in the community, using national central registers and a series of 2,230 adults hospitalized in Finland (Tiihonen et al., 2009). Initial use of clozapine, a perphenazine depot and olanzapine had the lowest rates of discontinuation associated with them, while that for oral haloperidol was higher, but the first-mentioned drugs carried the lowest risk of rehospitalization. Mortality was markedly higher in patients not taking antipsychotics, and the risk of suicide was also high in these cases. Among second-generation antipsychotic drugs, clozapine was associated with a substantially lower mortality than any other antipsychotics (Tiihonen et al., 2009).

Many large, epidemiological, genetic or imaging studies are based on clinical series or other samples where representativeness is compromised. In the *birth cohort* setting it is possible to pool register data with clinical and observational data and avoid this to a large extent. The aim of the Northern Finland 1966 Birth Cohort has been to analyse the developmental pathways of schizophrenic psychoses from the fetal period to adulthood, especially with respect to risk factors and outcomes, including genome-wide analyses and brain morphology. The cases for the cohort have been obtained from the FHDR (see above). One aim has been to determine whether adult-onset schizophrenia is associated with abnormalities during pregnancy, delivery or the neonatal period (Jones, Rantakallio, Hartikainen, Isohanni, & Sipilä, 1998). Low birth weight (< 2,500 g) and a combination of low birth weight and short gestation (< 37 weeks) were more common among the subjects with schizophrenia. The same cohort data have also been used to study register-based outcomes (e.g., Miettunen et al., 2007) such as work periods and disability pensions; almost half of the patients with schizophrenic psychoses had not been pensioned off after an average follow-up of 10 years.

The possible role of viral infections as contributors to the aetiology of schizophrenia has a long history beginning with clinical accounts and the enigma of the season of birth effect (reviewed by Murray, 1994). Viral and other environmental hypotheses received more direct epidemiological support from a number of landmark studies from the Nordic countries. A report by Mednick, Machon, Huttunen, and Bonett (1988) suggested a putative link with prenatal exposure to influenza. They observed a higher than expected prevalence of schizophrenia in the Helsinki population with birthdates indicating that they were *in utero* during the 1957 influenza pandemic. This excited a great deal of interest, with an influential report from Robin Murray's group (O'Callaghan, Sham, Takei, Glover, & Murray, 1991) demonstrating a similar ecological association in the UK. This was a heady period for causal research in schizophrenia when environmental factors that might account for neurodevelopmental characteristics of the illness had been supported by epidemiological data from Swedish conscripts on the role of cannabis use and a resurgence of interest in obstetric complications (see, e.g., Cannon et al., 2002, for a review). However, an association with viral infections in early life and later schizophrenia had not yet been demonstrated in the same individuals. The North Finland 1966 birth cohort was to make an important contribution, investigating the association between childhood CNS infections and later schizophrenia and other psychoses by piecing together a multitude of routinely collected data. The full story is described by Rantakallio, Jones, Moring, and Von Wendt (1997) and Koponen et al. (2004).

Data concerning CNS infections in the cohort members up to 14 years of age were collected in several ways during the period from 1966 until 1980. The most important sources were records of admissions to the four children's hospitals in the area from 1966 to 1972 and, thereafter, the Finnish Hospital Discharge Register (FHDR, described above) until 1980. The records of neurological outpatient clinics in particular yielded additional cases.

The psychiatric outcomes of those exposed and unexposed to the infections were defined up until age 31 years; that is 1997. All cohort members over 16 who appeared on the FHDR until the end of 1994 and 1997 for any mental disorder (i.e., ICD-8 diagnoses 290–309, DSM-III-R diagnoses 290–316, and ICD-10 diagnoses F00–F69, F99; American Psychiatric Association, 1987; World Health Organization, 1965, 1977, 1992) were identified. All their case records were scrutinized and diagnoses were checked against the DSM-III-R (Isohanni et al., 1997; Moilanen et al., 2003). Age of onset of schizophrenia was identified from the first psychotic symptoms recorded in case notes. Comorbid diagnoses of substance-use disorder (DSM-III-R codes 303.9 and 305) and mental retardation (including borderline intellectual functioning; IQ 50–84; DSM-III-R codes 317.00 and V40.00) were also recorded. A proxy measure for clinical severity was obtained from the number of hospital treatment periods and length of stay in hospital. Father's social class, perinatal brain damage, mental retardation and childhood epilepsy were also recorded as potential mediating and confounding factors. Children were considered to have perinatal brain damage if they had an Apgar score of zero at one minute or less than five at 15 minutes, convulsions during the neonatal period, or a diagnosis of asphyxia, brain injury, or intraventricular haemorrhage at discharge, but did not have CNS malformation, chromosomal aberrations, or hereditary CNS degeneration.

There were 145 verified childhood CNS infections in the study population; 102 of them had been viral. The diagnostic validation in 1997 (age 31) identified 100 people (65 men) with schizophrenia, four of whom had had a CNS viral infection. The cumulative incidence rate ratio for schizophrenia following any CNS infection was 3.2 (1.2–8.4) with a population attributable risk of 2.7% (0.7–10.6). There were 55 cases of other, non-schizophrenia psychoses, none of whom had suffered a viral CNS infection.

None of the schizophrenia cases and two of the patients with other psychosis had had a bacterial infection. In schizophrenia patients two cases had Coxsackie B5 infection, while adenovirus 7 and mumps were recorded in one case each; three of these four cases of CNS infections were male. Thus, the cumulative incidence ratio of schizophrenia was even higher among those with a past viral CNS infection; 4.5 (95% CI 1.6–12.6). The clinical course variables of schizophrenia did not differ between those with or without a previous CNS infection.

Almost beyond the limits of epidemiology of this kind is the intriguing observation that the two subjects with Coxsackie B5 infection who later grew up to develop schizophrenia were among an epidemic of 17 newborn cases of this infection identified from July to August 1966, all except one occurring in the same maternity unit. Sixteen of these 17 cases were included in the schizophrenia study, one having emigrated and so left the risk-set. This gives an incidence of adult onset schizophrenia of 2/16 (12.5%) among those with neonatal Coxsackie B meningitis; the difference between this figure and the risk of schizophrenia among the unexposed group 96/10,791 (0.9%) is highly statistically significant, despite few cases contributing to the calculation. This shows the power of population-based research, where record linkage is enhanced by precise measures of exposure such as viral titres, and transcends the numbers involved. The approach to what might be called the sero-epidemiology of schizophrenia that builds on Robin Murray's contribution to knowledge about the infectious aetiology of schizophrenia has now been taken up in recent research in other birth cohorts. This has been particularly successful in North America and Denmark where maternal sera and neonatal blood samples are available (e.g., Mortensen et al., 2007a, 2007b), and in Sweden (Dalman et al., 2008) where a study of over 1.2 million children confirmed the association between viral CNS infection in children and later schizophrenia and the broader group of non-affective psychoses. It should be noted that the associations in the replication studies was smaller than in the Northern Finnish cohort, while another analysis that overlapped with the original study was, essentially, negative (Suvisaari, Mautemps, Haukka, Hovi, & Lönnqvist, 2003). The hegemony of meta-analysis will one day deliver its judgement but, in fact, it remains a mystery as to whether the Northern Finnish nursery concealed a clue regarding the causes of schizophrenia or whether chance simply threw it a double six.

Birth cohorts can effectively be reconstructed from registers collected for other reasons, just as case-control studies are always, at least conceptually, nested within a hypothetical cohort. Birth, health, child development and school records have been routinely archived in Finland. Mary Cannon, Finnish colleagues and others from Robin Murray's group (Cannon et al., 1999) used this rich store to undertake a case-control study of school performance and later schizophrenia nested within the cohort of people born in Helsinki during the decade beginning in 1951. Much work had indicated that childhood IQ, measured directly or manifested through school performance, would be lower in the children who would, as adults, develop schizophrenia (e.g., Jones, Rodgers, Murray, & Marmot, 1994), findings that have been interpreted as cognitive precursors of the disorder within a neurodevelopmental framework. Intriguingly, Cannon and colleagues showed that it was a non-academic factor of school performance, on which loaded the motoric activities of sports and handicrafts, that was associated with schizophrenia. This may, to some extent, be due to the particular measurement by Finnish teachers of their students' abilities in the cognitive domain, but does presage new interest in the links between motor systems and the neural basis of psychotic symptoms that have, themselves, been investigated in the Northern Finland 1966 Birth Cohort, mentioned above (Isohanni et al., 2001; Ridler et al., 2006). This latter study has been influential in current formulations of the, so called, neurodevelopmental hypothesis of schizophrenia whereas Cannon's Helsinki study, in finding an unexpected lack of association between developmental factors and criminological outcomes in the disorder (Cannon et al., 2002), showed that there is much more to schizophrenia than this developmental aspect.

Another example of register linkage was the work by Gissler, Hemminki, and Lönnqvist (1996), who determined rates of suicide associated with pregnancy according to certain characteristics of pregnancy and its outcome. Information on suicides was linked with the Finnish birth, abortion and hospital discharge registers to find out how many women who committed suicide had had a completed pregnancy during their last year of life. Given a mean annual suicide rate of 11.3 per 100,000, the rate associated with birth was significantly lower (5.9) and those associated with miscarriage (18.1) and induced abortion (34.7) were significantly higher.

Register research in Norway

Early Norwegian studies using the Norwegian Psychiatric Case Register were focused on topics such as admission rates for schizophrenia (Ødegard, 1971). Hansen, Arnesen, and Jacobsen (1997) studied total mortality among people admitted to psychiatric hospitals and concluded that mortality among psychiatric patients is still unsatisfactorily high, and that men constitute a special high-risk group. Subsequently they also studied cause-specific mortality among psychiatric patients after deinstitutionalization and found more cardiovascular deaths and unnatural deaths among such cases, particularly among men. Strand and Kunst (2006) studied suicide mortality using registry data on 613,807 Norwegians born between 1955 and 1965. Suicide mortality was higher among women with a privileged childhood socioeconomic position than among those of lower status. They concluded that downward mobility and failure to meet the high demands set by their well-educated parents, psychological distress, mental disorder, gender differences and social networks and norms were all possible mechanisms for this finding. Tellnes and colleagues (1992) analysed long-term sickness certification up until the end of 1990, based on data recorded by the National Insurance Administration. Sickness absence due to mental disorders occurred in 31 per 10,000 employed persons.

Hagen, Stovner, Skorpen, Pettersen, and Zwart (2008) linked genetic data from the Nord-Trondelag Health Study with antipsychotic medication data from the Norwegian prescription database. The Val158Met polymorphism in the *COMT* gene had no major impact on the number of individuals who had been prescribed antipsychotic medication, but the subjects with the Met/Met genotype were receiving the highest median daily doses of antipsychotics. The Prescription Database has shown trends in the use of selective serotonin reuptake inhibitors (SSRIs; Bramness, Hausken, Sakshaug, Skurtveit, & Rønning, 2005) and has been used in the investigation of the abuse potential of the muscle relaxant carisoprodol (Bramness, Furu, Engeleand, & Skurtveit, 2007). The Norwegian Twin Registers have also been used for research in psychiatry (Bergem, 2002), Kringlen (1968) having undertaken the first Norwegian twin study based on the Norwegian Twin Registers and having demonstrated that sampling techniques of earlier studies of schizophrenia had resulted in an overemphasis of genetic contribution to the disorder, a conclusion neglected for thirty years until reinforced by work from the Murray stable (Cardno et al., 1999).

Register research in Sweden

Sweden took a step towards promoting the use of health-care registers for research purposes by founding the Swedish Centre for Epidemiology in 1992, and outstanding epidemiological research based on Swedish registers has been published during the past 15 years. In particular, there is a strong tradition of *risk factor research* in Sweden, work which has included several landmark studies.

The landmark study mentioned already was the longitudinal follow-up of a *Swedish conscript cohort* that suggested that cannabis use in adolescence or young adulthood is a risk factor for schizophrenia (Andréasson et al., 1987). A later follow-up of the same cohort showed that there was a linear trend in the frequency of cannabis use and the risk of schizophrenia, with a 3.1-fold higher risk of schizophrenia among those who had used cannabis over 50 times compared to those who had never used it (Zammit, Allebeck, Andréasson, Lundberg, & Lewis, 2002). Although there have been several investigations into cannabis and psychosis, this Swedish study is still the only one that has been able to use schizophrenia diagnosis as the outcome, due to its large sample size and register-based outcome assessment, and it has been the prototype for other studies in this field.

The conscript cohort has been put to other use. Investigations carried out in many countries had suggested that the incidence and prevalence of schizophrenia is higher in large cities than in rural areas, it was assumed for a long time that this had been caused by geographical drift of persons with a higher risk of schizophrenia from rural to urban areas. Follow-up of the 1969–1970 Swedish conscripts showed that it was urban upbringing, not urban residence that increased the risk of schizophrenia (Lewis, David, Andréasson, & Allebeck, 1992). Another Swedish study showed that the effect of urban place of birth was not related to obstetric complications or socioeconomic status in childhood (Harrison et al., 2003).

Swedish research groups have actively used the *Swedish birth register* to investigate pre- and perinatal risk factors for severe mental disorders. Two groups (Dalman, Allebeck, Cullberg, Grunewald, & Köster, 1999; Hultman, Sparen, Takei, Murray, & Cnattingius, 1999) showed that several specific obstetric complications increase the risk of schizophrenia and to some extent also the risk of affective and reactive psychoses attributable to multi-parity. Other Swedish studies on childhood risk factors for psychotic disorders have found that serious viral infections of the central nervous system (Dalman et al., 2008; see above for discussion of this association) and poor school performance both increase the risk of non-affective, schizophrenia-like psychosis (David, Malmberg, Brandt, Allebeck, & Lewis, 1997; MacCabe et al., 2008), but not bipolar disorder (MacCabe et al., 2010), though set in the context of a Finnish conscript study (Tiihonen et al., 2005) the situation is complex. These two studies were examples of only a few register studies to focus on bipolar disorder where, even with large populations the numbers of cases often restrict the possibilities for research. The Swedish sample has also been used to demonstrate the wide range of adverse pregnancy outcomes in mothers with affective psychosis (MacCabe et al., 2007) and in those with schizophrenia (Nilsson, Lichtenstein, Cnattingius, Murray, & Hultman, 2002).

A more recent Swedish family study has combined the multi-generation register and the hospital discharge register in order to investigate whether schizophrenia and bipolar disorder share any common genetic links (Lichtenstein et al., 2009). They reported 64% heritability for schizophrenia and a very similar level of 59% heritability for bipolar disorder. The genetic correlation between the two was high at .60. One key study concerning *mortality in cases of psychiatric disorders* was that published by Allebeck and Wistedt (1986), which showed that persons with schizophrenia have an increased risk of mortality from all causes of death and from suicide in particular. A recent Swedish follow-up study compared the risk of death by suicide after a suicide attempt in different psychiatric disorders, and found the highest risks of suicide to exist among patients with schizophrenia and unipolar depressive and bipolar disorders (Tidemalm, Långström, Lichtenstein, & Runeson, 2008). The Swedish Twin Registry has been used to investigate the heritability of major depression, Kendler, Gatz, Gardner, and Pederson (2006) demonstrating for the first time that the heritability of liability to major depression was significantly higher in women (42%) than men (29%).

Work in Iceland

We have not included here an account of Iceland's contribution (population of 0.3 million) of its own nationwide registers. The current focus there is on the anonymous Icelandic Healthcare Database, which has been constructed by a private company, deCODE Genetics. This database has opened unique possibilities for modelling disease risk as a function of genetic and environmental factors and has resulted in the identification of risk genes for several disorders, including schizophrenia (Stefansson et al., 2002, 2008).

Conclusions

Many investigators have used the unique resources of the Nordic registers to discover much about the occurrence, causes, natural history and treatments of psychiatric illness and the psychoses, in particular. That Robin Murray is among the authors of more than 10% of the studies cited in this review demonstrates his personal impact and perspicacity in this field. Nationwide hospital registers have been used to study admission rates and also, in combination with interview data, to assess the incidence and prevalence of certain disorders. Hospital registers have also commonly been used for case finding, especially in more severe disorders such as schizophrenia. Registers from early life, such as those of births, have been used as sources for exposure variables in connection with various register or interview outcomes (e.g., suicides), and registers have enabled hypotheses to be tested that otherwise would have been difficult to study reliably, e.g., due to the rarity of the events or disorders concerned. The registers have contributed to many areas of psychiatric epidemiology but perhaps most to schizophrenia where a number of themes, including cannabis, neurodevelopment, obstetric complications and early life viral infections have drawn upon and contributed to the work of Robin Murray and his colleagues both in England and abroad.

As in many areas of life, the devil is in the detail and there are major methodological and administrative challenges of this work. In principle (but not always in practice) it is easy to obtain, analyse and publish register data. In truth, though, the use of register data includes both practical and methodological tests (Gissler & Haukka, 2004), as well as being an honour and privilege for the researchers concerned. Register data are usually collected for administrative or clinical purposes, and not for scientific study. The data are often superficial, and exposure and outcome definitions may be imprecise. The variables used may reflect events that are easy to categorize, but not usually the detailed measures needed for analysing the psychological and qualitative traits necessary for some psychiatric research. Information on family and social environments is scarce and while we can obtain information on prescribed medication, we have no information on why the doctor chose this particular medication or, just as in clinical practice, whether patients took it or threw it away. Unidentified and residual confounding factors are major limitations of register-based research, though new modelling techniques can negate these, at least in part (Hernán, Cole, Margolick, Cohen, & Robins, 2005).

Are Nordic countries an epidemiologist's paradise?

A great supporter of European psychiatry and past president of the Association of European Psychiatrists (AEP), Robin Murray convened the 1996 Congress in London (http://www.europsy.net/what-we-do/past-congresses/) where he suggested that one of us (PBJ) organize a symposium on this title, "The Nordic countries: An epidemiologist's paradise". This title without the question mark seemed appropriate to the organizers whereas it drew wry smiles from the Nordic speakers and audience. In the real world, hard work, data processing, methodological skills, teamwork and diplomacy are needed for successful register-based studies.

At best, Nordic registers are population-based and achieve high levels of ascertainment so are ideal for epidemiological purposes with few of the usual biases inherent in many epidemiological surveys. Explanatory variables and outcome data are collected prospectively and the number of cases can be large, so that it is possible to investigate rare exposure events such as the Coxsackie B and schizophrenia story outlined above. In the future, increasing international collaboration and the combining of different registers within and between countries will lead to further possibilities for studying novel topics. Many of the investigations will have their origins in studies of schizophrenia, and many of those were shaped by Robin Murray's ideas.

Acknowledgements

This work has been supported by the Academy of Finland (#125 853, JM; #129 434, JS; #110 143, MI) and the Sigrid Jusélius Foundation (MI). PBJ acknowledges the support of the NIHR CLAHRC for Cambridgeshire & Peterborough and the Wellcome Trust.

References

Agerbo, E. (2007). High income, employment, postgraduate education, and marriage: A suicidal cocktail among psychiatric patients. *Archives of General Psychiatry*, *64*, 1377–1384.

Allebeck, P., & Wistedt, B. (1986). Mortality in schizophrenia. A ten-year follow-up based on the Stockholm County inpatient register. *Archives of General Psychiatry*, *43*, 650–653.

American Psychiatric Association. (1987). *Diagnostic and statistical manual of mental disorders* (3rd ed. revised; DSM-III-R). Washington, DC: American Psychiatric Association.

American Psychiatric Association. (1994). *Diagnostic and statistical manual of mental disorders* (4th ed.; DSM-IV). Washington, DC: American Psychiatric Association.

Andréasson, S., Allebeck, P., Engström, A., & Rydberg, U. (1987). Cannabis and schizophrenia. A Longitudinal study of Swedish conscripts. *Lancet*, *26*;2(8574), 1483–1486.

Arajärvi, L., Suvisaari, J., Suokas, J., Schreck, M., Haukka, J., Partonen, T., et al. (2005). Prevalence and diagnosis of schizophrenia based on register, case record and interview data in an isolated Finnish birth cohort born 1940–1969. *Social Psychiatry and Psychiatric Epidemiology*, *40*, 808–816.

Arseneault, L., Cannon, M., Witton, J., & Murray, R. M. (2004). Causal association between cannabis and psychosis: Examination of the evidence. *British Journal of Psychiatry*, *184*, 110–117.

Bennedsen, B. E., Mortensen, P. B., Olesen, A. V., & Henriksen, T. B. (2001). Congenital malformations, stillbirths, and infant deaths among children of women with schizophrenia. *Archives of General Psychiatry*, *58*, 674–679.

Bergem, A. L. (2002). Norwegian Twin Registers and Norwegian twin studies—An overview. *Twin Research*, *5*, 407–414.

Bloor, R. N. (1995). Setting up a psychiatric case register. *Advances in Psychiatric Treatment*, *1*, 86–91.

Bramness, J. G., Furu, K., Engeland, A., & Skurtveit, S. (2007). Carisoprodol use and abuse in Norway: A pharmaco-epidemiological study. *British Journal of Clinical Pharmacology, 64*, 210–218.

Bramness, J. G., Hausken, A. M., Sakshaug, S., Skurtveit, S., & Rønning, M. (2005). Prescription of selective serotonin reuptake inhibitors 1990–2004. *Tidsskrift for den Norske Laegeforening, 125*, 2470–2473.

Byrne, M., Agerbo, E., Ewald, H., Eaton, W. W., & Mortensen, P. B. (2003). Parental age and risk of schizophrenia. A case-control study. *Archives of General Psychiatry, 60*, 673–678.

Byrne, N., Regan, C., & Howard, L. (2005). Administrative registers in psychiatric research: A systematic review of validity studies. *Acta Psychiatrica Scandinavica, 112*, 409–414.

Cannon, M., Huttunen, M. O., Tanskanen, A. J., Arseneault L., Jones, P. B., & Murray, R. M. (2002). Perinatal and childhood risk factors for later criminality and violence in schizophrenia: Longitudinal, population-based study. *British Journal of Psychiatry, 180*, 496–501.

Cannon, M., Jones, P., Huttunen, M. O., Tanskanen, A., Huttunen, T., Rabe-Hesketh, S., et al. (1999). School performance in Finnish children and later development of schizophrenia: A population-based longitudinal study. *Archives of General Psychiatry, 56*, 457–463.

Cannon, T. D., Kaprio, J., Lönnqvist, J., Huttunen, M., & Koskenvuo, M. (1998). The genetic epidemiology of schizophrenia in a Finnish twin cohort. A population-based modeling study. *Archives of General Psychiatry, 55*, 67–74.

Cappelen, I., & Lyshol, H. (2004). An overview of the health registers in Norway [in Norwegian, with English abstract]. *Norsk Epidemiologi, 14*, 33–38.

Cardno, A. G., Marshall, E. J., Coid, B., Macdonald, A. M., Ribchester, T. R., Davies, N. J., et al. (1999). Heritability estimates for psychotic disorders: The Maudsley twin psychosis series. *Archives of General Psychiatry, 56*(2), 162–168.

Dalman, C., Allebeck, P., Cullberg, J., Grunewald, C., & Köster, M. (1999). Obstetric complications and the risk of schizophrenia. A longitudinal study of a national birth cohort. *Archives of General Psychiatry, 56*, 234–240.

Dalman, C., Allebeck, P., Gunnell, D., Harrison, G., Kristensson, K., Lewis, G., et al. (2008). Infections in the CNS during childhood and the risk of subsequent psychotic illness: A cohort study of more than one million Swedish subjects. *American Journal of Psychiatry, 165*, 59–65.

Dalman, C., Broms, J., Cullberg, J., & Allebeck, P. (2002). Young cases of schizophrenia identified in a national inpatient register. *Social Psychiatry and Psychiatric Epidemiology, 37*, 527–531.

David, A. S., Malmberg, A., Brandt, L., Allebeck, P., & Lewis, G. (1997). IQ and risk for schizophrenia: A population-based cohort study. *Psychological Medicine, 27*, 1311–1323.

de Graaf, R., Bijl, R. V., Smit, F., Ravelli, A., & Vollebergh, W. A. M. (2000). Psychiatric and sociodemographic predictors of attrition in a longitudinal study. *American Journal of Epidemiology, 152*, 1039–1047.

Der, G., Gupta, S., & Murray, R. M. (1990). Is schizophrenia disappearing? *Lancet, 335*, 513–516.

Eaton, W. W., Byrne, M., Ewald, H., Mors, O., Chen, C.-Y., Esben, A., et al. (2006). Association of schizophrenia and autoimmune diseases: Linkage of Danish national registers. *American Journal of Psychiatry, 163*, 521–528.

Elo, S. L., & Karlberg, I. H. (2009). Validity and utilization of epidemiological data: A study of ischaemic heart disease and coronary risk factors in a local population. *Public Health, 123*, 52–57.

Erlangsen, A., Canudas-Romo, V., & Conwell, Y. (2008). Increased use of antidepressants and decreasing suicide rates: A population-based study using Danish register data. *Journal of Epidemiology and Community Health*, *62*, 448–454.

Flay, B. R. (1986). Efficacy and effectiveness trials (and other phases of research) in the development of health promotion programs. *Preventive Medicine*, *15*, 451–474.

Furu, K. (2008). Establishment of the nationwide Norwegian prescription database (NorPD)—New opportunities for research in pharmaco-epidemiology in Norway. *Norsk Epidemiologi*, *18*, 129–136.

Gaist, D., Sørensen, H. T., & Hallas, J. (1997). The Danish prescription registries. *Danish Medical Bulletin*, *44*, 445–448.

Gissler, M., & Haukka, J. (2004). Finnish health and social welfare registers in epidemiological research. *Norsk Epidemiology*, *14*, 113–120.

Gissler, M., Hemminki, E., & Lönnqvist, J. (1996). Suicides after pregnancy in Finland, 1987–94: Register linkage study. *British Medical Journal*, *313*, 1431–1434.

Glintborg, B., Hillestrom, P. R., Olsen, L. H., Dalhoff, K. P., & Poulsen, H. E. (2007). Are patients reliable when self-reporting medication use? Validation of structured drug interviews and home visits by drug analysis and prescription data in acutely hospitalized patients. *Journal of Clinical Pharmacology*, *47*, 1440–1449.

Haapea, M., Miettunen, J., Veijola, J., Lauronen, E., Tanskanen, P., & Isohanni, M. (2007). Non-participation may bias the results of a psychiatric survey. An analysis from the survey including magnetic resonance imaging within the Northern Finland 1966 Birth Cohort. *Social Psychiatry and Psychiatric Epidemiology*, *42*, 403–409.

Häfner, H., & an der Heiden, W. (1986). The contribution of European case registers to research on schizophrenia. *Schizophrenia Bulletin*, *12*, 26–51.

Hagen, K., Stovner, L. J., Skorpen, F., Pettersen, E., & Zwart, J. A. (2008). *COMT* genotypes and use of antipsychotic medication: Linking population-based prescription database to the HUNT study. *Pharmaco-epidemiology and Drug Safety*, *17*, 372–377.

Hansen, V., Arnesen, E., & Jacobsen, B. K. (1997). Total mortality in people admitted to a psychiatric hospital. *British Journal of Psychiatry*, *170*, 186–190.

Harrison, G., Fouskakis, D., Rasmussen, F., Tynelius, P., Sipos, A., & Gunnell, D. (2003). Association between psychotic disorder and urban place of birth is not mediated by obstetric complications or childhood socio-economic position: A cohort study. *Psychological Medicine*, *33*, 723–731.

Haukka, J., Suominen, K., Partonen, T., & Lönnqvist, J. (2008). Determinants and outcomes of serious attempted suicide: A nationwide study in Finland, 1996–2003. *American Journal of Epidemiology*, *167*, 1155–1163.

Haukka, J., Suvisaari, J., Tuulio-Henriksson, A., & Lönnqvist, J. (2007). High concordance between self-reported medication and official prescription database information. *European Journal of Clinical Pharmacology*, *63*, 1069–1074.

Haukka, J., Suvisaari, J., Varilo, T., & Lönnqvist, J. (2001). Regional variation in the incidence of schizophrenia in Finland: A study of birth cohorts born from 1950 to 1969. *Psychological Medicine*, *31*, 1045–1053.

Heilä, H., Haukka, J., Suvisaari, J., & Lönnqvist, J. (2005). Mortality among patients with schizophrenia and reduced psychiatric hospital care. *Psychological Medicine*, *35*, 725–732.

Hernán, M. A., Cole, S. R., Margolick, J., Cohen, M., & Robins, J. M. (2005). Structural accelerated failure time models for survival analysis in studies with time-varying treatments. *Pharmaco-epidemiology and Drug Safety*, *14*, 477–491.

Hiroeh, U., Appleby, L., Mortensen, P. B., & Dunn, G. (2001). Death by homicide, suicide, and other unnatural causes in people with mental illness: A population-based study. *Lancet, 358*, 2110–2112.

Holl, K., Lundin, E., Kaasila, M., Grankvist, K., Afanasyeva, Y., Hallmans, G., et al. (2008). Effect of long-term storage on hormone measurements in samples from pregnant women: The experience of the Finnish maternity cohort. *Acta Oncologica, 47*, 406–412.

Hultman, C. M., Sparen, P., Takei, N., Murray, R. M., & Cnattingius, S. (1999). Prenatal and neonatal risk factors for schizophrenia, affective psychosis, and reactive psychosis of early onset: Case-control study. *British Medical Journal, 318*, 421–426.

Ingelsson, E., Arnlöv, J., Sundström, J., & Lind, J. (2005). The validity of a diagnosis of heart failure in a hospital discharge register. *European Journal of Heart Failure, 7*, 787–791.

Isohanni, I., Järvelin, M.-R., Nieminen, P., Jones, P., Rantakallio, P., Jokelainen, J., et al. (1998). School performance as a predictor of psychiatric hospitalization in adult life. A 28-year follow-up in the Northern Finland 1966 birth cohort. *Psychological Medicine, 28*, 967–974.

Isohanni, M., Jones, P. B., Moilanen, K., Rantakallio, P., Veijola, J., Oja, H., et al. (2001). Early developmental milestones in adult schizophrenia and other psychoses. A 31-year follow-up of the Northern Finland 1966 birth cohort. *Schizophrenia Research, 52*, 1–19.

Isohanni, M., Mäkikyrö, T., Moring, J., Räsänen, P., Hakko, H., Partanen, U., et al. (1997). Comparison of clinical and research DSM-III-R diagnoses of schizophrenia in a Finnish national birth cohort. *Social Psychiatry & Psychiatric Epidemiology, 32*, 303–308.

Johansson, L. A., & Westerling, R. (2000). Comparing Swedish hospital discharge records with death certificates: Implications for mortality statistics. *International Journal of Epidemiology, 29*, 495–502.

Jones, P., Rodgers, B., Murray, R., & Marmot, M. (1994). Child development risk factors for adult schizophrenia in the British 1946 birth cohort. *Lancet, 344*(8934), 1398–1402.

Jones, P. B., Barnes, T. R., Davies, L., Dunn, G., Lloyd, H., Hayhurst, K. P., et al. (2006). Randomized controlled trial of the effect on quality of life of second- vs. first-generation antipsychotic drugs in schizophrenia: Cost utility of the latest antipsychotic drugs in schizophrenia study (CUtLASS 1). *Archives of General Psychiatry, 63*, 1079–1087.

Jones, P. B., Rantakallio, P., Hartikainen, A. L., Isohanni, M., & Sipilä, P. (1998). Schizophrenia as a long-term outcome of pregnancy, delivery, and perinatal complications: A 28-year follow-up of the 1966 North Finland general population birth cohort. *American Journal of Psychiatry, 155*, 355–364.

Kaprio, J. (2006). Twin studies in Finland 2006. *Twin Research and Human Genetics, 9*, 772–777.

Kendler, K. S., Gatz, M., Gardner, C. O., & Pedersen, N. L. (2006). A Swedish national twin study of lifetime major depression. *American Journal of Psychiatry, 163*, 109–114.

Khashan, A. S., Abel, K. M., McNamee, R., Pedersen, M. G., Webb, R. T., Baker, P. N., et al. (2008). Higher risk of offspring schizophrenia following antenatal maternal exposure to severe adverse life events. *American Journal of Psychiatry, 65*, 146–152.

Kieseppä, T., Partonen, T., Haukka, J., Kaprio, J., & Lönnqvist, J. (2004). High concordance of bipolar I disorder in a nationwide sample of twins. *American Journal of Psychiatry, 161*, 1814–1821.

Kieseppä, T., Partonen, T., Kaprio, J., & Lönnqvist, J. (2000). Accuracy of register- and record-based bipolar I disorder diagnoses in Finland—A study of twins. *Acta Neuropsychiatrica, 12*, 106–109.

King-Hele, S. A., Abel, K. M., Webb, R. T., Mortensen, P. B., Appleby, L., & Pickles, A. R. (2007). Risk of sudden infant death syndrome with parental mental illness. *American Journal of Psychiatry*, *64*, 1323–1330.

Koponen, H., Rantakallio, P., Veijola, J., Jones, P., Jokelainen, J., & Isohanni, M. (2004). Childhood central nervous system infections and risk for schizophrenia. *European Archives Psychiatry and Clinical Neuroscience*, *254*, 9–13.

Kringlen, E. (1968). An epidemiological-clinical twin study on schizophrenia. *Journal of Psychiatry Research 6*(Suppl.. 1), 49–63.

Kristjansson, E., Allebeck, P., & Wistedt, B. (1987). Validity of the diagnosis schizophrenia in a psychiatric inpatient register. *Nordisk Psykiatrisk Tidsskrift*, *43*, 229–234.

Lahti, R. A., & Penttilä, A. (2001). The validity of death certificates: Routine validation of death certification and its effects on mortality statistics. *Forensic Science International*, *115*, 15–32.

Lewis, G., David, A., Andréasson, S., & Allebeck, P. (1992). Schizophrenia and city life. *Lancet*, *340*, 137–140.

Lichtenstein, P., De Faire, U., Floderus, B., Svartengren, M., Svedberg, P., & Pedersen, N. L. (2002). The Swedish Twin Registry: A unique resource for clinical, epidemiological and genetic studies. *Journal of Internal Medicine*, *252*, 184–205.

Lichtenstein, P., Yip, B., Björk, C., Pawitan, Y., Cannon, T. D., Sullivan, P. F., et al. (2009). Common genetic determinants of schizophrenia and bipolar disorder in Swedish families: A population-based study. *Lancet*, *373*, 234–239.

Lieberman, J. A., Stroup, T. S., McEvoy, J. P., Swartz, M. D., Rosenheck, M. D., Perkins, D. O., et al. (2005). Effectiveness of antipsychotic drugs in patients with chronic schizophrenia. *New England Journal of Medicine*, *353*, 1209–1223.

Löffler, W., Häfner, H., Fätkenheur, B., Maurer, K., Riecher-Rössier, A., Lutzhaft, S., et al. (1994). Validation of Danish case register diagnosis for schizophrenia. *Acta Psychiatrica Scandinavica*, *90*, 196–203.

MacCabe, J. H., Lambe, M. P., Cnattingius, S., Sham, P. C., David, A. S., Reichenberg, A., et al. (2010). Excellent school performance at age 16 and risk of adult bipolar disorder: National cohort study. *British Journal of Psychiatry*, *196*, 109–115.

MacCabe, J. H., Lambe, M. P., Cnattingius, S., Torräng, A., Bjork, C., Sham, P. C., et al. (2008). Scholastic achievement at age 16 and risk of schizophrenia and other psychoses: A national cohort study. *Psychological Medicine*, *38*, 1133–1140.

MacCabe, J. H., Martinsson, L., Lichtenstein, P., Nilsson, E., Cnattingius, S., Murray, R. M., et al. (2007). Adverse pregnancy outcomes in mothers with affective psychosis. *Bipolar Disorders*, *9*, 305–309.

Madsen, K. M., Hviid, A., Vestergaard, M., Schendel, D., Wohifahrt, J., Thorsen, P., et al. (2002). A population-based study of measles, mumps, and rubella vaccination and autism. *New England Journal of Medicine*, *347*, 1477–1482.

Mäkikyrö, T., Isohanni, M., Moring, J., Hakko, H., Hovatta, I., & Lönnqvist, J. (1998). Accuracy of register-based schizophrenia diagnoses in a genetic study. *European Psychiatry*, *13*, 57–62.

Mednick, S. A., Machon, R. A., Huttunen, M. O., & Bonett, D. (1988). Adult schizophrenia following prenatal exposure to an influenza epidemic. *Archives of General Psychiatry*, *45*, 189–192.

Miettunen, J., Lauronen, E., Veijola, J., Koponen, H., Saarento, O., Taanila, A., et al. (2007). Socio-demographic and clinical predictors of occupational status in schizophrenic psychoses—Follow-up within the Northern Finland 1966 birth cohort. *Psychiatry Research*, *150*, 217–225.

Miettunen, J., Suvisaari, J., Haukka, J., & Isohanni, M. (2011). Use of register data for psychiatric epidemiology in the Nordic countries. In M. Tsuang, M. Tohen, & P. B. Jones (Eds.), *Textbook in psychiatric epidemiology* (3rd ed.) (pp. 117–131). Oxford, UK: Wiley-Blackwell.

Moilanen, K., Veijola, J., Läksy, K., Mäkikyrö, T., Miettunen, J., Kantojärvi, L., et al. (2003). Reasons for the diagnostic discordance between clinicians and researchers in schizophrenia in the Northern Finland 1966 birth cohort. *Social Psychiatry & Psychiatric Epidemiology*, *38*, 305–310.

Mortensen, P. B. (2004). Register-based research in Denmark [in Danish, with English abstract]. *Norsk Epidemiologi*, *14*, 121–124.

Mortensen, P. B., Nørgaard-Pedersen, B., Waltoft, B. L., Sørensen, T. L., Hougaard, D., & Torrey, E. F. (2007a). *Toxoplasma gondii* as a risk factor for early onset schizophrenia: Analysis of filter paper blood samples obtained at birth. *Biological Psychiatry*, *61*, 688–693.

Mortensen, P. B., Nørgaard-Pedersen, B., Waltoft, B. L., Sørensen, T. L., Hougaard, D., & Yolken, R. H. (2007b). Early infections of *Toxoplasma gondii* and the later development of schizophrenia. *Schizophrenia Bulletin*, *33*, 741–744.

Mortensen, P. B., Pedersen, C. B., & Westergaard, T. (1999). Effects of family history and place and season of birth on the risk of schizophrenia. *New England Journal of Medicine*, *340*, 603–608.

Munk-Jørgensen, P., Kastrup, M., & Mortensen, P. B. (1993). The Danish psychiatric register as a tool in epidemiology. *Acta Psychiatrica Scandinavica*, *370*(Suppl.), 27–32.

Munk-Jørgensen, P., & Mortensen, P. B. (1992). Incidence and other aspects of the epidemiology of schizophrenia in Denmark, 1971–87. *British Journal of Psychiatry*, *161*, 489–495.

Murray, R. M. (1994). Neurodevelopmental schizophrenia: The rediscovery of dementia praecox. *British Journal of Psychiatry*, *25*(Suppl.), 6–12.

Nilsson, E., Lichtenstein, P., Cnattingius, S., Murray, R. M., & Hultman, C. M. (2002). Women with schizophrenia: Pregnancy outcome and infant death among their offspring. *Schizophrenia Research*, *58*, 221–229.

Nordentoft, M., Breum, L., Munck, L. K., Nordestgaard, A. G., Hunding, A., & Laursen Bjaeldager, P. A. (1993). High mortality by natural and unnatural causes: A 10 year follow-up study of patients admitted to a poisoning treatment centre after suicide attempts. *British Medical Journal*, *306*, 1637–1641.

O'Callaghan, E., Sham, P., Takei, N., Glover, G., & Murray, R. M. (1991). Schizophrenia after prenatal exposure to 1957 A2 influenza epidemic. *Lancet*, *337*(8752), 1248–1250.

Ødegard, Ø. (1971). Hospitalized psychoses in Norway: Time trends 1926–1965. *Social Psychiatry*, *6*, 53–58.

Oksbjerg Dalton, S., Mellemkjaer, L., Olsen, J. H., Mortensen, P. B., & Johansen, C. (2002). Depression and cancer risk: A register-based study of patients hospitalized with affective disorders, Denmark, 1969–1993. *American Journal of Epidemiology*, *155*, 1088–1095.

Pajunen, P., Koukkunen, H., Ketonen, M., Jerkkola, T., Immonen-Räihä, P., Kärjä-Koskekari, P., et al. (2005). The validity of the Finnish hospital discharge register and causes of death register data on coronary heart disease. *European Journal of Cardiovascular Prevention and Rehabilitation*, *12*, 132–137.

Pedersen, C. B., & Mortensen, P. B. (2001). Evidence of a dose–response relationship between urbanicity during upbringing and schizophrenia risk. *Archives of General Psychiatry*, *58*, 1039–1046.

Perälä, J., Saarni, S., Ostamo, A., Pirkola, S., Haukka, J., Härkänen, T., et al. (2008). Geographic variation and sociodemographic characteristics of psychotic disorders in Finland. *Schizophrenia Research*, *106*, 337–347.

Perälä, J., Suvisaari, J., Saarni, S. I., Kuoppasalmi, K., Isometsä, E., Pirkola, S., et al. (2007). Lifetime prevalence of psychotic and bipolar I disorders in a general population. *Archives of General Psychiatry*, *64*, 19–28.

Pihlajamaa, J., Suvisaari, J., Henriksson, M., Heilä, H., Karjalainen, E., Koskela, J., et al. (2008). The validity of schizophrenia diagnosis in the Finnish hospital discharge register: Findings from a 10-year birth cohort sample. *Nordic Journal of Psychiatry*, *62*, 198–203.

Qin, P., Mortensen, P. B., & Pedersen, C. B. (2009). Frequent change of residence and risk of attempted and completed suicide among children and adolescents. *Archives of General Psychiatry*, *66*, 628–632.

Rantakallio, P., Jones, P. B., Moring, J., & Von Wendt, L. (1997). Association between central nervous system infections during childhood and adult onset schizophrenia and other psychoses: A 28-year follow-up. *International Journal of Epidemiology*, *26*, 837–843.

Ridler, K., Veijola, J. M., Tanskanen, P., Miettunen, J., Chitnis, X., Suckling, J., et al. (2006). Fronto-cerebellar systems are associated with infant motor and adult executive functions in healthy adults but not in schizophrenia. *Proceedings of the National Academy of Sciences of the United States of America*, *103*, 15651–15656.

Rosenthal, D., Wender, P. H., Kety, S. S., Welner, J., & Schulsinger, F. (1971). The adopted-away offspring of schizophrenics. *American Journal of Psychiatry*, *128*, 307–311.

Skytthe, A., Kyvik, K., Bathum, L., Holm, N., Vaupel, J. W., & Christensen, K. (2006). The Danish twin registry in the new millennium. *Twin Research in Human Genetics*, *9*, 763–771.

Statistics Finland. (2004). *Use of register and administrative data sources for statistical purposes best practices of Statistics Finland.* Statistics Finland Handbooks 45. (Available in English at: www.stat.fi/tup/julkaisut/kasikirjoja_45_en.pdf)

Stefansson, H., Rujescu, D., Cichon, S., Pietiläinen, O. P., Ingason, A., Steinberg, S., et al. (2008). Large recurrent microdeletions associated with schizophrenia. *Nature*, *455*, 232–236.

Stefansson, H., Sigurdsson, E., Steinthorsdottir, V., Bjornsdottir, S., Sigmundsson, T., Ghosh, S., et al. (2002). Neuregulin 1 and susceptibility to schizophrenia. *American Journal of Human Genetics*, *71*, 877–892.

Strand, B. H., & Kunst, A. (2006). Childhood socioeconomic status and suicide mortality in early adulthood among Norwegian men and women. A prospective study of Norwegians born between 1955 and 1965 followed for suicide from 1990 to 2001. *Social Science and Medicine*, *63*, 2825–2834.

Suvisaari, J. M., Haukka, J. K., Tanskanen, A. J., & Lönnqvist, J. K. (1999). Decline in the incidence of schizophrenia in Finnish cohorts born from 1954 to 1965. *Archives of General Psychiatry*, *56*, 733–740.

Suvisaari, J. M., Mautemps, N., Haukka, J., Hovi, T., & Lönnqvist, J. (2003). Childhood central nervous system viral infections and adult schizophrenia. *American Journal of Psychiatry*, *160*, 1183–1185.

Taiminen, T., Ranta, K., Karisson, H., Lauerma, H., Leinonen, K. M., Wallenius, E., et al. (2001). Comparison of clinical and best-estimate research DSM-IV diagnoses in a

Finnish sample of first-admission psychosis and severe affective disorder. *Nordic Journal of Psychiatry, 55*, 107–111.

Tellnes, G., Mathisen, S., Skau, I., Thune, O., Ulsberg, S., & Berg, J. E. (1992). Who is long-term sick-listed in Norway? From the project evaluation of the follow-up of long-term sick-listed. *Tidsskrift for Norske Laegeforening, 112*, 2773–2778.

Tidemalm, D., Långström, N., Lichtenstein, P., & Runeson, B. (2008). Risk of suicide after suicide attempt according to coexisting psychiatric disorder: Swedish cohort study with long-term follow-up. *British Medical Journal, 337*, 2205.

Tienari, P., Wynne, L. C., Moring, J., Läksy, K., Nieminen, P., Sorri, A., et al. (2000). Finnish adoptive family study: Sample selection and adoptee DSM-III-R diagnoses. *Acta Psychiatrica Scandinavica, 101*, 433–443.

Tienari, P., Wynne, L. C., Sorri, A., Lahti, I., Läsky, K., Moring, J., et al. (2004). Genotype–environment interaction in schizophrenia-spectrum disorder. Long-term follow-up study of Finnish adoptees. *British Journal of Psychiatry, 184*, 216–222.

Tiihonen, J., Haukka, J., Henriksson, M., Cannon, M., Kieseppä, T., Laaksonen, I., et al. (2005). Premorbid intellectual functioning in bipolar disorder and schizophrenia: Results from a cohort study of male conscripts. *American Journal of Psychiatry, 162*, 1904–1910.

Tiihonen, J., Lönnqvist, J., Wahlbeck, K., Klaukka, T., Tanskanen, A., & Haukka, J. (2006). Antidepressants and the risk of suicide, attempted suicide, and overall mortality in a nationwide cohort. *Archives of General Psychiatry, 63*, 1358–1367.

Tiihonen, J., Lönnqvist, J., Wahlbeck, K., Klaukka, T., Tanskanen, A., & Haukka, J. (2009). 11-year follow-up of mortality in patients with schizophrenia: A population-based cohort study (FIN11 study). *Lancet, 374*, 620–627.

Webb, R. T., Pickles, A. R., Appleby, L., Mortensen, P. B., & Abel, K. M. (2007). Death by unnatural causes during childhood and early adulthood in offspring of psychiatric inpatients. *Archives of General Psychiatry, 64*, 345–352.

Westergaard, T., Mortensen, P. B., Pedersen, C. B., Wohlfahrt, J., & Melbye, M. (1999). Exposure to prenatal and childhood infections and the risk of schizophrenia. Suggestions from a study of sibship characteristics and influenza prevalence. *Archives of General Psychiatry, 56*, 993–998.

Wierdsma, A. I., Sytema, S., van Os, J. J., & Mulder, C. L. (2008). Case registers in psychiatry: Do they still have a role for research and service monitoring? *Current Opinion in Psychiatry, 21*, 379–384.

World Health Organization. (1965). *International classification of diseases* (ICD-8). Geneva, Switzerland: WHO.

World Health Organization. (1977). *International classification of diseases* (ICD-9). Geneva, Switzerland: WHO.

World Health Organization. (1992). *International classification of diseases* (ICD-10). Geneva, Switzerland: WHO.

World Health Organization. (2009). *International classification of diseases* (ICD-9-CM schizophrenic disorders). Geneva, Switzerland: WHO.

Zammit, S., Allebeck, P., Andréasson, S., Lundberg, I., & Lewis, G. (2002). Self-reported cannabis use as a risk factor for schizophrenia in Swedish conscripts of 1969: Historical cohort study. *British Medical Journal, 325*, 1199–1203.

Part II

Neuroscience

5 The search for madness

A metaphasical trip through the basal ganglia

Paul D. Morrison

The basal ganglia as a *super*-hub

The basal ganglia (striatum, globus pallidus, subthalamic nucleus, substantia-nigra and pedunculopontine nucleus) are a major functional "hub" within the CNS. The striatum receives massive input from the whole neocortex, from limbic and pre-limbic cortices and from the hippocampal complex and basolateral amygdala. In short, much of its input stems from other major CNS hubs. This indicates that the basal ganglia are involved in integrating highly pre-processed as opposed to "raw" sensory information. Although classically considered to have a role in motor processing, it has become clear that the basal ganglia are important in thinking and emotion (Pennartz et al., 2009).

Within the striatum, approximately 95% of neurons are medium spiny neurons (MSNs). The MSN constitutes the only output unit of the striatum. MSNs are GABAergic neurons, taking their name from a feature untypical of GABAergic neurons; That is, similar to pyramidal neurons, they express dendritic spines. Excitatory inputs from the cortex, the limbic system (*and the thalamus*) target the heads of dendritic spines. In total, each MSN receives excitatory inputs from tens of thousands of cortical neurons, whose fibres traverse the striatum as a longitudinal band. There is a massive convergence of information within the striatum. This so-called "funnelling" of information (from cortex to striatum) is repeated once more, in the projection of some 100 million MSNs onto a considerably smaller population of pallidal/nigral neurons. Thereafter, projections from the (internal) pallidum and substantia-nigra (pars-reticulata; SNpr) form the major outflow tracts of the basal ganglia, targeting the ventral, mediodorsal, intralaminar and midline thalamic nuclei. In turn, the thalamic nuclei project back to the neocortex and limbic system, effecting closure of the (cortico-basal ganglia-thalamo-cortical) loops. Classical accounts document a direct pathway (which amplifies regional cortical activity) and an indirect pathway (which dampens regional cortical activity). The division into direct and indirect pathways appears to hold for the ventral as well as dorsal divisions of the striatum. As discussed more fully below in the context of psychosis, the MSNs of the indirect pathway express dopamine (DA) receptors of the D2 subtype. Those of the direct pathway express D1 receptors (Nieuwenhuys, Voogd, & van Huijzen, 2008).

Three major parallel loops have been described corresponding to sensorimotor, cognitive and affective processing. Each loop is described in terms of specific cortical/limbic territories, corresponding subregions within the basal ganglia and distinct thalamic nuclei. But what has become clear is that the different loops are not isolated from each other (Nieuwenhuys et al., 2008; Pennartz et al., 2009). Integration at many levels within the basic architecture has been described. Consequently the realization that cortico-basal ganglia-thalamo-cortical loops can operate in series (and not just in parallel) has come to the fore.

Cognitions in the basal ganglia: *Embodiment* of a dominant psychomotor stream

Our understanding of the type of computations performed by the basal ganglia circuits and their functional correlates at a psychomotor level are still rudimentary. Nevertheless, influential models have been created. The idea of "funnelling" implies competition and the selection of a particular, dominant psychomotor stream at the expense of weaker or spurious inputs (Rolls & Treves, 1997). If at any time the striatum is literally bombarded by excitatory inputs, some sort of selection procedure becomes essential.

It has been proposed that the basal ganglia operate as a competitive network (Houk et al., 2007; Redgrave, Prescott, & Gurney, 1999; Rolls & Treves, 1997). MSNs are interconnected by recurrent inhibitory collaterals. These collaterals release GABA and target the dendrites of other MSNs. This is *lateral inhibition*. The strength of inhibitory feedback from one MSN to another is relatively weak, and, as will be described below, is subject to modulation by dopamine and other transmitters. The relative weakness of these inputs, however, may subserve fine-grained interactions between MSNs. The computations that determine whether a particular MSN is firing (or not), at any particular time-point, occur within the dendrites. It has been suggested that a currently dominant *assembly* of MSNs is, via lateral inhibition, able to "silence" competing assemblies (Houk et al., 2007; Redgrave et al., 1999; Rolls & Treves, 1997). The dominant stream may reverberate through the thalamus, cortices and basal ganglia in successive cycles.[1]

The MSN is also subject to *feed-forward* inhibition via GABAergic interneurons, themselves excited by cortical inputs. Those which express parvalbumin form baskets around the soma of MSNs (Nieuwenhuys et al., 2008). As is seen in other regions of the CNS, these interneurons may control the precise timing of action-potentials from principal neurons and help to synchronize an MSN assembly. But a role for feed-forward connections in competition between MSN assemblies has not been ruled out (Pennartz et al., 2009). A plethora of other interneuron types has been described, but their functional characteristics and roles are largely unknown. One point will be made here and returned to later. That is, among the diverse types of GABAergic terminals within the striatum, only the recurrent collaterals and parvalbumin-containing basket neurons express cannabinoid receptors (Freiman, Anton, Monyer, Urbanski, & Szabo, 2006).

In summary, the gross anatomy of the basal ganglia and their constituent circuitry indicate that one functional role is the selection of a dominant psychomotor stream(s) from competing streams. This dominant stream returns to higher centres, whereas competing streams are drowned out (*within the unconscious*). Houk and colleagues have proposed the term *embodiment*, which encompasses not just selection, but also the *initiation* of a particular psychomotor programme at the expense of others (Houk et al., 2007).

In people with Parkinson's disease (PD), it is well recognized that there is a progressive failure of the ability to convert thought into action (to initiate movement). This stems from the loss of dopaminergic innervation of the striatum. Similar phenomena are observed in animals depleted of brainstem dopamine. The Parkinsonian patient also has difficulty *switching* between different motor programmes. Finally, the expression of emotion and cognition can also be impaired. PD exemplifies the importance of the basal ganglia (and DA) in the embodiment of psychomotor behaviours.

As a further example, drugs that have the ability to block excitatory cortical/limbic inputs to the striatum can impair the embodiment of psychomotor programmes. The best exemplar is the N-methyl-D-aspartate (NMDA) channel blocker class of drug, typified by ketamine, a so-called dissociative anaesthetic. In humans, ketamine disrupts the embodiment of ideas and movement. This property is utilized in anaesthetic practice where it becomes possible to conduct major surgical operations, while the patient is still technically "awake" and able to support their own respiration. Ketamine has also been said to mimic the negative symptoms of schizophrenia (Javitt, 2007).[2] Almost by definition, the negative symptoms of schizophrenia reflect an impoverished ability to embody cognitive, motor and emotional programmes over an extended period of time.

Striatal learning: "The helping hand of things"

The human being is not "thrown" into the world with fully operational cortico-basal-ganglia loops. Instead the circuits are sculpted and refined over the course of a lifetime. Whereas Kant believed that basic mental faculties existed *prior* to perceptual experience, Hegel postulated a two-way dialectic between the *developing* mind and the outside world. What he termed as "the helping hand of things", our interaction with the world, was necessary for the emergence of our basic mental faculties; our concept of identity, time, causality, substance, and so on. For Hegel, knowledge was about *living*, rather than acquiring facts. Piaget's experimental work corresponds with Hegel's view. Piaget described how an individual *assimilates* the world and in so doing *accommodates* to the world, in successive stages, each building on the last—from the emergence of basic motor skills right up to the development of abstract reasoning (Hundert, 1989). What we are talking about is the development of those habits of mind, movement and emotion, that *make-up* an individual—which constitute the self, the personality. Four aspects of basal-ganglia function are particularly resonant with respect to the initial development of psychotic patterns of thought and action:

1 Learning in the basal ganglia is largely *unconscious*.
2 Learning is relatively *slow*.
3 New associations (action–outcome) routines become stubbornly *ingrained* as habits.
4 The basal ganglia *teach* the higher centres about new associations (rather than the other way around).

The corticostriatal loops subserving motor functions are probably the first to be sculpted. The type of learning initiated is believed to be of the trial-and-error type. Initially, movements are flailing and imprecise, but in the "right general territory" (Houk et al., 2007). Ultimately, and within a relatively short period, expertise is "attained". "Success" builds on success. In time psychomotor programmes can be selected and initiated effortlessly and automatically, given a particular context. Programmes can be combined in various sequences. And perhaps most fundamentally of all, the nervous system learns to discriminate between self-generated movement (*as well as speech and ideation*) and passive movement generated by an external agency. Put more succinctly, the nervous system comes to recognize its own will. Of course, the development of such CNS functions is not, at least in retrospect, a source of pride or an achievement for the subject, but as Piaget suggested, it is *taken-for-granted* as the natural way of *being-in-the-world*.

The role of the basal ganglia in discriminating between self-generated and externally generated movement has attracted recent attention among neuroscientists. Redgrave and Gurney have proposed a model in which, the *discovery of novel actions* and the *determination of agency* depend upon the type of phasic dopamine activity traditionally associated with reward-prediction errors (Redgrave & Gurney, 2006). They conjecture that the dopamine signal arrives in the striatum, coincident with a representation of a (just-performed) motor *act* and a sensory *outcome*. Over time an organism is said to build a "store" of action–outcome routines, which can then be deployed in a flexible manner. They argue that action–outcome learning is *intrinsically driven* (rather than reward driven) and take as an example the play of children.

One further point deserves comment; both the model of Redgrave and Gurney and the traditional theories that posit phasic DA as a reward signal, emphasize that dopamine affects change in synapses via the well-established mechanisms of neuronal plasticity. Specifically, this points to a role of dopamine in long-term potentiation (LTP) and long-term depression (LTD) of synapses (Wickens, 2009). Recent experimental work has shown that as animals learn and consolidate a new task, striatal circuits undergo a dynamic reorganization involving LTP of excitatory inputs from the cortex (Yin et al., 2009).

One can never "step-into" the same synapse twice

Plasticity describes a set of processes in which the synaptic connections between neurons adapt, becoming strengthened (LTP) or weakened (LTD) in response to the electrochemical input (or information) that they receive and process. Such changes can occur extremely rapidly, and be short-lived or maintained—the latter depending on new protein synthesis. There is now overwhelming evidence that experience-dependent plasticity underlies learning and memory in neuronal circuits, and spans relatively simple forms such as sensitization and habituation to more complex forms such as associative, procedural and declarative memory (Bailey, Giustetto, Huang, Hawkins, & Kandel, 2000). Initially (in the 1980s), plasticity focused on glutamate transmission and, in particular, the role of the NMDA receptor. But traditional monoamine transmitters are also intimately involved in plasticity and learning. The concept of plasticity has been expanded further and now encompasses not only biochemical modifications at synapses but also structural changes in the neuropil, that is to say, at dendrites, dendritic spines and axon terminals and modification of chromatin. Maturation and development are enveloped by the concept of plasticity.

The most commonly studied type of plasticity in the striatum is a depression of corticostriatal synapses (Calabresi, Picconi, Tozzi, & Di Filippo, 2007). However, cortical inputs to MSNs can be modified in either direction. At any time point, only those striatal synapses that are *currently active* are amenable to modification. The CNS might employ this mechanism to ensure that only a subpopulation of synapses change, while the majority of the network remains constant. Neuromodulators do not elicit change on their own, but appear to be involved in determining the overall direction of change within concurrently active circuits. Three modulators are especially important; dopamine, adenosine and the endocannabinoids (Wickens, 2009).

The MSN population consists of cells belonging to the direct pathway (D1 receptor expressing) and cells belonging to the indirect pathway (D2 expressing; Figure 5.1). The intricacies of plasticity differ between the two cell types. At both cell types, LTD is mediated by, so called, retrograde endocannabinoid signalling (retrograde because transmission occurs in the opposite direction from usual; from the dendrites to axon terminals; Shen, Flajolet, Greengard, & Surmeier, 2008). Depression at cortical inputs to MSNs of the indirect pathway requires D2 stimulation, for example it can be blocked by drugs like sulpiride (Kreitzer & Malenka, 2005). In agreement the activation of dopamine (DA) D2 receptors leads to the release of endocannabinoid (eCB) transmitters (Giuffrida et al., 1999). Here we predominantly focus on MSNs expressing D2 receptors because of links between the D2 receptor and psychotic illness. Opposing LTD, co-activation of adenosine A_{2A} and NMDA receptors elicits LTP at corticostriatal synapses of the indirect pathway (Shen et al., 2008).

In the absence of dopamine, LTD at corticostriatal synapses of the indirect pathway is absent. This is probably more than an electrophysiological curiosity. For example, in animals made Parkinsonian by depletion of brainstem DA stores, corticostriatal LTD is lost. Treatment of the animals with a D2 agonist restores LTD and motor functioning. But, interestingly, the addition of an inhibitor of endocannabinoid clearance further enhances motor function (Kreitzer & Malenka, 2007). Overall this suggests that the fine-tuning of cortical inputs by dopamine at

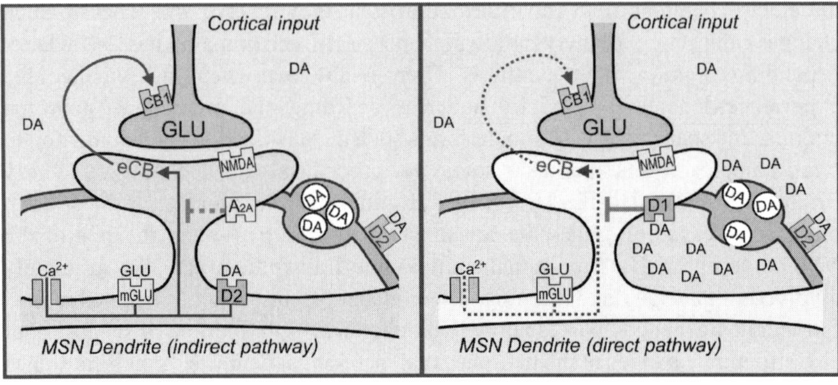

Figure 5.1 Bidirectional plasticity at cortical inputs to the striatum. Plasticity at corticostriatal synapses depends on the precise timing (pairing) of pre- and post-synaptic action potentials (APs), and extracellular concentrations of the neuromodulator dopamine. Unpaired APs are of no consequence to corticostriatal plasticity. *Left panel*: In medium spiny neurons belonging to the indirect pathway a convergence of signals; activation of voltage-operated calcium channels, type I metabotropic glutamate receptors (mGLU) and D2 dopamine receptors elicit retrograde endocannabinoid (eCB) mediated long-term depression (LTD) of excitatory cortical inputs. Long-term potentiation (LTP) of cortical synapses onto indirect pathway MSNs depends on the activation of adenosine A2A and NMDA receptors. *Right panel*: At MSNs belonging to the direct pathway, cortical inputs, which contribute to the generation of a post-synaptic AP, undergo NMDA-dependent LTP, but only in the presence of D1 dopamine receptor stimulation. In the absence of D1 receptor stimulation, paired firing of pre- and post-synaptic elements leads to LTD, which is mediated via retrograde endocannabinoid signalling. Bi-directional modifications of corticostriatal connections may be important in reward-related striatal learning and in the formation of habitual motor, cognitive and affective behaviours (CB1, cannabinoid type 1 receptor; GLU, glutamate).

D2 receptors and endocannabinoids at CB_1 receptors is important in the embodiment of psychomotor programmes.

The consolidation of a psychomotor behaviour, to the point where it becomes habitual corresponds with LTP of cortical inputs to MSNs of the indirect pathway, i.e., those expressing D2 receptors (Yin et al., 2009). Intact endocannabinoid signalling is also necessary for habit learning (Hilario, Clouse, Yin, & Costa, 2007). At present the precise mechanisms are unclear. One feasible scenario is that, because neighbouring GABAergic terminals are more sensitive to CB_1 agonists and express more CB_1 receptors than the adjacent, and less sensitive cortical input, a net strengthening of cortical inputs (LTP) occurs (Figure 5.2). This has been now been demonstrated within the striatum (Adermark & Lovinger, 2009), having initially been discovered within the hippocampus (Chevaleyre & Castillo, 2003)—and termed *heterosynaptic plasticity*. But further work is necessary to elucidate the mechanisms fully.

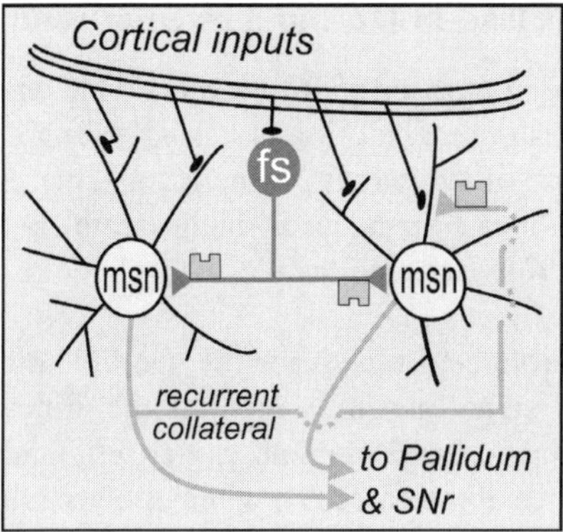

Figure 5.2 The role of CB_1 receptors at GABA-ergic synapses in the striatum. Two populations of GABA-ergic neurons express CB_1 receptors at their terminals. Fast-spiking (fs) interneurons synapse on the somata of medium-spiny neurons (MSNs). These interneurons are thought to synchronize spike discharges in groups of MSNs. Recurrent collaterals synapse on the dendrites of other MSNs. They are believed to mediate lateral inhibition between competing assemblies of MSNs, in a "winner-takes-all" scenario. Endocannabinoid (eCB)-mediated depression of recurrent collaterals might favour cooperation and new learning, rather than competition between MSNs. In support, recent findings show that eCBs signalling at CB_1 receptors in the striatum is essential for habit formation. Excessive, prolonged or sensitized CB_1 receptor signalling might favour connections between logically unrelated ideas.

Overall, there is now clear evidence that striatal learning is associated with change in the strength of cortical inputs. Neuromodulators such as dopamine and the endocannabinoids play a key role in shaping such change. Although our knowledge of striatal physiology has advanced rapidly, much remains to be discovered. It is clear that dopamine and the eCBs can regulate glutamate and GABA signalling within the striatum. But it remains largely unknown how such processes affect striatal output over both short and long durations and how this impacts upon the embodiment of ongoing psychomotor behaviour and new learning. Following a normal developmental trajectory, the striatum appears to seamlessly implement these two apparently conflicting functions (embodiment and new learning) within a single architecture. Experimental studies (fMRI and electrophysiology) have suggested that, in simple terms, the striatum "teaches" the cortex about new associations, rather than the other way around (Pasupathy & Miller, 2005; Seger & Cincotta, 2006). This echoes current theories of hippocampal function, where learning is first established in a subcortical processor, but the final memory trace is ultimately stored in the cortex.

We now focus on pharmacological manipulations of striatal neuromodulators. Drugs that target the dopamine, endocannabinoid and purinergic systems appear to have either pro- or antipsychotic effects in man. Moreover, the pharmacology between different drug classes shows a high degree of consistency.

Psychosis: All roads lead to D2, but a circular road never ends

Prolonged or excessive stimulation of D2 receptors is known to induce a psychosis. In people with pre-existing mental illness, a single drug dose can be enough to elicit a transient relapse of symptoms (Lieberman, Kane, & Alvir, 1987). Drugs which block D2 receptors are the mainstay in the treatment of schizophrenia. And dopamine depleting drugs are also, as the theory would predict, antipsychotic (McKenna, 2007).

There has been a prolonged search for the neurobiological underpinnings of excess D2-mediated signalling in schizophrenic illness. Initial reports of pathologically increased D2 receptor numbers were unfounded. But there has been more consistent evidence of increased DA within pre-synaptic terminals (Howes & Kapur, 2009). Moreover schizophrenic patients have been shown to release more DA following amphetamine, and have higher concentrations of striatal extracellular DA (Abi-Dargham et al., 1998, 2000). How this arises, e.g., inappropriate excitatory drive to DA neurons, pathological DA storage mechanisms, failure to transiently inhibit DA neuron firing following non-arrival of an anticipated reward, is unknown.

Until recently, there has been little attention paid to what excess dopamine and excess stimulation of D2 receptors actually does in the striatum, at the level of synapses. The introduction of transgenic fluorescence methods has made it possible to identify D2 and D1 expressing MSNs unequivocally in electropharmacological experiments. As outlined above, some of the roles of D2 receptors have become clearer. It has become apparent that many of the effects of D2 on glutamate and GABAergic terminals within the striatum depend upon the release of endocannabinoid transmitters (Calabresi et al., 2007; Kreitzer & Malenka, 2008; Wickens, 2009). This suggests that eCBs could be integral in dopamine-mediated psychoses.

Pro- and antipsychotic drugs explained!

Stimulant drugs and delta-9-tetrahydrocannabinol (THC), the major ingredient in cannabis, can elicit acute paranoid psychoses (Angrist, Sathananthan, Wilk, & Gershon, 1974; D'Souza et al., 2004; Morrison et al., 2009). Stimulant psychosis usually emerges in the context of repeated use, whereas THC can be psychotomimetic following a single exposure. Stimulant-associated psychoses can persist long after drug use has stopped, necessitating ongoing psychiatric treatment (McKenna, 2007) while cannabis, especially forms containing high concentrations of THC, can increase the risk for the emergence of chronic psychotic disorders (Di Forti et al., 2009; Murray, Morrison, Henquet, & Di Forti, 2007). For both classes of compound, earlier and heavier use carries more risk of chronic psychosis (Arseneault et al., 2002; Chen et al., 2003).

One outcome of repeated stimulant use is a functional up-regulation of CB_1 receptors in the striatum. This only occurs on GABAergic terminals, glutamate terminals appear to be unaffected (Centonze et al., 2007). Notably, CB_1 receptor knockout or potent CB_1 receptor antagonists impair stimulant sensitization (thought to be a necessary precursor of stimulant psychoses; Corbille et al., 2007; Thiemann, Di Marzo, Molleman, & Hasenohrl, 2008; Thiemann, van der Stelt et al., 2008). In a particularly elegant design it was demonstrated that microinjections of a potent CB_1 antagonist directly into the ventral striatum reduced the expression of behavioural sensitization to methamphetamine (Chiang & Chen, 2007). Findings with the first-generation CB_1 blocker rimonabant in sensitization paradigms have been inconsistent (Lesscher, Hoogveld, Burbach, van Ree, & Gerrits, 2005; Thiemann, van der Stelt et al., 2008). Indeed, rimonabant, as opposed to newer CB_1 antagonists, only partially blocks the effects of THC in humans (Huestis et al., 2001; Zuurman et al., 2008). This might explain why an early trial of rimonabant in schizophrenia failed.

Another cannabinoid manipulation is more promising. The molecule cannabidiol (CBD), a constituent of free-growing, natural *Cannabis sativa* (but bred out of skunk) appears to have antipsychotic properties in humans. At low doses, the receptor pharmacology of CBD involves pharmacological antagonism of CB_1 agonists (via an allosteric site) and inhibition of adenosine re-uptake (Pertwee, 2008). CBD displays efficacy against stimulant (Moreira & Guimaraes, 2005; Zuardi, Rodrigues, & Cunha, 1991) and NMDA models of psychosis in animals (Long, Malone, & Taylor, 2006), and against L-DOPA (Zuardi et al., 2009), ketamine (Bosi, Hallak, Dursun, Deakin, & Zuardi, 2003) and THC-elicited psychosis in humans (Bhattacharyya et al., 2010; Zuardi, Shirakawa, Finkelfarb, & Karniol, 1982). A head-to-head trial of CBD versus amisulpride in 42 schizophrenic patients found equivalent efficacy (Leweke et al., 2009), but further data, particularly over the longer term, is required.

Overall, activation of the D2→eCB→CB_1 axis leads to inhibition of local glutamate and GABA terminals within the striatum. In stark contrast, the adenosine signalling system strengthens the same synapses (Shen et al., 2008; Shindou, Arbuthnott, & Wickens, 2008; Figure 5.3). This begs the question as to whether manipulations of adenosine signalling have any pro- or antipsychotic effects. The main striatal adenosine receptor is the A_{2A} subtype (Dixon, Gubitz, Sirinathsinghji, Richardson, & Freeman, 1996). If excessive activity of the D2→eCB→CB_1 axis is propsychotic, does enhanced A_{2A} activity have antipsychotic effects? Accruing evidence appears to support this. First A_{2A} agonists are effective in animal models of psychosis (Andersen, Fuxe, Werge, & Gerlach, 2002; Sills, Azampanah, & Fletcher, 2001). Moreover, in humans, molecules that inhibit the breakdown of adenosine or its re-uptake have antipsychotic properties. There have now been three positive randomized controlled trials (RCTs) of allopurinol (Akhondzadeh, Safarcherati, & Amini, 2005; Brunstein, Ghisolfi, Ramos, & Lara, 2005; Dickerson et al., 2009), which inhibits the breakdown of adenosine (Schmidt et al., 2009), and one positive RCT of dipyridamole (Akhondzadeh, Shasavand, Jamilian, Shabestari, & Kamalipour, 2000), which inhibits adenosine re-uptake (Kim & Liao, 2008), in schizophrenic patients.

The contrasting pharmacological manipulation appears to fit within this overall scheme. Caffeine, a broad-spectrum antagonist at adenosine receptors, has been associated with a worsening of psychotic symptoms in patients and with clozapine

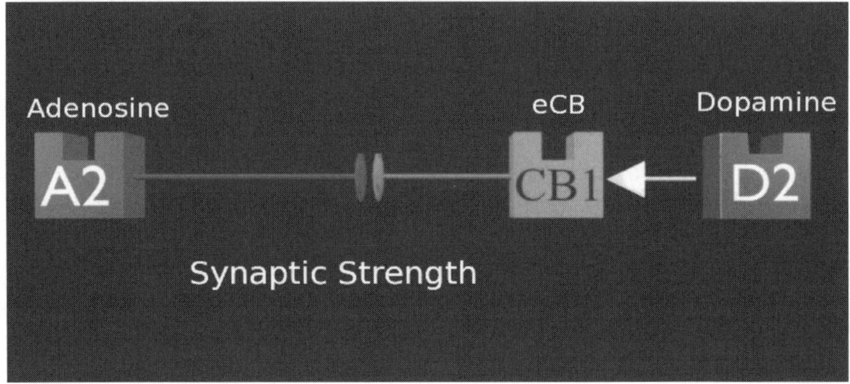

Figure 5.3 Opposition of the D2→CB_1 axis and adenosine receptors. Excitatory and inhibitory synapses within the striatum are modulated by the neuromodulators; dopamine, adenosine and the endocannabinoids (eCB). The strength of synapses is in dynamic flux. Activation of the D2→CB_1 axis leads to weakening of synaptic connections. Activation of A_{2A} receptors leads to strengthening of the same connections. Drugs that "push" the D_2→CB_1 axis have pro-psychotic properties, whereas drugs that "push" the opposing A_{2A} arm are antipsychotic. In agreement, blockers of the D_2→CB_1 axis are antipsychotic, while blockers of A_{2A} receptors may exacerbate psychosis.

resistance (Broderick & Benjamin, 2004; Caykoylu, Ekinci, & Kuloglu, 2008; Dratcu, Grandison, McKay, Bamidele, & Vasudevan, 2007). Most psychiatrists (including the present author), however, would have some difficulty in accepting the notion that a cup of coffee can elicit psychosis. Yet in a well-conducted placebo-controlled study under double-blind conditions, caffeine tablets exacerbated psychotic symptoms in schizophrenic patients (Lucas et al., 1990).

Spurious new connections?

Previously we have advanced a model that emphasizes the effects of the D2→eCB→CB_1 axis on GABAergic transmission within the striatum (Morrison & Murray, 2009; see Figure 5.2). This is underpinned by the observations that CB_1 receptors occur at considerably higher density on GABA compared to glutamatergic terminals, and also that CB_1 responses on GABAergic terminals are sensitized by repeated stimulant use.

The competitive network functions of the striatum are believed to depend upon mutual inhibition between MSN assemblies, through recurrent GABAergic synapses. Relaxation of mutual inhibition (via presynaptic CB_1 receptors) may favour associations between discrete, otherwise competing, psychomotor programmes.

Indeed, the earliest European descriptions of *Cannabis sativa* emphasized that the drug evoked an overabundance of meaningful connections within the mind, a property sought by a later generation (in the 1960s). At extremes, however, such hyper-associability may blur into psychotic thinking.

A drug-model can be regarded as a molecular "lesion" that disrupts circuit dynamics. Given that the surface features of an exogenous and endogenous psychosis are similar, the drug-model offers some insight into the neurobiology of endogenous psychoses. Thus, in the earliest stages of endogenous psychoses, coincident but logically unrelated ideas might be associated, when (in reality) competition and selection of content is demanded. This might initially manifest as a feeling, an awareness of certain coincidences or a conviction that the world has changed. Reiteration, via the highest faculties, which would normally lead to dampening of the new but patently false idea, instead heralds a gradual rewriting of reality into cortical memory stores. In time, existing corticostriatal circuits would be supplanted by a new network.

Acknowledgements

The author has received financial support from the BRC, MRC and Beckley Foundation.

Notes

1 Supplementary 3D animation for this text can be downloaded from http://vimeo.com/11955410.

2 In anaesthetic practice ketamine can also elicit a so-called *emergent-reaction*; an oneroid state characterized by euphoria/anxiety, spatio-temporal illusions, body image distortion and bizarre thinking in the context of overall clouding of consciousness (as plasma concentrations fall). Some have suggested that ketamine mimics some of the positive symptoms of schizophrenia.

References

Abi-Dargham, A., Gil, R., Krystal, J., Baldwin, R. M., Seibyl, J. P., Bowers, M., et al. (1998). Increased striatal dopamine transmission in schizophrenia: Confirmation in a second cohort. *American Journal of Psychiatry*, *155*(6), 761–767.

Abi-Dargham, A., Rodenhiser, J., Printz, D., Zea-Ponce, Y., Gil, R., Kegeles, L. S., et al. (2000). Increased baseline occupancy of D2 receptors by dopamine in schizophrenia. *Proceedings of the National Academy of Sciences of the United States of America*, *97*(14), 8104–8109.

Adermark, L., & Lovinger, D. M. (2009). Frequency-dependent inversion of net striatal output by endocannabinoid-dependent plasticity at different synaptic inputs. *Journal of Neuroscience*, *29*(5), 1375–1380.

Akhondzadeh, S., Safarcherati, A., & Amini, H. (2005). Beneficial antipsychotic effects of allopurinol as add-on therapy for schizophrenia: A double blind, randomized and placebo controlled trial. *Progress in Neuropsychopharmacology & Biological Psychiatry*, *29*(2), 253–259.

Akhondzadeh, S., Shasavand, E., Jamilian, H., Shabestari, O., & Kamalipour, A. (2000). Dipyridamole in the treatment of schizophrenia: Adenosine–dopamine receptor interactions. *Journal of Clinical Pharmacology & Therapeutics*, *25*(2), 131–137.

Andersen, M. B., Fuxe, K., Werge, T., & Gerlach, J. (2002). The adenosine A2A receptor agonist CGS 21680 exhibits antipsychotic-like activity in *Cebus apella* monkeys. *Behavioral Pharmacology*, *13*(8), 639–644.

Angrist, B., Sathananthan, G., Wilk, S., & Gershon, S. (1974). Amphetamine psychosis: Behavioral and biochemical aspects. *Journal of Psychiatric Research*, *11*, 13–23.

Arseneault, L., Cannon, M., Poulton, R., Murray, R., Caspi, A., & Moffitt, T. E. (2002). Cannabis use in adolescence and risk for adult psychosis: Longitudinal prospective study. *British Medical Journal*, *325*(7374), 1212–1213.

Bailey, C. H., Giustetto, M., Huang, Y. Y., Hawkins, R. D., & Kandel, E. R. (2000). Is heterosynaptic modulation essential for stabilizing Hebbian plasticity and memory? *Nature Reviews Neuroscience*, *1*(1), 11–20.

Bhattacharyya, S., Morrison, P. D., Fusar-Poli, P., Martin-Santos, R., Borgwardt, S., Winton-Brown, T., et al. (2010). Opposite effects of delta-9-tetrahydrocannabinol and cannabidiol on human brain function and psychopathology. *Neuropsychopharmacology*, *35*(3), 764–774.

Bosi, D. C., Hallak, J. E. C., Dursun, S. M., Deakin, J. F. W., & Zuardi, A. W. (2003). Effects of cannabidiol on (s)-ketamine-induced psychopathology in healthy volunteers. *Journal of Psychopharmacology*, *17*(Suppl.), A55.

Broderick, P., & Benjamin, A. B. (2004). Caffeine and psychiatric symptoms: A review. *Journal of the Oklahoma State Medical Association*, *97*(12), 538–542.

Brunstein, M. G., Ghisolfi, E. S., Ramos, F. L., & Lara, D. R. (2005). A clinical trial of adjuvant allopurinol therapy for moderately refractory schizophrenia. *Journal of Clinical Psychiatry*, *66*(2), 213–219.

Calabresi, P., Picconi, B., Tozzi, A., & Di Filippo, M. (2007). Dopamine-mediated regulation of corticostriatal synaptic plasticity. *Trends in Neuroscience*, *30*(5), 211–219.

Caykoylu, A., Ekinci, O., & Kuloglu, M. (2008). Improvement from treatment-resistant schizoaffective disorder, manic type after stopping heavy caffeine intake: A case report. *Progress in Neuropsychopharmacology & Biological Psychiatry*, *32*(5), 1349–1350.

Centonze, D., Rossi, S., De Chiara, V., Prosperetti, C., Battista, N., Bernardi, G., et al. (2007). Chronic cocaine sensitizes striatal GABAergic synapses to the stimulation of cannabinoid CB1 receptors. *European Journal of Neuroscience*, *25*(6), 1631–1640.

Chen, C. K., Lin, S. K., Sham, P. C., Ball, D., Loh, E. W., Hsiao, C. C., et al. (2003). Premorbid characteristics and co-morbidity of methamphetamine users with and without psychosis. *Psychological Medicine*, *33*(8), 1407–1414.

Chevaleyre, V., & Castillo, P. E. (2003). Heterosynaptic LTD of hippocampal GABAergic synapses: A novel role of endocannabinoids in regulating excitability. *Neuron*, *38*(3), 461–472.

Chiang, Y. C., & Chen, J. C. (2007). The role of the cannabinoid type 1 receptor and downstream cAMP/DARPP-32 signal in the nucleus accumbens of methamphetamine-sensitized rats. *Journal of Neurochemistry*, *103*(6), 2505–2517.

Corbille, A. G., Valjent, E., Marsicano, G., Ledent, C., Lutz, B., Herve, D., et al., (2007). Role of cannabinoid type 1 receptors in locomotor activity and striatal signaling in response to psychostimulants. *Journal of Neuroscience*, *27*(26), 6937–6947.

D'Souza, D. C., Perry, E., MacDougall, L., Ammerman, Y., Cooper, T., Wu, Y. T., et al. (2004). The psychotomimetic effects of intravenous delta-9-tetrahydrocannabinol in healthy individuals: Implications for psychosis. *Neuropsychopharmacology*, *29*(8), 1558–1572.

Dickerson, F. B., Stallings, C. R., Origoni, A. E., Sullens, A., Khushalani, S., Sandson, N., et al. (2009). A double-blind trial of adjunctive allopurinol for schizophrenia. *Schizophrenia Research*, *109*(1–3), 66–69.

Di Forti, M., Morgan, C., Dazzan, P., Pariante, C., Mondelli, V., Marques, T. R., et al. (2009). High-potency cannabis and the risk of psychosis. *British Journal of Psychiatry, 195*(6), 488–491.

Dixon, A. K., Gubitz, A. K., Sirinathsinghji, D. J., Richardson, P. J., & Freeman, T. C. (1996). Tissue distribution of adenosine receptor mRNAs in the rat. *British Journal of Pharmacology, 118*(6), 1461–1468.

Dratcu, L., Grandison, A., McKay, G., Bamidele, A., & Vasudevan, V. (2007). Clozapine-resistant psychosis, smoking, and caffeine: Managing the neglected effects of substances that our patients consume every day. *American Journal of Therapeutics, 14*(3), 314–318.

Freiman, I., Anton, A., Monyer, H., Urbanski, M. J., & Szabo, B. (2006). Analysis of the effects of cannabinoids on identified synaptic connections in the caudate-putamen by paired recordings in transgenic mice. *Journal of Physiology, 575*(3), 789–806.

Giuffrida, A., Parsons, L. H., Kerr, T. M., Rodriguez de Fonseca, F., Navarro, M., & Piomelli, D. (1999). Dopamine activation of endogenous cannabinoid signaling in dorsal striatum. *Nature Neuroscience, 2*(4), 358–363.

Hilario, M. R., Clouse, E., Yin, H. H., & Costa, R. M. (2007). Endocannabinoid signaling is critical for habit formation. *Frontiers in Integrative Neuroscience, 1*, 6.

Houk, J. C., Bastianen, C., Fansler, D., Fishbach, A., Fraser, D., Reber, P. J., et al. (2007). Action selection and refinement in subcortical loops through basal ganglia and cerebellum. *Philosophical Transactions of the Royal Society London B Biological Science, 362*(1485), 1573–1583.

Howes, O. D., & Kapur, S. (2009). The dopamine hypothesis of schizophrenia: Version III—The final common pathway. *Schizophrenia Bulletin, 35*(3), 549–562.

Huestis, M. A., Gorelick, D. A., Heishman, S. J., Preston, K. L., Nelson, R. A., Moolchan, E. T., et al. (2001). Blockade of effects of smoked marijuana by the CB1-selective cannabinoid receptor antagonist SR141716. *Archives of General Psychiatry, 58*(4), 322–328.

Hundert, E. M. (1989). *Philosophy, psychiatry and neuroscience: Three approaches to the mind*. Oxford, UK: Oxford University Press.

Javitt, D. C. (2007). Glutamate and schizophrenia: Phencyclidine, *N*-methyl-D-aspartate receptors, and dopamine–glutamate interactions. *International Review of Neurobiology, 78*, 69–108.

Kim, H. H., & Liao, J. K. (2008). Translational therapeutics of dipyridamole. *Arteriosclerosis Thrombosis & Vascular Biology, 28*(3), S39–42.

Kreitzer, A. C., & Malenka, R. C. (2005). Dopamine modulation of state-dependent endocannabinoid release and long-term depression in the striatum. *Journal of Neuroscience, 25*(45), 10537–10545.

Kreitzer, A. C., & Malenka, R. C. (2007). Endocannabinoid-mediated rescue of striatal LTD and motor deficits in Parkinson's disease models. *Nature, 445*(7128), 643–647.

Kreitzer, A. C., & Malenka, R. C. (2008). Striatal plasticity and basal ganglia circuit function. *Neuron, 60*(4), 543–554.

Lesscher, H. M., Hoogveld, E., Burbach, J. P., van Ree, J. M., & Gerrits, M. A. (2005). Endogenous cannabinoids are not involved in cocaine reinforcement and development of cocaine-induced behavioural sensitization. *European Neuropsychopharmacology, 15*(1), 31–37.

Leweke, F. M., Koethe, D., Pahlisch, F., Schreiber, D., Gerth, C. W., Nolden, B. M., et al. (2009). Antipsychotic effects of cannabidiol (17th EPA Congress, Lisbon, Portugal, January 2009). *European Psychiatry, 24*(Suppl. 1), s207.

Lieberman, J. A., Kane, J. M., & Alvir, J. (1987). Provocative tests with psychostimulant drugs in schizophrenia. *Psychopharmacology (Berlin), 91*(4), 415–433.

Long, L. E., Malone, D. T., & Taylor, D. A. (2006). Cannabidiol reverses MK-801-induced disruption of prepulse inhibition in mice. *Neuropsychopharmacology*, *31*(4), 795–803.

Lucas, P. B., Pickar, D., Kelsoe, J., Rapaport, M., Pato, C., & Hommer, D. (1990). Effects of the acute administration of caffeine in patients with schizophrenia. *Biological Psychiatry*, *28*(1), 35–40.

McKenna, P. (2007). *Schizophrenia and related syndromes*. London, UK: Routledge.

Moreira, F. A., & Guimaraes, F. S. (2005). Cannabidiol inhibits the hyperlocomotion induced by psychotomimetic drugs in mice. *European Journal of Pharmacology*, *512*(2–3), 199–205.

Morrison, P. D., & Murray, R. M. (2009). From real-world events to psychosis: The emerging neuropharmacology of delusions. *Schizophrenia Bulletin*, *35*(4), 668–674.

Morrison, P. D., Zois, V., McKeown, D. A., Lee, T. D., Holt, D. W., Powell, J. F., et al., (2009). The acute effects of synthetic intravenous Delta9-tetrahydrocannabinol on psychosis, mood and cognitive functioning. *Psychological Medicine*, *39*(10), 1607–1616.

Murray, R. M., Morrison, P. D., Henquet, C., & Di Forti, M. (2007). Cannabis, the mind and society: The hash realities. *Nature Reviews Neuroscience*, *8*(11), 885–895.

Nieuwenhuys, R., Voogd, J., & van Huijzen, C. (2008). *The human central nervous system*. Berlin, Germany: Springer-Verlag.

Pasupathy, A., & Miller, E. K. (2005). Different time courses of learning-related activity in the prefrontal cortex and striatum. *Nature*, *433*(7028), 873–876.

Pennartz, C. M., Berke, J. D., Graybiel, A. M., Ito, R., Lansink, C. S., van der Meer, M., et al. (2009). Corticostriatal interactions during learning, memory processing, and decision making. *Journal of Neuroscience*, *29*(41), 12831–12838.

Pertwee, R. G. (2008). The diverse CB1 and CB2 receptor pharmacology of three plant cannabinoids: Delta9-tetrahydrocannabinol, cannabidiol and delta9-tetrahydrocannabivarin. *British Journal of Pharmacology*, *153*(2), 199–215.

Redgrave, P., & Gurney, K. (2006). The short-latency dopamine signal: A role in discovering novel actions? *Nature Reviews Neuroscience*, *7*(12), 967–975.

Redgrave, P., Prescott, T. J., & Gurney, K. (1999). The basal ganglia: A vertebrate solution to the selection problem? *Neuroscience*, *89*(4), 1009–1023.

Rolls, E. T., & Treves, A. (1997). *Neural networks and brain function*. Oxford, UK: Oxford University Press.

Schmidt, A. P., Bohmer, A. E., Antunes, C., Schallenberger, C., Porciuncula, L. O., Elisabetsky, E., et al. (2009). Anti-nociceptive properties of the xanthine oxidase inhibitor allopurinol in mice: Role of A1 adenosine receptors. *British Journal of Pharmacology*, *156*(1), 163–172.

Seger, C. A., & Cincotta, C. M. (2006). Dynamics of frontal, striatal, and hippocampal systems during rule learning. *Cerebral Cortex*, *16*(11), 1546–1555.

Shen, W., Flajolet, M., Greengard, P., & Surmeier, D. J. (2008). Dichotomous dopaminergic control of striatal synaptic plasticity. *Science*, *321*(5890), 848–851.

Shindou, T., Arbuthnott, G. W., & Wickens, J. R. (2008). Actions of adenosine A2A receptors on synaptic connections of spiny projection neurons in the neostriatal inhibitory network. *Journal of Neurophysiology*, *99*(4), 1884–1889.

Sills, T. L., Azampanah, A., & Fletcher, P. J. (2001). The adenosine A2A agonist CGS 21680 reverses the reduction in prepulse inhibition of the acoustic startle response induced by phencyclidine, but not by apomorphine and amphetamine. *Psychopharmacology (Berlin)*, *156*(2–3), 187–193.

Thiemann, G., Di Marzo, V., Molleman, A., & Hasenohrl, R. U. (2008). The CB(1) cannabinoid receptor antagonist AM251 attenuates amphetamine-induced behavioural sensitization while causing monoamine changes in nucleus accumbens and hippocampus. *Pharmacology Biochemistry & Behaviour*, *89*(3), 384–391.

Thiemann, G., van der Stelt, M., Petrosino, S., Molleman, A., Di Marzo, V., & Hasenohrl, R. U. (2008). The role of the CB1 cannabinoid receptor and its endogenous ligands, anandamide and 2-arachidonoylglycerol, in amphetamine-induced behavioural sensitization. *Behavioural Brain Research*, *187*(2), 289–296.

Wickens, J. R. (2009). Synaptic plasticity in the basal ganglia. *Behavioural Brain Research*, *199*(1), 119–128.

Yin, H. H., Mulcare, S. P., Hilario, M. R., Clouse, E., Holloway, T., Davis, M. I., et al. (2009). Dynamic reorganization of striatal circuits during the acquisition and consolidation of a skill. *Nature Neuroscience*, *12*(3), 333–341.

Zuardi, A. W., Crippa, J. A., Hallak, J. E., Pinto, J. P., Chagas, M. H., Rodrigues, G. G., et al. (2009). Cannabidiol for the treatment of psychosis in Parkinson's disease. *Journal of Psychopharmacology*, *23*(8), 979–983.

Zuardi, A. W., Rodrigues, J. A., & Cunha, J. M. (1991). Effects of cannabidiol in animal models predictive of antipsychotic activity. *Psychopharmacology (Berlin)*, *104*(2), 260–264.

Zuardi, A. W., Shirakawa, I., Finkelfarb, E., & Karniol, I. G. (1982). Action of cannabidiol on the anxiety and other effects produced by delta 9-THC in normal subjects. *Psychopharmacology (Berlin)*, *76*(3), 245–250.

Zuurman, L., Roy, C., Schoemaker, R. C., Amatsaleh, A., Guimaeres, L., Pinquier, J. L., et al. (2008). Inhibition of THC-induced effects on the central nervous system and heart rate by a novel CB1 receptor antagonist AVE1625. *Journal of Psychopharmacology*, *24*(3), 363–371.

6 Neurophysiological endophenotypes for psychosis

Madiha Shaikh and Elvira Bramon

The endophenotype approach to psychosis

Using conventional clinical diagnoses as the sole phenotype may not be optimal for the genetic dissection of complex (non-Mendelian) psychiatric diseases such as schizophrenia, bipolar disorder or psychosis. Psychiatric diagnoses are based on symptomatic definitions that reflect much heterogeneity (Begleiter & Porjesz, 2006; Gottesman & Gould, 2003). There is a growing recognition that common mental disorders, such as schizophrenia, bipolar disorder, and depression, are caused by numerous genetic and environmental factors, each of which have individually small effects and which only result in overt disease expression if their combined effects cross a hypothetical "threshold of liability" (Falconer, 1965).

In recent decades, research has increasingly focused on identifying endophenotypes in subjects with psychiatric diseases as well as their relatives in order to understand the genetic factors underlying the pathogenesis of the disorders. Endophenotypes are biological or clinical characteristics associated with a disease that can be easily, objectively and reliably measured as quantitative traits. These are heritable traits, which lie on the pathway between the genes and the diagnosis in question (Gottesman & Gould, 2003). Crucially, endophenotypes are significantly closer to the action of genetic factors than a clinical diagnosis and consequently could be less genetically complex than the disorder itself (i.e., fewer genes will affect the trait, or the effect of a particular gene will be greater in relation to the trait than to the clinical syndrome; Gottesman & Gould, 2003).

Genes that influence liability to mental disorders are likely to impinge on multiple neural systems, including cortical and subcortical dopaminergic, serotonergic, and glutamatergic systems that mediate a number of neurocognitive and affective processes, such as attention, learning, memory, language, stress sensitivity, emotional regulation, and social cognition (Cannon, Gasperoni, van Erp, & Rosso, 2001; Heinz, Romero, Gallinat, Juckel, & Weinberger, 2003). Therefore, promising endophenotypes for psychosis syndromes may be found in direct physiological or anatomical assessments of brain systems. We believe that these endophenotypes provide a more powerful strategy in searching for the genes involved in the development of psychosis (Burmeister, McInnis, & Zollner, 2008; Gottesman & Gould, 2003) and compared to psychiatric syndromes, endophenotypes can be allied more easily to animal models of the disease (Gould & Gottesman, 2006).

Event-related potentials as endophenotypes for psychosis

Neurophysiological tests obtained through electroencephalogram (EEG) are one of the promising endophenotypes for psychosis syndromes. Event-related potentials (ERPs) are fluctuations in the EEG produced in response to stimuli that are time-locked to sensory, motor or cognitive events. ERPs provide a non-invasive way of assessing the underlying neural network activity during such sensory/cognitive events. An ERP waveform consists of a pattern of waves or components that can be characterized and quantified by their latency, amplitude and scalp distribution. These ERP components are understood to exist on a continuum between exogenous and endogenous potentials. Exogenous ERP components are elicited by external stimuli; their characteristics being dependent on the features of these stimuli. Endogenous potentials are cognitive components that index information processing in the brain (Picton et al., 2000). A number of ERP markers have been proposed to characterize schizophrenia and bipolar disorder such as P300, P50, MMN, N100 (Bramon et al., 2003, 2005; Bramon, Croft et al., 2004; Bramon, Rabe-Hesketh, Sham, Murray, & Frangou, 2004; Frangou et al., 1997; Schulze et al., 2007, 2008).

P50 waves as a measure of sensory gating in psychosis

Sensory gating refers to the pre-attentional habituation of responses to repeated exposure to the same sensory stimulus. The inhibition of responsiveness to repetitive stimulation provides humans with the ability to negotiate a sensory-laden environment by blocking out irrelevant, meaningless, or redundant stimuli (Potter, Summerfelt, Gold, & Buchanan, 2006). Sensory gating is impaired in schizophrenia resulting in some level of "flooding" through sensory information overload (Freedman, Adler, Waldo, Pachtman, & Franks, 1983; Freedman et al., 1987, 1996).

Event-related potentials, in particular the P50 paradigm, have been used to measure sensory gating and its deficits in psychosis by examining the amplitude of the P50 waveform to two consecutive auditory stimuli separated by several hundred milliseconds (Freedman et al., 1983; Siegel, Waldo, Mizner, Adler, & Freedman, 1984). The normal response is for subjects to have a reduced P50 response to the second stimulus, suggesting that this repeated stimulus is actively suppressed. The degree of each suppression is conventionally measured as the ratio of the test to the conditioning P50 amplitude.

There is some controversy regarding whether or not the schizophrenia-related deficit truly represents a "gating" impairment. Some studies have reported that the amplitude from the second stimulus is the same in patients and controls, while the amplitude and/or latency for the first stimulus is altered in patients (and perhaps accounting for the decreased ratio; Jin & Potkin, 1996; Jin et al., 1997). As in many other studies, we did not find this effect in our sample. Instead, we observed a gating phenomenon in which the response to the first stimulus does not differ between groups. However, response to the second stimulus is greater in patients and their unaffected relatives in comparison to controls (Schulze et al.,

2007; Shaikh et al., 2010). In addition, P50 suppression ratio components have demonstrated a high level of reliability (ICC = 0.66) and heritability (68%; Hall, Schulze, Rijsdijk et al., 2006), thus making P50 a promising endophenotype.

There have been several reports of impaired sensory gating in patients with schizophrenia and their unaffected first-degree relatives (Adler, Hoffer, Griffith, Waldo, & Freedman, 1992; Clementz, Geyer, & Braff, 1998; Freedman et al., 1996; Myles-Worsley, 2002; Siegel et al., 1984; Waldo et al., 1994). These findings are supported by a meta-analysis indicating that severe P50 gating deficits exist in schizophrenia compared to controls with a pooled effect size of 1.6 (standardized difference between the patient and control means as obtained by the meta-analysis of all included studies; Bramon, Rabe-Hesketh et al., 2004). In addition, abnormal P50 gating response is also found in patients with bipolar disorder (with psychotic symptoms) and their unaffected relatives (Lijffijt et al., 2009; Schulze et al., 2007). These findings suggest that P50 suppression may be associated with genetic liability to psychosis overall and that the suppression ratio is possibly a strong endophenotype, useful for genetic association studies.

P300 component in psychosis and populations at risk

P300 is probably the most widely studied ERP in psychosis research. It is a relatively low frequency wave of positive polarity that is largest in central-parietal scalp regions and like other ERPs can be triggered by stimuli in any sensory modality. The auditory P300 is typically elicited using an auditory "oddball" paradigm wherein a series of repetitive stimuli are presented in a pseudo-random order. To generate a P300 response subjects must actively discriminate infrequent ("oddball" or "target") stimuli from the frequent "standard" stimuli. Therefore the P300 ERP paradigm entails directed, effortful processing of stimuli by participants and an overt response (Turetsky et al., 2007). This necessitates activation of attention and memory processes and therefore it is thought that analysis of the P300 waveform can provide clues as to the timing and nature of the cognitive activity involved (Polich, 2007). According to Polich and Comerchero (2003), the P300 waveform can be viewed as a measure of central nervous system activity occurring when stimulus memory representations are generated, with component size reflecting the degree of information processing/amount of attention allocated.

P300 indices have consistently demonstrated a high level of heritability as reflected in greater similarities in monozygotic compared to dizygotic twins or unrelated individuals (Alexander et al., 1996; Eischen & Polich, 1994; Katsanis, Iacono, McGue, & Carlson, 1997; O'Connor, Morzorati, Christian, & Li, 1994; Polich & Burns, 1987; van Beijsterveldt, Molenaar, de Geus, & Boomsma, 1998; van Beijsterveldt & van Baal, 2002; Weisbrod, Hill, Niethammer, & Sauer, 1999). A study by our group examining the Maudsley twin series estimated the heritability of P300 amplitude to be 69%, which is in accordance to the above meta-analysis (Hall, Schulze, Rijsdijk et al., 2006). For P300 latency, the results showed evidence for the presence of familiarity but the sample lacked the power to distinguish between genetic and shared environmental influences (Hall, Schulze, Rijsdijk et al., 2006). By analysing the genetic overlap between ERP components in the same sample, P300 amplitude and latency were found to have a significant negative correlation mediated by genetic factors (− 0.40). Thus, about half of the genetic factors contributing to P300 amplitude also affect its latency (Hall, Schulze, Bramon et al., 2006). Furthermore, the P300 ERP exhibits very strong test–retest reliability: healthy twin pairs were tested twice with a mean inter-test interval of 17.8 days (7–56 days) and very high reliabilities of 0.86 for P300 amplitude and 0.87 for P300 latency were observed (Hall, Schulze, Rijsdijk et al., 2006) The high heritability and reliability of P300 indices provides support for their role as endophenotypes.

P300 indices, have been employed to characterize cognitive deficits in schizophrenia (Roth & Cannon, 1972). Reduced amplitude and delayed latency of the P300 component have been replicated in the Maudsley studies as well as in psychosis research globally (Blackwood, 2000; Blackwood, St Clair, Muir, & Duffy, 1991; Bramon et al., 2005; Frangou et al., 1997; van der Stelt, Lieberman, & Belger, 2005). In support of these findings, meta-analyses have confirmed that patients with schizophrenia have smaller P300 (p3b) amplitude and prolonged P300 latency in comparison to healthy controls (Bramon, Rabe-Hesketh et al., 2004; Jeon & Polich, 2003). The severity of the P300 amplitude and latency deficits described is comparable with the most robust findings reported for brain morphometric and neuropsychological abnormalities in schizophrenia (Bramon, Rabe-Hesketh et al., 2004).

Our meta-analysis of family studies (Blackwood et al., 1991, 2001; Frangou et al., 1997; Karoumi et al., 2000; Kidogami, Yoneda, Asaba, & Sakai, 1991; Kimble et al., 2000; Roxborough, Muir, Blackwood, Walker, & Blackburn, 1993; Schreiber, Stolzborn, Kornhuber, & Born, 1992; Turetsky, Cannon, & Gur, 2000; Weisbrod et al., 1999; Winterer et al., 2003) showed that unaffected relatives of patients with schizophrenia also suffer P300 deficits in both amplitude (Pooled Effect Size: 0.61; 95% CI: 0.30 to 0.91; $p < .001$) and latency (Pooled Effect Size: - 0.50; 95% CI: - 0.88 to - 0.13; $p = .009$; Bramon et al., 2005). P300 latency delays and amplitude reductions are also present in bipolar patients (Muir, St Clair, & Blackwood, 1991; O'Donnell, Vohs, Hetrick, Carroll, & Shekhar, 2004; Salisbury, Shenton, & McCarley, 1999; Schulze et al., 2008; Souza et al., 1995) and in relatives of patients with bipolar disorder, indicating that these may also serve as endophenotypes for psychosis in general (Bestelmeyer, Phillips, Crombie, Benson, & St Clair, 2009; Hall et al., 2007; Pierson, Jouvent, Quintin, Perez-Diaz, & Leboyer, 2000; Schulze et al., 2008).

Significant P300 amplitude reductions, similar to those observed in recent onset and chronically ill schizophrenia patients are observed in individuals who suffer prodromal psychotic symptoms and who are therefore at ultra-high risk (UHR) of developing a psychotic illness (van der Stelt et al., 2005). A more recent study by our group examined P300 in a sample of 35 prodromal individuals with at-risk mental states (ARMs) as defined by Yung and colleagues (Yung et al., 2005). We found significant P300 amplitude reductions in the ARM group compared to 57 healthy controls, but no changes in P300 latency in these "at risk" individuals were found (Bramon et al., 2008). This finding for P300 amplitude has since been replicated twice in independent samples of 54 (Özgürdal et al., 2008) and 100 (Frommann et al., 2008) prodromal patients. Longitudinal follow-up data and large patient samples are required to determine whether P300 actually has predictive validity for later schizophrenia or other psychiatric disorders in these UHR populations. Together these findings suggest that P300 may be associated with genetic liability to psychosis overall, making it a promising endophenotype for genetic studies as well as a potential biomarker for early detection of psychosis risk.

Association between sensory gating as measured by the P50 wave and psychosis candidate genes

Although the use of endophenotypes in genetic association studies has been proposed as a potential solution, to date only a few studies have examined the relationship between genetics and ERP endophenotypes for psychosis.

Neuregulin 1 *(NRG1)* is one of the promising candidate genes for schizophrenia with the discovery of a high-risk haplotype in the Icelandic population in 2002 on the 5′-end of the gene (Stefansson et al., 2002). Since then, the Icelandic *NRG1* haplotype has been associated with lower hippocampal volumes in schizophrenia patients and in non-affected family members (Gruber et al., 2008). One of its polymorphisms (SNP8NRG221533) has been reported to influence subcortical medial microstructure in the human brain (Winterer et al., 2008) while the other (SNP8NRG243177) contributes to the enlargement of lateral ventricles in first episode schizophrenia (Mata et al., 2009). A recent fMRI study of a working-memory task found differential brain activations in the left hippocampus, precuneus and cerebellum, as well as the right anterior cingulate between patients carrying an at-risk allele on the *NRG1* gene and patients without this genetic risk (Kircher, Thienel et al., 2009). Decreased activation of frontal and temporal lobe regions has also been associated with SNP8NRG243177 (Hall, Whalley et al., 2006). There have also been reports of *NRG1* being associated with psychotic symptoms, cognitive impairments in schizophrenia and semantic language capacities (Hall, Whalley et al., 2006; Kircher, Krug et al., 2009; Lawrie, Hall, McIntosh, Cunningham-Owens, & Johnstone, 2008). Therefore, we set out to investigate the association between *NRG1* and EEG endophenotypes for psychosis.

Another candidate gene proposed for schizophrenia is that encoding the brain-derived neurotrophic factor (BDNF); a neurotrophin located predominantly in the prefrontal cortex (PFC) and hippocampus (Pezawas et al., 2004; Yamada & Nabeshima, 2003), areas thought to be involved in P50 generation. *BDNF* is involved in learning and memory through its role in activity dependent neuroplasticity, including the modulation of synaptic changes such as hippocampal long-term potentiation (LTP; Altar et al., 1997; Poo, 2001). A genetic variant (Val^{66}Met) in the human pro-protein of BDNF, which alters intracellular trafficking and secretion of the protein, was associated with performance in memory (Chen et al., 2004; Dempster et al., 2005; Egan et al., 2003). Some studies have also reported an association between the Val^{66}Met polymorphism and schizophrenia (Hong, Yu, Lin, & Tsai, 2003; Neves-Pereira et al., 2005; Rosa et al., 2006); however, several independent studies and meta-analyses did not find any associations (Kanazawa, Glatt, Kia-Keating, Yoneda, & Tsuang, 2007; Zintzaras, 2007). Nonetheless, the Val^{66}Met genotype may be important for modulating several schizophrenia-related phenotypes including brain morphology, cognitive function and psychiatric symptoms (Dempster et al., 2005; Egan et al., 2003; Han et al., 2008; Hariri et al., 2003; Numata et al., 2006; Szeszko et al., 2005). Therefore, it would be of interest to investigate the association between *BDNF* and ERP endophenotypes.

The gene encoding catechol-O-methyltransferase (COMT) is a potentially strong candidate for schizophrenia susceptibility (Egan et al., 2001; Li et al., 1996, 2000; Lohmueller, Pearce, Pike, Lander, & Hirschhorn, 2003; Shifman et al., 2002), owing to the role of *COMT* in dopamine metabolism and the location of the gene within the deleted region in velocardiofacial syndrome; a disorder associated with high rates of schizophrenia. The *COMT* gene is thought to influence prefrontal cognition; in particular the *COMT* Val^{158}Met polymorphism has been associated to working memory deficits in schizophrenia (Bruder et al., 2005; Egan et al., 2001; Galderisi et al., 2005; Goldberg et al., 2003; Liao et al., 2009; Malhotra et al., 2002; Minzenberg et al., 2006; Rosa et al., 2004; Rybakowski et al., 2006). These memory deficits described in schizophrenia might well be expected to influence the P50 wave, which also in part reflects memory processes. Lu et al. (2007) using 62 participants, found that the valine homozygous carriers are likely to have the greatest gating deficits, supporting *COMT* as a genetic determinant of the P50 endophenotype, as well as a role for prefrontal dopamine in auditory filtering. As the evidence connecting P50 and *COMT* is limited, we considered it useful to test this association using a larger sample.

In our recent study, we examined the effect of polymorphisms in the *NRG1*, *COMT* and *BDNF* genes on the P50 endophenotype in a sample of 451 individuals and found no evidence for association between these polymorphisms and P50 (Shaikh et al., 2010). While *BDNF*, *COMT* and *NRG1* have been associated with psychosis and cognitive deficits in psychotic illness, our results suggest that variation in *BDNF* Val^{66}Met, *COMT* Val^{158}Met and *NRG1* does not affect the generation of the P50 gating deficit.

Despite their biological plausibility and many early encouraging findings, some recent large-scale genome-wide association studies of schizophrenia (Kirov et al., 2008; Sanders et al., 2008) and bipolar disorder (Sklar et al., 2008) and meta-analysis of association studies (Munafo, Bowes, Clark, & Flint, 2005; Okochi et al., 2009) have reported a lack of association with *COMT* Val^{158}Met and *BDNF* Val^{66}Met polymorphisms. Likewise, endophenotype studies exploring both functional and structural deficits of psychosis have failed to find any associations with *COMT* and *BDNF* (Bramon et al., 2006; Dutt et al., 2009). Similarly, recent meta-analyses and an association study concluded that *NRG1* markers do not contribute significantly to schizophrenia (Gong et al., 2009; Jonsson et al., 2009). Despite negative findings, there have been many positive reports of association replicating *NRG1* as a candidate gene for psychosis (Georgieva et al., 2008; Lewis et al., 2003; Li, Collier, & He, 2006; Munafo, Attwood, & Flint, 2008; Prata et al., 2009; Sanders et al., 2008; Stefansson et al., 2002, 2003; Stefansson, Steinthorsdottir, Thorgeirsson, Gulcher, & Stefansson, 2004; Williams et al., 2003). The evidence from our large study suggests that any such association between P50 indices and *NRG1*, *COMT* Val^{158}Met or *BDNF* Val^{66}Met genotypes, if present, must be very subtle (Shaikh et al., 2010). One point to consider is whether genes influencing each ERP endophenotype are at least partially distinct from each other. A study by our group investigating the genetic overlap between P300, MMN and P50 ERPs (Hall, Schulze, Bramon et al., 2006) found that each ERP serves to evaluate different information-processing functions that may be mediated by distinct neurobiological mechanisms, which in turn are influenced by different sets of genetic risk factors. In this light, it would be of interest to investigate other candidate genes/regions for schizophrenia, in particular the a7 nicotinic acetylcholine receptor gene (*CHRNA7*) located at 15q13–14 and its partial duplication *CHRFAM7A*, both of which are reported to influence P50 gating deficits (Freedman et al., 1997; Leonard et al., 2002; Martin et al., 2007; Raux et al., 2002).

Association between candidate genes for psychosis and the P300 endophenotype

The use of P300 as an endophenotype in genetic research is growing. The *COMT* gene, thought to play a role in schizophrenia and influence cognitive performance has been studied in relation to the P300 ERP. Tsai et al. (2003) in a study population of 120 healthy Han Chinese females, found the Met/Met genotype of the *COMT* Val^{158}Met to be associated with significantly shorter P300 latency across frontal and central sites. This is consistent with enhanced frontal dopaminergic neurotransmission and enhanced cognition in Met/Met individuals, compared to Val carriers. Gallinat et al. (2003) using European participants reported reductions in frontal P300 amplitude associated with the Met/Met genotype. Inheriting the Met/Met genotype did not influence P300 amplitudes at central or parietal sites. The smaller P300 wave in frontal regions was interpreted as "neuronal noise" reductions resulting from enhanced dopaminergic transmission in Met/Met carriers. The authors explained their different findings by region, by arguing that central and parietal P300 reflect stable P300 signals as opposed to frontal measurements representing "noise" (Gallinat et al., 2003). Golimbet and colleagues (2006) found higher P300 amplitudes for Met/Met individuals compared to a Val/Val group, although this effect was only significant in 35 healthy first-degree relatives of schizophrenic patients and not the patients themselves (Golimbet et al., 2006). Preliminary data from the Maudsley Family and Twin Study with 189 individuals failed to replicate either of these associations between *COMT* Val^{158}Met genotype and P300 (Bramon et al., 2006; Williams, 2009). While the previous studies by Tsai et al. (2003) and Gallinat et al. (2003) are of small sample sizes and are at least in part contradictory, there is certainly enough evidence to warrant further examination of the relationship between P300 indices and *COMT* Val^{158}Met.

NRG1 has been examined extensively in relation to schizophrenia and even bipolar disorder, but there is limited information about its association with psychosis endophenotypes. Our recent investigation into the effect of *NRG1* on the P300 endophenotype in psychosis revealed that SNP8NRG221533 contributes to the processing speed of auditory stimuli (Bramon et al., 2008). Consequently, it seems plausible that variation in *NRG1* may convey risk for schizophrenia by disrupting neural connectivity, possibly white matter integrity, and leading to a slower speed of cognitive processing (Bramon et al., 2008). Although the association between *NRG1* and P300 latency can only be regarded as preliminary and requires replication, ideally in a larger sample, these findings do suggest that variation in *NRG1* influences functional measures in psychosis. Our results provide support for *NRG1* as a plausible candidate gene.

Conclusions

To date our research has provided evidence for ERPs, namely P300 and P50, as neurophysiological endophenotypes for psychosis and has revealed an association between *NRG1* and P300 latency. This makes a strong case for the use of ERPs in genetic studies and has led our team to investigate other promising EEG endophenotypes such as MMN, N100 and quantitative EEG traits such as gamma oscillations and coherence of EEG signals in future work.

Future research building on the findings of work from our group should employ a more complex endophenotype approach to psychiatric genetics by integrating measures from a range of modalities including neurochemical, neuroanatomical and neuropsychological markers of psychosis risk. A comprehensive multi-modal endophenotype for psychosis may help to identify susceptibility genes for psychosis, and contribute to understanding the neurobiological basis of the disorder. It is also crucial to increase the sample sizes available for study, continue to develop and refine endophenotypes, and apply models of increased genetic complexity including gene–gene/environment interactions and genome-wide association studies.

The identification of susceptibility variants for schizophrenia and bipolar disorder and the confirmation of their functional impact on the disease or on its endophenotypes will help in defining the molecular and physiological pathways influencing disease risk. It is important to realize that even rare variants with a small effect on the population level or variants with small odds ratios can provide insight into pathogenic mechanisms, point to other transcripts related by sequence or function, and suggest interesting pharmaceutical targets. Also, the early identification (and treatment) of individuals at increased risk for the disease might become possible using multi-modal assessments as well as genetic screening. It is hoped that a better understanding of the genetic factors involved in the pathogenesis will also assist in the characterization of environmental risk factors that play a role, leading to preventative strategies.

References

Adler, L. E., Hoffer, L. J., Griffith, J., Waldo, M. C., & Freedman, R. (1992). Normalization by nicotine of deficient auditory sensory gating in the relatives of schizophrenics. *Biological Psychiatry*, *327*, 607–616.

Alexander, J. E., Bauer, L. O., Kuperman, S., Morzorati, S., O'Connor, S. J., Rohrbaugh, J., et al. (1996). Hemispheric differences for P300 amplitude form an auditory oddball task. *International Journal of Psychophysiology*, *21*, 189–196.

Altar, C. A., Cai, N., Bliven, T., Juhasz, M., Conner, J. M., Acheson, A. L., et al. (1997). Anterograde transport of brain-derived neurotrophic factor and its role in the brain. *Nature*, *389*, 856–860.

Begleiter, H., & Porjesz, B. (2006). Genetics of human brain oscillations. *International Journal of Psychophysiology*, *602*, 162–171.

Bestelmeyer, P. E., Phillips, L. H., Crombie, C., Benson, P., & St Clair, D. (2009). The P300 as a possible endophenotype for schizophrenia and bipolar disorder: Evidence from twin and patient studies. *Psychiatry Research*, *1693*, 212–219.

Blackwood, D. (2000). P300, a state and a trait marker in schizophrenia. *The Lancet*, *3554*, 771–772.

Blackwood, D. H., Fordyce, A., Walker, M. T., St Clair, D. M., Porteous, D. J., & Muir, W. J. (2001). Schizophrenia and affective disorders—Cosegregation with a translocation at chromosome 1q42 that directly disrupts brain-expressed genes: Clinical and P300 findings in a family. *American Journal of Human Genetics*, *692*, 428–433.

Blackwood, D. H., St Clair, D. M., Muir, W. J., & Duffy, J. C. (1991). Auditory P300 and eye tracking dysfunction in schizophrenic pedigrees. *Archives of General Psychiatry*, *4810*, 899–909.

Bramon, E., Croft, R. J., Arthur, M., McDonald, C., Frangou, S., & Murray, R. M. (2003). The P300 wave in schizophrenia: A family study. *Schizophrenia Research*, *60*, 248.

Bramon, E., Croft, R. J., McDonald, C., Virdi, G. K., Gruzelier, J. G., Baldeweg, T., et al. (2004). Mismatch negativity in schizophrenia: A family study. *Schizophrenia Research*, *671*, 1–10.

Bramon, E., Dempster, E., Frangou, S., McDonald, C., Schoenberg, P., MacCabe, J. H., et al. (2006). Is there an association between the *COMT* gene and P300 endophenotypes? *European Psychiatry*, *211*, 70–73.

Bramon, E., McDonald, C., Croft, R. J., Landau, S., Filbey, F., Gruzelier, J. H., et al. (2005). Is the P300 wave an endophenotype for schizophrenia? A meta-analysis and a family study. *NeuroImage*, *274*, 960–968.

Bramon, E., Rabe-Hesketh, S., Sham, P., Murray, R. M., & Frangou, S. (2004). Meta-analysis of the P300 and P50 waveforms in schizophrenia. *Schizophrenia Research*, *70*(2–3), 315–329.

Bramon, E., Shaikh, M., Broome, M., Lappin, J., Berge, D., Day, F., et al. (2008). Abnormal P300 in people with high risk of developing psychosis. *NeuroImage*, *412*, 553–560.

Bruder, G. E., Keilp, J. G., Xu, H., Shikhman, M., Schori, E., Gorman, J. M., et al. (2005). Catechol-O-methyltransferase (*COMT*) genotypes and working memory: Associations with differing cognitive operations. *Biological Psychiatry*, *5811*, 901–907.

Burmeister, M., McInnis, M. G., & Zollner, S. (2008). Psychiatric genetics: Progress amid controversy. *Nature Reviews Genetics*, *97*, 527–540.

Cannon, T. D., Gasperoni, T. L., van Erp, T. G. M., & Rosso, I. M. (2001). Quantitative neural indicators of liability to schizophrenia: Implications for molecular genetic studies. *American Journal of Medical Genetics*, *1051*, 16–19.

Chen, Z. Y., Patel, P. D., Sant, G., Meng, C. X., Teng, K. K., Hempstead, B. L., et al. (2004). Variant brain-derived neurotrophic factor (BDNF) (Met[66]) alters the intracellular trafficking and activity-dependent secretion of wild-type BDNF in neurosecretory cells and cortical neurons. *Journal of Neuroscience*, *2418*, 4401–4411.

Clementz, B., Geyer, M., & Braff, D. (1998). Poor P50 suppression among schizophrenia patients and their first-degree biological relatives. *American Journal of Psychiatry*, *15512*, 1691–1694.

Dempster, E., Toulopoulou, T., McDonald, C., Bramon, E., Walshe, M., Filbey, F., et al. (2005). Association between BDNF Val[66]Met genotype and episodic memory. *American Journal of Medical Genetics B Neuropsychiatric Genetics*, *134B1*, 73–75.

Dutt, A., McDonald, C., Dempster, E., Prata, D., Shaikh, M., Williams, I., et al. (2009). The effect of *COMT*, *BDNF*, 5-*HTT*, *NRG1* and *DTNBP1* genes on hippocampal and lateral ventricular volume in psychosis. *Psychological Medicine*, *39*, 1–15.

Egan, M. F., Goldberg, T. E., Kolachana, B. S., Callicott, J. H., Mazzanti, C. M., Straub, R. E., et al. (2001). Effect of COMT Val108/158 Met genotype on frontal lobe function and risk for schizophrenia. *Proceedings of the National Academy of Sciences of the USA*, *9812*, 6917–6922.

Egan, M. F., Kojima, M., Callicott, J. H., Goldberg, T. E., Kolachana, B. S., Bertolino, A., et al. (2003). The BDNF Val[66]Met polymorphism affects activity-dependent secretion of BDNF and human memory and hippocampal function. *Cell*, *1122*, 257–269.

Eischen, S., & Polich, J. (1994, July). P300 from families. *Electroencephalography & Clinical Neurophysiology*, *924*, 369–372.

Falconer, D. S. (1965). The inheritance of liability to certain diseases, estimated from the incidence among relatives. *Annals of Human Genetics*, *29*, 51–76.

Frangou, S., Sharma, T., Alarcon, G., Sigmudsson, T., Takei, N., Binnie, C., et al. (1997). The Maudsley family study, II: Endogenous event-related potentials in familial schizophrenia. *Schizophrenia Research*, *23*, 45–53.

Freedman, R., Adler, L., Myles-Worsley, M., Nagamoto, H., Miller, C., Kisley, M., et al. (1996). Inhibitory gating of an evoked response to repeated audiotry stimuli in schizophrenic and normal subjects. *Archives of General Psychiatry*, *53*, 1114–1121.

Freedman, R., Adler, L., Waldo, M., Pachtman, E., & Franks, R. (1983). Neurophysiological evidence for a defect in inhibitory pathways in schizophrenia: Comparison of medicated and drug-free patients. *Biological Psychiatry*, *18*, 537–551.

Freedman, R., Adler, L. E., Gerhardt, G. A., Waldo, M., Baker, N., Rose, G. M., et al. (1987). Neurobiological studies of sensory gating in schizophrenia. *Schizophrenia Bulletin*, *134*, 669–678.

Freedman, R., Coon, H., Myles-Worsley, M., Orr-Urtreger, A., Olincy, A., Davis, A., et al. (1997). Linkage of a neurophysiological deficit in schizophrenia to a chromosome 15 locus. *Proceedings of the National Academy of Sciences*, *94*, 587–592.

Frommann, I., Brinkmeyer, J., Ruhrmann, S., Hack, E., Brockhaus-Dumke, A., Bechdolf, A., et al. (2008). Auditory P300 in individuals clinically at risk for psychosis. *International Journal of Psychophysiology*, *70*, 192–205.

Galderisi, S., Maj, M., Kirkpatrick, B., Piccardi, P., Mucci, A., Invernizzi, G., et al. (2005). Catechol-O-methyltransferase Val[158]Met polymorphism in schizophrenia: Associations with cognitive and motor impairment. *Neuropsychobiology*, *522*, 83–89.

Gallinat, J., Bajbouj, M., Sander, T., Schlattmann, P., Xu, K., Ferro, E. F., et al. (2003). Association of the G1947A COMT (Val(108/158)Met) gene polymorphism with prefrontal P300 during information processing. *Biological Psychiatry*, *541*, 40–48.

Georgieva, L., Dimitrova, A., Ivanov, D., Nikolov, I., Williams, N. M., Grozeva, D., et al. (2008). Support for neuregulin 1 as a susceptibility gene for bipolar disorder and schizophrenia. *Biological Psychiatry*, *645*, 419–427.

Goldberg, T. E., Egan, M. F., Gscheidle, T., Coppola, R., Weickert, T., Kolachana, B. S., et al. (2003). Executive subprocesses in working memory—Relationship to catechol-O-methyltransferase Val^{158}Met genotype and schizophrenia. *Archives of General Psychiatry*, *609*, 889–896.

Golimbet, V., Gritsenko, I., Alfimova, M., Lebedeva, I., Lezheiko, T., Abramova, L., et al. (2006). Association study of *COMT* gene Val^{158}Met polymorphism with auditory P300 and performance on neurocognitive tests in patients with schizophrenia and their relatives. *World Journal of Biological Psychiatry*, *74*, 238–245.

Gong, Y. G., Wu, C. N., Xing, Q. H., Zhao, X. Z., Zhu, J., & He, L. (2009). A two-method meta-analysis of neuregulin 1(NRG1) association and heterogeneity in schizophrenia. *Schizophrenia Research*, *111*, 109–114.

Gottesman, I. I., & Gould, T. D. (2003). The endophenotype concept in psychiatry: Etymology and strategic intentions. *American Journal of Psychiatry*, *1604*, 636–645.

Gould, T. D., & Gottesman, I. I. (2006). Psychiatric endophenotypes and the development of valid animal models. *Genes Brain Behaviour*, *52*, 113–119.

Gruber, O., Falkai, P., Schneider-Axmann, T., Schwab, S. G., Wagner, M., & Maier, W. (2008). Neuregulin-1 haplotype HAP(ICE) is associated with lower hippocampal volumes in schizophrenic patients and in non-affected family members. *Journal of Psychiatric Research*, *431*, 1–6.

Hall, J., Whalley, H. C., Job, D. E., Baig, B. J., McIntosh, A. M., Evans, K. L., et al. (2006). A neuregulin 1 variant associated with abnormal cortical function and psychotic symptoms. *Nature Neuroscience*, *912*, 1477–1478.

Hall, M. H., Rijsdijk, F., Kalidindi, S., Schulze, K., Kravariti, E., Kane, F., et al. (2007). Genetic overlap between bipolar illness and event-related potentials. *Psychological Medicine*, *375*, 667–678.

Hall, M. H., Schulze, K., Bramon, E., Murray, R. M., Sham, P. & Rijsdijk, F. (2006). Genetic overlap between P300, P50, and duration mismatch negativity. *American Journal of Medical Genetics B Neuropsychiatric Genetics*, *141B*, 336–343.

Hall, M. H., Schulze, K., Rijsdijk, F., Picchioni, M., Ettinger, U., Bramon, E., et al. (2006). Heritability and reliability of P300, P50 and duration mismatch negativity. *Behavioural Genetics*, *366*, 845–857.

Han, D. H., Park, D. B., Choi, T. Y., Joo, S. Y., Lee, M. K., Park, B. R., et al. (2008). Effects of brain-derived neurotrophic factor–catecholamine-O-methyltransferase gene interaction on schizophrenic symptoms. *NeuroReport*, *1911*, 1155–1158.

Hariri, A. R., Goldberg, T. E., Mattay, V. S., Kolachana, B. S., Callicott, J. H., Egan, M. F., et al. (2003). Brain-derived neurotrophic factor Val^{66}Met polymorphism affects human memory-related hippocampal activity and predicts memory performance. *Journal of Neuroscience*, *2317*, 6690–6694.

Heinz, A., Romero, B., Gallinat, J., Juckel, G., & Weinberger, D. R. (2003). Molecular brain imaging and the neurobiology and genetics of schizophrenia. *Pharmacopsychiatry*, *36*, S152–S157.

Hong, C. J., Yu, Y. W., Lin, C. H., & Tsai, S. J. (2003). An association study of a brain-derived neurotrophic factor Val^{66}Met polymorphism and clozapine response of schizophrenic patients. *Neuroscience Letters*, *3493*, 206–208.

Jeon, Y. W., & Polich, J. (2003). Meta-analysis of P300 and schizophrenia: Patients, paradigms, and practical implications. *Psychophysiology*, *405*, 684–701.

Jin, Y., & Potkin, S. G. (1996). P50 changes with visual interference in normal subjects: A sensory distraction model for schizophrenia. *Clinical Electroencephalography*, *273*, 151–154.

Jin, Y., Potkin, S. G., Patterson, J. V., Sandman, C. A., Hetrick, W. P., & Bunney, J. W. E. (1997). Effects of P50 temporal variability on sensory gating in schizophrenia. *Psychiatry Research*, *70*, 71–81.

Jonsson, E. G., Saetre, P., Vares, M., Andreou, D., Larsson, K., Timm, S., et al. (2009). DTNBP1, NRG1, DAOA, DAO and GRM3 polymorphisms and schizophrenia: An association study. *Neuropsychobiology*, *593*, 142–150.

Kanazawa, T., Glatt, S. J., Kia-Keating, B., Yoneda, H., & Tsuang, M. T. (2007). Meta-analysis reveals no association of the Val^{66}Met polymorphism of brain-derived neurotrophic factor with either schizophrenia or bipolar disorder. *Psychiatric Genetics*, *173*, 165–170.

Karoumi, B., Laurent, A., Rosenfeld, F., Rochet, T., Brunon, A. M., Dalery, J., et al. (2000). Alteration of event related potentials in siblings discordant for schizophrenia. *Schizophrenia Research*, *412*, 325–334.

Katsanis, J., Iacono, W., McGue, M., & Carlson, S. (1997). P300 event-related potential heritability in monozygotic and dizygotic twins. *Psychophysiology*, *34*, 47–58.

Kidogami, Y., Yoneda, H., Asaba, H., & Sakai, T. (1991). P300 in 1st degree relatives of schizophrenics. *Schizophrenia Research*, *61*, 9–13.

Kimble, M., Lyons, M., O'Donnell, B., Nestor, P., Niznikiewicz, M., & Toomey, R. (2000). The effect of family status and schizotypy on electrophysiologic measures of attention and semantic processing. *Biological Psychiatry*, *475*, 402–412.

Kircher, T., Krug, A., Markov, V., Whitney, C., Krach, S., Zerres, K., et al. (2009). Genetic variation in the schizophrenia-risk gene neuregulin 1 correlates with brain activation and impaired speech production in a verbal fluency task in healthy individuals. *Human Brain Mapping*, *3010*, 3406–3416.

Kircher, T., Thienel, R., Wagner, M., Reske, M., Habel, U., Kellermann, T., et al. (2009). Neuregulin 1 ICE-single nucleotide polymorphism in first episode schizophrenia correlates with cerebral activation in fronto-temporal areas. *European Archives of Psychiatry and Clinical Neuroscience*, *2592*, 72–79.

Kirov, G., Zaharieva, I., Georgieva, L., Moskvina, V., Nikolov, I., Cichon, S., et al. (2008). A genome-wide association study in 574 schizophrenia trios using DNA pooling. *Molecular Psychiatry*, *148*, 796–803.

Lawrie, S. M., Hall, J., McIntosh, A. M., Cunningham-Owens, D. G., & Johnstone, E. C. (2008). Neuroimaging and molecular genetics of schizophrenia: Pathophysiological advances and therapeutic potential. *British Journal of Pharmacology*, *153*(Suppl. 1), S120–124.

Leonard, S., Gault, J., Hopkins, J., Logel, J., Vianzon, R., Short, M., et al. (2002). Association of promoter variants in the alpha 7 nicotinic acetylcholine receptor subunit gene with an inhibitory deficit found in schizophrenia. *Archives of General Psychiatry*, *5912*, 1085–1096.

Lewis, C. M., Levinson, D. F., Wise, L. H., DeLisi, L. E., Straub, R. E., Hovatta, I., et al. (2003). Genome scan meta-analysis of schizophrenia and bipolar disorder, part II: Schizophrenia. *American Journal of Human Genetics*, *731*, 34–48.

Li, D., Collier, D. A., & He, L. (2006). Meta-analysis shows strong positive association of the neuregulin 1 (NRG1) gene with schizophrenia. *Human Molecular Genetics*, *1512*, 1995–2002.

Li, T., Ball, D., Zhao, J., Murray, R. M., Liu, X., Sham, P. C., et al. (2000). Family based linkage disequilibrium mapping using SNP marker haplotypes: Application to a potential locus for schizophrenia at chromosome 22q11. *Molecular Psychiatry*, *5*, 452.

Li, T., Sham, P. C., Vallada, H., Xie, T., Tang, X., Murray, R. M., et al. (1996). Preferential transmission of the high activity allele of COMT in schizophrenia. *Psychiatric Genetics, 63*, 131–133.

Liao, S. Y., Lin, S. H., Liu, C. M., Hsieh, M. H., Hwang, T. J., Liu, S. K., et al. (2009). Genetic variants in COMT and neurocognitive impairment in families of patients with schizophrenia. *Genes Brain and Behaviour, 82*, 228–237.

Lijffijt, M., Moeller, F. G., Boutros, N. N., Steinberg, J. L., Meier, S. L., Lane, S. D., et al. (2009). Diminished P50, N100 and P200 auditory sensory gating in bipolar I disorder. *Psychiatry Research, 1673*, 191–201.

Lohmueller, K. E., Pearce, C. L., Pike, M., Lander, E. S., & Hirschhorn, J. N. (2003). Meta-analysis of genetic association studies supports a contribution of common variants to susceptibility to common disease. *Nature Genetics, 332*, 177–182.

Lu, B. Y., Martin, K. E., Edgar, J. C., Smith, A. K., Lewis, S. F., Escamilla, M. A., et al. (2007). Effect of catechol O-methyltransferase val(158)met polymorphism on the p50 gating endophenotype in schizophrenia. *Biological Psychiatry, 627*, 822–825.

Malhotra, A. K., Kestler, L. J., Mazzanti, C., Bates, J. A., Goldberg, T., & Goldman, D. (2002). A functional polymorphism in the *COMT* gene and performance on a test of prefrontal cognition. *American Journal of Psychiatry, 1594*, 652–654.

Martin, L. F., Leonard, S., Hall, M. H., Tregellas, J. R., Freedman, R., & Olincy, A. (2007). Sensory gating and alpha-7 nicotinic receptor gene allelic variants in schizoaffective disorder, bipolar type. *American Journal of Medical Genetics B Neuropsychiatric Genetics, 144B5*, 611–614.

Mata, I., Perez-Iglesias, R., Roiz-Santianez, R., Tordesillas-Gutierrez, D., Gonzalez-Mandly, A., Vazquez-Barquero, J. L., et al. (2009). A neuregulin 1 variant is associated with increased lateral ventricle volume in patients with first-episode schizophrenia. *Biological Psychiatry, 656*, 535–540.

Minzenberg, M. J., Xu, K., Mitropoulou, V., Harvey, P. D., Finch, T., Flory, J. D., et al. (2006). Catechol-O-methyltransferase Val^{158}Met genotype variation is associated with prefrontal-dependent task performance in schizotypal personality disorder patients and comparison groups. *Psychiatric Genetics, 163*, 117–124.

Muir, W., St Clair, D., & Blackwood, D. (1991). Long-latency auditory event-related potentials in schizophrenia and in bipolar and unipolar affective disorder. *Psychological Medicine, 21*, 867–879.

Munafo, M. R., Attwood, A. S., & Flint, J. (2008). Neuregulin 1 genotype and schizophrenia. *Schizophrenia Bulletin, 341*, 9–12.

Munafo, M. R., Bowes, L., Clark, T. G., & Flint, J. (2005). Lack of association of the *COMT* (Val158/108 Met) gene and schizophrenia: A meta-analysis of case-control studies. *Molecular Psychiatry, 108*, 765–770.

Myles-Worsley, M. (2002). P50 sensory gating in multiplex schizophrenia families from a Pacific Island isolate. *American Journal of Psychiatry, 15912*, 2007–2012.

Neves-Pereira, M., Cheung, J. K., Pasdar, A., Zhang, F., Breen, G., Yates, P., et al. (2005). *BDNF* gene is a risk factor for schizophrenia in a Scottish population. *Molecular Psychiatry, 102*, 208–212.

Numata, S., Ueno, S., Iga, J., Yamauchi, K., Hongwei, S., Ohta, K., et al. (2006). Brain-derived neurotrophic factor (BDNF) Val^{66}Met polymorphism in schizophrenia is associated with age at onset and symptoms. *Neuroscience Letters, 4011–12*, 1–5.

O'Connor, S., Morzorati, S., Christian, J. C., & Li, T. K. (1994). Heritable features of the auditory oddball event-related potential: Peaks, latencies, morphology and topography. *Electroencephalography and Clinical Neurophysiology, 922*, 115–125.

O'Donnell, B. F., Vohs, J. L., Hetrick, W. P., Carroll, C. A., & Shekhar, A. (2004). Auditory event-related potential abnormalities in bipolar disorder and schizophrenia. *International Journal of Psychophysiology*, *531*, 45–55.

Okochi, T., Ikeda, M., Kishi, T., Kawashima, K., Kinoshita, Y., Kitajima, T., et al. (2009). Meta-analysis of association between genetic variants in COMT and schizophrenia: An update. *Schizophrenia Research*, *110*, 140–148.

Özgürdal, S., Gudlowski, Y., Witthaus, H., Kawohl, W., Uhl, I., Hauser, M., et al. (2008). Reduction of auditory event-related P300 amplitude in subjects with at-risk mental state for schizophrenia. *Schizophrenia Research*, *105*, 272–278.

Pezawas, L., Verchinski, B. A., Mattay, V. S., Callicott, J. H., Kolachana, B. S., Straub, R. E., et al. (2004). The brain-derived neurotrophic factor Val^{66}Met polymorphism and variation in human cortical morphology. *Journal of Neuroscience*, *2445*, 10099–10102.

Picton, T. W., Bentin, S., Berg, P., Donchin, E., Hillyard, S. A., Johnson, R., Jr., et al. (2000). Guidelines for using human event-related potentials to study cognition: Recording standards and publication criteria. *Psychophysiology*, *372*, 127–152.

Pierson, A., Jouvent, R., Quintin, P., Perez-Diaz, F., & Leboyer, M. (2000). Information processing deficits in relatives of manic depressive patients. *Psychological Medicine*, *303*, 545–555.

Polich, J. (2007). Updating P300: An integrative theory of P3a and P3b. *Clinical Neurophysiology*, 11810, 2128–2148.

Polich, J., & Burns, T. (1987). P300 from identical twins. *Neuropsychologia*, *251B*, 299–304.

Polich, J., & Comerchero, M. D. (2003). P3a from visual stimuli: Typicality, task, and topography. *Brain Topography*, *153*, 141–152.

Poo, M. M. (2001). Neurotrophins as synaptic modulators. *Nature Reviews Neuroscience*, *21*, 24–32.

Potter, D., Summerfelt, A., Gold, J., & Buchanan, R. W. (2006). Review of clinical correlates of P50 sensory gating abnormalities in patients with schizophrenia. *Schizophrenia Bulletin*, *324*, 692–700.

Prata, D. P., Breen, G., Osborne, S., Munro, J., St Clair, D., & Collier, D. A. (2009). An association study of the neuregulin 1 gene, bipolar affective disorder and psychosis. *Psychiatric Genetics*, *193*, 113–116.

Raux, G., Bonnet-Brilhault, F., Louchart, S., Houy, E., Gantier, R., Levillain, D., et al. (2002). The-2 bp deletion in exon 6 of the "alpha 7-like" nicotinic receptor subunit gene is a risk factor for the P50 sensory gating deficit. *Molecular Psychiatry*, *79*, 1006–1011.

Rosa, A., Cuesta, M. J., Fatjo-Vilas, M., Peralta, V., Zarzuela, A., & Fananas, L. (2006). The Val^{66}Met polymorphism of the brain-derived neurotrophic factor gene is associated with risk for psychosis: Evidence from a family based association study. *American Journal of Medical Genetics B Neuropsychiatric Genetics*, *141B2*, 135–138.

Rosa, A., Peralta, V., Cuesta, M. J., Zarzuela, A., Serrano, F., Martinez-Larrea, A., et al. (2004). New evidence of association between *COMT* gene and prefrontal neurocognitive from sibling function in healthy individuals pairs discordant for psychosis. *American Journal of Psychiatry*, *1616*, 1110–1112.

Roth, W. T., & Cannon, E. H. (1972). Some features of the auditory evoked response in schizophrenics. *Archives of General Psychiatry*, *274*, 466–471.

Roxborough, H., Muir, W. J., Blackwood, D. H. R., Walker, M. T., & Blackburn, I. M. (1993). Neuropsychological and P300 abnormalities in schizophrenics and their relatives. *Psychological Medicine*, *232*, 305–314.

Rybakowski, J. K., Borkowska, A., Czerski, P. M., Dmitrzak-Weglarz, M., Skibinska, M., Kapelski, P., et al. (2006). Performance on the Wisconsin Card Sorting Test in schizophrenia and genes of dopaminergic inactivation (*COMT*, *DAT*, *NET*). *Psychiatry Research*, *1431*, 13–19.

Salisbury, D. F., Shenton, M. E., & McCarley, R. W. (1999). P300 topography differs in schizophrenia and manic psychosis. *Biological Psychiatry*, *451*, 98–106.

Sanders, A. R., Duan, J., Levinson, D. F., Shi, J., He, D., Hou, C., et al. (2008). No significant association of 14 candidate genes with schizophrenia in a large European ancestry sample: Implications for psychiatric genetics. *American Journal of Psychiatry*, *1654*, 497–506.

Schreiber, H., Stolzborn, G., Kornhuber, H. H., & Born, J. (1992). Event-related potential correlates of impaired selective attention in children at high-risk for schizophrenia. *Biological Psychiatry*, *328*, 634–651.

Schulze, K. K., Hall, M. H., McDonald, C., Marshall, N., Walshe, M., Murray, R. M., et al. (2007). P50 auditory evoked potential suppression in bipolar disorder patients with psychotic features and their unaffected relatives. *Biological Psychiatry*, *622*, 121–128.

Schulze, K. K., Hall, M. H., McDonald, C., Marshall, N., Walshe, M., Murray, R. M., et al. (2008). Auditory P300 in patients with bipolar disorder and their unaffected relatives. *Bipolar Disorder*, *103*, 377–386.

Shaikh, M., Hall, M. H., Schulze, K., Dutt, A., Walshe, M., Williams, I., et al. (2010). Do COMT, BDNF and NRG1 polymorphisms influence P50 sensory gating in psychosis? *Psychological Medicine*, *40*, 1–14.

Shifman, S., Bronstein, M., Sternfeld, M., Pisanté-Shalom, A., Lev-Lehman, E., Weizman, A., et al. (2002). A highly significant association between a COMT haplotype and schizophrenia. *American Journal of Human Genetics*, *716*, 1296–1302.

Siegel, C., Waldo, M., Mizner, G., Adler, L., & Freedman, R. (1984). Deficits in sensory gating in schizophrenic patients and their relatives. *Archives of General Psychiatry*, *41*, 607–612.

Sklar, P., Smoller, J. W., Fan, J., Ferreira, M. A., Perlis, R. H., Chambert, K., et al. (2008). Whole-genome association study of bipolar disorder. *Molecular Psychiatry*, *136*, 558–569.

Souza, V. B., Muir, W. J., Walker, M. T., Glabus, M. F., Roxborough, H. M., Sharp, C. W., et al. (1995). Auditory P300 event-related potentials and neuropsychological performance in schizophrenia and bipolar affective disorder. *Biological Psychiatry*, *375*, 300–310.

Stefansson, H., Sarginson, J., Kong, A., Yates, P., Steinthorsdottir, V., Gudfinnsson, E., et al. (2003). Association of neuregulin 1 with schizophrenia confirmed in a Scottish population. *American Journal of Human Genetics*, *721*, 83–87.

Stefansson, H., Sigurdsson, E., Steinthorsdottir, V., Bjornsdottir, S., Sigmundsson, T., Ghosh, S., et al. (2002). Neuregulin 1 and susceptibility to schizophrenia. *American Journal of Human Genetics*, *714*, 877–892.

Stefansson, H., Steinthorsdottir, V., Thorgeirsson, T. E., Gulcher, J. R., & Stefansson, K. (2004). Neuregulin 1 and schizophrenia. *Annals of Medicine*, *361*, 62–71.

Szeszko, P. R., Lipsky, R., Mentschel, C., Robinson, D., Gunduz-Bruce, H., Sevy, S., et al. (2005). Brain-derived neurotrophic factor Val^{66}Met polymorphism and volume of the hippocampal formation. *Molecular Psychiatry*, *107*, 631–636.

Tsai, S. J., Yu, Y. W. Y., Chen, T. J., Chen, J. Y., Liou, Y. J., Chen, M. C., et al. (2003). Association study of a functional catechol-O-methyltransferase-gene polymorphism and cognitive function in healthy females. *Neuroscience Letters*, *3382*, 123–126.

Turetsky, B. I., Calkins, M. E., Light, G. A., Olincy, A., Radant, A. D., & Swerdlow, N. R. (2007). Neurophysiological endophenotypes of schizophrenia: The viability of selected candidate measures. *Schizophrenia Bulletin*, *331*, 69–94.

Turetsky, B. I., Cannon, T. D., & Gur, R. E. (2000). P300 subcomponent abnormalities in schizophrenia: III. Deficits in unaffected siblings of schizophrenic probands. *Biological Psychiatry*, *475*, 380–390.

van Beijsterveldt, C. E. M., Molenaar, P. C. M., de Geus, E. J. C., & Boomsma, D. I. (1998). Individual differences in P300 amplitude: A genetic study in adolescent twins. *Biological Psychology*, *472*, 97–120.

van Beijsterveldt, C. E. M., & van Baal, G. C. M. (2002). Twin and family studies of the human electroencephalogram: A review and a meta-analysis. *Biological Psychology*, *611–12*, 111–138.

van der Stelt, O., Lieberman, J. A., & Belger, A. (2005). Auditory P300 in high-risk, recent-onset and chronic schizophrenia. *Schizophrenia Research*, *772–3*, 309–320.

Waldo, M. C., Cawthra, E., Adler, L. E., Dubester, S., Staunton, M., Nagamoto, H., et al. (1994). Auditory sensory gating, hippocampal volume, and catecholamine metabolism in schizophrenics and their siblings. *Schizophrenia Research*, *122*, 93–106.

Weisbrod, M., Hill, H., Niethammer, R., & Sauer, H. (1999). Genetic influence on auditory information processing in schizophrenia: P300 in monozygotic twins. *Biological Psychiatry*, *465*, 721–725.

Williams, I. S. (2009). *Genetic influences on neurophysiological endophenotypes for psychosis*. Psychological Medicine, London. University of London doctoral thesis.

Williams, N. M., Preece, A., Spurlock, G., Norton, N., Williams, H. J., Zammit, S., et al. (2003). Support for genetic variation in neuregulin 1 and susceptibility to schizophrenia. *Molecular Psychiatry*, *85*, 485–487.

Winterer, G., Egan, M. F., Raedler, T., Sanchez, C., Jones, D. W., Coppola, R., et al. (2003). P300 and genetic risk for schizophrenia. *Archives of General Psychiatry*, *6011*, 1158–1167.

Winterer, G., Konrad, A., Vucurevic, G., Musso, F., Stoeter, P., & Dahmen, N. (2008). Association of, 5′ end neuregulin-1 (NRG1) gene variation with subcortical medial frontal microstructure in humans. *NeuroImage*, *402*, 712–718.

Yamada, K., & Nabeshima, T. (2003). Brain-derived neurotrophic factor/TrkB signaling in memory processes. *Journal of Pharmacological Sciences*, *914*, 267–270.

Yung, A. R., Yuen, H. P., McGorry, P. D., Phillips, L. J., Kelly, D., Dell'Olio, M., et al. (2005). Mapping the onset of psychosis: The comprehensive assessment of at-risk mental states. *Australian and New Zealand Journal of Psychiatry*, *3911–12*, 964–971.

Zintzaras, E. (2007). Brain-derived neurotrophic factor gene polymorphisms and schizophrenia: A meta-analysis. *Psychiatric Genetics*, *172*, 69–75.

7 Glutamate and GABA transmitter systems

Post-mortem studies and the neuropathology of amino acids in schizophrenia

Paul J. Harrison

Introduction

Exploration of Planet Psychosis began with an expedition by Alzheimer over a hundred years ago. Like all subsequent visits over the following seventy years, it failed to find any convincing signs of life. This led one space commentator to describe the whole endeavour as a graveyard (Plum, 1972). However, reports that the planet was dead were premature. Later expeditions, using the more advanced techniques that have become available to collect and analyse samples, have begun to reveal evidence for traces of life. While these fall well short of a defining life form (i.e., a diagnostic neuropathology, or an unequivocal—and unequivocally interpretable—neuropathological correlate of schizophrenia), they do provide clues as to the nature of the planet and the type of life that characterizes it (Harrison, 1999; Harrison, Lewis, & Kleinman, 2011). As Dr McCoy might have said, "It's neuropathology, Jim (or Robin), but not as we know it."

The expeditions to be reviewed here are those that have sought the neurochemical pathology of schizophrenia, from direct examination of brain tissue, and which have focused on the amino acids glutamate and GABA. These are, respectively, the major excitatory and inhibitory transmitters of the brain. The resulting data complement those that have arisen from the various other approaches that have been adopted, and which also provide evidence for involvement of glutamate and GABA in schizophrenia, including pharmacological studies, animal models, neuroimaging modalities, peripheral markers, and neurophysiology (e.g., Bickel & Javitt, 2009; Blum & Mann, 2002; Charych, Liu, Moss, & Brandon, 2009; Coyle, Tsai, & Goff, 2003; Gonzales-Burgos & Lewis, 2008; Javitt & Zukin, 1991; Konradi & Heckers, 2003; Moghaddam, 2004; Olney & Farber, 1995). A simplified overview is shown in Figure 7.1.

Approaches to studying glutamate and GABA neuropathology in schizophrenia

Neuropathological studies of glutamate, or GABA (or, indeed, other transmitter) systems can be divided up into several categories, notwithstanding a degree of overlap between them.

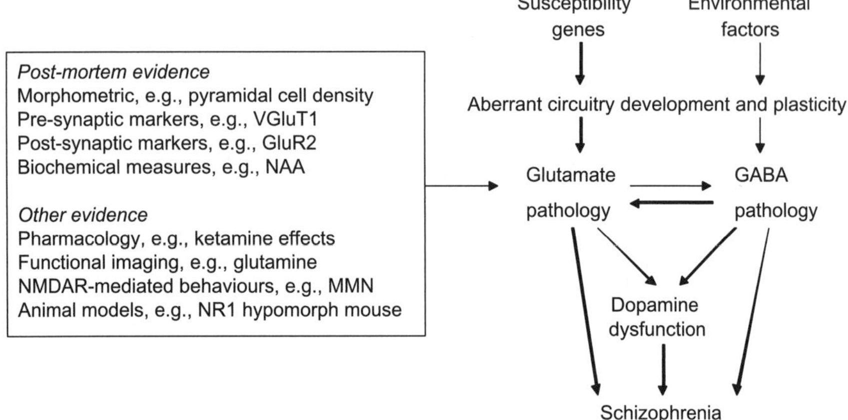

Figure 7.1 A simplified and speculative schematic of glutamate and GABA involvement in the pathogenesis and neuropathology of schizophrenia. The box summarizes the types of evidence that underlie such notions with regard to glutamate, and with the contribution of post-mortem studies highlighted. VGluT1: vesicular glutamate transporter 1; GluR2: AMPA receptor subunit 2; NAA: N-acetyl aspartate; MMN: mismatch negativity; NR1: NMDA receptor 1.

First, those that have used routine methods and stains to measure some aspect of neuron populations defined according to presumed transmitter phenotype. For example, pyramidal neurons in the cerebral cortex are readily identifiable using standard histological stains, and are unambiguously glutamatergic; similarly, cortical interneurons, defined by shape, size and laminar location, can be reasonably viewed as being mostly GABAergic.

Extending this approach, populations of neurons can be defined based upon the presence (expression) of specific mRNAs or proteins. For example, GABA interneurons can be identified and subdivided according to specific markers, as outlined below. In each case, the numerical density, size, shape, or spatial distribution of the neurons can be measured, and compared between schizophrenia and control subjects. Other markers localize to axons or pre-synaptic terminals (e.g., synaptophysin, synapsin, complexins), or to dendrites (e.g., MAP2, spinophilin), or demarcate glutamatergic and GABAergic synapses (e.g., VGluT1 or VGAT, respectively).

Another class of study measures individual glutamate or GABA receptors, or transporters, using mRNA or protein-based approaches; the corresponding binding sites can also be assessed using radioligand binding and autoradiography. Finally, there are biochemical indices of glutamate or GABAergic metabolites and enzymes.

Each of these approaches has pros and cons, related in part to the degree of confounding by peri-mortem and other variables (Harrison, 1996) and each has provided evidence for alterations in schizophrenia, as briefly summarized below. For detailed reviews and citations, see Harrison (1999) and Harrison et al. (2011).

Neuropathological studies of glutamate in schizophrenia

Several studies have found that pyramidal neurons are smaller, in terms of somal cross-sectional area or volume, in prefrontal cortex, hippocampus, and some other cortical regions. The packing density of cortical pyramidal neurons may be increased. Finally, the orientation and/or clustering of pyramidal neurons may differ in some regions. Insofar as these crude morphometric indices have functional correlates, they likely imply a difference in the afferent or efferent connectivity, or activity, of pyramidal neurons, which give rise to all the long corticocortical and cortico-subcortical, excitatory pathways in the brain. However, none of these morphometric findings is wholly established, nor their interpretation unambiguous; it is really when they are viewed in tandem with the other studies to be described below that their significance and robustness is more apparent.

Pre-synaptic markers of glutamatergic synapses, such as complexin II, synapsin, and VGluT1 are decreased in several studies, in hippocampus and neocortical areas (see Eastwood, 2004; Kao & Porton, 2009). To some extent, such decrements may reflect a lower density of synaptic connections (consistent with the limited ultrastructural data from electron microscopy), but they may also indicate a decrease in synaptic activity or release of glutamate. The latter interpretation particularly applies to VGluT1, for which there is a clear relationship between expression level and functional activity. Unfortunately, VGluT1 also highlights complexities in the data; that is, there are discrepancies between mRNA and protein data, as well as simply opposing results (Eastwood, Burnet, & Harrison, 2005; Eastwood & Harrison, 2010; Oni-Orisan, Kristiansen, Haroutunian, Ruff, & McCullumsmith, 2008; Talbot et al., 2004). It is unclear if these differing results reflect complexities of transcriptional versus (post)-translational regulation, anatomical localization, heterogeneity between cohorts, or are simply failures to replicate.

There are equivalent post-synaptic molecular markers, in particular spinophilin, a marker of dendritic spines, the protuberances upon which most glutamate synapses are apposed. Its expression is decreased in the hippocampus in schizophrenia (Law, Weickert, Hyde, Kleinman, & Harrison, 2004a), in keeping with the lower density of dendritic spines reported in several morphological studies (see Harrison et al., 2011).

It is impossible to summarize succinctly the many studies of individual glutamate receptors and transporters, their mRNAs, proteins, and binding sites. Suffice it to say that there are sporadic reports that the abundance of most are altered in schizophrenia, but with no clear consensus about the identity of those that change or do not change, nor the anatomical or cellular localization of the alterations. For reviews, see Harrison, Law, and Eastwood (2003), Konradi and Heckers (2003), and Kristiansen, Huerta, Beneyto, and Meador-Woodruff (2007). Similarly, there have been few recent biochemical studies of glutamate systems in schizophrenia, with the older data lacking firm conclusions. However, there are hints that overall transmission is decreased, including decrements in *N*-acetylaspartate and other indices, consistent with neuroimaging data.

Neuropathological studies of GABA in schizophrenia

An equivalent range of neuropathological findings—with arguably more compelling results overall—apply to GABA as to glutamate. The data arise largely from work pioneered by the groups of Benes (e.g., Benes & Berretta, 2001; Benes et al., 2007), Lewis (e.g., Hashimoto et al., 2008; Lewis, Hashimoto, & Volk, 2005; Volk, Austin, Pierri, Sampson, & Lewis, 2000), and others (Reynolds, Zhang, & Beasley, 2001).

Many studies have shown decreased expression of the GABA synthesizing enzyme glutamic acid decarboxylase (GAD), especially the 67 kDa isoform (GAD_{67}), whether measured as mRNA or number of GAD-immunoreactive (i.e., GABAergic) neurons. Not all GABA neurons are equally affected, and there is a preferential decrement in the subpopulation of parvalbumin-immunoreactive GABA interneurons, seen particularly in the dorsolateral prefrontal cortex, as well as in other regions. These cells, which include chandelier cells and basket cells, innervate the soma and proximal axons of pyramidal neurons, and inhibit their output. In this way they are increasingly appreciated to be key determinants of cortical gamma oscillations and network activity (Fuchs et al., 2007). The parvalbumin decrements likely reflect mainly a decreased activity, but possibly also the number, of these cells. Accompanying the decrease are reductions in markers of their synapses, e.g., the GABA transporter GAT and its mRNA, and a presumed compensatory up-regulation of the post-synaptic GABA receptor a2 subunit. There are also changes in expression of a range of other GABA receptor subunits, isoforms, and interacting proteins (Charych et al., 2009).

In summary, neuropathological studies provide good evidence that both the glutamate and GABA systems are affected in schizophrenia, whether assessed in terms of their neurons, synapses, molecular components, or metabolites. These effects are apparent in many brain regions, including hippocampus (Harrison, 2004), frontal cortex (Torrey et al., 2005), thalamus (Watis, Chen, Chua, Chong, & Sim, 2008), and cerebellum (e.g., Burnet, Eastwood et al., 2008; Burnet, Hutchinson et al., 2008; Eastwood, Cotter, & Harrison, 2001). The data also show that this relationship is complex and reciprocal. For example, GABA interneurons express, and are regulated by, NMDA receptors, responding to glutamate innervation from pyramidal and other excitatory neurons; equally, pyramidal neurons express GABA receptors (see Conn, Lindsley, & Jones, 2009). Hence, it is clearly over-simplistic to view glutamate and GABA pathologies as being distinct. Also, there are no simple conclusions as to the precise nature, distribution, cause, or consequences of the alterations. For example, as to the relationship between the various aspects of pathology: is one causally related or primary to the other, and if so which way round? Can "primary" be defined in terms of a specific population of cells, synapses, or receptors? Also, which of the alterations are intrinsic to schizophrenia and which are secondary to chronic illness and its sequelae? How does the amino-acid pathology interact with the dopaminergic component (Lisman et al., 2008; Stone, Morrison, & Pilowsky, 2007)? A final interpretational issue, to be considered next, concerns the extent to which the glutamate and GABA pathologies in schizophrenia may be a reflection of polymorphic—single nucleotide polymorphism (SNP) or copy number variation (CNV) related—variation in encoding genes. That is, the pathology is related to the genetic predisposition to schizophrenia rather than, or in addition to, the syndrome itself.

Glutamate, GABA and schizophrenia susceptibility genes

Both candidate gene and genome-wide approaches suggest that genes affecting synaptic development and function are overrepresented among schizophrenia risk genes (Guilmatre et al., 2009; Harrison & West, 2006; Walsh et al., 2008), and there is also evidence that this applies also to genes affecting glutamatergic function and, in particular, N-methyl-D-aspartate receptor (NMDAR) signalling (Allen et al., 2008; Collier & Li, 2003; Harrison & Owen, 2003; Harrison & Weinberger, 2005; Harrison & West, 2006). Whether this convergence is real or illusory remains to be determined (not least since the definition of such a gene is difficult, in addition to the problem of proving disease association for any gene), but in the meantime neuropathological studies of these genes are being carried out to provide some support for the notion. Several kinds of study design are being applied.

First, descriptive studies are important (and irreplaceable) for showing, or clarifying the details of, the expression of the genes in human brain. Hitherto, data for many genes only existed in rodent brains, or in vitro, or in peripheral tissues. It is increasingly apparent that there are unique expression profiles in human brain, affecting the localization, timing, distribution or relative abundance of the gene products. For example, neuregulin 1, which impacts on both glutamate and GABA synapses (Harrison & Law, 2006; Mei & Xiong, 2008) is widely expressed throughout life in human brain (Law, Weickert, Hyde, Kleinman, & Harrison, 2004b), including expression of an isoform, type IV, which (unlike all other neuregulin 1 isoforms) is specific to the brain, shows enrichment prenatally, and is related to a risk haplotype in the gene (Law et al., 2006; Tan et al., 2007). A second example is provided by serine racemase and D-amino acid oxidase (DAO), the enzymes which respectively synthesize and degrade the NMDA receptor modulator D-serine and which thus are directly relevant to NMDAR hypofunction theories of schizophrenia (Labrie, Clapcote, & Roder, 2009; Olney & Farber, 1995; Verrall, Betts, Burnet, & Harrison, 2010). Recent studies show that both these genes are expressed in human brain in a way that appears to differ from other species studied (Verrall et al., 2007), a difference which may (or may not) be important with regard to their roles in schizophrenia and its treatment. As a third example, metabotropic glutamate receptor 3 (GRM3; mGlu3), is a candidate gene that regulates glutamate release and indirectly modulates NMDA receptor function (Egan et al., 2004; Harrison, Lyon, Sartorius, Burnet, & Lane, 2008). It turns out that there are splice variants of this gene, which again may be unique to human brain, and which are predicted to give rise to a functionally distinct receptor subtype (Sartorius et al., 2006).

Second, there are quantitative studies that use the standard schizophrenia versus control group design, but where the molecular target happens to be a putative risk gene. Taking as examples the same genes introduced in the previous paragraph, the expression, and activity, of DAO is increased in schizophrenia (Burnet, Eastwood et al., 2008; Madeira, Freitas, Vargas-Lopes, Wolosker, & Panizzutti, 2008; Verrall et al., 2007), as may be the expression of a gene called *G72*, which regulates DAOA (and which is also a schizophrenia candidate gene in its own right; Korostishevsky et al., 2004). Expression of serine racemase (Steffek, Haroutunian, & Meador-Woodruff, 2006; Verrall et al., 2007) and GRM3 (Crook, Akil, Law, Hyde, & Kleinman, 2002; Ghose, Gleason, Potts, Lewis-Amezcua, & Tamminga, 2009; Gupta et al., 2005; Sartorius et al., 2008) do not show consistent alterations in the illness, although there may be a change in one of the GRM3 splice variants mentioned (Sartorius et al., 2008). These and other examples show that the expression and function of various glutamatergic and GABAergic candidate genes is altered in the brain in schizophrenia. However, like all case-control studies, especially of post-mortem brains, they cannot reveal causation. Hypothetically, equivalent studies of at-risk subjects and unaffected relatives could contribute, as they have in other research domains, but they are likely to remain impractical.

Instead, the third strategy, which is increasingly being implemented is to carry out “genetic neuropathology”, with the aim of identifying differences between subjects who do and who do not possess alleles reported as conferring risk of schizophrenia. This is conceptually akin to neuroimaging or neuropsychological studies where MRI or fMRI signals, or cognitive performance, is compared between groups based on genotype. The argument here is that most genetic-risk variants are non-coding polymorphisms and so any pathogenicity, if it exists, is likely to be via their effects on gene expression—in terms of quantity, splicing, or potentially timing or distribution (Harrison & Weinberger, 2005). For example, risk polymorphisms in the gene concerned predicts expression of the neuregulin type IV isoform mentioned earlier (Law et al., 2006), and of the GRM3 splice variant (Sartorius et al., 2008), as well as of GAD1 (Straub et al., 2007) and several other genes (e.g., Huffaker et al., 2009; Nakata et al., 2009). Conversely, some studies fail to find genotype effects on gene expression (e.g., Bristow et al., 2009; Burnet, Eastwood et al., 2008; Tang et al., 2009), and thus provide no evidence to support (and indeed provide some evidence against) a physiological or pathophysiological functionality of the polymorphisms. The key requirement of genetic neuropathology studies is sample size, to provide enough subjects in each genotype group to give at least some power. The positive examples given here mostly involve well over 100 brains, which for the field is a very large—indeed, previously unheard of—sample size, and predicates the continuing accrual of large and well characterized brain collections.

The fourth strategy, a variant of the third one, is to examine whether there is unequal expression of transcripts arising from each DNA strand in individuals who are heterozygous for transcribed risk alleles (Bray, 2008). The attraction is that this removes inter-subject variability, by simply measuring the ratio of the two mRNAs within each subject: if non-coding risk alleles are pathogenic by virtue of altering gene expression, as hypothesized, this method is a sensitive way to detect it. The downside is that allelic expression patterns may not be temporally or spatially consistent. The approach has been implemented for several schizophrenia risk genes (Bray, 2008), though not as yet for the leading glutamate or GABA gene candidates.

Summary

Further exciting episodes focusing on glutamate, GABA, and other transmitter systems in schizophrenia are to be anticipated. We need to keep going boldly where men (and women) have gone before, but to go to novel areas and undertake more detailed (and open-minded) explorations. The Prime Directive, apart from scientific understanding, is of course to improve the outcome for patients (Lewis & Sweet, 2009). A strong impetus to continue the search is provided by recent treatment trials, aimed at novel therapeutic targets that were identified, at least partly, based on neuropathological findings (Conn et al., 2009; Lewis, Volk, & Hashimoto, 2004; Patil et al., 2007).

Acknowledgements

Thanks to all past and present members of the Harrison glutamate expedition parties, notably First Officers Sharon Eastwood and Phil Burnet, who have led the crew since the group set off in 1992. Also thanks to all those back at Starfleet Command and other Earth stations who have supported the mission in one way or another, especially Commanders Dan Weinberger, Joel Kleinman, Fuller Torrey, Margaret Esiri, and the late Rob Kerwin. The missions have been generously funded by the Stanley Medical Research Institute and MRC, with additional support from the Wellcome Trust, NARSAD, and the British Medical Association.

References

Allen, N. C., Bagade, S., McQueen, M. B., Ioannidis, J. P. A., Kavvoura, F. K., Khoury, M. J., et al. (2008). Systematic meta-analyses and field synopsis of genetic association studies in schizophrenia: The SzGene database. *Nature Genetics*, *40*, 827–834.

Benes, F. M., & Berretta, S. (2001). GABAergic interneurons: Implications for understanding schizophrenia and bipolar disorder. *Neuropsychopharmacology*, *25*, 1–27.

Benes, F. M., Lim, B., Matzilevich, D., Walsh, J. P., Subburaju, S., & Minns, M. (2007). Regulation of the GABA cell phenotype in hippocampus of schizophrenics and bipolars. *Proceedings of the National Academy of Sciences USA*, *104*, 10164–10169.

Bickel, S., & Javitt, D. C. (2009). Neurophysiological and neurochemical animal models of schizophrenia: Focus on glutamate. *Behavioural Brain Research*, *204*, 352–362.

Blum, B. P., & Mann, J. J. (2002). The GABAergic system in schizophrenia. *International Journal of Neuropsychopharmacology*, *5*, 159–180.

Bray, N. J. (2008). Gene expression in the etiology of schizophrenia. *Schizophrenia Bulletin*, *34*, 412–418.

Bristow, G. C., Lane, T. A., Walker, M., Chen, L., Sei, Y., Hyde, T. M., et al. (2009). Expression of kinase interacting with stathmin (KIS, UMHK1) in human brain and lymphoblasts: Effects of schizophrenia and genotype. *Brain Research*, *1301*, 197–206.

Burnet, P. W. J., Eastwood, S. L., Bristow, G. C., Godlewska, B. R., Sikka, P., Walker, M., et al. (2008). D-amino acid oxidase activity and expression are increased in schizophrenia. *Molecular Psychiatry*, *13*, 658–660.

Burnet, P. W. J., Hutchinson, L., von Hesling, M., Gilbert, E. J., Brandon, N. J., Rutter, A. R., et al. (2008). Expression of D-serine and glycine transporters in the prefrontal cortex and cerebellum in schizophrenia. *Schizophrenia Research*, *102*, 283–294.

Charych, E. I., Liu, F., Moss, S. J., & Brandon, N. J. (2009). GABA(A) receptors and their associated proteins: Implications in the etiology and treatment of schizophrenia and related disorders. *Neuropharmacology*, *57*, 481–495.

Collier, D. A., & Li, T. (2003). The genetics of schizophrenia: Glutamate not dopamine? *European Journal of Pharmacology*, *480*, 177–184.

Conn, P. J., Lindsley, C. W., & Jones, C. K. (2009). Activation of metabotropic glutamate receptors as a novel approach for the treatment of schizophrenia. *Trends in Pharmacological Sciences*, *30*, 25–31.

Coyle, J. T., Tsai, G., & Goff, D. C. (2003). Converging evidence of NMDA receptor hypofunction in the pathophysiology of schizophrenia. *Annals of the New York Academy of Science*, *1003*, 318–327.

Crook, J. M., Akil, M., Law, B. C. W., Hyde, T. M., & Kleinman, J. E. (2002). Comparative analysis of group II metabotropic glutamate receptor immunoreactivity in Brodmann's area 46 of the dorsolateral prefrontal cortex from patients with schizophrenia and normal subjects. *Molecular Psychiatry*, *7*, 157–164.

Eastwood, S. L. (2004). The synaptic pathology of schizophrenia: Is aberrant neurodevelopment and plasticity to blame? In J. Smythies (Ed.), Disorders of synaptic plasticity and schizophrenia. *International Review of Neurobiology*, *59*, 47–72.

Eastwood, S. L., Burnet, P. W. J., & Harrison, P. J. (2005). Decreased hippocampal expression of the susceptibility gene PPP3CC and other calcineurin subunits in schizophrenia. *Biological Psychiatry*, *57*, 702–710.

Eastwood, S. L., Cotter, D., & Harrison, P. J. (2001). Cerebellar synaptic protein expression in schizophrenia. *Neuroscience*, *105*, 219–229.

Eastwood, S. L., & Harrison, P. J. (2010). Markers of glutamate synaptic transmission and plasticity are increased in the anterior cingulate cortex in bipolar disorder. *Biological Psychiatry*, *67*, 1010–1016.

Egan, M. F., Straub, R. E., Goldberg, T. E., Yakub, I., Callicott, J. H., Hariri, A. R., et al. (2004). Variation in GRM3 affects cognition, prefrontal glutamate, and risk for schizophrenia. *Proceedings of the National Academy of Sciences USA*, *101*, 12604–12609.

Fuchs, E. C., Zivkovic, A. R., Cunningham, M. O., Middleton, S., LeBeau, F. E. N., Bannerman, D., et al. (2007). Recruitment of parvalbumin-positive interneurons determines hippocampal function and associated behavior. *Neuron*, *53*, 591–604.

Ghose, S., Gleason, K. A., Potts, B. W., Lewis-Amezcua, K., & Tamminga, C. A. (2009). Differential expression of metabotropic glutamate receptors 2 and 3 in schizophrenia: A mechanism for antipsychotic drug action? *American Journal of Psychiatry*, *166*, 812–820.

Gonzalez-Burgos, G., & Lewis, D. A. (2008). GABA neurons and the mechanisms of network oscillations: Implications for understanding cortical dysfunction in schizophrenia. *Schizophrenia Bulletin*, *34*, 944–961.

Guilmatre, A., Dubourg, C., Mosca, A. L., Legallic, S., Goldenberg, A., Drouin-Garraud, V., et al. (2009). Recurrent rearrangements in synaptic and neurodevelopmental genes and shared biologic pathways in schizophrenia, autism, and mental retardation. *Archives of General Psychiatry*, *66*, 947–955.

Gupta, D. S., McCullumsmith, G. E., Beneyto, M., Haroutunian, V., Davis, K. L., & Meador-Woodruff, J. H. (2005). Metabotropic glutamate receptor protein expression in the prefrontal cortex and striatum in schizophrenia. *Synapse*, *57*, 123–131.

Harrison, P. J. (1996). Advances in post mortem molecular neurochemistry and neuropathology: Examples from schizophrenia research. *British Medical Bulletin*, *52*, 527–538.

Harrison, P. J. (1999). The neuropathology of schizophrenia—A critical review of the data and their interpretation. *Brain*, *122*, 593–624.

Harrison, P. J. (2004). The hippocampus in schizophrenia: A review of the neuropathological evidence and its pathophysiological implications. *Psychopharmacology*, *174*, 151–162.

Harrison, P. J., & Law, A. J. (2006). Neuregulin 1 and schizophrenia: Genetics, gene expression, and neurobiology. *Biological Psychiatry*, *60*, 132–140.

Harrison, P. J., Law, A. J., & Eastwood, S. L. (2003). Glutamate receptors and transporters in the hippocampus in schizophrenia. *Annals of the New York Academy of Sciences USA*, *1003*, 94–101.

Harrison, P. J., Lewis, D. A., & Kleinman, J. E. (2011). Neuropathology of schizophrenia. In D. R. Weinberger & P. J. Harrison (Eds.), *Schizophrenia* (3rd ed., pp. 372–392). Oxford, UK: Wiley-Blackwell.

Harrison, P. J., Lyon, L., Sartorius, L. J., Burnet, P. W. J., & Lane, T. A. (2008). The group II metabotropic glutamate receptor 3 (mGluR3, mGlu3, GRM3): Expression, function and involvement in schizophrenia. *Journal of Psychopharmacology*, *22*, 308–322.

Harrison, P. J., & Owen, M. J. (2003). Genes for schizophrenia? Recent findings and their pathophysiological implications. *Lancet*, *361*, 417–419.

Harrison, P. J., & Weinberger, D. R. (2005). Schizophrenia genes, gene expression, and neuropathology: On the matter of their convergence. *Molecular Psychiatry*, *10*, 40–68.

Harrison, P. J., & West, V. A. (2006). Six degrees of separation: On the prior probability that schizophrenia susceptibility genes converge on synapses, glutamate and NMDA receptors. *Molecular Psychiatry*, *11*, 981–983.

Hashimoto, T., Bazmi, H. H., Mirnics, K., Wu, Q., Sampson, A. R., & Lewis, D. A. (2008). Conserved regional patterns of GABA-related transcript expression in the neocortex of subjects with schizophrenia. *American Journal of Psychiatry*, *165*, 479–489.

Huffaker, S. J., Chen, J. S., Nicodemus, K. K., Sambataro, F., Yang, F., Mattay, V., et al. (2009). A primate-specific, brain isoform of KCNH2 affects cortical physiology, cognition, neuronal repolarization and risk of schizophrenia. *Nature Medicine*, *15*, 509–518.

Javitt, D. C., & Zukin, S. R. (1991). Recent advances in the phencyclidine model of schizophrenia. *American Journal of Psychiatry*, *148*, 1301–1308.

Kao, K. T., & Porton, B. (2009). Synaptic vesicle associated proteins and schizophrenia. In D. C. Javitt & J. Kantrowitz (Eds.), *Handbook of neurochemistry and molecular neurobiology. Vol. 27: Schizophrenia* (3rd ed., pp. 2–12). New York, NY: Springer Science.

Konradi, C., & Heckers, S. (2003). Molecular aspects of glutamate dysregulation: Implications for schizophrenia and its treatment. *Pharmacology and Therapeutics*, *97*, 153–179.

Korostishevsky, M., Kaganovich, M., Cholostoy, A., Ashkenazi, M., Ratner, Y., Dahary, D., et al. (2004). Is the G72/G30 locus associated with schizophrenia? Single nucleotide polymorphisms, haplotypes, and gene expression analysis. *Biological Psychiatry*, *56*, 169–176.

Kristiansen, L. V., Huerta, I., Beneyto, M., & Meador-Woodruff, J. H. (2007). NMDA receptors and schizophrenia. *Current Opinion in Pharmacology*, *7*, 48–55.

Labrie, V., Clapcote, S. J., & Roder, J. C. (2009). Mutant mice with reduced NMDA-NR1 glycine affinity or lack of D-amino acid oxidase function exhibit altered anxiety-like behaviors. *Pharmacology Biochemistry and Behavior*, *91*, 610–620.

Law, A. J., Lipska, B. K., Weickert, C. S., Hyde, T. M., Straub, R. E., Hashimoto, R., et al. (2006). Neuregulin 1 transcripts are differentially expressed in schizophrenia and regulated by 5′ SNPs associated with the disease. *Proceedings of the National Academy of Sciences USA*, *103*, 6747–6752.

Law, A. J., Weickert, C. S., Hyde, T. M., Kleinman, J. E., & Harrison, P. J. (2004a). Reduced spinophilin but not microtubule-associated protein 2 expression in the hippocampal formation in schizophrenia and mood disorders: Molecular evidence for a pathology of dendritic spines. *American Journal of Psychiatry*, *161*, 1848–1855.

Law, A. J., Weickert, C. S., Hyde, T. M., Kleinman, J. E., & Harrison, P. J. (2004b). Neuregulin-1 (NRG-1) mRNA and protein in the adult human brain. *Neuroscience*, *127*, 125–136.

Lewis, D. A., Hashimoto, T., & Volk, D. W. (2005). Cortical inhibitory neurons and schizophrenia. *Nature Reviews Neuroscience*, *6*, 312–324.

Lewis, D. A., & Sweet, R. A. (2009). Schizophrenia from a neural circuitry perspective: Advancing toward rational pharmacological therapies. *Journal of Clinical Investigation*, *119*, 706–716.

Lewis, D. A., Volk, D. W., & Hashimoto, T. (2004). Selective alterations in prefrontal cortical GABA neurotransmission in schizophrenia: A novel target for the treatment of working memory dysfunction. *Psychopharmacology*, *174*, 143–150.

Lisman, J. E., Coyle, J. T., Green, R. W., Javitt, D. C., Benes, F. M., Heckers, S., et al. (2008). Circuit-based framework for understanding neurotransmitter and risk gene interactions in schizophrenia. *Trends in Neurosciences*, *31*, 234–242.

Madeira, C., Freitas, M. E., Vargas-Lopes, C., Wolosker, H., & Panizzutti, R. (2008). Increased brain D-amino acid oxidase (DAAO) activity in schizophrenia. *Schizophrenia Research*, *101*, 76–83.

Mei, L., & Xiong, W. C. (2008). Neuregulin 1 in neural development, synaptic plasticity and schizophrenia. *Nature Reviews Neuroscience*, *9*, 437–452.

Moghaddam, B. (2004). Targeting metabotropic glutamate receptors for treatment of the cognitive symptoms of schizophrenia. *Psychopharmacology*, *174*, 39–44.

Nakata, K., Lipska, B. K., Hyde, T. M., Ye, T. Z., Newburn, E. N., Morita, Y., et al. (2009). DISC1 splice variants are up-regulated in schizophrenia and associated with risk polymorphisms. *Proceedings of the National Academy of Sciences USA*, *106*, 15873–15878.

Olney, J. W., & Farber, N. B. (1995). Glutamate receptor dysfunction and schizophrenia. *Archives of General Psychiatry*, *52*, 998–1007.

Oni-Orisan, A., Kristiansen, L. V., Haroutunian, V., Ruff, J. H. M. W., & McCullumsmith, R. E. (2008). Altered vesicular glutamate transporter expression in the anterior cingulate cortex in schizophrenia. *Biological Psychiatry*, *63*, 766–775.

Patil, S. T., Zhang, L., Martenyi, F., Lowe, S. L., Jackson, K. A., Andreev, B. V., et al. (2007). Activation of mGlu2/3 receptors as a new approach to treat schizophrenia: A randomized Phase 2 clinical trial. *Nature Medicine*, *13*, 1102–1107.

Plum, F. (1972). Prospects for research on schizophrenia. Neuropathological findings. *Neuroscience Research Program Bulletin*, *10*, 384–388.

Reynolds, G. P., Zhang, Z., & Beasley, C. M. (2001). Neurochemical correlates of cortical GABAergic deficits in schizophrenia: Selective losses of calcium binding protein immunoreactivity. *Brain Research Bulletin*, *55*, 579–584.

Sartorius, L. J., Nagappan, G., Lipska, B. K., Lu, B., Sei, Y., Ren-Patterson, R., et al. (2006). Alternative splicing of human metabotropic glutamate receptor 3. *Journal of Neurochemistry*, *96*, 1139–1148.

Sartorius, L. J., Weinberger, D. R., Hyde, T. M., Harrison, P. J., Kleinman, J. E., & Lipska, B. K. (2008). Expression of a GRM3 splice variant is increased in the dorsolateral prefrontal cortex of individuals carrying a schizophrenia risk SNP. *Neuropsychopharmacology*, *33*, 2626–2634.

Steffek, A. E., Haroutunian, V., & Meador-Woodruff, J. H. (2006) Serine racemase protein expression in cortex and hippocampus in schizophrenia. *NeuroReport*, *17*, 1181–1185.

Stone, J. M., Morrison, P. D., & Pilowsky, L. S. (2007). Glutamate and dopamine dysregulation in schizophrenia—A synthesis and selective review. *Journal of Psychopharma-cology*, *21*, 440–452.

Straub, R. E., Lipska, B. K., Egan, M. F., Goldberg, T. E., Callicott, J. H., Mayhew, M. B., et al. (2007). Allelic variation in GAD1 (GAD(67)) is associated with schizophrenia and influences cortical function and gene expression. *Molecular Psychiatry*, *12*, 854–869.

Talbot, K., Eidem, W. L., Tinsley, C. L., Benson, M. A., Thompson, E. W., Smith, R. J., et al. (2004). Dysbindin-1 is reduced in intrinsic, glutamatergic terminals of the hippocampal formation in schizophrenia. *Journal of Clinical Investigation*, *113*, 1353–1363.

Tan, W., Wang, Y. H., Gold, B., Chen, J. S., Dean, M., Harrison, P. J., et al. (2007). Molecular cloning of a brain-specific, developmentally regulated neuregulin 1 (NRG1) isoform and identification of a functional promoter variant associated with schizophrenia. *Journal of Biological Chemistry*, *282*, 24343–24351.

Tang, J. X., Legros, R. P., Louneva, N., Yeh, L., Cohen, J. W., Hahn, C. G., et al. (2009). Dysbindin-1 in dorsolateral prefrontal cortex of schizophrenia cases is reduced in an isoform-specific manner unrelated to dysbindin-1 mRNA expression. *Human Molecular Genetics*, *18*, 3851–3863.

Torrey, E. F., Barci, B. M., Webster, M. J., Bartko, J. J., Meador-Woodruff, J. H., & Knable, M. B. (2005). Neurochemical markers for schizophrenia, bipolar disorder, and major depression in postmortem brains. *Biological Psychiatry*, *57*, 252–260.

Verrall, L., Walker, M., Rawlings, N., Benzel, I., Kew, J. N. C., Harrison, P. J., et al. (2007). D-amino acid oxidase and serine racemase in human brain: Normal distribution and altered expression in schizophrenia. *European Journal of Neuroscience*, *26*, 1657–1669.

Verrall, L. J., Betts, J. F., Burnet, P. W. J., & Harrison, P. J. (2010). The neurobiology of D-amino acid oxidase (DAO) and its involvement in schizophrenia. *Molecular Psychiatry*, *15*, 122–137.

Volk, D. W., Austin, M. C., Pierri, J. N., Sampson, A. R., & Lewis, D. A. (2000). Decreased glutamic acid decarboxylase$_{67}$ messenger RNA expression in a subset of prefrontal cortical gamma-aminobutyric acid neurons in subjects with schizophrenia. *Archives of General Psychiatry*, *57*, 237–245.

Walsh, T., McClellan, J. M., McCarthy, S. E., Addington, A. M., Pierce, S. B., Cooper, G. M., et al. (2008). Rare structural variants disrupt multiple genes in neurodevelopmental pathways in schizophrenia. *Science*, *320*, 539–543.

Watis, L., Chen, S. H., Chua, H. C., Chong, S. A., & Sim, K. (2008). Glutamatergic abnormalities of the thalamus in schizophrenia: A systematic review. *Journal of Neural Transmission*, *115*, 493–511.

8 Animal models of schizophrenia revisited

Trevor W. Robbins

Introduction

Perhaps no other topic in behavioural neuroscience or psychopharmacology has been so controversial or maligned; yet the validity of animal models of schizophrenia remains one of the most important and contemporary issues in the entire field of translational and clinical neuroscience. This paradoxical position has arisen partly from the reappraisal of the significance of the cognitive deficits in schizophrenia and from a perception of the need to pursue new hypotheses concerning the understanding of the positive and negative symptoms of this disorder, as well as their neural and neurochemical substrates. When considering the concept of "animal models" of human neurological or neuropsychiatric disorders, there are several considerations that need to be taken into account, particularly in the case of schizophrenia. Animal "models" of neurodegenerative diseases such as Huntington's and Alzheimer's diseases will ultimately have been indispensable for defining the causal role of specific forms of molecular pathology and also for assessment of new therapeutic strategies based, for example, on neuroprotection. Some of these diseases have a clear genetic basis, and may even be monogenic in nature; hence genetic models are plausible and are also more than likely to be useful. But this is not the case in schizophrenia. Although much is known about the neurobiological correlates of the disorder, these do not include any reliable information about its molecular pathology, and, like many neuropsychiatric disorders, its genetic involvement is complex, generally depending on multiple genes, each likely to have only small effects. Thus modelling a single genetic change using transgenic preparations is unlikely to capture any of the complexity of the complex syndrome that is schizophrenia. An additional problem concerns the bizarre and subjective nature of many of the symptoms in schizophrenia such as hallucinations and delusions; it is notoriously difficult to relate such symptoms to what is likely to be observed in, for example, a murine model. Understandably, these difficulties have led to assertions that it is impossible to provide an animal model of schizophrenia.

There is evidently much support for such a position. But this should not be taken to mean that basic neuroscience studies using experimental animals have no place in schizophrenia research. Much of what we know about the structure and functioning of the mammalian brain has, after all, derived from animal studies. This includes, for example, wiring diagrams of such structures as the cortico-striatal pathways and the hippocampus, which we know to be implicated in schizophrenia. It includes detailed knowledge of the workings of the ascending dopamine systems, which are dysregulated in schizophrenia. Such studies have led to the development and clinical application of dopamine D2 receptor antagonists, which are used to control the positive symptoms in schizophrenia—and still form the basis of new drug discovery programmes. Moreover, much is known about the behavioural and cognitive functions subserved by these structures in experimental animals, and this can be related to human studies by the use of similar means for testing them cross-species.

Cognitive deficits in schizophrenia

The outstanding success of cognitive neuroscience has found an immediate application to schizophrenia because of the definition of its profile of cognitive deficits, for example, through such schemes as the MATRICS project (Marder & Fenton, 2004). In fact, it is possible to measure some aspects of cognition in experimental animals that are relevant to the generally more powerful and sophisticated systems observed in humans (see Table 8.1). This applies, for example, to studies of "working memory", set-shifting and other aspects of cognitive flexibility, inhibitory control, associative learning, and aspects of "declarative memory" such as recognition memory, as well as basic attentional capabilities. Many of these domains of cognition are affected in schizophrenia and can be related to the seven so-called domains of deficits of the MATRICS project depicted in Table 8.1. It follows that animal studies of impaired cognition in these domains may well be relevant to the search for therapies through "cognitive enhancement".

Table 8.1 MATRICS: Translating the seven domains of disturbed cognitive function in schizophrenia into tests for experimental animals

	Domain	*Example*
1	Speed of processing	Reaction time
2	Attention/vigilance	Five-choice serial reaction-time task
3	Working memory	Delayed response, delayed alternation
4	Verbal learning and memory	Not available
5	Visual learning and memory	Object recognition memory
		Paired associates learning
6	Reasoning and problem solving	Attentional set-shift/reversal learning
7	Social cognition	Social interaction test

Working memory

A landmark study in the field was that of Brozoski, Brown, Rosvold, and Goldman (1979), who showed that the midbrain dopamine projections to the prefrontal cortex had important functions in "working memory", as measured by the spatial delayed response test in rhesus monkeys. Depletion of prefrontal dopamine produced deficits every bit as large as those resulting from ablation of the frontal lobe on performance on the spatial delayed response task—and this deficit could be reversed by dopamine receptor agonists. Further work showed that a similar spatial memory deficit could be measured by means of saccadic eye movements and could be manipulated by dopamine D1 receptor agonist or antagonists (Goldman-Rakic, 1998). The immediate significance of these discoveries for schizophrenia was first of all that schizophrenics were shown to have working-memory deficits, either for spatial working memory using the CANTAB test of self-ordered spatial working memory (e.g., Pantelis et al., 1999) or based on the delayed saccade methods (Park & Holzman, 1992).

Of even more direct relevance to schizophrenia, use of the spatial delayed response paradigm in monkeys has led to a greater theoretical understanding of the role that antipsychotic agents such as haloperidol may play in the cognitive deficits in schizophrenia. Castner, Williams, and Goldman-Rakic (2000) showed that chronic treatment with haloperidol, which is a dopamine D2 receptor antagonist, actually produced substantial impairments in working memory performance in otherwise normal rhesus monkeys. Intriguingly, separate neuropharmacological studies had shown that the chronic haloperidol treatment produces a down-regulation of the dopamine D1 receptor, which could conceivably underlie the cognitive impairment; treatment with a full D1 agonist reversed the deficits, lending some support to this hypothesis. In considering the utility of this experiment, one has to ask how else it would have been possible to show that chronic haloperidol treatment potentially induces cognitive deficits in schizophrenia. This antipsychotic treatment is usually inextricably confounded with possible chronic disease processes in schizophrenia, and so it is impossible to unravel them, especially when one also considers the impossibility of forming a control group of non-schizophrenic volunteers receiving chronic haloperidol. It could, of course, be argued that haloperidol may impair performance in intact monkeys, but could conceivably have a reduced effect (or even an improvement) in a preparation more akin to human schizophrenia. We thus return to the issue of whether one can induce in experimental animals a suitable pathological state that simulates human schizophrenia. Such induction is likely to be difficult in rhesus monkeys for a host of practical and ethical reasons, and opportunities have to be taken to translate paradigms used in non-human primates to rodents. This can be done for working memory to some extent, but the concept of cross-species translation will be illustrated by reference to work done on another prominent cognitive deficit in schizophrenia, in performing the Wisconsin Card Sort Test.

Attentional set-shifting and reversal learning

The Wisconsin Card Sort Test (WCST) is a complex test of cognitive flexibility, much used in the clinical testing of frontal lobe damaged patients, as well as in schizophrenia itself. The WCST is, in fact, related to a paradigm from animal learning theory called the extra-dimensional shift. This theoretical analysis suggests that attention to stimuli with several perceptual dimensions can be allocated to just one of the dimensions on the basis of reinforcement, but then may be shifted to other previously irrelevant dimensions, upon a change in the reinforcement contingencies. This form of extra-dimensional shifting may be contrasted with a transfer of attention to novel exemplars within the same perceptual dimension (intra-dimensional shift, related to abstract rule learning) and reversal learning, where the identify of which object is rewarded is shifted, so that the animal now has to select the previously incorrect option. These different aspects of cognitive flexibility were originally shown by Dias, Robbins, and Roberts (1996) to depend on two different sectors of the marmoset prefrontal cortex (extra-dimensional shift, lateral prefrontal cortex; reversal learning, orbitofrontal cortex). However, recent work has shown that this double dissociation also probably applies to the human prefrontal cortex, on the basis of neuroimaging (Hampshire & Owen, 2006) as well as lesion studies.

The relevance to schizophrenia has been shown by a number of studies describing impairments in this task at a number of stages, especially the reversal learning and extra-dimensional set-shifting components (e.g., Leeson et al., 2009; Pantelis et al., 1999).

However, a recent study by Ceaser et al. (2008) has found that first-degree relatives of schizophrenics do not show specific deficits at the extra-dimensional shift stage, suggesting that failure to shift at this stage is not an endophenotype of schizophrenia. Nonetheless, these first-degree relatives did exhibit some apparent cumulative impairments in performance at other stages of the test and there is no doubt that the test is highly sensitive to the cognitive deficits present in first-episode and chronic schizophrenia.

The top-down translation of this test to animal "models" of schizophrenia has been enhanced by the development of a rodent version (Birrell & Brown, 2000), which is based not on visual dimensions but on texture and smell. Thus, the same learning theory logic can be applied to the test, whether employed for mice or rats. And, remarkably, the same apparent neural dissociation exists between the extra-dimensional shift and reversal stages, being dependent on the medial and orbitofrontal cortex, respectively (Bissonette et al., 2008; McAlonan & Brown, 2003). The exciting consequence of these findings is that it is now feasible to attempt a vertical translation from human patients, through non-human primates, to rodents. Rats have been commonly used to screen new procognitive drugs that may be suitable for schizophrenia and mice preferentially for testing suitable genetic models. Both of these areas have recently been the focus of enormous research activity. For example, improvements in extra-dimensional set-shifting in the rat have been observed by candidate cognitive enhancing agents including the catechol-O-methyltransferase (COMT) inhibitor talcapone (Tunbridge,

Bannerman, Sharp, & Harrison, 2004), a D1 receptor agonist (Fletcher, Tenn, Rizos, Lovic, & Kapur, 2005), alpha-7 nicotinic agonists (J. Vivian, September 2007, personal communication), a PDE10A inhibitor (Rodefer, Murphy, & Baxter, 2005) and 5-HT6 receptor antagonists (Hatcher et al., 2005). In the mouse, effects of genetic manipulation of the *COMT* gene have been shown to have predictable effects (Papaleo et al., 2008) and the paradigm has evident relevance to studies of some of the genes implicated in schizophrenia including, for example, neuroregulin and DISC1 (Arguello & Gogos, 2006; Ayhan, Sawa, Ross, & Pletnikov, 2009).

The beneficial effects on attentional set-shifting of some of the agents mentioned have been shown either in normal, intact animals or in preparations that have been "disturbed" or manipulated in some way to mimic salient aspects of schizophrenia. It may be crucial to examine the validation of these various "models" in order to determine the potential relevance of the drug effect to schizophrenia.

There is, for example, the issue of possible "false positives" in applying this and other cognitive paradigms to the search for new therapeutic agents to treat cognitive deficits in schizophrenia—it is obvious that not all of the agents that have yielded positive effects so far will prove clinically efficacious. Why should this be? In the case of many cognitive processes it is evident that these are controlled by a complex neurocircuitry that is modulated in very many different ways—and thus is susceptible to many different forms of disruption and influence. A deficit such as extra-dimensional shifting, in common with virtually all of the other symptoms of schizophrenia, is not simply unique to schizophrenia. Moreover, we do not know the precise neuropathology underlying deficits on such attentional set-shifting in schizophrenia—if we did, then it would be possible to predict which drug would be efficacious in remediating this cognitive impairment. Similarly, if a drug restores a deficit in an animal model of schizophrenia, such as chronic phencyclidine (PCP) treatment, a genetic mutation or social isolation, then the utility of such an effect would depend on the validity of the animal model—and these issues are only now becoming considered as will become evident below. It is possible, therefore, that a drug that is "cognitive enhancing" in overcoming deficits in one model might be irrelevant to schizophrenia (but possibly relevant to treatment of another disorder). Therefore, it will not be feasible to determine whether a cognitive test in animals is relevant to the search for medications in schizophrenia until we have further feedback, and hence back-translation, from clinical trials. One set of relevant observations demonstrating "back-translation" comes from the study by Goetghebeur and Dias (2009), which is described in the next section.

"Model manipulations" relevant to schizophrenia

The nature and validity of the various manipulations have been extensively reviewed by Lipska and Weinberger (2000) and also by Robbins (2004) and Robbins and Moore (2008). They can be divided broadly into pharmacological, neurodevelopmental and genetic models, but we will only be able to cover a selection of the paradigms listed in Table 8.2.

Table 8.2 Models of schizophrenia

- ***Genetic manipulation/linkage***
  (e.g., neuroregulin k.d.; a-7 nicotinic receptor/q15/P50 responses: DISC1 k.d.; COMT polymorphisms)
- ***Neurodevelopmental models***
  - *Lesions* (e.g., neonatal hippocampal)
  - *Disrupted neurogenesis*
    - MAM-mitotic neurotoxin exposed in utero
    - Gestational X-irradiation
  - *Early stress*
    - Maternal deprivation
    - Isolation-rearing (from 21 days)
    - (deprivation of social play)
- ***Pharmacological models***
    - Amphetamine (dopamine indirect agonist)
    - Phencyclidine/ketamine (NMDA receptor antagonist)
    - Psilocybin (5-HT_{2A} receptor agonist)

Note: See also Lipska and Weinberger (2000).

Pharmacological models

The main pharmacological models are based on two key hypotheses concerning schizophrenia, each of which is supported by considerable evidence: the dopamine over-activity hypothesis and the N-methyl-D-aspartate (NMDA) glutamate receptor deficit hypothesis. The former is the rationale for the amphetamine model, generally using chronic (and sensitizing) regimens—in human drug abusers, symptoms of paranoid schizophrenia quite frequently result from chronic amphetamine abuse (Snyder, 1973). The latter model is generally explored through regimens of treatment with NMDA receptor antagonists, such as PCP or ketamine. The latter agent is well-known to produce several of the subjective and cognitive symptoms that are observed in schizophrenia, including apparent delusional phenomena and negative symptoms (Krystal et al., 1994). In the animal models chronic regimens of PCP are most often employed, although ketamine is the preferred agent in experimental studies in human volunteers. The NMDA receptor model runs into a number of problems beginning with the fact that it is not entirely clear what are the underlying mechanisms of the drug effects. One consequence of chronic PCP, for example, is obviously that of NMDA receptor blockade, but this can additionally have counterintuitive effects such as an up-regulation of extracellular glutamate, caused by blockade of the NMDA receptor on GABA-containing inhibitory interneurons, that normally regulate cortical glutamate release. Thus, one surprising side-effect of PCP and ketamine is an apparent enhancement of glutamatergic activity, which makes it difficult to be sure whether the effects are the result of glutamate hypo- or hyperfunction. Clearly, either hypo- or hyper-glutamatergic activity could lead to detrimental symptoms. Chronic PCP additionally causes a depletion of prefrontal cortical dopamine, which, as we have seen, may have cognitive effects of its own. A further problem for this model is that different NMDA receptor agents can have drastically differing effects on behaviour in rodents for reasons that are not easily understood at present, but possibly result from actions due to different NMDA receptor subtypes (see Gilmour et al., 2009).

At present, the utility of these pharmacological models is somewhat in doubt; they are easy to implement but may only result in the production of agents that affect dopamine or NMDA receptor function. On the other hand, it is of interest that the chronic PCP model has been used to achieve a notable recent example "back-translation", using the extra-dimensional shift paradigm described above. An experimental medicine study showed that the atypical stimulant, anti-narcoleptic drug modafinil rather surprisingly improved set-shifting performance when administered to high–functioning schizophrenic patients as an adjunct to their antipsychotic medication (Turner et al., 2004). In the rat version of this paradigm, an analogous effect was shown when modafinil reversed the deficits caused in extra-dimensional set-shifting by a chronic regimen of PCP treatment (Goetghebeur & Dias, 2009).

Neurodevelopmental models

The main motivation for these manipulations is the realization by Robin Murray and others during the 1980s (e.g., Murray & Lewis, 1987) that the evidence for neurodevelopmental factors in schizophrenia had become overwhelming. These models are based on a number of criteria, other than being simply developmental in nature. Thus, they capitalize on the fact that forebrain networks involving structures such as the hippocampus and prefrontal cortex are particularly prone to disruption in schizophrenia (possibly due to early trauma or anoxia) as well as possible consequences of any developmental dysplasia in these structures, including a cortically imposed dysregulation of the ascending dopamine systems. A classic example is the neonatal hippocampal lesion introduced by Lipska, Jaskiw, and Weinberger (1993), which led not only to a developmentally specific hippocampal impairment, but also to an accompanying set of neural deficits resulting from developmental abnormalities of the prefrontal cortex and an up-regulation of mesolimbic dopamine. This preparation thus resulted in heightened responses to amphetamine, and other behavioural sequelae associated with dopamine malfunction, such as impaired pre-pulse inhibition ("sensory gating") of the startle response, which is also impaired in schizophrenia itself, under certain conditions (Geyer, Krebs-Thomson, Braff, & Swerdlow, 2001).

An alternative method of disrupting the balance and coordination of hippocampal and cortical development can be achieved by treating rats at a particular developmental stage (E17) with the mitotic neurotoxin MAM (methylazoxymethanol acetate). At this particular age this otherwise rather non-selective means of retarding neural development has remarkably specific effects that lead to changes in brain weight, especially as a consequence of reduced hippocampal and (less obviously) cortical volume, with the size of structures such as the cerebellum being normal. Talamini, Koch, Ter Horst, and Korf

(1998) reported parallels with morphological findings for the entorhinal cortex in MAM-treated rats with what is also observed in the brains of schizophrenic patients. Additionally, there are the same dysregulatory effects on subcortical and cortical dopamine function, and a range of behavioural and cognitive deficits, including impairments in delayed alternation ("working memory") and attentional set-shifting and reversal learning (Featherstone, Rizos, Nobrega, Kapur, & Fletcher, 2007; Moore, Jentsch, Ghajarnia, Geyer, & Grace, 2006). The MAM model is currently the focus of considerable efforts to characterize the molecular, cellular, anatomical as well as functional, deficits, which are beyond the scope of this brief review.

A final method to be described here of impairing development in a manner relevant to that observed in schizophrenia can be achieved by variations in early social experience. One approach is to employ early maternal separation, which results in a number of behavioural, neural and endocrine impairments during adulthood (Matthews, 2003). However, while maternal separation leads to important emotional sequelae, possibly relevant for affective changes in schizophrenia, these effects of early social stress are perhaps most relevant for general depressive disorders. By contrast, social isolation at the weaning age (i.e., just prior to adolescence) can reproduce many of the molecular and neuronal, as well as behavioural, changes observed, for example, following neonatal hippocampal lesions (Fone & Porkess, 2008). Thus, these rats exhibit typical locomotor hyperactivity associated with heightened response to amphetamine and an up-regulation of midbrain dopamine activity, as well as cognitive deficits in spatial working memory and set-shifting behaviour and reversal learning. They are not unduly stressed, at least in endocrine terms, the main effect of the isolation appearing to be a deprivation of social play and its impact on normal cortical development.

Impairments in pre-pulse inhibition in socially isolated rats are remediated by dopamine D2 receptor antagonists and are developmentally specific, not occurring, for example, in rats housed in isolation for equivalent periods as adults (Geyer, Wilkinson, Humby, & Robbins, 1993). Moreover, they show neurochemical changes in such regions as the hippocampus and prefrontal cortex (e.g., Varty, Marsden, & Higgins, 1999). Epidemiological studies of schizophrenia suggest that adolescents at risk for mental disorders may amplify their propensity for a first psychotic episode by social withdrawal (Cannon et al., 1997) and it is possible that social isolation in adolescent rats helps to model this aspect. Figure 8.1 depicts the cascade of processes occurring in the aetiology of schizophrenia, including the "social withdrawal loop". It is notable that the first obvious behavioural signs in rats with neonatal hippocampal lesions are those of social withdrawal (Lipska & Weinberger, 2000), so it is of interest to speculate how much of this syndrome similarly depends on a disruption of the neural plasticity in development normally conferred by social play. Combining early social isolation with other manipulations such as the use of MAM or transgenesis may lead to more robust models of schizophrenia as a consequence of taking into account these social factors.

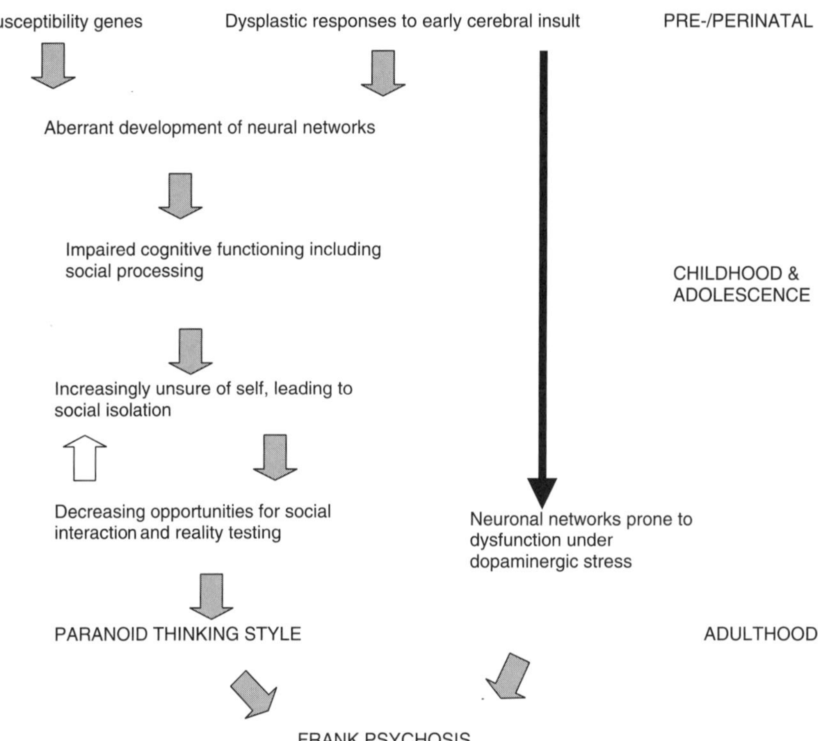

Figure 8.1 The aetiology of schizophrenia: A neurodevelopmental cascade.

Genetic models

As knowledge about the genetic bases of schizophrenia accumulates, we can be sure that analyses of animal models will increasingly focus on genetic manipulations (Ayhan et al., 2009). Of course, although the techniques for knocking-in and out specific genes are well developed in the mouse, the genetic manipulations required may well have to be much more selective and sophisticated in order to mimic the exact nature of genetic mutations observed in schizophrenia. The problem of genes having relatively small effects has already been raised; if one observes only a small fraction of effects (e.g., cognitive impairments) relevant to schizophrenia, is this to be expected? If, alternatively, one observes an entire spectrum of plausible effects, should this be a cause for scepticism? It can be predicted that combinations of genes will be manipulated in order to test for epistatic (i.e., synergistic) effects, and also that possible epigenetic factors will be carefully scrutinized.

One of the most fundamental attempts to grapple with possible candidate genes in schizophrenia has been to over-express the D2 receptor, given that an increase in dopamine D2 receptor numbers is a common symptom, even in the earliest stages of stages of schizophrenia. This treatment in mice produces a number of cognitive deficits including reversal learning and working memory, that have been speculated to result from a down-regulation of the dopamine D1 receptor, in a way similar to that hypothesized to occur following chronic haloperidol treatment (see Castner et al., 2000). However, this over-expression of D2 receptors surprisingly did not reproduce a pre-pulse inhibition deficit, which is so frequently observed in many of the other putative models (Kellendonk et al., 2006).

Positive and negative symptoms of schizophrenia

Whereas it has proven feasible to analyse specific cognitive symptoms in schizophrenia in terms of some of the building blocks of cognition identified in other species, the attempt to analyse the much more problematic positive and negative symptoms in the same way has traditionally been difficult. Is it possible, for example, to identify hallucinatory or delusional phenomena in animals, following some of the manipulations described above? There have been a number of pioneering attempts, notably using non-human primates, to address this issue. For example, Nielsen, Lyon, and colleagues were able to describe complex sequences of bizarre behaviour in monkeys exposed to chronic amphetamine treatment, which were most easily explicable if one assumed that the animal was hallucinating about the presence of certain visual or auditory stimuli (Nielsen, Lyon, & Ellison, 1983). Recently, Kapur (2003) has introduced an "aberrant stimulus salience" notion that has been borrowed by a careful and original reading of the animal literature of the effects of amphetamine-like drugs and on the functions of the midbrain dopamine systems. Amphetamine is well-known to exacerbate control over responding by reward-related stimuli termed conditioned reinforcers, this behaviour depending on dopaminergic mechanisms of the nucleus accumbens (e.g., Taylor & Robbins, 1986) and by limbic afferents conveying information on stimulus–reward associations to this structure. Moreover, Schultz and colleagues (e.g., Schultz, Dayan, & Montague, 1997) have discovered that midbrain dopamine neurons fire in fast phasic bursts to stimuli predicting food reward in rhesus monkeys. Such effects can easily be related to the "incentive salience" hypothesis of accumbens dopamine by Berridge (2007), which emphasizes the normal role of this projection in motivational processes governed by Pavlovian conditioning. Kapur's insight has been to suggest that the dopamine hyperactivity in schizophrenia results in inappropriate salience being attributed to environmental stimuli. This inappropriate salience triggers an attributional system, presumably of cortical origin, which constructs a delusional hypothesis to account for it. Thus, the therapeutic influence of neuroleptic drugs can be put down to their capacity to extinguish, or at least blunt, this maladaptive salience.

A key problem remains that of understanding why the delusions in schizophrenia are typically of the paranoid type, given that these presumably result from too much salience accruing to stimuli with aversive effects. Intriguingly, however, d-amphetamine enhances the potency of conditioned *punishing* as well as conditioned reinforcing stimuli in rats (Killcross, Everitt, & Robbins, 1997), and so its effects on stimulus salience, presumably mediated by striatal dopamine, are independent of affective valence—thus showing that it might be an entirely plausible substrate for the type of process postulated by Kapur. Further plausibility has been provided by a recent functional imaging study by G. Murray et al. (2008), which shows that schizophrenics exposed to a simple discrimination learning schedule while being scanned in a magnet show abnormal behavioural and BOLD responses to the least rewarded option, suggesting that they are allocating inappropriate salience to these largely irrelevant stimuli. It will be interesting in future work to determine whether this aberrant stimulus salience can occur in the way suggested above for aversive, as well as irrelevant, stimuli. At any rate, in addition to a possibly overactive ascending dopamine system, impaired salience is also presumably the consequence of a malfunctioning cortical system which is responsible for processing salient information and providing subjective hypotheses to rationalize unusual events. Investigating further this cortical–subcortical interaction may prove to be crucial in future attempts to define the neural substrates of positive symptoms in animal models.

Conclusion: Synthesizing the symptoms in schizophrenia

This brief survey of positive symptoms cannot disguise our relative inability to understand, as well as characterize, the negative symptoms of schizophrenia and our limited capacity to model and quantify these in experimental animals. As with the previous advances described, this will depend on the provision of a detailed description of negative symptoms in schizophrenia and an analysis in terms of cognitive processes and their interaction with motivational factors. At present, negative symptoms have been considered in terms of impaired social interactions among animals, and possible changes in "reward threshold" as quantified, for example, using brain stimulation reward. Many of these behavioural changes do, in fact, occur in the "models" described, such as the neonatal hippocampal lesioning paradigm (Lipska & Weinberger, 2000), so this perhaps represents a promising start. It is perhaps surprising that cognitive deficit, positive and negative symptoms can apparently co-exist in a "model" of schizophrenia, especially given the present focus on modelling specific symptoms, rather than the entire schizophrenic syndrome. On the other hand, a tripartite division along these lines, although apparently supported by several distinct forms of analysis, may be more artificial than is commonly supposed. The positive symptoms of delusions certainly appear to involve pathological processing by cognitive mechanisms that are recruited to meet the demands of subcortical activations, for example conveyed by the ascending dopamine system. It may be more accurate to think of schizophrenia as a collection of cognitive symptoms that have some common elements, probably focused on cortical mechanisms. The impairments in attention and working memory, the delusional phenomena and even the negative symptoms could all result from a common cortical dysplasia or hypoconnectivity. The symptoms of schizophrenia, then, result from a lack of balancing among various processing mechanisms, most obviously disrupting that between subcortical (especially striatal) and cortical (most especially hippocampal and frontal) regions. An animal model strategy based on what is known about the various pathologies that occur to these neural systems in schizophrenia may thus yet set the stage for a further analysis of the aetiological factors that we assume will soon be guiding the search for novel therapeutic strategies to ameliorate this crippling disorder.

Acknowledgements

The Behavioural and Clinical Neuroscience Institute is supported by a joint award from the MRC and the Wellcome Trust. Nicola Richmond is thanked for her help with the manuscript.

References

Arguello, P. A., & Gogos, J. A. (2006). Modeling madness in mice: One piece at a time. *Neuron*, *52*, 179–196.

Ayhan, Y., Sawa, A., Ross, C. A., & Pletnikov, M. V. (2009). Animal models of gene–environment interactions in schizophrenia. *Behavioural Brain Research*, *204*, 274–281.

Berridge, K. (2007). What is the role of dopamine in reward today? *Psychopharmacology (Berlin)*, *191*, 391–432.

Birrell, J. M., & Brown, V. J. (2000). Medial frontal cortex mediates perceptual attentional set shifting in the rat. *Journal of Neuroscience*, *20*, 4320–4324.

Bissonette, G. B., Martins, G. J., Franz, T. M., Harper, E. S., Schoenbaum, G., & Powell, E. M. (2008). Double dissociation of the effects of medial and orbital prefrontal cortical lesions on attentional and affective shifts in mice. *Journal of Neuroscience*, *28*, 11124–11130.

Brozoski, T. J., Brown, R. M., Rosvold, H. E., & Goldman, P. S. (1979). Cognitive deficit caused by regional depletion of dopamine in prefrontal cortex of rhesus monkey. *Science*, *205*, 929–932.

Cannon, M., Jones, P., Gilvarry, C., Rifkin, L., Mckenzie, K., Foerster, A., et al. (1997). Premorbid social functioning in schizophrenia and bipolar disorder: Similarities and differences. *American Journal of Psychiatry*, *154*, 1544–1550.

Castner, S. A., Williams, G. V., & Goldman-Rakic, P. S. (2000). Reversal of antipsychotic-induced working memory deficits by short-term dopamine D1 receptor stimulation. *Science*, *287*, 2020–2022.

Ceaser, A. E., Goldberg, T. E., Egan, M. F., McMahon, R. P., Weinberger, D. R., & Gold, J. M. (2008). Set-shifting ability and schizophrenia: A marker of clinical illness or an intermediate phenotype? *Biological Psychiatry*, *64*, 782–788.

Dias, R., Robbins, T. W., & Roberts, A. C. (1996). Dissociation in prefrontal cortex of affective and attentional shifts. *Nature*, *380*, 69–72.

Featherstone, R. E., Rizos, Z., Nobrega, J. N., Kapur, S., & Fletcher, P. J. (2007). Gestational methylazoxymethanol acetate treatment impairs select cognitive functions: Parallels to schizophrenia. *Neuropsychopharmacology*, *32*, 483–492.

Fletcher, P. J., Tenn, C. C., Rizos, Z., Lovic, V., & Kapur, S. (2005). Sensitization to amphetamine, but not PCP, impairs attentional set shifting: Reversal by a D1 receptor agonist injected into the medial prefrontal cortex. *Psychopharmacology (Berlin)*, *183*, 190–200.

Fone, K. C., & Porkess, M. V. (2008). Behavioural and neurochemical effects of post-weaning social isolation in rodents—Relevance to developmental neuropsychiatric disorders. *Neuroscience and Biobehavioral Reviews*, *32*, 1087–1102.

Geyer, M. A., Krebs-Thomson, K., Braff, D. L., & Swerdlow, N. R. (2001). Pharmacological studies of prepulse inhibition models of sensorimotor gating deficits in schizophrenia: A decade in review. *Psychopharmacology (Berlin)*, *156*, 117–154.

Geyer, M. A., Wilkinson, L. S., Humby, T., & Robbins, T. W. (1993). Isolation rearing of rats produces a deficit in prepulse inhibition of acoustic startle similar to that in schizophrenia. *Biological Psychiatry*, *34*, 361–372.

Gilmour, G., Pioli, E. Y., Dix, S. L., Smith, J. W., Conway, M. W., Jones, W. T., et al. (2009). Diverse and often opposite behavioural effects of NMDA receptor antagonists in rats: Implications for "NMDA antagonist modelling" of schizophrenia. *Psychopharmacology (Berlin)*, *205*, 203–216.

Goetghebeur, P., & Dias, R. (2009). Comparison of haloperidol, risperidone, sertindole, and modafinil to reverse an attentional set-shifting impairment following subchronic PCP administration in the rat—A back translational study. *Psychopharmacology (Berlin)*, *202*, 287–293.

Goldman-Rakic, P. S. (1998). The prefrontal landscape: Implications of functional architecture for understanding human mentation and the central executive. In A. C. Roberts, T. W. Robbins, & L. Weiskrantz (Eds.), *The prefrontal cortex: Executive and cognitive functions* (pp. 97–102). Oxford, UK: Oxford University Press.

Hampshire, A., & Owen, A. M. (2006). Fractionating attentional control using event-related fMRI. *Cerebral Cortex*, *16*, 1679–1689.

Hatcher, P. D., Brown, V. J., Tait, D. S., Bate, S., Overend, P., Hagan, J. J., et al. (2005). 5-HT6 receptor antagonists improve performance in an attentional set shifting task in rats. *Psychopharmacology (Berlin)*, *181*, 253–259.

Kapur, S. (2003). Psychosis as a state of aberrant salience: A framework linking biology, phenomenology, and pharmacology in schizophrenia. *American Journal of Psychiatry*, *160*, 13–23.

Kellendonk, C., Simpson, E. H., Polan, H. J., Malleret, G., Vronskaya, S., Winiger, V., et al. (2006). Transient and selective overexpression of dopamine D2 receptors in the striatum causes persistent abnormalities in prefrontal cortex functioning. *Neuron*, *49*, 603–615.

Killcross, A. S., Everitt, B. J., & Robbins, T. W. (1997). Symmetrical effects of amphetamine and alpha-flupenthixol on conditioned punishment and conditioned reinforcement: Contrasts with midazolam. *Psychopharmacology (Berlin)*, *129*, 141–152.

Krystal, J. H., Karper, L. P., Seibyl, J. P., Freeman, G. K., Delaney, R., Bremner, J. D., et al. (1994). Subanesthetic effects of the noncompetitive NMDA antagonist, ketamine, in humans. Psychotomimetic, perceptual, cognitive, and neuroendocrine responses. *Archives of General Psychiatry*, *51*, 199–214.

Leeson, V. C., Robbins, T. W., Matheson, E., Hutton, S. B., Ron, M. A., Barnes, T. R., et al. (2009). Discrimination learning, reversal, and set-shifting in first-episode schizophrenia: Stability over six years and specific associations with medication type and disorganization syndrome. *Biological Psychiatry*, *66*, 586–593.

Lipska, B. K., Jaskiw, G. E., & Weinberger, D. R. (1993). Postpubertal emergence of hyperresponsiveness to stress and to amphetamine after neonatal excitotoxic hippocampal damage: A potential animal model of schizophrenia. *Neuropsychopharmacology*, *9*, 67–75.

Lipska, B. K., & Weinberger, D. R. (2000). To model a psychiatric disorder in animals: Schizophrenia as a reality test. *Neuropsychopharmacology*, *23*, 223–239.

Marder, S. R., & Fenton, W. (2004). Measurement and treatment research to improve cognition in schizophrenia: NIMH MATRICS initiative to support the development of agents for improving cognition in schizophrenia. *Schizophrenia Research*, *72*, 5–9.

Matthews, K. (2003). Social separation models of depression. In M. A. Ron & T. W. Robbins (Eds.), *Disorders in brain and mind* (pp. 338–371). Cambridge, UK: Cambridge University Press.

McAlonan, K., & Brown, V. J. (2003). Orbital prefrontal cortex mediates reversal learning and not attentional set shifting in the rat. *Behavioural Brain Research*, *146*, 97–103.

Moore, H., Jentsch, J. D., Ghajarnia, M., Geyer, M. A., & Grace, A. A. (2006). A neurobehavioral systems analysis of adult rats exposed to methylazoxymethanol acetate on E17: Implications for the neuropathology of schizophrenia. *Biological Psychiatry*, *60*, 253–264.

Murray, G. K., Cheng, F., Clark, L., Barnett, J. H., Blackwell, A. D., Fletcher, P. C., et al. (2008). Reinforcement and reversal learning in first-episode psychosis. *Schizophrenia Bulletin*, *34*, 848–855.

Murray, R. M., & Lewis, S. W. (1987). Is schizophrenia a neurodevelopmental disorder? *British Medical Journal (Clinical Research Edition)*, *295*, 681–682.

Nielsen, E. B., Lyon, M., & Ellison, G. (1983). Apparent hallucinations in monkeys during around-the-clock amphetamine for seven to fourteen days. Possible relevance to amphetamine psychosis. *Journal of Nervous and Mental Diseases*, *171*, 222–233.

Pantelis, C., Barber, F. Z., Barnes, T. R., Nelson, H. E., Owen, A. M., & Robbins, T. W. (1999). Comparison of set-shifting ability in patients with chronic schizophrenia and frontal lobe damage. *Schizophrenia Research*, *37*, 251–270.

Papaleo, F., Crawley, J. N., Song, J., Lipska, B. K., Pickel, J., Weinberger, D. R., et al. (2008). Genetic dissection of the role of catechol-O-methyltransferase in cognition and stress reactivity in mice. *Journal of Neuroscience*, *28*, 8709–8723.

Park, S., & Holzman, P. S. (1992). Schizophrenics show spatial working memory deficits. *Archives of General Psychiatry*, *49*, 975–982.

Robbins, T. W. (2004). Animal models of psychosis. In D. Charney & E. Nestler (Eds.), *The neurobiology of mental illness* (pp. 263–286). New York, NY: Oxford University Press.

Robbins, T. W., & Moore, H. (2008). Modelling psychiatric disorders in experimental animals. In A. Tasman, J. K. Lieberman, M. First, & M. Maj (Eds.), *Psychiatry* (3rd ed., pp. 275–288). Chichester, UK: Wiley.

Rodefer, J. S., Murphy, E. R., & Baxter, M. G. (2005). PDE10A inhibition reverses subchronic PCP-induced deficits in attentional set-shifting in rats. *European Journal of Neuroscience*, *21*, 1070–1076.

Schultz, W., Dayan, P., & Montague, P. R. (1997). A neural substrate of prediction and reward. *Science*, *275*, 1593–1599.

Snyder, S. H. (1973). Amphetamine psychosis: A "model" schizophrenia mediated by catecholamines. *American Journal of Psychiatry*, *130*, 61–67.

Talamini, L. M., Koch, T., Ter Horst, G. J., & Korf, J. (1998). Methylazoxymethanol acetate-induced abnormalities in the entorhinal cortex of the rat: Parallels with morphological findings in schizophrenia. *Brain Research*, *789*, 293–306.

Taylor, J. R., & Robbins, T. W. (1986). 6-Hydroxydopamine lesions of the nucleus accumbens, but not of the caudate nucleus, attenuate enhanced responding with reward-related stimuli produced by intra-accumbens d-amphetamine. *Psychopharmacology (Berlin)*, *90*, 390–397.

Tunbridge, E. M., Bannerman, D. M., Sharp, T., & Harrison, P. J. (2004). Catechol-O-methyltransferase inhibition improves set-shifting performance and elevates stimulated dopamine release in the rat prefrontal cortex. *Journal of Neuroscience*, *24*, 5331–5335.

Turner, D. C., Clark, L., Pomarol-Clotet, E., Mckenna, P., Robbins, T. W., & Sahakian, B. J. (2004). Modafinil improves cognition and attentional set shifting in patients with chronic schizophrenia. *Neuropsychopharmacology*, *29*, 1363–1373.

Varty, G. B., Marsden, C. A., & Higgins, G. A. (1999). Reduced synaptophysin immunoreactivity in the dentate gyrus of prepulse inhibition-impaired isolation-reared rats. *Brain Research*, *824*, 197–203.

Part III

Neuroimaging

9 Application of neuroimaging to the study of psychosis

Philip McGuire

Introduction

Robin Murray's department pioneered the application of neuroimaging to the study of psychosis. This work helped to improve our understanding of the mechanisms that underlie psychotic symptoms and psychotic disorders. In this chapter, I will first focus on neuroimaging studies that investigated the pathophysiology of auditory hallucinations, and then describe how neuroimaging was used to examine the mechanisms underlying the onset of psychotic disorders.

Neuroimaging studies of psychosis in the Department of Psychological Medicine

Shared environmental factors

Both Robin Murray and I shared some surprisingly similar environmental influences. We were both born in Glasgow, and we both moved to Edinburgh as children, and went to the same school—the Royal High School. I first met Robin when I came to the Maudsley Hospital for an interview for the psychiatric training scheme. During the interview, Robin took what seemed to be an unusual interest in one of the very few awards mentioned on my c.v., the Sir David Yule Scholarship. He asked me what exactly it had been awarded for. I knew that, despite its rather grand title, it was automatically given to any pupil who simply remained at the school for the sixth and final year. Although briefly tempted to invent some more impressive reason, I nevertheless explained its disappointing provenance. This was fortunate, as it was at this point that Robin revealed that he knew very well what it was awarded for, as he had attended the same school. The interview ended with him asking if I had any questions. As the first neuroimaging studies in psychiatry had recently appeared, I enquired whether the Institute had any plans to invest in a positron emission tomography (PET) scanner. Robin said that he wasn't convinced that neuroimaging would prove much use to psychiatry, cited the methodological problems associated with a recent study of dopamine receptors, and concluded that it might turn out to be a bit of a waste of money. Despite this, his enthusiasm and charm was such that I was easily persuaded to join him at the Maudsley.

When I first visited Robin's department, I was sent to go and chat to the researchers in his group. Almost everyone I met was either involved in genetic association studies or epidemiology—neuroimaging research at that time had a very low profile. There was very little in the way of local scanning facilities, so structural imaging data had to be acquired at St Georges Hospital or at the National Hospital at Queen Square, and although there was a PET scanner at the Hammersmith Hospital, nobody from the Institute had access to it. However, there was a single photon emission tomography (SPET) camera in the Department of Nuclear Medicine at King's College Hospital, which was mainly used for clinical purposes in medicine and surgery. Robin encouraged me to talk to the physicist there, and see if it was possible to do some research on schizophrenia. This led to a SPET study, and then a series of subsequent studies using other techniques that focused on understanding the mechanisms underlying auditory hallucinations.

Using neuroimaging to study psychotic symptoms

This first study used SPET to measure cerebral blood flow when patients were experiencing auditory verbal hallucinations. Patients were scanned on two occasions, once when they were actually experiencing hallucinations, and on another occasion when the same patient was hallucination free. Comparison of the images from the two states, within each subject, thus revealed the pattern of cerebral blood flow associated with hallucinations of speech. We found that hallucinations were particularly associated with increased blood flow in the left inferior frontal gyrus (McGuire, Shah, & Murray, 1993). This was interesting, as it suggested that auditory verbal hallucinations might be related to the generation of inner speech. We went on to examine this hypothesis using the PET scanner at the MRC Cyclotron Unit at the Hammersmith Hospital, in collaboration with Professor Chris Frith. In this study, patients were scanned while performing tasks that involved either the generation of inner speech, or both the generation and monitoring of inner speech. Patients with schizophrenia who were especially prone to auditory verbal hallucinations were compared with a matching group of patients who had never experienced auditory hallucinations, and healthy controls. All three groups engaged the left inferior frontal cortex when generating inner speech. However, when monitoring their own inner speech, controls and patients with no history of hallucinations engaged the left temporal cortex, whereas the hallucination-prone patients did not (McGuire et al., 1995). These data suggested that auditory verbal hallucinations might be related to a problem with the monitoring, rather than the generation, of inner speech. Further studies using functional MRI confirmed and extended these initial findings. They revealed that the perception of auditory hallucinations was associated with activity in a network of language-related areas, that included the inferior frontal cortex, but also the anterior cingulate and superior temporal cortex (Shergill, Bullmore, Simmons, Murray, & McGuire, 2000). The vulnerability to hallucinations was associated with altered activation within this network when subjects were monitoring their own verbal output, and a tendency to attribute their own verbal material to an alien, external source, when it was acoustically distorted (Allen et al., 2007; Fu et al., 2006, 2008; Johns & McGuire, 1999; Shergill, Brammer, Williams, Murray, & McGuire, 2000).

Further work examined whether these findings were related to faulty communication between brain areas that generated and monitored inner speech. In patients who were prone to hallucinations, the effective connectivity between these areas appears to be different to that in controls or patients who didn't experience auditory hallucinations (Mechelli et al., 2007) and an alteration in the integrity of the fasciculi that anatomically connect these regions (Shergill et al., 2007).

One of the commonest causes of psychotic symptoms in the general population, particularly in South London, is cannabis use. While this relationship is long established, how cannabis acts on the brain to induce psychotic phenomena is less clear. In the 1990s, Robin Murray played a key role in highlighting the aetiological contribution of cannabis use to psychosis, and in changing the views of the psychiatric community and the government about its importance as a risk factor for schizophrenia. In this context, we used functional magnetic resonance imaging (fMRI) to examine the acute effect of tetrahydrocannabidiol (THC) and cannabidiol (CBD), the two main psychoactive constituents of cannabis, on brain function. This work indicated that the acute induction of psychotic symptoms by THC was related to its effect on activation in the striatum, consistent with evidence that these effects may be mediated through an effect of THC on dopamine release (Bhattacharyya et al., 2009; Plate 9.1). In contrast, CBD had effects on regional activation that were opposite to those of THC, consistent with evidence that it has antipsychotic effects (Bhattacharyya et al., 2010).

Neuroimaging studies of the early phase of psychosis

Robin's department has had a long-standing interest in studies of the early phase of psychosis, and conducted one of the first large-scale studies of first-episode psychosis, the AESOP (Aetiology and Ethnicity of Schizophrenia and Other Psychoses) study. Although primarily an epidemiological study, it also included a neuroimaging component, which produced a series of publications on brain structure in first-episode psychosis (Lappin et al., 2007; Morgan et al., 2007), and the effects of treatment on this (Dazzan et al., 2005). Remarkably, this and other first-episode studies were completed in the absence of any local clinical services for carly intervention in psychosis, which made recruitment of subjects for research in this area difficult. This was especially true for studies on people with prodromal symptoms of psychosis, who are not usually managed by conventional mental health services. Neuroimaging studies in this population have particular research potential, as it is possible to examine brain structure, function and chemistry in a prospective fashion, before and after the onset of psychosis, in the same individual. Moreover, as the subjects are usually medication naïve, the results are not confounded by effects of antipsychotic treatment. The department's first neuroimaging research in prodromal subjects involved samples that had been recruited in specialized early intervention services in Australia and Switzerland (Borgwardt et al., 2007; Pantelis et al., 2003). However, over the last decade, staff in Robin Murray's department have played a key role in helping to develop early intervention services in South London, including the Lambeth Early Onset (LEO) service for patients with first-episode psychosis (Power et al., 2007), and OASIS (Outreach and Support In South London), a service for people with prodromal signs of psychosis (Broome et al., 2005). These services have permitted a programme of research in the clinical populations that would otherwise have been difficult to recruit.

Neuroimaging studies in people with prodromal signs of psychosis have provided new information on grey matter volume, neurocognitive function, dopamine activity, and glutamate levels before the first episode of psychosis. Grey matter volume is reduced in a set of brain areas that is similar to that showing grey matter volume reductions in patients with schizophrenia, even though most of the sample will never go on to develop psychosis (Borgwardt et al., 2007; Pantelis et al., 2003; Stone et al., 2009). Functional MRI studies of cognitive processes implicated in psychosis, such as executive functions, working memory, episodic memory and salience processing, indicate that this group show functional alterations in the brain areas that are normally critical for these processes, including the prefrontal, anterior cingulate and medial temporal cortex, and the striatum (Allen et al., 2010; Broome et al., 2009; Plate 9.2). In addition, the functional connectivity between these regions appears to be perturbed (Benetti et al., 2009; Crossley et al., 2009). Again, these findings are qualitatively similar to those seen in patients with established psychosis (Fusar-Poli et al., 2007). Dopamine and glutamate are the two neurotransmitters that are most strongly implicated in psychosis, but the stage of illness at which these transmitter systems are perturbed is unclear. Using the PET scanner at the Hammersmith Hospital, we found that subjects with prodromal symptoms have elevated dopamine function in the striatum, and that the magnitude of this elevation was correlated to the severity of their prodromal symptoms (Howes et al., 2009). A study using MR spectroscopy found that prodromal subjects have reduced levels of thalamic glutamate compared to controls, but higher levels of glutamate in the anterior cingulated cortex (Stone et al., 2009; Plate 9.3). By combining different neuroimaging techniques in the same individuals, it has also been possible to examine the relationship between the findings in this population. Thus, application of fMRI and PET in the same sample of prodromal subjects revealed that the degree of altered prefrontal activation in this group during a verbal fluency task, and during a working-memory task was directly correlated with the severity of the striatal dopamine dysfunction (Fusar-Poli et al., 2010a, 2010b; Plate 9.4), consistent with evidence that dopamine dysfunction is correlated with the impairment in verbal fluency performance at the behavioural level (Howes et al., 2009). Future studies may clarify whether the dopaminergic abnormalities are secondary to changes in prefrontal function, or vice versa. The combination of MR spectroscopy and volumetric MRI in the same prodromal subjects indicated that the reduction in cortical grey matter volume in this group was correlated with the lowering of thalamic glutamate levels (Stone et al., 2009; Plate 9.5). This finding raises the possibility that the process underlying the reduction in grey matter volume in this group may involve glutamate dysfunction.

Because some people with prodromal symptoms progress to a full-blown psychotic disorder but others do not, comparison of neuroimaging data from these two subgroups can identify features that predict a later transition to psychosis. Follow-up of subjects subsequent to MRI scanning suggests that within this population, reduced right inferior frontal volume at first clinical presentation is associated with the subsequent onset of psychosis (Borgwardt et al., 2007; Pantelis et al., 2003). Longitudinal neuroimaging studies in this group can reveal within-subject brain changes that are associated with the transition from the prodromal to the first-episode state. MRI studies that have assessed grey matter volume at baseline and after the onset of illness indicate that this is associated with longitudinal volume reductions in the medial temporal, cingulate and prefrontal cortex (Borgwardt et al., 2008; Pantelis et al., 2003). Neuroimaging findings that are specific to the onset of psychosis provide clues as to which neurobiological changes are correlates of psychotic illness, as opposed to an increased vulnerability to psychosis. A key future goal for neuroimaging work in the department is to use these research findings to inform the clinical application of neuroimaging in the development of tools that can help to predict which individuals at high risk of psychosis are most likely to go on to develop the disorder (McGuire, Howes, Stone, & Fusar-Poli, 2008).

Conclusion

Neuroimaging has made a major contribution to the work of Robin Murray's department on research on psychosis. The fact that this happened despite an initial lack of technical infrastructure is a testament to Robin's enthusiasm, support and ability to inspire his staff.

References

Allen, P., Amaro, E., Fu, C. H., Williams, S. C., Brammer, M. J., Johns, L. C., et al. (2007). Neural correlates of the misattribution of speech in schizophrenia. *British Journal of Psychiatry*, *190*, 162–169.

Allen, P., Seal, M. L., Valli, I., Fusar-Poli, P., Perlini, C., Day, F., et al. (2009). Altered prefrontal and hippocampal function during verbal encoding and recognition in people with prodromal symptoms of psychosis. *Schizophrenia Bulletin* 2009 Nov 23. (doi:10.1093/schbul/sbp113). [Epub ahead of print].

Allen, P., Stephan, K. E., Mechelli, A., Day, F., Ward, N., Dalton, J., et al. (2010). Cingulate activity and fronto-temporal connectivity in people with prodromal signs of psychosis. *NeuroImage*, *49*(1), 947–955.

Benetti, S., Mechelli, A., Picchioni, M., Broome, M., Williams, S., & McGuire, P. (2009). Functional integration between the posterior hippocampus and prefrontal cortex is impaired in both first episode schizophrenia and the at risk mental state. *Brain*, *132*(9), 2426–2436.

Bhattacharyya, S., Fusar-Poli, P., Borgwardt, S., Martin-Santos, R., Nosarti, C., O'Carroll, C., et al. (2009). Modulation of mediotemporal and ventrostriatal function in humans by delta-9-tetrahydrocannabinol: A neural basis for the effects of *Cannabis sativa* on learning and psychosis. *Archives of General Psychiatry*, *66*(4), 442–451.

Bhattacharyya, S., Morrison, P. D., Fusar-Poli, P., Martin-Santos, R., Borgwardt, S., Winton-Brown, T., et al. (2010). Opposite effects of delta-9-tetrahydrocannabinol and cannabidiol on human brain function and psychopathology. *Neuropsychopharmacology*, *35*(3), 764–774.

Borgwardt, S. J., McGuire, P. K., Aston, J., Gschwandtner, U., Pfluger, M. O., Stieglitz, R. D., et al. (2008). Reductions in frontal, temporal and parietal volume associated with the onset of psychosis. *Schizophrenia Research*, *106*(2–3), 108–114.

Borgwardt, S. J., Riecher-Rossler, A., Dazzan, P., Chitnis, X., Aston, J., Drewe, M., et al. (2007). Regional gray matter volume abnormalities in the at risk mental state. *Biological Psychiatry*, *61*(10), 1148–1156.

Broome, M., Woolley, J., Johns, L., Valmaggia, L., Tabraham, P., Bramon, E., et al. (2005). Outreach And Support In South London (OASIS): Clinical audit of a service for people with prodromal symptoms. *European Psychiatry*, *20*(5–6), 372–378.

Broome, M. R., Matthiasson, P., Fusar-Poli, P., Woolley, J. B., Johns, L. C., Tabraham, P., et al. (2009). Neural correlates of executive function and working memory in the "at-risk mental state". *British Journal of Psychiatry*, *194*(1), 25–33.

Crossley, N. A., Mechelli, A., Fusar-Poli, P., Broome, M. R., Matthiasson, P., Johns, L. C., et al. (2009). Superior temporal lobe dysfunction and frontotemporal dysconnectivity in subjects at risk of psychosis and in first-episode psychosis. *Human Brain Mapping*, *30*(12), 4129–4137.

Dazzan, P., Morgan, K. D., Orr, K., Hutchinson, G., Chitnis, X., Suckling, J., et al. (2005). Different effects of typical and atypical antipsychotics on grey matter in first episode psychosis: The AESOP study. *Neuropsychopharmacology*, *30*(4), 765–774.

Fu, C. H., Brammer, M. J., Yaguez, L., Allen, P., Matsumoto, K., Johns, L., et al. (2008). Increased superior temporal activation associated with external misattributions of self-generated speech in schizophrenia. *Schizophrenia Research*, *100*(1–3), 361–363.

Fu, C. H., Vythelingum, G. N., Brammer, M. J., Williams, S. C., Amaro, E., Jr., Andrew, C. M., et al. (2006). An fMRI study of verbal self-monitoring: Neural correlates of auditory verbal feedback. *Cerebral Cortex*, *16*(7), 969–977.

Fusar-Poli, P., Howes, O., Allen, P., Broome, M., Valli, I., Asselin, M.-C., et al. (2010a). Altered prefrontal activation directly related to striatal dopamine dysfunction in people with prodromal symptoms of schizophrenia. *Molecular Psychiatry*, *16*(1), 67–75.

Fusar-Poli, P., Howes, O., Allen, P., Broome, M., Valli, I., Asselin, M.-C., et al. (2010b). Abnormal frontostriatal interactions in people with prodromal signs of psychosis: A multimodal imaging study. *Archives of General Psychiatry*, *67*(7), 683–691.

Fusar-Poli, P., Perez, J., Broome, M., Borgwardt, S., Placentino, A., Caverzasi, E., et al. (2007). Neurofunctional correlates of vulnerability to psychosis: A systematic review and meta-analysis. *Neuroscience and Biobehavioral Reviews*, *31*(4), 465–484.

Howes, O. D., Montgomery, A. J., Asselin, M.-C., Murray, R. M., Valli, I., Tabraham, P., et al. (2009). Elevated striatal dopamine function linked to prodromal signs of schizophrenia. *Archives of General Psychiatry*, *66*(1), 13–20.

Johns, L. C., & McGuire, P. K. (1999). Verbal self-monitoring and auditory hallucinations in schizophrenia. *Lancet*, *353*(9151), 469–470.

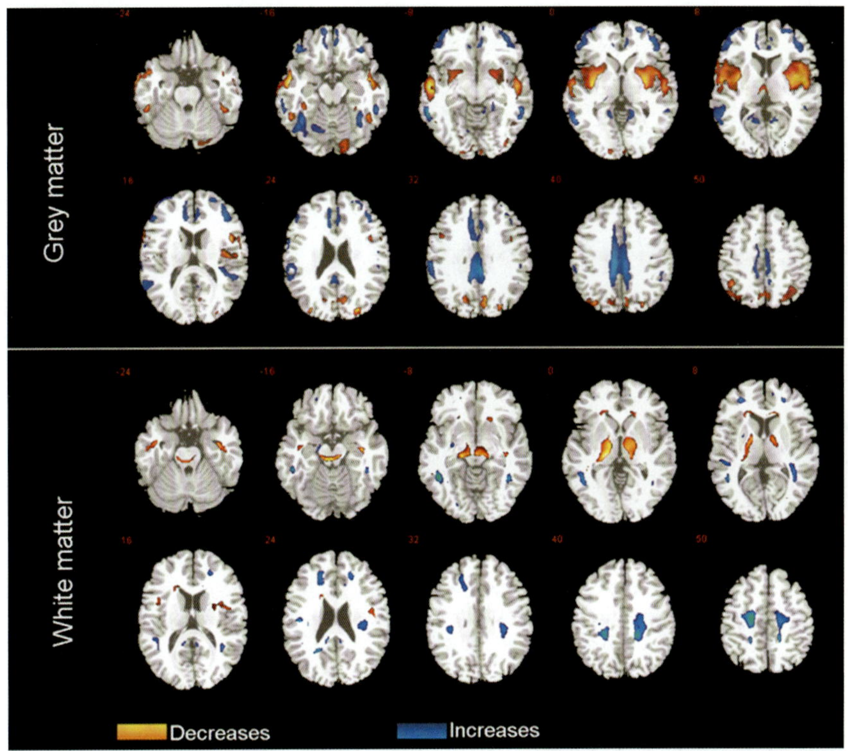

Plate 3.1 Decreased (orange) and increased (blue) grey matter and white matter volume in VPT adolescents compared to controls (adapted from Nosarti, Giouroukou et al., 2008, *Brain, 131*, 205–217, by permission of Oxford University Press).

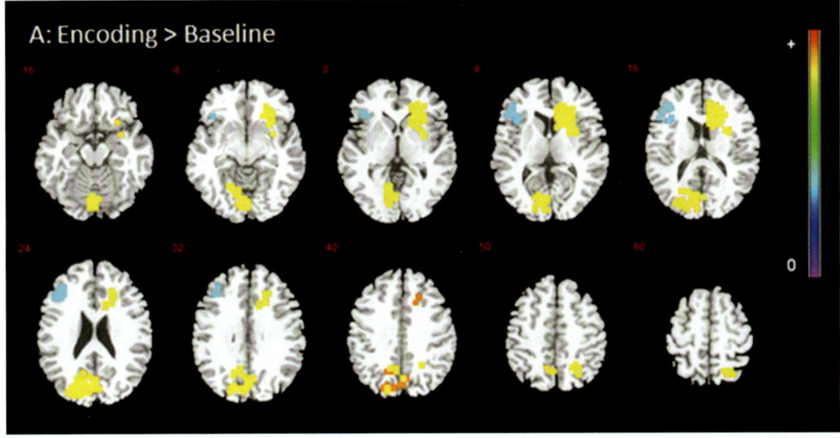

Plate 3.2 Increased (yellow) and decreased (blue) regional brain activation in preterm-born young adults compared to controls during the encoding phase of a visual paired associates task (adapted from Narberhaus et al., 2009, *NeuroImage, 47*, 1884–1893, by permission of Elsevier).

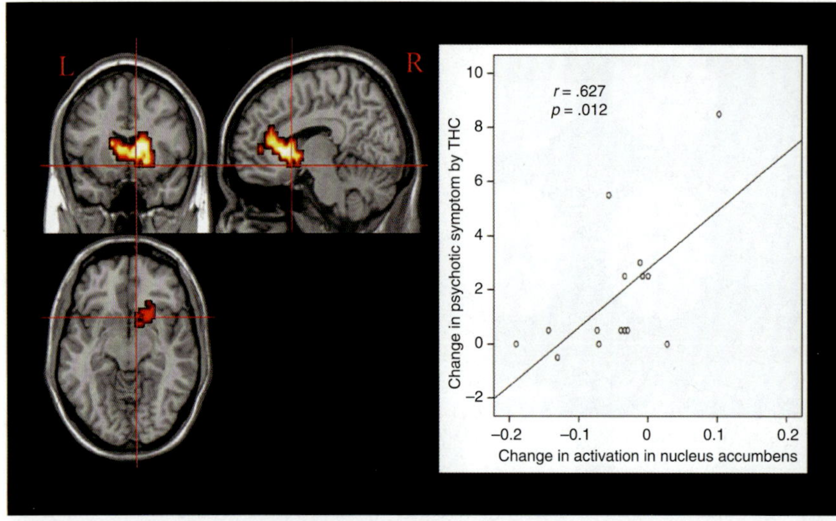

Plate 9.1 Acute induction of psychotic symptoms by tetrahydrocannabidiol (THC). In healthy subjects, administration of THC modulated activation in the ventral striatum, and the magnitude of this effect was correlated with the severity of the psychotic symptoms it induced.

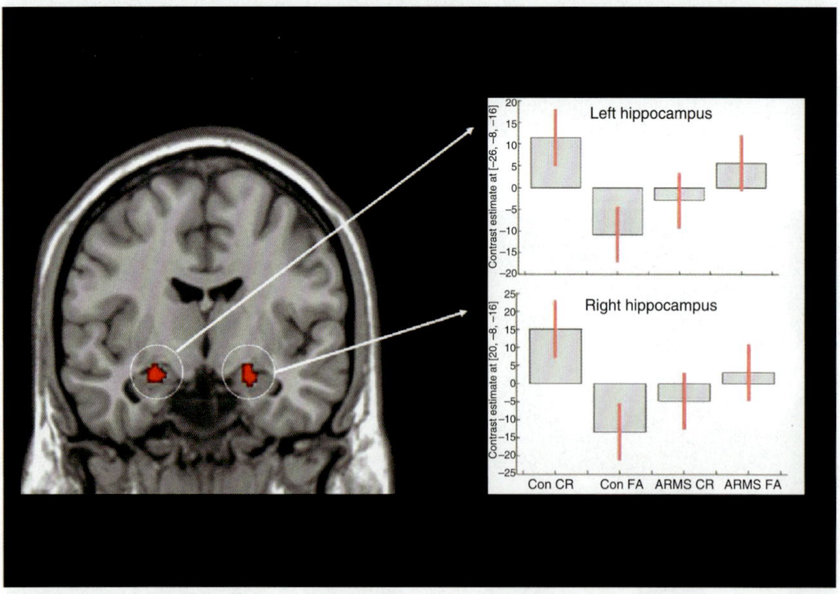

Plate 9.2 Altered hippocampal function in subjects with prodromal signs of psychosis. In controls, the hippocampus is activated when subjects correctly recognize a previously presented word (Con CR), but not when they think they incorrectly report having seen a word that had not been shown before (Con FA). This difference in hippocampal response is significantly attenuated in prodromal subjects (ARMS CR and ARMS FA).

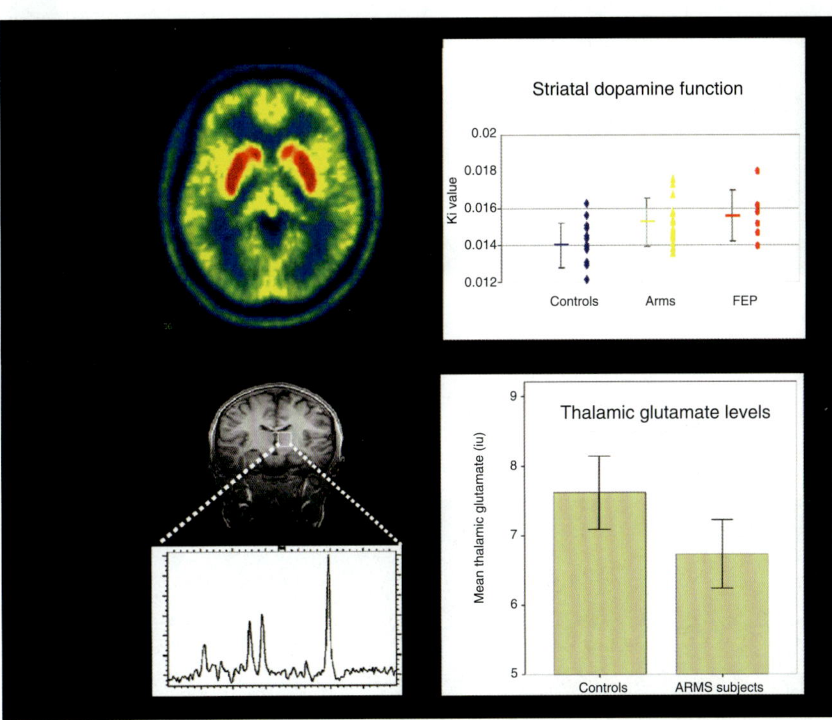

Plate 9.3 Neurochemical dysfunction in subjects with prodromal signs of psychosis. PET and MR spectroscopy data showing that subjects at ultra high risk of psychosis have elevated dopamine synthesis capacity in the striatum (upper part of figure), and reduced levels of glutamate in the thalamus (lower part).

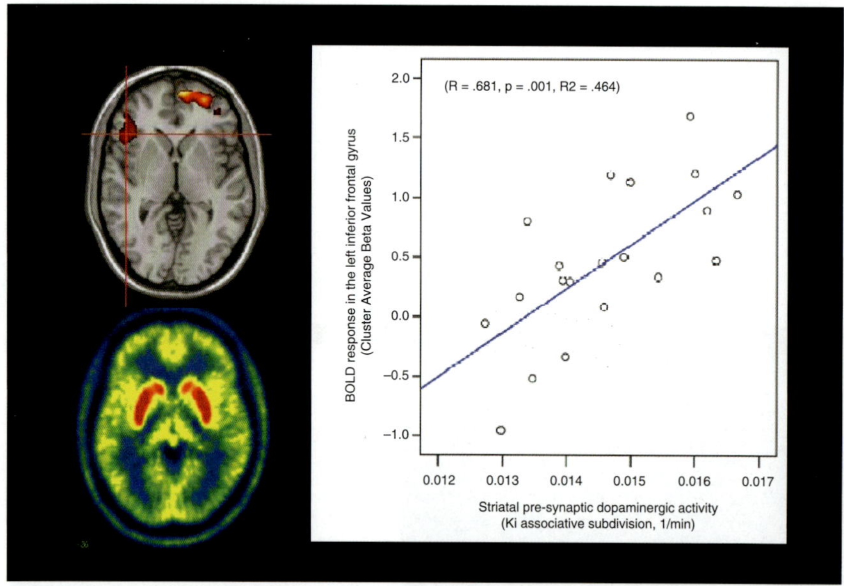

Plate 9.4 Correlation between subcortical dopamine dysfunction and altered cortical activation in subjects with prodromal symptoms of psychosis. In these subjects, the greater the elevation of striatal dopamine function, the greater the alteration in prefrontal response during a verbal fluency task.

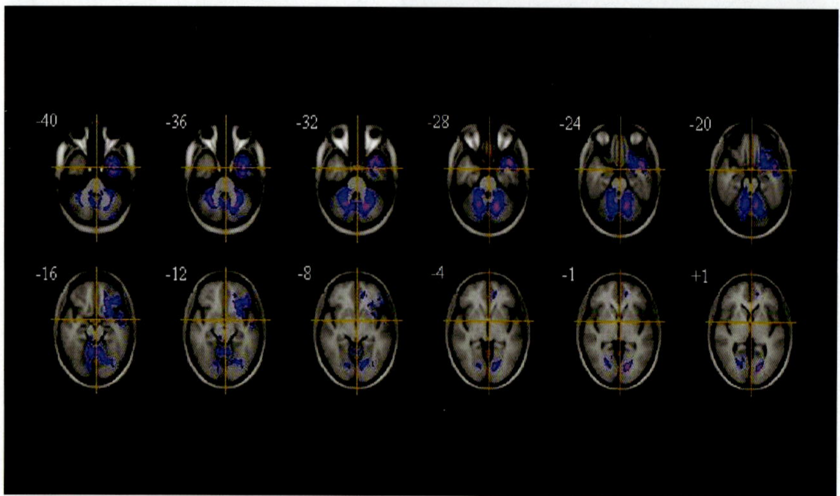

Plate 9.5 Brain areas in subjects with prodromal symptoms where grey matter volume was related to thalamic glutamate levels. Reduced volume in medial temporal, inferior frontal, insular and cerebellar cortex was correlated with a reduction in glutamate levels in the thalamus.

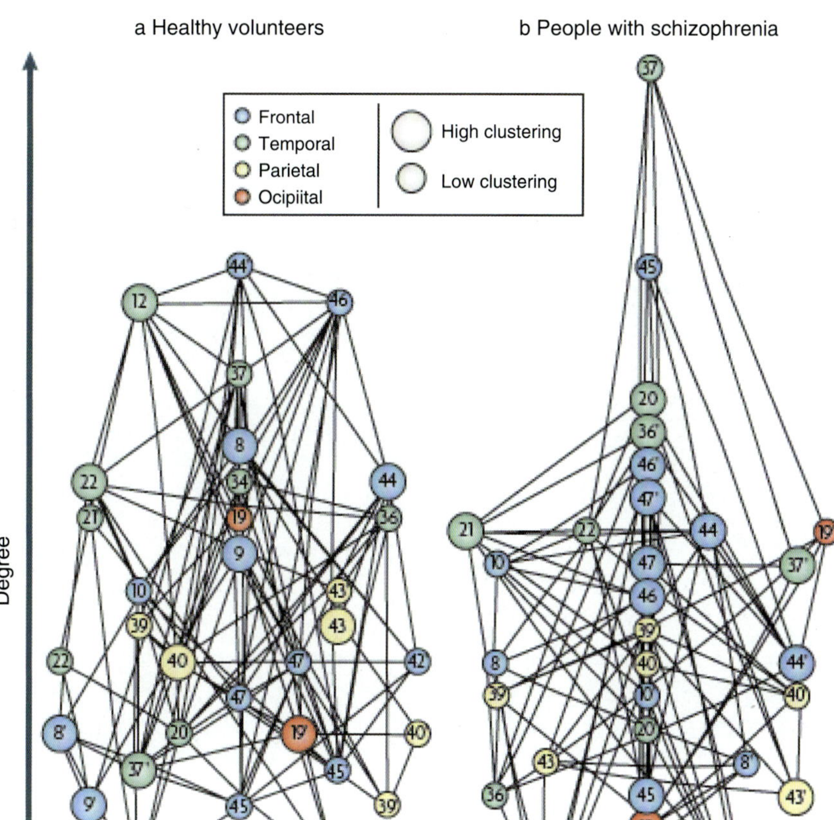

Plate 10.1 Disease-related disorganization of brain anatomical networks derived from structural MRI data. In both parts, the nodes (circles) represent cortical regions and the connections represent high correlation in grey matter density between nodes. The nodes are arranged vertically by degree (number of connections) and are separated horizontally for clarity of representation. The numbers indicate approximate Brodmann area and the prime symbols (′) denote left-sided regions. The clustering coefficient of each node, a measure of its local connectivity, is indicated by its size; nodes with high clustering are larger. (a) The brain anatomical network of the healthy volunteers has a hierarchical organization characterized by low clustering of high degree nodes. (b) the equivalent network constructed from MRI data on people with schizophrenia shows loss of this hierarchical organization—high-degree nodes are more often highly clustered. (Reproduced from Bullmore and Sporns, 2009, *Nature Reviews Neuroscience, 10*, 186–198.)

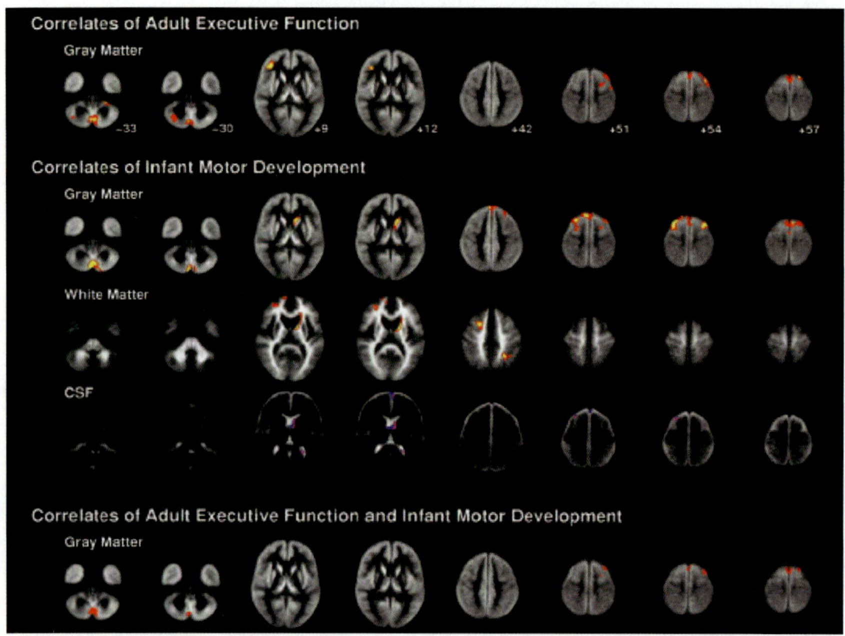

Plate 10.2 Developmental antecedents of adult human brain structure. Adult executive function (top row) and infant motor development (rows 2–4) were positively correlated with grey matter volume in partially overlapping regions (row 5) of brain images collected from non-psychotic adults drawn from the 1966 Northern Finland birth cohort. These normal developmental continuities between timing of infant motor skills milestones and adult anatomy of premotor, striatal and cerebellar regions were disrupted in patients with schizophrenia, who had been relatively slow to acquire basic motor skills in infancy and had relatively poor executive function as adults. (Reproduced from Ridler et al., 2006, *Proceedings of the National Academy of Sciences of the United States of America, 103*, 15651–15656.)

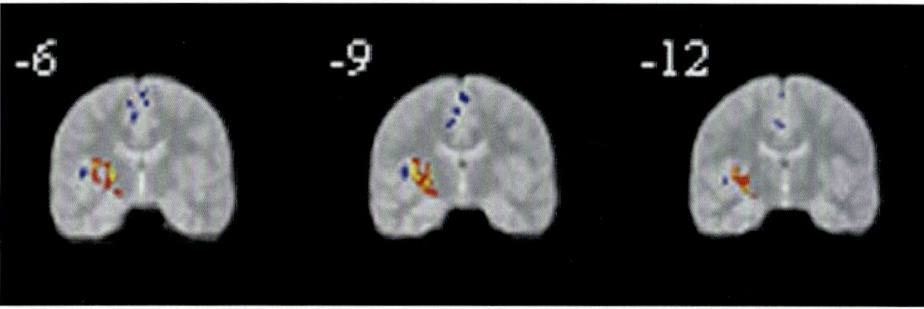

(B)

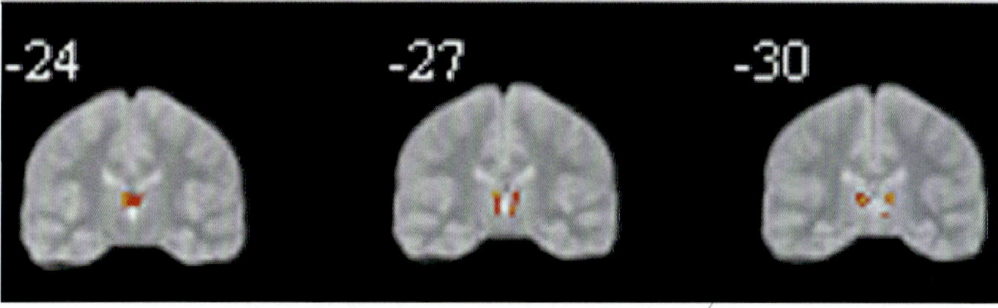

Plate 11.1 (A) Brain changes in subjects on typical antipsychotics versus drug-free subjects. Some regions of deficits (blue) and excesses (red) for grey matter in subjects taking typicals. (B) Brain changes in subjects on atypical antipsychotics versus drug-free subjects. Regions of excesses (red) for grey matter in subjects taking atypicals. Results are displayed on an averaged grey and white matter map. The left side of the image corresponds to the right side of the brain. Numbers refer to the approximate y coordinates in the standard space of Talairach and Tournoux.

Lappin, J. M., Dazzan, P., Morgan, K., Morgan, C., Chitnis, X., Suckling, J., et al. (2007). Duration of prodromal phase and severity of volumetric abnormalities in first-episode psychosis. *British Journal of Psychiatry, 51*(Suppl.), S123–127.

McGuire, P., Howes, O. D., Stone, J., & Fusar-Poli, P. (2008). Functional neuroimaging in schizophrenia: Diagnosis and drug discovery. *Trends in Pharmacological Sciences, 29*(2), 91–98.

McGuire, P. K., Shah, G. M., & Murray, R. M. (1993). Increased blood flow in Broca's area during auditory hallucinations in schizophrenia. *Lancet, 342*(8873), 703–706.

McGuire, P. K., Silbersweig, D. A., Wright, I., Murray, R. M., David, A. S., Frackowiak, R. S., et al. (1995). Abnormal monitoring of inner speech: A physiological basis for auditory hallucinations. *Lancet, 346*(8975), 596–600.

Mechelli, A., Allen, P., Amaro, E., Jr., Fu, C. H., Williams, S. C., Brammer, M. J., et al. (2007). Misattribution of speech and impaired connectivity in patients with auditory verbal hallucinations. *Human Brain Mapping, 28*(11), 1213–1222.

Morgan, K. D., Dazzan, P., Orr, K. G., Hutchinson, G., Chitnis, X., Suckling, J., et al. (2007). Grey matter abnormalities in first-episode schizophrenia and affective psychosis. *British Journal of Psychiatry, 51*(Suppl.), S111–116.

Pantelis, C., Velakoulis, D., McGorry, P. D., Wood, S. J., Suckling, J., Phillips, L. J., et al. (2003). Neuroanatomical abnormalities before and after onset of psychosis: A cross-sectional and longitudinal MRI comparison. *Lancet, 361*(9354), 281–288.

Power, P., Iacoponi, E., Reynolds, N., Fisher, H., Russell, M., Garety, P., et al. (2007). The Lambeth Early Onset Crisis Assessment Team Study: General practitioner education and access to an early detection team in first-episode psychosis. *British Journal of Psychiatry, 51*(Suppl.), S133–139.

Shergill, S. S., Brammer, M. J., Williams, S. C., Murray, R. M., & McGuire, P. K. (2000). Mapping auditory hallucinations in schizophrenia using functional magnetic resonance imaging. *Archives of General Psychiatry, 57*(11), 1033–1038.

Shergill, S. S., Bullmore, E., Simmons, A., Murray, R., & McGuire, P. (2000). Functional anatomy of auditory verbal imagery in schizophrenic patients with auditory hallucinations. *American Journal of Psychiatry, 157*(10), 1691–1693.

Shergill, S. S., Kanaan, R. A., Chitnis, X. A., O'Daly, O., Jones, D. K., Frangou, S., et al. (2007). A diffusion tensor imaging study of fasciculi in schizophrenia. *American Journal of Psychiatry, 164*(3), 467–473.

Stone, J. M., Day, F., Tsagaraki, H., Valli, I., McLean, M. A., Lythgoe, D. J., et al. (2009). Glutamate dysfunction in people with prodromal symptoms of psychosis: Relationship to gray matter volume. *Biological Psychiatry, 66*(6), 533–539.

10 Brain networks and schizophrenia

Ed Bullmore

Introduction

One of Robin Murray's greatest scientific influences has been and continues to be his advocacy of neurodevelopmental theories of schizophrenia. These ideas inevitably have stimulated major efforts by his research group at the Institute of Psychiatry to use neuroimaging to map brain abnormalities in adults with schizophrenia and to understand the causes and generative mechanisms of these imaging phenotypes in terms of genetic effects and brain developmental processes. Here I briefly review some of the relevant "School of Murray" and other magnetic resonance imaging (MRI) studies addressing these issues and conclude that: (i) there is now strong evidence that human brain structure is normally organized in the form of complex networks, which show developmental changes in their organization; and (ii) that brain structure is abnormal in schizophrenia, and these abnormalities exist at the level of systems or networks rather than single regions. There is also some good but limited evidence that abnormalities of brain structure are linked to genetic risk for schizophrenia, may arise early in development, and show dynamic or progressive changes in the period around the onset of the psychotic syndrome in early adults. This is a scientific direction of travel that still has some way to go but has already made a substantial difference to how we think about schizophrenia, as an adult outcome of abnormal neurocognitive network formation.

One of the many ways Robin Murray strongly supported and influenced generations of training psychiatrists, psychologists and other scientists was by encouraging us all to think about psychosis as an adult syndrome emerging on the basis of long-standing prior disorders of brain development (Murray & Lewis, 1987). In the late 1980s, when Murray and colleagues at the Institute of Psychiatry, and Weinberger (1987) at the US National Institute of Mental Health, first articulated this idea persuasively, it was somewhat insurgent in the context of prior theories of schizophrenia, which either ignored brain mechanisms entirely or supposed that they were ill-defined degenerative processes like the Kraepelinian concept of schizophrenia as a precocious dementia.

The aspect of Robin Murray's theory that always most interested me was how it could be visualized by the methods of neuroimaging, or mapped in terms of brain systems. What does the brain look like in adult patients with schizophrenia or their first-degree relatives? How can abnormalities of adult brain organization be explained in terms of developmental processes, dating back probably to antenatal life? How can putatively abnormal development of neurocognitive systems in schizophrenia be related to genetic or other causal factors? In what follows, I will give a brief account of some of the relevant work that has been done to address these broad questions, focusing on studies where I have had the benefit of collaborating with Robin Murray and/or fellow "graduates" of his highly productive school of schizophrenia research at the Institute of Psychiatry.

Is there good evidence that the brain looks structurally abnormal in schizophrenia?

The answer to this question is now clearly yes. It was not always so. One of the first and most powerful neuroimaging studies of schizophrenia, by Johnstone, Crow, Frith, Husband, and Kreel (1976) using X-ray computed tomography at the MRC Unit in Northwick Park, showing clear evidence of ventricular enlargement associated with poor cognitive function in chronic patients with schizophrenia, was greeted with a high degree of scepticism. The immediate reaction was disbelieving because the prevailing orthodoxy of the time was that schizophrenia, like bipolar disorder, was a "functional" psychosis in contrast to "organic" disorders like Alzheimer's disease. It was thus axiomatic that schizophrenia could not be associated with structural brain abnormalities akin to those seen in neurodegenerative disorders (Bullmore, Fletcher, & Jones, 2009).

This previously mainstream position has now been abandoned in the light of overwhelming evidence to the contrary. Meta-analytic studies have provided some of the clearest evidence for consistent and statistically robust brain abnormalities in adult schizophrenia. Ian Ellison-Wright and colleagues published one of the first MRI meta-analyses of schizophrenia, confirming ventricular enlargement (about +10%), cortical grey matter attenuation (about -5% globally), and basal ganglia enlargement (Wright et al., 2000). This region-by-region approach to MRI meta-analysis has since been followed-up at a more fine-grained level of anatomical resolution, mapping meta-analytic group differences at each voxel of whole brain maps (Ellison-Wright, Glahn, Laird, Thelen, & Bullmore, 2008). Schizophrenia is associated with replicable grey matter reduction in bilateral prefrontal, anterior cingulate, insular and lateral temporal cortex, and thalamus. Meta-analytic maps of the diffusion tensor imaging (DTI) literature identified significant reduction of fractional anisotropy of white matter in left frontal and temporal lobes (Ellison-Wright & Bullmore, 2009). The most parsimonious explanation is that schizophrenia is associated with abnormal organization of one or more large-scale brain structural networks, comprising multiple "processing nodes" of cortical or subcortical grey matter and the white matter tracts of "wiring" that interconnect them (Sigmundsson et al., 2001).

Inevitably, once we start talking about brain abnormality in terms of systems, rather than a single brain region such as hippocampus, we have to start using correlational and multivariate methods of analysis to understand how different components of the system interact with each other. Peter Woodruff and colleagues were among the first to do this for regional grey matter volume measurements, showing that there were generally strong positive correlations between different brain regions in terms of brain volume, e.g., a big temporal cortex tends to go with a big frontal cortex, and some of these fronto-temporal correlations were abnormally reduced in schizophrenia (Woodruff et al., 1997). Using principal components (PC) analysis to reduce the dimensionality of correlational analysis over a larger number of regions, Wright and colleagues later found that much of the variation and covariation of about 100 regional grey matter volume measurements was attributable to a few major PCs, and that patients with schizophrenia had abnormally low scores on the first (global grey matter) and third (fronto-temporal grey matter) components (Wright et al., 1999).

Although these findings of grey matter volume covariation between anatomically separated regions are quite robust empirically, and have been replicated and extended, their anatomical interpretation remains debatable. In a developmental frame of mind, we noted that afferentation of cortex tends to favour the growth and survival of cortical neurons: cells that become connected are more likely to survive, and reciprocal connectivity confers trophic benefits on both cells. On this basis, one can imagine that establishment of early axonal connectivity between distributed cortical regions could encourage their shared growth, leading to the observed pattern of correlated regional volumes across adult brain images (Wright et al., 2000). By the same account, attenuation of grey matter covariation could be interpreted as indicating that early cortico-cortical afferentation processes were abnormal in individuals who were much later diagnosed as having schizophrenia. To my mind, this neurodevelopmental interpretation of adult grey matter volume covariation in MRI, and its utility as a marker of much earlier developmental aberration in schizophrenia, remains plausible but not yet proven (Bullmore, Frangou, & Murray, 1997). The proposed links—from early foetal processes of cortical afferentation by axonal projections, and formation of primary trophic synapses between cortical neurons, to variation of large-scale grey and white structures in the adult brain—need to be tested more directly, e.g., by longitudinal MRI studies of mammalian brain development. Without better prospectively generated knowledge of the imaging markers of normal brain development, it will remain difficult to refute backward-looking developmental interpretations of abnormal adult brain structure in schizophrenia.

However, one recent development in support of the more general proposition that patterns of grey matter regional covariation in MRI are biologically and pathophysiologically significant has been the application of graph theoretical methods to analysis of inter-regional covariation matrices (see Bassett & Bullmore, 2009; Bullmore & Sporns, 2009, for reviews). These studies have shown that anatomical networks derived from MR imaging data on large samples of healthy volunteers demonstrate a number of non-random or complex topological properties. For example, human brain anatomical networks have the "small world" property of high local clustering of connections combined with a short path length between any possible pair of regions. This architecture theoretically favours both segregated and integrated modes of information processing, nearly minimizes wiring costs, and is characteristic also of other nervous systems including the inter-regional wiring diagram of the macaque cortex and the cellular connectome of the nematode worm *Caenorhabditis elegans* (Bassett et al., 2010; Sporns, Tononi, & Edelman, 2000). The economical small-world properties of human anatomical networks derived from structural MRI data are also convergent with homologous properties reported in anatomical networks derived from DTI data and functional networks derived from functional MRI data.

This remarkable convergence of results across species and modalities strongly suggests that grey matter covariation in MRI is measuring a biologically important aspect of brain organization. Moreover, Dani Bassett and colleagues at the National Institute of Mental Health (NIMH) used similar methods to show that anatomical networks derived from structural MRI data on a large sample of patients with schizophrenia were topologically abnormal—multimodal cortex was less hierarchically connected, and physically inefficient—the total wiring length or distance between connected regions was greater in schizophrenia (Bassett et al., 2008; see Plate 10.1).

In short, we can conclude that there is good neuroimaging evidence for abnormalities of large-scale anatomical systems or networks in schizophrenia. It is also important to acknowledge that the earliest ideas about anatomical dysconnectivity in psychosis date back to the nineteenth-century work of Carl Wernicke and that the more modern concept of anatomically abnormal neurocognitive networks is closely related to seminal theories of functional dysconnectivity (Friston 1996; Stephan, Friston, & Frith, 2009) and psychological dysmodularity (David, 1994) in schizophrenia.

What are the developmental antecedents of brain abnormality in schizophrenia?

This is a much more challenging experimental question than the relatively simple question of whether abnormalities exist in the adult brain. It would obviously be very difficult for many reasons to make serial imaging measurements on individuals from early infancy to the early adult age range of maximum risk for psychosis, which is one theoretically direct way of addressing the question. Here I will briefly describe three rather different approaches that have been experimentally tractable, although of course they also raise a number of subsidiary questions.

The first approach adopts the directness of a longitudinal imaging design but makes it tractable by truncating the period of pre-psychotic measurement. Chris Pantelis and colleagues in Melbourne, together with Philip McGuire and John Suckling at the Institute of Psychiatry, produced one of the first major MRI studies on longitudinal brain changes in young people with symptoms indicating a high risk of incipient psychosis, but not yet satisfying formal diagnostic criteria for a psychotic disorder (Pantelis et al., 2003). MRI data were collected at baseline on all subjects, and again after a period of 12 + months. It was found that high-risk patients destined to develop a formal psychotic disorder, compared to those patients who did not later develop psychosis, had less grey matter in the right medial temporal, lateral temporal, and inferior frontal cortex, and in the cingulate cortex bilaterally in the baseline imaging data. In the longitudinal comparison, when rescanned, individuals who had developed psychosis showed a reduction in grey matter in the left parahippocampal, fusiform, orbitofrontal and cerebellar cortices, and the cingulate gyri. In those who had not become psychotic, longitudinal changes were restricted to the cerebellum. Thus it seems that it might be possible to identify MRI markers predicting clinical outcome in young people at high risk of psychotic disorder and, more fundamentally, that the clinical process of becoming psychotic is associated with an underlying process of abnormal change in brain structural organization. It remains an important, largely unsolved question to consolidate these and other early MRI reports of progressive brain structural change in schizophrenia, and to understand more clearly what cellular, molecular or genomic processes might be driving such changes in MRI phenotype around the moment of first psychotic crisis.

The second approach, developed by Peter Jones in Cambridge, UK, and Matti Isohanni in Oulu, Finland, leveraged the power of a population birth cohort to explore more distant developmental antecedents of abnormal brain structure in people with psychosis (Ridler et al., 2006; see Plate 10.2). Representative samples of non-psychotic adults ($n = 93$) and people with schizophrenia ($n = 49$) were drawn from the Northern Finland 1966 general population birth cohort. Infant motor development (IMD) was prospectively assessed at age 1 year; executive function testing and MRI scans were completed at age 33–35 years. We found that earlier motor development in infancy was correlated with superior executive function in non-psychotic subjects. Earlier motor development was also normally associated with increased grey matter density in adult premotor cortex, striatum, and cerebellum and increased white matter density in frontal and parietal lobes. Adult executive function was normally associated with increased grey matter density in a fronto-cerebellar system that partially overlapped, but was not identical to, the grey matter regions normally associated with IMD. People with schizophrenia had relatively delayed IMD and impaired adult executive function in adulthood. Furthermore, they demonstrated no normative associations between fronto-cerebellar structure, IMD, or executive function. We concluded that frontal cortico-cerebellar systems correlated with adult executive function are anatomically related to systems associated with normal infant motor development. As previously anticipated by theories of schizophrenia as a "cognitive dysmetria" syndrome (Andreasen, Paradiso, & O'Leary, 1998), abnormalities of cortico-cerebellar networks may thus underlie both the early developmental and adult cognitive abnormalities in schizophrenia. More generally, this study illustrates the feasibility and added value of incorporating well-tolerated and increasingly affordable MRI measurements in large-scale epidemiologically principled longitudinal studies.

The third approach, pioneered by Colm McDonald, Pak Sham and colleagues, intended to reach back further still by understanding the genetic causes of MRI phenotypes (McDonald et al., 2004). We collected MRI data on patients with schizophrenia and their first-degree relatives, and likewise on patients with bipolar disorder and their first-degree relatives. Each participant was assigned a genetic liability score, based on standard threshold-liability modelling of genetic risk for psychotic spectrum disorders, and this was correlated with local grey and white matter measurements. Imaging markers significantly associated with variation in genetic liability were defined as grey matter or white matter endophenotypes for schizophrenia or bipolar disorder. Genetic risk for schizophrenia was specifically associated with distributed grey matter volume deficits in the bilateral fronto-striato-thalamic and left lateral temporal regions, whereas genetic risk for bipolar disorder was specifically associated with grey matter deficits only in the right anterior cingulate gyrus and ventral striatum. A generic association between genetic risk for both disorders and white matter volume reduction in the left frontal and temporoparietal regions was consistent with left frontotemporal disconnectivity as a genetically controlled brain structural abnormality common to both psychotic disorders. Genetic risks for schizophrenia and bipolar disorder were thus associated with specific grey matter but generic white matter endophenotypes. We concluded that the classical dichotomy of functional psychosis, into distinct disease entities of schizophrenia and bipolar disorder, was neither wholly right nor wholly wrong: the two major psychoses show both distinctive and similar patterns of brain structural abnormality related to variable genetic risk. Recent meta-analysis has confirmed generic as well as specific profiles of anatomical abnormality in case-control studies of schizophrenia and bipolar disorder (Ellison-Wright & Bullmore, 2010). It is also interesting to note that some recent major genetic studies combining data on patients with schizophrenia and bipolar disorder have identified multiple risk alleles common to both disorders, especially in the major histocompatibility complex (International Schizophrenia Consortium, 2009), further prompting theoretical revision of the distinction between classical types of psychosis (Craddock & Owen, 2010). It will be very interesting in future to see if molecular genetics can be more directly associated with putative imaging endophenotypes of psychotic disorders.

Conclusions

The neurodevelopmental model of schizophrenia is certainly not refuted by recent decades of progress in neuroimaging research. Rather there is now strong evidence for abnormality of large-scale anatomical networks in adult patients with psychosis, which may be attributable to much earlier developmental antecedents and under strong genetic control. The next generation of challenges is broadly to link this emerging large-scale network phenotype to both micro-scale (cellular or gene expression) phenotypes and clinical aspects of the disorder, such as cognitive impairment and progression through acute psychotic episodes.

References

Andreasen, N. C., Paradiso, S., & O'Leary, D. S. (1998). Cognitive dysmetria as an integrative theory of schizophrenia: A dysfunction in cortico-subcortical-cerebellar circuitry? *Schizophrenia Bulletin*, *24*, 203–218.

Bassett, D. S., & Bullmore, E. T. (2009). Human brain networks in health and disease. *Current Opinion in Neurology*, *22*, 340–347.

Bassett, D. S., Bullmore, E. T., Verchinski, B. A., Mattay, V. S., Weinberger, D. R., & Meyer-Lindenberg. A. (2008). Hierarchical organization of human cortical networks in health and schizophrenia. *Journal of Neuroscience*, *28*, 9239–9248.

Bassett, D. S., Greenfield, D. L., Meyer-Lindenberg, A., Weinberger, D. R., Moore, S. W., & Bullmore, E. T. (2010). Efficient physical embedding of topologically complex information processing networks in brains and computer circuits. *PLoS Computational Biology*, *6*, e10000748.

Bullmore, E., Fletcher, P. C., & Jones, P. B. (2009). Why psychiatry can't afford to be neurophobic. *British Journal of Psychiatry*, *194*, 293–295.

Bullmore, E., & Sporns, O. (2009). Complex brain networks: Graph theoretical analysis of structural and functional systems. *Nature Reviews Neuroscience*, *10*, 186–198.

Bullmore, E. T., Frangou, S., & Murray, R. M. (1997). The dysplastic net hypothesis: An integration of developmental and dysconnectivity theories of schizophrenia. *Schizophrenia Research*, *28*, 143–156.

Craddock, N., & Owen, M. J. (2010). The Kraepelinian dichotomy—going, going ... but still not gone. *British Journal of Psychiatry*, *196*, 92–95.

David, A. S. (1994). Dysmodularity: A neurocognitive model for schizophrenia. *Schizophrenia Bulletin*, *20*, 249–255.

Ellison-Wright, I. C., & Bullmore, E. (2009). Meta-analysis of diffusion tensor imaging studies in schizophrenia. *Schizophrenia Research*, *108*, 3–10.

Ellison-Wright, I. C., & Bullmore, E. (2010). Anatomy of bipolar disorder and schizophrenia: A meta-analysis. *Schizophrenia Research*, *117*, 1–12.

Ellison-Wright, I. C., Glahn, D. C., Laird, A. R., Thelen, S. M., & Bullmore, E. (2008). The anatomy of first-episode and chronic schizophrenia: An anatomical likelihood estimation meta-analysis. *American Journal of Psychiatry*, *165*, 1015–1023.

Friston, K. J. (1996). Theoretical neurobiology and schizophrenia. *British Medical Bulletin*, *52*, 644–655.

International Schizophrenia Consortium. (2009). Common polygenic variation contributes to risk of schizophrenia and bipolar disorder. *Nature*, *460*, 748–752.

Johnstone, E. C., Crow, T. J., Frith, C. D., Husband, J., & Kreel, L. (1976). Cerebral ventricular size and cognitive impairment in chronic schizophrenia. *Lancet*, *2*(7992), 924–926.

McDonald, C., Bullmore, E. T., Sham, P. C., Chitnis, X., Wickham, H., Bramon, E., et al. (2004). Association of genetic risks for schizophrenia and bipolar disorder with specific and generic brain structural endophenotypes. *Archives of General Psychiatry*, *61*, 974–984.

Murray, R. M., & Lewis, S. W. (1987). Is schizophrenia a neurodevelopmental disorder? *British Medical Journal*, *295*, 681–682.

Pantelis, C., Velakoulis, D., McGorry, P. D., Wood, S. J., Suckling, J., Phillips, L. J., et al. (2003). Neuroanatomical abnormalities before and after onset of psychosis: A cross-sectional and longitudinal MRI comparison. *Lancet*, *361*, 281–288.

Ridler, K., Veijola, J. M., Tanskanen, P., Mietunnen, J., Chitnis, X., Suckling, J., et al. (2006). Fronto-cerebellar systems are associated with infant motor and adult executive functions in healthy adults but not in schizophrenia. *Proceedings of the National Academy of Sciences of the United States of America*, *103*, 15651–15656.

Sigmundsson, T., Suckling, J., Maier, M., Williams, S. C. R., Bullmore, E. T., Greenwood, K. E., et al. (2001). Structural abnormalities in frontal, temporal and limbic regions and interconnecting white matter tracts in schizophrenic patients with prominent negative symptoms. *American Journal of Psychiatry*, *158*, 234–243.

Sporns, O., Tononi, G., & Edelman, G. M. (2000). Theoretical neuroanatomy: Relating anatomical and functional connectivity in graphs and cortical connection matrices. *Cerebral Cortex*, *10*, 127–141.

Stephan, K., Friston, K. J., & Frith, C. D. (2009). Dysconnection in schizophrenia: From abnormal synaptic plasticity to failures of self-monitoring. *Schizophrenia Bulletin*, *35*, 509–527.

Weinberger, D. R. (1987). Implications of normal brain development for the pathogenesis of schizophrenia. *Archives of General Psychiatry*, *44*, 660–669.

Woodruff, P. W., Wright, I. C., Shuriquie, N., Russouw, H., Rushe, T., Howard, R. J., et al. (1997). Structural brain abnormalities in male schizophrenics reflect fronto-temporal dissociation. *Psychological Medicine*, *27*, 1257—1266.

Wright, I. C., Rabe-Hesketh, S., Woodruff, P. W., David, A. S., Murray, R. M., & Bullmore, E. T. (2000). Meta-analysis of regional brain volumes in schizophrenia. *American Journal of Psychiatry*, *157*, 16–25.

Wright, I. C., Sharma, T., Ellison, Z. R., McGuire, P. K., Friston, K. J., Brammer, M. J., et al. (1999). Supra-regional brain systems and the neuropathology of schizophrenia. *Cerebral Cortex*, *9*, 366–378.

11 Neuroimaging and psychosis

Are brain changes in individuals with psychosis neurodevelopmental for some and progressive for others?

Paola Dazzan, Kevin Morgan, Julia Lappin and Paul Fearon

Schizophrenia is a disorder that presents with problems in perception, structure of thought, concepts of self, cognitive functions, volition, and emotions. It often evolves into a chronic disorder, with highly damaging effects on personal functioning. More than 100 years ago Kraepelin proposed that schizophrenia might result from an underlying organic brain disorder (Kraepelin, 1919). In their seminal paper in 1987, Murray and Lewis formulated a neurodevelopmental theory for schizophrenia, suggesting that an abnormal development of the central nervous system is in fact central to the pathogenesis of this illness (Murray & Lewis, 1987). As posited by this hypothesis, alterations in brain morphology would be present in the earliest stage of schizophrenia, and not be progressive, as sequelae of earlier events of aetiological importance.

Brain structure in schizophrenia

Over the last 30 years, the in vivo investigation of the brain in schizophrenia has indeed flourished, since the pivotal computerized tomography (CT) report of Johnstone and colleagues on the presence of enlarged ventricles in patients with established schizophrenia (Johnstone, Crow, Frith, Husband, & Kreel, 1976). With the subsequent advent of magnetic resonance imaging (MRI), a large number of studies have investigated the possible anatomical and functional changes that may underlie the pathogenesis of schizophrenia, in an attempt to identify a neuroanatomical marker for this disorder.

The first body of literature in this area investigated mostly patients with an established illness. This literature was reviewed in an excellent and comprehensive paper by Shenton, Dickey, Frumin, and McCarley (2001), and re-evaluated in a meta-analysis by Wright et al. (2000). The most consistently reported alterations observed in these studies were the enlargement of the lateral, and, to a lesser extent, third ventricles, and the reduction in whole brain volume, in comparison to healthy controls. Ventricular enlargement is a change that could occur in the context of tissue loss in surrounding regions, and, indeed, volume reductions have been reported in grey matter, with a distributed pattern of regional reductions. These have been located in medial temporal areas, such as the hippocampus, the amygdala, and the superior temporal gyrus. Reductions have also been located in the frontal lobe, particularly in the prefrontal and orbitofrontal parts. It is not surprising that these areas are reported as affected in this illness. In fact, parts of the temporal lobe, such as the superior temporal gyrus, are involved in auditory and language processes, visual information, visual recognition and audio-visual integration (Calvert, 2001), functions altered in schizophrenia. Similarly for the frontal lobe, deficits in frontal functions, such as working memory, executive function, and attention, are considered trait markers for schizophrenia, and psychoses in general (Brewer et al., 2003; Cornblatt, Obuchowski, Roberts, Pollack, & Erlenmeyer-Kimling, 1999; Glahn et al., 2007; Morey et al., 2005; Wood et al., 2003).

Unfortunately, studies conducted in patients with an established illness suffer from many limitations. For example, patients may have suffered many illness relapses, may have been hospitalized for long periods of time, and the changes observed might be a reflection of neurodegenerative processes. Another limitation is the fact that subjects may have been exposed to the effects of antipsychotic medications for prolonged periods of time. It would therefore be difficult, from these studies, to disentangle which brain neuroanatomical alterations are part of the pathophysiology of schizophrenia, and which result from other factors.

In an attempt to address these issues, more recent studies have evaluated individuals at illness onset, never exposed to antipsychotic medications, or exposed for relatively brief periods of time. A large body of evidence has therefore emerged from research on individuals evaluated at their first psychotic episode, or while still in the prodromal phase. The following sections will focus on literature on first-episode psychosis, as evidence from studies on prodromal subjects who have not yet developed psychosis is beyond the scope of this chapter. Consistently with previous literature, first-episode psychosis research has confirmed that at least some of the brain abnormalities previously reported in chronic individuals, are present already at the time of illness onset. In particular, meta-analyses of region-of-interest studies that evaluated patients with first-episode schizophrenia (Steen, Mull, McClure, Hamer, & Lieberman, 2006; Vita, De, Silenzi, & Dieci, 2006) confirm ventricular volume is increased, and hippocampus (but not amygdala) is reduced, at illness onset. Another meta-analysis, which evaluated studies that used a voxel-based morphometry approach, thus evaluating the brain as a whole, identified more distributed grey matter reductions, involving the thalamus, the uncus and amygdala region, the insulae, the anterior cingulate, and the inferior frontal gyrus (Ellison-Wright, Glahn, Laird, Thelen, Bullmore, 2008).

Of note, the number of subjects included in the studies subject to these meta-analyses needs to be considered before concluding that brain abnormalities are already present at illness onset. For example, the excellent meta-analysis quoted earlier in this chapter on studies on chronic patients (Wright et al., 2000) evaluated 58 studies, including a total of 1,588 patients. In contrast, studies in first-episode psychosis have sample sizes much smaller than the average size of 33 patients used in chronic studies. One of the largest first-episode psychosis imaging studies in the literature was lead by Robin Murray, and the contribution of this work should be considered when attempting to interpret the findings of the first-episode psychosis imaging literature.

The contribution of the AESOP study

AESOP (Aetiology and Ethnicity in Schizophrenia and Other Psychoses) was the first epidemiological study to evaluate both the biological and social risk factors that could explain an increased incidence of psychosis across certain ethnic groups in the United Kingdom (Fearon et al., 2006). As part of this study, brain structure, neurodevelopmental indices, ethnicity, and environmental factors, were evaluated in individuals who consecutively presented to the psychiatric services over a period of two years. The imaging arm of the study used: (i) a case-control design, comparing patients with healthy controls from the same population; and (ii) a within-group design to explore the association between brain structure and potential risk factors.

In the AESOP sample, a total of 97 patients and a similar number of controls received an MRI scan. Both patients with schizophrenia and patients with affective psychosis showed larger lateral and third ventricle volumes than controls (Morgan et al., 2007). Interestingly, regional cortical grey matter reductions (anterior cingulate gyrus, insula and fusiform gyrus) were evident in affective psychosis but not in schizophrenia, although patients with schizophrenia displayed decreased hippocampal volume and larger basal ganglia volume. The absence of more widespread differences in patients with schizophrenia might have been due to the specific recruitment strategy. One of the strengths of this study was in fact its epidemiological design, with patients included independently of factors such as illness severity and family history. Many previous studies on patients with first-episode schizophrenia came from in-patient samples, or university clinics, which attracted subjects not necessarily representative of first-episode schizophrenia in general (Job et al., 2002; Pantelis et al., 2003). Furthermore, in AESOP patients and controls were recruited from the same catchment area, and therefore had the same socioeconomic background. Socioeconomic factors are often not taken into account in comparison samples used in imaging studies, while these factors may well affect brain development, and therefore the resulting findings. These AESOP data appear consistent with existing literature showing that morphological changes are present at illness onset, but are not marked (Ellison-Wright et al., 2008; Velakoulis et al., 2006).

Factors, both neurodevelopmental and environmental, that could explain some of the morphological differences observed in first-episode psychosis were also assessed in AESOP. For example, a known index of neurodevelopmental aberration in psychosis is the presence of minor neurological signs in motor and sensory functions (Dazzan et al., 2008). In this sample, higher rates of neurological signs (both motor and sensory) in patients were associated with volume reduction of subcortical structures (putamen, globus pallidus and thalamus; Dazzan et al., 2004). Signs of sensory integration deficits were additionally associated with volume reduction in the cerebral cortex, including the precentral, superior and middle temporal, and lingual gyri. Interestingly, even in the controls, sensory integrative deficits were associated with a reduction of these cortical areas (Dazzan, Morgan, Chitnis et al., 2005). These data were the first to suggest that these cortical brain structural changes represent a common neuroanatomical substrate of a minor neurological dysfunction, across healthy individuals and patients with psychosis, while subcortical basal ganglia changes might be a specific correlate of the pathogenesis of psychosis, and as such be found in those patients with motor deficits.

Although this evidence points to a possible neurodevelopmental origin for brain changes at psychosis onset, other findings from this study suggest that environmental factors may also play a role in possibly inducing morphological brain changes. For example, exposure to typical antipsychotics seemed to affect more extensively the basal ganglia (with an enlargement of the putamen) and cortical areas (reductions of anterior cingulate gyrus, superior and medial frontal gyri, superior and middle temporal gyri, insula, and precuneus), while atypical antipsychotics seemed particularly associated with enlargement of the thalami (Dazzan, Morgan, Orr et al., 2005; see Plate 11.1). In fact, the study showed that morphological changes result from even short-term treatment with antipsychotics, and therefore treatment needs to be considered even in the evaluation of brain structure at illness onset.

Ethnicity is a socially relevant aspect that was uniquely investigated in the AESOP study in relation to brain structure. African-Caribbean and Black African people living in the UK have a higher incidence of diagnosed psychosis compared to White British people (Fearon et al., 2006). It has been argued this may be a consequence of misdiagnosis. If this were true, African-Caribbean and Black African people would be less likely to show the patterns of structural brain abnormalities reported in White British patients. This study therefore investigated whether there were differences in the prevalence of structural brain abnormalities in White and Black first-episode psychosis patients (Morgan et al., 2009). The results showed that both White British patients and African-Caribbean/Black African patients had larger ventricles and larger basal ganglia volume when compared to their respective ethnic controls. However, only the African-Caribbean/Black African patients additionally showed smaller global grey matter than their ethnically matched controls. While groups did not differ for sociodemographic characteristics, the African-Caribbean/Black African patients were receiving a significantly higher dosage of antipsychotic medication. It is therefore possible that the observed smaller grey matter volume is at least in part a drug effect, or even the marker of a more severe illness that was being treated with higher doses of antipsychotics (Dorph-Petersen et al., 2005; Lieberman et al., 2005).

Taken together, the findings from AESOP suggest that psychosis is associated with brain changes at illness onset, and that these are less marked than those observed in the chronic illness. Furthermore, it suggests that while some of these changes may have a neurodevelopmental basis, others may well be the result of environmental insults, like the effect of antipsychotic treatment.

Are the changes progressive?

The evidence reviewed suggests that there are abnormalities in the brain structure of patients with psychosis. These abnormalities, according to a "neurodevelopmental" model, are already present at illness onset, to indicate the presence of an alteration in the central nervous system concomitant, or antecedent to, the onset of the disorder. However, this evidence also suggests that these abnormalities may be less marked than those observed in the more advanced illness stages. This hypothesis is supported by a meta-analysis of voxel-based morphometry studies, which compared findings from studies that performed a brain-wide evaluation of structure in first-episode patients, in comparison with those that used the same approach in chronic patients (Ellison-Wright et al., 2008). This meta-analysis showed an overlap between regions that were reduced in both first-episode and chronic patients. These included the thalamus, the left uncus/amygdala region, the left and right insulae, the anterior cingulate, and the left inferior frontal gyrus. Notably, the authors also found that individuals with chronic schizophrenia had more extensive grey matter reductions in the frontal cortex (medial frontal gyrus and left dorsolateral prefrontal cortex), the right insula cortex, and the left and right temporal cortex. These findings point to the presence of a progressive process that affects the brain even after illness onset.

The issue of whether brain changes progress during illness course is best addressed by a longitudinal evaluation of the brain, repeated in the same subjects over time. Unfortunately, there have been relatively few longitudinal studies of brain structure in psychosis, and reports of progressive changes have not been consistent. A review by Hulshoff Pol and Kahn (2008) identified 11 longitudinal MRI studies investigating patients with schizophrenia who were beyond the first two years of illness, to explore whether there are brain dynamic changes after the first illness phase (Hulshoff Pol & Kahn, 2008). The follow-up interval between assessments in the studies included varied between 1 and 10 years. The review indicated that global brain volume decreased in patients by -0.5% per year, in comparison to - 0.2% per year in healthy controls. The findings also indicated that grey matter reduction was particularly evident in the frontal and temporal regions.

Since clinical deterioration is particularly marked in the early illness phases, it might be expected that some of these brain changes would have been more likely to occur soon after illness onset. In a one-year follow-up, Cahn and colleagues (2002) evaluated a group of patients with schizophrenia, at onset and again after one year (Cahn, Hulshoff Pol, Lems et al., 2002). They indeed found that patients, in comparison to controls, displayed significantly greater reductions of total brain volume (-1.2%) and grey matter volume of the cerebrum (-2.9%), and significant increases of lateral ventricle volume (7.7%), thus suggesting that the first year after illness onset is a crucial period of vulnerability. Therefore, the question remains as to whether this progression particularly occurs in those individuals who also experience a more severe illness. Some, but not all, studies investigating this aspect suggest that in fact more pronounced changes are associated with a poorer clinical and functional outcome, and possibly also with a more marked decline in cognitive function (Cahn, Hulshoff Pol, Lems et al., 2002; Cahn, Hulshoff Pol, Bongers et al., 2002; van Haren et al., 2003). Consistent with these studies, a six-year follow-up of the AESOP first-episode sample showed that a more marked grey matter reduction was present in those individuals who had been more exposed to antipsychotic medications, and who had a more severe and continuous illness course (data available from the authors on request).

The pathophysiological process underlying these progressive brain changes remains to be established. It has been suggested, from post-mortem studies, that progressive brain reductions could results from a myelin-related dysfunction (Davis et al., 2003). Also, reductions may represent aberrant dynamics of functional neural networks (Hulshoff Pol & Kahn, 2008). Finally, some of these brain changes may depend on whether patients have been exposed to treatment with conventional or atypical antipsychotic drugs, since conventional antipsychotics may be particularly associated with whole brain grey matter reductions, particularly in some cortical areas (Dazzan, Morgan, Orr et al., 2005; Lieberman et al., 2005).

In conclusion, data from AESOP and other studies suggest that there is a "neurodevelopmental" vulnerability to schizophrenia, which is manifested in an excess of neurodevelopmental indices such as minor neurological signs, and in brain tissue reduction in areas relevant to the pathophysiology of this illness, such as the temporal and frontal lobes. The onset of psychosis, and the progression of the illness, may involve a superimposed degenerative process, which would cause these abnormalities to become more marked over time. This progression in brain alterations may reflect a continuous pathophysiological process, and the question remains as to whether this occurs in all individuals with psychosis, or in a specific subgroup of individuals, perhaps vulnerable to a more severe illness or to environmental insults such as exposure to antipsychotics.

References

Brewer, W. J., Wood, S. J., McGorry, P. D., Francey, S. M., Phillips, L. J., Yung, A. R., et al. (2003). Impairment of olfactory identification ability in individuals at ultra-high risk for psychosis who later develop schizophrenia. *American Journal of Psychiatry*, *160*, 1790–1794.

Cahn, W., Holshoff Pol, H. E., Bongers, M., Schnack, H. G., Mandl, R. C., van Haren, N. E., et al. (2002). Brain morphology in antipsychotic-naive schizophrenia: A study of multiple brain structures. *British Journal of Psychiatry*, *43*(Suppl.), S66–S72.

Cahn, W., Hulshoff Pol, H. E., Lems, E. B., van Haren, N. E., Schnack, H. G., Van Der Linden, J. A., et al. (2002). Brain volume changes in first-episode schizophrenia: A 1-year follow-up study. *Archives of General Psychiatry*, *59*, 1002–1010.

Calvert, G. A. (2001). Crossmodal processing in the human brain: Insights from functional neuroimaging studies. *Cerebral Cortex*, *11*, 1110–1123.

Cornblatt, B., Obuchowski, M., Roberts, S., Pollack, S., & Erlenmeyer-Kimling, L. (1999). Cognitive and behavioral precursors of schizophrenia. *Development and Psychopathology*, *11*, 487–508.

Davis, K. L., Stewart, D. G., Friedman, J. I., Buchsbaum, M., Harvey, P. D., Hof, P. R., et al. (2003). White matter changes in schizophrenia: Evidence for myelin-related dysfunction. *Archives of General Psychiatry, 60*, 443–456.

Dazzan, P., Lloyd, T., Morgan, K. D., Zanelli, J., Morgan, C., Orr, K., et al. (2008). Neurological abnormalities and cognitive ability in first-episode psychosis. *British Journal of Psychiatry, 193*, 197–202.

Dazzan, P., Morgan, K. D., Chitnis, X., Suckling, J., Morgan, C., Fearon, P., et al. (2005). The structural brain correlates of neurological soft signs in healthy individuals. *Cerebral Cortex, 16*, 1225–1231.

Dazzan, P., Morgan, K. D., Orr, K. G., Hutchinson, G., Chitnis, X., Suckling, J., et al. (2004). The structural brain correlates of neurological soft signs in AESOP first-episode psychoses study. *Brain, 127*, 143–153.

Dazzan, P., Morgan, K. D., Orr, K. G., Hutchinson, G., Chitnis, X., Suckling, J., et al. (2005). Different effects of typical and atypical antipsychotics on grey matter in first episode psychosis: The AESOP study. *Neuropsychopharmacology, 30*, 765–774.

Dorph-Petersen, K. A., Pierri, J. N., Perel, J. M., Sun, Z., Sampson, A. R., & Lewis, D. A. (2005). The influence of chronic exposure to antipsychotic medications on brain size before and after tissue fixation: A comparison of haloperidol and olanzapine in macaque monkeys. *Neuropsychopharmacology, 30*, 1649–1661.

Ellison-Wright, I., Glahn, D. C., Laird, A. R., Thelen, S. M., & Bullmore, E. (2008). The anatomy of first-episode and chronic schizophrenia: An anatomical likelihood estimation meta-analysis. *American Journal of Psychiatry, 165*, 1015–1023.

Fearon, P., Kirkbride, J. B., Morgan, C., Dazzan, P., Morgan, K., Lloyd, T., et al. (2006). Incidence of schizophrenia and other psychoses in ethnic minority groups: Results from the MRC AESOP Study. *Psychological Medicine, 36*, 1541–1550.

Glahn, D. C., Bearden, C. E., Barguil, M., Barrett, J., Reichenberg, A., Bowden, C. L., et al. (2007). The neurocognitive signature of psychotic bipolar disorder. *Biological Psychiatry, 62*, 910–916.

Hulshoff Pol, H. E., & Kahn, R. S. (2008). What happens after the first episode? A review of progressive brain changes in chronically ill patients with schizophrenia. *Schizophrenia Bulletin, 34*, 354–366.

Job, D. E., Whalley, H. C., McConnell, S., Glabus, M., Johnstone, E. C., & Lawrie, S. M. (2002). Structural gray matter differences between first-episode schizophrenics and normal controls using voxel-based morphometry. *NeuroImage, 17*, 880–889.

Johnstone, E. C., Crow, T. J., Frith, C. D., Husband, J., & Kreel, L. (1976). Cerebral ventricular size and cognitive impairment in chronic schizophrenia. *Lancet, 2*, 924–926.

Kraepelin, E. (1919). *Dementia praecox and paraphrenia*. Edinburgh, UK: Livingston.

Lieberman, J. A., Tollefson, G. D., Charles, C., Zipursky, R., Sharma, T., Kahn, R. S., et al. (2005). Antipsychotic drug effects on brain morphology in first-episode psychosis. *Archives of General Psychiatry, 62*, 361–370.

Morey, R. A., Inan, S., Mitchell, T. V., Perkins, D. O., Lieberman, J. A., & Belger, A. (2005). Imaging frontostriatal function in ultra-high-risk, early, and chronic schizophrenia during executive processing. *Archives of General Psychiatry, 62*, 254–262.

Morgan, K. D., Dazzan, P., Morgan, C., Lappin, J., Hutchinson, G., Chitnis, X., et al. (2009). Differing patterns of brain structural abnormalities between black and white patients with their first episode of psychosis. *Psychological Medicine, 40*, 1–11.

Morgan, K. D., Dazzan, P., Orr, K. G., Hutchinson, G., Chitnis, X., Suckling, J., et al. (2007). Grey matter abnormalities in first-episode schizophrenia and affective psychosis. *British Journal of Psychiatry, 51*(Suppl.), S111–S116.

Murray, R. M., & Lewis, S. W. (1987). Is schizophrenia a neurodevelopmental disorder? *British Medical Journal, 295*, 681–682.

Pantelis, C., Velakoulis, D., McGorry, P. D., Wood, S. J., Suckling, J., Phillips, L. J., et al. (2003). Neuroanatomical abnormalities before and after onset of psychosis: A cross-sectional and longitudinal MRI comparison. *Lancet, 361*, 281–288.

Shenton, M. E., Dickey, C. C., Frumin, M., & McCarley, R. W. (2001). A review of MRI findings in schizophrenia. *Schizophrenia Research, 49*, 1–52.

Steen, R. G., Mull, C., McClure, R., Hamer, R. M., & Lieberman, J. A. (2006). Brain volume in first-episode schizophrenia: Systematic review and meta-analysis of magnetic resonance imaging studies. *British Journal of Psychiatry, 188*, 510–518.

van Haren, N. E., Cahn, W., Hulshoff Pol, H. E., Schnack, H. G., Caspers, E., Lemstra, A., et al. (2003). Brain volumes as predictor of outcome in recent-onset schizophrenia: A multi-center MRI study. *Schizophrenia Research, 64*, 41–52.

Velakoulis, D., Wood, S. J., Wong, M. T. H., McGorry, P. D., Yung, A., Phillips, L., et al. (2006). Hippocampal and amygdala volumes according to psychosis stage and diagnosis: A magnetic resonance imaging study of chronic schizophrenia, first-episode psychosis, and ultra-high-risk individuals. *Archives of General Psychiatry, 63*, 139–149.

Vita, A., De, P. L., Silenzi, C., & Dieci, M. (2006). Brain morphology in first-episode schizophrenia: A meta-analysis of quantitative magnetic resonance imaging studies. *Schizophrenia Research, 82*, 75–88.

Wood, S. J., Pantelis, C., Proffitt, T., Phillips, L. J., Stuart, G. W., Buchanan, J. A., et al. (2003). Spatial working memory ability is a marker of risk-for-psychosis. *Psychological Medicine, 33*, 1239–1247.

Wright, I. C., Rabe-Hesketh, S., Woodruff, P. W., David, A. S., Murray, R. M., & Bullmore, E. T. (2000). Meta-analysis of regional brain volumes in schizophrenia. *American Journal of Psychiatry, 157*, 16–25.

12 Gray matter alterations in schizophrenia

Are they reversible?

Matcheri S. Keshavan and Tejas Bhojraj

Introduction

It is unclear which of the inhabitants of gray matter (neuronal bodies and dendrites, glia, and the blood vessels) contribute to volume losses in schizophrenia, and whether they "die out". First, substantial data provide evidence for reduced gray matter volumes in schizophrenia across a wide range of brain regions. Second, longitudinal imaging studies suggest that the gray matter losses are not only seen before and early in the course of the illness, but also continue to progress during the chronic phases of the illness, contributing to clinical worsening. Third, neuropathological evidence points to reductions in glial numbers, neuronal somal volume and dendrite density, but not neuronal loss. Finally, clinical studies are inconclusive about whether antipsychotics contribute to or mitigate gray matter loss in schizophrenia. The absence of reduced neuronal numbers may suggest the benefit of hypothesis-driven pharmacological and cognitive remediations on neuroplasticity. Reassuringly, while the neuronal inhabitants of gray matter may be moribund, they may at least in part be revived with appropriate therapeutic interventions.

Schizophrenia is associated with widespread alterations in gray matter (GM) and white matter (WM; Shenton, Dickey, Frumin, & McCarley, 2001). GM alterations, which are the focus of this chapter, appear to be stable and trait related, may be related to the genetic susceptibility in this illness and present in the premorbid (Keshavan, Diwadkar, Montrose, Rajarethinam, & Sweeney, 2005) and prodromal phases of the disorder (Keshavan, Diwadkar, & Rosenberg, 2005; Pantelis et al., 2003). The structural alterations are associated with the symptomatic manifestations of the illness (Gur et al., 2000; Gur, Keshavan, & Lawrie, 2007; Lacerda et al., 2007; Sun, Maller, Guo, & Fitzgerald, 2009), and neurocognitive deficits (Antonova et al., 2005; Antonova, Sharma, Morris, & Kumari, 2004) and may predict poor outcome (Mitelman et al., 2007; Prasad, Sahni, Rohm, & Keshavan, 2005). What remains unclear is the nature of the impairments and whether gray matter volume loss reflects neuronal loss, loss of other GM constituents, or a combination. Gray matter is composed of neuronal cell bodies as well as their axonal and dendrite processes, glia and the vasculature collectively termed "neuropil" (Crutcher, 1989; Kobayashi et al., 2006; Lovick, 1993; Marin-Padilla, Tsai, King, & Roper, 2003; Narr et al., 2005; Sweet et al., 2004; Vercellino et al., 2009; Wakita et al., 2002). Which of these constituents might account for the observed structural alterations in schizophrenia?

The first author's work in schizophrenia was inspired by Professor Robin Murray when he was in training at the Maudsley Hospital and the Institute of Psychiatry, London, where he was involved in a small study examining differences in cerebral ventricular size in patients with schizophrenia with and without family histories of psychotic and affective disorders (Keshavan & Toone, 1988). His subsequent work involved investigation of the schizophrenia brain in patients in the first psychotic episode and those at familial risk for this illness using magnetic resonance imaging (MRI), and magnetic resonance spectroscopy (MRS) studies. In this chapter, we first briefly review the extant literature (including our studies) on the current state of our understanding of gray matter losses in schizophrenia and the implications of these changes to the clinical manifestations and outcome of this illness. Second, we review the question of what constituents of gray matter might contribute to the observed gray-matter deficits, and whether these alterations reflect neuronal loss or simply impaired neuronal viability. Third, we discuss the pathophysiological processes that might underlie reductions in neuropil, and the time course when these processes might set in. Finally, we argue that the impaired neuronal viability in schizophrenia is potentially reversible, and suggest future directions of research.

Are gray matter volume reductions a core aspect of the pathophysiology of schizophrenia?

Beginning in the early part of the twentieth century it has been known that schizophrenia is characterized by loss of brain parenchyma and enlarged cerebral ventricles, as evidenced by pneumo-encepholographic studies (Vogel & Lange, 1966) and post-mortem brain studies (Harrison, 1999). Computed tomography (CT) scan studies confirmed these findings in the late 1970s (Johnstone, Crow, Frith, Husband, & Kreel, 1976; Johnstone et al., 1978; Reveley, Reveley, Clifford, & Murray, 1982; Reveley, Reveley, & Murray, 1983, 1984). Magnetic resonance imaging (MRI) studies showed robust evidence of widespread gray matter (GM) reductions notably in the heteromodal association cortex and limbic regions (Ellison-Wright, Glahn, Laird, Thelen, & Bullmore, 2008; Honea, Crow, Passingham, & Mackay, 2005; Shenton et al., 2001; Wright, Ellison et al., 1999; Wright et al., 2000; Wright, Sharma et al., 1999). There is evidence for progressive GM reductions during the prodromal phase (Pantelis et al., 2003), early psychotic phase (P. Thompson, Cannon, & Toga, 2002) and during the chronic phases of schizophrenia (DeLisi & Nasrallah, 2008). Gray-matter reductions have also been reported in adolescents at familial risk for schizophrenia, who may be presumably in a premorbid phase of this illness (Keshavan et al., 1997; Lawrie et al., 1999).

Brain structural alterations may possibly contribute to altered brain function (Buckholtz et al., 2007; Lv et al., 2008; Park et al., 2006). Functional MRI studies (Kindermann, Karimi, Symonds, Brown, & Jeste, 1997; Zakzanis, Poulin, Hansen, & Jolic, 2000) have shown evidence of impaired regional brain function consistent with the observed structural alterations. Taken together, imaging studies strongly point to reductions in one or more neuronal elements in the schizophrenia brain. It is, however, difficult to draw conclusions about the nature of neuropathological alterations based on structural imaging studies alone.

What constituents of gray matter might be predominately affected?

Early neuropathological studies were generally inconclusive about the nature of cerebral pathology in schizophrenia, showing decreases, increases or no change (Christensen, Moller, & Faurbye, 1970; Plum, 1972). Recent post-mortem studies using immunohistochemical methods and sophisticated cell-counting techniques have relatively consistently revealed neuropathological abnormalities suggesting that GM decrements in schizophrenia may be related to reductions of synapto-dendritic arborization (neuropil) and somal size and/or also from microglial abnormalities. A large body of evidence implicates a reduction of somal and neuropil size, without neuronal loss in schizophrenia (Dorph-Petersen et al., 2009; Pierri, Volk, Auh, Sampson, & Lewis, 2001; Rajkowska, Selemon, & Goldman-Rakic, 1998; Selemon, Rajkowska, & Goldman-Rakic, 1998). The reduced somal size notwithstanding, reduced synaptic and dendritic density may cause neuronal density to be either normal or actually increased in cortical GM (Dorph-Petersen et al., 2009; Selemon, Mrzljak, Kleinman, Herman, & Goldman-Rakic, 2003). The limbic, temporal and dorsal cortices, regions volumetrically compromised in patients, also show neuropathological changes on post-mortem studies. The dorsal prefrontal cortical layer III cells, in addition to showing somal size reductions, also show decreased synaptic density, putatively due to reduced density of pre-synaptic (axon terminals of cortical afferents) and/or post-synaptic (dendritic) components (Lewis, Glantz, Pierri, & Sweet, 2003). Studies show reduced dendritic arborization, dendritic spinal density and MAP2 (microtubule associated protein, a post-synaptically localized molecule) immunoreactivity suggesting post-synaptic compromise in Brodmann Areas (BA) 9 and 32 (Broadbelt & Jones, 2008).

Immunohistochemical studies assaying axonal terminal molecular markers like syntaxin, synaptophysins and synaptosomal proteins (e.g., SNAP25) found reduced immunoreactivity suggesting reduced pre-synaptic axonal density in the dorsal prefrontal cortex (Halim et al., 2003; Honer et al., 2002; Karson et al., 1999; P. M. Thompson, Sower, & Perrone-Bizzozero, 1998). Functional alterations of these molecules including those of intracellular phosphorylation dependent signaling further suggest pre-synaptic compromise (Castillo, Ghose, Tamminga, & Ulery-Reynolds, 2010). Pre-synaptic reductions may be most prominent in the cortical layer III (Glantz & Lewis, 2000) pyramidal neurons, the main afferents of which are from the medial dorsal thalamus and which are interconnected by GABAergic inhibitory interneurons (chandelier cells). Reduced synaptic density may stem from reduced chandelier-cell arborization as prefrontal GAT immunoreactivity (a marker of GABA-bearing axon terminals) is reduced (Lewis & Hashimoto, 2007; Lewis,

Hashimoto, & Volk, 2005; Lewis, Volk, & Hashimoto, 2004). Decreased reelin (produced by GABAergic interneurons) may also suggest chandelier-cell alterations (Caruncho, Dopeso-Reyes, Loza, & Rodriguez, 2004; Costa et al., 2002). Thalamic afferents may also be decreased as parvalbumin immunoreactivity (a marker of thalamic axon terminals) is reduced (Bernstein et al., 2007; Lewis, Cruz, Melchitzky, & Pierri, 2001). This may be tentatively explained by alterations of glutamatergic transmission and glutamatergic receptor intra-cellular signaling in thalamic neuronal bodies, possibly leading to a distal axonal compromise (Meador-Woodruff, Clinton, Beneyto, & McCullumsmith, 2003; Smith, Haroutunian, Davis, & Meador-Woodruff, 2001a, 2001b; Watis, Chen, Chua, Chong, & Sim, 2008). A structural thalamic defect, however, remains conjectural as a study did not report medio dorsal thalamic neuropathological alterations (Kreczmanski et al., 2007). Temporal neocortices (superior temporal and auditory cortices) also show reduced somal size, reelin labeled cell numbers, synaptophysin immunoreactivity, MAP immunoreactivity and dendritic arborization in layer III pyramidal cells (Jonsson, Luts, Guldberg-Kjaer, & Brun, 1997; Lewis et al., 2003; Sweet et al., 2004; Torrey et al., 2005; Young et al., 1998). The anatomically non-contiguous neuropathological alterations of prefrontal and temporal neocortices suggests cell-specific, rather than region-specific abnormalities (Lewis et al., 2003). Studies of the limbic cortex finding reduced pre-synaptic components like GAP (growth associated proteins) and synaptophysins and reduced somal size within the anterior cingulate cortex, hippocampus and dentate gyrus, suggest reduced synaptic density possibly due to decreased pre-synaptic components (Chambers, Thomas, Saland, Neve, & Perrone-Bizzozero, 2005; Eastwood & Harrison, 1998; Honer et al., 1997; Webster, Shannon Weickert, Herman, Hyde, & Kleinman, 2001; Weinberger, 1999; Young et al., 1998). Although the limbic cortex receives afferents from a number of brain regions, those contributing to this pre-synaptic deficit are unclear. Significant post-synaptic deficits (reduced MAP expression, dendritic arborization and dendritic and neuronal disarray) are noted for the hippocampus (Broadbelt, Byne, & Jones, 2002; D. Cotter, Kerwin, Doshi, Martin, & Everall, 1997; D. Cotter, Wilson, Roberts, Kerwin, & Everall, 2000; Eastwood et al., 2007; Rosoklija et al., 2005).

Microglial (astrocytes and oligodendrocytes) abnormalities have also been invoked to explain a host of neuropathological alterations in the schizophrenia brain. Evidence for microglial alterations is, however, not regionally specific and somewhat limited compared to that for neuronal and synaptic deficits. Reduced microglial (including astrocytes and oligodendrocytes) numbers, in addition to the reduced dendritic and synaptic density may explain the increased somal density in the context of normal neuronal numbers in schizophrenia. Since astrocytes play a key role in the synapto-dendritic integrity and metabolism of neurotransmitters, their reduced numbers, altered function and gene expression may underlie the compromised synaptic and dendritic integrity (Barley, Dracheva, & Byne, 2009; Bernstein, Steiner, & Bogerts, 2009; De Keyser, Mostert, & Koch, 2008). Decreased astrocyte numbers may also be partly responsible for reduced neuronal integrity and somal size (D. R. Cotter, Pariante, & Everall, 2001). As astrocytes bear receptors for interleukins and other immuno-modulators, they may mediate the relation of immunological dysfunction and schizophrenic brain alterations (De Keyser et al., 2008; Muller, Myint, & Schwarz, 2009; Muller & Schwarz, 2008). Reduced numbers of, and altered gene expression in oligodendrocytes may alter myelin synthesis and underlie white matter deficits and axonal abnormalities in schizophrenia (Bernstein et al., 2009; Bertram et al., 2007; Hoistad et al., 2009; Parlapani et al., 2009). This oligodendrocyte/myelin dysfunction in schizophrenia is consistent with a neurodevelopmental basis and may potentially explain structural and functional disconnectivity documented in schizophrenia (Haroutunian & Davis, 2007; Haroutunian, Katsel, Dracheva, Stewart, & Davis, 2007; Hoistad et al., 2009). In summary, the dorsal prefrontal, temporal and limbic cortices (most notably the hippocampus), show decreased dendritic and synaptic density and somal size and may underlie GM loss. Microglial abnormalities, albeit not regionally resolved by studies, have been implicated in schizophrenia and their reduced numbers may also contribute to GM volume and density deficits in this illness.

What pathophysiological processes might underlie reductions of neuropil and somal size?

Brain changes observed in schizophrenia, like any other neurologic illness, could be a result of the causative factors that may underlie the etiology of schizophrenia, the consequences of the illness and/or its treatment or compensatory phenomena secondary to the underlying pathophysiology. Specific microneuroanatomical alterations implicate early neurodevelopmental migratory failure mainly during the first and second trimesters (gestation) in the neuropathological alterations in schizophrenia (see Figure 12.1). Entorhinal, anterior cingulate, hippocampal and prefrontal cortical neurons are more numerous in the deep compared to superficial cortical layers, and may be abnormally present in subcortical regions in patients compared to controls. This suggests an incomplete, or even a failure of, "inside-out" migration of neuronal precursor cells from the subcortical regions towards the cortical surface (Akil & Lewis, 1997; Arnold, 1999; Arnold, Ruscheinsky, & Han, 1997; Benes, 1993; Hennah, Thomson, Peltonen, & Porteous, 2006; Jones, 1995; Kovalenko et al., 2003; Rioux, Nissanov, Lauber, Bilker, & Arnold, 2003; Tabares-Seisdedos et al., 2006). Neuronal disarray in the hippocampal and anterior cingulate layer II also implicates early neurodevelopmental insults during neuronal migration (Conrad, Abebe, Austin, Forsythe, & Scheibel, 1991; Conrad & Scheibel, 1987; Harrison, 1999; Jonsson et al., 1997; Kovelman & Scheibel, 1984).

What may underlie altered neuronal migration? Current evidence implicates genes coding for intracellular signaling molecules involved in the *early* developmental processes of neuronal migration, guidance and differentiation such as *DISC1* (Disrupted in Schizophrenia), neural adhesion molecules, NRG (neuregulins), those involved in GABAergic transmission and reelin (Bertram et al., 2007; Caruncho et al., 2004; Cox et al., 2009; Di Cristo, 2007; Hennah et al., 2006; Meyer & Morris, 2009; Murray, Jones, & O'Callaghan, 1991) in schizophrenia. Although genes directly involved in dopaminergic transmission may not mediate neuronal migration, abnormal migration of GABAergic neurons due to altered dopaminergic signaling has been suggested (Benes & Berretta, 2001). Genetic polymorphisms of the glutamic acid decarboxylase (GAD_{67}) gene (the GABA synthetic enzyme) in chandelier cells have been associated with schizophrenia and prefrontal GM loss (Addington et al., 2005; Akbarian & Huang, 2006; Akbarian et al., 1995). Some genes like *DISC1* and neuregulin (*NRG*-1) may also be involved in oligodendrocyte integrity and their polymorphisms may explain both neuronal and microglial compromise (Bertram et al., 2007; Schmitt, Parlapani, Gruber, Wobrock, & Falkai, 2008; Wood, Bonath, Kumar, Ross, & Cunliffe, 2009). Migratory failure (see Figure 12.1) possibly due to a genetic diathesis expressed during early neurodevelopment may be only one of the candidates for explaining neuronal alterations in schizophrenia. Maternally deprived rats, showing a "schizophrenia like" phenotype, have altered neuropil receptor expression suggesting a role for early neurodevelopmental environmental insults (Suarez et al., 2009). Individuals with a familial diathesis for schizophrenia have altered BDNF (Brain Derived Neurotrophic Factor) responses to early neurodevelopmental alterations such as perinatal hypoxia. Specifically, those at familial risk respond to hypoxia by a decrease in BDNF levels, rather than an increase, as in healthy controls (Cannon, Yolken, Buka, & Torrey, 2008). This suggests a possible role for gene–environmental interactions in causing early neurodevelopmental deficits.

Neuropil reductions in schizophrenia have also been considered to result from an exaggeration of normative development pruning processes that happen *later* in development, i.e., around adolescence (see Figure 12.1). Glutamatergic hypofunction has been posited to account for a host of alterations such as disinhibition of mesocortical dopaminergic tone and for negative symptoms and cognitive deficits by causing prefrontal cortical dysfunction and has become one of the commonly accepted models of schizophrenia (Goff & Coyle, 2001; Lindsley et al., 2006). Glutamate, via N-methyl D-aspartate (NMDA) activity may be important for late neurodevelopmental processes like apoptosis and synaptic pruning (Goff & Coyle, 2001; Lindsley et al., 2006). Recent evidence has implicated NMDA receptor hypofunction in excessive synaptic pruning causing altered synaptic plasticity and hence to account for neuropil reductions in schizophrenia (Goff & Coyle, 2001; Lindsley et al., 2006). Normal adolescent neuronal apoptosis may be dysregulated in schizophrenia. Adolescent neurodevelopment normally involves neuronal apoptosis ("programmed" cell death) and synaptic pruning (Keshavan, Anderson, & Pettegrew, 1994). Altered neuronal apoptosis has been implicated in reduced neuropil size and viability in schizophrenia (Glantz, Gilmore, Lieberman, & Jarskog, 2006). Specifically, a "non-lethal", attenuated apoptosis may reduce neuronal viability and decrease neuropil and somal size without inducing cell death (Jarskog, Glantz, Gilmore, & Lieberman, 2005). As some studies also report reduced neuron numbers in patients (Berger, Wood, & McGorry, 2003), exaggerated "lethal" apoptotic processes are also presumably involved in schizophrenia. Neurochemical imaging studies involving phosphorus magnetic resonance spectroscopy (31p MRS) have shown evidence of impaired prefrontal membrane phospholipid metabolism, and proton MRS studies suggest deficits in *N*-acetyl aspartate, a marker of neuronal viability (Keshavan, Sanders, Pettegrew, Dombrowsky, & Panchalingam, 1993; Keshavan, Stanley, Montrose, Minshew, & Pettegrew, 2003; Keshavan, Stanley, & Pettegrew, 2000). As synaptic and dendritic density may correlate with somal volume (Lewis et al., 2003), reduced dendrites and synapses per neuron (decreased neuropil volume) reported in schizophrenia (Arnold, 1999; Barley et al., 2009; Bernstein et al., 2009; De Keyser et al., 2008), may be possibly due to and/or excessive peri-adolescent synaptic pruning (Keshavan et al., 1994). Astrocytes may also be responsible for neuronal and neuropil integrity and their decreased numbers have been thought to play a role in reduced somal size (Barley et al., 2009; Bernstein et al., 2009; D. R. Cotter et al., 2001; De Keyser et al., 2008). Reductions of somal size have been mainly noted within the dorsal prefrontal cortical and auditory cortical layer III pyramidal cells (Lewis et al., 2003; Pierri et al., 2001; Pierri, Volk, Auh, Sampson, & Lewis, 2003). These reductions are noted for layer III pyramidal neurons involved in glutamate transmission and may be cell-type specific rather than region specific (Lewis et al., 2003).

Gray matter reductions in schizophrenia may also result from excitotoxic processes. One possibility is disinhibition of glutamatergic projections (Deutsch, Rosse, Schwartz, & Mastropaolo, 2001) to layer III cells (Lewis et al., 2003), which may induce excitotoxic damage. The α-amino-3-hydroxy-5-methyl-4-isoxazolepropionic acid (AMPA) glutamatergic receptors may also be abnormally permeable to the excitotoxigenic Ca^{++} ions in schizophrenia and hence sensitize cells to glutamatergic toxicity (Goff & Coyle, 2001). Absence of gliosis in the schizophrenic brain suggests that the reduced neuropil size may result from early (gestational) and late neurodevelopmental insults rather than inflammatory or degenerative processes (Falkai et al., 1999; Harrison, 1999, 2004). Although evidence points more toward a neurodevelopmental rather than a neurodegenerative model of schizophrenia (Fatemi & Folsom, 2009), some post-mortem analyses, however, show evidence of neurodegenerative processes including microglial alterations in schizophrenia (Bayer, Buslei, Havas, & Falkai, 1999; Halliday, 2001; Iritani, 2007). Also SB100 levels in the CSF (a putative marker of active brain changes) is elevated in chronic, elderly patients (Schmitt et al., 2005), suggesting to a neurodegenerative process lasting until the final stages of the illness rather than a neurodevelopmental etiology. Disease-related (state-dependent) neurodegenerative processes may also set in during the nascent stages of the illness and may be unrelated to medication as shown by longitudinal GM decline in medication naïve first-episode patients (Mane et al., 2009). Progressive GM loss in patients, hypothesized to occur due to excessive apoptosis also points to a neurodegenerative etiology in schizophrenia (Csernansky, 2007). Evidence has suggested alterations of genes involved in apoptosis in neurodegeneration, GM loss and the attendant ventricular enlargement in patients (Jarskog, Selinger, Lieberman, & Gilmore, 2004; Papiol et al., 2005). Progressive neurodegenerative brain changes may be region specific, with some regions remaining stable while some actively deteriorate over time on GM (O'Donnell et al., 1995; Takahashi et al., 2007). As the premorbid GM deficit may correlate with the post-onset decline, it seems likely that a neurodegenerative process may be superimposed on, and be proportional in its severity to an initial GM deficit caused by a neurodevelopmental alteration (Farrow, Whitford, Williams, Gomes, & Harris, 2005; see Figure 12.1).

Gray-matter decrements, probably a reflection of reduced somal and neuropil size, are related to psychopathology and clinical worsening. Reductions in neuropil and somal size in the layer III pyramidal cells, which send efferent glutamatergic projections to the striatal and subcortical dopaminergic cells may play a key role in the pathophysiology of schizophrenia. Glutamatergic connections from cortical pyramidal cells to subcortical dopaminergic neurons (Lewis et al., 2003) may reciprocally regulate mesocortical and mesolimbic dopaminergic transmission. This regulation of mesocortical and mesolimbic dopaminergic transmission may be altered in schizophrenia (Del Arco & Mora, 2009; Seeman, 2009; Seeman & Guan, 2009; Tanaka, 2006; Winterer & Weinberger, 2004). Increased dopaminergic transmission in the mesolimbic pathway may account for positive symptoms including paranoia while a hypodopaminergic mesocortical

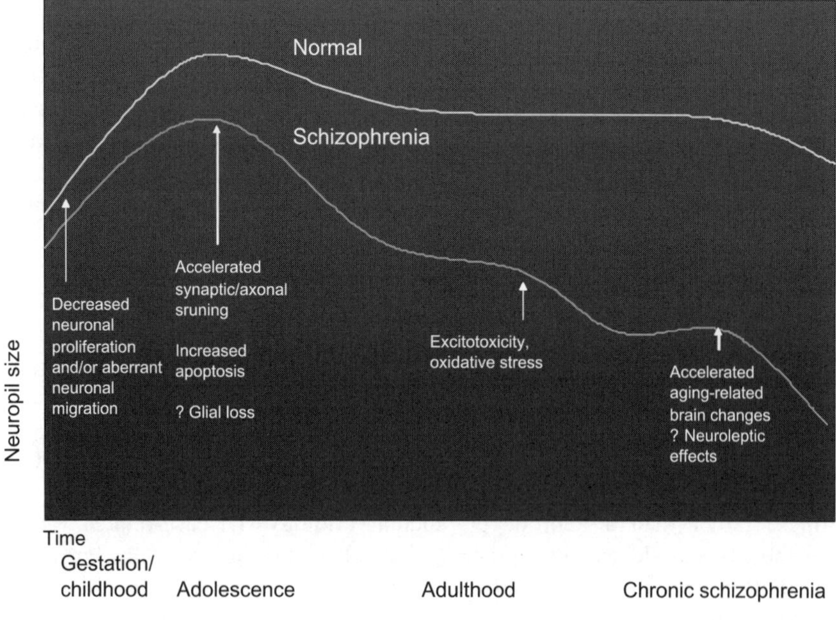

Figure 12.1 A schematic representation of putative causes of neuropil reduction in schizophrenia acting at different points throughout the lifetime. The *Y*-axis plots neuropil size, which is seen to show an exaggerated decline in schizophrenia compared to healthy individuals over time, which is represented on the *X*-axis. This exaggeration may be ascribed to neurodevelopmental insults and neurodegenerative processes acting during the course of the illness.

transmission may cause cognitive deficits and negative symptoms including avolition, anhedonia and apathy (Deutch, 1992; Kapur, 2003).

Gray-matter reductions in schizophrenia may also result from processes other than the pathophysiological substrate of the illness. Schizophrenia is associated with high rates of alcohol- and nicotine-use disorders, both of which may have the consequence of brain structural alterations (Brody et al., 2004; Nesvag, Frigessi, Jonsson, & Agartz, 2007). Cannabis may also increase GM volume loss (Bangalore et al., 2008). The processes of age-related cognitive decline and brain change may also be amplified in schizophrenia (Dickerson, 2007; see Figure 12.1). Psychosocial impoverishment, which characterizes many patients with prominent negative symptoms and institutionalization, may also contribute to brain volume loss secondary to disuse atrophy as is seen in neuromuscular disorders (Antonini et al., 2004).

Finally, antipsychotics may have important effects on brain structure and function (see Figure 12.1). While antipsychotic drugs remain the mainstay of treatment in schizophrenia, they do not address some core aspect of the illness, notably negative symptoms and cognitive impairment. Dopamine, acting through D2 receptors may contribute to stable (increased signal to noise ratio) coding of both external and internal stimuli in recurrent cortical microcircuits composed of pyramidal cells and interneurons (Tanaka, 2006; Winterer, 2006; Winterer & Weinberger, 2004). It is hence possible that D2 blocking effects of antipsychotics will worsen some aspects of neurocognition and precipitate negative symptoms (Reilly, Harris, Khine, Keshavan, & Sweeney, 2007). By contrast, other studies suggest a modest, but significant beneficial effect of atypical antipsychotics compared to typical antipsychotics (Bilder et al., 2002). Typical antipsychotics may reduce BDNF levels, possibly contributing to reduced neuronal viability (Angelucci, Mathe, & Aloe, 2000). For these reasons, the potential distinctions between the effects on brain structures by typical and atypical antipsychotics have been actively investigated. Gray-matter reductions during follow-up in first-episode schizophrenia are prominent in haloperidol-treated patients, but not seen in those treated with olanzapine (Lieberman, Stroup et al., 2005; Lieberman, Tollefson et al., 2005). By contrast, however, primate studies suggest reductions in cortical volume and glial density following treatment with both haloperidol and olanzapine (Konopaske et al., 2007, 2008). The question of whether antipsychotics are neuro-protective or neuro-toxic therefore remains a matter of debate. Preliminary findings suggest that antipsychotic medications may increase astrocyte numbers, alter their neurotransmitter uptake activity and/or alter their gene expression (Jiang, Saetre, Jazin, & Carlstrom, 2009; Matute, Melone, Vallejo-Illarramendi, & Conti, 2005; Qi et al., 2009), potentially contributing to the effect of antipsychotics on GM volume (Lieberman, Tollefson et al., 2005).

Are neuropil reductions in schizophrenia reversible?

It is crucial to explore possible avenues of ameliorating, or possibly stemming, neuropil and somal size reductions (GM decrements) in schizophrenia. The lack of marked neuronal loss and synaptic plasticity (albeit attenuated; Daskalakis,

Christensen, Fitzgerald, & Chen, 2002; Fitzgerald et al., 2004; Frantseva et al., 2008) in schizophrenia justify an investigation into possible avenues of halting, or even reversing, the neuropathological changes in schizophrenia.

Brain derived neurotrophic factor (BDNF), a key regulator of synaptic plasticity and neuronal viability is reduced in schizophrenia (Angelucci, Brene, & Mathe, 2005; Cannon et al., 2008; Chen et al., 2009; Guillin, Demily, & Thibaut, 2007; Lu & Martinowich, 2008) and may underlie reduced plasticity in this illness (Daskalakis et al., 2002; Fitzgerald et al., 2004; Frantseva et al., 2008). Genetic polymorphisms in BDNF may covary with brain regional volumes for the prefrontal and hippocampal regions (Szeszko et al., 2005; Varnas et al., 2008), further underlining its probable role in maintaining synaptic plasticity and hence neuropil volume. Subjects with a familial diathesis also have altered BDNF responses to neuronal insults such as hypoxia (Cannon et al., 2008). This suggests that inherited BDNF polymorphisms (Szeszko et al., 2005; Varnas et al., 2008) may possibly synergistically interact with and sensitize the brain to environmental insults and may contribute to premorbid risk for schizophrenia. Increasing BDNF activity or release, possibly through neuroplasticity based cognitive therapies (Vinogradov et al., 2009) and even physical exercise (Ferris, Williams, & Shen, 2007; Gomez-Pinilla, Vaynman, & Ying, 2008; Griffin, Bechara, Birch, & Kelly, 2009; Komulainen et al., 2008; White & Castellano, 2008; Winter et al., 2007) may possibly protect against neuropil and somal alterations in patients and their "high-risk" relatives. Reduced BDNF levels and/or reduced BDNF receptor concentrations may contribute to reduced cortical inhibitory neuronal (chandelier cells) activity (Hashimoto et al., 2005). Reduced chandelier-cell activity, together with a hypodopaminergic tone, may be central to cognitive dysfunction in schizophrenia by reducing the prefrontal cortical pyramidal cell layer's signal-to-noise ratio.

While antipsychotic drugs are highly effective in treating psychotic symptoms, their beneficial effects in ameliorating cognitive deficits, which are the core, lasting features of schizophrenia, are unclear. However, atypical antipsychotics may have modest benefits in cognition (Bilder et al., 2002). By contrast, psychosocial cognitive remediation has robust efficacy for improving executive and social cognitive deficits (Fisher, Holland, Merzenich, & Vinogradov, 2009). Interestingly cognitive remediation appears to enhance cortical thickness as well as BDNF release (Vinogradov et al., 2009). Atypical antipsychotics may also be associated with less GM loss during follow-up (Lieberman, Stroup et al., 2005) and may increase BDNF release (Pillai & Mahadik, 2006). BDNF may also mediate increase in cortical plasticity with repetitive transcranial magnetic stimulation (TMS) a treatment increasingly used in psychiatric disorders (Cheeran et al., 2008; Freitas, Fregni, & Pascual-Leone, 2009). Future therapeutic research, therefore, needs to capitalize on these observations, and develop pharmacological and psychotherapeutic interventions that enhance neuroplasticity and thereby at least in part reverse the neuropathological alterations in schizophrenia. Pharmacological approaches have thus far been unsatisfactory, but cognitive remediation has shown some promise. In a recent study in early schizophrenia patients we showed cognitive enhancement therapy to blunt the GM loss in limbic and cingulate cortices when compared to supportive care and psychoeducation (Eack et al., 2010). This suggests that the potentially neuroprotective effects of brain plasticity may be invoked by cognitive enhancement to mitigate the GM loss in schizophrenia.

References

Addington, A. M., Gornick, M., Duckworth, J., Sporn, A., Gogtay, N., Bobb, A., et al. (2005). GAD1 (2q31.1), which encodes glutamic acid decarboxylase (GAD67), is associated with childhood-onset schizophrenia and cortical gray matter volume loss. *Molecular Psychiatry*, *10*(6), 581–588.

Akbarian, S., & Huang, H. S. (2006). Molecular and cellular mechanisms of altered GAD1/GAD67 expression in schizophrenia and related disorders. *Brain Research Reviews*, *52*(2), 293–304.

Akbarian, S., Kim, J. J., Potkin, S. G., Hagman, J. O., Tafazzoli, A., Bunney, W. E., Jr., et al. (1995). Gene expression for glutamic acid decarboxylase is reduced without loss of neurons in prefrontal cortex of schizophrenics. *Archives of General Psychiatry*, *52*(4), 258–266.

Akil, M., & Lewis, D. A. (1997). Cytoarchitecture of the entorhinal cortex in schizophrenia. *American Journal of Psychiatry*, *154*(7), 1010–1012.

Angelucci, F., Brene, S., & Mathe, A. A. (2005). BDNF in schizophrenia, depression and corresponding animal models. *Molecular Psychiatry*, *10*(4), 345–352.

Angelucci, F., Mathe, A. A., & Aloe, L. (2000). Brain-derived neurotrophic factor and tyrosine kinase receptor TrkB in rat brain are significantly altered after haloperidol and risperidone administration. *Journal of Neuroscience Research*, *60*(6), 783–794.

Antonini, G., Mainero, C., Romano, A., Giubilei, F., Ceschin, V., Gragnani, F., et al. (2004). Cerebral atrophy in myotonic dystrophy: A voxel based morphometric study. *Journal of Neurology, Neurosurgery & Psychiatry*, *75*(11), 1611–1613.

Antonova, E., Kumari, V., Morris, R., Halari, R., Anilkumar, A., Mehrotra, R., et al. (2005). The relationship of structural alterations to cognitive deficits in schizophrenia: A voxel-based morphometry study. *Biological Psychiatry*, *58*(6), 457–467.

Antonova, E., Sharma, T., Morris, R., & Kumari, V. (2004). The relationship between brain structure and neurocognition in schizophrenia: A selective review. *Schizophrenia Research*, *70*(2–3), 117–145.

Arnold, S. E. (1999). Neurodevelopmental abnormalities in schizophrenia: Insights from neuropathology. *Developmental Psychopathology*, *11*(3), 439–456.

Arnold, S. E., Ruscheinsky, D. D., & Han, L. Y. (1997). Further evidence of abnormal cytoarchitecture of the entorhinal cortex in schizophrenia using spatial point pattern analyses. *Biological Psychiatry*, *42*(8), 639–647.

Bangalore, S. S., Prasad, K. M., Montrose, D. M., Goradia, D. D., Diwadkar, V. A., & Keshavan, M. S. (2008). Cannabis use and brain structural alterations in first episode schizophrenia—A region of interest, voxel based morphometric study. *Schizophrenia Research*, *99*(1–3), 1–6.

Barley, K., Dracheva, S., & Byne, W. (2009). Subcortical oligodendrocyte- and astrocyte-associated gene expression in subjects with schizophrenia, major depression and bipolar disorder. *Schizophrenia Research*, *112*(1–3), 54–64.

Bayer, T. A., Buslei, R., Havas, L., & Falkai, P. (1999). Evidence for activation of microglia in patients with psychiatric illnesses. *Neuroscience Letters*, *271*(2), 126–128.

Benes, F. M. (1993). The relationship between structural brain imaging and histopathologic findings in schizophrenia research. *Harvard Review of Psychiatry*, *1*(2), 100–109.

Benes, F. M., & Berretta, S. (2001). GABAergic interneurons: Implications for understanding schizophrenia and bipolar disorder. *Neuropsychopharmacology*, *25*(1), 1–27.

Berger, G. E., Wood, S., & McGorry, P. D. (2003). Incipient neurovulnerability and neuroprotection in early psychosis. *Psychopharmacology Bulletin*, *37*(2), 79–101.

Bernstein, H. G., Krause, S., Krell, D., Dobrowolny, H., Wolter, M., Stauch, R., et al. (2007). Strongly reduced number of parvalbumin-immunoreactive projection neurons in the mammillary bodies in schizophrenia: Further evidence for limbic neuropathology. *Annals of the New York Academy of Sciences*, *1096*, 120–127.

Bernstein, H. G., Steiner, J., & Bogerts, B. (2009). Glial cells in schizophrenia: Pathophysiological significance and possible consequences for therapy. *Expert Review of Neurotherapeutics*, *9*(7), 1059–1071.

Bertram, I., Bernstein, H. G., Lendeckel, U., Bukowska, A., Dobrowolny, H., Keilhoff, G., et al. (2007). Immunohistochemical evidence for impaired neuregulin-1 signaling in the prefrontal cortex in schizophrenia and in unipolar depression. *Annals of the New York Academy of Sciences*, *1096*, 147–156.

Bilder, R. M., Goldman, R. S., Volavka, J., Czobor, P., Hoptman, M., Sheitman, B., et al. (2002). Neurocognitive effects of clozapine, olanzapine, risperidone, and haloperidol in patients with chronic schizophrenia or schizoaffective disorder. *American Journal of Psychiatry*, *159*(6), 1018–1028.

Broadbelt, K., Byne, W., & Jones, L. B. (2002). Evidence for a decrease in basilar dendrites of pyramidal cells in schizophrenic medial prefrontal cortex. *Schizophrenia Research*, *58*(1), 75–81.

Broadbelt, K., & Jones, L. B. (2008). Evidence of altered calmodulin immunoreactivity in areas 9 and 32 of schizophrenic prefrontal cortex. *Journal of Psychiatric Research*, *42*(8), 612–621.

Brody, A. L., Mandelkern, M. A., Jarvik, M. E., Lee, G. S., Smith, E. C., Huang, J. C., et al. (2004). Differences between smokers and nonsmokers in regional gray matter volumes and densities. *Biological Psychiatry*, *55*(1), 77–84.

Buckholtz, J. W., Meyer-Lindenberg, A., Honea, R. A., Straub, R. E., Pezawas, L., Egan, M. F., et al. (2007). Allelic variation in RGS4 impacts functional and structural connectivity in the human brain. *Journal of Neuroscience*, *27*(7), 1584–1593.

Cannon, T. D., Yolken, R., Buka, S., & Torrey, E. F. (2008). Decreased neurotrophic response to birth hypoxia in the etiology of schizophrenia. *Biological Psychiatry*, *64*(9), 797–802.

Caruncho, H. J., Dopeso-Reyes, I. G., Loza, M. I., & Rodriguez, M. A. (2004). A GABA, reelin, and the neurodevelopmental hypothesis of schizophrenia. *Critical Review of Neurobiology*, *16*(1–2), 25–32.

Castillo, M. A., Ghose, S., Tamminga, C. A., & Ulery-Reynolds, P. G. (2010). Deficits in syntaxin 1 phosphorylation in schizophrenia prefrontal cortex. *Biological Psychiatry*, *67*(3), 208–216.

Chambers, J. S., Thomas, D., Saland, L., Neve, R. L., & Perrone-Bizzozero, N. I. (2005). Growth-associated protein 43 (GAP-43) and synaptophysin alterations in the dentate gyrus of patients with schizophrenia. *Progress in Neuro-Psychopharmacology and Biological Psychiatry*, *29*(2), 283–290.

Cheeran, B., Talelli, P., Mori, F., Koch, G., Suppa, A., Edwards, M., et al. (2008). A common polymorphism in the brain-derived neurotrophic factor gene (*BDNF*) modulates human cortical plasticity and the response to rTMS. *Journal of Physiology*, *586*(23), 5717–5725.

Chen, D. C., Wang, J., Wang, B., Yang, S. C., Zhang, C. X., Zheng, Y. L., et al. (2009). Decreased levels of serum brain-derived neurotrophic factor in drug-naive first-episode schizophrenia: Relationship to clinical phenotypes. *Psychopharmacology (Berlin)*, *207*(3), 375–380.

Christensen, E., Moller, J. E., & Faurbye, A. (1970). Neuropathological investigation of 28 brains from patients with dyskinesia. *Acta Psychiatrica Scandinavica*, *46*(1), 14–23.

Conrad, A. J., Abebe, T., Austin, R., Forsythe, S., & Scheibel, A. B. (1991). Hippocampal pyramidal cell disarray in schizophrenia as a bilateral phenomenon. *Archives of General Psychiatry*, *48*(5), 413–417.

Conrad, A. J., & Scheibel, A. B. (1987). Schizophrenia and the hippocampus: The embryological hypothesis extended. *Schizophrenia Bulletin*, *13*(4), 577–587.

Costa, E., Chen, Y., Davis, J., Dong, E., Noh, J. S., Tremolizzo, L., et al. (2002). REELIN and schizophrenia: A disease at the interface of the genome and the epigenome. *Molecular Interventions*, *2*(1), 47–57.

Cotter, D., Kerwin, R., Doshi, B., Martin, C. S., & Everall, I. P. (1997). Alterations in hippocampal non-phosphorylated MAP2 protein expression in schizophrenia. *Brain Research*, *765*(2), 238–246.

Cotter, D., Wilson, S., Roberts, E., Kerwin, R., & Everall, I. P. (2000). Increased dendritic MAP2 expression in the hippocampus in schizophrenia. *Schizophrenia Research*, *41*(2), 313–323.

Cotter, D. R., Pariante, C. M., & Everall, I. P. (2001). Glial cell abnormalities in major psychiatric disorders: The evidence and implications. *Brain Research Bulletin*, *55*(5), 585–595.

Cox, E. T., Brennaman, L. H., Gable, K. L., Hamer, R. M., Glantz, L. A., Lamantia, A. S., et al. (2009). Developmental regulation of neural cell adhesion molecule in human prefrontal cortex. *Neuroscience*, *162*(1), 96–105.

Crutcher, K. A. (1989). Tissue sections from the mature rat brain and spinal cord as substrates for neurite outgrowth in vitro: Extensive growth on gray matter but little growth on white matter. *Experimental Neurology*, *104*(1), 39–54.

Csernansky, J. G. (2007). Neurodegeneration in schizophrenia: Evidence from in vivo neuroimaging studies. *Scientific World Journal*, *7*, 135–143.

Daskalakis, Z. J., Christensen, B. K., Fitzgerald, P. B., & Chen, R. (2002). Transcranial magnetic stimulation: A new investigational and treatment tool in psychiatry. *Journal of Neuropsychiatry and Clinical Neuroscience*, *14*(4), 406–415.

De Keyser, J., Mostert, J. P., & Koch, M. W. (2008). Dysfunctional astrocytes as key players in the pathogenesis of central nervous system disorders. *Journal of Neurological Science*, *267*(1–2), 3–16.

Del Arco, A., & Mora, F. (2009). Neurotransmitters and prefrontal cortex-limbic system interactions: Implications for plasticity and psychiatric disorders. *Journal of Neural Transmission*, *116*(8), 941–952.

DeLisi, L. E., & Nasrallah, H. A. (2008). Celebrating twenty years of schizophrenia research. *Schizophrenia Research*, *100*(1–3), 1–3.

Deutch, A. Y. (1992). The regulation of subcortical dopamine systems by the prefrontal cortex: Interactions of central dopamine systems and the pathogenesis of schizophrenia. *Journal of Neural Transmission Supplement*, *36*, 61–89.

Deutsch, S. I., Rosse, R. B., Schwartz, B. L., & Mastropaolo, J. (2001). A revised excitotoxic hypothesis of schizophrenia: Therapeutic implications. *Clinical Neuropharmacology, 24*(1), 43–49.

Di Cristo, G. (2007). Development of cortical GABAergic circuits and its implications for neurodevelopmental disorders. *Clinical Genetics, 72*(1), 1–8.

Dickerson, F. B. (2007). Women, aging, and schizophrenia. *Journal of Women and Aging, 19*(1–2), 49–61.

Dorph-Petersen, K. A., Delevich, K. M., Marcsisin, M. J., Zhang, W., Sampson, A. R., Gundersen, H. J., et al. (2009). Pyramidal neuron number in layer 3 of primary auditory cortex of subjects with schizophrenia. *Brain Research, 1285*, 42–57.

Eack, S. M., Hogarty, G. E., Cho, R. Y., Prasad, K. M., Greenwald, D. P., Hogarty, S. S., et al. (2010). Neuroprotective effects of cognitive enhancement therapy against gray matter loss in early schizophrenia: Results from a 2-year randomized controlled trial. *Archives of General Psychiatry, 67*(7), E1–E10.

Eastwood, S. L., & Harrison, P. J. (1998). Hippocampal and cortical growth-associated protein-43 messenger RNA in schizophrenia. *Neuroscience, 86*(2), 437–448.

Eastwood, S. L., Lyon, L., George, L., Andrieux, A., Job, D., & Harrison, P. J. (2007). Altered expression of synaptic protein mRNAs in STOP (MAP6) mutant mice. *Journal of Psychopharmacology, 21*(6), 635–644.

Ellison-Wright, I., Glahn, D. C., Laird, A. R., Thelen, S. M., & Bullmore, E. (2008). The anatomy of first-episode and chronic schizophrenia: An anatomical likelihood estimation meta-analysis. *American Journal of Psychiatry, 165*(8), 1015–1023.

Falkai, P., Honer, W. G., David, S., Bogerts, B., Majtenyi, C., & Bayer, T. A. (1999). No evidence for astrogliosis in brains of schizophrenic patients. A post-mortem study. *Neuropathology and Applied Neurobiology, 25*(1), 48–53.

Farrow, T. F., Whitford, T. J., Williams, L. M., Gomes, L., & Harris, A. W. (2005). Diagnosis-related regional gray matter loss over two years in first episode schizophrenia and bipolar disorder. *Biological Psychiatry, 58*(9), 713–723.

Fatemi, S. H., & Folsom, T. D. (2009). The neurodevelopmental hypothesis of schizophrenia, revisited. *Schizophrenia Bulletin, 35*(3), 528–548.

Ferris, L. T., Williams, J. S., & Shen, C. L. (2007). The effect of acute exercise on serum brain-derived neurotrophic factor levels and cognitive function. *Medicine and Science in Sports and Exercise, 39*(4), 728–734.

Fisher, M., Holland, C., Merzenich, M. M., & Vinogradov, S. (2009). Using neuroplasticity-based auditory training to improve verbal memory in schizophrenia. *American Journal of Psychiatry, 166*(7), 805–811.

Fitzgerald, P. B., Brown, T. L., Marston, N. A., Oxley, T., De Castella, A., Daskalakis, Z. J., et al. (2004). Reduced plastic brain responses in schizophrenia: A transcranial magnetic stimulation study. *Schizophrenia Research, 71*(1), 17–26.

Frantseva, M. V., Fitzgerald, P. B., Chen, R., Moller, B., Daigle, M., & Daskalakis, Z. J. (2008). Evidence for impaired long-term potentiation in schizophrenia and its relationship to motor skill learning. *Cerebral Cortex, 18*(5), 990–996.

Freitas, C., Fregni, F., & Pascual-Leone, A. (2009). Meta-analysis of the effects of repetitive transcranial magnetic stimulation (rTMS) on negative and positive symptoms in schizophrenia. *Schizophrenia Research, 108*(1–3), 11–24.

Glantz, L. A., Gilmore, J. H., Lieberman, J. A., & Jarskog, L. F. (2006). Apoptotic mechanisms and the synaptic pathology of schizophrenia. *Schizophrenia Research, 81*(1), 47–63.

Glantz, L. A., & Lewis, D. A. (2000). Decreased dendritic spine density on prefrontal cortical pyramidal neurons in schizophrenia. *Archives of General Psychiatry, 57*(1), 65–73.

Goff, D. C., & Coyle, J. T. (2001). The emerging role of glutamate in the pathophysiology and treatment of schizophrenia. *American Journal of Psychiatry*, *158*(9), 1367–1377.

Gomez-Pinilla, F., Vaynman, S., & Ying, Z. (2008). Brain-derived neurotrophic factor functions as a metabotrophin to mediate the effects of exercise on cognition. *European Journal of Neuroscience*, *28*(11), 2278–2287.

Griffin, E. W., Bechara, R. G., Birch, A. M., & Kelly, A. M. (2009). Exercise enhances hippocampal-dependent learning in the rat: Evidence for a BDNF-related mechanism. *Hippocampus*, *19*(10), 973–980.

Guillin, O., Demily, C., & Thibaut, F. (2007). Brain-derived neurotrophic factor in schizophrenia and its relation with dopamine. *International Review of Neurobiology*, *78*, 377–395.

Gur, R. E., Cowell, P. E., Latshaw, A., Turetsky, B. I., Grossman, R. I., Arnold, S. E., et al. (2000). Reduced dorsal and orbital prefrontal gray matter volumes in schizophrenia. *Archives of General Psychiatry*, *57*(8), 761–768.

Gur, R. E., Keshavan, M. S., & Lawrie, S. M. (2007). Deconstructing psychosis with human brain imaging. *Schizophrenia Bulletin*, *33*(4), 921–931.

Halim, N. D., Weickert, C. S., McClintock, B. W., Hyde, T. M., Weinberger, D. R., Kleinman, J. E., et al. (2003). Presynaptic proteins in the prefrontal cortex of patients with schizophrenia and rats with abnormal prefrontal development. *Molecular Psychiatry*, *8*(9), 797–810.

Halliday, G. M. (2001). A review of the neuropathology of schizophrenia. *Clinical and Experimental Pharmacology and Physiology*, *28*(1–2), 64–65.

Haroutunian, V., & Davis, K. L. (2007). Introduction to the special section: Myelin and oligodendrocyte abnormalities in schizophrenia. *International Journal of Neuropsychopharmacology*, *10*(4), 499–502.

Haroutunian, V., Katsel, P., Dracheva, S., Stewart, D. G., & Davis, K. L. (2007). Variations in oligodendrocyte-related gene expression across multiple cortical regions: Implications for the pathophysiology of schizophrenia. *International Journal of Neuropsychopharmacology*, *10*(4), 565–573.

Harrison, P. J. (1999). The neuropathology of schizophrenia. A critical review of the data and their interpretation. *Brain*, *122*(4), 593–624.

Harrison, P. J. (2004). The hippocampus in schizophrenia: A review of the neuropathological evidence and its pathophysiological implications. *Psychopharmacology (Berlin)*, *174*(1), 151–162.

Hashimoto, T., Bergen, S. E., Nguyen, Q. L., Xu, B., Monteggia, L. M., Pierri, J. N., et al. (2005). Relationship of brain-derived neurotrophic factor and its receptor TrkB to altered inhibitory prefrontal circuitry in schizophrenia. *Journal of Neuroscience*, *25*(2), 372–383.

Hennah, W., Thomson, P., Peltonen, L., & Porteous, D. (2006). Genes and schizophrenia. Beyond schizophrenia: The role of DISC1 in major mental illness. *Schizophrenia Bulletin*, *32*(3), 409–416.

Hoistad, M., Segal, D., Takahashi, N., Sakurai, T., Buxbaum, J. D., & Hof, P. R. (2009). Linking white and grey matter in schizophrenia: Oligodendrocyte and neuron pathology in the prefrontal cortex. *Frontiers in Neuroanatomy*, Vol. *3*, Article 9.

Honea, R., Crow, T. J., Passingham, D., & Mackay, C. E. (2005). Regional deficits in brain volume in schizophrenia: A meta-analysis of voxel-based morphometry studies. *American Journal of Psychiatry*, *162*(12), 2233–2245.

Honer, W. G., Falkai, P., Bayer, T. A., Xie, J., Hu, L., Li, H. Y., et al. (2002). Abnormalities of SNARE mechanism proteins in anterior frontal cortex in severe mental illness. *Cerebral Cortex*, *12*(4), 349–356.

Honer, W. G., Falkai, P., Young, C., Wang, T., Xie, J., Bonner, J., et al. (1997). Cingulate cortex synaptic terminal proteins and neural cell adhesion molecule in schizophrenia. *Neuroscience*, *78*(1), 99–110.

Iritani, S. (2007). Neuropathology of schizophrenia: A mini review. *Neuropathology*, *27*(6), 604–608.

Jarskog, L. F., Glantz, L. A., Gilmore, J. H., & Lieberman, J. A. (2005). Apoptotic mechanisms in the pathophysiology of schizophrenia. *Progress in Neuro-Psychopharmacology and Biological Psychiatry*, *29*(5), 846–858.

Jarskog, L. F., Selinger, E. S., Lieberman, J. A., & Gilmore, J. H. (2004). Apoptotic proteins in the temporal cortex in schizophrenia: High Bax/Bcl-2 ratio without caspase-3 activation. *American Journal of Psychiatry*, *161*(1), 109–115.

Jiang, L., Saetre, P., Jazin, E., & Carlstrom, E. L. (2009). Haloperidol changes mRNA expression of a QKI splice variant in human astrocytoma cells. *BMC Pharmacology*, Vol. *9*, Article 6.

Johnstone, E. C., Crow, T. J., Frith, C. D., Husband, J., & Kreel, L. (1976). Cerebral ventricular size and cognitive impairment in chronic schizophrenia. *Lancet*, *2*(7992), 924–926.

Johnstone, E. C., Crow, T. J., Frith, C. D., Stevens, M., Kreel, L., & Husband, J. (1978). The dementia of dementia praecox. *Acta Psychiatrica Scandinavica*, *57*(4), 305–324.

Jones, E. G. (1995). Cortical development and neuropathology in schizophrenia. *Ciba Foundation Symposium Journal*, *193*, 277–295.

Jonsson, S. A., Luts, A., Guldberg-Kjaer, N., & Brun, A. (1997). Hippocampal pyramidal cell disarray correlates negatively to cell number: Implications for the pathogenesis of schizophrenia. *European Archives of Psychiatry and Clinical Neuroscience*, *247*(3), 120–127.

Kapur, S. (2003). Psychosis as a state of aberrant salience: A framework linking biology, phenomenology, and pharmacology in schizophrenia. *American Journal of Psychiatry*, *160*(1), 13–23.

Karson, C. N., Mrak, R. E., Schluterman, K. O., Sturner, W. Q., Sheng, J. G., & Griffin, W. S. (1999). Alterations in synaptic proteins and their encoding mRNAs in prefrontal cortex in schizophrenia: A possible neurochemical basis for "hypofrontality". *Molecular Psychiatry*, *4*(1), 39–45.

Keshavan, M. S., Anderson, S., & Pettegrew, J. W. (1994). Is schizophrenia due to excessive synaptic pruning in the prefrontal cortex? The Feinberg hypothesis revisited. *Journal of Psychiatric Research*, *28*(3), 239–265.

Keshavan, M. S., Diwadkar, V., & Rosenberg, D. R. (2005). Developmental biomarkers in schizophrenia and other psychiatric disorders: Common origins, different trajectories? *Epidemiologia e Psichiatria Sociale*, *14*(4), 188–193.

Keshavan, M. S., Diwadkar, V. A., Montrose, D. M., Rajarethinam, R., & Sweeney, J. A. (2005). Premorbid indicators and risk for schizophrenia: A selective review and update. *Schizophrenia Research*, *79*(1), 45–57.

Keshavan, M. S., Montrose, D. M., Pierri, J. N., Dick, E. L., Rosenberg, D., Talagala, L., et al. (1997). Magnetic resonance imaging and spectroscopy in offspring at risk for schizophrenia: Preliminary studies. *Progress in Neuro-Psychopharmacology and Biological Psychiatry*, *21*(8), 1285–1295.

Keshavan, M. S., Sanders, R. D., Pettegrew, J. W., Dombrowsky, S. M., & Panchalingam, K. S. (1993). Frontal lobe metabolism and cerebral morphology in schizophrenia: 31P MRS and MRI studies. *Schizophrenia Research*, *10*(3), 241–246.

Keshavan, M. S., Stanley, J. A., Montrose, D. M., Minshew, N. J., & Pettegrew, J. W. (2003). Prefrontal membrane phospholipid metabolism of child and adolescent offspring at risk for schizophrenia or schizoaffective disorder: An in vivo 31P MRS study. *Molecular Psychiatry*, *8*(3), 316–323, 251.

Keshavan, M. S., Stanley, J. A., & Pettegrew, J. W. (2000). Magnetic resonance spectroscopy in schizophrenia: Methodological issues and findings—Part II. *Biological Psychiatry*, *48*(5), 369–380.

Keshavan, M. S., & Toone, B. S. (1988). Heterogeneity in sporadic schizophrenia. *British Journal of Psychiatry*, *152*, 573–575.

Kindermann, S. S., Karimi, A., Symonds, L., Brown, G. G., & Jeste, D. V. (1997). Review of functional magnetic resonance imaging in schizophrenia. *Schizophrenia Research*, *27*(2–3), 143–156.

Kobayashi, K., Fukuoka, T., Yamanaka, H., Dai, Y., Obata, K., Tokunaga, A., et al. (2006). Neurons and glial cells differentially express P2Y receptor mRNAs in the rat dorsal root ganglion and spinal cord. *Journal of Comparative Neurology*, *498*(4), 443–454.

Komulainen, P., Pedersen, M., Hanninen, T., Bruunsgaard, H., Lakka, T. A., Kivipelto, M., et al. (2008). BDNF is a novel marker of cognitive function in ageing women: The DR's EXTRA study. *Neurobiology of Learning and Memory*, *90*(4), 596–603.

Konopaske, G. T., Dorph-Petersen, K. A., Pierri, J. N., Wu, Q., Sampson, A. R., & Lewis, D. A. (2007). Effect of chronic exposure to antipsychotic medication on cell numbers in the parietal cortex of macaque monkeys. *Neuropsychopharmacology*, *32*(6), 1216–1223.

Konopaske, G. T., Dorph-Petersen, K. A., Sweet, R. A., Pierri, J. N., Zhang, W., Sampson, A. R., et al. (2008). Effect of chronic antipsychotic exposure on astrocyte and oligodendrocyte numbers in macaque monkeys. *Biological Psychiatry*, *63*(8), 759–765.

Kovalenko, S., Bergmann, A., Schneider-Axmann, T., Ovary, I., Majtenyi, K., Havas, L., et al. (2003). Regio entorhinalis in schizophrenia: More evidence for migrational disturbances and suggestions for a new biological hypothesis. *Pharmacopsychiatry*, *36*(Suppl. 3), S158–161.

Kovelman, J. A., & Scheibel, A. B. (1984). A neurohistological correlate of schizophrenia. *Biological Psychiatry*, *19*(12), 1601–1621.

Kreczmanski, P., Heinsen, H., Mantua, V., Woltersdorf, F., Masson, T., Ulfig, N., et al. (2007). Volume, neuron density and total neuron number in five subcortical regions in schizophrenia. *Brain*, *130*(3), 678–692.

Lacerda, A. L., Hardan, A. Y., Yorbik, O., Vemulapalli, M., Prasad, K. M., & Keshavan, M. S. (2007). Morphology of the orbitofrontal cortex in first-episode schizophrenia: Relationship with negative symptomatology. *Progress in Neuro-Psychopharmacology and Biological Psychiatry*, *31*(2), 510–516.

Lawrie, S. M., Whalley, H., Kestelman, J. N., Abukmeil, S. S., Byrne, M., Hodges, A., et al. (1999). Magnetic resonance imaging of brain in people at high risk of developing schizophrenia. *Lancet*, *353*(9146), 30–33.

Lewis, D. A., Cruz, D. A., Melchitzky, D. S., & Pierri, J. N. (2001). Lamina-specific deficits in parvalbumin-immunoreactive varicosities in the prefrontal cortex of subjects with schizophrenia: Evidence for fewer projections from the thalamus. *American Journal of Psychiatry*, *158*(9), 1411–1422.

Lewis, D. A., Glantz, L. A., Pierri, J. N., & Sweet, R. A. (2003). Altered cortical glutamate neurotransmission in schizophrenia: Evidence from morphological studies of pyramidal neurons. *Annals of the New York Academy of Sciences*, *1003*, 102–112.

Lewis, D. A., & Hashimoto, T. (2007). Deciphering the disease process of schizophrenia: The contribution of cortical GABA neurons. *International Review of Neurobiology*, *78*, 109–131.

Lewis, D. A., Hashimoto, T., & Volk, D. W. (2005). Cortical inhibitory neurons and schizophrenia. *Nature Reviews Neuroscience*, *6*(4), 312–324.

Lewis, D. A., Volk, D. W., & Hashimoto, T. (2004). Selective alterations in prefrontal cortical GABA neurotransmission in schizophrenia: A novel target for the treatment of working memory dysfunction. *Psychopharmacology (Berlin)*, *174*(1), 143–150.

Lieberman, J. A., Stroup, T. S., McEvoy, J. P., Swartz, M. S., Rosenheck, R. A., Perkins, D. O., et al. (2005). Effectiveness of antipsychotic drugs in patients with chronic schizophrenia. *New England Journal of Medicine*, *353*(12), 1209–1223.

Lieberman, J. A., Tollefson, G. D., Charles, C., Zipursky, R., Sharma, T., Kahn, R. S., et al. (2005). Antipsychotic drug effects on brain morphology in first-episode psychosis. *Archives of General Psychiatry*, *62*(4), 361–370.

Lindsley, C. W., Shipe, W. D., Wolkenberg, S. E., Theberge, C. R., Williams, D. L., Jr., Sur, C., et al. (2006). Progress towards validating the NMDA receptor hypofunction hypothesis of schizophrenia. *Current Topics in Medicinal Chemistry*, *6*(8), 771–785.

Lovick, T. A. (1993). The periaqueductal gray-rostral medulla connection in the defence reaction: Efferent pathways and descending control mechanisms. *Behavioral Brain Research*, *58*(1–2), 19–25.

Lu, B., & Martinowich, K. (2008). Cell biology of BDNF and its relevance to schizophrenia. *Novartis Foundation Symposium*, *289*, 119–129; discussion 129–135, 193–115.

Lv, Y. T., Yang, H., Wang, D. Y., Li, S. Y., Han, Y., Zhu, C. Z., et al. (2008). Correlations in spontaneous activity and gray matter density between left and right sensoritmotor areas of pianists. *NeuroReport*, *19*(6), 631–634.

Mane, A., Falcon, C., Mateos, J. J., Fernandez-Egea, E., Horga, G., Lomena, F., et al. (2009). Progressive gray matter changes in first episode schizophrenia: A 4-year longitudinal magnetic resonance study using VBM. *Schizophrenia Research*, *114*(1–3), 136–143.

Marin-Padilla, M., Tsai, R. J., King, M. A., & Roper, S. N. (2003). Altered corticogenesis and neuronal morphology in irradiation-induced cortical dysplasia: A Golgi-Cox study. *Journal of Neuropathology and Experimental Neurology*, *62*(11), 1129–1143.

Matute, C., Melone, M., Vallejo-Illarramendi, A., & Conti, F. (2005). Increased expression of the astrocytic glutamate transporter GLT-1 in the prefrontal cortex of schizophrenics. *Glia*, *49*(3), 451–455.

Meador-Woodruff, J. H., Clinton, S. M., Beneyto, M., & McCullumsmith, R. E. (2003). Molecular abnormalities of the glutamate synapse in the thalamus in schizophrenia. *Annals of New York Academy of Sciences*, *1003*, 75–93.

Meyer, K. D., & Morris, J. A. (2009). Disc1 regulates granule cell migration in the developing hippocampus. *Human Molecular Genetics*, *18*(17), 3286–3297.

Mitelman, S. A., Brickman, A. M., Shihabuddin, L., Newmark, R. E., Hazlett, E. A., Haznedar, M. M., et al. (2007). A comprehensive assessment of gray and white matter volumes and their relationship to outcome and severity in schizophrenia. *NeuroImage*, *37*(2), 449–462.

Muller, N., Myint, A. M., & Schwarz, M. J. (2009). The impact of neuroimmune dysregulation on neuroprotection and neurotoxicity in psychiatric disorders—Relation to drug treatment. *Dialogues in Clinical Neurosciences*, *11*(3), 319–332.

Muller, N., & Schwarz, M. J. (2008). COX-2 inhibition in schizophrenia and major depression. *Current Pharmaceutical Design*, *14*(14), 1452–1465.

Murray, R. M., Jones, P., & O'Callaghan, E. (1991). Fetal brain development and later schizophrenia. *Ciba Foundation Symposium*, *156*, 155–163; discussion 163–170.

Narr, K. L., Bilder, R. M., Toga, A. W., Woods, R. P., Rex, D. E., Szeszko, P. R., et al. (2005). Mapping cortical thickness and gray matter concentration in first episode schizophrenia. *Cerebral Cortex*, *15*(6), 708–719.

Nesvag, R., Frigessi, A., Jonsson, E. G., & Agartz, I. (2007). Effects of alcohol consumption and antipsychotic medication on brain morphology in schizophrenia. *Schizophrenia Research*, *90*(1–3), 52–61.

O'Donnell, B. F., Faux, S. F., McCarley, R. W., Kimble, M. O., Salisbury, D. F., Nestor, P. G., et al. (1995). Increased rate of P300 latency prolongation with age in schizophrenia. Electrophysiological evidence for a neurodegenerative process. *Archives of General Psychiatry*, *52*(7), 544–549.

Pantelis, C., Velakoulis, D., McGorry, P. D., Wood, S. J., Suckling, J., Phillips, L. J., et al. (2003). Neuroanatomical abnormalities before and after onset of psychosis: A cross-sectional and longitudinal MRI comparison. *Lancet*, *361*(9354), 281–288.

Papiol, S., Molina, V., Desco, M., Rosa, A., Reig, S., Gispert, J. D., et al. (2005). Ventricular enlargement in schizophrenia is associated with a genetic polymorphism at the interleukin-1 receptor antagonist gene. *NeuroImage*, *27*(4), 1002–1006.

Park, H. J., Lee, J. D., Chun, J. W., Seok, J. H., Yun, M., Oh, M. K., et al. (2006). Cortical surface-based analysis of 18F-FDG PET: Measured metabolic abnormalities in schizophrenia are affected by cortical structural abnormalities. *NeuroImage*, *31*(4), 1434–1444.

Parlapani, E., Schmitt, A., Erdmann, A., Bernstein, H. G., Breunig, B., Gruber, O., et al. (2009). Association between myelin basic protein expression and left entorhinal cortex pre-alpha cell layer disorganization in schizophrenia. *Brain Research*, *1301*, 126–134.

Pierri, J. N., Volk, C. L., Auh, S., Sampson, A., & Lewis, D. A. (2001). Decreased somal size of deep layer 3 pyramidal neurons in the prefrontal cortex of subjects with schizophrenia. *Archives of General Psychiatry*, *58*(5), 466–473.

Pierri, J. N., Volk, C. L., Auh, S., Sampson, A., & Lewis, D. A. (2003). Somal size of prefrontal cortical pyramidal neurons in schizophrenia: Differential effects across neuronal subpopulations. *Biological Psychiatry*, *54*(2), 111–120.

Pillai, A., & Mahadik, S. P. (2006). Differential effects of haloperidol and olanzapine on levels of vascular endothelial growth factor and angiogenesis in rat hippocampus. *Schizophrenia Research*, *87*(1–3), 48–59.

Plum, F. (1972). Prospects for research on schizophrenia. 3. Neurophysiology. Neuropathological findings. *Neurosciences Research Program Bulletin*, *10*(4), 384–388.

Prasad, K. M., Sahni, S. D., Rohm, B. R., & Keshavan, M. S. (2005). Dorsolateral prefrontal cortex morphology and short-term outcome in first-episode schizophrenia. *Psychiatry Research*, *140*(2), 147–155.

Qi, L. Y., Xiu, M. H., Chen da, C., Wang, F., Kosten, T. A., Kosten, T. R., et al. (2009). Increased serum S100B levels in chronic schizophrenic patients on long-term clozapine or typical antipsychotics. *Neuroscience Letters*, *462*(2), 113–117.

Rajkowska, G., Selemon, L. D., & Goldman-Rakic, P. S. (1998). Neuronal and glial somal size in the prefrontal cortex: A postmortem morphometric study of schizophrenia and Huntington disease. *Archives of General Psychiatry*, *55*(3), 215–224.

Reilly, J. L., Harris, M. S., Khine, T. T., Keshavan, M. S., & Sweeney, J. A. (2007). Antipsychotic drugs exacerbate impairment on a working memory task in first-episode schizophrenia. *Biological Psychiatry*, *62*(7), 818–821.

Reveley, A. M., Reveley, M. A., Clifford, C. A., & Murray, R. M. (1982). Cerebral ventricular size in twins discordant for schizophrenia. *Lancet*, *1*(8271), 540–541.

Reveley, A. M., Reveley, M. A., & Murray, R. M. (1983). Enlargement of cerebral ventricles in schizophrenics is confined to those without known genetic predisposition [letter]. *Lancet*, *2*(8348), 525.

Reveley, A. M., Reveley, M. A., & Murray, R. M. (1984). Cerebral ventricular enlargement in non-genetic schizophrenia: A controlled twin study. *British Journal of Psychiatry*, *144*, 89–93.

Rioux, L., Nissanov, J., Lauber, K., Bilker, W. B., & Arnold, S. E. (2003). Distribution of microtubule-associated protein MAP2-immunoreactive interstitial neurons in the parahippocampal white matter in subjects with schizophrenia. *American Journal of Psychiatry*, *160*(1), 149–155.

Rosoklija, G., Keilp, J. G., Toomayan, G., Mancevski, B., Haroutunian, V., Liu, D., et al. (2005). Altered subicular MAP2 immunoreactivity in schizophrenia. *Prilozi*, *26*(2), 13–34.

Schmitt, A., Bertsch, T., Henning, U., Tost, H., Klimke, A., Henn, F. A., et al. (2005). Increased serum S100B in elderly, chronic schizophrenic patients: Negative correlation with deficit symptoms. *Schizophrenia Research*, *80*(2–3), 305–313.

Schmitt, A., Parlapani, E., Gruber, O., Wobrock, T., & Falkai, P. (2008). Impact of neuregulin-1 on the pathophysiology of schizophrenia in human post-mortem studies. *European Archives of Psychiatry Clinical Neurosciences*, *258*(Suppl. 5), 35–39.

Seeman, P. (2009). Glutamate and dopamine components in schizophrenia. *Journal of Psychiatry Neurosciences*, *34*(2), 143–149.

Seeman, P., & Guan, H. C. (2009). Glutamate agonists for treating schizophrenia have affinity for dopamine D2High and D3 receptors. *Synapse*, *63*(8), 705–709.

Selemon, L. D., Mrzljak, J., Kleinman, J. E., Herman, M. M., & Goldman-Rakic, P. S. (2003). Regional specificity in the neuropathologic substrates of schizophrenia: A morphometric analysis of Broca's area 44 and area 9. *Archives of General Psychiatry*, *60*(1), 69–77.

Selemon, L. D., Rajkowska, G., & Goldman-Rakic, P. S. (1998). Elevated neuronal density in prefrontal area 46 in brains from schizophrenic patients: Application of a three-dimensional, stereologic counting method. *Journal of Comprehensive Neurology*, *392*(3), 402–412.

Shenton, M. E., Dickey, C. C., Frumin, M., & McCarley, R. W. (2001). A review of MRI findings in schizophrenia. *Schizophrenia Research*, *49*(1–2), 1–52.

Smith, R. E., Haroutunian, V., Davis, K. L., & Meador-Woodruff, J. H. (2001a). Expression of excitatory amino acid transporter transcripts in the thalamus of subjects with schizophrenia. *American Journal of Psychiatry*, *158*(9), 1393–1399.

Smith, R. E., Haroutunian, V., Davis, K. L., & Meador-Woodruff, J. H. (2001b). Vesicular glutamate transporter transcript expression in the thalamus in schizophrenia. *NeuroReport*, *12*(13), 2885–2887.

Suarez, J., Llorente, R., Romero-Zerbo, S. Y., Mateos, B., Bermudez-Silva, F. J., de Fonseca, F. R., et al. (2009). Early maternal deprivation induces gender-dependent changes on the expression of hippocampal CB(1) and CB(2) cannabinoid receptors of neonatal rats. *Hippocampus*, *19*(7), 623–632.

Sun, J., Maller, J. J., Guo, L., & Fitzgerald, P. B. (2009). Superior temporal gyrus volume change in schizophrenia: A review on region of interest volumetric studies. *Brain Research Review*, *61*(1), 14–32.

Sweet, R. A., Bergen, S. E., Sun, Z., Sampson, A. R., Pierri, J. N., & Lewis, D. A. (2004). Pyramidal cell size reduction in schizophrenia: Evidence for involvement of auditory feedforward circuits. *Biological Psychiatry*, *55*(12), 1128–1137.

Szeszko, P. R., Lipsky, R., Mentschel, C., Robinson, D., Gunduz-Bruce, H., Sevy, S., et al. (2005). Brain-derived neurotrophic factor val66met polymorphism and volume of the hippocampal formation. *Molecular Psychiatry*, *10*(7), 631–636.

Tabares-Seisdedos, R., Escamez, T., Martinez-Gimenez, J. A., Balanza, V., Salazar, J., Selva, G., et al. (2006). Variations in genes regulating neuronal migration predict reduced prefrontal cognition in schizophrenia and bipolar subjects from mediterranean Spain: A preliminary study. *Neuroscience*, *139*(4), 1289–1300.

Takahashi, T., Suzuki, M., Tanino, R., Zhou, S. Y., Hagino, H., Niu, L., et al. (2007). Volume reduction of the left planum temporale gray matter associated with long duration of untreated psychosis in schizophrenia: A preliminary report. *Psychiatry Research*, *154*(3), 209–219.

Tanaka, S. (2006). Dopaminergic control of working memory and its relevance to schizophrenia: A circuit dynamics perspective. *Neuroscience*, *139*(1), 153–171.

Thompson, P., Cannon, T. D., & Toga, A. W. (2002). Mapping genetic influences on human brain structure. *Annals of Medicine*, *34*(7–8), 523–536.

Thompson, P. M., Sower, A. C., & Perrone-Bizzozero, N. I. (1998). Altered levels of the synaptosomal associated protein SNAP-25 in schizophrenia. *Biological Psychiatry*, *43*(4), 239–243.

Torrey, E. F., Barci, B. M., Webster, M. J., Bartko, J. J., Meador-Woodruff, J. H., & Knable, M. B. (2005). Neurochemical markers for schizophrenia, bipolar disorder, and major depression in postmortem brains. *Biological Psychiatry*, *57*(3), 252–260.

Varnas, K., Lawyer, G., Jonsson, E. G., Kulle, B., Nesvag, R., Hall, H., et al. (2008). Brain-derived neurotrophic factor polymorphisms and frontal cortex morphology in schizophrenia. *Psychiatric Genetics*, *18*(4), 177–183.

Vercellino, M., Masera, S., Lorenzatti, M., Condello, C., Merola, A., Mattioda, A., et al. (2009). Demyelination, inflammation, and neurodegeneration in multiple sclerosis deep gray matter. *Journal of Neuropathology and Experimental Neurology*, *68*(5), 489–502.

Vinogradov, S., Fisher, M., Holland, C., Shelly, W., Wolkowitz, O., & Mellon, S. H. (2009). Is serum brain-derived neurotrophic factor a biomarker for cognitive enhancement in schizophrenia? *Biological Psychiatry*, *66*(6), 549–553.

Vogel, T., & Lange, H. J. (1966). [Pneumoencephalographic and psychopathological pictures in endogenous psychoses. Statistical study on the material published by G. Huber in 1957]. *Archive für Psychiatrie und Nervenkrankheiten*, *208*(4), 371–384.

Wakita, H., Tomimoto, H., Akiguchi, I., Matsuo, A., Lin, J. X., Ihara, M., et al. (2002). Axonal damage and demyelination in the white matter after chronic cerebral hypoperfusion in the rat. *Brain Research*, *924*(1), 63–70.

Watis, L., Chen, S. H., Chua, H. C., Chong, S. A., & Sim, K. (2008). Glutamatergic abnormalities of the thalamus in schizophrenia: A systematic review. *Journal of Neural Transmission*, *115*(3), 493–511.

Webster, M. J., Shannon Weickert, C., Herman, M. M., Hyde, T. M., & Kleinman, J. E. (2001). Synaptophysin and GAP-43 mRNA levels in the hippocampus of subjects with schizophrenia. *Schizophrenia Research*, *49*(1–2), 89–98.

Weinberger, D. R. (1999). Cell biology of the hippocampal formation in schizophrenia. *Biological Psychiatry*, *45*(4), 395–402.

White, L. J., & Castellano, V. (2008). Exercise and brain health—Implications for multiple sclerosis: Part 1—Neuronal growth factors. *Sports Medicine*, *38*(2), 91–100.

Winter, B., Breitenstein, C., Mooren, F. C., Voelker, K., Fobker, M., Lechtermann, A., et al. (2007). High impact running improves learning. *Neurobiology of Learning and Memory*, *87*(4), 597–609.

Winterer, G. (2006). Cortical microcircuits in schizophrenia—The dopamine hypothesis revisited. *Pharmacopsychiatry*, *39*(Suppl. 1), S68–71.

Winterer, G., & Weinberger, D. R. (2004). Genes, dopamine and cortical signal-to-noise ratio in schizophrenia. *Trends in Neuroscience*, *27*(11), 683–690.

Wood, J. D., Bonath, F., Kumar, S., Ross, C. A., & Cunliffe, V. T. (2009). Disrupted-in-schizophrenia 1 and neuregulin 1 are required for the specification of oligodendrocytes and neurones in the zebrafish brain. *Human Molecular Genetics*, *18*(3), 391–404.

Wright, I. C., Ellison, Z. R., Sharma, T., Friston, K. J., Murray, R. M., & McGuire, P. K. (1999). Mapping of grey matter changes in schizophrenia. *Schizophrenia Research*, *35*(1), 1–14.

Wright, I. C., Rabe-Hesketh, S., Woodruff, P. W., David, A. S., Murray, R. M., & Bullmore, E. T. (2000). Meta-analysis of regional brain volumes in schizophrenia. *American Journal of Psychiatry*, *157*(1), 16–25.

Wright, I. C., Sharma, T., Ellison, Z. R., McGuire, P. K., Friston, K. J., Brammer, M. J., et al. (1999). Supra-regional brain systems and the neuropathology of schizophrenia. *Cerebral Cortex*, *9*(4), 366–378.

Young, C. E., Arima, K., Xie, J., Hu, L., Beach, T. G., Falkai, P., et al. (1998). SNAP-25 deficit and hippocampal connectivity in schizophrenia. *Cerebral Cortex*, *8*(3), 261–268.

Zakzanis, K. K., Poulin, P., Hansen, K. T., & Jolic, D. (2000). Searching the schizophrenic brain for temporal lobe deficits: A systematic review and meta-analysis. *Psychological Medicine*, *30*(3), 491–504.

Part IV

Genetics

13 A short (and partial) history of genetics at the Institute of Psychiatry

Peter McGuffin

The principal aim of this chapter is to give an overview of the history of genetics at the Institute of Psychiatry with a special emphasis on the role, over the past three decades, of Robin Murray. However, in order to set this in its proper context it is necessary to go back a little further and take a look at the history of the comparatively new science of genetics and the beginnings of its applications in the study of mental disorders.

The beginnings of psychiatric genetics

The notion that mental disorders have a tendency to run in families is almost certainly an ancient one. However, the first recorded examples that I have been able to find of doctors systematically noting their psychiatrically ill patients' family histories come from the Bethlem Royal Hospital Museum. Here one can see the "front sheets" of patients case notes dating from 1823 when the hospital began to require the admitting doctor to fill in a box entitled "whether hereditary". The idea evidently caught on. For example, on a recent visit to St Andrews Hospital in Northampton I was able to view case notes from 1838, the year the hospital was opened as the Northamptonshire County General Lunatic Asylum, where the front sheets posed exactly the same question. These are examples, then, of the prehistory of psychiatric genetics, for it was in the time before doctors specializing in mental illness were yet known as psychiatrists and some years before genetics came into being as a branch of the biological sciences. Indeed, the term "genetics" did not even exist until coined by the English biologist William Bateson (1861–1926) in 1905.

Bateson invented the name, genetics, for a new and burgeoning field that had been stimulated by the rediscovery in 1900 of Gregor Mendel's research papers. These had been published more than 30 years earlier but had been virtually completely ignored by his fellow biologists. Bateson also proposed the terms heterozygote and homozygote for individuals carrying one of each or two of the same "elements", as Mendel called them, that underlie a trait. A little later, in 1908, the Danish biologist Wilhelm Johannesson invented the term "gene" for Mendel's elements and was the first to distinguish between observed phenotypes and the inferred, at that time unmeasurable, genotypes.

Almost certainly one of the reasons why Mendel's discoveries had not caught on earlier was that his studies focused on dichotomous traits in plants (e.g., smooth versus wrinkled peas) whereas, most individual difference within human and other animal species appear quantitative (e.g., height, weight). The great proponent of studies of the inheritance of quantitative traits was the English polymath (and one-time medical student at Denmark Hill) Francis Galton (1822–1911), who founded the National eugenics laboratory at University College London in 1904. Galton and his followers such as Karl Pearson (1857–1936) also founded modern statistics and behavioural genetics and were at first antagonistic to Mendelism, which they thought was incompatible with their biometric approach to quantitative traits. This remained the case until R. A. Fisher (1890–1962) brilliantly showed, in a paper published in 1918—the first exposition on polygenic inheritance, that such traits could in fact result from the combined small effects of multiple genes acting in a way that was compatible with Mendelian laws (Fisher, 1918).

The systematic study of what we now call psychiatric genetics began in earnest around the same time in 1917 when the German Research Institute for Psychiatry (*Deutsche Forschungsanstalt fur Psychiatrie*) was established in Munich. Its founding director was Emil Kraepelin (1856–1926). Kraepelin is of course remembered as the father of the modern classification of psychiatric disorders and his writings remain influential in current schemes such as ICD-10 (World Health Organization, 1992) and DSM-IV (American Psychiatric Association, 1994). However, in his work at the Universities of Heidelberg and, later, Munich he also laid the basis for a distinctly biomedical model of psychiatry, rooted in new areas such as neurobiology and genetics.

One of Kraepelin's protégés at Heidelberg was Alois Alzheimer (1864–1915), after whom the illness is named, and who first described its characteristic neuropathology. Kraepelin's dream was that all mental illness would eventually turn out to be like Alzheimer's disease with specific chemical and/or anatomical abnormalities being discovered for each of the major categories of disorder. He also saw great potential in the new science of genetics and Ernst Rüdin (1874–1952), who in 1916 had published the first large-scale study looking at the familial transmission of schizophrenia (Rüdin, 1916), was placed in charge of the "genealogical-demographic department" of Kraepelin's institute. In the years between the two world wars this department, the world's first devoted to psychiatric genetics, thrived, producing the first twin studies in psychiatry and attracting many of the brightest visiting fellows from other countries. One of these was Eliot Slater (1904–1983).

Genetics at the Maudsley

Aubrey Lewis (1900–1975) was the dominant intellectual star when the young Dr Eliot Slater arrived to commence his postgraduate psychiatric training in 1931 (Gottesman & McGuffin, 1996). Lewis was a great admirer of the Munich Institute and saw that, if the Maudsley Hospital was ever going to rival Munich, it would need to develop technical expertise in a range of areas including genetics. Together with Edward Mapother (1881–1940), then medical superintendent of the Maudsley, Lewis encouraged Slater to apply for a Rockefeller foundation Fellowship to study genetics in Munich. The application was successful and Slater set off for Germany in the autumn of 1934. In Munich he carried out one of the first case-notes-based family studies of bipolar disorder (then called manic-depressive insanity) and introduced the innovation of having judges rate case histories in a "blindfold" fashion. He developed his new skills rapidly and when Slater returned to the Maudsley in 1936 he received a grant from the Medical Research Council (MRC) to perform a twin study.

Slater's progress was in spite of the fact that he scarcely met his head of department in the Munich Institute, Ernst Rüdin. This was perhaps just as well since Rüdin was a staunch supporter of the National Socialist (Nazi) party while Slater liked to fraternize with Jewish intellectuals, one of whom, Lydia Pasternak, sister of the novelist Boris Pasternak, he married. Rüdin was also a convinced eugenicist and became a major figure in the German racial hygiene movement. Subsequent atrocities by the Nazis in the name of eugenics had enormous repercussions for the image of psychiatric genetics, which virtually ceased to exist as a branch of science in Germany and much of mainland Europe in the aftermath of World War II (1939–1945).

The war also interrupted the further development of genetics at the Maudsley as the hospital evacuated to two sites away from inner London, at Sutton under the leadership of Lewis and at Mill Hill under Slater. The next major Slater study was the now classic investigation of psychotic and neurotic illness in twins, commenced in 1947 with the assistance of a new research worker, James (Jerry) Shields (1918–1978). Shields had an, at first sight, unlikely background for such a post, having been trained as a social worker. However, he was to become a highly influential figure in psychiatric and behavioural genetics, going on to publish a classic study of volunteer twins reared together and apart (Shields, 1962) and later key studies and theoretical papers with Irving Gottesman on schizophrenia.

The year after Shields' arrival, 1948, three important events took place. The Maudsley Hospital Medical School was renamed the Institute of Psychiatry and became a founding member of the British Postgraduate Medical Federation (along with the Institute of Neurology and several other sister institutes in London). The Maudsley amalgamated with the Bethlem Royal Hospital (founded 1247) to form the "Joint Hospital" and the Maudsley Twin Register was established. The idea of the latter was simple in essence; every patient registered at the Joint Hospital was asked, "Are you a twin?" and if they answered yes and their twin was alive they were entered on the register. The Twin Register formed the basis for many subsequent postgraduate theses and important published papers. (Slater's only real oversight was in not registering opposite-sex dizygotic twins. This was because there was at that time no established statistical method for analysing such data and combining them with same-sex twin data.)

Slater's group gradually expanded to include Valerie Cowie, a psychiatrist specializing in mental handicap who was also trained at the Galton Laboratory (as the Eugenics Institute came to be known), University College London, in the new field of cytogenetics. There were also small numbers of non-medically qualified research assistants who were invariably women and paid on secretarial grades. In 1959 the MRC thought that the group had sufficiently become a going concern for it to be made into the MRC Psychiatric Genetics Unit. The unit was housed in modest prefabricated building, ever after known as the "Genetics Hut", which was intended to be temporary, but which long outlived the MRC Unit itself, being eventually demolished in 1989.

The unit was never large. There were only three senior staff, Slater, Cowie and Shields, but it was one of the few research units of its kind in the world and it attracted many academic visitors from overseas. Notable among these were Ming T. Tsuang, a psychiatrist from Taiwan who came to do a PhD with Slater on a sibling study of schizophrenia (Tsuang, 1967), and Irving I. Gottesman, a post-doctoral fellow from the United States who with James Shields completed a landmark twin study of schizophrenia (Shields & Gottesman, 1972). Gottesman and Shields (Gottesman & Shields, 1967) also went on to apply a polygenic-threshold model of schizophrenia using an approach model proposed by the Edinburgh geneticist D. S. Falconer (1913–2004; Falconer, 1965). This was effectively an update of the Fisher approach, mentioned earlier, but adapted for "all or nothing" traits such as being affected or unaffected by schizophrenia. Formal statistical methods for testing the fit of models did not really exist at this time but the Gottesman–Shields application appeared very plausible and for the first time provided estimates, under varying assumptions, of the heritability of schizophrenia, i.e., the proportion of variation in liability attributable to genes. These were uniformly high and of this Slater must surely have approved for he was convinced of the very substantial genetic contribution to the disorder. To Slater's credit he appears not to have objected to Gottesman and Shields' high-profile advocacy of polygenic inheritance despite the fact that it was in direct contradiction of his own hypothesis that the inheritance of schizophrenia could be explained by a single gene with incomplete penetrance (Slater, 1958).

Interestingly, Slater did not welcome all potential academic visitors with open arms. The late Theodore (Ted) Reich (1938–2003) used to tell of how he wrote a letter of application to Slater in 1967, or thereabouts, asking if he could join his unit as a visiting fellow fully funded by the United States National Institutes of Health (NIH). Slater turned him down and Reich instead began his illustrious research career in psychiatric genetics by going to Edinburgh to study with D. S. Falconer. Slater's reluctance to take on a new fellow was perhaps because he was approaching the usual age of retirement for MRC Directors, 65. When he reached retirement in 1969 the MRC decided not to appoint a new director and instead closed the unit. Soon after this Valerie Cowie left and James Shields was now the only remaining member of staff of what then became a section of the Institute's Department of Psychiatry.

The 1970s

Almost inevitably the next few years were a period of decline for genetics at the Maudsley. The often brilliant but always modest and self-effacing Shields was no empire builder and social psychiatry was the ascendant and fashionable discipline. The centres of gravity for psychiatric genetics were now all in the USA. Opinion among many leading American psychiatric researchers had turned in favour of genetics in the 1960s and early 1970s with publication of adoption studies of schizophrenia by Heston (1966) based in Oregon and the US–Danish studies led by Kety, Rosenthal, Wender, and Schulsinger (1968). These showed, in ways that many found more tangible than twin studies, that schizophrenia is substantially genetic.

Gottesman had returned to work at the University of Minnesota, where he helped establish in the Department of Psychology one of the most influential behaviour genetics groups in the USA. Tsuang had moved to the University of Iowa where he established a very successful research programme in the Psychiatry Department led by one of the then champions of biological psychiatry, George Winokur. Ted Reich went back to Washington University, St Louis, where he set about building up one of the largest critical masses of talented psychiatric genetics researchers anywhere with a particular emphasis on developing quantitative methods led by, for example John Rice, Brian Suarez and Robert Cloninger. Around the same time a highly successful section was set up by an Elliot Gershon at the National Institute of Mental Health (NIMH) at Bethesda. Indeed, in the mid-to-late 1970s the NIMH was the place to be in biological psychiatry for any aspiring clinician scientist and one of the most promising of these from the UK was Robin Murray who obtained leave of absence from his senior registrar training at the Maudsley to visit the USA as a Lilly MRC Travelling Fellow in 1977.

Meanwhile the decline of psychiatric genetics in the UK had been noted by senior figures and it seemed sufficiently concerning that an internal working party was set up at the institute in 1975 and a national working party was convened by the MRC in 1977. The MRC working party concluded that the MRC should "encourage promising research workers to put forward specific research proposals" and that an "earmarked" training fellowship should be set up (Murray, 1979).

In March of the same year, 1977, I arrived at the Joint Hospital as a senior house officer to join the psychiatry training scheme. I had already spent two years after house jobs in Leeds training in internal medicine followed by just over a year in psychiatry there. During a period working on the coronary care unit at St James's Hospital, Leeds, I became involved in a study on myocardial infarction looking at the possible aetiological role of food antibodies and the moderating effects of human leukocyte antigen (HLA) type (Scott, McGuffin, Rajah, Stoker, & Losowsky, 1976; Scott, McGuffin, Swinburne, & Losowsky, 1976). The results were entirely negative but I became intrigued by the HLA system and its associations with other common diseases. When I switched to psychiatry my wife, Anne Farmer (already a trainee psychiatrist), and I designed a study with the generous support of Dr S. M. Rajah, who ran the Leeds HLA lab, to look at schizophrenia. The study seemed promising. There were speculations at the time that schizophrenia might involve immunological disturbances and a group from Milan had already had the same idea and had published a paper on HLA and schizophrenia in the *British Journal of Psychiatry* (Smeraldi, Bellodi, Sacchetti, & Cazzullo, 1976).

By the time I moved to the Maudsley our association study paper was already in press, also in the *British Journal of Psychiatry* (McGuffin, Farmer, & Rajah,

1978), and I determined to follow this up for my MPhil. The problem was who could I persuade to be my supervisor? Only James Shields had expressed genuine interest in our HLA paper when it came out but he was reluctant to offer supervision. Always frail, his health was deteriorating and he died later that same year.

My only remaining hope was Paul Mullen, a clinical lecturer on the Metabolic Ward in Mapother House wing of the Maudsley where I was then based. Mullen had the most impressive grasp of biological psychiatry of any of the rising stars around the Maudsley at that time, early 1978, and he agreed to take me on, on the basis that I was not to hold him to task as an expert on the finer points of genetics and the HLA system. It was a good partnership and my MPhil part one essay, which contained what nowadays would be called a meta-analysis of the handful of published association studies and a proposal to do a linkage study, was well received by the examiners—although, as I have reported elsewhere (McGuffin, Owen, O'Donovan, Thapar, & Gottesman, 1994), one very eminent social psychiatrist discouragingly remarked that it was all "very arcane".

It was about this time that Robin Murray, who I had never previously met, returned to the UK to resume a position as senior registrar. A little later two vacancies arose for clinical senior lectureships at the Institute. Paul Mullen was appointed to one and Robin Murray to the other. Mullen at this stage suggested that I should go and talk to Murray about my research plans with a view to Murray taking over as my supervisor. Murray, said Mullen, although not a card-carrying geneticist, had much more specialist interest and knowledge about the field than he did. Professor Sir Denis Hill, the Head of the Department of Psychiatry, obviously had the same idea because soon after James Shields' sad demise Murray was called in to the professor's office. Hill invited him to take over as head of the now virtually defunct Genetics Section and to produce a written plan for its redevelopment.

The renaissance of the Genetics Section

The Murray proposals, dated January 1979, were set out in a succinct three sides of A4 (Murray, 1979). The document started off by noting the reports of the recent institute and MRC working parties and Murray's own findings in "informal discussions within the institute" of "no overtly expressed opposition to the idea that the Institute should continue to have a genetic section or sub-section". He noted that in general the Institute's resources concerning genetics were "somewhat meagre" but that we did have a psychologist, David Fulker (1937–1998), who was an international authority on statistical genetics (a fact probably unrecognized at that stage by anyone else in the Department of Psychiatry). The Maudsley twin register was an obvious asset that needed to be kept going and was then being supervised in her semi-retirement by Vera Seal, one of the "secretaries"/research workers from the MRC Unit days. It would also be important, said Dr Murray, to respond to the MRC working party's proposal for a research training fellowship by finding a suitable candidate. There were, he noted, not many around "but we are fortunate in that Dr P. McGriffin [sic] who is currently a senior registrar at the Joint Hospital has a long-standing interest in genetics and would like such a training".

It was my turn to be called in by Sir Denis, who instructed me that I was to phone the MRC and request the application forms for a training fellowship. I duly did so and completed the forms with Robin Murray's guidance, and I also followed up on his suggestions that I should apprentice myself part-time to David Fulker, who was then running the animal lab at the Royal Bethlem Hospital, the hospital where I was coincidentally based as a senior registrar. I should also try to visit Cedric ("CO") Carter (1917–1984), one of the doyennes of UK clinical genetics and director of the MRC Unit at Great Ormond Street. I did so and he was kindly encouraging. My other mentor at this stage was Professor Hilliard ("H") Festenstein (1930–1989) who headed the Major Histocompatibility Antigens (MHC) Group at the Royal London Hospital and who invited me to talk about my proposed study at one of his lab meetings and subsequently offered me collaboration and training should my MRC application be successful. I was duly interviewed by the MRC panel with CO Carter being the main inquisitor and was offered a fellowship, which was to be spent partly at major genetics centres in London and partly in the USA (both part of the Murray document's proposals).

The other two major proposals in the Murray document were that a three-year lectureship should be set up for a basic scientist with expertise in "biological markers" who would be a link person between the genetics section and the Department of Neurochemistry and that there "should be closer liaison between the proposed genetic section (or sub-section) and Dr Fulker's group in Psychology" (with whom Murray was already jointly supervising a PhD student). The other request and the only one to have major cost implications apart from the temporary lecturer was for a half-time secretary. Despite the fact the Murray proposals were drawn up in the middle of the Callaghan government's "winter of discontent" (when the UK was in an economic turmoil that felt much worse to most than the recent recession), they received the go ahead from Sir Denis and the one and a half new posts were funded. Iain Campbell, a young biochemist and fellow Scot who Robin had met at NIMH, was appointed to the lecturer post and Maureen Titmuss became our new half-time secretary.

Everything then began to move remarkably swiftly. By the time I took up my MRC fellowship and moved into the Hut in October 1979 it was nearly full. Christine Clifford, Fulker and Murray's PhD student, had been given a desk. She was a bright psychology graduate who after a spell of bad luck had really landed on her feet. The bad luck was that shortly after starting an animal behaviour genetic study at Fulker's Bethlem laboratory she had begun coming out in rashes. It turned out that she was horribly allergic to the rodents she was studying and needed a rapid change of project. The good fortune was that Fulker and Murray were just in the process of designing a twin study of obsessionality and neuroticism, the first study of its kind, with the aim of applying up-to-the-minute model fitting. This led not only to Clifford's thesis but to some oft-cited papers (e.g., Clifford, Murray, & Fulker, 1984).

The other new arrivals, each with their own office, were two young psychiatrists of about my own vintage, Hugh Gurling and Adrienne Reveley. Gurling I knew well as a near contemporary of mine on the Maudsley training scheme. He was employed on a new grant of Murray's as a research senior registrar to perform a twin study of alcoholism using the Maudsley twin register. Reveley, an Anglo-Irish medical graduate of Trinity College Dublin, had recently completed her postgraduate psychiatric training at Washington University, St Louis, and, while a chief resident there, had become interested in genetics. She was at this stage exploring the possibilities for a Wellcome Trust or MRC fellowship and was veering toward a new twin study of schizophrenia.

I also was given my own office. This was a great privilege for a senior registrar-level researcher at the Institute in those days and I felt very proud, especially when I noted on the sunny autumn day that I entered the Hut that it was one of the larger individual offices and just next to the entrance. My pride turned to dismay a few days later when it began to rain and I discovered that my office was the one with the leakiest roof. This required strategic placement of buckets and other containers around the room and books, files and papers that could be potentially damaged had to be stored in the dry spots. The other unnerving experience was that the floor of the office had a habit of buckling slightly whenever anyone entered through the front door of the Hut. I went to see Dr Murray who himself had a proper, if modest, office in the main building. He advised me to be patient and that he was doing all he could to address the lamentable state of repair of the Hut. Eventually we were visited by the dean, Dr Jim Birley, who pronounced the Hut uninhabitable and in need of refurbishment. As a result, the Hut researchers were decanted to the primate house next door. This was also a prefabricated building but in a much better state than the Genetics Hut. Why were there no nonhuman primates living there? The Home Office had recently declared it to be substandard accommodation in which to house experimental animals and ordered that the monkeys should be given somewhere better to live. We human primates, on the other hand, found our dry, warm, temporary home to be the embodiment of luxury.

Meanwhile, research progressed well. Gurling's twin study of alcoholism was well underway and he was successful in gaining a Wellcome Trust Fellowship, part of which was to be spent in the USA. My own collection of families multiply affected by schizophrenia was also running nicely and, partly on Adrienne Reveley's advice, I managed to enrol on a set of courses that she herself had earlier taken at the Galton laboratory. These proved invaluable and enabled me to introduce myself to the late Dr Peter Cook who was then running the MRC Biochemical Genetics Unit, one of the best genetic marker/linkage analysis labs in the world, and he agreed to help me extend my study to include nearly 30 other polymorphisms in addition to HLA. Another spin-off of working next to Dr Reveley was an overlap between her work on expanding the Maudsley schizophrenia twin studies and my own family-linkage studies. One of the families that I came across was in her series too. It contained a set of triplets (the "Z triplets") one of whom had been treated mainly at the Maudsley and had been diagnosed as manic depressive while the other two, mainly treated at hospitals elsewhere, had been diagnosed as schizophrenic. They looked identical and we subsequently showed by statistically analysing the blood group markers typed in Ruth Sanger's (1918–2001) lab at the Galton Laboratory, that they were indeed monozygotic. If we had the diagnoses "correct" then anything we wrote on the Z triplets would represent either a heretical challenge or a black swan (depending on whether one takes a religious or a Popperian stance on Kraepelin's dichotomy). We showed the diagnoses were descriptively accurate by performing two types of research interview, the Present State Examination (PSE) and the Schedule for Affective Disorders and Schizophrenia (SADS), and by having abstracts, interspersed with "dummy" abstracts, blindly rated by experts. The paper, written jointly with a new recruit to the Hut, Tony Holland, provoked some interest when it was first published (McGuffin, Reveley, & Holland, 1982) but enjoyed a new lease of life more recently when the updated twin study evidence began to converge with molecular genetic studies showing a marked overlap genetically between schizophrenia and bipolar disorder (Craddock, O'Donovan, & Owen, 2006).

However another study around this time that achieved much more contemporary exposure was a joint brainwave between Drs Murray and Reveley. Computerized Tomographic brain scanning was all the rage in the early 1980s with most studies confirming the original finding of Johnstone, Crow, Frith, Husband, and Kreel (1976) that schizophrenics have larger lateral cerebral ventricles than controls. Was this genetic or environmental or a combination of two? The answer was unknown until Reveley, Reveley, and Murray (1983) published their results on identical twins discordant for diagnosis of schizophrenia where it was clear that enlarged ventricles were found only in the affected twins suggesting that the enlargement was a result of the disease process rather than genetic predisposition.

New directions: Molecular genetics and gene–environment interplay

In 1981 I moved to the United States to complete part of my MRC fellowship, as planned, at Washington University, St Louis. Some months later, Hugh Gurling made his journey to Stanford University to complete the overseas part his Wellcome Trust Fellowship. To each of us remarkable things happened. Gurling, who had previously been doing a twin study, became engrossed in molecular genetics whereas I, until then a dyed-in-the-wool genetic markers researcher, became entranced with quantitative genetics, which was all round me at "Wash U". Washington University had now recruited Irv Gottesman to add to their array of quantitative talent in the psychiatry department and there were regular joint seminars with the Mathematics Department and the Biostatistics Department, headed by D. C. Rao. I had taken all of my linkage data from London with me and had been working through the analyses, as one did in those days, using pencil and paper, a hand-held calculator and a set of tables. I also had help and advice from Brian Suarez, who was the linkage expert at Wash U and whose papers I had studied while I was still in London. Suarez introduced me to the LIPED program written in FORTRAN by Jurg Ott. I had heard about LIPED and had had some discussions about using it, or her own FORTRAN programme, with Elizabeth Sturt, a statistician who worked in the MRC Social Psychiatry Unit at the Institute of Psychiatry. However now was a chance to actually apply LIPED, as far as I knew for the first time, on a psychiatric data set.

My data (McGuffin, Festenstein, & Murray, 1983) consisted entirely of what are now called "classical markers", HLA and blood types and various protein polymorphisms that could be measured in peripheral blood. But now the "New Genetics" (Comings, 1980) of DNA markers was suddenly upon us. These consisted of potentially hundreds of restriction fragment length polymorphisms (RFLPs) that would enable an entire linkage map spanning the human genome to be produced with 100% coverage (as opposed to the few percent coverage achieved in a study such as mine). While I was dallying with stats, Gurling saw the real potential of the New Genetics for psychiatry and gained the training at Stanford that would enable him to exploit this on return to the UK.

With Robin Murray's blessing and encouragement, on his return Hugh Gurling teamed up with Roger Marchbanks, a reader in the Neurochemistry Department, to set up molecular genetics in earnest at the Institute. I had returned to the UK at around the same time in the summer of 1982 and was subsequently awarded an MRC senior fellowship to carry out a study on the interplay between familial factors and psychosocial adversity in depression. This again followed on from a Murray suggestion and was a collaboration with Paul Bebbington and others in the MRC Social Psychiatry Unit. It involved, something fairly novel for me, no molecules at all. It did, however, help me to renew collaboration with Elizabeth "Pip" Sturt (1944–1985), who was working in the MRC unit as a general statistician, there being no decent jobs at this stage in London for statistical geneticists. Sturt had completed a PhD in linkage analysis with C. A. B. Smith (1917–2002) at the Galton lab and was keen to return to full-time genetics research. We worked on a couple of review and theoretical papers together and Murray, keen to expand the expertise of the genetic section in statistics, managed to "find" funding (something at which he has been amazingly adept) for a statistical genetic post. Sturt was duly appointed and immediately had an impact on the section. Tragically, before her research programme really got going she was killed in a road traffic accident while on a cycling holiday with her boyfriend. This came on top of another setback for statistical genetics at the Institute when, in 1985, David Fulker was recruited to a senior position at the Institute for Behavioural Genetics in Boulder, Colorado, USA.

The following year Hugh Gurling also left the Institute for a senior lectureship at University College London and the opportunity to set up his own laboratory. In collaboration with Hannes Petursson, one of his contemporaries on the Maudsley psychiatric training scheme and now a senior figure in Icelandic psychiatry, Gurling began to study Icelandic families multiply affected by schizophrenia in the hope of locating susceptibility loci by linkage analysis. Almost immediately, the collaboration appeared to strike lucky, finding an apparently significant linkage peak on the short arm of chromosome 5. This led to a paper in *Nature*

(Sherrington et al., 1988), which received a great deal of attention but, unfortunately, could not be replicated in any of the schizophrenia linkage studies that followed. This was among the first, then, of a sadly familiar pattern in psychiatric molecular genetics of high profile positive findings followed by non replication. Many of us thought (and this was explicitly articulated in a paper by Sturt & McGuffin, 1985) that part of the problem was to do with statistical power and that vastly larger sample sizes than those currently available would be required.

With the aim of collecting family samples on a Europe-wide front, Marchbanks and I wrote a preliminary proposal to the European Science Foundation to set up a network on the Molecular Neurobiology of Mental Illness (MNMI). A full application was invited and was subsequently successful and in 1987 the network was launched with its steering committee chaired by the French neurobiologist Jacques Mallet, and with members including some of the brightest up-and-coming geneticists in Europe including Francoise Clerget-Darpoux (Paris), Kay Davies (Oxford) and Leena Peltonen (Helsinki).

I had by this stage, 1987, left the Institute myself to go to the University of Wales College of Medicine, Cardiff, but the Genetic Section at the Institute continued to thrive with new Murray recruits such as Mike Owen, Pak Sham, David Collier and John Powell, all of them ensuring a high-profile presence of the institute in the ESF MNMI network. Indeed, UK psychiatric genetics was now benefiting from an Institute of Psychiatry diaspora generally. The group in Edinburgh were beginning to make their mark with Douglas Blackwood, an institute alumnus, one of their leading lights. Gurling's group at University College London continue to attract attention and my own group in Cardiff greatly benefited from being alongside one of the best medical genetics unit in the country led by Peter Harper. Elsewhere in Europe molecular psychiatric genetics was also beginning to take off. The MNMI was soon upgraded to an ESF programme. This had only a fairly modest amount of central money for meetings and fostering collaborations but it helped groups, particularly in France, Germany and Scandinavia as well as in the UK, to leverage national funding. Ultimately, the MNMI programme, which went on over a decade and involved more than a dozen countries, never really resulted in a "big" discovery that matched its ambition to take psychiatry into an era of "big science". It did, however, kick-start psychiatric genetics throughout Europe and arguably the Psychiatric Genetics Section at the Institute played a key role in the whole process. Remarkably, during this whole time Robin Murray, as well as being head of the genetic section, was also dean of the Institute, a post he held by-election from 1982 to 1989.

Here and now: The psychosis IRG and the SGDP

Following a review by the British Postgraduate Medical Federation (BPMF) in 1989, Murray's successor as dean, Stuart Checkley, set about reorganizing the Institute's research strategy. The BPMF review group had recommended that the Institute structures were too fragmented and that although there were many highly successful individuals the resultant overall performance of the Institute summed to less than the potential of its individual components. More needed to be done to encourage interdisciplinary work and so a series of interdisciplinary research groups (IRGs) were established. One of these covered the territory of schizophrenia and related disorders and Murray, by now one of the best established psychosis researchers on the world stage, was put in charge of the psychosis IRG. His interests had already gone well beyond genetics, to cover such areas as neuroimaging, epidemiology and the effects of social stressors and illicit drug use as factors in psychosis.

Elsewhere in the Institute interest in genetics was growing in a rather different direction. In particular the Child Psychiatry Department under Michael Rutter had been acquiring expertise in the genetics of autism and other developmental disorders beginning in the late 1970s with Folstein and Rutter's (1977) seminal twin-study paper showing that autism, far from being caused, as was once thought, by emotionally icy parenting, was almost certainly a substantially genetic disorder. A small but effective genetics theme grew within the Child Psychiatry Department and was enhanced by the establishment of an MRC Child Psychiatry Unit. By contrast in 1994 a sister unit, the MRC Social Psychiatry Unit, was wound down following a review and recommendation of the MRC Neuroscience and Mental Health Board. However, the board expressed disquiet that social psychiatry now appeared to be on the wane and advised that maybe the way ahead lay in greater partnership with biology and, particularly, genetics. This chimed well with Rutter's view and, following successful programme grant application, the Social Genetic and Developmental Psychiatry (SGDP) MRC Centre was established, which, as its name suggests, aimed to combine the study of nature and nurture in the development of psychiatric disorders and related traits. This is not the place to describe the history of the SGDP further and it has been outlined in papers by Rutter and McGuffin (2004) and by McGuffin and Plomin (2004) but suffice it to say that the establishment of this new MRC Centre paved the way for recruitment from the USA to the Institute of social and developmental experts such as Judy Dunn, Avshalom Caspi and Terry Moffitt as well as leading geneticists such as Robert Plomin and, from within the UK, Ian Craig from Oxford and up-and-comings such as Philip Asherson from Cardiff. In 1998 the SGDP Centre and the Child Psychiatry Unit were amalgamated and Anne Farmer and I were allowed back from exile in Wales.

Although the formation of the MRC SGDP Centre arguably represented a shift in the centre of gravity of genetics at the Institute many joint links between the MRC Centre and the psychosis IRG flourished, led by, for example, Pak Sham and David Collier who held joint appointments between the Department of Psychiatry, which from 1998 Murray also headed, and the SGDP. As noted he has now long engaged in many other aspects of psychosis research, but Murray has continued to contribute to genetics in the form of highly cited twin studies (e.g., Cardno et al., 1999; Cardno, Rijsdijk, Sham, Murray, & McGuffin, 2002) and to the present version of "big science" in psychiatry, genome-wide association studies (e.g., Stefansson et al., 2009). Therefore it is a fitting tribute to Murray's twin roles in nurturing genetics through its lean period and growing the subject at the Institute of Psychiatry to a position of strength and then subsequently building up a psychosis IRG, that the psychosis IRG and the SGDP were two areas of research highlighted by the higher education funding councils' 2008 Research Assessment Exercise as being outstanding on a world scale.

References

American Psychiatric Association. (1994). *Diagnostic and statistical manual of mental disorders* (4th ed.). Washington, DC: APA.

Cardno, A. G., Marshall, E. J., Coid, B., Macdonald, A. M., Ribchester, T. R., Davies, N. J., et al. (1999). Heritability estimates for psychotic disorders: The Maudsley twin psychosis series. *Archives of General Psychiatry*, *56*(2), 162–168.

Cardno, A. G., Rijsdijk, F. V., Sham, P. C., Murray, R. M., & McGuffin, P. (2002). A twin study of genetic relationships between psychotic symptoms. *American Journal of Psychiatry*, *159*(4), 539–545.

Clifford, C. A., Murray, R. M., & Fulker, D. W. (1984). Genetic and environmental influences on obsessional traits and symptoms. *Psychological Medicine*, *14*(4), 791–800.

Comings, D. E. (1980). Prenatal diagnosis and the "new genetics". *American Journal of Human Genetics*, *32*(3), 453–454.

Craddock, N., O'Donovan, M. C., & Owen, M. J. (2006). Genes for schizophrenia and bipolar disorder? Implications for psychiatric nosology. *Schizophrenia Bulletin*, *32*(1), 9–16.

Falconer, D. (1965). The inheritance of liability to certain diseases, estimated from the incidence among relatives. *Annals of Human Genetics*, *29*, 51–76.

Fisher, R. (1918). The correlation between relatives on the supposition of Mendelian inheritance. *Philosophical Transactions of the Royal Society of Edinburgh*, *52*, 399–433.

Folstein, S., & Rutter, M. (1977). Infantile autism: A genetic study of 21 twin pairs. *Journal of Child Psychology and Psychiatry*, *18*(4), 297–321.

Gottesman, I., & McGuffin, P. (1996). Eliot Slater and the birth of psychiatric genetics in Great Britain. In H. Freeman & G. Berrios (Eds.), *150 Years of British psychiatry* (Vol. II, pp. 537–548). London, UK: Gaskell (an imprint of the Royal College of Psychiatrists).

Gottesman, I. I., & Shields, J. (1967). A polygenic theory of schizophrenia. *Proceedings of the National Academy of Sciences of the United States of America*, *58*(1), 199–205.

Heston, L. (1966). Psychiatric disorders in foster home reared children of schizophrenic mothers. *British Journal of Psychiatry*, *112*, 819–825.

Johnstone, E. C., Crow, T. J., Frith, C. D., Husband, J., & Kreel, L. (1976). Cerebral ventricular size and cognitive impairment in chronic schizophrenia. *Lancet*, *2*(7992), 924–926.

Kety, S., Rosenthal, D., Wender, P. & Schulsinger, F. (1968). The types and prevalence of mental illness in the biological and adoptive families of adopted schizophrenics. In D. Rosenthal & S. Kety (Eds.), *The transmission of schizophrenia* (pp. 345–362). Oxford, UK: Pergamon Press.

McGuffin, P., Farmer, A., & Rajah, S. (1978). Histocompatibility antigens in schizophrenia. *British Journal of Psychiatry*, *132*, 149–151.

McGuffin, P., Festenstein, H., & Murray, R. (1983). A family study of HLA antigens and other genetic markers in schizophrenia. *Psychological Medicine*, *13*, 31–43.

McGuffin, Owen, M., O'Donovan, M., Thapar, A., & Gottesman, I. (1994). *Seminars in psychiatric genetics*. London, UK: Gaskell (an imprint of the Royal College of Psychiatrists).

McGuffin, P., & Plomin, R. (2004). A decade of the Social, Genetic and Developmental Psychiatry Centre at the Institute of Psychiatry. *British Journal of Psychiatry, 185*, 280–282.

McGuffin, P., Reveley, A., & Holland, A. (1982). Identical triplets: Non-identical psychosis? *British Journal of Psychiatry, 140*, 1–6.

Murray, R. M. (1979). *Discussion paper on psychiatric genetics at the Institute of Psychiatry*. Unpublished ms, Institute of Psychiatry, London.

Reveley, A. M., Reveley, M. A., & Murray, R. M. (1983). Enlargement of cerebral ventricles in schizophrenics is confined to those without known genetic predisposition. *Lancet, 2*(8348), 525.

Rüdin, E. (1916). *Studien über Vererbung und Entstehung geistiger Störungen. Vol 1: Zur Vererbung und Neuentstehung der Dementia praecox* [*Studies on the inheritance and etiology of mental disorders. Vol. 1: The inheritance and etiology of schizophrenia*]. Berlin, Germany: Springer.

Rutter, M., & McGuffin, P. (2004). The Social, Genetic and Developmental Psychiatry Centre: Its origins, conception and initial accomplishments. *Psychological Medicine, 34*, 933–947.

Scott, B., McGuffin, P., Rajah, S., Stoker, J., & Losowky, M. (1976). Dietary antibodies in myocardial infarction. *Lancet, 2*(7977), 125–126.

Scott, B., McGuffin, P., Swinburne, L., & Losowsky, M. (1976). Histocompatibility antigens and myocardial infarction. *Tissue Antigens, 7*, 187–188.

Sherrington, R., Brynjolfsson, J., Petursson, H., Potter, M., Dudleston, K., Barraclough, B., et al. (1988). Localization of a susceptibility locus for schizophrenia on chromosome 5. *Nature, 336*(6195), 164–167.

Shields, J. (1962). *Monozygotic twins*. London, UK: Oxford University Press.

Shields, J., & Gottesman, I. I. (1972). Cross-national diagnosis of schizophrenia in twins. The heritability and specificity of schizophrenia. *Archives of General Psychiatry, 27*(6), 725–730.

Slater, E. (1958). The monogenic theory of schizophrenia. *Acta Genetica et Statistica Medica, 8*, 50–56.

Smeraldi, E., Bellodi, L., Sacchetti, E., & Cazzullo, C. L. (1976). The HLA system and the clinical response to treatment with chlorpromazine. *British Journal of Psychiatry, 129*, 486–489.

Stefansson, H., Ophoff, R., Steinberg, S., Andreassen, O., Cichon, S., Rujescu, D., et al. (2009). Common variants conferring risk of schizophrenia. *Nature, 460*, 744–747.

Sturt, E., & McGuffin, P. (1985). Can linkage and marker association resolve the genetic aetiology of psychiatric disorders? Review and argument. *Psychological Medicine, 15*, 455–462.

Tsuang, M. T. (1967). A study of pairs of sibs both hospitalized for mental disorder. *British Journal of Psychiatry, 113*(496), 283–300.

World Health Organization. (1992). *ICD-10 Classifications of mental and behavioural disorder: Clinical descriptions and diagnostic guidelines*. Geneva, Switzerland: WHO.

14 From first contact to the final frontier

A star trek along the DISC1 pathway to schizophrenia

David Porteous

First contact

It was in the late 1980s that Professor H. John Evans, Director of the MRC Clinical and Population Cytogenetics Unit (now Human Genetics Unit) encouraged psychiatrists David St Clair, Walter Muir and Douglas Blackwood to trawl the registry of cytogenetic records accumulated over the years by the unit for possible cases with psychiatric phenotypes. In the intervening years this simple, but effective, strategy has reaped several notable successes, none more so than through the Scottish family that lead to the discovery of DISC1. In 1990, St Clair, Muir, Blackwood, Evans and colleagues first reported a Scottish family with a high loading of psychiatric illness, which co-segregated with a balanced translocation between chromosomes 1 and 11 (log of the odds, LOD, = 3.4; St Clair et al., 1990). A decade or so later, Blackwood et al. (2001) published a major update, now reporting on 87 family members of who 37 carried the translocation. Of 29 individuals carrying the translocation and for whom a psychiatric assessment was possible, 7 had a diagnosis of schizophrenia (SCZ), 1 had a diagnosis of bipolar disorder (BP) and there were 10 cases of recurrent major depression (MDD). Thus, 18 of 29 (62%) translocation carriers had a diagnosis of major mental illness whereas none of 38 non-translocation carriers had such a diagnosis, compelling statistical evidence for a causal link between the t(1;11) and the psychiatric liability in this unique family. Indeed, the updated LOD score of 3.6 for schizophrenia alone and of 7.1 for the broad diagnosis of major mental illness remains to this day one of the single most striking linkage findings in the psychiatric field. Importantly, the psychiatric presentations were typical with no other distinguishing clinical features. Moreover, Blackwood et al. (2001) also reported that the latency and amplitude of the event related potential (ERP) P300, a measure of the speed and efficiency of information processing, was indistinguishable between unaffected and affected translocation carriers and that as a group the translocation carriers showed the characteristic abnormal ERP P300 associated with SCZ and with BP. The pattern of inheritance in the Scottish t(1;11) family was thus consistent with a simple dominant mode of inheritance for a broad spectrum of major psychiatric illness, with incomplete penetrance, and with altered ERP P300 as a correlated endophenotype. Secondary and independently segregating genetic risk factors, variable environmental exposures and/or stochastic events may influence the presence or absence of clinical signs and the specific psychiatric diagnosis at the age of ascertainment, but it is clear that in this family the t(1;11) accounts for essentially all of the transmitted genetic risk. At the time, this finding was viewed sceptically by many as it challenged two fervently held precepts—on the clinical side, the aetiological distinction between schizophrenia, bipolar disorder and major depressive disorder, and on the genetic side, the notion that these psychiatric conditions were "always" complex, non-Mendelian disorders. While the biological explanation remained uncertain, the evidence for a simple, shared genetic liability for a broad spectrum of mental illness in this particular family was beyond challenge.

The undiscovered country

Molecular cytogenetics is a powerful and under-utilized tool for gene finding (Pickard, Millar, Porteous, Muir, & Blackwood, 2005). With dogged, yet very modestly funded effort by comparison to the vast resources thrown at large-scale association studies, the Edinburgh laboratory alone has been able to report on the positional cloning and subsequent genetic and biological validation of *DISC1* (Millar et al., 2000), *PDE4B* (Millar et al., 2005), *GRIK4* (Pickard et al., 2006), *NPAS3* (Pickard et al., 2009) and *ABCA13* (Knight et al., 2009) by this method. In the post-genome era, mapping a translocation is now facile by fluorescently labelled in situ hybridization of genomic clones of known map location to spreads of metaphase chromosomes from patient blood samples. Polymerase chain reaction (PCR) mapping and sequencing of the breakpoint can quickly follow. But in the pre-genome era, all the mapping reagents, including human-mouse somatic cell hybrids and dedicated clone libraries, had to built from scratch (Evans et al., 1995; Fletcher et al., 1993). Consequently, it was a full decade before the t(1;11) translocation was finally cloned and analysed (Millar et al., 2000). What did sequencing of the translocation breakpoint reveal? The answer was not one, but two genes, both novel. The first, coding for a protein, which took the name Disrupted in Schizophrenia 1, or *DISC1*, the second, an RNA-only gene, named *DISC2*.

DISC2 is a very large, spliced RNA-only gene that runs anti-parallel to *DISC1* on chromosome 1. In common with other RNA-only genes, it is only moderately conserved across species (Taylor, Devon, Millar, & Porteous, 2003) and its function was then and still remains uncertain, but by analogy with other examples, it may regulate *DISC1* expression. On first discovery, the function of *DISC1* was also far from clear as it showed no obvious similarity to other known genes or proteins. De novo biochemical and expression studies have since established that DISC1 is a multifunctional, neurodevelopmentally regulated scaffold protein (see Chubb, Bradshaw, Soares, Porteous, & Millar, 2008, for a comprehensive review and references therein).

The scaffold function of DISC1 helps resolve the genetics paradox. The multiple proteins shown to interact with DISC1 are enriched for proteins known to have a role in neurodevelopment, neurosignalling, cytoskeletal, centrosomal and synaptic function (Camargo et al., 2007), thus having the potential to simultaneously affect a wide range of plausible risk processes in susceptibility (Chubb et al., 2008). And, indeed, several of these DISC1 interactors, such as NDE1, PDE4B, PDE4D, LIS1 and PCM1, turn out to be co-dependent or independent genetic risk factors (see Chubb et al., 2008, for a review).

Star Trek

As the likely biological function of *DISC1* was being elucidated, so the genetics community started to report evidence in support of a role for *DISC1* not just in the original Scottish family, but also in the generalized population. Again, statistical support came not just from studies of schizophrenia, but also bipolar and unipolar disorder (see Chubb et al., 2008, for a review). Indeed, the spectrum of disorders in which *DISC1* appeared to play a role extended to include schizoaffective disorder (Hamshere et al., 2005), autism spectrum disorder (Kilpinen et al., 2008) and possibly also Alzheimer's disease (Beecham et al., 2009). There is evidence, too, from brain-imaging studies that common genetic variants of *DISC1* explain variation in hippocampal and cortical function (Callicott et al., 2005; Di Giorgio et al., 2008; Prata et al., 2008; Szeszko et al., 2008).

But as for all putative risk factors in major mental illness, the picture is still complex. *DISC1* is a large gene, extending over some 450 kb of genomic DNA and is poorly tagged by first-generation Affymetrics and Illumina genome-wide association study (GWAS) chips. It is therefore somewhat of a surprise that the *DISC1* locus generated any association signal in GWAS studies (Sullivan et al., 2008). To illustrate the point, Hennah et al. (2009) recently reported a detailed association study of the *DISC1* locus in four European cohorts and reported association for BP in the Finnish cohort at rs1538979 (odds ratio = 2.73; CI 1.42–5.27) and at rs821577 in the London cohort (odds ratio = 1.64; CI 1.2–2.19). Conditioning on these two single nucleotide polymorphisms (SNPs) revealed a third significant SNP association at rs821633, which modified risk depending upon the presence or absence of the other two SNPs. None of these three are on the Illumina550 chip and only rs821577 is present on the Affy500 chip, therefore this finding would be missed using these platforms, likewise if these specific SNPs were not tested in a locus specific association study. This rather novel concept of intergenic allelic interplay has its antecedent in an earlier study by Hennah et al. (2007), which identified a *DISC1* risk haplotype by genome-wide linkage analysis and repeated the analysis conditioned for its presence or absence, thus identifying a second *DISC1*-dependent locus in the form of NDE1, a known DISC1 interactor. NDE1 and NDEL1 are two highly related neurodevelopmental proteins that dimerize and heteromultimerize when binding to DISC1 (Bradshaw et al., 2009). Burdick et al. (2008) reported evidence for a genetic and biological interaction between the common *DISC1* missense mutation S704C and differential binding of NDE1 and NDEL1. There is growing evidence that the common *DISC1* missense variants L607F and S704C may modify *DISC1* function in SCZ, BP and, indeed, normal individuals (Eastwood, Hodgkinson, & Harrison, 2009; Leliveld et al., 2008, 2009; Thomson et al., 2005). Song et al. (2008) reported the results of genomic resequencing of *DISC1* coding sequence and splice junctions in 288 SCZ samples and identified 8 new, ultra-rare variants that were not seen in controls. They estimated that 2% of all SCZ subjects had *DISC1* missense mutations. Large-scale resequencing studies are under way in our laboratory and others and will no doubt firm up (or refute) the softer end of current genetic evidence, but it is now beyond debate that there are several *DISC1* variants, both coding and non-coding, which do influence brain function and personality within the psychopathic and normal range.

The real catalysts for taking *DISC1* seriously as a telling light upon the aetiology of psychotic and mood disorders came from two highly complementary research directions in 2005, which were highlighted that year by *Science* magazine as "scientific breakthroughs". The first introduced a critical new genetic player and direct protein interactor with DISC1. A fragment of the phosphodiesterase gene type 4B, PDE4B, was one in a very long list of putative protein interactors identified by Camargo et al. (2007) in their comprehensive yeast-2-hybrid screen. In parallel, the Edinburgh laboratory identified a single case of schizophrenia and a cousin with psychotic disorder in whom the *PDE4B* gene was disrupted by a cytogenetic breakpoint (Millar et al., 2005), genetic evidence that was subsequently substantiated by association analysis (Nakata et al., 2008; Pickard et al., 2007; Tomppo et al., 2009). Importantly, Millar et al. (2005) showed that DISC1 interacted dynamically with PDE4B to modulate cAMP in a protein kinase A (PKA) and phosphorylation-dependent fashion. Phosphodiesterases, of which there are over 20 different forms, are the sole means of catabolizing cAMP, a key signalling molecule in the brain (see Mackie, Millar, & Porteous, 2007, for a review). The PDE4 isoforms (A, B, C and D) had already been linked to memory formation and mood disorder through cognate fly mutants and from knock-out studies of the B and D isoforms in the mouse, and PDE4 was the known target for rolipram, a well-known antidepressant and mood stabilizer (see Mackie et al., 2007, for a review). Subsequent peptide mapping studies identified both consensus and PDE4 isoform specific binding domains on DISC1 (Murdoch et al., 2007), about which a little more later.

At the same time, Akira Sawa's laboratory at Johns Hopkins University was undertaking a novel approach to modelling *DISC1* gene modulation in the mouse by electroporation of gene constructs in utero and studying the effects on early postnatal brain development (Kamiya et al., 2005). They showed that short hairpin loop RNA oligonucleotides could transiently repress expression of endogenous mouse *DISC1*. Down regulation of *DISC1* resulted in a striking phenotype of reduced migration out of the sub-ventricular zone to the cortical plate. This was accompanied by altered cell polarity and reduced arborization. They reported a similar phenotype when truncated human DISC1 cDNA was over expressed. This study demonstrated for the first time in vivo a direct role for DISC1 in early brain development, consistent with the neurodevelopmental hypothesis in schizophrenia, as originally and independently proposed by Weinberger (1987) and by Jones and Murray (1991).

Shortly thereafter, a series of transgenic and mutant mouse models of DISC1 were reported, each of which gave rise to developmental and behavioural phenotypes that modelled important aspects of the human conditions (see Chubb et al., 2008, for a review). Intriguingly, two independent ethylnitrosourea (ENU) mutagen-induced, missense mouse models of DISC1, Q31L and L100P were shown to exhibit rather different behaviours in standardized tests, suggesting a depression-like and schizophrenia-like phenotype respectively (Clapcote et al., 2007). These mutation-specific behaviours responded differentially to typical and atypical antipsychotics and to antidepressants (Clapcote et al., 2007). It turned out that the Q31L and L100P mutations map to two distinct DISC1–PDE4B selective binding domains (Murdoch et al., 2007). Does this provide a mechanistic explanation for their differential behaviours and responses to antipsychotic and antidepressant treatment? It is an attractive suggestion, which demands further study.

The final frontier

It may be somewhat premature to describe the current state of play with DISC1 as the "final" frontier, but in the last two years several new groups have joined the DISC1 field and made a major impact, collectively sealing the case for the DISC1 pathway as worthy of detailed study in relation to basic neuroscience and biological psychiatry.

Taking the next big step beyond the work of Sawa and colleagues, Duan et al. (2007) used an elegant retrovirally mediated, single-cell RNAi strategy to selectively suppress mouse *DISC1* expression in vivo in differentiating hippocampal neuronal precursor cells. They made the striking observation that *DISC1* suppression in neuronal precursors resulted in over migration, aberrant integration and misfiring. But by what means? In a follow-up study, Kim et al. (2009) demonstrated that the critical function of DISC1 in postnatal hippocampal neurogenesis is mediated in large part by interaction with KIA1212, known also and more evocatively as Girdin (girders of actin filaments). Parallel work by Enomoto et al. (2009) suggested much the same. Kim et al. (2009) further demonstrated that this interaction with Girdin suppresses v-akt murine thymoma viral oncogene homologue (AKT) signalling and, remarkably, that the gross effects of *DISC1* suppression could be largely rescued by rapamycin, which inhibits mTOR, an effector pathway activated by AKT signalling. There are important points of difference between these two studies (Porteous & Millar, 2009) that only further investigation will resolve, but this potential link between DISC1 and AKT1, and thus a second major brain-signalling pathway, is tantalizing. Indeed, Enomoto and colleagues (2005) had previously reported that AKT1, a key serine/threonine specific kinase with multiple signalling properties, regulates actin organization and cell motility via Girdin, which directly binds actin at the leading edge of migrating cells. The genetic evidence for AKT being a risk factor for schizophrenia is modest by comparison to DISC1, but there is a growing body of evidence from human and mouse studies that the AKT pathway may indeed be important (see Arguello & Gogos, 2008, for a review). Genetic variants in AKT1 have been reported associated with schizophrenia. AKT1 activity and AKT-dependent phosphorylation of GSK3β is decreased in post-mortem schizophrenic brains. *AKT1* knock-out mice show impaired pre-pulse inhibition of the startle response, a corollary of the altered salience typifying schizophrenia. Both typical and atypical antipsychotics enhance AKT signalling by activating AKT or by increasing phosphorylation of GSK3β.

This brings us neatly to GSK3β itself, which a little earlier Mao et al. (2009) had identified as a novel DISC1 interactor, bringing the *wnt* pathway and β-catenin neurosignalling firmly to the fore. GSK3β is inhibited by both AKT signalling and by DISC1. It is a known target for lithium chloride, still widely used to treat bipolar disorder. Mao et al. (2009) further reported that administration of the GSK3β-specific inhibitor SB216763 could rescue the behavioural effects of lentivirus-induced *DISC1* suppression in the adult dentate gyrus.

If the rather remarkable effects of rolipram and other psychiatric drugs on *DISC1* missense mouse mutants reported by Clapcote et al. (2007), of rapamycin reported by Kim et al. (2009), and of SB216763 (and lithium chloride) reported by Mao et al. (2009) are positive portents of future therapeutic strategies, it will nevertheless be critical to determine exactly which aspects of the DISC1 pathway phenotype must be corrected and when during brain development. What should not be underestimated, however, is the value of this recent research to future DISC1 pathway research and biological psychiatry in general as a consequence of landing on signalling pathways that are the subject of intense interest and substantial research and development investment by academia and industry in relation to cancer, cardiovascular and inflammatory disease.

Fully understanding structure–function relationships of the DISC1 complex and the impact of genetic variation awaits more detailed biophysical characterization. We know that DISC1 comprises a highly disordered N-terminal head domain and a C-terminal tail with multiple coiled-coil domains and we also know that almost the entire length of DISC1 interacts with one protein or another (see Chubb et al., 2008, for a review). The binding domains for PDE4, GSK3β and Girdin at least partially overlap. Both DISC1 and Girdin dimerize and both bind NDEL1, which in turn binds NDE1 and thus LIS1, yet another key protein in brain development. In post-mortem brains, significant fractions of DISC1 form higher order aggregates in chronic psychiatric cases, but not in normal controls (Leliveld et al., 2008). Moreover, DISC1 aggregation appears to abrogate the binding of NDE1 (Leliveld et al., 2008) and is sensitive to polymorphic variation at the Ser704Cys position (Leliveld et al., 2009). This is the same polymorphism previously related by structural and functional magnetic resonance imaging (MRI) to altered brain function (Callicott et al., 2005; Di Giorgio et al., 2008; Prata et al., 2008; Szeszko et al., 2008) and also to altered brain expression of DISC1 partners (Lipska et al., 2006).

Does all this imply a need for DISC1 pathway and mutation-specific, bespoke drug treatments? There is little doubt in my mind that drug effectiveness and thus compliance will be highly influenced by genetic factors. As genetics supplants classical *Diagnostic and Statistical Manual* (DSM) diagnostic criteria (as surely it must do) then we may well see a shift towards individualized treatments for "DISCopathies" and other "geneopathies". The study of Song et al. (2008) puts a lower estimate of 2% for "DISCopathies", but this figure does not take account of genetic association studies that point to the additional effect of common, non-coding variants of DISC1, PDE4B, PDE4D, NDE1, LIS1 (see Chubb et al., 2008, for a review) and PCM1 (Gurling et al., 2006; Kamiya et al., 2008). Moreover, we have recently shown that common cis-variants of DISC1 significantly alter the expression levels of the *DISC1* gene by up to 20% of normal (Hennah & Porteous, 2009). Through the hub function of DISC1, these modest reductions of *DISC1* gene expression levels may exert subtle, but pervasive effects on neurodevelopment and neurophysiology. We could also show that common variants in DISC1, PDE4B, PDE4D and NDE1 are transcriptional modulators of cAMP signalling, cytoskeletal, synaptogenic, neurodevelopmental and sensory perception proteins (Hennah & Porteous, 2009). Furthermore, this set of regulated proteins is significantly enriched (5% of total, $p = .007$) for current targets of psychiatric drug development (Hennah & Porteous, 2009). Thus, the dual impact of rare, highly penetrant and of common, low penetrant gene variants within the DISC1 pathway may contribute to a sizeable net fraction of the genetic variance in schizophrenia and related major mental disorders. Could this match, or possibly exceed, the 3% variance that may be accounted for by the "polygenes" identified through the much vaunted genome-wide association studies for schizophrenia (Purcell et al., 2009)? Time will tell.

When considering which proteins DISC1 interacts with, where and when in the developing and adult brain, it is important also to take account of the growing evidence for multiple transcripts and protein isoforms of DISC1 and their developmental regulation (see Chubb et al., 2008, for a review). This has taken on a further significance in light of recent evidence for as many as 50 different isoforms and for a dramatic difference in their pre- and postnatal brain expression profile (Nakata et al., 2009), evidence that once again harks back to the prescient neurodevelopmental hypothesis in schizophrenia (Jones & Murray, 1991; Weinberger, 1987).

Studying DISC1–protein interactions in pair-wise fashion is bound to oversimplify and potentially deceive. Defining the DISC1 proteome by cell type and lineage during pre- and postnatal development and in the adult brain may be necessary for a full understanding of the multiplicity of DISC1 functions, how these relate to the full spectrum of DISC1-related psychopathology and of variation within the normal range of personality and cognition. As recently proposed (Porteous & Millar, 2009), the emerging picture is of DISC1 as the "orchestrator of a suite of protein–protein interactions harmonized in time and space". The conventional models of signal transduction and metabolic flux, depicted as linear pathways, feedback loops and "upstream/downstream" molecules, fail to convey the highly structured and compartmentalized nature of cells. This new concept (Porteous & Millar, 2009) of "the DISC1 complex as the pathway", whether in the nucleus, at the growth cone, the centromere, the mitochondria, the pre- or postsynaptic density, has each "pathway" defined by local and locally determined isoforms, interactions, cAMP concentrations and phosphorylation states. It is around this concept that we would seek and expect to devise evidence-based molecular therapies, of relevance to a sizeable fraction of those suffering from psychotic and/or mood disorders, that are both effective and safe.

Acknowledgements

I thank the MRC, Wellcome Trust and NARSAD for grant-aided support, my colleagues in the Medical Genetics Section for all their contributions to the science discussed here and last, but not least to Prof. Robin Murray for sharing his unique insight into schizophrenia and constructively challenging the genetic evidence on DISC1.

References

Arguello, P. A., & Gogos, J. A. (2008). A signaling pathway AKTing up in schizophrenia. *Journal of Clinical Investigation*, *118*(6), 2018–2021.

Beecham, G. W., Martin, E. R., Li, Y. J., Slifer, M. A., Gilbert, J. R., Haines, J. L., et al. (2009). Genome-wide association study implicates a chromosome 12 risk locus for late-onset Alzheimer disease. *American Journal of Human Genetics*, *84*(1), 35–43.

Blackwood, D. H., Fordyce, A., Walker, M. T., St Clair, D. M., Porteous, D. J., & Muir, W. J. (2001). Schizophrenia and affective disorders—Cosegregation with a translocation at chromosome 1q42 that directly disrupts brain-expressed genes: Clinical and P300 findings in a family. *American Journal of Human Genetics*, *69*(2), 428–433.

Bradshaw, N. J., Christie, S., Soares, D. C., Carlyle, B. C., Porteous, D. J., & Millar, J. K. (2009). NDE1 and NDEL1: Multimerisation, alternate splicing and DISC1 interaction. *Neuroscience Letters*, *449*(3), 228–233.

Burdick, K. E., Kamiya, A., Hodgkinson, C. A., Lencz, T., DeRosse, P., Ishizuka, K., et al. (2008). Elucidating the relationship between DISC1, NDEL1 and NDE1 and the risk for schizophrenia: Evidence of epistasis and competitive binding. *Human Molecular Genetics*, *17*(16), 2462–2473.

Callicott, J. H., Straub, R. E., Pezawas, L., Egan, M. F., Mattay, V. S., Hariri, A. R., et al. (2005). Variation in DISC1 affects hippocampal structure and function and increases risk for schizophrenia. *Proceeding of the National Academy of Sciences of the USA*, *102*(24), 8627–8632.

Camargo, L. M., Collura, V., Rain, J. C., Mizuguchi, K., Hermjakob, H., Kerrien, S., et al. (2007). Disrupted in schizophrenia 1 interactome: Evidence for the close connectivity of risk genes and a potential synaptic basis for schizophrenia. *Molecular Psychiatry*, *12*(1), 74–86.

Chubb, J. E., Bradshaw, N. J., Soares, D. C., Porteous, D. J., & Millar, J. K. (2008). The DISC locus in psychiatric illness. *Molecular Psychiatry*, *13*(1), 36–64.

Clapcote, S. J., Lipina, T. V., Millar, J. K., Mackie, S., Christie, S., Ogawa, F., et al. (2007). Behavioral phenotypes of Disc1 missense mutations in mice. *Neuron*, *54*(3), 387–402.

Di Giorgio, A., Blasi, G., Sambataro, F., Rampino, A., Papazacharias, A., Gambi, F., et al. (2008). Association of the SerCys DISC1 polymorphism with human hippocampal formation gray matter and function during memory encoding. *European Journal of Neuroscience*, *28*(10), 2129–2136.

Duan, X., Chang, J. H., Ge, S., Faulkner, R. L., Kim, J. Y., Kitabatake, Y., et al. (2007). Disrupted-in-schizophrenia 1 regulates integration of newly generated neurons in the adult brain. *Cell*, *130*(6), 1146–1158.

Eastwood, S. L., Hodgkinson, C. A., & Harrison, P. J. (2009). DISC-1 Leu607Phe alleles differentially affect centrosomal PCM1 localization and neurotransmitter release. *Molecular Psychiatry*, *14*(6), 556–557.

Enomoto, A., Asai, N., Namba, T., Wang, Y., Kato, T., Tanaka, M., et al. (2009). Roles of disrupted-in-schizophrenia 1-interacting protein girdin in postnatal development of the dentate gyrus. *Neuron*, *63*(6), 774–787.

Enomoto, A., Murakami, H., Asai, N., Morone, N., Watanabe, T., Kawai, K., et al. (2005). Akt/PKB regulates actin organization and cell motility via Girdin/APE. *Developmental Cell*, *9*(3), 389–402.

Evans, K. L., Brown, J., Shibasaki, Y., Devon, R. S., He, L., Arveiler, B., et al. (1995). A contiguous clone map over 3 Mb on the long arm of chromosome 11 across a balanced translocation associated with schizophrenia. *Genomics*, *28*(3), 420–428.

Fletcher, J. M., Evans, K., Baillie, D., Byrd, P., Hanratty, D., Leach, S., et al. (1993). Schizophrenia-associated chromosome 11q21 translocation: Identification of flanking markers and development of chromosome 11q fragment hybrids as cloning and mapping resources. *American Journal of Human Genetics*, *52*(3), 478–490.

Gurling, H. M., Critchley, H., Datta, S. R., McQuillin, A., Blaveri, E., Thirumalai, S., et al. (2006). Genetic association and brain morphology studies and the chromosome 8p22 pericentriolar material 1 (PCM1) gene in susceptibility to schizophrenia. *Archives of General Psychiatry*, *63*(8), 844–854.

Hamshere, M. L., Bennett, P., Williams, N., Segurado, R., Cardno, A., Norton, N., et al. (2005). Genomewide linkage scan in schizoaffective disorder: Significant evidence for linkage at 1q42 close to DISC1, and suggestive evidence at 22q11 and 19p13. *Archives of General Psychiatry*, *62*(10), 1081–1088.

Hennah, W., & Porteous, D. (2009). The DISC1 pathway modulates expression of neurodevelopmental, synaptogenic and sensory perception genes. *PLoS One*, *4*(3), e4906.

Hennah, W., Thomson, P., McQuillin, A., Bass, N., Loukola, A., Anjorin, A., et al. (2009). DISC1 association, heterogeneity and interplay in schizophrenia and bipolar disorder. *Molecular Psychiatry*, *14*(9), 865–873.

Hennah, W., Tomppo, L., Hiekkalinna, T., Palo, O. M., Kilpinen, H., Ekelund, J., et al. (2007). Families with the risk allele of DISC1 reveal a link between schizophrenia and another component of the same molecular pathway, NDE1. *Human Molecular Genetics*, *16*(5), 453–462.

Jones, P., & Murray, R. M. (1991). The genetics of schizophrenia is the genetics of neurodevelopment. *British Journal of Psychiatry*, *158*, 615–623.

Kamiya, A., Kubo, K., Tomoda, T., Takaki, M., Youn, R., Ozeki, Y., et al. (2005). A schizophrenia-associated mutation of DISC1 perturbs cerebral cortex development. *Nature Cell Biology*, *7*(12), 1167–1178.

Kamiya, A., Tan, P. L., Kubo, K., Engelhard, C., Ishizuka, K., Kubo, A., et al. (2008). Recruitment of PCM1 to the centrosome by the cooperative action of DISC1 and BBS4: A candidate for psychiatric illnesses. *Archives of General Psychiatry*, *65*(9), 996–1006.

Kilpinen, H., Ylisaukko-Oja, T., Hennah, W., Palo, O. M., Varilo, T., Vanhala, R., et al. (2008). Association of DISC1 with autism and Asperger syndrome. *Molecular Psychiatry*, *13*(2), 187–196.

Kim, J. Y., Duan, X., Liu, C. Y., Jang, M. H., Guo, J. U., Pow-anpongkul, N., et al. (2009). DISC1 regulates new neuron development in the adult brain via modulation of AKT-mTOR signaling through KIAA1212. *Neuron*, *63*(6), 761–773.

Knight, H. M., Pickard, B. S., Maclean, A., Malloy, M. P., Soares, D. C., McRae, A. F., et al. (2009). A cytogenetic abnormality and rare coding variants identify ABCA13 as a candidate gene in schizophrenia, bipolar disorder, and depression. *American Journal of Human Genetics*, *85*(6), 833–846.

Leliveld, S. R., Bader, V., Hendriks, P., Prikulis, I., Sajnani, G., Requena, J. R., et al. (2008). Insolubility of disrupted-in-schizophrenia 1 disrupts oligomer-dependent interactions with nuclear distribution element 1 and is associated with sporadic mental disease. *Journal of Neuroscience*, *28*(15), 3839–3845.

Leliveld, S. R., Hendriks, P., Michel, M., Sajnani, G., Bader, V., Trossbach, S., et al. (2009). Oligomer assembly of the C-terminal DISC1 domain (640–854) is controlled by self-association motifs and disease-associated polymorphism S704C. *Biochemistry*, *48*(32), 7746–7755.

Lipska, B. K., Peters, T., Hyde, T. M., Halim, N., Horowitz, C., Mitkus, S., et al. (2006). Expression of DISC1 binding partners is reduced in schizophrenia and associated with DISC1 SNPs. *Human Molecular Genetics*, *15*(8), 1245–1258.

Mackie, S., Millar, J. K., & Porteous, D. J. (2007). Role of DISC1 in neural development and schizophrenia. *Current Opinions in Neurobiology*, *17*(1), 95–102.

Mao, Y., Ge, X., Frank, C. L., Madison, J. M., Koehler, A. N., Doud, M. K., et al. (2009). Disrupted in schizophrenia 1 regulates neuronal progenitor proliferation via modulation of GSK3beta/beta-catenin signaling. *Cell*, *136*(6), 1017–1031.

Millar, J. K., Pickard, B. S., Mackie, S., James, R., Christie, S., Buchanan, S. R., et al. (2005). DISC1 and PDE4B are interacting genetic factors in schizophrenia that regulate cAMP signaling. *Science*, *310*(5751), 1187–1191.

Millar, J. K., Wilson-Annan, J. C., Anderson, S., Christie, S., Taylor, M. S., Semple, C. A., et al. (2000). Disruption of two novel genes by a translocation co-segregating with schizophrenia. *Human Molecular Genetics*, *9*(9), 1415–1423.

Murdoch, H., Mackie, S., Collins, D. M., Hill, E. V., Bolger, G. B., Klussmann, E., et al. (2007). Isoform-selective susceptibility of DISC1/phosphodiesterase-4 complexes to dissociation by elevated intracellular cAMP levels. *Journal of Neuroscience*, *27*(35), 9513–9524.

Nakata, K., Lipska, B. K., Hyde, T. M., Ye, T., Newburn, E. N., Morita, Y., et al. (2008). Positive association of the PDE4B (phosphodiesterase 4B) gene with schizophrenia in the Japanese population. *Journal of Psychiatric Research*, *43*(1), 7–12.

Nakata, K., Lipska, B. K., Hyde, T. M., Ye, T., Newburn, E. N., Morita, Y., et al. (2009). DISC1 splice variants are upregulated in schizophrenia and associated with risk polymorphisms. *Proceeding of the National Academy of Sciences of the USA*, *106*(37), 15873–15878.

Pickard, B. S., Christoforou, A., Thomson, P. A., Fawkes, A., Evans, K. L., Morris, S. W., et al. (2009). Interacting haplotypes at the NPAS3 locus alter risk of schizophrenia and bipolar disorder. *Molecular Psychiatry*, *14*(9), 874–884.

Pickard, B. S., Malloy, M. P., Christoforou, A., Thomson, P. A., Evans, K. L., Morris, S. W., et al. (2006). Cytogenetic and genetic evidence supports a role for the kainate-type glutamate receptor gene, GRIK4, in schizophrenia and bipolar disorder. *Molecular Psychiatry*, *11*(9), 847–857.

Pickard, B. S., Millar, J. K., Porteous, D. J., Muir, W. J., & Blackwood, D. H. (2005). Cytogenetics and gene discovery in psychiatric disorders. *Pharmacogenomics Journal*, *5*(2), 81–88.

Pickard, B. S., Thomson, P. A., Christoforou, A., Evans, K. L., Morris, S. W., Porteous, D. J., et al. (2007). The PDE4B gene confers sex-specific protection against schizophrenia. *Psychiatric Genetics*, *17*(3), 129–133.

Porteous, D., & Millar, K. (2009). How DISC1 regulates postnatal brain development: Girdin gets in on the AKT. *Neuron*, *63*(6), 711–713.

Prata, D. P., Mechelli, A., Fu, C. H., Picchioni, M., Kane, F., Kalidindi, S., et al. (2008). Effect of disrupted-in-schizophrenia-1 on pre-frontal cortical function. *Molecular Psychiatry*, *13*(10), 909, 915–917.

Purcell, S. M., Wray, N. R., Stone, J. L., Visscher, P. M., O'Donovan, M. C., Sullivan, P. F., et al. (2009). Common polygenic variation contributes to risk of schizophrenia and bipolar disorder. *Nature*, *460*(7256), 748–752.

Song, W., Li, W., Feng, J., Heston, L. L., Scaringe, W. A., & Sommer, S. S. (2008). Identification of high risk DISC1 structural variants with a 2% attributable risk for schizophrenia. *Biochemical and Biophysical Research Communications*, *367*(3), 700–706.

St Clair, D., Blackwood, D., Muir, W., Carothers, A., Walker, M., Spowart, G., et al. (1990). Association within a family of a balanced autosomal translocation with major mental illness. *Lancet*, *336*(8706), 13–16.

Sullivan, P. F., Lin, D., Tzeng, J. Y., van den Oord, E., Perkins, D., Stroup, T. S., et al. (2008). Genomewide association for schizophrenia in the CATIE study: Results of stage 1. *Molecular Psychiatry*, *13*(6), 570–584.

Szeszko, P. R., Hodgkinson, C. A., Robinson, D. G., Derosse, P., Bilder, R. M., Lencz, T., et al. (2008). DISC1 is associated with prefrontal cortical gray matter and positive symptoms in schizophrenia. *Biological Psychology*, *79*(1), 103–110.

Taylor, M. S., Devon, R. S., Millar, J. K., & Porteous, D. J. (2003). Evolutionary constraints on the disrupted in schizophrenia locus. *Genomics*, *81*(1), 67–77.

Thomson, P. A., Harris, S. E., Starr, J. M., Whalley, L. J., Porteous, D. J., & Deary, I. J. (2005). Association between genotype at an exonic SNP in DISC1 and normal cognitive aging. *Neuroscience Letters*, *389*(1), 41–45.

Tomppo, L., Hennah, W., Lahermo, P., Loukola, A., Tuulio-Henriksson, A., Suvisaari, J., et al. (2009). Association between genes of disrupted in schizophrenia 1 (DISC1) interactors and schizophrenia supports the role of the DISC1 pathway in the etiology of major mental illnesses. *Biological Psychiatry*, *65*(12), 1055–1062.

Weinberger, D. R. (1987). Implications of normal brain development for the pathogenesis of schizophrenia. *Archives of General Psychiatry*, *44*(7), 660–669.

15 Dopamine gene variants and schizophrenia

A scheme for investigating nominally significant or discrepant associations

Vishwajit L. Nimgaonkar, Kodavali V. Chowdari, Konasale M. Prasad, Annie M. Watson, Hader Mansour, Joel A. Wood and A. Javier Lopez

Introduction

Environmentalists and geneticists alike agree that a unitary causation for schizophrenia (SZ) is unlikely (Gottesman, 1994; Jablensky & Kalaydjieva, 2003). The attraction of gene-mapping studies is the prospect of invoking causation through associations, in contrast to classical epidemiological studies. Recent schizophrenia gene-mapping efforts have identified several putative risk variants, but they have not been replicated widely. The main obstacle is the relatively modest risk conferred by individual variants (odds ratios, OR, ~ 1.2–1.5), making replication difficult. Though larger effects have been reported with some rare variants, the precise risk variants are unknown and many await replication. Additional variants with larger effects may not be detected. Thus, it may be difficult to fulfill classical criteria for causation. These problems are shared with other common, genetically complex disorders.

We suggest a practical framework to deal with this conundrum, that we call *recursive functional analysis* (RFA). We propose two iterative elements: (i) attempts at replication (with further analysis of non-replicating samples); and (ii) evaluation of the function of putative risk variants, the latter dictated by the nature of the risk variant. These interactive activities would refine and inform further genetic association analyses. The RFA scheme relies heavily on, and could even be "embedded" in other basic studies of gene function and neuroscience. Thus, a thread connecting key variables may be generated and help understand pathogenesis.

We describe our ongoing work with dopaminergic genes as an example. Having consistently detected associations with schizophrenia in some, but not all samples, we are now querying putative risk alleles at the dopamine transporter (*SLC6A3*) in addition to cellular assays and complementary phenotypes. Samples that did not replicate the initial associations are also being evaluated. Synthesis of these analyses will help determine whether dopaminergic genes contribute to schizophrenia risk.

In the following sections, we first review gene-mapping studies of SZ. We argue that genome-wide association studies (GWAS) may not solve the dual problems of modest effect size and proof of causality. We propose an interactive framework grounded in biological research to assist with this effort. As illustration, we review our ongoing work with dopaminergic gene variants. We end by raising questions about our proposed framework, in the hopes of refining it further.

Early gene-mapping studies

The relatively high heritability of schizophrenia (~ 70–80%) and recent advances in genomics have spurred an unprecedented increase in gene-mapping efforts; these efforts have been undeterred by repeated segregation analyses that suggest complex inheritance and the likely presence of several risk variants, with possible interactive effects (epistasis; Purcell et al., 2009; Risch, 1990). Linkage has been reported in several regions, though inconsistency is often the norm (Lewis et al., 2003). If the genes underlying liability to SZ have a small direct impact, or risk is conferred by common alleles, the power to detect linkage is limited (O'Donovan & Owen, 1999; Petronis et al., 2003; Risch & Merikangas, 1996). Thus, we expect highly variable findings. This has been borne out by recent association studies utilizing panels of single nucleotide polymorphisms (SNPs) in functional or positional candidate genes, e.g., dysbindin (*DTNBP*), neuregulin 1, regulator of G protein signaling 4 (*RGS4*), G72 and D-amino-acid oxidase (*DAOA*; Norton, Williams, & Owen, 2006; Owen, Craddock, & O'Donovan, 2005; http://www.szgene.org). The risk conferred by individual SNPs is modest (OR ~ 1.2; Shirts & Nimgaonkar, 2004).

The promise of genome-wide association studies (GWAS)

Several technological advancements have recently enabled GWAS for genetically complex disorders (Altshuler, Daly, & Lander, 2008). The prime attraction of GWAS, in contrast to candidate gene analyses, is the facile analysis of the entire genome and the ability to rank risk due to individual polymorphisms. GWAS can also enable analysis of epistatic interactions. However, sample size is a major constraint. As statistical analyses require penalties for multiple comparisons, insufficiently sized samples run the risk of false-negative results (the current convention requires p values of 1×10^{-8} or better with individual variants).

GWAS and common polymorphisms

Understandably, the first published report (which used pooled DNA samples from 645 participants) reported only suggestive, albeit consistent, associations (Mah et al., 2006). A later study that individually assayed 178 cases and 144 controls also reported a suggestive association ($p = 3.7 \times 10^{-7}$; Lencz et al., 2007). Another study performed GWAS on 479 cases and 2,937 controls, but associations with genome-wide significance could not be detected (Sullivan et al., 2008). Subsequent GWAS studies were considerably larger. Still, samples of 871 cases and 863 controls did not detect genome-wide significant associations (Need et al., 2009). Three other larger GWAS samples similarly did not individually yield genome-wide significant results, though a significant result emerged in the chromosome 6p21.3–22.1 region when all three were pooled (ISC (International Schizophrenia Consortium); Purcell et al., 2009; Shi et al., 2009; Stefansson et al., 2009). Another meta-analysis involving overlapping samples indicated significant associations with an intronic SNP in the zinc-finger protein gene 804A (*ZNF804A*, OR 1.12, $p = 1.61 \times 10^{-7}$; O'Donovan et al., 2008). The biological function of the human leukocyte antigen (HLA) polymorphisms implicated in schizophrenia and the ZNF804A SNP is unknown. Thus, genome-wide significant results are emerging, but they explain only a small fraction of the substantial heritability of SZ.

GWAS and rare polymorphisms

Recently, a hypothesis linking rare mutations to psychiatric disorders has come to the fore (McClellan, Susser, & King, 2007). Interest has increasingly centered on relatively large, submicroscopic chromosomal aberrations such as copy number variants (CNVs). CNVs are segments of DNA 1 kilobase (kb) or larger, for which copy number differences have been revealed by comparison of individual genomes (Feuk, Carson, & Scherer, 2006). They include copy number duplications or deletions, combinations of duplications and deletions at the same locus, or even multi-allelic, complex rearrangements (Redon et al., 2006). Not only can such changes directly affect transcription of particular genes in the deleted/duplicate genes, they can also affect transcription of more remotely located genes. Moreover, they can lead to genomic instability in future generations (Cook & Scherer, 2008). Interest in CNVs in psychiatric disorders was sparked by case-control studies of autism spectrum disorder (ASD; Cusco et al., 2009; Marshall et al., 2008; Sebat et al., 2007; Szatmari et al., 2007). Recently, an excess of CNVs has also been reported in schizophrenia (Kirov et al., 2008; Rujescu et al., 2009; Vrijenhoek et al., 2008; Walsh et al., 2008; Xu et al., 2009). The most notable associations involved being deletions on chromosome 1q21.1 and 15q13.3 (OR > 6; Consortium, 2008), that were also noted in a schizophrenia and psychosis study (Stefansson et al., 2008).

The substantial risks conferred by individual CNVs are clearly important, but there are several unresolved issues. First, clear identification of CNVs is challenging. Second, due to their relative rarity, the "true" prevalence of many CNVs is unknown. Though CNVs may confer substantive risk, they may individually be very rare (Consortium, 2008; Cook & Scherer, 2008). A CNV may not be completely penetrant, as many inherited CNVs are noted among parents who are normal (Cook & Scherer, 2008). Though CNVs such as a ch15q11-q13 repeat and a deletion at chromosome 16p11 have been documented repeatedly in ASD, there is considerable diversity in the location of other CNVs that differentiate cases and controls in other studies (Abrahams & Geschwind, 2008). Finally, CNVs in the same region can lead to overlapping or very different phenotypes (Cook & Scherer, 2008).

Epistatic interactions

SZ is likely to be caused by multiple etiological agents, raising the possibility of interactions between individual risk factors and the further possibility that the joint risk is elevated multiplicatively. The interactions between genetic risk factors (epistasis) and/or interactions between genetic and non-genetic or environmental risk factors (G/E interactions) need not be restricted to pairs of factors but higher order interactions between numerous risk factors are more likely. Several candidate studies predating GWAS have reported on pair-wise and three-way interactions between SNPs localized to several SZ candidate genes, reviewed by Prasad and colleagues (2010). Most of the analyses were restricted to 2–3 genes, but some reported on SNPs that individually were not associated with SZ. Epistatic interactions in relation to intermediate phenotype (magnetic resonance imaging, MRI, morphometric measures) have also been noted (Zinkstok et al., 2008). A "gene–environment" interaction model in relation to obstetric complications (OCs) and a set of selected schizophrenia candidate genes also suggested interactions (Nicodemus et al., 2008).

Such exploratory analyses can be hampered by false-positive and false-negative results. Further, individual risk factors may not have statistically detectable main effects. If such main effects are modified by another environmental or genetic variant, the power to detect it may be reduced (Cordell & Clayton, 2002). Efforts at replication may be hampered if the ascertainment schemes for replicate samples alter the impact or frequency of individual risk factors. Conventional statistical approaches that depend on hierarchical model building may fail to detect interaction effects in the absence of main effects (Culverhouse, Suarez, Lin, & Reich, 2002). Several novel analytic approaches are being developed (Martin, Ritchie, Hahn, Kang, & Moore, 2006; Ritchie, Hahn, & Moore, 2003; Velez et al., 2007; Zhang & Liu, 2007). Some methods focus on case-only designs (Cui et al., 2008; Kang et al., 2008). A restricted partition method is also being developed for quantitative traits (Cockerham & Weir, 1984). Genetic and statistical models are developed to align the locus by "genetic background interaction concept" with more standard concepts of epistasis, when genetic background is modeled using an additive relationship matrix (Culverhouse, Klein, & Shannon, 2004; Jannink, 2007). Application of these approaches to GWAS datasets is awaited.

Summary of current SZ gene-mapping studies

Though encouraging replications have been observed in genetic-association studies, the primary associations have not been identified consistently at most of these loci for SZ, either because the pattern of linkage disequilibrium (LD) makes it difficult to assign primacy, or because of the associations interactions between polymorphisms. The majority of associations occur in untranslated regions, so the functional impacts of the associations are unclear.

Can GWAS explain SZ genetics?

GWAS have attained spectacular success for identifying novel genetic risk factors for a host of common, multi-factorial diseases; some of these studies have illuminated novel causative genes (Altshuler et al., 2008; Manolio et al., 2009). There have also been less spectacular results for many other disorders, including SZ. Skeptics have argued that the genetic architecture of polygenic/multi-factorial disorders may be too complex to dissect effectively, in view of likely environmental variation (Dermitzakis & Clark, 2009). The possible reasons for the "dark matter" of unidentified genetic risk have recently been elaborated (Manolio et al., 2009). They include overestimation of heritability, inadequate control samples, undetermined polymorphisms, including rare variants and epistasis. All these factors arguably play a role (and are being addressed) in ongoing SZ studies. The results of additional GWAS studies, numbering many thousands of participants are awaited (Cichon et al., 2009).

Proving causation

Even if credible statistical associations are found from GWAS, they will only provide probabilistic evidence. Convincing demonstration of etiology will arguably require other lines of evidence, particularly functional evidence. The original Koch's postulates were framed for infectious agents and are less relevant for chronic, non-infectious disorders (Koch, 1882). The Bradford Hill criteria are more suitable. They include establishment of a temporal relationship, strength of the association, demonstration of a dose–response relationship, consistency, plausibility, consideration of alternate explanations, specificity and coherence (Hill, 1965). It has been argued that they, too, may be difficult to fulfill when a genetic variant has modest effect (Hill, 1965; Page, George, Go, Page, & Allison, 2003). Page and colleagues argue that in such a context, the researcher is forced to argue for "probabilistic" causation (Page et al., 2003). They suggest that acceptance of a genetic variant as a causative factor should occur by a process of elimination of plausible artifacts. They also require "biological plausibility", a condition that may be difficult to fulfill for disorders of unknown etiology such as SZ.

Proof of causation may ultimately have to rest on prospective cohort-based studies. Such studies are difficult. Given the relatively low incidence of SZ, it may be very expensive to recruit and prospectively evaluate sufficiently large cohorts. Perhaps the most compelling proof for causation will emerge if and when rational therapies designed on the basis of the genetic information are shown to be efficacious. Hence alternative strategies are necessary.

A proposed framework for SZ gene-mapping studies

In view of the inconsistencies and the anticipated difficulty in proving causation solely through gene-mapping efforts, we suggest a scheme that may be of practical use. Our suggested approach will help identify additional information that may be useful for building pathogenic models for SZ and allied disorders. We propose "recursive functional analysis" (RFA), a modification of our earlier design for evaluating epistatic interactions (Prasad et al., 2010). It entails complementary cellular, *in vitro* and *in vivo* studies to investigate the impact of variation at risk loci. Such studies would proceed in tandem with replicate analyses, each set of studies informing the other (see Figure 15.1). Once an association is detected, our design calls for additional replicate studies. If a statistically satisfactory replication is detected, further fine mapping work as well as functional analyses are suggested. The fine mapping would be dictated by available information; it could include evaluation of additional polymorphisms through "deep" sequencing, analyses of haplotypes and epistatic interactions. The functional analyses would also be dictated by the nature of the associated allele, and would entail interlocking, iterative evaluations of the putative risk allele in relation to mRNA/protein levels, selected cellular assays, animal models and key human quantitative traits. In addition, experiments exclusive of the genetic variants may also be necessary, e.g., eliciting gene function, bioassays and interactional networks. Thus, a thread connecting pairs of key variables could be generated that may help explain pathogenesis more comprehensively. The essential goal is to understand how the impact of the genetic variation is propagated spatially and temporally from the DNA level to the level of overt behavior (Dermitzakis, 2008).

Even if replication is available, the other arm of the RFA scheme requires analyses of as many additional samples as possible. While meta-analysis would

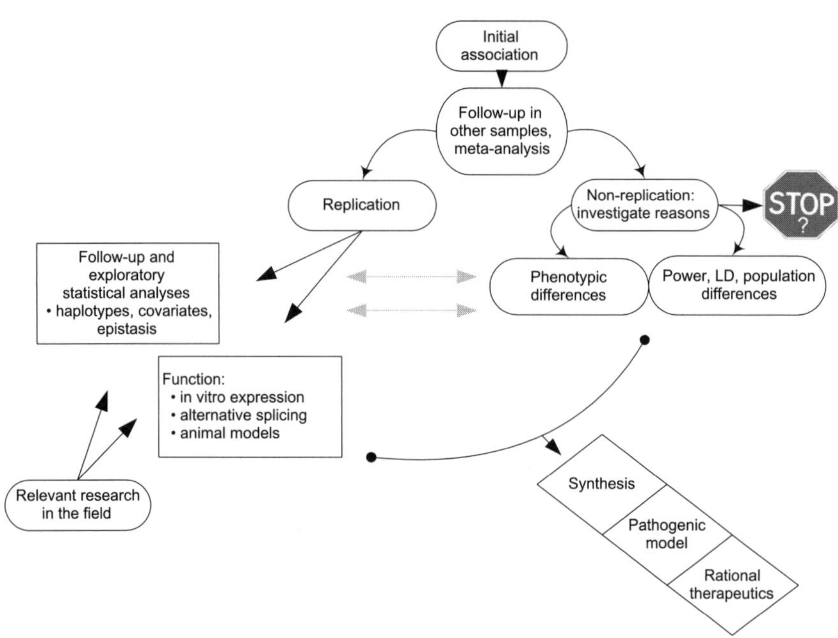

Figure 15.1 Recursive functional analysis (RFA).

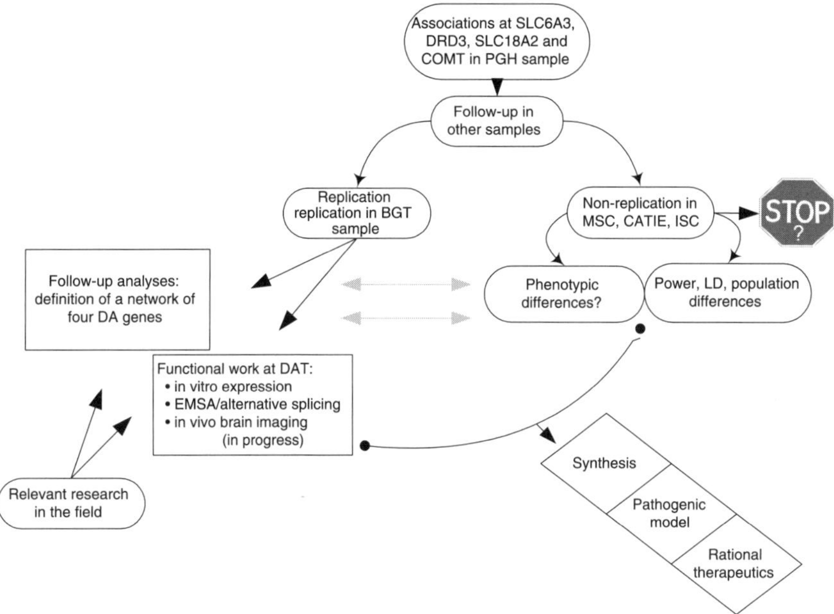

Figure 15.2 Progress with dopamine gene-association studies using RFA.

naturally be considered, one would also analyze additional samples that ideally have adequate power to detect the association. Analysis of additional ethnic groups would be considered important not only to assist with fine mapping, but also to evaluate the role of environmental risk factors in the future. Based on prior evidence, one may anticipate one or more non-replicating samples. We view the non-replicating samples as potentially being important for refining hypotheses stemming from the initial association. Analysis of available genomic and phenotypic information in conjunction with the replicating samples may show reasons for the lack of replication. Such information would be woven into the original observations, and, in conjunction with the functional analyses, may help refine models of pathogenesis, thus possibly paving the way for rational therapeutics. In the following section, we describe our ongoing work with dopamine gene variants, with a focus on dopamine transporter gene (*SLC6A3*) variants (see Figure 15.2).

Testing the dopamine (DA) hypothesis with genetic variants: Application of the RFA scheme

A number of neurotransmitters have been implicated in SZ, potentially suggesting a very large number of candidate genes. A considerable portion of SZ research has involved dopamine (DA) dysfunction, stemming from a heuristic "DA hypothesis"

(Carlsson, 1988). The hypothesis has been progressively refined since its simplistic invocation of a hyper-dopaminergic state (Crow, 1981; Howes & Kapur, 2009; Lang, Puls, Muller, Strutz-Seebohm, & Gallinat, 2007). Numerous DA polymorphisms have been investigated in SZ, with inconsistent results (Talkowski, Bamne, Mansour, & Nimgaonkar, 2007). Our review suggested that a significant proportion of common variation in the DA pathway has not been considered in past genetic-association studies, possibly contributing to the lack of consistency between studies (Talkowski et al., 2007). Since different DA gene variants have typically been evaluated in each study, it has often been difficult to conduct meaningful meta-analyses (Allen et al., 2008).

Recognizing that DA dysfunction is unlikely to explain a major portion of etiology, we have conducted multi-stage analyses of independent samples. We have emphasized joint analyses across independent samples (Talkowski et al., 2008). We initially screened 18 dopamine-related genes using two independent Caucasian samples from the USA: a family-based sample and a case-control sample. To improve power, we evaluated the joint distribution of test statistics from both samples (Skol, Scott, Abecasis, & Boehnke, 2006). Nominally significant associations were detected with *SLC6A3* (aka *DAT*), *DRD3*, *COMT*, and *SLC18A2* (aka *VMAT2*). Systematic analyses were then conducted for these four genes using tag SNPs in an extended US case-control sample (478 cases and 501 controls). Pair-wise epistatic interactions were also modeled for selected SNPs. The results were next tested in an independent Caucasian family-based sample from Bulgaria (n = 659 case–parent trios). Joint analyses of the US and the Bulgarian samples identified nominally significant association at all four genes ($p_{joint} < .05$). We tested 29 putative interactions from the initial study and detected replication between 7 locus pairs ($p < .05$ in both samples). Simulations suggested our interaction results were unlikely to have occurred by chance (p = .008 and .001, respectively; Talkowski et al., 2008). Based on the suggestive associations, an additional set of 24 DA genes were analyzed among the US Caucasian cases and screened adult controls. Some case-control differences were noted at individual SNPs, but no significant associations were detected following gene-based tests (Hoteling's T2 or Tmax) and appropriate corrections for multiple comparisons. Thus, the results supported a continued focus on the DA genes of interest. We subsequently proposed a network of risk alleles at four DA genes that together confer risk for SZ.

Further analysis of the DA network hypothesis: Focus on the dopamine transporter (*SLC6A3, DAT*)

The DA genetic-association studies pointed us towards a limited set of genes, but the interactions are only statistical in nature. As enunciated in our RFA scheme, they would be more plausible if there was functional evidence, particularly at the allelic level. In addition, the associations were detected with representative tag SNPs; the true risk variants may not have been analyzed. Indeed, our analyses focused exclusively on common polymorphisms. The impact of rare variants is still unknown. To enable systematic analyses, we have evaluated additional polymorphisms individually at the genes of interest, with an initial focus on the *DAT* (*SLC6A3*; Talkowski et al., 2010). We prioritized *SLC6A3* because polymorphisms at this locus appeared to contribute a significant number of epistatic interactions, so it might be a "hub" for a set of causative variants. We aim to extend our analyses to the other three genes once additional, convincing data are available.

We initially analyzed rs3756450, a SNP that is associated with SZ in our samples and is localized 5′ to the promoter sequences of *SLC6A3* (Kelada et al., 2005). We conducted electrophoretic mobility shift assays (EMSA) and found that allele-specific effects are detectable (Talkowski et al., 2008). As this genomic region may represent a novel promoter regulatory domain for *DAT* transcription, we investigated the impact of common SNPs in a 2.8 kb region flanking the core promoter region (- 2.7 kb to + 63 bp) in the neuroblastoma cell line SH-SY5Y, using dual luciferase promoter assays. Haplotypes generated by site-directed mutagenesis revealed varying impact of individual SNPs on promoter activity using dual luciferase assays. Analyses in silico also predicted allele-specific binding of transcription factors for some of these SNPs. Though EMSA assays indicated several factors that appeared to bind to specific sites within this region, allele-specific binding was not detected for any SNP apart from rs3756450. We have thus identified novel putative regulatory domains flanking the core promoter of *DAT* that merit further investigation (Bamne, Talkowski, Chowdari, & Nimgaonkar, 2010).

Representative common polymorphisms of *SLC6A3* were next identified (Talkowski et al., 2010). Analysis of these polymorphisms in the US and Bulgarian samples identified replicable associations with SZ. Most of the associated SNPs were localized to the third and fourth introns. Computational modeling of genomic sequences at introns 3 and 4 predicted a novel cassette exon within intron 3, designated E3b. E3b is conserved among primates and many other mammalian groups. Alternative splicing of E3b was confirmed in a region-specific manner in post-mortem human brain. In mini-gene constructs, the extent of E3b splicing varies between two common haplotypes, one of which confers risk for SZ in the initial samples. As E3b introduces multiple early in-frame stop codons, it truncates the *SLC6A3* open-reading frame and may cause the mRNA to undergo nonsense-mediated decay. Thus, genomic variants that increase E3b splicing could reduce the amount of productive mRNA available for translation. We have begun to test this hypothesis using post-mortem brain samples. Eventually, we also hope to test this model as a pathogenic mechanism for schizophrenia.

Following our RFA scheme, we also evaluated whether the initial genetic associations could be observed in other cohorts. We accessed *SLC6A3* SNP data from three independent case-control GWAS, namely the Molecular Genetics of Schizophrenia (MGS; Shi et al., 2009), the Clinical Antipsychotic Trials of Intervention Effectiveness (CATIE; Stroup et al., 2003), and the International Schizophrenia Consortium (ISC; Purcell et al., 2009). Analysis of genotyped and imputed SNPs did not show significant associations consistent with those detected in our samples, though some nominally significant associations were detected in the ISC samples.

In view of the discrepancies between our initial results and the later GWAS analyses, we are now evaluating phenotypic variation as a possible source for the discrepancy. This is difficult as the studies used different interview schedules. However, some compatible data are available from our initial Pittsburgh samples and the MGS dataset. Initial analyses reveal highly significant differences in demographic features, as well as the prevalence of different psychotic phenomena (Talkowski et al., 2010).

Further steps to analyze the DA network hypothesis

Having consistently detected associations with schizophrenia in some but not all samples, we are now querying putative risk alleles using additional cellular assays and complementary phenotypes. Consistent with the RFA scheme, we are also investigating correlates between individual polymorphisms and brain-imaging variables. Finally, through multivariate analyses of clinical variables, we are attempting to unravel variables contributing to the discrepant associations across well-powered samples. Since meta-analyses of all available samples do not support the initial replicable associations, the null hypothesis deserves serious consideration (vide infra).

Conclusions

Our studies with DA gene polymorphisms illustrate the integrated RFA approach that we advocate for understanding genetically complex disorders. In contrast to many other investigators, we are conducting genetic associations and functional studies in tandem. These studies are woven into complementary investigations by other groups. The goal is to motivate further focused searches and ultimately to develop rational therapies. Still, our studies continue to beg two important questions: (i) When should studies such as ours be abandoned in view of non-replications?; (ii) When is a polymorphism accepted definitively as a causative factor? These questions need to be debated. While p-values from genetic-association studies provide defined benchmarks, an iron clad set of criteria that include functional studies may be difficult to arrive at. The ultimate evidence may be the development of effective, rational therapies.

Acknowledgements

This work was supported by National Institutes of Health (Grant numbers MH56242, MH63480 to VLN, GM081293 to AJL), NSF (grant 0821202 to AJL) and Pennsylvania Department of Health (SAP# 4100043365; PI, R. Loeber).

References

Abrahams, B. S., & Geschwind, D. H. (2008). Advances in autism genetics: On the threshold of a new neurobiology. *Nature Review of Genetics*, *9*(5), 341–355.

Allen, N. C., Bagade, S., McQueen, M. B., Ioannidis, J. P., Kavvoura, F. K., Khoury, M. J., et al. (2008). Systematic meta-analyses and field synopsis of genetic association studies in schizophrenia: The SzGene database. *Nature Genetics*, *40*(7), 827–834.

Altshuler, D., Daly, M. J., & Lander, E. S. (2008). Genetic mapping in human disease. *Science*, *322*(5903), 881–888.

Bamne, M. N., Talkowski, M. E., Chowdari, K. V., & Nimgaonkar, V. L. (2010). Functional analysis of upstream common polymorphisms of the dopamine transporter gene. *Schizophrenia Bulletin*, *36*(5), 977–982.

Carlsson, A. (1988). The current status of the dopamine hypothesis of schizophrenia. *Neuropsychopharmacology*, *1*(3), 179–186.

Cichon, S., Craddock, N., Daly, M., Faraone, S. V., Gejman, P. V., Kelsoe, J., et al. (2009). Genomewide association studies: History, rationale, and prospects for psychiatric disorders. *American Journal of Psychiatry*, *166*(5), 540–556.

Cockerham, C. C., & Weir, B. S. (1984). Covariances of relatives stemming from a population undergoing mixed self and random mating. *Biometrics*, *40*(1), 157–164.

Consortium, T. I. S. (2008). Rare chromosomal deletions and duplications increase risk of schizophrenia. *Nature*, *455*(7210), 237–241.

Cook, E. H., Jr., & Scherer, S. W. (2008). Copy-number variations associated with neuropsychiatric conditions. *Nature*, *455*(7215), 919–923.

Cordell, H. J., & Clayton, D. G. (2002). A unified stepwise regression procedure for evaluating the relative effects of polymorphisms within a gene using case/control or family data: Application to HLA in type 1 diabetes. *American Journal of Human Genetics*, *70*(1), 124–141.

Crow, T. J. (1981). Positive and negative schizophrenia symptoms and the role of dopamine. *British Journal of Psychiatry*, *139*, 251–254.

Cui, Y., Kang, G., Sun, K., Qian, M., Romero, R., & Fu, W. (2008). Gene-centric genomewide association study via entropy. *Genetics*, *179*(1), 637–650.

Culverhouse, R., Klein, T., & Shannon, W. (2004). Detecting epistatic interactions contributing to quantitative traits. *Genetic Epidemiology*, *27*(2), 141–152.

Culverhouse, R., Suarez, B. K., Lin, J., & Reich, T. (2002). A perspective on epistasis: Limits of models displaying no main effect. *American Journal of Human Genetics*, *70*(2), 461–471.

Cusco, I., Medrano, A., Gener, B., Vilardell, M., Gallastegui, F., Villa, O., et al. (2009). Autism-specific copy number variants further implicate the phosphatidylinositol signaling pathway and the glutamatergic synapse in the etiology of the disorder. *Human Molecular Genetics*, *18*(10), 1795–1804.

Dermitzakis, E. T. (2008). From gene expression to disease risk. *Nature Genetics*, *40*(5), 492–493.

Dermitzakis, E. T., & Clark, A. G. (2009). Genetics. Life after GWA studies. *Science*, *326*(5950), 239–240.

Feuk, L., Carson, A. R., & Scherer, S. W. (2006). Structural variation in the human genome. *Nature Review of Genetics*, *7*(2), 85–97.

Gottesman, I. I. (1994). Complications to the complex inheritance of schizophrenia [Review]. *Clinical Genetics*, *46*(1 Spec. No.), 116–123.

Hill, A. (1965). The environment and disease: Association or causation? *Proceedings of the Royal Society of Medicine*, *58*, 295–300.

Howes, O. D., & Kapur, S. (2009). The dopamine hypothesis of schizophrenia: Version III—The final common pathway. *Schizophrenia Bulletin*, *35*(3), 549–562.

Jablensky, A. V., & Kalaydjieva, L. V. (2003). Genetic epidemiology of schizophrenia: Phenotypes, risk factors, and reproductive behavior. *American Journal of Psychiatry*, *160*(3), 425–429.

Jannink, J. L. (2007). Identifying quantitative trait locus by genetic background interactions in association studies. *Genetics*, *176*(1), 553–561.

Kang, G., Yue, W., Zhang, J., Huebner, M., Zhang, H., Ruan, Y., et al. (2008). Two-stage designs to identify the effects of SNP combinations on complex diseases. *Journal of Human Genetics*, *53*(8), 739–746.

Kelada, S. N., Costa-Mallen, P., Checkoway, H., Carlson, C. S., Weller, T. S., Swanson, P. D., et al. (2005). Dopamine transporter (SLC6A3) 5′ region haplotypes significantly affect transcriptional activity in vitro but are not associated with Parkinson's disease. *Pharmacogenetic Genomics.*, *15*(9), 659–668.

Kirov, G., Gumus, D., Chen, W., Norton, N., Georgieva, L., Sari, M., et al. (2008). Comparative genome hybridization suggests a role for NRXN1 and APBA2 in schizophrenia. *Human Molecular Genetics*, *17*(3), 458–465.

Koch, R. (Ed.). (1882). *Die Aetiologie der Tuberculose*. New York, NY: Dover.

Lang, U. E., Puls, I., Muller, D. J., Strutz-Seebohm, N., & Gallinat, J. (2007). Molecular mechanisms of schizophrenia. *Cell Physiology and Biochemistry*, *20*(6), 687–702.

Lencz, T., Morgan, T. V., Athanasiou, M., Dain, B., Reed, C. R., Kane, J. M., et al. (2007). Converging evidence for a pseudoautosomal cytokine receptor gene locus in schizophrenia. *Molecular Psychiatry*, *12*(6), 572–580.

Lewis, C. M., Levinson, D. F., Wise, L. H., DeLisi, L. E., Straub, R. E., Hovatta, I., et al. (2003). Genome scan meta-analysis of schizophrenia and bipolar disorder, part II: Schizophrenia. *American Journal of Human Genetics*, *73*(1), 34–48.

Mah, S., Nelson, M. R., Delisi, L. E., Reneland, R. H., Markward, N., James, M. R., et al. (2006). Identification of the semaphorin receptor PLXNA2 as a candidate for susceptibility to schizophrenia. *Molecular Psychiatry*, *11*(5), 471–478.

Manolio, T. A., Collins, F. S., Cox, N. J., Goldstein, D. B., Hindorff, L. A., Hunter, D. J., et al. (2009). Finding the missing heritability of complex diseases. *Nature*, *461*(7265), 747–753.

Marshall, C. R., Noor, A., Vincent, J. B., Lionel, A. C., Feuk, L., Skaug, J., et al. (2008). Structural variation of chromosomes in autism spectrum disorder. *American Journal of Human Genetics*, *82*(2), 477–488.

Martin, E. R., Ritchie, M. D., Hahn, L., Kang, S., & Moore, J. H. (2006). A novel method to identify gene–gene effects in nuclear families: The MDR-PDT. *Genetic Epidemiology*, *30*(2), 111–123.

McClellan, J. M., Susser, E., & King, M. C. (2007). Schizophrenia: A common disease caused by multiple rare alleles. *British Journal of Psychiatry*, *190*, 194–199.

Need, A. C., Ge, D., Weale, M. E., Maia, J., Feng, S., Heinzen, E. L., et al. (2009). A genome-wide investigation of SNPs and CNVs in schizophrenia. *Public Library of Science Genetics*, *5*(2), e1000373.

Nicodemus, K. K., Marenco, S., Batten, A. J., Vakkalanka, R., Egan, M. F., Straub, R. E., et al. (2008). Serious obstetric complications interact with hypoxia-regulated/vascular-expression genes to influence schizophrenia risk. *Molecular Psychiatry*, *13*(9), 873–877.

Norton, N., Williams, H. J., & Owen, M. J. (2006). An update on the genetics of schizophrenia. *Current Opinions in Psychiatry*, *19*(2), 158–164.

O'Donovan, M. C., Craddock, N., Norton, N., Williams, H., Peirce, T., Moskvina, V., et al. (2008). Identification of loci associated with schizophrenia by genome-wide association and follow-up. *Nature Genetics*, *40*(9), 1053–1055.

O'Donovan, M. C., & Owen, M. J. (1999). Candidate gene-association studies of schizophrenia. *American Journal of Human Genetics*, *65*(3), 587–592.

Owen, M. J., Craddock, N., & O'Donovan, M. C. (2005). Schizophrenia: Genes at last? *Trends in Genetics*, *21*(9), 518–525.

Page, G. P., George, V., Go, R. C., Page, P. Z., & Allison, D. B. (2003). "Are we there yet?": Deciding when one has demonstrated specific genetic causation in complex diseases and quantitative traits. *American Journal of Human Genetics*, *73*(4), 711–719.

Petronis, A., Gottesman, I. I., Kan, P., Kennedy, J. L., Basile, V. S., Paterson, A. D., et al. (2003). Monozygotic twins exhibit numerous epigenetic differences: Clues to twin discordance? *Schizophrenia Bulletin*, *29*(1), 169–178.

Prasad, K. M., Talkowski, M. E., Chowdari, K. V., McClain, L., Yolken, R. H., & Nimgaonkar, V. L. (2010). Candidate genes and their interactions with other genetic/environmental risk factors in the etiology of schizophrenia. *Brain Research Bulletin*, *83*(3–4), 86–92.

Purcell, S. M., Wray, N. R., Stone, J. L., Visscher, P. M., O'Donovan, M. C., Sullivan, P. F., et al. (2009). Common polygenic variation contributes to risk of schizophrenia and bipolar disorder. *Nature*, *460*(7256), 748–752.

Redon, R., Ishikawa, S., Fitch, K. R., Feuk, L., Perry, G. H., Andrews, T. D., et al. (2006). Global variation in copy number in the human genome. *Nature*, *444*(7118), 444–454.

Risch, N. (1990). Linkage strategies for genetically complex traits. II. The power of affected relative pairs. *American Journal of Human Genetics*, *46*, 229–241.

Risch, N., & Merikangas, K. (1996). The future of genetic studies of complex human diseases. *Science*, *273*(13), 1516–1517.

Ritchie, M. D., Hahn, L. W., & Moore, J. H. (2003). Power of multifactor dimensionality reduction for detecting gene–gene interactions in the presence of genotyping error, missing data, phenocopy, and genetic heterogeneity. *Genetic Epidemiology*, *24*(2), 150–157.

Rujescu, D., Ingason, A., Cichon, S., Pietilainen, O. P., Barnes, M. R., Toulopoulou, T., et al. (2009). Disruption of the neurexin 1 gene is associated with schizophrenia. *Human Molecular Genetics*, *18*(5), 988–996.

Sebat, J., Lakshmi, B., Malhotra, D., Troge, J., Lese-Martin, C., Walsh, T., et al. (2007). Strong association of de novo copy number mutations with autism. *Science*, *316*(5823), 445–449.

Shi, J., Levinson, D. F., Duan, J., Sanders, A. R., Zheng, Y., Pe'er, I., et al. (2009). Common variants on chromosome 6p22.1 are associated with schizophrenia. *Nature*, *460*(7256), 753–757.

Shirts, B. H., & Nimgaonkar, V. (2004). The genes for schizophrenia: Finally a breakthrough? *Current Psychiatry Reports*, *6*(4), 303–312.

Skol, A. D., Scott, L. J., Abecasis, G. R., & Boehnke, M. (2006). Joint analysis is more efficient than replication-based analysis for two-stage genome-wide association studies. *Nature Genetics*, *38*(2), 209–213.

Stefansson, H., Ophoff, R. A., Steinberg, S., Andreassen, O. A., Cichon, S., Rujescu, D., et al. (2009). Common variants conferring risk of schizophrenia. *Nature*, *460*(7256), 744–747.

Stefansson, H., Rujescu, D., Cichon, S., Pietilainen, O. P., Ingason, A., Steinberg, S., et al. (2008). Large recurrent microdeletions associated with schizophrenia. *Nature*, *455*(7210), 232–236.

Stroup, T. S., McEvoy, J. P., Swartz, M. S., Byerly, M. J., Glick, I. D., Canive, J. M., et al. (2003). The National Institute of Mental Health Clinical Antipsychotic Trials of Intervention Effectiveness (CATIE) project: Schizophrenia trial design and protocol development. *Schizophrenia Bulletin*, *29*(1), 15–31.

Sullivan, P. F., Lin, D., Tzeng, J. Y., van den Oord, E., Perkins, D., Stroup, T. S., et al. (2008). Genomewide association for schizophrenia in the CATIE study: Results of stage 1. *Molecular Psychiatry*, *13*(6), 570–584.

Szatmari, P., Paterson, A. D., Zwaigenbaum, L., Roberts, W., Brian, J., Liu, X. Q., et al. (2007). Mapping autism risk loci using genetic linkage and chromosomal rearrangements. *Nature Genetics*, *39*(3), 319–328.

Talkowski, M. E., Bamne, M., Mansour, H., & Nimgaonkar, V. L. (2007). Dopamine genes and schizophrenia: Case closed or evidence pending? *Schizophrenia Bulletin*, *33*(5), 1071–1081.

Talkowski, M. E., Kirov, G., Bamne, M., Georgieva, L., Torres, G., Mansour, H., et al. (2008). A network of dopaminergic gene variations implicated as risk factors for schizophrenia. *Human Molecular Genetics*, *17*(5), 747–758.

Talkowski, M. E., McCann, K. L., Chen, M., McClain, L., Bamne, M., Wood, J., et al. (2010). Fine-mapping reveals novel alternative splicing of the dopamine transporter. *American Journal of Medical Genetics Part B: Neuropsychiatric Genetics*, *153B*(8), 1434–1447.

Velez, D. R., White, B. C., Motsinger, A. A., Bush, W. S., Ritchie, M. D., Williams, S. M., et al. (2007). A balanced accuracy function for epistasis modeling in imbalanced datasets using multifactor dimensionality reduction. *Genetic Epidemiology*, *31*(4), 306–315.

Vrijenhoek, T., Buizer-Voskamp, J. E., van der Stelt, I., Strengman, E., Sabatti, C., Geurts van Kessel, A., et al. (2008). Recurrent CNVs disrupt three candidate genes in schizophrenia patients. *American Journal of Human Genetics*, *83*(4), 504–510.

Walsh, T., McClellan, J. M., McCarthy, S. E., Addington, A. M., Pierce, S. B., Cooper, G. M., et al. (2008). Rare structural variants disrupt multiple genes in neurodevelopmental pathways in schizophrenia. *Science*, *320*(5875), 539–543.

Xu, B., Woodroffe, A., Rodriguez-Murillo, L., Roos, J. L., van Rensburg, E. J., Abecasis, G. R., et al. (2009). Elucidating the genetic architecture of familial schizophrenia using rare copy number variant and linkage scans. *Proceedings of the National Academy of Sciences USA*, *106*(39), 16746–16751.

Zhang, Y., & Liu, J. S. (2007). Bayesian inference of epistatic interactions in case-control studies. *Nature Genetics*, *39*(9), 1167–1173.

Zinkstok, J., Schmitz, N., van Amelsvoort, T., Moeton, M., Baas, F., & Linszen, D. (2008). Genetic variation in COMT and PRODH is associated with brain anatomy in patients with schizophrenia. *Genes Brain and Behavior*, *7*(1), 61–69.

16 Ebb and flow in biological psychiatry

Tim J. Crow

One day early in 1966 I met the physician Sir John Ellis, for whom I had acted as houseman at the London Hospital, in the corridor. He asked me what I wanted to do. I already had a job arranged in the Physiology Department of the University of Aberdeen in the autumn of that year. I said I was interested in psychiatry, but had six months to spare. He contacted his friend Sir Aubrey Lewis and at short notice I was appointed by Gerald Russell and Michael Gelder to work on the professorial unit under Sir Aubrey in the six months before he retired. It turned out to be a most educational experience for a bewildered psychiatric tyro.

Sir Aubrey was a singular figure. He had the capacity to instil fear in the registrars on the Maudsley rotation by the threat of exposure of their intellectual nakedness with an erudite question. He was of a notably sceptical disposition. I have adapted the title of one of his essays "Ebb and Flow in Social Psychiatry", to "Biological Psychiatry" in honour of his successor Robin Murray, with whom I have enjoyed scientific controversy for nearly 30 years.

At the time of which I write the *Lancet* published an editorial, entitled "Pink Spots and Red Herrings", on the subject of whether schizophrenia was associated with excretion of dimethyl-phenyl-ethylamine (DMPE) in the urine, as had been proposed a year earlier by authors including two fellows of the Royal Society, one president of the College of Physicians, following work by A. J. Friedhoff in the USA. The paper proposed DMPE as the key to the chemistry of schizophrenia. The *Lancet* leader writer believed otherwise and turned out to be right. The researchers had ignored dietary variation and apparently detected a component of coffee.

Dopamine and laterality

Therefore I have taken "pink spots" and "red herrings" as categories for putative advances in biological psychiatry (see Table 16.1). The field is full of claims for genuine associations, many of which most workers in the field will regard as spurious, but to demonstrate this fact to the satisfaction of all is problematic.

The DMPE story therefore turned out to be a red herring. But it was followed in 1967 by what all agree is a genuine pink spot, the dopamine hypothesis of schizophrenia. This I think should properly be accredited to Randrup and Munkvad

Table 16.1 Ebb ("pink spots" or hopeful theories) and flow ("red herrings" or discarded theories) in biological psychiatry

Year	*Pink spot*	*Red herring*
1966		DMPE
1967	Dopamine hypothesis	
1969	Laterality and psychosis	
1972		Platelet MAO
1976	Ventricular size in schizophrenia	
1979		Virus-like agent
1983		Contagion
1985	Genetic psychoses	Non-genetic psychoses
1986	(1) Continuum of psychosis	
1987	Neurodevelopmental theory	Obstetric complications Prenatal influenza Polygenes (e.g., *ZNF804A*)
1989	(2) X–Y linked gene	
1995	(3) Sapiens-specific	
2000	(4) Germinal cell layer of the cortex	

(1967), two workers in Sct. Hans Hospital in Roskilde, Denmark. This has had a lasting influence, particularly in explaining the mode of action of neuroleptic drugs. It has been less successful in unravelling pathogenesis.

It can be contrasted with the second of my examples, the discovery of laterality in relation to psychosis, which took place at the Maudsley at the time I was there. Pierre Flor Henry reported that in temporal lobe epilepsy when psychosis develops and the lesion is on the left side it is schizophrenic in form, whereas when the lesion is on the right side it is affective in form (Flor-Henry, 1969). Few people believed Pierre at the time, perhaps in part because his presentation was "continental" in style. But in due course he was proven right, particularly by the work of Lindsay, Ounsted, and Richards (1979) in a follow-up of individuals diagnosed with epilepsy in childhood. It is an important finding. It reintroduced the question of laterality in relation to psychosis, which had been discussed but had lain dormant at the end of the nineteenth century.

Now I want to suggest that you can put the dopamine hypothesis and laterality together to solve the problem of how ascending monoaminergic neurones interact with laterality in the cortex, an interaction that has hitherto been obscure but relevant to the pathogenesis of psychotic symptoms. The key is the paper by Hsiao, Lin, Liu, Tzen, and Yen (2003). These authors investigated the dopamine uptake process with a ligand called 3H-TRODAT. They did not find an overall change in dopamine uptake in patients with schizophrenia but they did find a marked asymmetry—to the right in controls, that was absent in patients. With respect to this asymmetry there was a clear separation of patient and control populations such as has not been seen in the literature elsewhere.

What this indicates is that there is an interaction between ascending dopaminergic neurones, and asymmetries in the cortex. I think the interaction must occur at the level of the D2 receptors located on the cortico-striatal terminals in the corpus striatum. It has recently been shown that a representation of a word in the cerebral cortex is dependent on cortical width, the wider representation being on the side with the thinner cortex. This reflects the most recent evolutionary development within the human brain—the cortex on one side is thinned relative to the other. By contrast with this asymmetry, which is recent, the dopaminergic projections are ancient. This interaction shows us the way in which long established motivational systems influence the human capacity for language. The word, as De Saussure emphasized is bipartite, comprising a sound pattern (the "signifier") and its associations (the "signifieds"). One, presumably the signifier, is located in the dominant hemisphere, and one in the non-dominant hemisphere, and it is this that gives the capacity for language its characteristic flexibility, and its bi-hemispheric disposition.

Thus we have a framework for understanding the interaction between dopaminergic mechanisms and the symptoms of schizophrenia, encoded as they are in the structure of language. Recently I have discussed with Shitij Kapur the relationship between the learning theory concept of "incentive" and the concept that he has used in his discussions of the pathophysiology of schizophrenic symptoms of "salience". Are these the same concepts? The problem is that one (incentive) is derived from the animal literature, and one has been applied to human cognition, which as is well known is conducted in terms of symbolic representations, and these may have no manifestation in behaviour.

The resolution I suggest can be represented in the formula:

Salience = Incentive + Laterality.

I claim to be the first researcher to associate dopamine with reward processes (Crow, 1972) in the experiments that I conducted in physiology in Aberdeen and to be the first to associate dopaminergic processes with the type of reward referred to as "incentive" (Crow, 1973). I express the hope that the above formula will facilitate the application of the concept of incentive to the phenomena of human language including psychotic symptoms.

Platelet MAO

The next significant event that I identify is the discovery that the activity of the enzyme monoamine-oxidase (MAO) was reduced in the platelets of patients suffering from schizophrenia (Murphy & Wyatt, 1972). This was a striking finding repeated by a number of different groups working independently and apparently representing a genetically determined correlate of schizophrenia. A substantial literature was fairly soon generated and created considerable excitement. Reduced activity of monoamine degrading enzyme activity appeared consistent with over-activity of monoaminergic transmission, as for example in the dopamine over-activity hypothesis.

The literature might have been even larger had it not been for two reports. The first (Owen et al., 1976) was that in an unusual population of patients who had been free of neuroleptics enzyme activity was not reduced. The second (DeLisi et al., 1981) was that as patients were started on neuroleptics for the first time enzyme activity in their platelets progressively declined. It was clear that the reduction reported was a consequence, albeit slowly developing, of neuroleptic administration. Once this was appreciated the excitement rapidly abated. Platelet MAO was a red herring.

Ventricular size in schizophrenia

In 1976 my colleagues, Eve Johnstone, Chris Frith and I in the Division of Psychiatry at the Clinical Research Centre at Northwick Park Hospital collaborating with Louis Kreel and Janet Husband in the Division of Radiology and, making use of one of the first computerized tomographic machines to be deployed in clinical investigation, reported that the ventricles of a group of chronically hospitalized patients with schizophrenia were larger than those of an age- and pre-morbid-occupation-matched group of well individuals (Johnstone, Crow, Frith, Husband, & Kreel, 1976).

This finding was received with interest at the Institute of Psychiatry on the other side of London. From the internet it is possible to retrieve a copy of the second page of our paper. It is apparent that this particular cyber-page had been torn out of the journal *Lancet*, had been well fingered and had "rubbish" written in the margin. I had heard that the original had been taken from the library copy of the *Lancet* at the institute. I confirm this, as evidence of my interpretation of the sequence of events—that the finding was greeted as a red herring at the institute.

Word passed up through the hierarchy to Sir Denis Hill, then occupant of the chair of psychiatry, who wrote in a letter to the *Lancet* expressed with considerable civility:

> These findings are of such importance that every effort must be made to examine this work for possible sources of bias or error which could lead to erroneous conclusions. Johnstone et al. (1976) are aware of this but have not considered all the possibilities … .

In particular he suggested we had overlooked the possibility of diagnostic error. Nevertheless Sir Denis concluded that the findings "will prove a great stimulus to research in schizophrenia".

Prof David Marsden, at the time chair of the Department of Neurology at the Institute of Psychiatry, also wrote and expressed the opinion that the effect of neuroleptics (which we had actually documented) had been neglected. There is little doubt that opinion at the institute was that the finding was a red herring.

Thirty-three years later I think it is well accepted that this was not the case. An increase in ventricular size is one of the best replicated findings in schizophrenia research. Why it should be so is still obscure, but that it is so and is not due to physical treatment or other exogenous factors is established.

At this time a new face appeared on the research scene. Daniel Weinberger from the National Institute of Mental Health in Washington published a paper (Weinberger, Torrey, Neophytides, & Wyatt, 1979) in which he and his colleagues documented in a large series, decade by decade of age, and with even more extensive control of medication and other treatments, that indeed there was enlargement of the ventricles, relatively uniform and unrelated to extraneous factors. The important point that is now secure is that the change is uniform across populations and individuals, that is to say that there is a mean increase in ventricular volume without an increase in variance. This indicates that ventricular enlargement is characteristic of the group of diseases described as schizophrenia as a whole and that this group is therefore associated with structural brain change.

The viral theory

What was the change due to? The possibility that my colleagues and I, in association with David Tyrrell who played a significant part in the discovery of rhinoviruses, took seriously was that psychosis could be a type of viral encephalopathy, doubtless with slow progression and perhaps following a latent period, and that such an exogenous agent was responsible for damage to the tissues of the brain reflected in ventricular enlargement. There were precedents, for example in relation to the influenza pandemic of 1918, Vilyuisk encephalitis, and some other viral illnesses. We arranged for a battery of relevant investigations including lumbar punctures. After a time the researchers examining tissue cultures reported cytopathic effects that appeared to be prevented by a passage through filters of a certain pore size. The effect apparently could be transmitted from one cell culture to another although definitive identification as due to a virus was lacking. Tyrrell thought that it reflected the presence of a small virus, perhaps ribonucleic acid dependent, that was replicating with difficulty in the culture conditions. The findings were published in the *Lancet* (Tyrrell, Parry, Crow, Johnstone, & Ferrier, 1979). We also had some animal transmission experiments that yielded what we thought were interesting anomalies (Baker et al., 1983).

But the programme got not much further than this. Viral replication was not established, and in due course Taylor et al. (1982) were able to show that the cytopathic effect, although real, was not due to a replicating agent on the basis that it was not stopped by nucleic acid or protein synthesis inhibitors. Moreover, careful reduplication of the conditions of the transmission experiments failed to replicate the initial findings (Baker, Ridley,Crow, & Tyrrell, 1989). We concluded that although the cytopathogenic agent had not been identified it was not likely to be a virus, and the causes of schizophrenia had to be sought elsewhere.

Schizophrenia as contagion

Meantime another line of thought apparently consistent with the viral hypothesis had been developing. Torrey and Peterson (1973) argued that the epidemiology of psychosis was consistent with viral infection, and Hare (1983) presented the case that schizophrenia was a condition that increased in incidence in the nineteenth century. These authors suggested that the observations were consistent with an infection that was horizontally transmitted.

Impressed with these arguments I sought in the literature evidence in support of the contagion theory (Crow, 1983) and thought I had found it in the case of same-sex concordance in siblings, increased concordance in twins reared together compared to those reared apart, and a report of unusual incidences within apartment blocks in Moscow. The editor of the *Lancet* accepted the argument for publication with some foreboding, and was rewarded with a quick response in the correspondence columns. Among the contributions was one from Murray and Reveley (1983), who argued that it was not necessary to invoke a common pathogenic agent to explain concordance in monozygotic (MZ) twins because those who were more severely affected were more likely to be living together and concordant than those who were less severely affected. They further argued that:

> ... it seems unreasonable to suppose that any single factor will turn out to be implicated in all cases of schizophrenia ... strategies designed to highlight differences ... rather than to identify common aetiology, appear to hold the greatest promise.

I recollect dismissing the argument concerning MZ twins without too much embarrassment at the time, but was forced to recant nine months later for reasons that I explain below. On the question of heterogeneity of form of psychosis and its relationship to aetiological agent, there is also more to say later.

Meantime, Done and I (Crow & Done, 1983) thought we had found a new approach to the problem. When psychosis occurs in pairs of siblings if it is due to the passage of some agent from one to the other sibling, or if both encounter the agent from a third source, they should on the whole be affected at the same time. We therefore examined all the data we could find on sibling pairs with psychosis and, wonderful to relate, it confirmed the prediction. When siblings developed psychosis it appeared that they did so at the same time and not the same age. I was delighted, and harvested some notoriety from the propagation of the contagion theory. But then, as I recollect in the middle of the night, I saw the fly in the ointment. When one collects sibling pairs one does so at the time of admission to hospital: one hears about elder siblings who are already ill, one hears less about younger siblings who are yet to become ill. Selective bias enters the assessment. Age of onset must be taken into account. When this is done the findings appear quite contrary to the prediction—on the whole onsets occurred at the same age and not the same time (Crow & Done, 1986).

This finding, together with the negative findings of the search for a viral agent, finally convinced me we were mistaken. A viral theory provides no general account of the phenomena of psychosis.

Thus, with some regret (see e.g. Crow, 1993b), I had to place the viral hypothesis and the contagion theory in the class of red herrings.

Aetiological diversity and the continuum concept

The next event that I judge, at least in retrospect, to be of general interest emerged in the mid 1980s. Murray, Lewis, and Reveley (1985) developed the notion that the psychoses are intrinsically heterogeneous, and that this is the clue to their aetiological basis, many different aetiologies are expected. This view has had a considerable influence on the subsequent literature.

In contrast, although as far as I know the polarity was not noted at the time, is the concept that the psychoses constitute a continuum from typical schizophrenic illnesses with degeneration at one end, through schizoaffective and bipolar affective to unipolar affective illnesses at the other. I put this forward in a review (Crow, 1986), although, as is now well known, Emil Kraepelin himself had doubts as early as 1920 about the categorical nature of the dichotomy between schizophrenia and affective psychoses with which he is usually credited. Moreover the category of schizoaffective psychoses (Kasanin, 1933) challenged the original binary system, and this is particularly thrown into doubt by the reanalysis of data from the US/UK diagnostics study carried out by Kendell and Gourlay (1970). In a discriminant function analysis these authors failed to find the bimodal distribution predicted by the original binary system but found rather that the peak of distribution lay between the two classical entities. My paper drew attention to these earlier contributions and placed them alongside data from family studies (e.g., Angst, Felder, & Lohmeyer, 1979; Gershon et al., 1982), surveys (e.g., Odegaard, 1972; Penrose, 1991) and data on season of birth and incidence (on which I would now place less emphasis than I did then) to support the continuum viewpoint. I argued for a genetic continuum, and that this has implications for the structure of the gene (specifically that the nature of the variation was continuous and non-Mendelian, in form). An editorial in the *Lancet* (1987) commented on the issue.

As I now see it the concepts of aetiological diversity and continuity of form of psychosis are at least in part in conflict. If one believes there is more than one aetiological agent one is inclined to believe that the form of psychosis will reflect this diversity and to hope that the heterogeneity can be recognized clinically. Thus have some major advances in medicine taken place. By contrast if one is disposed to the view that there are no discontinuities in the clinical picture and that there is an underlying homogeneity, then one is drawn to the view that the variations in form of psychosis that are apparent to every clinician reflect a single spectrum of variation at the level of aetiology, and that in this case it has to be genetic. According to this view the phenomena of psychosis from this perspective raised fundamental questions about the nature of cross-species genetic variation.

The neurodevelopmental concept

In 1987 two papers appeared (Murray & Lewis, 1987; Weinberger, 1987) that formulated a viewpoint that previously had not been explicit in the literature, that the psychoses represent deviations of the development of the brain with age. Looking back one wonders to what extent one had considered this viewpoint previously. It can be argued that the notion is present in the literature, for example in some of the writings of Kraepelin and Bleuler, and particularly those of Kretschmer, but it seems these had not really been formulated as an aetiological theory. It is true that several authors including, for example, Gittelman-Klein and Klein (1969), who described a class of "childhood socials" who later developed psychosis, had considered the problem on a much longer time course than, for example, had we at the time we entertained the viral hypothesis. Such illnesses, perhaps unparsimoniously were regarded as exceptional. It is clear that they are inconsistent with a late environmental aetiology.

Weinberger writes of his theory that it "is a … model in which a fixed 'lesion' from early in life interacts with normal brain maturation events that occur much later … ". Murray and Lewis say that "the lesion lies dormant until the brain matures sufficiently to call into operation the damaged systems … ". Thus both are committed, at least in part, to an environmental aetiology.

The question is what such aetiologies are there? One possibility, introduced in both papers, is that complications of pregnancy and parturition are relevant, and this has precedent in the literature. It is now possible to come to a firm conclusion. The National Child Developmental Survey (Done et al., 1991) focused on the causes of perinatal mortality. Neither the individual causes of morbidity or mortality, nor a combined index had any success in predicting later onset of psychosis. R. E. Kendell's contributions to this debate are notable. Initially from a survey in Scotland he had come to the conclusion that some complications of pregnancy, e.g., pre-eclamptic toxaemia, predisposed to later psychosis. But then he appreciated that the first records to be returned to the Scottish office following births were those with the least complications. When he had corrected this bias in his control population, the association disappeared. His conclusion was that the role of birth complications had been overestimated. Most recently the meta-analysis by Cannon, Jones, and Murray (2002) of case-control series yielded substantially negative findings. The authors concluded, perhaps against their initial predictions, that "the findings from the population-based studies were mostly negative and surprisingly contradictory" and asked to comment on the specific issue of which complication was most relevant "at no stage did we suggest that a causal relationship has been established to any one obstetric risk factor".

This leaves prenatal exposure to influenza in the second trimester of pregnancy as the leading aetiological runner, as suggested by Mednick, Machon, Huttunen, and Bonett (1988) and supported by O'Callagan, Sham, Takei, Murray, and Glover (1991) and Sham et al. (1992). It is not widely appreciated that it was possible to subject this concept to a relatively stringent test in the National Child Development Survey data because many of the mothers had encountered influenza in the 1957 epidemic in the course of their pregnancies. The predictions of the influenza hypothesis were that among the 985 mothers who were exposed in the second trimester there should have been 28.5 children who developed psychosis, whereas there were in fact two, a figure consistent with the predictions of the hypothesis that prenatal influenza and schizophrenia are unrelated (e.g., Crow, 1997).

Thus we are left with few early environmental insults with which to support the original formulation of a neurodevelopmental theory. It is arguable that cannabis is an exception, but the evidence is much controverted, and might disappear in a puff of smoke!

The role of polygenes

As environmental factors fall away, a genetic predisposition becomes more attractive and has always been supported by evidence from family, twin and adoption studies. There are many supporters of the polygene theory, that many genes each of small effect are relevant, but as linkage (Crow, 2007) and association studies (Sanders et al., 2008) fail to reveal consistent effects of specific genes this concept becomes increasingly strained.

The paradigm case is *ZNF804A*, nominated by the reputable group of genetic workers in Cardiff as the salient finding from the most extensive survey (O'Donovan, Craddock, & Owens, 2008). Careful scrutiny of their table indicates that the *p*-values and odds ratios do not separate this gene from others selected on the basis that they form the positive tail of the stochastic distribution of the very large numbers of comparisons generated in association studies.

This leaves us with the rather awkward conclusion that we have no environmental precipitants and no genetic factors with which to bolster a neurodevelopmental theory.

The nature of the variation

If we return to the clinical phenomena that we wish to account for, and the functions with which they are associated, it is difficult to avoid the conclusion that we are dealing with intellectual ability and the capacity for language on the one hand and the full range of emotional expression on the other. Overall we are concerned with the capacity to develop beliefs about the external world and to interpret it in terms of the framework of human society. In other words these are species-specific capacities. Why should they be invariant with respect to gene sequence variation and the environment?

When one considers the phenomena are expressed in terms of age of onset across the reproductive phase of life one can see that there are large and homogeneous variations most unlikely to be accounted for by small effects of many genes (Marneros, Diester, & Rohde, 1991). Thus, earlier onsets are characteristic of states that are more schizophrenic in form and later onsets are affective in form: schizoaffective illnesses occur with a mean age of onset ten years later than schizophrenic and bipolar affective ten years later than this. Moreover the relationship between age of onset and sex is approximately linear over the age range from 3–60 years—20% are in females at the childhood end and 30% are in males at the age of 60 (Crow, 1993a). How are such uniformities to be accounted for in terms of multiple unrelated genes?

William Bateson (1909) considered that there was a form of variation that was intrinsic to a species, and that this had characteristics that distinguished it from Mendelian variation, which he in particular had introduced to the English-speaking scientific world. If not in the sequence where could such variation arise? We have to account for sex differences and that the distinction between species is related to the capacity for mate recognition, and this in turn depends on the sex chromosomes. Haldane's rule indicates that the X chromosome is intimately involved in the speciation process (Presgraves, 2008).

What change occurred on the sex chromosomes between the chimpanzee and man? The answer is clear; a small 3.5 megabase block on the X chromosome long arm was reduplicated on the Y chromosome short arm. This event occurred 6 million years ago (Williams, Close, Giouzeli, & Crow, 2006). Within this block of homology are located three genes, one of which has been eliminated and one probably inactivated by a frame shift mutation. This leaves the *Protocadherin11X/Y* gene pair as the explanation for the survival of the transposed block on the Y and as a possible explanation of species-specific differences. Of particular importance is the fact that there is an epigenetic interaction between the X and the Y (referred to as meiotic suppression of unpaired chromosomes—MSUC).

Such a mechanism must in some way regulate the expression of the Protocadherin gene pair. Such variation would thus depend upon the adhesive forces between the histone structures that make up the two chromosomes and are subject to methylation, phosphorylation and acetylation. The potential of such epigenetic diversity to account for variation that relates to cerebral asymmetry is illustrated by twin studies (Steinmetz, Herzog, Schlaug, Huang, & Jancke, 1995).

On this basis let us attempt to construct a hypothesis that might account for the genetic substructure of the neurodevelopmental hypothesis:

1. That a continuum of psychotic illness stretches from typically schizophrenic through schizoaffective and bipolar to unipolar affective psychoses.
2. That genetic variation is dependent upon a sex-chromosomal locus, specifically that it is X and Y linked.
3. The variation is sapiens-specific and relates to those characteristics that distinguish this species from the great apes.
4. The gene involved influences the germinal cell layer of the cerebral cortex.

As a cell surface adhesion factor that has changed in the course of hominid evolution the *Protocadherin11X/Y* gene pair fulfils these criteria (Williams et al., 2006).

References

Angst, J., Felder, W., & Lohmeyer, B. (1979). Schizoaffective disorders. I. Results of a genetic investigation. *Journal of Affective Disorders*, *1*, 139–153.

Baker, H. F., Ridley, R. M., Crow, T. J., Bloxham, C. A., Parry, R. P., & Tyrrell, D. A. J. (1983). An investigation of the effects of intracerebral injection in the marmoset of cytopathic cerebrospinal fluid from patients with schizophrenia or neurological disease. *Psychological Medicine*, *13*, 449–511.

Baker, H. F., Ridley, R. M., Crow, T. J., & Tyrrell, D. A. (1989). A re-investigation of the behavioural effects of intracerebral injection in marmosets of cytopathic cerebrospinal fluid from patients with schizophrenia or neurological disease. *Psychological Medicine*, *19*, 325–329.

Bateson, W. (1909). *Mendel's principles of heredity*. Cambridge, UK: Cambridge University Press.

Cannon, M., Jones, P. B., & Murray, R. M. (2002). Obstetric complications and schizophrenia: Historical and meta-analytic review. *American Journal of Psychiatry*, *159*, 1080–1092.

Crow, T. J. (1972). A map of the rat mesencephalon for electrical self-stimulation. *Brain Research*, *36*, 265–273.

Crow, T. J. (1973). Catecholamine-containing neurones and electrical self-stimulation. II. Theoretical considerations. *Psychological Medicine*, *3*, 66–73.

Crow, T. J. (1983). Is schizophrenia an infectious disease? *Lancet*, *342*, 173–175.

Crow, T. J. (1986). The continuum of psychosis and its implication for the structure of the gene. *British Journal of Psychiatry*, *149*, 419–429.

Crow, T. J. (1993a). Sexual selection, Machiavellian intelligence and the origins of psychosis. *Lancet*, *342*, 594–598.

Crow, T. J. (1993b). Should contagion be resurrected? A response to Butler and Stieglitz. *Schizophrenia Bulletin*, *19*, 455–459.

Crow, T. J. (1997). What was the evidence that prenatal exposure to influenza causes schizophrenia? *British Journal of Psychiatry*, *169*, 790–791.

Crow, T. J. (2007). How and why genetic linkage has not solved the problem of psychosis: Review and hypothesis. *American Journal of Psychiatry*, *164*, 13–21.

Crow, T. J., & Done, D. J. (1983). Schizophrenia is infectious. *American College of Neuropsychopharmacology Annual Meeting*, p. 53.

Crow, T. J., & Done, D. J. (1986). Age of onset of schizophrenia in siblings: A test of the contagion hypothesis. *Psychiatry Research*, *18*, 107–117.

DeLisi, L. E., Wise, C. D., Bridge, T. P., Rosenblatt, J. E., Wagner, R. L., Morihisa, J., et al. (1981). A probable neuroleptic effect on platelet monamine oxidase in chronic schizophrenic patients. *Psychiatry Research*, *4*, 95–107.

Done, D. J., Johnstone, E. C., Frith, C. D., Golding, J., Shepherd, P. M., & Crow, T. J. (1991). Complications of pregnancy and delivery in relation to psychosis in adult life: Data from the British perinatal mortality survey sample. *British Medical Journal*, *302*, 1576–1580.

Editorial. (1987). A continuum of psychosis? *Lancet*, *330*, 889–890.

Flor-Henry, P. (1969). Psychosis and temporal lobe epilepsy, a controlled investigation. *Epilepsia*, *10*, 363–395.

Gershon, E. S., Hamovit, J., Guroff, J. J., Dibble, E., Leckmann, J. F., Sceery, W., et al. (1982). A family study of schizo-affective, bipolar I, bipolar II, unipolar and normal control patients. *Archives of General Psychiatry*, *39*, 1157–1167.

Gittleman-Klein, R., & Klein, D. F. (1969). Premorbid asocial adjustment and prognosis in schizophrenia. *Journal of Psychiatric Research*, *7*, 35–53.

Hare, E. H. (1983). Was insanity on the increase? *British Journal of Psychiatry*, *142*, 439–455.

Hsiao, K., Lin, K.-J., Liu, C.-Y., Tzen, K.-Y., & Yen, T.-C. (2003). Dopamine transporter change in drug-naïve schizophrenia: An imaging study with Tc-99m-TRODAT-1. *Schizophrenia Research*, *65*, 39–46.

Johnstone, E. C., Crow, T. J., Frith, C. D., Husband, J., & Kreel, L. (1976). Cerebral ventricular size and cognitive impairment in chronic schizophrenia. *Lancet*, *ii*, 924–926.

Kasanin, J. (1933). The acute schizo-affective psychoses. *American Journal of Psychiatry*, *90*, 97–126.

Kendell, R. E., & Gourlay, J. (1970). The clinical distinction between the affective psychoses and schizophrenia. *British Journal of Psychiatry*, *117*, 261–266.

Lindsay, J., Ounsted, C., & Richards, P. (1979). Long-term outcome in children with temporal lobe seizure. *Developmental Medicine and Child Neurolology*, *21*, 630–636.

Marneros, A., Diester, A., & Rohde, A. (1991). *Affektive, Schizoaffektive und Schizophrene Psychosen* (*Ein Vergleichende Langseitstudie*). Berlin, Germany: Springer.

Mednick, S. A., Machon, R. A., Huttunen, M. O., & Bonett, D. (1988). Adult schizophrenia following prenatal exposure to an influenza epidemic. *Archives of General Psychiatry*, *45*, 189–192.

Murphy, D. L., & Wyatt, R. J. (1972). Reduced MAO activity in blood platelets from schizophrenic patients. *Nature*, *238*, 225–226.

Murray, R. M., & Lewis, S. W. (1987). Is schizophrenia a neurodevelopmental disorder? *British Journal of Psychiatry*, *295*, 681–682.

Murray, R. M., Lewis, S. W., & Reveley, A. M. (1985). Towards an aetiological classification of schizophrenia. *Lancet*, *325*, 1023–1026.

Murray, R. M., & Reveley, A. M. (1983). Genetics of schizophrenia. *Lancet*, *i*, 1159–1160.

O'Callaghan, E., Sham, P., Takei, N., Murray, R. M., & Glover, G. (1991). Schizophrenia after prenatal exposure to the 1957 A2 influenza epidemic. *Lancet*, *337*, 1248–1250.

O'Donovan, M. C., Craddock, N., & Owens, M. J. (2008). Strong evidence for multiple psychosis susceptibility genes—A rejoinder to Crow. *Psychological Medicine*, *38*, 1681–1685.

Odegaard, O. (1972). The multifactorial inheritance of predisposition to schizophrenia. In A. R. Kaplan (Ed.), *Genetic factors in schizophrenia* (pp. 256–275). Springfield, IL: Thomas.

Owen, F., Bourne, R. C., Crow, T. C., Johnstone, E. C., Bailey, A. R., & Hershon, H. I. (1976). Platelet monoamine oxidase in schizophrenia. An investigation in drug-free chronic hospitalized patients. *Archives of General Psychiatary*, *33*, 1370–1373.

Penrose, L. S. (1991). Survey of cases of familial mental illness. *European Archives of Psychiatry and Clinical Neuroscience*, *240*, 315–324.

Presgraves, D. C. (2008). Sex chromosomes and speciation in *Drosophila*. *Trends in Genetics*, *24*, 336–343.

Randrup, A., & Munkvad, I. (1967). Stereotyped activities produced by amphetamine in several animal species and man. *Psychopharmacologia*, *11*, 300–310.

Sanders, A. R., Duan, J., Levinson, D. F., Shi, J., He, D., Hou, C., et al. (2008). No significant association of 14 candidate genes with schizophrenia in a large European ancestry sample: Implications for psychiatric genetics. *American Journal of Psychiatry*, *165*, 497–506.

Sham, P., O'Callaghan, E., Takei, N., Murray, G. K., Hare, E. H., & Murray, R. M. (1992). Schizophrenia following prenatal exposure to influenza epidemics between 1939 and 1960. *British Journal of Psychiatry*, *160*, 461–466.

Steinmetz, H., Herzog, A., Schlaug, G., Huang,Y., & Jancke, L. (1995). Brain (a)symmetry in monozygotic twins. *Cerebral Cortex*, *5*, 296–300.

Taylor, G. R., Crow, T. J., Ferrier, I. N., Johnstone, E. C., Parry, R. P., & Tyrrell, D. A. J. (1982). Virus-like agent in schizophrenia and some neurological disorders. *Lancet*, *ii*, 1166–1167.

Torrey, E. F., & Peterson, M. R. (1973). Slow and latent viruses in schizophrenia. *Lancet*, *ii*, 22–24.

Tyrrell, D. A. J., Parry, R. P., Crow, T. J., Johnstone, E. C., & Ferrier, I. N. (1979). Possible virus in schizophrenia and some neurological disorders. *Lancet*, *i*, 839–841.

Weinberger, D. R. (1987). Implications of normal brain developments for the pathogenesis of schizophrenia. *Archives of General Psychiatry*, *44*, 660–669.

Weinberger, D. R., Torrey, E. F., Neophytides, A. N., & Wyatt, R. J. (1979). Lateral cerebral ventricular enlargement in chronic schizophrenia. *Archives of General Psychiatry*, *36*, 735–739.

Williams, N. A., Close, J., Giouzeli, M., & Crow, T. J. (2006). Accelerated evolution of *Protocadherin11X/Y*: A candidate gene-pair for cerebral asymmetry and language. *American Journal of Medical Genetics (Neuropsychiatric Genetics)*, *141B*, 623–633.

Part V

Cognition

17 Cognitive models of psychosis, the jumping to conclusions reasoning bias and improving psychological treatment for delusions

Philippa Garety, Daniel Freeman, Suzanne Jolley, Kerry Ross, Helen Waller and Graham Dunn

Cognitive models of psychosis

Cognitive models of the positive symptoms of psychosis specify the cognitive, social and emotional processes hypothesized to contribute to their occurrence and persistence (Bentall, Corcoran, Howard, Blackwood, & Kinderman, 2001; Birchwood, 2003; Fowler, 2000; Freeman, Garety, Kuipers, Fowler, & Bebbington, 2002; Garety, Bebbington, Fowler, Freeman, & Kuipers, 2007; Garety, Kuipers, Fowler, Freeman, & Bebbington, 2001; Morrison, 2001). In 2001, we proposed that psychotic symptoms might be better understood by linking social, psychological and neurobiological attempts at explaining the phenomenological experiences (Garety et al., 2001). We argued that cognitive models are an important link in the chain from phenotype to genotype, providing a psychological description of the phenomena from which hypotheses concerning causal processes implicated in specific symptoms can be derived and tested.

Shortly after our cognitive model was published in 2001, I (Philippa Garety) bumped into Robin (Murray) in the Institute of Psychiatry canteen. The paper had been well received, and since it represented a culmination of our group's work and thinking over about ten years, we were rather pleased with it. He smiled quizzically and ventured, "That paper of yours in *Psychological Medicine*, you know, it would have been quite good ... if only you had mentioned the brain!" The chapter that follows describes an approach to psychosis that focuses unashamedly on cognitive processes. We hope to show how these cognitive processes are relevant to understanding the phenomenon of delusion and are important in developing new psychological treatments. In 2007, however, prompted by Robin's challenge, we felt we could ignore the brain no longer and attempted to integrate the neurobiological with the cognitive; interested readers are directed to this later review (Garety et al., 2007). It is therefore a great pleasure to contribute from a cognitive perspective to this Festschrift to honour the work and career of a giant of research in schizophrenia.

Cognitive models share the common proposition that pre-existing beliefs and ongoing appraisals of experiences are crucial for the development and persistence of positive symptoms of psychosis, specifically delusions and hallucinations. In our model, psychosis is considered to be complex and multi-factorial (Fowler, 2000; Freeman et al., 2002; Garety et al., 2001, 2007). Building on the highly influential work of Robin Murray and others in proposing the neurodevelopmental hypothesis, we adopted the widely accepted proposal that a person who develops psychosis has a premorbid vulnerability of biopsychosocial origin (e.g., Jones, Rodgers, Murray, & Marmot, 1994; Murray & Lewis, 1987). In the vulnerable individual, stress triggers particular emotional and cognitive changes, resulting in anomalies of conscious experience, for example hallucinatory voices. These anomalous experiences have been linked to information processing and neurobiological disturbances (Frith, 1992, 2005; Gray, Feldon, Rawlins, Hemsley, & Smith, 1991; Hemsley, 1993, 2005; Kapur, 2003). We further proposed that specific reasoning and information-processing biases, pre-existing schematic beliefs about the self and others, current emotional disturbance and social factors (such as isolation and adversity) both singly and in combination facilitate *appraisals* of the origins of these anomalous mental states as external. This results in the abnormal beliefs and hallucinations becoming symptomatic. Thus, the experience, for example, of a voice does not necessarily develop into a full-blown psychotic symptom. This only occurs when an individual appraises the voice in particular ways—such as that it comes from an external source, and is personally significant and uncontrollable. It is the particular interpretation or *appraisal* that causes the associated distress and disability, rather than the experience itself (Chadwick & Birchwood, 1994; Morrison & Baker, 2000). This emphasis on the role of appraisal is in common with cognitive models of other disorders, such as Beck et al.'s cognitive model of depression (Beck, Rush, Shaw, & Emery, 1979). The cognitive model of Garety et al. (2001) is represented schematically in Figure 17.1.

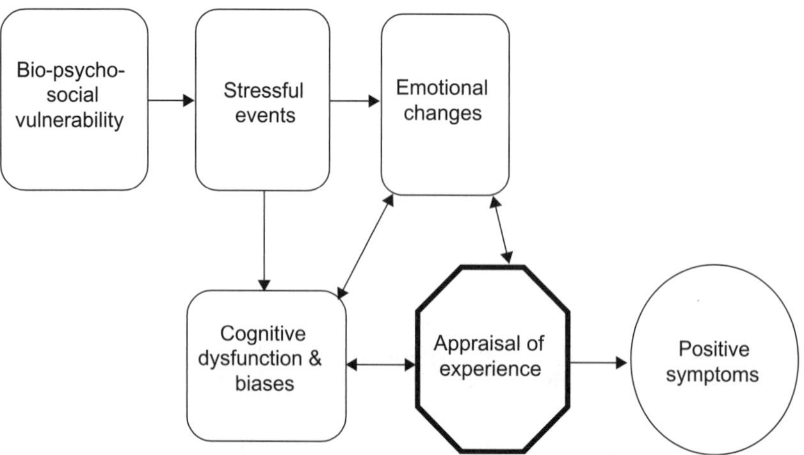

Figure 17.1 A cognitive model of the positive symptoms of psychosis (as discussed in Garety, Kuipers, Fowler, Freeman, & Bebbington, 2001).

There are thus four central propositions of cognitive models of psychosis. First, that cognitive and affective processes act synergistically or interactively to contribute to the development and persistence of positive psychotic symptoms. Second, that psychotic experiences in themselves are not pathological; they are present in a substantial minority of the general population (5–30%) without necessitating a need for care (Freeman et al., 2005; Johns et al., 2004; van Os, Hannssen, Bijl, & Ravelli, 2000; van Os, Hannssen, Bijl, & Vollebergh, 2001). Third, that it is *the appraisal* of these experiences that is central to the development of pathological symptoms. Finally, based on epidemiological and experimental evidence, a number of processes are hypothesized to contribute to this biased appraisal: reasoning and attribution biases; dysfunctional beliefs about the self and the world; isolation and adverse social environments; emotional processes associated with anxiety and depression; and aspects of the psychotic experience itself, such as novelty and aberrant salience (see Garety et al., 2001, 2007, for reviews of the relevant literature).

Treatment of delusions

Although many patients with psychosis benefit from antipsychotic medication, a substantial proportion show a relatively poor response (Jones et al., 2006; Lieberman et al., 2005), with approximately 50% of patients demonstrating persistent delusions even after the first acute psychotic episode has abated (Craig et al., 2004). Recent research indicates that the effects of antipsychotic medication on delusional conviction, in particular, are less marked than on other aspects of delusions, such as associated distress and behavioural response (Mizrahi et al., 2006). If, as we argue, appraisals are central to the development and persistence of delusions and hallucinations, there is a clear implication for treatment: treatment may be effective if it assists with reappraisal. Cognitive-behavioural therapy (CBT) for psychosis was initially developed to improve the treatment of persistent distressing delusions and hallucinations, and meta-analyses consistently indicate that this intervention does show efficacy, but that the effects are small to moderate (Pilling et al., 2002; Wykes, Steel, Everitt, & Tarrier, 2008; Zimmermann, Favrod, Trieu, & Pomini, 2005). Although antipsychotic medication and CBT, therefore, both have benefits, the goal of delivering sustained improvement in delusions remains. Better treatments are needed, based on a sound understanding of cause and maintenance.

Delusions and reasoning biases: Data gathering (jumping to conclusions) and belief inflexibility

Cognitive models propose that a number of processes contribute to biased appraisals leading to the development of delusions and hallucinations. One factor that has been highlighted is reasoning biases (Bentall et al., 2001; Garety et al., 2005; Moritz & Woodward, 2007; Rector & Beck, 2001). Delusions have been shown with particular consistency to be associated with reduced data gathering and belief inflexibility (see Fine, Gardner, Craigie, & Gold, 2007; Freeman 2007; Garety & Freeman, 1999, for reviews). Reduced data gathering in individuals with delusions has been repeatedly demonstrated using probabilistic reasoning tasks based on a Bayesian model of probabilistic inference (Dudley, John, Young, & Over, 1997; Garety, Hemsley, & Wessely, 1991; Menon, Mizrahi, & Kapur, 2008; Moritz & Woodward, 2005; Peters & Garety, 2006; Peters, Thornton, Skisou, Linney, & MacCabe, 2008; van Dael et al., 2006).

On a typical probabilistic reasoning task (the beads task), participants are asked to request as many pieces of evidence (coloured beads) as they would like before making a decision (from which of two hidden jars the beads are drawn). The participants are shown that the jars have beads of two different colours and are informed of the proportions of each coloured bead in the jars. In the original version of the task, one jar has 85 black beads and 15 yellow beads, and the other jar has the opposite ratio of black and yellow beads. In a more difficult version the beads are in the ratio 60 : 40. The key variable employed is the number of items requested before making a decision. Individuals with delusions request fewer beads before making their decision than psychiatric or non-clinical controls. The extreme form of the bias—"jumping to conclusions" (JTC)—has been operationalized as when a decision is made after two or fewer beads. Fifty to seventy percent of people with delusions jump to conclusions when the beads are in the ratio of 85 : 15 compared with 10% of non-clinical controls (Freeman, 2007) and approximately 40% of people with delusions jump to conclusions even when the beads are in the difficult ratio of 60 : 40 (Garety et al., 2005).

The JTC bias has been replicated widely, using various modifications of the basic paradigm, not only in people with delusions, but also in people who have recovered from delusions, people at risk of delusions, and people with delusion proneness in the general population (see Freeman, 2007; Fine et al., 2007; Moritz & Woodward, 2007, for recent reviews). That the bias is present in at-risk populations and in remitted groups, although in an attenuated form, suggests it is a trait representing liability to delusions, but that it may in addition be exacerbated in acute delusional states (Broome et al., 2007; Garety et al., 2005; Peters & Garety, 2006; van Dael et al., 2006). Taken together, this research indicates that this bias is a trait that may contribute to both delusion formation and persistence. The evidence also shows that this is a data-gathering bias rather than a deficit in probabilistic reasoning (Garety & Freeman, 1999). The reasoning bias is specifically associated with level of delusional conviction (Freeman, Pugh, & Garety, 2008; Garety et al., 2005; Moritz & Woodward, 2005).

Possible mechanisms for the jumping to conclusions bias

The mechanism for the JTC bias is not yet clear, and a wide variety of proposals have been made. Some hypotheses involve motivation, affect or further-thinking biases, for all of which, at present, inconclusive evidence exists, while others invoke neurocognitive deficits (Fine et al., 2007; Freeman, 2007; Lincoln, Lange, Burau, Exner, & Moritz, 2010; Merrin, Kinderman, & Bentall, 2007; Moritz,

Woodward, & Lambert, 2007; So, Freeman, & Garety, 2008). The evidence with respect to neurocognition is quite limited. Broome et al. (2007) have found an association of JTC with impaired working memory. Furthermore, Young and Bentall, in 1995, noted that patients with delusions have a difficulty processing sequential information. More recently, Bentall et al. (2009), using structural equation modelling, found that JTC appeared to be related to paranoia via a cognitive functioning factor, which was partially comprised of tests they considered to reflect executive functioning, including a test of working memory (backward digit span). There is, therefore, emerging evidence of a link with working memory. However, associations between jumping to conclusions and working memory or other cognitive impairments have not been consistently shown (e.g., Dudley et al., 1997; Langdon, Ward, & Coltheart, 2010; Moritz & Woodward, 2005; van Hooren et al., 2008). The relationship of JTC to the well-attested cognitive impairments of schizophrenia (such as attention, memory and executive function deficits) has yet to be examined systematically. It should be noted that JTC differs from these cognitive impairments in schizophrenia in that, unlike them, it has been shown to be specifically related to delusional symptoms. The mechanism for JTC may therefore involve working memory, but at present it remains an open question.

Reasoning biases and response to treatment

In a novel line of research, it has recently been shown that JTC may moderate the response to antipsychotic treatments in a drug-naïve group of patients with a first episode of psychosis, such that those with an extreme JTC bias showed a poorer treatment response (Menon et al., 2008). The bias was not changed, in this acute sample, following administration of antipsychotic medication (Menon et al., 2008). JTC also does not appear to change in response to standard CBT approaches. Both Brakioulas et al. (2008) and Garety et al. (2008) reported that it was not changed following a course of CBT. Thus, on the present evidence, JTC does not appear to mediate treatment, whether psychological or pharmacological, but it might moderate treatment effects.

A related empirical literature shows that many individuals with delusions produce few alternative explanations for the evidence cited for their beliefs (Freeman et al., 2004), do not think that they could be mistaken in their belief (Garety et al., 1997), and report that they would not change their belief in a hypothetical contradiction task (Wessely et al., 1993). These findings have recently been incorporated into the concept of belief flexibility. Belief flexibility refers to "a meta-cognitive process about thinking about one's own delusional beliefs, changing them in the light of reflection and evidence and generating and considering alternatives" (Garety et al., 2005, p. 374). Jumping to conclusions and belief flexibility are related (Freeman et al., 2004; Garety et al., 2005). There have been indications that belief flexibility predicts a positive response to both antipsychotic medication (Brett-Jones, Garety, & Hemsley, 1987) and CBT (Chadwick & Lowe, 1990; Garety et al., 1997; Sharp et al., 1996). We recently

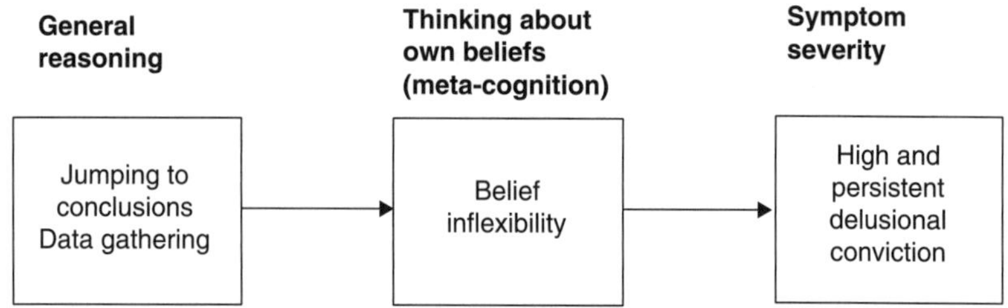

Figure 17.2 Reasoning processes in delusional conviction.

found evidence that belief inflexibility mediates the effect of jumping to conclusions on delusional conviction (Garety et al., 2005). It is proposed that jumping to conclusions limits belief flexibility thereby maintaining and escalating levels of delusional conviction (see Figure 17.2).

Thus there is ample evidence that JTC is associated with delusions, and further evidence that it is related to belief flexibility, that it is not typically changed by treatment, whether pharmacological or psychological, and there are indications that it moderates treatment effects. We therefore conclude that JTC is a key target for treatment: novel strategies aimed at reducing jumping to conclusions and improving data gathering are likely to be beneficial in enhancing belief flexibility and thereby assisting reappraisal of delusional beliefs.

Developing a new treatment approach for delusions: Reasoning training

We have therefore embarked on a programme of treatment development, targeted at the JTC bias, to aim to improve the effectiveness of treatment for delusions. In the first study (Ross, Freeman, Dunn, & Garety, 2009), we sought to demonstrate, employing a brief computerized reasoning training, that it is possible to improve data gathering (reduce JTC) in people with delusions. A secondary aim was to explore whether improvements in reasoning would lead to improvements in flexibility in thinking about delusions. It was also planned to examine whether training reduced delusional conviction. However, since delusional beliefs are strongly and persistently held, it was considered unlikely that a brief training would lead to significant and immediate reductions in delusion conviction. Finally, it was also a test of the cognitive model; if changing reasoning style alters delusional ideation, this will support the claims of cognitive models which hypothesize that reasoning has a causal role in delusions.

A new reasoning training intervention: Two studies

In the first study (Ross et al., 2009), a computerized training programme was developed, designed to use engaging material of a neutral content, and aimed to convey the overall idea that it is preferable not to reach a decision too quickly.

Participants were presented with three training tasks, each lasting fifteen minutes, which illustrated the targeted reasoning biases and ways of correcting them. It focused on data gathering, generation and consideration of alternative ideas and the use of confirmatory and disconfirmatory evidence. Two of the tasks (Object Identification and Picture Interpretation) were adapted from previously devised modules of the meta-cognitive training (MCT) package, designed for group administration by Moritz, Burlon, and Woodward (2007); described also in Moritz and Woodward (2007). The third task, Visual Illusions, was designed specifically for this study. The whole training was presented using Microsoft™ PowerPoint® during a single session lasting approximately 45 minutes. At no time was the content of training discussed in relation to the participants' delusions or any aspect of the clinical assessment. This was because we wished to establish whether an intervention that solely targeted the reasoning process and not the content of delusions would have the hypothesized effects on data gathering and belief flexibility. Each task had three phases: presentation of stimuli and free response, review of initial responses and instruction in reasoning, and further practice with additional stimuli. Further detailed descriptions of the training tasks are given in Ross et al. (2009).

We recruited 34 people with a diagnosis of schizophrenia spectrum disorder and current delusions, held with at least 75% conviction. They were randomly allocated to the 45 minute reasoning training or to an attention control condition (neuropsychological testing). In terms of results, the brief, single session training intervention had an effect on data gathering, reflected in a significant increase immediately post-training in the number of beads requested on both versions of the beads task. The study therefore demonstrates that it is possible to change the data gathering of people with delusions, in the short term. Another finding was that JTC at baseline moderated the effects of training: those with an extreme JTC style benefited less from the training. As noted above, a prior JTC bias has recently been found to moderate change in response to antipsychotic medication (Menon et al., 2008); in this study, a prior JTC bias moderated the effects of reasoning training. It was clear that training improved data gathering more among those individuals with delusions who did not show the JTC bias at the outset. This leads to the conclusion that JTC in people with delusions is a strong bias that is somewhat unresponsive to only a brief training intervention. There were also improvements in the training group on belief flexibility and delusional conviction, though these fell short of significance.

The results of this first study were sufficiently encouraging to justify further development of this training approach. Our second study is now nearing completion and includes 13 participants with delusions assessed in detail—pre- and post-training and at two weeks' follow-up (Waller, in press). The training intervention has been substantially developed. It is more interactive and makes use of humour and multi-media, with film clips and especially commissioned video material. It emphasizes reasoning processes, but, in order to attempt to have a greater impact and relevance, it incorporates socially ambiguous and delusion relevant content. This newer training package has five modules, lasting about 2–3 hours in total, addressing data gathering, inhibition of hasty responses, and belief flexibility, including generating alternatives. Two modules are from Ross et al. (2009), one a modification of Moritz, Burlon, and Woodward (2007), while three completely new modules were developed. Since this package includes paranoia and other delusion-relevant material, we gathered feedback from participants as to its acceptability. Participants with delusions overwhelmingly reported that they found it acceptable and helpful:

- "The programme was easy to follow. It makes you think carefully about what you're doing. I learnt to slow down to make judgements, looking closely at arguments, and not reacting immediately but gathering evidence" (Participant A, post-training).
- "I noticed myself jumping to conclusions—I saw a woman walking around the housing estate. Under normal circumstances I would have found this really dodgy, but I asked neighbour who'd been out gardening about her and she was looking for her lost cat. I felt a lot better then" (Participant B, at 2 weeks' follow-up).

Preliminary results also suggest that the training, as intended, is more effective than Ross et al. (2009) at improving data gathering and belief flexibility and also that it reduces delusional conviction, both post-training and at two weeks' follow-up (Waller, in press).

Conclusions

We have presented in this chapter the initial stages of a programme of translational research aimed at treatment development. From our cognitive model, we identified a key theoretically derived and empirically validated process, the JTC reasoning bias. We have developed a targeted intervention for this bias and evaluated it in pilot studies. The results of these studies are fully consistent with the hypothesis that JTC reasoning bias has a causal role in delusional conviction by influencing appraisals, as proposed by the cognitive model. We consider that the intervention has the potential of improving outcomes for people with delusions, and we are now investigating it in a large-scale randomized study. If positive effects are confirmed, we then plan to incorporate and test the intervention as one component of a personalized CBT for delusions, and in combination with a trial of antipsychotic medication.

Acknowledgement

The authors thank Steffan Moritz and Todd Woodward for permission to use and adapt two of their group training modules. Daniel Freeman is supported by a Wellcome Trust Fellowship. Philippa Garety is a Senior Investigator of the National Institute of Health Research, and affiliated to the Biomedical Research Centre, King's College London. The work presented is carried out as part of the

Wellcome funded Psychosis Research Partnership (PRP) project (085396); we acknowledge the intellectual contribution of other members of the Partnership, Elizabeth Kuipers, Paul Bebbington, and David Fowler.

References

Beck, A. T., Rush, A. J., Shaw, B. F., & Emery, G. (1979). *Cognitive therapy of depression*. New York, NY: Guilford Press.

Bentall, R. P., Corcoran, R., Howard, R., Blackwood, N., & Kinderman, P. (2001). Persecutory delusions: A review and theoretical integration. *Clinical Psychology Review*, *21*, 1143–1192.

Bentall, R. P., Rowse, G., Shryane, N., Kinderman, P., Howard, R., Blackwood, N., et al. (2009). The cognitive and affective structure of paranoid delusions: A transdiagnostic investigation of patients with schizophrenia spectrum disorders and depression. *Archives of General Psychiatry*, *66*, 236–247.

Birchwood, M. (2003). Pathways to emotional dysfunction in first-episode psychosis. *British Journal of Psychiatry*, *182*, 373–375.

Brakioulas, V., Langdon, R., Sloss, G., Coltheart, M., Meares, R., & Harris, A. (2008). Delusions and reasoning: A study involving cognitive behavioural therapy. *Cognitive Neuropsychiatry*, *13*, 148–165.

Brett-Jones, J., Garety, P., & Hemsley, D. (1987). Measuring delusional experiences: A method and its application. *British Journal of Clinical Psychology*, *26*, 257–265.

Broome, M., Johns, L. C., Valli, I., Woolley, J. B., Tabraham, P., Brett, C., et al. (2007). Delusion formation and reasoning biases in those at clinical risk for psychosis. *British Journal of Psychiatry*, *191*, s38–s42.

Chadwick, P., & Birchwood, M. (1994). The omnipotence of voices. A cognitive approach to auditory hallucinations. *British Journal of Psychiatry*, *164*, 190–201.

Chadwick, P. D., & Lowe, C. F. (1990). Measurement and modification of delusional beliefs. *Journal of Consulting & Clinical Psychology*, *58*, 225–232.

Craig, T., Garety, P., Power, P., Rahaman, N., Colbert, S., Fornells-Ambrojo, M., et al. (2004). The Lambeth Early Onset (LEO) Team: Randomised controlled trial of the effectiveness of specialised care for early psychosis. *British Medical Journal*, *329*, 1067–1071.

Dudley, R. E., John, C. H., Young, A. W., & Over, D. E. (1997). Normal and abnormal reasoning in people with delusions. *British Journal of Clinical Psychology*, *36*, 243–258.

Fine, C., Gardner, M., Craigie, J., & Gold, I. (2007). Hopping, skipping or jumping to conclusions? Clarifying the role of the JTC bias in delusions. *Cognitive Neuropsychiatry*, *12*, 46–77.

Fowler, D. (2000). Cognitive behaviour therapy for psychosis: From understanding to treatment. *Psychiatric Rehabilitation Skills*, *4*, 199–215.

Freeman, D. (2007). Suspicious minds: The psychology of persecutory delusions. *Clinical Psychology Review*, *4*, 425–457.

Freeman, D., Garety, P. A., Bebbington, P. E., Smith, B., Rollinson, R., Fowler, D., et al. (2005). Psychological investigation of the structure of paranoia in a non-clinical population. *British Journal of Psychiatry*, *186*, 427–435.

Freeman, D., Garety, P. A., Fowler, D., Kuipers, E., Bebbington, P. E., & Dunn, G. (2004). Why do people with delusions fail to choose more realistic explanations for their experiences? An empirical investigation. *Journal of Consulting & Clinical Psychology*, *72*, 671–680.

Freeman, D., Garety, P. A., Kuipers, E., Fowler, D., & Bebbington, P. (2002). A cognitive model of persecutory delusions. *British Journal of Clinical Psychology*, *41*, 331–347.

Freeman, D., Pugh, K., & Garety, P. (2008). Jumping to conclusions and paranoid ideation in the general population. *Schizophrenia Research*, *102*, 254–260.

Frith, C. (2005). The neural basis of hallucinations and delusions. *Comptes Rendus Biologies*, *328*, 169–175.

Frith, C. D. (1992). *The cognitive neuropsychology of schizophrenia*. Hove, UK: Lawrence Erlbaum Associates, Ltd.

Garety, P., Bebbington, P., Fowler, D., Freeman, D., & Kuipers, E. (2007). Implications for neurobiological research of cognitive models of psychosis: A theoretical paper. *Psychological Medicine*, *37*, 1377–1391.

Garety, P. A., Fowler, D. G., Freeman, D., Bebbington, P., Dunn, G., & Kuipers, E. (2008). Cognitive behavioural therapy and family intervention for relapse prevention and symptom reduction in psychosis: Randomised controlled trial. *British Journal of Psychiatry*, *192*, 412–423.

Garety, P. A., Fowler, D., Kuipers, E., Freeman, D., Dunn, G., Bebbington, P., et al. (1997). The London-East Anglia Randomised Controlled Trial of Cognitive Behaviour Therapy for Psychosis II: Predictors of outcome. *British Journal of Psychiatry*, *171*, 420–426.

Garety, P. A., & Freeman, D. (1999). Cognitive approaches to delusions: A critical review of theories and evidence. *British Journal of Clinical Psychology*, *38*, 113–154.

Garety, P. A., Freeman, D., Jolley, S., Dunn, G., Bebbington, P. E., Fowler, D. G., et al. (2005). Reasoning, emotions and delusional conviction in psychosis. *Journal of Abnormal Psychology*, *114*, 373–384.

Garety, P. A., Hemsley, D. R., & Wessely, S. (1991). Reasoning in deluded schizophrenic and paranoid patients: Biases in performance on a probabilistic inference task. *Journal of Nervous & Mental Disease*, *179*, 194–201.

Garety, P. A., Kuipers, E., Fowler, D., Freeman, D., & Bebbington, P. (2001). Theoretical paper: A cognitive model of the positive symptoms of psychosis. *Psychological Medicine*, *31*, 189–195.

Gray, J., Feldon, J., Rawlins, J., Hemsley, D., & Smith, A. (1991). The neuropsychology of schizophrenia. *Behavioural and Brain Sciences*, *14*, 1–84.

Hemsley, D. R. (1993). A simple (or simplistic?) cognitive model for schizophrenia. *Behaviour Research & Therapy*, *31*, 633–645.

Hemsley, D. R. (2005). The schizophrenic experience: Taken out of context? *Schizophrenia Bulletin*, *31*(1), 43–53.

Johns, L. C., Cannon, M., Singleton, N., Murray, R. M., Farrell, M., Brugha, T., et al. (2004). Prevalence and correlates of self-reported psychotic symptoms in the British population. *British Journal of Psychiatry*, *185*, 298–305.

Jones, P., Rodgers, B., Murray, R., & Marmot, M. (1994). Child development risk factors for adult schizophrenia in the British 1946 birth cohort. *Lancet*, *344*, 1398–1402.

Jones, P. B., Barnes, T. R., Davies, L., Dunn, G., Lloyd, H., Hayhurst, K. P., et al. (2006). Randomized controlled trial of the effect on quality of life of second- vs. first-generation antipsychotic drugs in schizophrenia: Cost Utility of the Latest Antipsychotic Drugs in Schizophrenia Study (CUtLASS1). *Archives of General Psychiatry*, *63*, 1079–1087.

Kapur, S. (2003). Psychosis as a state of aberrant salience: A framework linking biology, phenomenology, and pharmacology in schizophrenia. *American Journal of Psychiatry, 160*, 13–23.

Langdon, R., Ward, P. B., & Coltheart, M. (2010). Reasoning anomalies associated with delusions in schizophrenia. *Schizophrenia Bulletin. 326*, 321–330.

Lieberman, J. A., Stroup, T. S., McEvoy, J. P., Swartz, M. S., Rosenheck, R. A., Perkins, D. O., et al. (Clinical Antipsychotic Trials of Intervention Effectiveness, CATIE, Investigators). (2005). Effectiveness of anti-psychotic drugs in patients with chronic schizophrenia. *New England Journal of Medicine, 353*, 1209–1223.

Lincoln, T. M., Lange, J., Burau, J., Exner, C., & Moritz, S. (2010). The effect of state anxiety on paranoid ideation and jumping to conclusions. An experimental investigation. *Schizophrenia Bulletin, 36*, 1140–1148.

Menon, M., Mizrahi, R., & Kapur, S. (2008). "Jumping to conclusions" and delusions in psychosis: Relationship and response to treatment. *Schizophrenia Research, 98*, 225–231.

Merrin, J., Kinderman, P., & Bentall, R. P. (2007). Jumping to conclusions and attributional style in patients with persecutory delusions. *Cognitive Therapy & Research, 31*, 741–758.

Mizrahi, R., Kiang, M., Mamo, D., Arenovich, T., Bagby, R., Zipursky, R., et al. (2006). The selective effect of antipsychotics on the different dimensions of the experience of psychosis in schizophrenia spectrum disorders. *Schizophrenia Research, 88*, 111–118.

Moritz, S., Burlon, M., & Woodward, T. S. (2007). *Metacognitive skill training for patients with schizophrenia (MCT)*. Hamburg, Germany: VanHam Campus Press.

Moritz, S., & Woodward, T. S. (2005). Jumping to conclusions in delusional and non delusional schizophrenic patients. *British Journal of Clinical Psychology, 44*, 193–207.

Moritz, S., & Woodward, T. S. (2007). Metacognitive training in schizophrenia: From basic research to knowledge translation and intervention. *Current Opinion in Psychiatry, 20*, 619–625.

Moritz, S., Woodward, T. S., & Lambert, M. (2007). Under what circumstances do patients with schizophrenia jump to conclusions? A liberal acceptance account. *British Journal of Clinical Psychology, 46*, 127–137.

Morrison, A. P. (2001). The interpretation of intrusions in psychosis: An integrative cognitive approach to hallucinations and delusions. *Behavioural & Cognitive Psychotherapy, 29*, 257–276.

Morrison, A. P., & Baker, C. A. (2000). Intrusive thoughts and auditory hallucinations: A comparative study of intrusions in psychosis. *Behaviour Research & Therapy, 38*, 1097–1106.

Murray, R. M., & Lewis, S. W. (1987). Is schizophrenia a neurodevelopmental disorder? *British Medical Journal (Clinical Research Edition), 295*(6600), 681–682.

Peters, E., & Garety, P. A. (2006). Cognitive functioning in delusions: A longitudinal examination. *Behaviour Research & Therapy, 44*, 481–514.

Peters, E. R., Thornton, P., Siksou, L., Linney, Y., & MacCabe, J. H. (2008). Specificity of the "jump-to-conclusions" bias in deluded patients. *British Journal of Psychology, 47*, 239–244.

Pilling, S., Bebbington, P., Kuipers, E., Garety, P., Geddes, J., Orbach, G., et al. (2002). Psychological treatments in schizophrenia: I. Meta-analysis of family intervention and cognitive behaviour therapy. *Psychological Medicine, 32*, 763–782.

Rector, N. A., & Beck, A. T. (2001). Cognitive behavioural therapy for schizophrenia: An empirical review. *Journal of Nervous & Mental Disease, 189*, 278–287.

Ross, K., Freeman, D., Dunn, G., & Garety, P. (2009). A randomized experimental investigation of reasoning training for people with delusions. *Schizophrenia Bulletin* [Epub ahead of print]. (doi:10.1093/schbul/sbn165)

Sharp, H. M., Fear, C. F., Williams, M. G., Healy, D., Lowe, C. F., Yeadon, H., et al. (1996). Delusional phenomenology—Dimensions of change. *Behaviour Research & Therapy*, *34*, 123–142.

So, S. H., Freeman, D., & Garety, P. (2008). Impact of state anxiety on the jumping to conclusions delusion bias. *Australia & New Zealand Journal of Psychiatry*, *42*, 879–886.

van Dael, F., Versmissen, D., Janssen, I., Myen-Germeys, I., van Os, J., & Krabbendam, L. (2006). Data gathering: Biased in psychosis? *Schizophrenia Bulletin*, *32*, 341–351.

van Hooren, S., Versmissen, D., Janssen, I., Myin-Germeys, I., a Campo, J., Mengelers, R., et al. (2008). Social cognition and neurocognition as independent domains in psychosis. *Schizophrenia Research*, *103*, 257–265.

van Os, J., Hanssen, M., Bijl, R. V., & Ravelli, A. (2000). Strauss (1969) revisited: A psychosis continuum in the general population? *Schizophrenia Research*, *45*, 11–20.

van Os, J., Hanssen, M., Bijl, R. V., & Vollebergh, W. (2001). Prevalence of psychotic disorder and community level of psychotic symptoms: An urban–rural comparison. *Archives of General Psychiatry*, *58*, 663–668.

Waller, H., Freeman, D., Jolley, S., Dunn, G., & Garety, P. (in press). Targeting reasoning biases in delusions: A pilot study of the Maudsley Review Training Programme for individuals with persistent, high conviction delusions. *Journal of Behavior Therapy and Experimental Psychiatry*.

Wessely, S., Buchanan, A., Reed, A., Cutting, J., Everitt, B., Garety, P., et al. (1993). Acting on delusions (1): Prevalence. *British Journal of Psychiatry*, *163*, 69–76.

Wykes, T., Steel, C., Everitt, B., & Tarrier, N. (2008). Cognitive behaviour therapy for schizophrenia: Effect sizes, clinical models, and methodological rigor. *Schizophrenia Bulletin*, *34*, 523–537.

Young, H. F., & Bentall, R. P. (1995). Hypothesis testing in patients with persecutory delusions: Comparison with depressed and normal subjects. *British Journal of Clinical Psychology*, *34*, 353–369.

Zimmermann, G., Favrod, J., Trieu, V., & Pomini, V. (2005). The effects of cognitive behavioural treatment on the positive symptoms of schizophrenia spectrum disorders: A meta-analysis. *Schizophrenia Research*, *77*, 1–9.

18 Giftedness and psychosis

James H. MacCabe

The fine line between genius and psychosis: Myth or reality?

I am struck by how many non-specialists, on learning that I study the relationship between intelligence and risk for mental disorders, immediately cite an example of a friend or relative who has achieved great intellectual success, but then developed a devastating psychotic illness. Many people assume that a link between genius and madness is well established, and are surprised to hear that the bulk of the evidence is very much to the contrary—most psychiatric conditions, in particular psychotic disorders, are associated with poor performance on cognitive tests.

In 1997, I underwent almost exactly the opposite revelation. Robin Murray's research had drawn me to train in psychiatry at the Maudsley, and by a combination of serendipity, scheming and supplication, I had managed to secure a six-month post as Robin's Senior House Officer at the National Psychosis Unit, a tertiary referral centre for treatment-resistant psychosis. I knew, of course, that people with psychosis tended to perform poorly on cognitive tests—the result, probably, of neurodevelopmental damage (Murray & Lewis, 1987). I expected that patients with more severe forms of psychosis would have even greater impairment.

I was astonished, however, to find that many of the patients had extraordinarily high levels of pre-morbid academic achievement—a Cambridge medical student, a high-flying lawyer, a rocket scientist with the European Space Agency: yet all were receiving treatment for severe psychosis. Furthermore, their families were often high achievers as well. "How could this be possible?", I asked Robin. Did these patients have a different disorder that was somehow mimicking schizophrenia? Did they have cognitive deficits that did not affect their academic achievement? Was the neurodevelopmental hypothesis false? I kept this last question to myself.

Epidemiological explanations

As my understanding of epidemiology developed, I began to realize that some of the apparent association could be explained by selection bias. Although the unit was a National Health Service (NHS) facility, freely available to any patient in the UK, the reality was that the patients were not a random selection of individuals with treatment-refractory psychosis. The patients and families with the greatest levels of knowledge, motivation and eloquence were probably more likely than average to convince their local teams to refer them. Like me, these patients were on the unit because of Robin Murray; they were therefore self-selected to be more motivated, and, probably, more intelligent than average.

Nevertheless, the existence of these patients proves that it is at least possible for people with a high level of intelligence or academic achievement to develop severe psychosis. If neurocognitive deficits are a result of abnormal neurodevelopment, then it follows that these patients may represent a non-neurodevelopmental subgroup.

Graduates with psychosis

The first question to address was whether these patients could be distinguished from the cognitively impaired patients on measures other than cognitive impairment. If so, this would suggest that cognitively intact patients were an aetiologically distinct group. As so often in these situations, Robin had access to data that would shed light on this question. Elham Aldouri, senior trainee psychiatrist at the Maudsley, had recently abstracted data on 46 university-educated patients and 48 non-university-educated patients, with schizophrenia, schizoaffective disorder or non-specific functional psychosis according to research diagnostic criteria (Spitzer, Endicott, & Robins, 1978), using the OPCRIT checklist (McGuffin, Farmer, & Harvey, 1991). University education is only a crude measure of pre-morbid academic attainment, but seemed acceptable for a preliminary study.

Using these data, I conducted a principal components analysis (closely related to factor analysis), deriving a factor structure for psychosis. Four principal components emerged: mania; biological depressive symptoms; core schizophrenic symptoms; and psychological depressive symptoms. I then compared the factor scores for each principal component between university-educated and non-university-educated groups (MacCabe, Aldouri, Fahy, Sham, & Murray, 2002).

The university-educated patients scored significantly higher on the psychological depression principal component, and lower on the core schizophrenic symptoms principal component, than the non-university-educated patients. My tentative interpretation of these results was that cognitively intact patients may represent an aetiologically distinct subgroup, with a stronger affective component to their illness.

A seductive idea

The main question, however, is whether the purported association between "genius" and "madness" has any truth. It is certainly a very ancient belief, and can be traced back to the writings of Aristotle, Plato and Socrates (Hershman & Lieb, 1998). In popular culture, the mad scientist and the tortured artistic genius are common stereotypes.

Before examining the evidence, it is important to explore why the idea of such an association has such a strong appeal. There is some evidence that people are particularly receptive to ideas that seem counterintuitive, selectively remembering information that is surprising or paradoxical (Boyer & Ramble, 2001). Thus, although many people with below-average intellectual abilities develop psychosis, this does not generate much discussion. However, when an Oxbridge graduate becomes ill, the apparent inconsistency arouses interest, and news of his misfortune quickly spreads. Indeed, it may be that the achievements of such people are exaggerated in the re-telling, accentuating the newsworthiness of the story. The discussion is then likely to turn to other such examples, and to the question of a possible causal link. In this way, a perception is generated that there is an association between academic success and psychosis.

The genius/madness association may also be an inherently attractive concept. The prospect that mental illness may be caused by superior abilities can be a way of understanding or even normalizing the experience of mental illness, for the patient or their relatives. There is also something appealing about the related idea that creativity and mental disorder are interlinked. The model of the anguished genius, as personified by Lord Byron, Vincent van Gogh and others (Jamison, 1993), has served as a romantic ideal for generations of artists.

Difficulties with studying the association

Much of the work investigating links between mental disorder and exceptional ability comprises biographical studies of eminent individuals. But these studies can be biased in two ways. The individuals chosen for study can be "cherry picked", such that people who have mental disorders are more likely to be studied. This type of selection bias may occur prior to the researcher's involvement—the fact that an individual has a mental disorder may make him more likely to be the subject of a biography. Further bias can be introduced by the biographer, in deciding which information to include or emphasize in the biography, and by the researcher, in deciding which of this material is relevant.

An example was the study of Jamison (1989), which described the biographies of 47 writers and artists and found that 38% had received treatment for mood disorders at some time in their lives. Indeed, almost all biographical studies have found greater than expected rates of mental illness in gifted or creative people, but had severe methodological flaws (Waddell, 1998).

Nancy Andreasen (1987) and colleagues were the first to undertake a modern study using detailed psychiatric assessments and standardized diagnostic criteria. The authors compared a group of 30 writers on the prestigious Iowa Writers' Workshop with a group of age-, education- and sex-matched controls. They found much higher rates of affective disorder generally, particularly bipolar disorder (13/30 versus 3/30, $p = .01$) and alcoholism, among the writers than the controls. There were no cases of schizophrenia in either group. Another study (Ludwig, 1994) compared 59 female writers with 59 members of a matched comparison group, using interviews and questionnaires. The writers were more likely than the comparison group to suffer from mood disorders, and similar effects were seen for substance misuse and anxiety disorders.

Population-based studies

As noted above, selection bias is a serious problem in studying links between psychosis and cognitive abilities. The challenge, then, is to test the evidence for an association between exceptional ability and psychosis in a representative sample of a population. This raises a further problem—in order to study an association between two rare characteristics, very large samples are required. Both of these problems have been overcome relatively recently, using population-based studies.

Icelandic studies

Jon Karlsson has used Icelandic case registers to study associations between mental illness and a number of measures of high functioning (Karlsson, 2004). In his most recent study, he compared individuals with exceptionally good academic functioning (the top two individuals in the country each year) at approximately age 18, with the remainder of the population. These individuals were at increased risk of psychosis, as were their first-degree relatives. A subsequent analysis showed that high achievers in mathematics and their relatives were at particularly high risk. However, despite using the entire Icelandic population, these studies were relatively underpowered, and of borderline statistical significance, and it was not clear whether the associations were with bipolar disorder or non-affective psychosis.

The 1966 Northern Finland Birth Cohort study

This is a cohort of 11,000 individuals, with prospectively collected data on school performance, followed until age 28 using the Finnish Hospital Discharge Register for schizophrenia, other psychoses and non-psychotic psychiatric disorders.

Boys with excellent school performance at age 16 had a fourfold increased risk of schizophrenia compared with controls. However, like the Icelandic studies, the numbers were small, and the effect was completely absent in girls (Isohanni, Jarvelin, Jones, Jokelainen, & Isohanni, 1999).

Israeli studies

In 1999, Michael Davidson and colleagues published a nested case-control study, in which 509 men with schizophrenia were matched on age, gender and school to 9,215 male controls; each case was matched to the mean score of the remainder of his class, and the analysis was a matched design using conditional logistic regression. Conscription occurred at age 16–17 between 1985 and 1991 and follow-up continued until 1995, when the cohort were aged approximately 20–27.

The proportion of pre-schizophrenia cases falling within the highest IQ category among the cases was six times higher than that among the comparison subjects (Davidson et al., 1999), but again the number in this category was very small.

Dunedin cohort

In the Dunedin Multidisciplinary Health and Development Study, a birth cohort from 1972–73 was assessed regularly through childhood and into early adulthood (Cannon et al., 2002). The participants were questioned about psychotic symptoms at age 11 and were screened for mental-health problems at age 26. Children who would develop mania in adulthood had significantly higher IQs than the remainder of the cohort, but the sample was very small, with only 8 pre-manic children (Koenen et al., 2009).

Pre-morbid school performance in schizophrenia and other psychoses: A national cohort study

From the foregoing review, we can conclude that there is suggestive evidence of associations between high achievement in various domains and psychosis. Although both affective or non-affective psychoses have been linked to high achievement in previous studies, the evidence for bipolar disorder and other affective psychoses is somewhat stronger. However, much of the research is potentially biased, and/or based on very small samples. Furthermore, none of the previous studies has been able to adjust adequately for familial factors such as socioeconomic group and education level. We therefore set out to examine the relationship between scholastic achievement at age 16 and risk for both affective and non-affective psychoses in adulthood, controlling for potential confounders including socioeconomic group and parental education. The research summarized here has been published in two peer-reviewed papers (MacCabe et al., 2008, 2010), and also in greater detail in a previous Maudsley publication (MacCabe, 2010).

By combining data obtained from seven Swedish national registers, we constructed a national cohort, with almost complete coverage of the Swedish population within a defined age range. We obtained the individual school grades for all pupils graduating from compulsory education (at age 15–16) between 1988 until 1997 inclusive, from the Swedish National School Register, which has almost universal coverage of Swedish children. School grades were nationally peer referenced, such that grades were comparable throughout Sweden. The Swedish authorities calculated a grade point average (GPA) for each pupil, which was used to determine that pupil's eligibility for upper secondary education from age 16–18. Using Swedish personal identification numbers, we linked data from the National School Register to that of the Hospital Discharge Register, which contains discharge diagnoses for hospital admissions, using the International Classification of Diseases (World Health Organization, 1992) versions 9 and 10. We included the following ICD codes: schizophrenia (ICD-9 codes 295.A–G, W,

X; ICD-10 codes F20.0–F20.9), schizoaffective disorder (ICD-9 code 295.H; ICD-10 codes F25.0–F25.9), bipolar disorder (ICD-9 codes 296, 296.A, C–E, W, X; ICD-10 codes F300–319) and other non-affective psychoses (ICD-9 codes 293, 294, 297, 298; ICD-10 codes F22.0–F24.9, F28.9, F29.9). We made further linkages, via the parents, to other population registers, which included information on the parents' socioeconomic status, education level, country of origin and citizenship.

The study population comprised all Swedish-born individuals in the National School Register from year 1988 through year 1997 inclusive, whose parents were also born in Sweden. We excluded individuals who developed any psychotic disorder before, or within one year of taking their examinations. Since the grade point average followed a normal distribution, it lent itself easily to conversion to *z*-scores. *Z*-score of grade point average was used as the exposure variable. We conducted a survival analysis, using Cox proportional hazards modelling, in which observations were censored when they ceased to be at risk of hospitalization for psychosis in Sweden—either because they had died, emigrated, or developed psychosis already.

Of 715,401 individuals in the sample, 1,805 developed a psychotic disorder during the follow-up period. Of these, there were 493 cases of schizophrenia, 95 cases of schizoaffective disorder, 280 cases of bipolar disorder and 937 cases of other psychotic disorders. Figure 18.1 shows the incidence rates of psychoses by grade point average. Both schizophrenia and schizoaffective disorder have similar patterns; individuals with the lowest school grades have the highest risk of psychosis, and there are no cases of either disorder among individuals in the highest category of school performance.

In the case of bipolar disorder, however, the pattern is completely different, with the highest incidence rate for bipolar disorder occurring in the best performing students. The hazard ratio (HR) for excellent school performance (more than two standard deviations, *SD*, above the population mean) versus average performance (within 1 *SD* of the population mean) was 3.79, 95% confidence interval (95% CI) = 2.11, 6.82. In other words, people in the excellent category of school performance are almost four times more likely to develop bipolar disorder than those with average scores. We adjusted for gender, socioeconomic group, advanced paternal and maternal age, parental education level and spring birth (January–April), but this had little effect on the hazard ratio (adjusted HR = 3.34, 95% CI = 1.82, 6.11), indicating that these factors were not confounding the association.

If excellent performance is associated with increased risk for bipolar disorder, the question arises: is bipolar disorder associated with general high performance, or with excellence in particular school subjects—creative subjects, for example? We therefore analysed the associations between "A" grades in individual school subjects and risk for bipolar disorder. "A" grades in Swedish, childcare, geography, music, religion, biology and history were strongly associated with increased risk for bipolar disorder at the $p < .001$ level, all with hazard ratios around two. "A" grades in engineering, civics, English, chemistry and mathematics were associated at the $p < .05$ level. "A" grades in art, physics and handicraft had non-significant

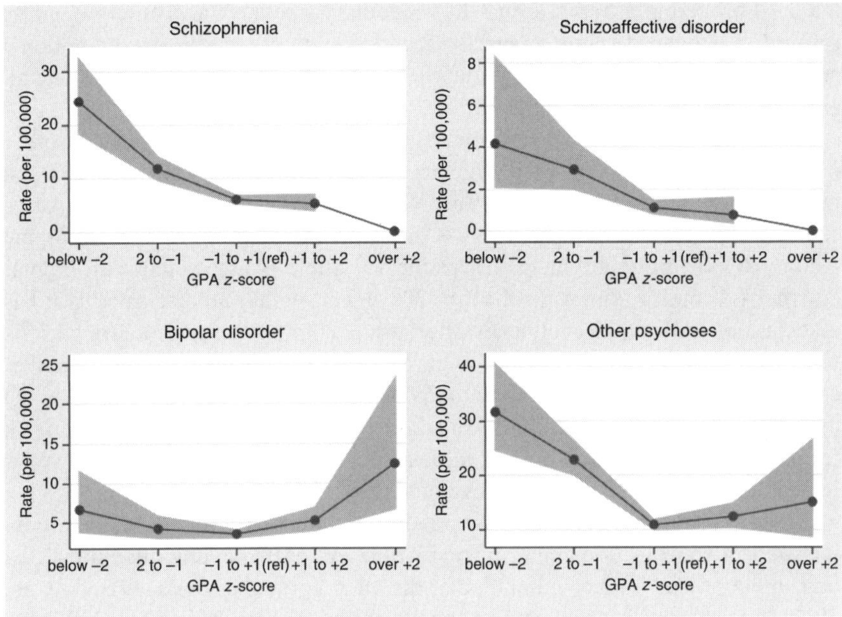

Figure 18.1 Rates of psychosis, by grade point average (ref = reference category).

associations with risk for bipolar disorder, but these association were all in the same direction—achieving an "A" grade was associated with an increased risk. Sport was unique in having an inverse association (HR = 0.42, p = .003), such that scoring an "A" grade was protective against bipolar disorder.

Discussion

I believe that this study provides strong evidence of an association between excellent academic achievement and risk for bipolar disorder. The other evidence reviewed in this chapter seems to be consistent with this conclusion. But how could school performance and bipolar disorder be related?

The question can be approached on at least four levels: at the population genetic level; the psychological level; the molecular genetic level; and the neurobiological level. At the level of population genetics, it has been suggested that selection pressure against psychosis-predisposing genetic variants may be counteracted by a selective advantage in unaffected relatives, conferred through increased creativity or intelligence (Keller & Miller, 2006). Although this is likely to be less relevant for bipolar disorder than for schizophrenia, as no overall fertility disadvantage in bipolar disorder has been found (MacCabe, Koupil, & Leon, 2009), it remains possible that certain genetically determined cognitive traits may be advantageous in some situations yet predispose to bipolar disorder—particularly mania. For example, rapid access to vocabulary, memory and other cognitive resources, enhanced stamina, sustained concentration and enhanced emotional reactivity may all be beneficial for intellectual performance or creativity, and all are also common features of mania.

At the level of individual risk alleles, these traits, as well as bipolar disorder itself, are likely to be under polygenic control, with significant epistasis and interaction with environmental factors. Nevertheless, there are some speculative candidate genes. One putative locus is the val66met brain-derived neurotrophic factor (BDNF) polymorphism, where the val allele is associated with bipolar disorder (Farmer, Elkin, & McGuffin, 2007), and within bipolar patients it has associations with rapid cycling (Muller et al., 2006) and superior frontal lobe functioning (Rybakowski, Borkowska, Skibinska, & Hauser, 2006). Another candidate is the SNP8NRG243177/rs6994992; C vs. T polymorphism of the promoter region of neuregulin 1, where the TT genotype, previously linked to risk for psychosis, was recently shown to be associated with creative thinking styles in people with high academic achievement (Keri, 2009).

At the level of neurobiology, one possibility is that both mania and creativity are associated with dopamine dysregulation. A recent review concluded that dopamine may be implicated in bipolar disorder, particularly mania (Berk et al., 2007). Case reports have emerged of poetic ability (Schrag & Trimble, 2001) and artistic creativity (Chatterjee, Hamilton, & Amorapanth, 2006; Kulisevsky, Pagonabarraga, & Martinez-Corral, 2009; Walker, Warwick, & Cercy, 2006) in Parkinsonian patients treated with dopamine agonists. Furthermore, in one case, this was accompanied by overt manic symptoms (Schrag & Trimble, 2001).

The mechanisms proposed here are, of course, speculative, but they provide us with a direction for future research into the putative links between intelligence, creativity and bipolar disorder.

Acknowledgements

The research in this chapter was made possible by Christina Hultman and her colleagues at Karolinska Institutet, Tony David, Pak Sham and Elham Aldouri. It was funded primarily through a research training fellowship from the MRC.

One of Robin Murray's many likeable qualities is his self-effacing modesty and indifference to praise. We therefore all felt for him as he bravely endured an onslaught of flattery at his Festschrift. Even his family were merciless in their adulation. I am afraid I can't pass up this opportunity to add my own tribute—I will try not to make it too fulsome but superlatives are entirely appropriate in this case.

Robin leaves a lasting impression on everybody fortunate enough to come within his orbit—his independence of thought, hard work, enthusiasm, energy, wisdom and integrity are formidable. But it is the combination of these merits with his human qualities of compassion, warmth, humour, and buoyant optimism that is truly inspiring. We will all carry some of Robin's virtues forward in our own careers—but none of us can ever hope to embody them all. Thank goodness he has no intention of retiring gracefully!

References

Andreasen, N. C. (1987). Creativity and mental illness: Prevalence rates in writers and their first-degree relatives. *American Journal of Psychiatry*, *144*(10), 1288–1292.

Berk, M., Dodd, S., Kauer-Sant'anna, M., Malhi, G. S., Bourin, M., Kapczinski, F., et al. (2007). Dopamine dysregulation syndrome: Implications for a dopamine hypothesis of bipolar disorder. *Acta Psychiatrica Scandinavica (Supplement)*, *434*, 41–49.

Boyer, P., & Ramble, C. (2001). Cognitive templates for religious concepts: Cross-cultural evidence for recall of counter-intuitive representations. *Cognitive Science*, *25*, 535–564.

Cannon, M., Caspi, A., Moffitt, T. E., Harrington, H., Taylor, A., Murray, R. M., et al. (2002). Evidence for early childhood, pan-developmental impairment specific to schizophreniform disorder: Results from a longitudinal birth cohort. *Archives of General Psychiatry*, *59*(5), 449–456.

Chatterjee, A., Hamilton, R. H., & Amorapanth, P. X. (2006). Art produced by a patient with Parkinson's disease. *Behavioural Neurology*, *17*(2), 105–108.

Davidson, M., Reichenberg, A., Rabinowitz, J., Weiser, M., Kaplan, Z., & Mark, M. (1999). Behavioral and intellectual markers for schizophrenia in apparently healthy male adolescents. *American Journal of Psychiatry*, *156*(9), 1328–1335.

Farmer, A., Elkin, A., & McGuffin, P. (2007). The genetics of bipolar affective disorder. *Current Opinion in Psychiatry*, *20*(1), 8–12.

Hershman, D. J., & Lieb, J. (1998). *Manic depression and creativity*. Amherst, MA: Prometheus Books.

Isohanni, I., Jarvelin, M. R., Jones, P., Jokelainen, J., & Isohanni, M. (1999). Can excellent school performance be a precursor of schizophrenia? A 28- year follow-up in the Northern Finland 1966 birth cohort [see comments]. *Acta Psychiatrica Scandinavica*, *100*(1), 17–26.

Jamison, K. R. (1989). Mood disorders and patterns of creativity in British writers and artists. *Psychiatry*, *52*(2), 125–134.

Jamison, K. R. (1993). *Touched with fire: Manic depressive illness and the artistic temperament*. New York, NY: Simon & Schuster.

Karlsson, J. L. (2004). Psychosis and academic performance. *British Journal of Psychiatry*, *184*, 327–329.

Keller, M. C., & Miller, G. (2006). Resolving the paradox of common, harmful, heritable mental disorders: Which evolutionary genetic models work best? *Behavioral and Brain Sciences*, *29*(4), 385–404.

Keri, S. (2009). Genes for psychosis and creativity: A promoter polymorphism of the neuregulin 1 gene is related to creativity in people with high intellectual achievement. *Psychological Science*, *20*(9), 1070–1073.

Koenen, K. C., Moffitt, T. E., Roberts, A. L., Martin, L. T., Kubzansky, L., Harrington, H., et al. (2009). Childhood IQ and adult mental disorders: A test of the cognitive reserve hypothesis. *American Journal of Psychiatry*, *166*(1), 50–57.

Kulisevsky, J., Pagonabarraga, J., & Martinez-Corral, M. (2009). Changes in artistic style and behaviour in Parkinson's disease: Dopamine and creativity. *Journal of Neurology*, *256*(5), 816–819.

Ludwig, A. M. (1994). Mental illness and creative activity in female writers. *American Journal of Psychiatry*, *151*(11), 1650–1656.

MacCabe, J. H. (2010). *The extremes of the bell curve: Excellent and poor school performance and risk for severe mental disorders*. Hove, UK: Psychology Press.

MacCabe, J. H., Aldouri, E., Fahy, T. A., Sham, P. C., & Murray, R. M. (2002). Do schizophrenic patients who managed to get to university have a non-developmental form of illness? *Psychological Medicine*, *32*(3), 535–544.

MacCabe, J. H., Koupil, I., & Leon, D. A. (2009). Lifetime reproductive output over two generations in patients with psychosis and their unaffected siblings: The Uppsala 1915–1929 Birth Cohort Multigenerational Study. *Psychological Medicine*, *39*, 1667–1676.

MacCabe, J. H., Lambe, M. P., Cnattingius, S., Sham, P. C., David, A. S., Reichenberg, A., et al. (2010). Excellent school performance at age 16 and risk of adult bipolar disorder: National cohort study. *British Journal of Psychiatry*, *196*(2), 109–115.

MacCabe, J. H., Lambe, M. P., Cnattingius, S., Torrang, A., Bjork, C., Sham, P. C., et al. (2008). Scholastic achievement at age 16 and risk of schizophrenia and other psychoses: A national cohort study. *Psychological Medicine*, *38*(8), 1133–1140.

McGuffin, P., Farmer, A., & Harvey, I. (1991). A polydiagnostic application of operational criteria in studies of psychotic illness. Development and reliability of the OPCRIT system [news]. *Archives of General Psychiatry*, *48*(8), 764–770.

Muller, D. J., de Luca, V., Sicard, T., King, N., Strauss, J., & Kennedy, J. L. (2006). Brain-derived neurotrophic factor (*BDNF*) gene and rapid-cycling bipolar disorder: Family based association study. *British Journal of Psychiatry*, *189*, 317–323.

Murray, R. M., & Lewis, S. W. (1987). Is schizophrenia a neurodevelopmental disorder? [editorial]. *British Medical Journal (Clinical Research Edition)*, *295*(6600), 681–682.

Rybakowski, J. K., Borkowska, A., Skibinska, M., & Hauser, J. (2006). Illness-specific association of val66met BDNF polymorphism with performance on Wisconsin Card Sorting Test in bipolar mood disorder. *Molecular Psychiatry*, *11*(2), 122–124.

Schrag, A., & Trimble, M. (2001). Poetic talent unmasked by treatment of Parkinson's disease. *Movement Disorders*, *16*(6), 1175–1176.

Spitzer, R. L., Endicott, J., & Robins, E. (1978). Research diagnostic criteria: rationale and reliability. *Archives of General Psychiatry*, *35*(6), 773–782.

Waddell, C. (1998). Creativity and mental illness: Is there a link? *Canadian Journal of Psychiatry*, *43*(2), 166–172.

Walker, R. H., Warwick, R., & Cercy, S. P. (2006). Augmentation of artistic productivity in Parkinson's disease. *Movement Disorders*, *21*(2), 285–286.

World Health Organization. (1992). *International statistical classification of diseases and related health problems* (ICD). Geneva, Switzerland: WHO.

Part VI

Social psychiatry

19 Towards a social aetiology of psychosis

The case of child sexual abuse

Paul Bebbington

Introduction

Robin Murray and I are exact contemporaries: we joined the Maudsley Hospital together in October 1972. Our research careers took different tracks, but have been in many ways complementary, and I have always been aware of his direction of travel in a way that has been useful to me. It is a pleasure to me to write this chapter in tribute to his enormous and thoughtful productivity, and in acknowledgement of his influence on my thinking.

Robin and I share a preoccupation with psychosis, and I have chosen to write about a topic that raises central questions about its nature. This is the relationship between psychosis and major disruptions in childhood. I will examine specifically the case of child sexual abuse. In addition to providing a plausible social cause of psychosis, it illuminates the possibilities and limitations of causal inference.

Social influences on psychosis

Social psychiatrists have, to their own satisfaction at least, been persuaded for several decades that there are major social influences on the emergence and maintenance of psychotic symptoms. This is a view shared by many psychologists working with people with psychosis. However, the dominant paradigm in psychosis remains that of neuroscience, and while neuroscientists will, when pressed, acknowledge a potential role for social factors, the focus of their attention is clearly elsewhere. The neuroscientific view is shared by psychiatrists at large, as revealed in a recent survey by Baillie, McCabe, and Priebe (2009; Figure 19.1).

In fact the evidence for social influences on the experiences, beliefs and behaviour of people with psychosis is strong and well established. Early attempts to demonstrate a causal function for social factors in psychosis involved the relationship between the social environment and the level of negative symptoms in schizophrenia (Brown, Bone, Dalison, & Wing, 1966; Wing & Brown, 1970; Wing & Freudenberg, 1961). These authors showed that the social poverty of the hospital environment was associated with the level of negative symptoms in long-term patients. Moreover, these phenomena showed concomitant variation: as the environment changed for the better, so did the patients. The relationship between environmental stimulation and the condition of patients was equally evident when

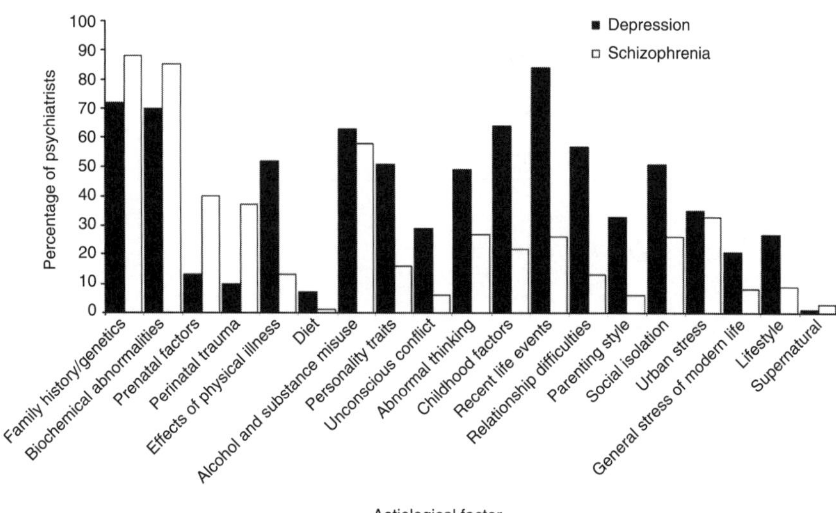

Figure 19.1 Percentage of responding psychiatrists rating each factor as relevant to the aetiology of depression or schizophrenia (Reproduced from Baillie et al., 2009, *Psychiatric Bulletin, 33*, 374–377, with permission of The Royal College of Psychiatrists).

they were living at home (Brown et al.,1966). Further, it was argued that negative symptoms were adaptive, reflecting a withdrawal from levels of stimulation that in themselves might have adverse affects. Rehabilitation programmes designed to reduce withdrawal and apathy would sometimes reactivate delusions and hallucinations (Stevens, 1973; Stone & Eldrid, 1959; Wing, Monck, Brown, & Carstairs, 1964). This early work has become less clinically relevant with the development of community psychiatric programmes designed to maintain the engagement of people with psychosis with their community. While these do not eliminate the problem of negative symptoms, they do remove their worst effects. However, at a theoretical level these findings are still very relevant.

The fifties and sixties of the last century also saw the development of scientific methods for assessing the effects of the family environment on psychosis. This body of work is now particularly well founded, and is of central clinical relevance (Kuipers, Onwumere, & Bebbington, 2010). Much of it hinges on the success of the measure *expressed emotion* in tapping into family environments and quantifying their adverse effects (Brown, Birley, & Wing, 1972). In a large number of prospective studies, people with psychosis living with family members rated high on expressed emotion are much more likely to experience a relapse (Bebbington & Kuipers, 1994). This finding led naturally to the use of family intervention in reducing relapse in people with psychosis (Pilling et al., 2002). The success of therapeutic intervention makes very plausible the idea that an adverse atmosphere at home actually causes the re-emergence of positive symptoms of schizophrenia.

The third theme relating to the effects of stress on psychosis concerns so-called stressful life events. These were seen as having a role in moving someone with a propensity for psychosis into a state of manifest disorder. The underlying assumptions were made most explicit as the stress–vulnerability model (Zubin & Spring, 1977). This was based on the idea that the stress of the event would have an imminent impact on the patient. The development of adequate technical methods for eliciting histories of life events, and of adequate designs for testing the hypotheses linking them to psychiatric disorder led to a fair number of studies devoted to demonstrating the link between stress and the emergence of psychotic symptoms.

The inaugural, and still seminal, study in this area is that of Brown and Birley (1968). They found a significantly raised rate of life events, although this seemed to be limited to the three weeks before the onset or relapse of schizophrenic illness. Under one definition, 46% of cases had an event in this three-week period compared to around 12% in more distant periods. By the mid-1990s, sixteen systematic studies had been published (Bebbington, Bowen, Hirsch, & Kuipers, 1995). However, they provide inconsistent support for the initial findings of Brown and Birley (1968). Some yielded negative results, while others suggested that the critical period for the impact of life events was longer than three weeks, and might be as long as a year. One of these life-events studies formed part of the Camberwell Collaborative Psychosis Study, which I worked on in association with Robin Murray and his colleagues (Bebbington et al., 1993). This study, which used methodology similar to Brown and Birley (1968), strongly suggested that events do increase before onset, and that, if this is of aetiological significance, the effect sometimes acts across a sizeable interval, up to several months.

However, the study of relatively every-day stressful life events is bedevilled by several methodological and inferential difficulties. As suggested above, a proportion of people with psychosis may withdraw socially, perhaps as a coping strategy. Depending on whether they have done so, particular individuals may have more, or less, events than members of the general population, and they may respond to the events they do experience more, or less, strongly than people without the propensity to psychosis. This makes the relatively straightforward epidemiological demonstration of an association more difficult. The methodological demands and the unimpressive results have reduced enthusiasm. The heyday of life-event studies in psychosis has passed: only two have been reported since the mid-1990s (Raune, Bebbington, & Kuipers, 2009; see Bebbington & Kuipers, 2011).

In summary, if the results of the available studies are taken as indicating some causal effect of recent stressful events, this effect is not major, is relatively non-specific (being seen in most psychiatric disorders), and is limited to a triggering role.

This is in very marked contrast to the strong association of psychosis with severely traumatic early events. In what follows, I will take childhood sexual abuse as a paradigm of such early trauma. Compared with most other putative aetiological agents in psychosis, including biological ones, child sexual abuse

(CSA) has two attributes that in combination make it stand out. The first is that it is common, and the second that the association with psychosis is very strong. These attributes mean that the population attributable risk fraction (PAF) is large. This in turn suggests that the public-health implications may also be major.

The frequency of child sexual abuse

While the prevalence of sexual abuse depends on the definition and on how the information is obtained, there is little doubt that it is a common phenomenon. Thus, a recent UK survey obtained a prevalence of 11% (May-Chahal & Cawson, 2005). Estimates from around the world have been in the same range (Dinwiddie et al., 2000; Friedman et al., 2002).

To these can now be added data from the 2007 Adult Psychiatric Morbidity Survey (APMS 2007; McManus, Meltzer, Brugha, Bebbington, & Jenkins, 2009). This psychiatric survey of a random sample of the English population included detailed questions about physical and sexual abuse. It was possible to date these forms of abuse, and therefore to identify sexual abuse in childhood. In addition to the level of detail, the survey included an innovation designed to improve the quality of the information elicited. This was computer-assisted self-interview (CASI), whereby participants responded to questions presented on a laptop. Interviews were carried out by professional survey interviewers, but they had no access to the responses in the CASI section of the interview. Participants knew this beforehand. There is evidence that CASI generally elicits franker responses to what is undoubtedly a sensitive topic than face-to-face questioning (Tourangeau, Rips, & Rasinski, 2000).

In APMS 2007, non-consensual sexual intercourse before the age of 16 was reported by 1.9% of the sample, unwanted sexual touching by 8.2%, and uncomfortable sexual talk by 10.3%; the experience of each form of abuse was considerably more frequent in women (Bebbington et al., 2011; see Figure 19.2). This discrimination between different forms of sexual abuse allows investigation of the effect of increasing severity of abuse on psychiatric outcomes.

Epidemiology and the limits of aetiological inference

Epidemiological studies are invaluable for establishing robust associations between variables, but the inference of causality must always be tentative, and depends on the ability to build up plausibility. Statistical tests of association have relevance for causal inference, but largely in a negative sense—causal possibilities can be eliminated. More elaborate tests such as latent variable analysis enable statements about the relative plausibility of competing models, but again these statements are tentative. Clearly the more ways a causal hypothesis can be tested, and the more times it is corroborated, the more allowable the causal inference.

Consider the hypothesis that the relationship between CSA and psychosis is causal. One way of testing this is by establishing cases of psychosis in an epidemiological sample and asking the whole sample about their experience of

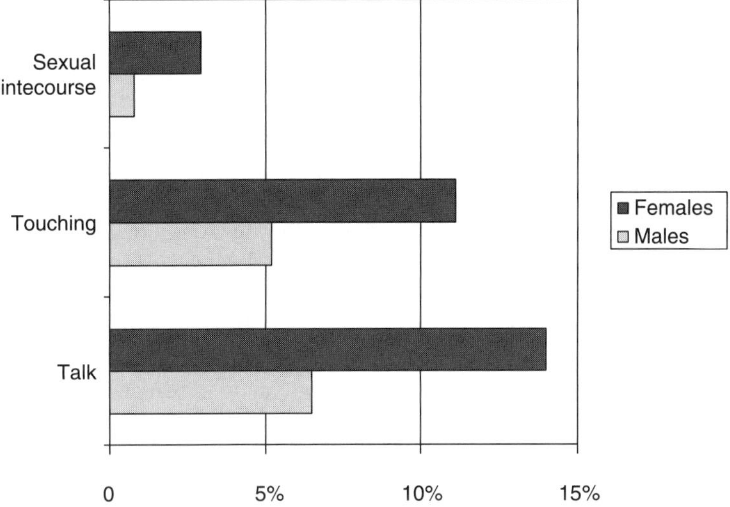

Figure 19.2 Frequency of CSA in the English national population (source of data APMS 2007).

CSA. The onset of psychosis and the experience of CSA can both be dated. Because most cases of psychosis start in adulthood (occasionally in the late teens), they will post-date any experience of CSA. Thus a causal effect of CSA has more plausibility than the reverse (that adult psychosis causes CSA). However, reverse causality cannot be ruled out, because the information establishing psychosis and CSA was gathered at the same time, and having psychosis might distort reportage of CSA. This may be particularly so in the case of a disorder accompanied by delusions. It is also possible that the salience of sexual abuse for the individual and the willingness to report it may be greater if that individual has a psychiatric disorder.

However, it is equally important not to discount reports of sexual abuse too readily. Goodman et al. (1999) showed that psychiatric patients' accounts of sexual abuse were consistent over time, concluding that the information obtained is sufficiently reliable to allow research in this area. Fergusson, Horwood, and Woodward (2000) assessed the stability of reports of CSA in a non-clinical sample over a three-year gap. They concluded that people did not falsely report that they had been abused, although positive reports were unstable, with false negatives reaching a prevalence as high as 50%. All in all, it does not seem likely that the effect of psychiatric disorder on reports of abuse are major, and the idea that CSA causes psychosis remains the more plausible. The sheer consistency of the evidence does suggest that the association is genuine and large, even though there may be dispute about its actual size.

Nevertheless, the aetiological standing of CSA would be increased if the history of CSA were established some time before the definitive identification of psychosis. However, it is widely regarded as unethical to quiz children in a random sample about their experience of CSA, and there are no such studies. One way round this is to identify CSA through contemporaneous official records, but this is likely to miss many cases, with unknown effects on the apparent association with psychosis (Spataro, Mullen, Burgess, Wells, & Moss, 2004).

Another difficulty for causal inference is the third variable problem—the idea that the link between CSA and psychosis is spurious, as each is caused by a third, unmeasured, variable. One example would be if psychosis in parents increased the risk both of CSA and of psychosis in their offspring. Again this has superficial plausibility, but it does not seem likely to account for much of the association in a general-population sample. One study adjusted for parental psychiatric disturbance still yielded very high relative odds linking CSA with psychotic symptoms (Janssen et al., 2004).

Other circumstantial factors make more convincing third-variable candidates: thus CSA often occurs in the context of other very adverse circumstances that might be responsible both for the CSA and for the later development of psychosis. Again this is something that needs to be considered, but it is actually an argument for broadening the category of social causes of psychosis while retaining essentially social hypotheses of causation. Moreover, without precise dating of the different variables, it is not possible to distinguish between spurious correlation and mediation. CSA in this context is most simply seen as a proxy for the wider social context. Bebbington and his colleagues (2004) found that sexual abuse was associated with a relative odds of psychosis of 15, but also with a wide range of other traumatic events and adverse circumstances. After adjustment for these, the odds ratio (OR) was reduced to around 3, but the association was still strongly significant.

A further aspect of the relationship between CSA and psychosis that supports the plausibility of a causal effect is that of dose–response. If psychosis is most common in people with the most severe forms of CSA, this is easiest to explain if the CSA causes the psychosis.

Finally, one of the strongest arguments for an aetiological effect is the identification of mediating processes, particularly if they are consistent with an overall theoretical model. In this context, such mediators might have both psychological and behavioural components. The psychological consequences of CSA may thereby become the psychological antecedents of psychosis. Alternatively, the psychological damage caused by CSA may in turn lead to unwise behaviour that leaves the victim open to further abuse. Severe trauma may also modify the physiological stress response in deleterious ways that may have later consequences (Driessen et al., 2000; Heim et al., 2000; Read, van Os, Morrison, & Ross, 2005; Spauwen, Krabbendam, Lieb, Wittchen, & van Os, 2006).

Child sexual abuse and psychosis

Links between CSA and psychosis have been increasingly noted since the 1990s. Ellason and Ross (1997) found a significant association, confirmed by Mueser et al. (1998), while Lysaker, Meyer, Evans, Clements, and Marks (2001) reported that 40% of their sample of people with schizophrenia acknowledged the experience of CSA. Given some level of sexual abuse, the OR of psychosis was extremely high in the British National Psychiatric Morbidity Survey carried out in 2000 (Bebbington et al., 2004), although no distinction was made between childhood and adult sexual abuse. The major association of CSA with psychosis has been affirmed in two recent reviews, although methodological caveats remain (Morgan & Fisher, 2007; Read et al., 2005). The sheer consistency of the evidence suggests that the association is genuine and large, even though there may be dispute about its actual size.

However, as with recent life events, the association is remarkably non-specific. Thus, following CSA, there appears to be an enhanced risk of adult depression, personality disorder, PTSD, drug and alcohol abuse, bulimia and suicidality (Bebbington et al., 2009; Dinwiddie et al., 2000; Kendler et al., 2000; Nelson et al., 2006; Putnam, 2003). This non-specificity is also apparent from the results of APMS 2007 (Bebbington et al., in press; Jonas et al., 2011; see Figure 19.3). A full aetiological account of sexual abuse and psychosis requires an explanation of this non-specificity.

A number of studies have reported a dose–response relationship linking child abuse with psychosis (see Read, Bentall, & Fosse, 2009, for a review), although this has been based on increasing combinations of abuse types (e.g., sexual abuse plus neglect plus physical abuse). There has been only one study (based on APMS 2007 data) of dose responsiveness in relation to the severity of the sexual abuse itself (Bebbington et al., in press). This found little evidence for a gradual progression. The study distinguished three categories of abuse: uncomfortable sexual talk, unwanted sexual touching and non-consensual sexual intercourse.

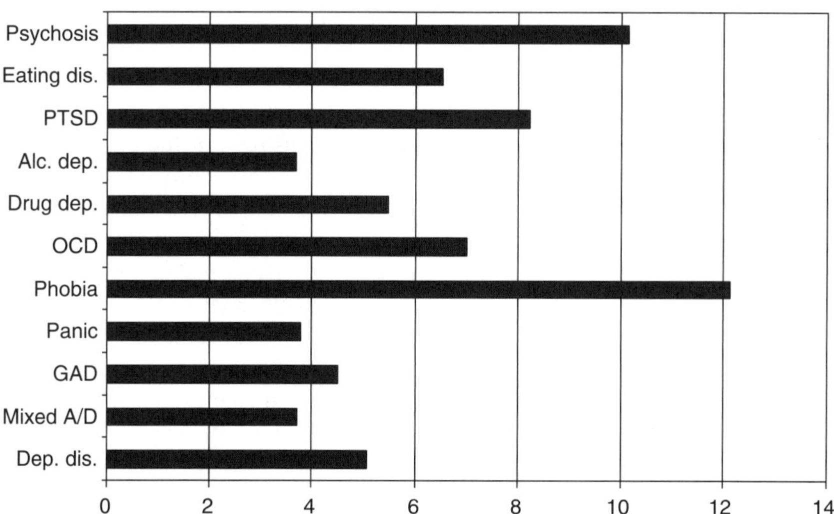

Figure 19.3 CSA involving intercourse: Relative odds of psychiatric disorders.

Those who had experienced only sexual talk or touching had a small and non-significant increase in the prevalence of psychosis, while those reporting sexual intercourse without consent had a very significantly increased risk (OR: 10.7). In these data, the association with psychosis therefore seems to be limited to childhood sexual intercourse. This finding is novel (Read et al., 2009). Although the less severe forms of abuse were not associated with psychosis, they were clearly linked to other disorders (Jonas et al., 2011). If so, this may offer some explanation of why the outcome of CSA may in particular cases be psychosis. In order to lead to psychosis, it is apparently necessary that CSA be in its most severe form, but the psychiatric outcome of this most severe form is not necessarily psychosis.

Mediation of the abuse–psychosis relationship

If we accept tentatively that the association between the CSA and psychosis represents a causal link, it leaves us with the problem of explaining how an early event can lead to a late consequence over a considerable period of time. If the relationship is causal, how might it be mediated?

From clinical and theoretical perspectives, it is relatively easy to see traumatic experiences like CSA leading directly to mental representations and dispositions that set a course for the subsequent development of even a complex mental disorder like psychosis. Likely candidates are mentally intrusive reminders of the abusive experience, psychological processes involving attitudes and beliefs, styles of coping that may impair the processing of the original abuse, and propensities towards mood disturbance, perhaps in the face of subsequent experience.

There is also evidence for mediation by other psychological processes, albeit mainly from studies of female college students in the USA. This suggests that the link between CSA and later psychiatric disorder operates at least partly through coping styles (O'Leary, 2009). People who have been sexually abused have generally been found to display avoidant coping (Cortes & Justicia, 2008; O'Leary 2009). When a history of CSA is associated with avoidant coping, the latter increases both trauma symptoms and levels of distress (Littleton, Horsley, John, & Nelson, 2007). It appears to prevent the resolution of dysfunctional cognitions. CSA also seems to be associated with reduced specificity of autobiographical memory (Sinclair, Crane, Hawton, & Williams, 2007), itself linked to continuing vulnerability for depression (Williams et al., 2007).

One putative pathway is that CSA sets up fundamental but dysfunctional schemas about oneself and the world—that the world is a dangerous place, that one is oneself blameworthy, or has no-one to help. CSA, by definition, occurs at a time of development when emotional responses and cognitive understanding may diverge. It is often reported as being accompanied by requirements of secrecy, and threats if the secret is broken. Thus no alternative views or explanations can be sought to disconfirm such schemas. CSA seems to have extreme adverse effects on self-esteem and psychological well-being (Banyard, Williams, & Siegel, 2001; Kamsner & McCabe, 2000; Murthi & Espelage, 2005). It results in self-blaming attributions (Mannarino & Cohen, 1996), and Arata (1999) reported that increased self-blame was associated with later psychopathology. CSA is also associated with insecure attachment styles (Alexander,1993).

Negative schemas about oneself and the world, and accompanying emotional disorders of depression and anxiety, are now known to exist in psychosis (Fowler et al., 2006), and to relate to the development of "at risk" mental states (Birchwood, 2003), and continuing vulnerability and symptom maintenance in those who have already developed positive symptoms of psychosis (Garety, Bebbington, Fowler, Freeman, & Kuipers, 2007; Garety, Kuipers, Fowler, Freeman, & Bebbington, 2001; Krabbendam, 2008; Krabbendam et al., 2005; Kuipers et al., 2006; Smith et al., 2006). It seems likely that such pre-setting of emotional dysfunction and negative schemas provides an easily triggered negative cognitive pathway. Along this pathway further life events and stresses will lead to unusual experiences and emotional problems, which may be appraised as external and then understood as symptoms of psychosis (Garety et al., 2001). There is some evidence for this when individuals have intrusive life events (Raune et al., 2009).

In addition to cognitive mechanisms, there appear to be major affective components in the development of psychosis. Factor analyses suggest that abuse is associated with anxiety, and that anxiety is in turn associated with more severe symptoms, including the development and persistence of positive symptoms of psychosis (Garety et al., 2005; Lysaker & Salyers, 2007). Such pathways are in principle amenable to empirical testing and to psychological intervention.

The findings of Bebbington et al. (in press) do suggest a strong affective component in the pathway between CSA and psychosis. Anxiety and depression were examined as potential mediators. There were differences in the size of the effect, and in most analyses mediation was only partial. In other words, the relationship between CSA and psychosis remained significant after adjustment for affect. Overall, controlling for depression showed the greatest impact on this relationship, although the results for anxiety were broadly similar.

CSA is strongly associated with revictimization (Classen, Palesh, & Aggarwal, 2005; Cloitre, Tardiff, Marzuk, Leon, & Portera, 1996; Coxell, King, Mezey, & Gordon, 1999; Muenzenmaier, Meyer, Struening, & Ferber, 1993). This has implications for the links between CSA and subsequent disorder, and suggests both the establishment of a persistent vulnerability, and the possible involvement of chains of adversity in generating outcomes. For example, one prospective study found that the effects of early abuse were mediated by subsequent life events (Horwitz, Widom, McLaughlin, & White, 2001), while an Australian twin study suggested that the effects of sexual abuse are moderated by other family factors, in women at any rate (Dinwiddie et al., 2000).

There has been very little investigation of the effects of repeated abuse. People who are abused as adults are reported to have higher rates of mental illness, especially schizophrenia, and psychiatric patients are reported to suffer significantly higher levels of adult abuse (Cloitre, Cohen, Edelman, & Han, 2001; Goodman et al., 2001). These findings support the idea that repeated abuse may be a significant factor, but, given the association between sexual assault as an adult and psychiatric diagnosis, it is not clear whether the repetition is a mark of illness rather than a risk factor.

In the data from APMS 2007, revictimization was defined as a sexual abuse in adulthood following CSA (Bebbington et al., in press). Such adult sexual abuse did not meet criteria for mediation, as it was not of itself related to psychosis. It did, however, augment the impact of CSA: people who reported further abuse after experiencing sexual intercourse without consent under the age of 16 were found to be the most vulnerable to psychosis, with an OR greater than 15. It should be noted that revictimization may merely be a marker for severity of abuse. It is also possible that the increment due to adult sexual abuse in the relationship between CSA and psychosis arises from confounding by abuse secondary to adult mental illness.

While Bebbington and colleagues (in press) found evidence that anxiety and depression may mediate the psychosis–abuse relationship, there are many other candidates, and complex models need to be retained (Garety et al., 2001, 2005, 2007).

The current standing of child sexual abuse in the aetiology of psychosis

We have good and insistent evidence that there is a strong association between CSA and adult psychosis. The most plausible explanation for this association is that in some way the CSA creates changes that are then responsible for the later emergence of psychosis. There is accumulating evidence for the necessary mediating mechanisms. Nevertheless, further research is needed to establish the way in which mediators operate. By triangulating the relationship between CSA and psychosis, such research increases the plausibility of a putative aetiological function for CSA. In the meantime, the significance of CSA for psychosis and for virtually every other psychiatric disorder indicates that the sequelae of CSA should be specifically targeted both in clinical assessment and in therapy. Cognitive-behaviour therapy techniques like imagery rescripting are likely to offer benefits, both in survivors of abuse generally, and in people whose psychosis has developed in the context of a history of abuse (Holmes, Arntz, & Smucker, 2007; Linden & Zehner, 2007).

References

Alexander, P. C. (1993). The differential effects of abuse characteristics and attachment in the prediction of long-term effects of sexual abuse. *Journal of Interpersonal Violence*, *8*, 346–362.

Arata, C. M. (1999). Coping with rape: The roles of prior sexual abuse and attributions of blame. *Journal of Interpersonal Violence*, *14*, 62–78.

Baillie, D., McCabe, R., & Priebe, S. (2009). Aetiology of depression and schizophrenia: Current views of British psychiatrists. *Psychiatric Bulletin*, *33*, 374–377.

Banyard, V. L., Williams, L. M., & Siegel, J. A. (2001). The long-term mental health consequences of child sexual abuse: An exploratory study of the impact of multiple traumas in a sample of women. *Journal of Traumatic Stress*, *14*, 697–715.

Bebbington, P. E., Bhugra, D., Brugha, T., Farrell, M., Lewis, G., Meltzer, H., et al. (2004). Psychosis, victimisation and childhood disadvantage: Evidence from the Second British National Survey of Psychiatric Epidemiology. *British Journal of Psychiatry, 185*, 220–226.

Bebbington, P. E., Bowen, J., Hirsch, S. R., & Kuipers, L. (1995). Schizophrenia and psychosocial stressors. In S. R. Hirsch & D. Weinberger (Eds.), *Schizophrenia* (pp. 587–604). Oxford, UK: Blackwell Science.

Bebbington, P. E., Cooper, C., Minot, S., Brugha, T. S., Jenkins, R., Meltzer, H., et al. (2009). Suicide attempts, gender and sexual abuse: Data from the British Psychiatric Morbidity Survey 2000. *American Journal of Psychiatry, 166*, 1135–1140.

Bebbington, P. E., Jonas, S., Brugha, T., Meltzer, H., Jenkins, R., Cooper, C., et al. (2011). Child sexual abuse reported by an English national sample: Characteristics and demography. *Social Psychiatry and Psychiatric Epidemiology, 46*, 255–262.

Bebbington, P. E., Jonas, S., Kuipers, E., King, M., Cooper, C., Brugha, T., et al. (in press). Sexual abuse and psychosis: Data from an English national survey. *British Journal of Psychiatry.*

Bebbington, P. E., & Kuipers, E. (2011). Schizophrenia and psychosocial stresses. In D. Weinberger & P. Harrison (Eds.), *Schizophrenia* (3rd ed., pp. 601–624). Oxford, UK: Blackwell Publishing.

Bebbington, P. E., & Kuipers, L. (1994). The predictive utility of expressed emotion in schizophrenia: An aggregate analysis. *Psychological Medicine, 24*, 707–718.

Bebbington, P. E., Wilkins, S., Jones, P., Foerster, A., Murray, R. M., Toone, B., et al. (1993). Life events and psychosis: Initial results from the Camberwell Collaborative Psychosis study. *British Journal of Psychiatry, 162*, 72–79.

Birchwood, M. (2003). Pathways to emotional dysfunction in first-episode psychosis. *British Journal of Psychiatry, 182*, 373–375.

Brown, G., Bone, M., Dalison, B., & Wing, J. (1966). *Schizophrenia and social care.* London, UK: Oxford University Press.

Brown, G. W., & Birley, J. L. T. (1968). Crises and life changes and the onset of schizophrenia. *Journal of Health and Social Behavior, 9*, 203–214.

Brown, G. W., Birley, J. L. T., & Wing, J. K. (1972). Influence of family life on the cause of schizophrenic disorders: A replication. *British Journal of Psychiatry, 121*, 241–258.

Classen, C. C., Palesh, O. G., & Aggarwal, R. (2005). Sexual revictimization: A review of the empirical literature. *Trauma Violence & Abuse. 6*, 103–129.

Cloitre, M., Cohen, L. R., Edelman, R. E., & Han, H. (2001). Posttraumatic stress disorder and extent of trauma exposure as correlates of medical problems and perceived health among women with childhood abuse. *Women's Health, 34*, 1–17.

Cloitre, M., Tardiff, K., Marzuk, P. M., Leon, A. C., & Portera, L. (1996). Childhood abuse and subsequent sexual assault among female inpatients. *Journal of Traumatic Stress, 9*, 473–482.

Cortes, D. C., & Justicia, F. J. (2008). Child sexual abuse coping and long term psychological adjustment. *Psicothema, 20*, 509–515.

Coxell, A., King, M., Mezey, G., & Gordon, D. (1999). Lifetime prevalence, characteristics and associated problems of non-consensual sex in men: A cross-sectional survey. *British Medical Journal, 318*, 846–850.

Dinwiddie, S., Heath, A. C., Dunne, M. P., Bucholz, K. K., Madden, P. A. F., Slutske, W. S., et al. (2000). Early sexual abuse and lifetime psychopathology: A co-twin-control study. *Psychological Medicine, 30*, 41–52.

Driessen, M., Herrmann, J., Stahl, K., Zwaan, M., Meier, S., Hill, A., et al. (2000). Magnetic resonance imaging volumes of the hippocampus and the amygdala in women with borderline personality disorder and early traumatization. *Archives of General Psychiatry*, *57*, 1115–1122.

Ellason, J. E., & Ross, C. A. (1997). Childhood trauma and psychiatric symptoms. *Psychological Reports*, *80*, 447–450.

Fergusson, D. M., Horwood, L. J., & Woodward, L. J. (2000). The stability of child abuse reports: A longitudinal study of the reporting behaviour of young adults. *Psychological Medicine*, *30*, 529–544.

Fowler, D., Freeman, D., Smith, B., Kuipers, E., Bebbington, P., Bashforth, H., et al. (2006). The Brief Core Schema Scales (BCSS): Psychometric properties and associations with paranoia and grandiosity in non-clinical and psychosis samples. *Psychological Medicine*, *36*, 749–759.

Friedman, S., Smith, L., Fogel, D., Paradis, C., Viswanathan, R., Ackerman, R., et al. (2002). The incidence and influence of early traumatic life events in patients with panic disorder: A comparison with other psychiatric outpatients. *Journal of Anxiety Disorders*, *16*, 259–272.

Garety, P. A., Bebbington, P., Fowler, D., Freeman, D., & Kuipers, E. (2007). Implications for neurobiological research of cognitive models of psychosis: A theoretical paper. *Psychological Medicine*, *37*, 1377–1391.

Garety, P. A., Freeman, D., Jolley, S., Dunn, G., Bebbington, P. E., Fowler, D., et al. (2005). Reasoning, emotions and delusional conviction in psychosis. *Journal of Abnormal Psychology*, *114*, 373–384.

Garety, P., Kuipers, E., Fowler, D., Freeman, D., & Bebbington, P. (2001). Theoretical paper: A cognitive model of the positive symptoms of psychosis. *Psychological Medicine*, *31*, 189–195.

Goodman, L. A., Salyers, M. P., Mueser, K. T., Rosenberg, S. D., Swartz, M., Essock, S. M., et al. (2001). 5 Site Health and Risk Study Research Committee. Recent victimization in women and men with severe mental illness: Prevalence and correlates. *Journal of Traumatic Stress*, *14*, 615–632.

Goodman, L. A., Thompson, K. M., Weinfurt, K. Corl, S., Acker, P., Mueser, K. T., et al. (1999). Reliability of reports of violent victimization and posttraumatic stress disorder among men and women with serious mental health. *Journal of Trauma and Stress*, *12*, 587–599.

Heim, C., Newport, D. J., Heit, S., Graham, Y. P., Wilcox, M., Bonsall, R., et al. (2000). Pituitary–adrenal and autonomic responses to stress in women after sexual and physical abuse in childhood. *Journal of American Medical Association*, *284*, 592–597.

Holmes, E. A., Arntz, A., & Smucker, M. R. (2007). Imagery rescripting in cognitive behaviour therapy: Images, treatment techniques and outcomes. *Journal of Behavior Therapy and Experimental Psychiatry*, *38*, 297–305.

Horwitz, A. V., Widom, C. S., McLaughlin, J., & White, H. R. (2001). The impact of childhood abuse and neglect on adult mental health: A prospective study. *Journal of Health and Social Behavior*, *42*, 184–201.

Janssen, I., Krabbendam, L., Bak, M., Hanssen, M., Vollebergh, W., de Graaf, R., et al. (2004). Childhood abuse as a risk factor for psychotic experiences. *Acta Psychiatrica Scandinavica*, *109*, 38–45.

Jonas, S., Bebbington, P. E., McManus, S., Meltzer, H., Jenkins, R., Kuipers, E., et al. (2011). Sexual abuse and psychiatric disorder in England: Results from the 2007 Adult Psychiatric Morbidity Survey. *Psychological Medicine*, *41*, 709–720.

Kamsner, S., & McCabe, M. P. (2000). The relationship between adult psychological adjustment and childhood sexual abuse, childhood physical abuse, and family of origin characteristics. *Journal of Interpersonal Violence*, *15*, 1243–1261.

Kendler, K. S., Bulik, C. M., Silberg, J., Hettema, J. M., Myers, J., & Prescott, C. A. (2000). Childhood sexual abuse and adult psychiatric and substance use disorders in women—An epidemiological and co-twin control analysis. *Archives of General Psychiatry*, *57*, 953–959.

Krabbendam, L. (2008). Childhood psychological trauma and psychosis. *Psychological Medicine*, *38*, 1405–1408.

Krabbendam, L., Myin-Germeys, I., Hanssen, M., de Graaf, R., Vollebergh, W., Bak, M., et al. (2005). Development of depressed mood predicts onset of psychotic disorder in individuals who report hallucinatory experiences. *British Journal of Clinical Psychology*, *44*, 113–125.

Kuipers, E., Garety, P., Fowler, D., Freeman, D., Dunn, G., & Bebbington, P. (2006). Cognitive, emotional and social processes in psychosis: Refining cognitive behavioural therapy for persistent positive symptoms. *Schizophrenia Bulletin*, *32*, S24–S31.

Kuipers, E., Onwumere, J., & Bebbington, P. (2010). A cognitive model of caregiving in psychosis. *British Journal of Psychiatry*, *196*, 259–264.

Linden, M., & Zehner, A. (2007). The role of childhood sexual abuse (CSA) in adult cognitive behaviour therapy. *Behavioural and Cognitive Psychotherapy*, *35*, 447–455.

Littleton, H., Horsley, S., John, S., & Nelson, D. V. (2007). Trauma coping strategies and psychological distress: A meta-analysis. *Journal of Traumatic Stress*, *20*, 977–988.

Lysaker, P. H., Meyer, P. S., Evans, J. D., Clements, C. A., & Marks, K. A. (2001). Childhood sexual trauma and psychosocial functioning in adults with schizophrenia. *Psychiatric Services*, *52*, 1485–1488.

Lysaker, P. H., & Salyers, M. P. (2007). Anxiety symptoms in schizophrenia spectrum disorders: Associations with social function, positive and negative symptoms, hope and trauma history. *Acta Psychiatrica Scandinavica*, *116*, 290–298.

Mannarino, A. P., & Cohen, J. A. (1996). Abuse-related attributions and perceptions, general attributions, and locus of control in sexually abused girls. *Journal of Interpersonal Violence*, *11*, 162–180.

May-Chahal, C., & Cawson, P. (2005). Measuring child maltreatment in the United Kingdom: A study of the prevalence of child abuse and neglect. *Child Abuse and Neglect*, *29*, 943–1070.

McManus, S., Meltzer, H., Brugha, T., Bebbington, P., & Jenkins, R. (2009). *Adult psychiatric morbidity in England, 2007: Results of a household survey*. London, UK: National Centre for Social Research.

Morgan, C., & Fisher, H. (2007). Environment and schizophrenia: Environmental factors in schizophrenia: Childhood trauma—A critical review. *Schizophrenia Bulletin*, *33*, 3–10.

Muenzenmaier, K., Meyer, I., Struening, E., & Ferber, J. (1993). Childhood abuse and neglect among women outpatients with chronic mental illness. *Hospital and Community Psychiatry*, *44*, 666–670.

Mueser, K. T., Goodman, L. B., Trumbetta, S. L., Rosenberg, S. D., Osher, F. C., Vidaver, R., et al. (1998). Trauma and post-traumatic stress disorder in severe mental illness. *Journal of Consulting and Clinical Psychology*, *66*, 493–499.

Murthi, M., & Espelage, D. L. (2005). Childhood sexual abuse, social support, and psychological outcomes: A loss framework. *Child Abuse & Neglect*, *29*, 1215–1231.

Nelson, E. C., Heath, A. C., Lynskey, M. T., Bucholz, K. K., Madden, P. A. F., Statham, D. J., et al. (2006). Childhood sexual abuse and risks for licit and illicit drug related outcomes: A twin study *Psychological Medicine*, *36*, 1473–1483.

O'Leary, P. J. (2009). Men who were sexually abused in childhood: Coping strategies and comparisons in psychological functioning. *Child Abuse and Neglect*, *33*, 471–479.

Pilling, S., Bebbington, P., Kuipers, E., Garety, P., Geddes, J., Martindale, B., et al. (2002). Psychological treatments in schizophrenia. I: Meta-analysis of family intervention and cognitive behaviour therapy. *Psychological Medicine*, *32*, 763–782.

Putnam, F. W. (2003). Ten-year research update review: Child sexual abuse. *Journal of the American Academy of Child and Adolescent Psychiatry*, *42*, 269–278.

Raune, D., Bebbington, P. E., & Kuipers, E. A. (2009). Stressful and intrusive life events preceding first episode psychosis. *Epidemiologia e Psichiatria Sociale*, *18*, 221–228.

Read, J., Bentall, R. P., & Fosse, R. (2009). Time to abandon the bio-bio-bio model of psychosis: Exploring the epigenetic and psychological mechanisms by which adverse life events lead to psychotic symptoms. *Epidemiologia e Psichiatria Sociale*, *18*, 299–310.

Read, J., van Os, J., Morrison, A. P., & Ross, C. A. (2005). Childhood trauma, psychosis and schizophrenia: A literature review with theoretical and clinical implications. *Acta Psychiatrica Scandinavica*, *112*, 330–350.

Sinclair, J., Crane, C., Hawton, K., & Williams, J. (2007). The role of autobiographical memory specificity in deliberate self-harm: Correlates and consequences. *Journal of Affective Disorders*, *102*, 11–18.

Smith, B., Fowler, D. G., Freeman, D., Bebbington, P., Bashforth, H., Garety, P., et al. (2006). Emotion and psychosis: Links between depression, self-esteem, negative schematic beliefs and delusions and hallucinations. *Schizophrenia Research*, *86*, 181–188.

Spataro, J., Mullen, P. E., Burgess, P. M., Wells, D. L., & Moss, S. A. (2004). Impact of child sexual abuse on mental health. Prospective study in males and females. *British Journal of Psychiatry*, *184*, 416–421.

Spauwen, J., Krabbendam, L., Lieb, R., Wittchen, H. U., & van Os, J. (2006). Impact of psychological trauma on the development of psychotic symptoms: Relationship with psychosis proneness. *British Journal of Psychiatry*, *188*, 527–533.

Stevens, B. C. (1973). Evaluation of rehabilitation for psychotic patients in the community. *Acta Psychiatrica Scandinavica*, *46*, 136–140.

Stone, A. A., & Eldrid, S. H. (1959). Delusion formation during the activation of chronic psychiatric patients. *Archives of General Psychiatry*, *1*, 177–179.

Tourangeau, R., Rips, L. J., & Rasinski, K. (2000). *The psychology of survey response*. Cambridge, UK: Cambridge University Press.

Williams, J. M., Barnhofer, T., Crane, C., Herman, D., Raes, F., Watkins, E., et al. (2007). Autobiographical memory specificity and emotional disorder. *Psychological Bulletin*, *133*, 122–148.

Wing, J. K., & Brown, G. W. (1970). *Institutionalism and schizophrenia*. Cambridge UK: Cambridge University Press.

Wing, J. K., & Freudenberg, R. K. (1961). The response of severely ill chronic schizophrenic patients to social stimulation. *American Journal of Psychiatry*, *118*, 311–322.

Wing, J. K., Monck, E., Brown, G. W., & Carstairs, G. M. (1964). Morbidity in the community of schizophrenic patients discharged from London mental hospitals in 1959. *British Journal of Psychiatry*, *110*, 10–21.

Zubin, J., & Spring, B. (1977). Vulnerability: A new view of schizophrenia. *Journal of Abnormal Psychology*, *86*, 103–126.

20 Does urban density matter?

Jane Boydell and Judith Allardyce

Introduction

In the study of the epidemiology of schizophrenia a consensus has emerged that urban living is associated with an excess of psychosis. Robin Murray was instrumental in the early studies investigating this phenomenon. This chapter will review the findings and discuss possible explanations for the urbanicity effect.

Urbanization

In an ingenious study, Torrey, Bowler, and Clark (1997) used the comprehensive 1880 census of the "insane" in the USA, to examine the association between urbanicity and severe mental illness. "Insanity" in 1880 included people who would be considered to have a psychotic illness today but, of course, also many others. Torrey et al. calculated prevalence rates for different degrees of urbanicity, then using *completely rural* as the baseline comparator odds ratios (OR) were estimated that showed a strong linear trend (OR urban 1.66, semi-urban 1.46, semi-rural 1.44, rural 1.37). This is fascinating because a gradient was found between different degrees of rural. Lundberg, Cantor-Graae, Kabakyenga, Rukundo, and Ostergren (2004) also found psychotic phenomena to be more prevalent in a town as compared to a rural setting in Uganda and similarly Kebede et al. (2004) demonstrated an urban–rural gradient in Ethiopia (which was more pronounced in single people). The generalizability of this urban effect suggests that social factors influence the urban–rural gradient, as the physical environment of cities is so different in Western and developing countries and has changed considerably over the last century.

Several studies have come from northern Europe, where good-quality national records have made large-scale epidemiological studies possible. Lewis, David, Andreasson, and Allebeck (1992) investigated the association between place of upbringing and incidence of schizophrenia in a cohort of over 49,000 male Swedish conscripts, linking it to the Swedish national psychiatric register. There was a strong significant linear trend ($\chi^2 = 9.9$, $p = .002$) with the highest rate of schizophrenia in those who had mostly lived in cities (Stockholm, Goteborg, Malmo) while they were growing up, crude OR 1.65. There were intermediate rates in large towns (> 50,000), crude OR 1.39, and small towns (< 50,000), crude

OR 1.28, with the lowest rates found in country areas, which were taken as baseline. Adjusting for family finances, parental divorce and family psychiatric history, had little effect on the estimates. Adjusting for cannabis use and any psychiatric disorder at conscription (as these may have been part of a prodrome) attenuated but did not eliminate the associations.

Mortensen et al. (1999) investigated the effect of place of birth on risk of admission with ICD-8 schizophrenia in a large Danish population-based cohort of 1.75 million. The relative risk associated with being born in Copenhagen as compared to birth in rural areas was 2.40 (95% CI 2.13–2.7), with a clear dose–response relationship for urbanicity, that is the larger the town of birth, the greater the risk of later developing schizophrenia. A family history of schizophrenia did not explain the results. The population attributable risk (PAF) for urban birth was 34.6%, which compared with 9% and 7%, respectively, for having a mother or father who had schizophrenia. The incidence of manic depression was fairly evenly distributed throughout the urban–rural gradient.

Peen and Dekker (1997) also found a significant positive correlation between admission rates for clinically diagnosed ICD-9 schizophrenia and degree of urbanization. This correlation did not seem to be accounted for by differences in the availability of psychiatric services as the average length of hospital admission and average number of readmissions did not differ between urban and rural areas. Similarly, Sundquist, Frank, and Sundquist (2004) found a dose–response relationship between level of urbanization and admission for psychosis in Sweden.

Most of the studies investigating urbanicity and psychosis have used admission data to measure incidence, and relied on national case registers of clinical diagnoses. This enables wide coverage but leaves the possibility that bias (referral, admission, diagnostic practice, etc.) may have affected the results. Robin Murray designed and supervised one of the few studies not to do this: Allardyce et al. (2001) compared all incident cases (admitted and not admitted) of psychosis from two areas in the UK, a largely rural part of southwest Scotland and urban south London. Computer-generated diagnoses of schizophrenia according to research diagnostic criteria (RDC) were used, avoiding potential bias introduced by different admission policies and diagnostic traditions. The incidence was 61% higher in the urban area compared to the rural area (standardized incidence ratio, SIR, 1.61, 95% CI 1.42–1.81), and once again the urban excess was more marked in males than females. An improvement on this study came from the AESOP (Aetiology and Ethnicity in Schizophrenia and Other Psychoses) study, again with Robin Murray as principal investigator, a multi-centre first onset psychosis study covering one million six hundred thousand person years, in that each case was interviewed (admitted or not) and a gold standard consensus diagnosis based on a standardized instrument was made. This found a marked difference between the study area in the capital city (London), where the age and sex standardized incidence for all psychosis was 49 per 100,000 and two other smaller cities, Nottingham (23.9 per 100,000) and Bristol (20.4 per 100,000; Kirkbride et al., 2006).

Overall a remarkable consensus has emerged in that more than 10 recent studies, reviewed by Krabbendam and van Os (2005), have shown an effect of urbanicity on rates of schizophrenia (overall pooled effect size from meta-analysis 1.72, 95% CI 1.53–1.92) with many showing a dose–response relationship. The effect seems to be greater in younger people and more recent birth cohorts (Haukka, Suvisaari, Varilo, & Lönnqvist, 2001; Marcelis, Navarro-Mateu, Murray, Selten, & van Os, 1998). The effect of urbanicity seems to be stronger for schizophrenia than for other psychotic disorders. Around 30% of schizophrenia cases can be accounted for by urban birth and upbringing, assuming causality, in Western countries (Krabbendam & van Os, 2005).

What could cause the urban effect?

Several studies have found an association of deprivation and low social class with psychosis risk (Croudace, Kayne, Jones, & Harrison, 2000; J. Harrison, Barrow, & Creed, 1995; Koppel & McGuffin, 1999), and so the question arises as to whether the urbanicity effect is explained by these factors, assuming they are more prevalent or more pernicious in urban environments. Ohta, Nakane, Nishihara, and Takemoto (1992) did not find a significant urban–rural difference in Nagasaki, Japan, and attributed this to there being few social-class differences between areas. G. Harrison et al. (2003) carried out a case-control study to separate and test for interaction between social class and deprivation of area of residence. People of lower social class origin and those born into deprived areas had higher odds of developing schizophrenia but those with both risk indices had eight times the odds of developing the disorder. Boydell et al. (2003) found that the incidence rate of RDC schizophrenia in deprived (but not in affluent) areas in London increased as inequality within the local area increased (Incidence Rate Ratio 3.79) after adjusting for age, sex, absolute deprivation and ethnicity. This suggests that perception of social status is important and it is possible, although speculative, that this differs in urban and rural areas. This perception might influence cognitive processes relevant to psychosis.

It is unlikely, however, that the entire urban effect can be attributed to social class and deprivation as some of the positive findings have come from countries where there is a higher standard of living in cities than in the rural areas. Furthermore, in the Swedish Conscript study of Lewis et al. (1992), the urban effect remained after adjusting for "family finances". G. Harrison et al. (2003) addressed this question using a Swedish birth cohort and found that the effect of urbanicity was not affected by social class at birth (measured as maternal educational level).

Several studies have tested whether the known biological risk factors for psychosis could explain the effect of urbanicity. These have found that adjusting for obstetric complications does not significantly attenuate the findings of an urban excess (Eaton, Mortensen, & Frydenberg, 2000; G. Harrison et al., 2003). Infectious disease does not seem to be a likely explanation as household overcrowding and season of birth do not interact with urbanicity (Agerbo,

Torrey, & Mortensen, 2001; Wahlbeck, Osmond, Forsen, Barker, & Eriksson, 2001). Traffic pollution does not seem to explain the urban excess (Pedersen & Mortensen, 2006). Substance misuse is important but does not explain the whole effect as it has been adjusted for in most studies (van Os, 2004). The aetiological factors for which urbanicity is a proxy remain unknown and negative biological studies do not in themselves point to a social explanation. The pervasive nature of the exposure involved in urbanicity is evidenced by studies showing a cumulative effect throughout childhood with no particular "at-risk age" (Pedersen & Mortensen, 2001a), the similar findings in non-developed countries, and the increase in isolated psychotic symptoms in urban dwellers who are not psychotic (van Os, Hanssen, Bijl, & Vollebergh, 2001). Krabbendam and van Os (2005) reviewed the evidence that the effect of urbanicity is conditional upon genetic risk as three studies have showed synergism between urbanicity and various measures of genetic risk. This does not contradict the earlier findings that the effect of urbanicity remained after adjusting for family history but rather that those with some genetic risk are more susceptible to the aetiological factors in the urban environment.

Social causation and social selection

When considering the effect of urbanicity, it is important to acknowledge the possible effects of "social drift", i.e., people with pre- or prodromal schizophrenia move into less-desirable social environments. Furthermore, people who are at risk of developing schizophrenia are more likely to have a lower IQ and poor interpersonal skills and may not be as able to leave an area when it deteriorates. This was thought to account for the increased rates of psychosis in cities and disorganized areas. However, this effect cannot account for the results of studies that looked at place of birth and upbringing. A variant of the social-drift theories is that the genes carried by the parents of people who became psychotic made them less able to compete and live in a good social environment. However, some studies have addressed this issue and suggested that it is unlikely that drift occurred in the previous parental generation, as the magnitude of this movement would need to have been extremely high to explain the findings (Mortensen et al., 1999).

Social isolation

Since the earliest observations of schizophrenia, researchers have noticed that sufferers tend to be more isolated than other people. The findings have generally been taken to indicate premorbid abnormalities but it is also possible that the isolation itself is a mediator for other aetiological factors or a factor on the causal path to psychosis. If social isolation is more prevalent in cities this might contribute to the urban excess. A fascinating finding to emerge from a whole-population Danish incidence study (Pederson & Mortenson, 2001b), was that change in municipality (and therefore school) increased the risk of schizophrenia whereas change of address during childhood within the municipality (usually therefore without changing school) was not associated with increased risk. Moves during early teenage years appeared to have the greatest effect, and the greater the number of moves, the greater the risk.

Studies have also investigated social isolation at the time of onset of psychosis. In 1956, when living alone was unusual, Hare (1956) found that areas with greater numbers of single-person households had a higher incidence of schizophrenia and this was not accounted for by movement of people with, or developing, schizophrenia into the area. He found that in half of the cases, living alone was due to interpersonal difficulties but, in a quarter of cases "force of circumstance" had occurred. He concluded that isolation was probably a cause and an effect of psychosis. Thornicroft, Bisoffi, De Salvia, and Tansella (1993) noted that clustering of individuals with schizophrenia in deprived areas occurs only in urban areas and suggested that social isolation is an important mediator of this. Related to these ideas is the theory that disruption of social networks decreases an individual's capacity to cope with psychosocial stress and increases the risk of schizophrenia. Van Os, Driessen, Gunther, and Delespaul (2000) found that people who were single had a slightly higher risk of developing psychosis if they lived in a neighbourhood with fewer single people, compared to a neighbourhood with many other single people. The authors suggested that single status might give rise to perceived (or actual) social isolation if most other people are living with a partner.

Social adversity and social defeat

Social adversity in many forms (poor housing, unemployment, low income, single-parent household) has been suggested as the explanation for the increased incidence of schizophrenia in urban populations. Wicks, Hjern, Gunnell, Lewis, and Dalman (2005) found a dose–response effect with increasing risk of schizophrenia with increasing number of adversities.

The social defeat hypothesis proposes that a chronic and long-term experience of social defeat may lead to sensitization of the mesolimbic dopamine system (and/or to increased baseline activity of this system) and thereby increase the risk for schizophrenia. Social defeat is defined as being in a subordinate position or "outsider status". The proponents Selten and Cantor-Graae (2005) point to the evidence that urban areas, migration, low IQ and the use of illicit drugs double or triple the risk of schizophrenia and suggest that social defeat is a unifying mechanism in the causation of the psychosis.

In urban areas greater population density leads to higher levels of social competition and hence more experience of social defeat. The proponents argue that genetic vulnerability to schizophrenia might be reasonably common and social defeat could act upon that vulnerability.

The social defeat hypothesis is an attractive explanation for many of the associations that have been found between social adversities (and by implication urbanicity) and increased risk of schizophrenia. The definition of the risk factor is, however, vague and could incorporate virtually any adversity. It is also a somewhat circular argument, for example if "outsider status" is included as "social defeat" then the hypothesis is effectively saying: outsiders are known to be more likely to develop psychosis so outsider status is a risk factor for psychosis.

The social context

The social context includes factors that only exist at the group (or ecological) level such as inequality, crime levels, relative socioeconomic status factors, and social cohesion. These can have a direct effect or might modify an individual-level risk factor.

Allardyce et al. (2005) characterized the whole of Scotland (by very small areas) in terms of social fragmentation, deprivation and urbanicity. Social fragmentation was measured using an index based on residential mobility, rented properties, single-person households and number of unmarried people. This study found a strong ecological effect of social fragmentation and deprivation and, importantly, that there was no effect of urbanicity on admission rates of psychosis after adjusting for fragmentation and deprivation. Although these findings are impressive it was not possible to adjust for individual-level risk factors, a common problem in ecological studies (Allardyce & Boydell, 2006). In a rare study that was able to adjust for individual economic situation, Silver, Mulvey, and Swanson (2002) found that neighbourhood residential mobility was still associated with schizophrenia. Kirkbride et al. (2007) also adjusted for a range of individual-level risk factors and found that 23% of the variance in incidence of schizophrenia could still be attributed to neighbourhood-level risk factors (including ethnic segregation and voter turnout). It has been suggested that many of these neighbourhood-level factors evolve around the presence of a high proportion of isolated individuals and could be proxy variables for low social cohesion (Krabbendam & van Os, 2005). Furthermore, social cohesion might modify some of the other neighbourhood variables such as deprivation. Differing levels of cohesion in urban and rural areas might contribute to the urban excess of psychosis.

Conclusion

The effect of urban density on incidence rates of psychosis is now well established but the explanation is still unclear. There is some evidence that social factors are important but much work needs to be done to identify a mechanism. This could potentially prevent 30% of new cases of schizophrenia.

References

Agerbo, E., Torrey, E. F., & Mortensen, P. B.(2001). Household crowding in early adulthood and schizophrenia are unrelated in Denmark: A nested case-control study. *Schizophrenia Research*, *47*, 243–246.

Allardyce, J., & Boydell, J. (2006). Review: The wider social environment and schizophrenia. *Schizophrenia Bulletin*, *32*, 592–598.

Allardyce, J., Boydell, J., van Os, J., Morrison, G., Castle, D., Murray, R. M., et al. (2001). Comparison of the incidence of schizophrenia in rural Dumfries and Galloway and urban Camberwell. *British Journal of Psychiatry*, *179*, 335–339.

Allardyce, J., Gilmour, H., Atkinson, J., Rapson, T., Bishop, J., & McCreadie, R. G. (2005). Social fragmentation, deprivation and urbanicity: Relation to first-admission rates for psychoses. *British Journal of Psychiatry*, *187*, 401–406.

Boydell, J., van Os, J., Lambri, M., Castle, D., Allardyce, J., McCreadie, R. G., et al. (2003). Incidence of schizophrenia in south-east London between 1965 and 1997. *British Journal of Psychiatry*, *182*, 45–49.

Croudace, T. J., Kayne, R., Jones, P. B., & Harrison, G. L. (2000). Non-linear relationship between an index of social deprivation, psychiatric admission prevalence and the incidence of psychosis. *Psychological Medicine*, *30*, 177–185.

Eaton, W., Mortensen, P. B., & Frydenberg, M. (2000). Obstetric factors, urbanization and psychosis. *Schizophrenia Research*, *43*, 117–123.

Hare, E. H. (1956). Family setting and the urban distribution of schizophrenia. *Journal of Mental Science*, *102*, 753–760.

Harrison, G., Fouskakis, D., Rasmussen, F., Tynelius, P., Sipos, A., & Gunnell, D. (2003). Association between psychotic disorder and urban place of birth is not mediated by obstetric complications or childhood socio-economic position: A cohort study. *Psycholological Medicine*, *33*, 723–731.

Harrison, J., Barrow, S., & Creed, F. (1995). Social deprivation and psychiatric admission rates among different diagnostic groups. *British Journal of Psychiatry*, *167*, 456–462.

Haukka, J., Suvisaari, J., Varilo, T., & Lönnqvist, J. (2001). Regional variation in the incidence of schizophrenia in Finland: A study of birth cohorts born from 1950 to 1969. *Psychological Medicine*, *31*, 1045–1053.

Kebede, D., Alem, A., Shibre, T., Negash, A., Deyassa, N., & Beyero, T. (2004). The sociodemographic correlates of schizophrenia in Butajira, rural Ethiopia. *Schizophrenia Research*, *69*, 133–141.

Kirkbride, J. B., Fearon, P., Morgan, C., Dazzan, P., Morgan, K., Murray, R. M., et al. (2007). Neighbourhood variation in the incidence of psychotic disorders in southeast London. *Social Psychiatry Psychiatric Epidemiology*, *42*, 438–445.

Kirkbride, J. B., Fearon, P., Morgan, C., Dazzan, P., Morgan, K., Tarrant, J., et al. (2006). Heterogeneity in incidence rates of schizophrenia and other psychotic syndromes: Findings from the 3-center AESOP study. *Archives of General Psychiatry*, *63*, 250–258.

Koppel, S., & McGuffin, P. (1999). Socio-economic factors that predict psychiatric admissions at a local level. *Psychological Medicine*, *29*, 1235–1241.

Krabbendam, L., & van Os, J. (2005). Schizophrenia and urbanicity: A major environmental influence conditional on genetic risk. *Schizophrenia Bulletin*, *31*, 795–799.

Lewis, G., David, A., Andreasson, S., & Allebeck, P. (1992). Schizophrenia and city life. *Lancet*, *340*, 137–140.

Lundberg, P., Cantor-Graae, E., Kabakyenga, J., Rukundo, G., & Ostergren, P. O. (2004). Prevalence of delusional ideation in a district in southwestern Uganda. *Schizophrenia Research*, *71*, 27–34.

Marcelis, M., Navarro-Mateu, F., Murray, R., Selten, J. P., & van Os, J. (1998). Urbanization and psychosis: A study of 1942–1978 birth cohorts in the Netherlands. *Psychological Medicine*, *28*, 871–879.

Mortensen, P. B., Pedersen, C. B., Westergaard, T., Wohlfahrt, J., Ewald, H., Mors, O., et al. (1999). Effects of family history and place and season of birth on the risk of schizophrenia. *New England Journal of Medicine*, *340*, 603–608.

Ohta, Y., Nakane, Y., Nishihara, J., & Takemoto, T. (1992). Ecological structure and incidence rates of schizophrenia in Nagasaki city. *Acta Psychiatrica Scandinavia, 86,* 113–120.

Pedersen, C. B., & Mortensen, P. B. (2001a). Evidence of a dose–response relationship between urbanicity during upbringing and schizophrenia risk. *Archives of General Psychiatry, 58,* 1039–1046.

Pedersen, C. B., & Mortensen, P. B. (2001b). Family history, place and season of birth as risk factors for schizophrenia in Denmark: A replication and reanalysis. *British Journal of Psychiatry, 179,* 46–52.

Pedersen, C. B., & Mortensen, P. B. (2006). Urbanization and traffic related exposures as risk factors for schizophrenia. *BMC Psychiatry,* Vol. *6,* Article 2.

Peen, J., & Dekker, J. (1997). Admission rates for schizophrenia in the Netherlands: An urban/rural comparison. *Acta Psychiatrica Scandinavia, 96,* 301–305.

Selten, J. P., & Cantor-Graae, E. (2005). Social defeat: Risk factor for schizophrenia? *British Journal of Psychiatry, 187,* 101–102.

Silver, E., Mulvey, E. P., & Swanson, J. W. (2002). Neighborhood structural characteristics and mental disorder: Faris and Dunham revisited. *Social Science Medicine, 55,* 1457–1470.

Sundquist, K., Frank, G., & Sundquist, J. (2004). Urbanisation and incidence of psychosis and depression: Follow-up study of 4.4 million women and men in Sweden. *British Journal of Psychiatry, 184,* 293–298.

Thornicroft, G., Bisoffi, G., De Salvia, D., & Tansella, M. (1993). Urban–rural differences in the associations between social deprivation and psychiatric service utilization in schizophrenia and all diagnoses: A case-register study in northern Italy. *Psychological Medicine, 23,* 487–496.

Torrey, E. F., Bowler, A. E., & Clark, K. (1997). Urban birth and residence as risk factors for psychoses: An analysis of 1880 data. *Schizophrenia Research, 25,* 169–176.

van Os, J. (2004). Does the urban environment cause psychosis? *British Journal of Psychiatry, 184,* 287–288.

van Os, J., Driessen, G., Gunther, N., & Delespaul, P. (2000). Neighbourhood variation in incidence of schizophrenia: Evidence for person–environment interaction. *British Journal of Psychiatry, 176,* 243–248.

van Os, J., Hanssen, M., Bijl, R. V., & Vollebergh, W. (2001). Prevalence of psychotic disorder and community level of psychotic symptoms: An urban–rural comparison. *Archives of General Psychiatry, 58,* 663–668.

Wahlbeck, K., Osmond, C., Forsen, T., Barker, D. J., & Eriksson, J. G. (2001). Associations between childhood living circumstances and schizophrenia: A population-based cohort study. *Acta Psychiatrica Scandinavia, 104,* 356–360.

Wicks, S., Hjern, A., Gunnell, D., Lewis, G., & Dalman, C. (2005). Social adversity in childhood and the risk of developing psychosis: A national cohort study. *American Journal of Psychiatry, 162,* 1652–1657.

21 Does higher potency cannabis mean higher risk for psychosis?

Marta Di Forti, Alessandra Paparelli and Paola Casadio

Introduction

The greatest consumers of cannabis round the world come from Western Europe, Australia and North America. In Europe, the UK has among the highest lifetime prevalence for cannabis use in young adolescents. Nevertheless, recent data show a slow decline in its consumption. This would be a reassuring prospect if at the same time significant changes had not been reported on the type of cannabis that is taking over the UK market (United Nations Office on Drugs and Crime, 2009). Sensimilla, street name skunk, is the most potent type of cannabis and now covers 70% of the cannabis UK market share. If a person was to ask for cannabis in southeast London, they would be 7 times out of 10 more likely to be offered skunk than traditional hash (resin) or traditional herbal cannabis (Hardwick & King, 2008).

Cannabis, intended as the drug, is obtained from different types of preparation derived from the plant *Cannabis sativa*, which contains the cannabinoids, the chemicals responsible for the drug's effects when consumed. The two known principal cannabinoids contained in the available types of cannabis are D9-tetrahydrocannabinol (D9-THC) and cannabidiol (CBD; Potter, Clark, & Brown, 2008). The skunk seized from the streets of England in 2008 by the police had an average D9-THC concentration of 12–18% with virtually no CBD compared to cannabis resin (hash) with a 2–4% D9-THC and a similar proportion of CBD, and compared to herbal cannabis, which has a similar percentage of D9-THC to hash but no or very little CBD (Potter et al., 2008).

D9-THC is the cannabis psychoactive ingredient, widely used in experimental studies that have investigated its ability to produce, in healthy volunteers, transient psychotic symptoms and impaired memory in a dose-dependent manner (D'Souza et al., 2004; Morrison et al., 2009). Furthermore, a positron emission tomography (PET) study has shown that inhalation of D9-THC acutely increases striatal dopamine (DA), which is thought to underlie psychotic symptoms (Bossong et al., 2009). These interesting findings were followed by another PET study where D9-THC was administered orally and which did not replicate Bossong et al.'s results. In fact, Stokes, Mehta, Curran, Breen, and Grasby (2009) found only a weak and non-significant effect of D9-THC on striatal DA release. It could be argued that the different means of administration of D9-THC might have influenced the strength of the effect on DA release. In contrast, CBD does not induce hallucinations or delusions, and it seems to ameliorate the cognitive impairment as well as the psychotic symptoms induced by D9-THC (Leweke, 2007; Murray, Morrison, Henquet, & Di Forti, 2008). Both D9-THC and CBD bind to the cannabinoid receptor 1 (CB1), which is widely expressed in the hippocampus, amygdala, cerebellum, basal ganglia and prefrontal cortex (Herkenham et al., 1991). However, the pharmacological mechanism underlying the interaction between D9-THC and CBD at the receptor site remains unclear (Pertwee, 2008).

A simple guide to understanding the cannabis and psychosis story

It has been known for many years that cannabis intoxication can lead to acute psychosis (Methers & Ghodse 1992; Negrete, Knapp, Douglas, & Smith, 1986; Thornicroft, 1990) and that cannabis use is associated with poor outcome in patients already suffering from psychotic illnesses (Grech, van Os, Jones, Lewis, & Murray, 2005; Linszen, Dingemans, & Lenior, 1994). Moreover, population-based longitudinal cohort studies have been carried out to understand the role of cannabis use as a causal risk factor for later schizophrenia, because of its potential impact on public health in many countries, given its widespread use, particularly among adolescents.

The first study to indicate a significant association between cannabis use and later onset of schizophrenia spectrum psychosis, was a Swedish cohort study of almost 50,000 conscripts followed up for 15 and 27 years (Andreasson, Allebeck, Engstrom, & Rydberg, 1987; Zammit, Allebeck, Andreasson, Lundberg, & Lewis, 2002). The study findings showed that conscripts who had smoked cannabis by the time of induction into the army were twice as likely to have developed schizophrenia at the 15-year follow-up than those who never used cannabis (Odds Ratio, OR, = 2.3, 95% CI = 1.0–5.3). This pioneering study also suggested that the magnitude of the risk of developing psychosis also depended upon the amount of cannabis consumed, measured as how many times conscripts had ever used it. Those subjects who had used cannabis more than 50 times, classified as heavy users, were six times more likely than non-users to receive a later diagnosis of schizophrenia. This dose–response relationship was later confirmed at the 27-year follow-up. Nevertheless, only 3% of those classified as heavy users went on to develop schizophrenia, indicating that the amount of cannabis consumed alone does not explain why only some users develop psychosis, suggesting a role for individual vulnerability to the drug effect. Many other prospective studies investigating the association between cannabis and psychosis have followed (see Table 21.1) to be later summarized in two meta-analyses. The first, by Henquet, Murray, Linszen, and van Os (2005), reported a pooled OR of 2.1 (95% CI = 1.7–2.5) and the most recent, by Moore et al. (2007), a pooled OR of 1.41 (95% CI = 1.20–1.65). Among these studies some have also explored the role played by the individual psychosis vulnerability, in moderating the variability of the

Table 21.1 Longitudinal studies in the general population: Strength of the association between cannabis use and onset of later schizophrenia spectrum disorders

Country where study was carried out (reference)	*Study design*	*Sample size*	*Length of follow -up*	*OR (95%CI)**
The Netherlands (NEMESIS; van Os et al., 2002)	Population based	4,045	3 years	2.8 (1.2–6.5)
Israel (Weiser, Knobler, Noy, & Kaplan, 2002)	Population based	9,724	4–15 years	2.0 (1.3–3.1)
New Zealand, Christchurch (Fergusson, Horwood, & Swain-Campbell, 2003)	Birth cohort	1,265	3 years	1.8 (1.2–2.6)
New Zealand, Dunedin (Arseneault et al., 2002)	Birth cohort	1,034	15 years	4.5 (1.11–18.21)**
The Netherlands (Ferdinand et al., 2005)	Population based	1,580	14 years	2.8 (1.79–4.43)
Germany (EDSP; Henquet et al., 2005)	Population based	2,437	4 years	1.7 (1.1–1.5)
United Kingdom (Wiles et al., 2006)	Population based	8,580	18 months	1.5 (0.55–3.94)
Greece (Stefanis et al., 2004)	Birth cohort	3,500	NA	4.3 (1.0–17.9)

Note: *OR = Odds Ratio. **Referring to exposure to cannabis use at age 15

response to cannabis use in the population. Across studies "psychosis vulnerability" has been defined either as a positive family history for psychosis or by a history of minor psychotic experiences occurring before onset of cannabis use. These minor psychotic experiences are usually collected by validated instruments to measure psychotic symptoms in the general population such as the Community Assessment of Psychic Experiences or CAPE (Stefanis et al., 2002). For instance, in a prospective study of 2,437 young German individuals with a 4-year follow-up, Henquet, Krabbendam et al. (2005) showed that cannabis use increases the risk of psychotic symptoms in young people (OR = 1.7, 95% CI = 1.1–1.5) but it has a much stronger effect in those with psychosis vulnerability at baseline, even though this did not significantly predict cannabis use at follow-up, therefore rejecting the self-medication hypothesis. This study also described a dose–response relationship with the increasing frequency of cannabis use.

Caspi et al. (2005) were the first to relate psychosis liability to a specific genetic mutation. In the Dunedin birth cohort study, they showed that among cannabis users, carries of one copy, and even more so of two copies, of the catecholamine-O-methyl transferase (COMT) Val^{158} allele were at significantly higher risk of developing a schizophreniform psychosis than COMT Met/Met carriers. COMT is the key enzyme involved in the pre-frontal cortex metabolism of dopamine (DA) release into synapses, and contains a G to A missense mutation that generates a valine (Val) to methionine (Met) substitution at codon 158 ($Val^{158}Met$). Individuals homozygotic for Val produce more enzymatic activity and consequently a quicker break down of DA opposite to the effect seen in those who are Met/Met. There has not yet been a clear replication of this intriguing gene by environment interaction study. Nevertheless, Henquet et al. (2009), using the experience sampling method (ESM), collected data on cannabis use and the occurrence of psychotic symptoms in daily life as well as samples of DNA from healthy volunteers. Her results indicated that the COMT Val^{158}Met polymorphism moderates the association between cannabis and psychotic symptoms in the flow of daily life in psychosis-prone people. COMT Val/Val carriers were in fact more likely to report hallucinatory experiences than COMT Val/Met carriers and even more than Met/Met, supporting the Caspi et al. findings.

Another important factor, which might impact on the strength of the association between cannabis use and psychosis, is the age at first use of cannabis. Once again, the Dunedin cohort study showed that individuals using cannabis at age 15 had a statistically significant fourfold increased risk of being diagnosed with a schizophreniform disorder at age 26 (OR = 4.50, 95% CI 1.11–18.21) compared with controls. Those who started using cannabis at age 18 also had an increased risk of developing a schizophreniform disorder at age 26, though it was not significant (OR = 1.65, 95% CI 0.65–4.18). In this study the authors were also able to demonstrate that early adolescence cannabis use was associated with an increased risk of schizophreniform disorder later in life even after psychotic symptoms preceding the onset of cannabis use were controlled for, even though this association was no longer significant (OR = 3.12, 95% CI 0.73–13.29; Arseneault et al., 2002).

Pattern of use and cannabis potency: The neglected players

The causal role that cannabis use might play in the development of psychotic disorders, despite the above evidence, remains controversial, leading the UK Government, for example, to repeatedly review cannabis safety (Advisory Council on the Misuse of Drugs, 2005). The debate over this issue has involved both groups of scientists and politicians still puzzled by the observation that, though consistent across all the reviewed studies, the effect of cannabis use on risk of psychosis is modest and confined to a minority of users. However, until now none of the studies carried out have collected detailed data on the pattern of cannabis use or its potency, which may be important factors moderating the associated risk to psychosis. A study by Smith (2005) has suggested that high-potency cannabis might be more harmful. Types of cannabis such as skunk, which contains very high concentration of D9-THC, might have a greater psychogenic effect because it also lacks CBD, which, as mentioned above, is thought to have antipsychotic properties (Leweke, Schneider, Radwan, Schmidt, & Emrich, 2000).

A very interesting study by Morgan and Curran (2008) measured cannabinoid traces in the hair of three groups of normal volunteers, and found that those with "D9-THC only" had higher level of schizophrenia-like symptoms than the "D9-THC plus CBD" and "no cannabinoids at all" groups (Morgan & Curran, 2008).

Furthermore, a recently published study by Di Forti et al. (2009) has collected and analysed detailed data on pattern of cannabis use (ever used, age at first use, duration and frequency of use) and potency from a sample of 280 first-episode psychosis patients and 174 population healthy controls. Di Forti's findings indicated that first-episode psychosis patients were neither more likely to have ever taken cannabis nor to have started in earlier adolescence than the control group. This was not surprising given that at least 40% of British 15- to 16-year-olds report having used cannabis, the most widely used illicit drug in the UK (United Nations Office on Drugs and Crime, 2009).

Nevertheless, their data on pattern of cannabis use and potency showed that among those who used cannabis, the first-episode psychosis patients group were almost twice as likely to have used it for more than five years compared to controls. When potential confounders (age, gender, ethnicity, use of stimulants, level of education achieved and employment status) were controlled for, this difference was slightly reduced (adjusted OR = 2.1, 95% CI 0.9–8.4) but no longer statistically significant. Moreover, first-episode psychosis patients were over six times more likely than the control group to use cannabis every day, even after adjusting for the above potential confounders (OR = 6.4, 95% CI 3.2–28.6). More interestingly, the data showed a striking difference between cases and controls in the type of cannabis the two groups preferentially used. As summarized in Table 21.2, patients with a first episode of psychosis were almost seven times more likely to choose high-potency cannabis preparations such as skunk than controls (adjusted OR = 6.8, 95% CI 2.6–25.4), who seemed to prefer the much less potent variety (Table 21.2). Overall these findings suggest that the potency and frequency of cannabis use may play a crucial role in further increasing the risk of psychosis.

This has potentially serious public-health implications given how the availability of skunk on the UK market, as mentioned in the introduction, is steadily increasing. Furthermore, from the study described above, Di Forti et al. calculated a PAF (population attributable fraction) of 27% for skunk use, which indicates the proportion of first-episode psychosis cases that could be prevented in southeast London if skunk use was abolished (unpublished data).

However, the above data are not limitation free. For instance, it is possible that those subjects who later develop a psychotic disorder during their prodromos choose high-potency cannabis to self-medicate. It remains paradoxical why anyone already experiencing prodomal and/or psychotic symptoms should choose to use a potent type of cannabis such as skunk, the high level of D9-THC of which is likely to exacerbate their symptoms, rather than ameliorating them with, perhaps, hash, which contains CBD, as well as low levels of D9-THC (Miettunen et al., 2008).

In addition, in the above case-control-design study the information on pattern of cannabis use was collected retrospectively by interviewing study participants and not validated by biological measures of the type of cannabis used in urine, blood or hair samples. Although, these biological methods might prove helpful in validating the evidence of current use, they would not add value in determining the pattern of use over time.

Table 21.2 Differences in pattern of use and potency of cannabis chosen between cases and controls, in a first-episode psychosis study from southeast London

Among cannabis users	*Cases (n = 159)*		*Controls (n = 109)*		*Adjusted OR*†	*95%CI*
	n	*(%)*	*n*	*(%)*		
Duration of use						
0–5 years	65	(40.8)	68	(62.5)	1.0	—
Over 5 years	94	(59.2)	41	(37.5)	2.1	0.9–5.3
Frequency of use						
Less than everyday	37	(23.1)	73	(66.7)	1.0	—
Everyday	122	(76.9)	36	(33.3)	6.6	3.8–31.6*
Type of cannabis used						
Traditional hash and imported herbal (THC/CBD = 1%)	34	(21.6)	68	(62.6)	1.0	—
Sensimilla or skunk (THC 12–18%; CBD = 0.5%)	125	(78.4)	41	(37.4)	6.8	1.6–22.8*

Notes: †Adjusted for: age, gender, ethnicity, other stimulants use, level of education achieved and employment status. *$p < .05$.

Conclusions

In conclusion, is cannabis potency important?

Anybody who enjoys drinking alcohol would know how, for example, the pattern of drinking and the strength of the wine chosen make the difference between its pleasurable use or harmful consequences. It is generally accepted that drinking a glass of wine every day is less likely to be associated with long-standing health problems than drinking a daily bottle of strong spirits. Unfortunately, most of the studies which have reported evidence of an association between cannabis use and psychosis have not collected detailed information on the patterns of use or on the potency of the cannabis smoked. So far, only one published study has been able to explore how differences in pattern of use and cannabis potency can affect the risk for psychosis. Hopefully, further research will investigate the impact of cannabis potency on mental health and, more widely, on health in general. This is an issue of great concern given that skunk is conquering the UK market, a worrying change that hopefully will provoke the development of more public education aiming to explain the available evidence on risks of regular use of high-potency cannabis.

References

Advisory Council on the Misuse of Drugs. (2005). *The classification of cannabis under the Misuse of Drugs Act 1971*. London, UK: Home Office.

Andreasson, S., Allebeck, P., Engstrom, A., & Rydberg, U. (1987). Cannabis and schizophrenia. A longitudinal study of Swedish conscripts. *Lancet*, *2*, 1483–1486.

Arseneault, L., Cannon, M., Poulton, R., Murray, R., Caspi, A., & Moffitt, T. E. (2002). Cannabis use in adolescence and risk for adult psychosis: Longitudinal prospective study. *British Medical Journal*, *325*, 1212–1213.

Bossong, M. G., van Berckel, B. N., Boellaard, R., Zuurman, L., Schuit, R. C., Windhorst, A. D., et al. (2009). Delta 9-tetrahydrocannabinol induces dopamine release in the human striatum. *Neuropsychopharmacology*, *34*, 759–766.

Caspi, A., Moffitt, T. E., Cannon, M., McClay, J., Murray, R., Harrington, H., et al. (2005). Moderation of the effect of adolescent-onset cannabis use on adult psychosis by a functional polymorphism in the catechol-O-methyltransferase gene: longitudinal evidence of a gene environment interaction. *Biological Psychiatry*, *57*, 1117–1127.

Di Forti, M., Morgan, C., Dazzan, P., Pariante, C., Mondelli, V., Reis Marques, T., et al. (2009). Use of high potency cannabis is associated with a greater risk of psychosis. *British Journal of Psychiatry*, *195*, 488–491.

D'Souza, D. C., Perry, E., MacDougall, L., Ammerman, Y., Cooper, T., Wu, Y. T., et al. (2004). The psychotomimetic effects of intravenous delta-9-tetrahydrocannabinol in healthy individuals: Implications for psychosis. *Neuropsychopharmacology*, *29*, 1558–1572.

Ferdinand, R. F., Sondeijker, F., van der Ende, J., Selten, J. P., Huizink, A., & Verhulst, F. C. (2005). Cannabis use predicts future psychotic symptoms, and vice versa. *Addiction*, *100*(5), 612–618.

Fergusson, D. M., Horwood, L. J., & Swain-Campbell, N. R. (2003). Cannabis dependence and psychotic symptoms in young people. *Psychological Medicine*, *33*(1), 15–21.

Grech, A., van Os, J., Jones, P. B., Lewis, S. W., & Murray, R. M. (2005). Cannabis use and outcome of recent onset psychosis. *European Psychiatry*, *20*(4), 349–353.

Hardwick, S., & King, L. (2008). *Home Office Cannabis Potency Study*. London, UK: Home Office. (available at: http://drugs.homeoffice.gov.uk/publication-search/cannabis/potency)

Henquet, C., Krabbendam, L., Spauwen, J., Kaplan, C., Lieb, R., Wittchen, H. U., et al. (2005). Prospective cohort study of cannabis use, predisposition for psychosis, and psychotic symptoms in young people. *British Medical Journal*, *330*(7481), 11.

Henquet, C., Murray, R., Linszen, D., & van Os, J. (2005). The environment and schizophrenia: The role of cannabis use. *Schizophrenia Bulletin*, *31*, 608–612.

Henquet, C., Rosa, A., Delespaul, P., Papiol, S., Fananas, L., van Os, J., et al. (2009). COMT Val/Met moderation of cannabis-induced psychosis: A momentary assessment study of "switching on" hallucinations in the flow of daily life. *Acta Psychiatrica Scandinava*, *119*, 156–160.

Herkenham, M., Lynn, A. B., Johnson, M. R., Melvin, L. S., de Costa, B. R., & Rice, K. C. (1991). Characterization and localization of cannabinoid receptors in rat brain: A quantitative in vitro autoradiographic study. *Journal of Neuroscience*, *11*(2), 563–583.

Leweke, F. M. (2007). Antipsychotic effects of cannabidiol. *European Psychiatry*, *s39*, 02.

Leweke, F. M., Schneider, U., Radwan, M., Schmidt, E., & Emrich, H. M. (2000). Different effects of nabilone and cannabidiol on binocular depth inversion in man. *Pharmacology Biochemistry Behaviour*, *66*, 175–181.

Linszen, D. H., Dingemans, P. M., & Lenior, M. E. (1994). Cannabis abuse and the course of recent-onset schizophrenic disorders. *Archives of General Psychiatry*, *51*, 273–279.

Methers, D. C., & Ghodse, A. H. (1992). Cannabis and psychotic illness. *British Journal of Psychiatry*, *161*, 648–653.

Miettunen, J., Tormanen, S., Murray, G. K., Jones, P. B., Maki, P., Ebeling, H., et al. (2008). Association of cannabis use with prodromal symptoms of psychosis in adolescence. *British Journal of Psychiatry*, *192*, 470–471.

Moore, T. H., Zammit, S., Lingford-Hughes, A., Barnes, T. R., Jones, P. B., Burke, M., et al. (2007). Cannabis use and risk of psychotic or affective mental health outcomes: A systematic review. *Lancet*, *370*, 319–328.

Morgan, C. J. A., & Curran, H. V. (2008). Effects of cannabidiol on schizophrenia-like symptoms in people who use cannabis. *British Journal of Psychiatry*, *192*, 306–307.

Morrison, P. D., Zois, V., McKeown, D. A., Lee, T. D., Holt, D. W., Powell, J. F., et al. (2009). The acute effects of synthetic intravenous delta9-tetrahydrocannabinol on psychosis, mood and cognitive functioning. *Psychological Medicine*, *39*(10), 1607–1616.

Murray, M. R., Morrison, P. D., Henquet, C., & Di Forti, M. (2008). Cannabis, the mind and society: The hash realities. *Nature Review Neuroscience*, *8*, 885–895.

Negrete, J. C., Knapp, W. P., Douglas, D. E., & Smith, W. B. (1986). Cannabis affects the severity of schizophrenic symptoms: Results of a clinical survey. *Psychological Medicine*, *16*, 515–520.

Pertwee, R. G. (2008). The diverse CB(1) and CB(2) receptor pharmacology of three plant cannabinoids: Delta(9)-tetrahydrocannabinol, cannabidiol and delta(9)-tetrahydrocannabivarin. *British Journal of Pharmacology*, *153*(2), 199–215.

Potter, D. J., Clark, P., & Brown, M. B. (2008). Potency of D9–THC and other cannabinoids in cannabis in England in 2005: Implications for psychoactivity and pharmacology. *Journal of Forensic Science*, *53*, 90–94.

Smith, N. (2005). High potency cannabis: The forgotten variable. *Addiction*, *100*, 1558–1559.

Stefanis, N. C., Delespaul, P., Henquet, C., Bakoula, C., Stefanis, C. N., & van Os, J. (2004). Early adolescent cannabis exposure and positive and negative dimensions of psychosis. *Addiction*, *99*(10), 1333–1341.

Stefanis, N. C., Hanssen, M., Smirnis, N. K., Avramopoulos, D. A., Evdokimidis, I. K., Stefanis, C. N., et al. (2002). Evidence that three dimensions of psychosis have a distribution in the general population. *Psychological Medicine*, *32*, 347–358.

Stokes, P. R., Mehta, M. A., Curran, H. V., Breen, G., & Grasby, P. M. (2009). Can recreational doses of THC produce significant dopamine release in the human striatum? *NeuroImage*, *48*(1), 186–190.

Thornicroft, G. (1990). Cannabis and psychosis: Is there epidemiological evidence for an association? *British Journal of Psychiatry*, *157*, 25–33.

United Nations Office on Drugs and Crime. (2009). *UNODC World Drug Report 2009*. (available at: http://www.unodc.org/unodc/en/world_drug_report_2009.htm)

van Os, J., Bak, M., Hanssen, M., Bijl, R. V., de Graaf, R., & Verdoux, H. (2002). Cannabis use and psychosis: A longitudinal population-based study. *American Journal of Epidemiology*, *156*, 319–327.

Weiser, M., Knobler, H. Y. , Noy, S., & Kaplan, Z. (2002). Clinical characteristics of adolescents later hospitalized for schizophrenia. *American Journal of Medical Genetics*, *114*(8), 949–955.

Wiles, N. J., Zammit, S., Bebbington, P., Singleton, N., Meltzer, H., & Lewis, G. (2006). Self-reported psychotic symptoms in the general population: Results from the longitudinal study of the British National Psychiatric Morbidity Survey. *British Journal of Psychiatry*, *188*, 519–526.

Zammit, S., Allebeck, P., Andreasson, S., Lundberg, I., & Lewis, G. (2002). Self-reported cannabis use as a risk factor for schizophrenia in Swedish conscripts of 1969: Historical cohort study. *British Medical Journal*, *325*, 1199.

22 The social determinants of psychosis in migrant and minority ethnic populations

Craig Morgan, Gerard Hutchinson, Paola Dazzan, Kevin Morgan and Paul Fearon

One of the most consistent and controversial findings in the epidemiology of schizophrenia and other psychoses is the high incidence of these disorders in migrant and minority ethnic populations. This has been found for a wide range of groups in a number of countries, e.g., migrant and minority ethnic groups in the UK, the Netherlands, Sweden, Denmark, Australia, and the USA (Bresnahan et al., 2007; Fearon & Morgan, 2006). In the UK attention has focused particularly on the Black Caribbean population, and in 1997 the AESOP[1] study—an incidence and case-control study of first-episode psychosis led by Robin Murray, Julian Leff, Peter Jones and Glynn Harrison—was established to investigate in detail the apparent high rates of schizophrenia and other psychoses in this and other minority ethnic populations. All authors of this chapter have been involved with this study since, or from shortly after, its inception. Here, we outline some of the key findings to emerge from the AESOP study and attempt to draw out their implications for our understanding of psychosis and for public health. In doing this, it is impossible to avoid mention of the political and ideological context within which this and related research has been conducted and interpreted.

Incidence rates, methods and misdiagnosis

In studies of migration, ethnicity and psychosis most attention, until recently at least, has focused on the Black Caribbean population in the UK (Sharpley, Hutchinson, McKenzie, & Murray, 2001). The migration of substantial numbers of people from the English-speaking Caribbean (mainly Jamaica, Barbados and Trinidad) to the UK, particularly to urban conurbations such as London and Birmingham, occurred largely in the 1940s and 1950s. For most, post-war economic prosperity in the UK and the promise of work was the primary reason for the decision to migrate, often with family migrating later.[2] However, rather than acceptance and prosperity, the overwhelming experience for most was one of rejection and discrimination, the majority securing only low-paid, low-status jobs and poor housing, the consequence being that substantial numbers settled in the poorer areas where accommodation was cheap but poorly maintained. Chronic discrimination and racial prejudice has limited economic and educational opportunities, the result being that many Caribbean migrants, and now their children and grandchildren born in the UK, continue to live in economically deprived urban areas. The earliest studies reporting rates of mental disorder in the UK among migrants from the Caribbean were published in the early 1960s. Since then there have been over twenty studies (most from London, Nottingham and Birmingham) that have investigated the incidence of psychosis or, more specifically, schizophrenia in this population (including both first-generation migrants and their children and grandchildren born in the UK; Fearon & Morgan, 2006). Without exception, each has reported higher incidence rates than in the White population—between two (Bhugra et al., 1997) and fourteen times higher (Harrison, Owens, Holton, Neilson, & Boot, 1988).

These findings, however, have been the subject of intense and often acrimonious debate, the critique being that they are either a methodological artefact or a consequence of misdiagnosis. Particularly in relation to early studies (i.e., pre-1991), a number of practical methodological considerations raised doubts about the validity of the findings (e.g., problems with accuracy of denominator data for migrant and minority ethnic groups; uncertain completeness of case identification; and reliance on routine clinical diagnoses). More fundamentally, there have been persistent arguments that the apparent high rates are a function of misdiagnosis. In brief, the argument is that emotional distress arising from difficult life circumstances in Black populations is misconstrued as psychosis by predominantly White psychiatrists influenced by negative cultural stereotypes of Black people (Fernando, 1991). This perspective has also influenced debate and research in other countries, including the Netherlands and the USA. As we have commented elsewhere (C. Morgan & Hutchinson, 2010a), in the UK this issue has become further entangled with discussions of access to, and quality of, care for Black Caribbean patients. There is equally consistent evidence that patients from these groups are more likely to access mental health care via a criminal justice agency and to be compulsorily admitted to hospital, with further suggestions of dissatisfaction with, and disengagement from, ongoing care (C. Morgan, Mallett, Hutchinson, & Leff, 2004). For some, perceived misdiagnosis and poor quality care are part of the same problem—institutional racism in psychiatry (Patel & Hegginbotham, 2007).

It was within this contentious context that the AESOP study (funded by the UK Medical Research Council) was established in 1997 and within which its findings have been interpreted and debated.

The AESOP study

AESOP, a multi-centre population-based incidence and case-control study of first-episode psychosis, conducted initially over a three-year period from September 1997 to August 2000, was set up with the following aims:

1 To establish a large population-based, first contact case-control study of psychosis in which to test hypotheses concerning social and biological factors that might explain the increased incidence of schizophrenia in the Black Caribbean population in the UK.
2 By determining the causes of the high incidence in this population, to throw light on the aetiology of schizophrenia in general.

The study sample comprised: (i) all cases with a first episode of psychosis (F10–F29 and F30–F33, psychotic codings, in ICD-10; World Health Organization, 1992) who presented to secondary and tertiary services within tightly defined catchment areas in the UK (southeast London, Nottingham, Bristol) over defined time periods; (ii) where possible, a close relative of each case; and (iii) a random sample of healthy community controls. Data were collected from cases, relatives, and controls in a range of domains: demographic, social (e.g., indicators of childhood and adult disadvantage), psychological (e.g., self-esteem), neurocognitive and biological (e.g., structural magnetic resonance imaging, neurological soft-signs).

The study was designed, as far as possible, to address the methodological limitations highlighted above. In particular, case-finding methods were based on, and extended, those used by the WHO in its 10-country study (Jablensky et al., 1992). A team of researchers covered all potential points of contact with health services for those with a first episode of psychosis within each catchment area, including community-based services. At the end of the periods of case recruitment, comprehensive leakage studies were conducted to identify all first-episode cases of psychosis who presented within the time frames of the study but who were not initially identified by study researchers. This yielded a further 60 cases, or 12% of the total final sample. Diagnoses were made with clinical information collected using the Schedules for Clinical Assessment in Neuropsychiatry (SCAN) on the basis of consensus meetings involving one of the AESOP study's principal investigators (JL, RM or PJ) and other members of the research team. All diagnoses were made with the principal investigator blind to the ethnicity of the case. In a similar vein, in assigning cases and controls to ethnic groups, any ambiguity was resolved through consensus. This process always included those with long-standing expertise in the study of ethnicity and mental health.

During the study period, we identified 592 cases (330 over 3 years in southeast London; 205 over 3 years in Nottingham; 57 over 9 months in Bristol) and 412 controls (183 in southeast London; 208 in Nottingham; 21 in Bristol), a total of 1004 subjects. Table 22.1 provides an overview of the basic characteristics of the sample.

Table 22.1 Basic characteristics of the AESOP sample

	London		*Nottingham*		*Bristol*	
	Cases	*Controls*	*Cases*	*Controls*	*Cases*	*Controls*
Age (Mean ± *SD*)	31.0 ± 10.5	36.1 ± 11.3	30.3 ± 11.2	38.4 ± 13.4	30.7 ± 10.8	31.5 ± 9.4
Male, *N* (%)	186 (56.7)	67 (36.6)	122 (59.5)	95 (45.7)	39 (68.4)	9 (42.9)
White British, *N* (%)	78 (23.6)	76 (41.5)	151 (73.7)	164 (78.9)	37 (64.9)	19 (90.5)
African Caribbean, *N* (%)	126 (38.2)	51 (27.9)	27 (13.2)	23 (11.1)	10 (17.5)	1 (4.8)
Black African, *N* (%)	66 (20.0)	21 (11.5)	3 (1.5)	1 (0.5)	5 (8.8)	0 (0.0)

Incidence rates and misdiagnosis (again)

As a first step in the detailed analysis of the extensive data collected, the incidence of all psychoses, and the various diagnostic subgroups, was calculated for all ethnic groups using 2001 UK census data (which has the most accurate information ever on the sizes of minority ethnic populations). In line with previous research, we found that the incidence of all psychoses was over six times higher in the Black Caribbean and four times higher in the Black African (i.e., migrants from sub-Saharan Africa, and their children and grandchildren born in the UK) populations (Fearon et al., 2006; Table 22.2). The findings for the Black African population are relatively novel and particularly important because this is a more recent migrant group with a very different background trajectory to that of the Caribbean population. When considered by diagnosis, the incidence of schizophrenia and manic psychosis were particularly elevated in the Black Caribbean and Black African populations (Table 22.2). Further, the incidence was raised in all other ethnic groups (including non-British White), albeit more modestly, with incidence rate ratios ranging from 1.5 to 2.7 for all psychoses (not shown in Table 22.2). As the number of cases from these other ethnic groups form a smaller proportion of the sample, these estimates are less robust. In the main these findings held in all three study centres, for men and women, and for all age bands. It is important to note, moreover, that the majority of cases in this study of Black Caribbean ethnicity were born in the UK (approx. 70%), which confirms that these high rates are now clearly evident in second and subsequent generation migrants.

These findings closely reflect those of a meta-analytic review of 18 studies of migration and psychosis by Cantor-Graae and Selten (2005). They found a weighted relative risk for schizophrenia of 2.7 for all migrant (vs. non-migrant) groups, with this increasing to around 4.8 for migrants (first and subsequent generation) from countries where the majority population is Black. Other recent reviews, not surprisingly, have produced similar conclusions, and more recent studies continue to suggest elevated incidence rates in migrant and minority ethnic populations (e.g., African Americans in the USA; Bresnahan et al., 2007). The degree of increased risk, however, is not consistent across migrant and minority ethnic groups—as hinted at in the meta-analysis conducted by Cantor-Graae and

Table 22.2 Incidence rates and rate ratios by ethnic group in the AESOP study

	All psychoses		*Schizophrenia*		*Manic psychosis*	
	IR	*RR*	*IR*	*RR*	*IR*	*RR*
White British	20	1.0	7	1.0	2	1.0
Black Caribbean	141	6.7	71	9.1	16	8.0
Black African	81	4.1	40	5.8	12	6.2

IR = incidence rate per 100,000 person years; age standardized; RR = incidence rate ratio.
From Fearon et al., 2006, *Psychological Medicine*, *36*(11), 1541–1550, reprinted with permission of Cambridge University Press.

Selten (2005) and findings from the AESOP study (Fearon et al., 2006). In a recent study in east London, the incidence was again found to be higher in most migrant and minority ethnic groups (Kirkbride et al., 2008). However, in Pakistani and Bangladeshi populations, this appeared to be evident for women only. In the Netherlands, the incidence appears to be highest in Moroccan migrants (Veling et al., 2006).

As these new data and meta-analyses have emerged, from more robust studies, the possibility that the reported high rates can be fully accounted for by methodological problems or misdiagnosis has receded. This is not to simply sweep away important questions about, for example, the cross-cultural validity of psychiatric diagnoses. However, all the relevant evidence points away from misdiagnosis as the primary explanation of reported high incidence rates. In the AESOP study, the incidence was raised for all diagnostic groups (Fearon et al., 2006). There is some evidence that persecutory delusions were more common in the Black Caribbean and Black African cases (Demjaha et al., 2006), but this may reflect the greater impact of social risk factors in these populations (see below) and there was certainly no evidence to suggest markedly different clinical profiles across each ethnic group. This mirrors findings from earlier studies (e.g., Harrison et al., 1988). Further, one of the few studies that has sought to investigate directly whether schizophrenia is frequently misdiagnosed in patients of Black Caribbean ethnicity in the UK did not find compelling evidence to support this (Hickling, McKenzie, Mullen, & Murray, 1999). Finally, there is no consistent evidence that clinical outcomes following a first episode of psychosis vary by ethnic group (e.g., Goater et al., 1999; Harrison, Amin, Singh, Croudace, & Jones, 1999), which would be expected if misdiagnosis was responsible for the inclusion of large numbers of cases from Black Caribbean and other minority ethnic populations in incidence studies. To be sure, the evidence on this is limited, and we are in the process of following all AESOP cases at 10 years to further investigate this, with additional support from the UK Medical Research Council.

These ongoing debates notwithstanding, research has increasingly moved on to investigate the substantive factors that may explain high rates of schizophrenia and other psychoses in migrant and minority ethnic populations, again with most information to date relating to the UK Black Caribbean population.

Social determinants

To cut a long story short, all findings have converged on the conclusion that the high rates are likely to be a consequence of exposure to adverse social contexts and experiences, broadly defined.

Childhood and adult adversity

A series of findings from the AESOP study, for example, link indicators of childhood and adult disadvantage with psychosis in general and further suggest the greater prevalence of adversity in the Caribbean population over the life course may contribute to the higher rates of psychosis (C. Morgan et al., 2007, 2008). To take one example (Kirkbride, Fearon et al., 2007), this study found that long-term (over one year) separation from a parent before the age of 16 (a marker of childhood disadvantage, indexing exposure to intra-familial conflict, financial hardship, and housing instability) was around three-times more common in those with a first episode of psychosis compared with our population-based controls, after taking account of possible confounders including a family history of psychosis. Most importantly, while the effect of separation on the odds of psychosis was similar for White British and Black Caribbean individuals, separations were much more common for Black Caribbean individuals (both cases and controls, e.g., 31% of Black Caribbean controls vs. 18% of White British controls, $p = .03$). This replicates an earlier, smaller study (Mallett, Leff, Bhugra, Pang, & Zhao, 2002).

This pattern was also evident for a number of indicators of adult social disadvantage and isolation (both recent and long standing), including unemployment, housing instability, and limited social networks (C. Morgan et al., 2008). When considered as an index by simply counting the number of indicators of disadvantage present, we found evidence of robust, independent and linear associations with odds of psychosis in both White British and Black Caribbean groups (Figure 22.1), i.e., a similar effect in both groups. But, not surprisingly, each form of adversity and cumulative adversity was much more common in the Black Caribbean population, again reflecting what is known more generally. These patterns are important as they are consistent with the high rates being a function of the greater prevalence of social risk factors in the Black Caribbean population. That is, if social experiences indexed by childhood separation and adult disadvantage are important in the aetiology of psychosis (and there is growing evidence for this), their greater prevalence in the Black Caribbean population may be one factor increasing rates.

There is a further set of analyses of AESOP data that support these conclusions. In recent years, there has been renewed interest in whether psychosis is more usefully conceptualized as categorical or dimensional, i.e., as lying on a continuum with normality (Verdoux & van Os, 2002). This is fuelled by research showing that psychosis-like experiences (i.e., low-level and transitory odd ideas, hallucinatory experiences, strange behaviour) are common in the general population and that the factors associated with these experiences are similar to those associated with clinically diagnosed psychotic disorders (van Os, Linscott, Myin-Germeys, Delespaul, & Krabbendam, 2009). In the AESOP control group, we had relevant data on such experiences from the psychosis screen we used, the Psychosis Screening Questionnaire (PSQ), and were consequently able to investigate whether the associations detailed above between ethnicity, indicators of childhood and adult disadvantage and psychosis held for psychosis-like experiences in our control sample (C. Morgan et al., 2009).

In a sample of 372 controls, the weighted prevalence of psychosis-like experiences was 19% (C. Morgan et al., 2009), well within the range of what has been reported in previous studies (C. Morgan et al., 2009). Three findings are particularly pertinent. First, separation from a parent during childhood for one-year or more due to family breakdown was associated with endorsement of

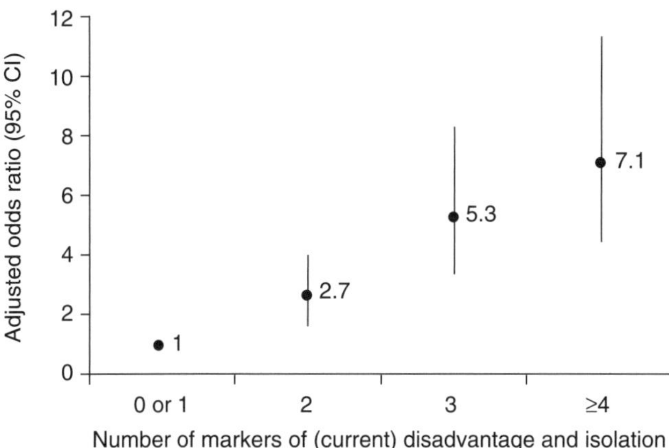

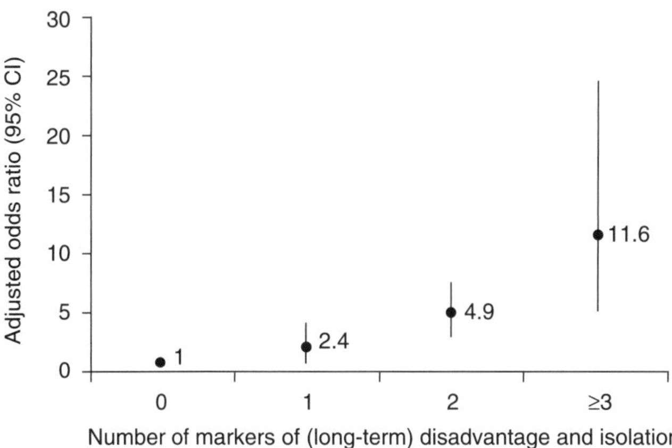

Figure 22.1 Adjusted odds ratios for each level of social disadvantage and isolation, current and long term (from C. Morgan et al., 2008, *Psychological Medicine, 38*(12), 1701–1715, reprinted with permission of Cambridge University Press).

psychosis-like experiences. That is, those who were separated were two times more likely to respond positively to a follow-up question on the PSQ (indicating fairly strong presence of anomalous experiences) than others, a finding that held after adjusting for potential confounders. Second, indicators of social disadvantage and isolation were associated with psychosis-like experiences. Third, the prevalence of psychosis-like experiences were higher in the Black Caribbean (Odds Ratio, OR, 2.1) and the Black African (OR 4.6) groups compared with the White British. When indicators of social disadvantage and, in particular, separation were adjusted for in analyses, the strength of the associations with ethnicity reduced and, for the Black Caribbean group, was no longer significant. In other words, the association between psychosis-like experiences and Black Caribbean ethnicity was explained by higher levels of disadvantage and separations.

Racism and discrimination

Further speculation has focused on exposure to racism and discrimination. There is some suggestive evidence from the AESOP study implicating perceptions of disadvantage as a possible contributory factor (Cooper et al., 2008), and Karlsen and Nazroo (2002), in an analysis of data from the UK Fourth National Survey of Ethnic Minorities, found that both socioeconomic position and the experience of discrimination were independent predictors of psychosis in Black and minority ethnic groups. Perhaps the most direct evidence comes from a study by Veling, Hoek, and Mackenbach (2008), who used general population data on perceptions of discrimination in the Netherlands to order migrant and minority ethnic groups according to levels of exposure to discrimination. Using this index of discrimination, they found clear evidence of a linear relationship with schizophrenia, such that the incidence increased in line with level of exposure to discrimination, the highest rates being in those with highest levels of perceived discrimination (i.e., Moroccan: incidence rate ratio, IRR, 4.82). The findings from the meta-analysis by Cantor-Graae and Selten (2005) that risk is highest in those migrants from countries where the majority population is Black may also be relevant here. It is worth noting at this point, moreover, that future research directly examining why some migrant and minority ethnic groups appear to be more at risk than others may be particularly instructive in further understanding this phenomenon.

Ethnic density

Perhaps most intriguing is the now replicated finding that the relative risk of schizophrenia increases as Black Caribbean people form a decreasing proportion of the local population (Boydell et al., 2001; Kirkbride, Morgan et al., 2007; Veling, Susser et al., 2008). That is, the less ethnically dense an area, the higher the rates of psychosis (see Figure 22.2). This possibly implicates both characteristics of the wider social environment (which ties in with other recent research linking area- and neighbourhood-level characteristics with risk; van Os, Driessen, Gunther, & Delespaul, 2000) and greater exposure to discrimination in areas with fewer minority groups. One further plausible mechanism underpinning this is that those who live in areas of low ethnic density have fewer available social supports or others with whom they can identify to buffer the impact of adverse social experiences. In other words, individual experience and the wider social context within which individuals live may interact to compound risk. It is noteworthy, moreover, that such a social patterning of risk defies ready explanation in terms of social drift or known biological risk factors.

Biological markers

At the same time as more evidence has emerged concerning social contexts, there has been no similar accumulation of evidence implicating known biological risk factors. For example, data from the AESOP study does not show either a greater

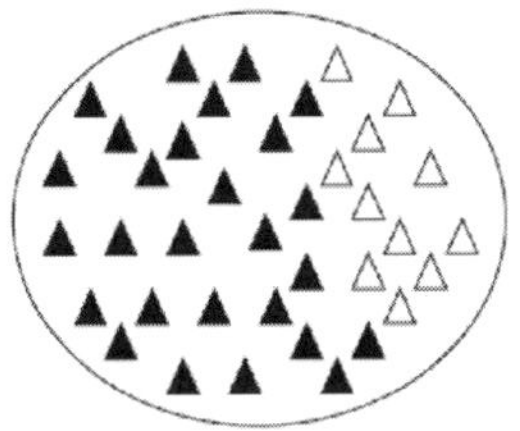
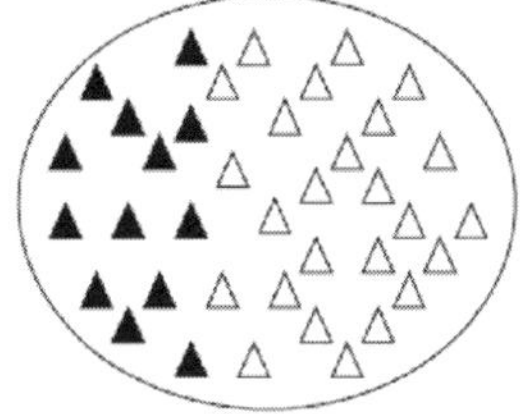
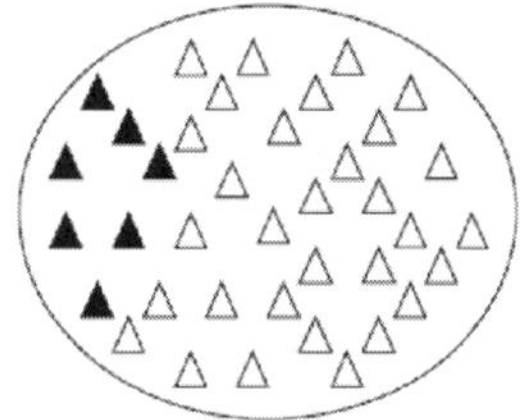

High % minority population	Medium % minority population	Low % minority population
RR 2.4[a]	RR 3.6[a]	RR 4.4[a]
RR 3.8[b]	RR 2.1[b]	RR 6.5[b]
RR 1.3[c]	–	RR 2.4[c]

Figure 22.2 Rate ratios for schizophrenia by ethnic density in recent studies. RR = rate ratio, Black versus White; [a]Boydell et al., 2001; [b]Kirkbride et al., 2007; [c]Veling et al., 2008 (from Morgan & Hutchinson, 2010a, *Psychological Medicine, 40*, 705–709, reprinted with permission of Cambridge University Press).

effect for neurodevelopmental markers or a greater prevalence in the Black Caribbean group (e.g., minor physical anomalies; Dean et al., 2007) and there is no evidence from other studies that obstetric complications are more common in the Caribbean population (Hutchinson et al., 1997). There is some evidence from AESOP neuroimaging data that structural brain abnormalities may be more marked in Black Caribbean cases relative to Black Caribbean controls (K. Morgan et al., 2010). This could, however, be a reflection of the impact of chronic adversity over the life course (see below). Finally, family studies suggest that schizophrenia is no more familial (genetic) in Caribbean than in White groups, the implication being that the excess rates must be environmentally driven (Hutchinson et al., 1996; Sugarman & Crawford, 1994). In addition, the risk appears to be higher still in second and subsequent generation migrants, i.e., those born in Britain (Cantor-Graae & Selten, 2005). Related to this, rates of schizophrenia in the Caribbean, i.e., Barbados (Mahy, Mallett, Leff, & Bhugra, 1999), Trinidad (Bhugra et al., 1996), Jamaica (Hickling & Rodgers-Johnson, 1995), are significantly lower than those reported in the UK Black Caribbean population, findings which suggest population variations in genetic risk cannot account for the observed disparities.

The sociodevelopmental origins of psychosis

This summary of findings from the AESOP study, and other relevant research, suggests two broad conclusions: (i) there is a genuinely increased incidence of schizophrenia and other psychoses in many migrant and minority ethnic groups, particularly in the UK Black Caribbean population; and (ii) the most likely explanation for this increased incidence is greater exposure, over the life course, to social disadvantage and adversity (broadly defined). The analyses and dissemination of data from the AESOP study have coincided with, and contributed to, a shift in our understanding of the basic epidemiology of schizophrenia and other psychoses and a resurgence of interest in the role of social experiences and contexts in the aetiology of these disorders (McGrath, 2007; McGrath et al., 2004). It is now broadly accepted, for example, that the incidence of schizophrenia is not uniform (as was often inferred from the WHO 10-country study; Jablensky et al., 1992) but varies markedly by place and social group (McGrath, 2007). In addition to our findings concerning ethnicity, other analyses of AESOP data comparing the incidence of psychoses by place (southeast London vs. Nottingham and Bristol) support this (Kirkbride et al., 2006). Perhaps more importantly, advances in genetics, neuroscience and cognitive psychology have suggested a number of plausible mechanisms through which social adversities may impact on development in such ways as to increase risk of schizophrenia and other psychoses, e.g., gene–environment interaction (van Os, Rutten, & Poulton, 2008), sensitization of the dopaminergic system (Collip, Myin-Germeys, & van Os, 2008), development of cognitive schema and affective processes (Garety, Kuipers, Fowler, Freeman, & Bebbington, 2001). It now seems likely that psychosis is the end product of a series of complex interactions between genes, biology and society (Howes & Kapur, 2009). In light of this, it is plausible that, from a similar base level of biological and genetic risk, greater exposure to social adversity (or social defeat; Selten & Cantor-Graae, 2005) over the life course, in the absence of supportive buffers, could substantially increase population rates of psychosis—as in the Black Caribbean population (and indeed other migrant groups around the world). This life course exposure would also explain why the second generation is at increased risk compared to their first-generation parents.

Conclusions

This is not simply an academic issue. What lies behind the often sterile epidemiological data on incidence and odds ratios are stories of distress and suffering that all too frequently devastate individuals and their families. And this returns us to where we began, with debates about whether the reported high rates are real or artefact. The evidence invariably points to there being a genuinely increased incidence, often to varying degrees, in migrant and ethnic minority groups. To persist in arguing otherwise, in the absence of any robust evidence to the contrary, runs the very real risk of diverting much needed attention from a major public-health problem. Data from AESOP and other recent studies strongly implicate aspects of the social environment and exposure to social adversity over the life course in the genesis of these high rates, particularly in the UK Black Caribbean population. These findings are contributing to a re-evaluation of the importance of social factors in the aetiology of schizophrenia and other psychoses in general. But, more importantly, it is by understanding what gives rise to such high rates in certain populations that we can move beyond futile ideological debates to an urgent consideration of appropriate and effective social and public health responses (C. Morgan & Hutchinson, 2010a).

Acknowledgements

In preparing this chapter, we have drawn from the following previous summaries and reviews of AESOP data and of migration and psychosis: Fearon & Morgan, 2006; C. Morgan & Fearon, 2007; C. Morgan & Hutchinson, 2010a, 2010b. We thank all of those who have been involved in the AESOP study over the past ten years.

Further details are available at: http://www.iop.kcl.ac.uk/departments/?locator = 398&context = 997.

Notes

1 AESOP: Aetiology and Ethnicity in Schizophrenia and Other Psychoses.
2 This was a period of significant migration from many former colonies of the British Empire, most notably India and Pakistan.

References

Bhugra, D., Hilwig, M., Hossein, B., Marceau, H., Neehall, J., Leff, J., et al. (1996). First-contact incidence rates of schizophrenia in Trinidad and one-year follow-up. *British Journal of Psychiatry*, *169*, 587–592.

Bhugra, D., Leff, J., Mallett, R., Der, G., Corridan, B., & Rudge, S. (1997). Incidence and outcome of schizophrenia in Whites, African-Caribbeans and Asians in London. *Psychological Medicine*, *27*, 791–798.

Boydell, J., van Os, J., McKenzie, K., Allardyce, J., Goel, R., McCreadie, R. G., et al. (2001). Incidence of schizophrenia in ethnic minorities in London, UK: Ecological study into interactions with environment. *British Medical Journal*, *323*, 1336–1338.

Bresnahan, M., Begg, M. D., Brown, A., Schaefer, C., Sohler, N., Insel, B., et al. (2007). Race and risk of schizophrenia in a US birth cohort: Another example of health disparity? *International Journal of Epidemiology*, *36*(4), 751–758.

Cantor-Graae, E., & Selten, J. P. (2005). Schizophrenia and migration: A meta-analysis and review. *American Journal of Psychiatry*, *162*, 12–24.

Collip, D., Myin-Germeys, I., & van Os, J. (2008). Does the concept of "sensitization" provide a plausible mechanism for the putative link between the environment and schizophrenia? *Schizophrenia Bulletin*, *34*(2), 220–225.

Cooper, C., Morgan, C., Byrne, M., Dazzan, P., Morgan, K., Hutchinson, G., et al. (2008). Perceptions of disadvantage, ethnicity and psychosis. *British Journal of Psychiatry*, *192*(3), 185–190.

Dean, K., Dazzan, P., Lloyd, T., Morgan, C., Morgan, K., Doody, G. A., et al. (2007). Minor physical anomalies across ethnic groups in a first-episode psychosis sample. *Schizophrenia Research*, *89*(1–3), 86–90.

Demjaha, A., Morgan, K., Morgan, C., Dazzan, P., Landau, S., Dean, K., et al. (2006). Symptom dimensions and ethnicity in the AESOP first onset psychosis study. *Schizophrenia Research*, *81*, 233–233.

Fearon, P., Kirkbride, J. B., Morgan, C., Dazzan, P., Morgan, K., Lloyd, T., et al. (2006). Incidence of schizophrenia and other psychoses in ethnic minority groups: Results from the MRC AESOP Study. *Psychological Medicine*, *36*(11), 1541–1550.

Fearon, P., & Morgan, C. (2006). Environmental factors in schizophrenia: The role of migrant studies. *Schizophrenia Bulletin*, *32*(3), 405–408.

Fernando, S. (1991). *Mental health, race and culture*. London, UK: Macmillan.

Garety, P. A., Kuipers, E., Fowler, D., Freeman, D., & Bebbington, P. E. (2001). A cognitive model of the positive symptoms of psychosis. *Psychological Medicine*, *31*(2), 189–195.

Goater, N., King, M., Cole, E., Leavey, G., Johnson-Sabine, E., Blizard, R., et al. (1999). Ethnicity and outcome of psychosis. *British Journal of Psychiatry*, *175*, 34–42.

Harrison, G., Amin, S., Singh, S. P., Croudace, T., & Jones, P. (1999). Outcome of psychosis in people of African-Caribbean family origin: A population-based first episode study. *British Journal of Psychiatry*, *175*, 43–49.

Harrison, G., Owens, D., Holton, A., Neilson, D., & Boot, D. (1988). A prospective study of severe mental disorder in Afro-Caribbean patients. *Psychological Medicine*, *18*, 643–657.

Hickling, F., & Rodgers-Johnson, P. (1995). The incidence of first-contact schizophrenia in Jamaica. *British Journal of Psychiatry*, *167*, 193–196.

Hickling, F. W., McKenzie, K., Mullen, R., & Murray, R. (1999). A Jamaican psychiatrist evaluates diagnoses at a London psychiatric hospital. *British Journal of Psychiatry*, *175*, 283–285.

Howes, O. D., & Kapur, S. (2009). The dopamine hypothesis of schizophrenia: Version III—The final common pathway. *Schizophrenia Bulletin*, *35*(3), 549–562.

Hutchinson, G., Takei, N., Bhugra, D., Fahy, T. A., Gilvarry, C., Mallett, R., et al. (1997). The increased rate of psychosis among African-Caribbeans in Britain is not due to an excess of pregnancy and birth complications. *British Journal of Psychiatry*, *171*, 145–147.

Hutchinson, G., Takei, N., Fahy, T. A., Bhugra, D., Gilvarry, C., Moran, P., et al. (1996). Morbid risk of schizophrenia in first-degree relatives of White and African-Caribbean patients with psychosis. *British Journal of Psychiatry*, *169*, 776–780.

Jablensky, A., Sartorius, N., Ernberg, G., Anker, M., Korten, A., Cooper, J. E., et al. (1992). Schizophrenia: Manifestations, incidence and course in different cultures: A World Health Organization ten-country study. *Psychological Medicine*, *20*(Suppl. 20), 1–97.

Karlsen, S., & Nazroo, J. (2002). Relation between racial discrimination, social class and health among ethnic minority groups. *American Journal of Public Health*, *92*, 624–631.

Kirkbride, J. B., Barker, D., Cowden, F., Stamps, R., Yang, M., Jones, P. B., et al. (2008). Psychoses, ethnicity and socio-economic status. *British Journal of Psychiatry*, *193*(1), 18–24.

Kirkbride, J. B., Fearon, P., Morgan, C., Dazzan, P., Morgan, K., Murray, R. M., et al. (2007). Neighbourhood variation in the incidence of psychotic disorders in southeast London. *Social Psychiatry and Psychiatric Epidemiology*, *42*(6), 438–445.

Kirkbride, J. B., Fearon, P., Morgan, C., Dazzan, P., Morgan, K., Tarrant, J., et al. (2006). Heterogeneity in incidence rates of schizophrenia and other psychotic syndromes: Findings from the 3-center AESOP study. *Archives of General Psychiatry*, *63*(3), 250–258.

Kirkbride, J. B., Morgan, C., Fearon, P., Dazzan, P., Murray, R. M., & Jones, P. B. (2007). Neighbourhood-level effects on psychoses: Re-examining the role of context. *Psychological Medicine*, *37*(10), 1413–1425.

Mahy, G., Mallett, R., Leff, J., & Bhugra, D. (1999). First-contact incidence rate of schizophrenia in Barbados. *British Journal of Psychiatry*, *175*, 28–33.

Mallett, R., Leff, J., Bhugra, D., Pang, D., & Zhao, J. H. (2002). Social environment, ethnicity and schizophrenia. *Social Psychiatry and Psychiatric Epidemiology*, *37*, 329–335.

McGrath, J., Saha, S., Welham, J., El Saadi, O., MacCauley, C., & Chant, D. (2004). A systematic review of the incidence of schizophrenia: The distribution of rates and the influence of sex, urbanicity, migrant status and methodology. *BMC Medicine*, *2*(1), 1–22.

McGrath, J. J. (2007). The surprisingly rich contours of schizophrenia epidemiology. *Archives of General Psychiatry*, *64*(1), 14–16.

Morgan, C., & Fearon, P. (2007). Social experience and psychosis insights from studies of migrant and ethnic minority groups. *Epidemiologia e Psichiatria Sociale*, *16*(2), 118–123.

Morgan, C., Fisher, H., Hutchinson, G., Kirkbride, J., Craig, T. K., Morgan, K., et al. (2009). Ethnicity, social disadvantage and psychotic-like experiences in a healthy population based sample. *Acta Psychiatrica Scandinavica*, *119*(3), 226–235.

Morgan, C., & Hutchinson, G. (2010a). The social determinants of psychosis in migrant and ethnic minority populations: A public health tragedy. *Psychological Medicine*, *40*, 705–709.

Morgan, C., & Hutchinson, G. (2010b). The sociodevelopmental origins of psychosis. In C. Morgan & D. Bhugra (Eds.), *Principles of social psychiatry* (2nd ed., pp. 193–213). London, UK: Wiley-Blackwell.

Morgan, C., Kirkbride, J., Hutchinson, G., Craig, T., Morgan, K., Dazzan, P., et al. (2008). Cumulative social disadvantage, ethnicity and first-episode psychosis: A case-control study. *Psychological Medicine*, *38*(12), 1701–1715.

Morgan, C., Kirkbride, J., Leff, J., Craig, T., Hutchinson, G., McKenzie, K., et al. (2007). Parental separation, loss and psychosis in different ethnic groups: A case-control study. *Psychological Medicine*, *37*(4), 495–503.

Morgan, C., Mallett, R., Hutchinson, G., & Leff, J. (2004). Negative pathways to psychiatric care and ethnicity: The bridge between social science and psychiatry. *Social Science and Medicine*, *58*(4), 739–752.

Morgan, K. D., Dazzan, P., Morgan, C., Lappin, J. M., Hutchinson, G., Chitnis, X., et al. (2010). Differing patterns of brain structural abnormalities between Black and White patients with their first episode of psychosis. *Psychological Medicine*, *40*, 1137–1147.

Patel, K., & Hegginbotham, C. (2007). Institutional racism in psychiatry does not imply racism in individual psychiatrists: Commentary on Institutional racism in psychiatry. *Psychiatric Bulletin*, *31*, 367–368.

Selten, J. P., & Cantor-Graae, E. (2005). Social defeat: Risk factor for schizophrenia? *British Journal of Psychiatry*, *187*, 101–102.

Sharpley, M., Hutchinson, G., McKenzie, K., & Murray, R. (2001). Understanding the excess of psychosis among the African-Caribbean population in England. *British Journal of Psychiatry*, *178*(Suppl. 40), s60–s68.

Sugarman, P. A., & Crawford, D. (1994). Schizophrenia in the Afro-Caribbean community. *British Journal of Psychiatry*, *164*, 474–480.

van Os, J., Driessen, G., Gunther, N., & Delespaul, P. (2000). Neighbourhood variation in incidence of schizophrenia. Evidence for person–environment interaction. *British Journal of Psychiatry*, *176*, 243–248.

van Os, J., Linscott, R. J., Myin-Germeys, I., Delespaul, P., & Krabbendam, L. (2009). A systematic review and meta-analysis of the psychosis continuum: Evidence for a psychosis proneness-persistence-impairment model of psychotic disorder. *Psychological Medicine*, *39*(2), 179–195.

van Os, J., Rutten, B. P., & Poulton, R. (2008). Gene–environment interactions in schizophrenia: Review of epidemiological findings and future directions. *Schizophrenia Bulletin*, *34*(6), 1066–1082.

Veling, W., Hoek, H. W., & Mackenbach, J. P. (2008). Perceived discrimination and the risk of schizophrenia in ethnic minorities: A case-control study. *Social Psychiatry and Psychiatric Epidemiology*, *43*(12), 953–959.

Veling, W., Selten, J. P., Veen, N., Laan, W., Blom, J. D., & Hoek, H. W. (2006). Incidence of schizophrenia among ethnic minorities in the Netherlands: A four-year first-contact study. *Schizophrenia Research*, *86*(1–3), 189–193.

Veling, W., Susser, E., van Os, J., Mackenbach, J. P., Selten, J. P., & Hoek, H. W. (2008). Ethnic density of neighborhoods and incidence of psychotic disorders among immigrants. *American Journal of Psychiatry*, *165*(1), 66–73.

Verdoux, H., & van Os, J. (2002). Psychotic symptoms in non-clinical populations and the continuum of psychosis. *Schizophrenia Research*, *54*(1–2), 59–65.

World Health Organization. (1992). *The ICD-10 classification of mental and behavioural disorders* (International Classification of Diseases, 10th ed.). Geneva, Switzerland: WHO.

23 Stress and psychosis

Professor Murray's contribution (so far) to the vulnerability–stress model

Valeria Mondelli and Carmine M. Pariante

The vulnerability–stress model and Robin's epidemiological studies

Previous studies in patients with psychosis have demonstrated that stress is an important factor in the development of psychosis, but the biological mechanisms by which stress affects psychosis remain unclear. One model of psychosis, the vulnerability–stress model, posits that predisposing biological factors increase the sensitivity of some individuals to stress and thus make them more vulnerable to develop psychosis under stressful circumstances (Broome et al., 2005; Walker & Diforio, 1997).

Work conducted by Professor Murray and co-workers in the early 1990s has shown that an excess of stressful life events precedes the onset of psychosis and psychotic relapse in patients with schizophrenia (Bebbington et al., 1993), a finding later replicated by other researchers (Walker, Mittal, & Tessner, 2008). Moreover, childhood adversities have also been linked to an increased risk for development of psychiatric disorders, and have been reported to be more frequent in patients with psychosis than in the general population (Read, van Os, Morrison, & Ross, 2005); and Professor Murray has also addressed this question within the AESOP study, a large epidemiologically based study of first-episode psychosis. This research has shown that an excess of both physical and sexual abuse is particularly present in female patients (Fisher et al., 2009). Interestingly, healthy women controls also show an association between childhood trauma and psychotic-like experience (Fisher et al., 2009). Finally, other studies conducted by Professor Murray within the AESOP sample have shown an increased risk of psychosis in individuals who have social and environmental risk factors associated with a more stressful daily life, like being a migrant, belonging to an ethnic minority, and living in a densely populated inner city area (Boydell et al., 2003; Fearon et al., 2006; Kirkbride et al., 2006). Again, these findings are consistent with evidence from other studies showing that patients with psychosis perceive daily hassles as more stressful than healthy subjects (Myin-Germeys, Delespaul, & van Os, 2005), indicating that they may have a higher sensitivity to stress.

But only biological studies can elucidate the mechanisms underlying the association between stress and psychosis.

The hypothalamic–pituitary–adrenal axis in psychosis and Robin's first biological study on stress and schizophrenia

The hypothalamic–pituitary–adrenal (HPA) axis is the most important component of the stress response system, and the object of many studies in biological psychiatry, including in psychosis. The HPA axis activity is governed by the secretion of adrenocorticotrophic hormone-releasing hormone (CRH) and vasopressin (AVP) from the hypothalamus, which in turn activate the secretion of adrenocorticotrophic hormone (ACTH) from the pituitary, which finally stimulates the secretion of the glucocorticoids (cortisol in humans and corticosterone in rodents) from the adrenal cortex (see Figure 23.1; Pariante & Lightman, 2008). Glucocorticoids then interact with their receptors in multiple-target tissues including the HPA axis, where they are responsible for feedback inhibition both on CRH and AVP from the hypothalamus and directly on the secretion of ACTH from pituitary cells.

Considering its role at the interface between stress and brain functioning, it is perhaps not surprising that the HPA axis has been found abnormal in psychiatric disorders, and in particular in major depression. For example, a significant percentage of depressed patients have increased levels of cortisol in the saliva, plasma and urine, and increased size (as well as activity) of the pituitary and adrenal glands (Pariante & Lightman, 2008). The picture in patients with psychosis, as discussed below, is far more complicated. The increased activity of the HPA axis in depression is thought to be related, at least in part, to reduced feedback inhibition by endogenous glucocorticoids. Through binding to their cognate receptors in the HPA axis—the glucocorticoid receptor (GR) and the mineralocorticoid receptor (MR)—endogenous glucocorticoids serve as potent negative regulators of HPA axis activity, in particular inhibiting the synthesis and release of CRH in the paraventricular nucleus and pro-opiomelanocortin (POMC)/ACTH in the pituitary (see Figure 23.1). Data supporting the notion that glucocorticoid-mediated feedback inhibition is impaired in major depression comes from a multitude of studies demonstrating that the HPA is not suppressed by pharmacological stimulation of the GR with an oral dose of the synthetic glucocorticoid dexamethasone (dexamethasone non-suppression); in contrast, even a small dose of dexamethasone induces a potent feedback inhibition of the HPA axis in healthy subjects, leading to reduced cortisol levels for up to 24 hours.

Studies in patients with psychosis have shown that patients who are in the acute phase of a psychotic disorder, with florid symptoms, newly hospitalized or unmedicated, also have clear evidence of hyperactivity of the HPA axis (Tandon et al., 1991). The hyperactivity of the HPA axis in psychosis is particularly evident at the illness onset, which is often described as a most distressing time. Indeed, studies in subjects experiencing their first psychotic episode have shown increased circulating levels of cortisol and ACTH (Ryan, Collins, & Thakore, 2003; Ryan, Sharifi, Condren, & Thakore, 2004) and higher rate of dexamethasone non-suppression (Ceskova, Kasparek, Zourkova, & Prikryl, 2006).

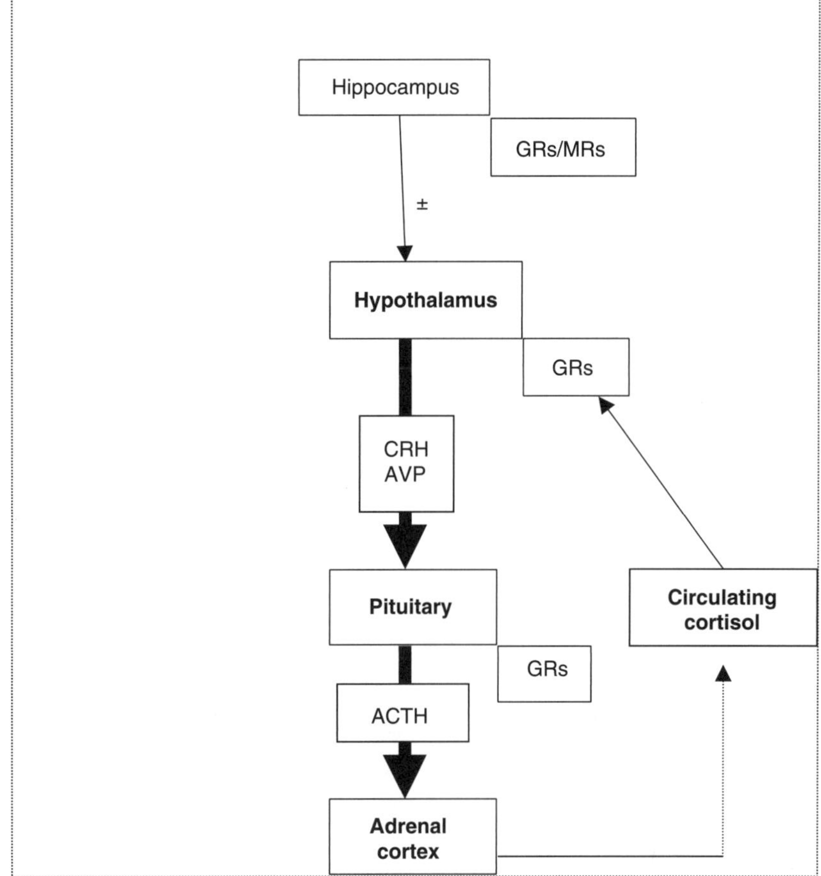

Figure 23.1 Schematic diagram of the hypothalamic–pituitary–adrenal (HPA) axis, including putative pathways leading to hyperactivity in psychosis. CRH = adrenocorticotrophic hormone-releasing hormone; AVP = vasopressin; ACTH = adrenocorticotrophic hormone; GRs = glucocorticoid receptors; MRs = mineralocorticoid receptors.

In contrast, data in patients with established psychosis show that long-term antipsychotic treatment normalizes HPA axis hyperactivity, and that patients with established diagnosis have a normal HPA axis (Tandon et al., 1991). Professor Murray's first study on HPA axis and psychosis, in the late 1990s, confirmed this evidence, by demonstrating that patients with established schizophrenia do not show any evidence of dexamethasone non-suppression (Ismail, Murray, Wheeler, & O'Keane, 1998).

But only a systematic approach to examination of the biological correlates of stress in different clinical samples of patients with psychosis can really elucidate the role of stress.

The beginning of a research programme: Robin's interest in pituitary volume

The first systematic effort by Professor Murray's group (and by the authors of this chapter in particular) to investigate HPA axis activity in relation to psychosis is represented by a series of studies (some conducted in close collaboration with the University of Melbourne) using the measurement of the pituitary volume using structural magnetic resonance imaging (MRI; see Figure 23.2) in a variety of samples of patients, controls, prodromals and relatives.

In major depression, HPA axis hyperactivity has been linked to an increased volume of the pituitary gland (Axelson et al., 1992). The pituitary gland regulates HPA axis activity by secreting ACTH, and its increased volume has been interpreted as reflecting an increase in the size and number of cells producing ACTH (Axelson et al., 1992). Is HPA axis hyperactivity in psychosis also associated with an increased volume of the pituitary gland, especially in subjects at their first episode of psychosis?

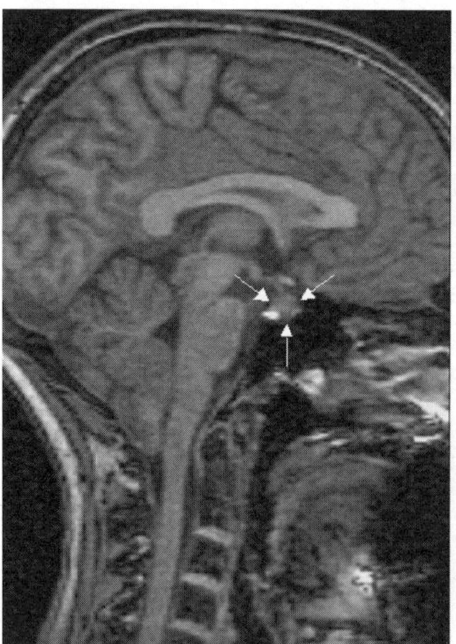

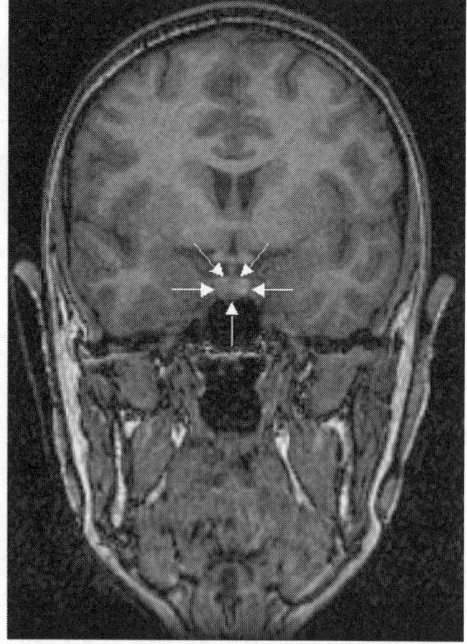

Figure 23.2 The pituitary gland visualized using MRI. The pituitary gland in a sagittal (left) and coronal (right) MRI image. Coronal slices are normally used for the tracing of the pituitary, and the pituitary boundaries are indicated by the arrows: the diaphragma sellae, superiorly; the sphenoid sinus, inferiorly; and the cavernous sinuses, bilaterally. The posterior bright spot, corresponding to the posterior pituitary (the intensity of which is thought to reflect vasopressin concentrations), is usually included in the tracing, while the pituitary stalk is not included.

The studies conducted so far, by us and others, clearly indicate that the pituitary is a dynamic organ, which changes differently at different stages of the psychotic disorder, in response to both the disorder itself and the treatment with antipsychotics. Specifically, these studies have shown that the pituitary volume increases during the prodromal phase leading to psychosis onset (Garner et al., 2005), and it is larger (+10–20% compared to controls) if assessed during the first 2–6 months after the psychosis onset (Pariante et al., 2004, 2005). This effect is not due to antipsychotic treatments as it has also been shown in neuroleptic-naïve prodromal subjects (Garner et al., 2005) as well as in neuroleptic-free patients with (first-episode) psychosis (Pariante et al., 2005). We believe that this effect likely reflects "stress-related" HPA axis hyperactivity. This notion is consistent with another study (on the "Maudsley Family Study" cohort) that has demonstrated a larger pituitary volume in healthy relatives of patients with schizophrenia, suggesting additionally that a genetically driven susceptibility to over activate the HPA axis could be part of the biological pathway leading to psychosis (Mondelli et al., 2008).

Other studies have also shown that, following this initial enlargement, the pituitary of patients with psychosis tends to become smaller. We have found a reduction of -17% in patients with established schizophrenia and an average of 19 years of duration of illness (Pariante et al., 2004); interesting, similar findings have been described by others in (neuroleptic-naïve) patients who have been psychotic for an average of 2 years (or of 6 years if the duration of prodromal symptoms is also included; Upadhyaya, El-Sheikh, MacMaster, Diwadkar, & Keshavan, 2007).

On top of these dynamic changes that are linked to the course of the disorder, antipsychotics, and especially antipsychotics inducing hyperprolactinemia, exert an additional enlarging effect on pituitary volume. This has been clearly shown in first-episode psychosis, where we have also found that subjects on typical antipsychotics have the largest pituitary volume (+30% vs. controls) when compared with those who are neuroleptic free (+15%) or on atypical antipsychotics (mostly olanzapine in this study, +17%; Pariante et al., 2005). Therefore, this additional enlarging effect of some antipsychotics is present even above the "stress-related" enlargement linked to the onset of the disorder. Considering the interaction between the changes in pituitary volume due to the disorder (acute enlargement followed by progressive reduction) and those due to the antipsychotics (stable enlargement), it is possible to explain the results from yet another study (on the "Maudsley Family Study" cohort), showing, in patients with an average duration of illness of 12–14 years, that pituitary volume is not different to controls, while a subgroup of patients with schizophrenia and receiving prolactin-elevating antipsychotics has an increased pituitary volume (Mondelli et al., 2008).

How to interpret the results from this series of studies? We believe that the increased pituitary volume associated with the development of psychosis—in prodromal subjects assessed *immediately before* the psychosis onset (Garner et al., 2005), in first-episode subjects assessed *immediately after* the psychosis onset (Pariante et al., 2005), and in *healthy relatives* of subjects with schizophrenia

(Mondelli et al., 2008)—is due to activation of the hormonal stress response, and, specifically, to an increase in the size and number of pituitary cells producing ACTH. Interestingly, as mentioned above, HPA axis hyperactivity in depressed patients has been interpreted as showing a lack of negative inhibitory feedback by circulating glucocorticoid hormones on the HPA axis, especially at the level of the pituitary (glucocorticoid resistance; Pariante & Lightman, 2008). Indeed, increased size and number of pituitary cells and increased volume of the pituitary are present also in subjects with a lack of negative inhibitory feedback by circulating glucocorticoid hormones because of Addison's disease (Mineura et al., 1987).

We also show that patients with an established diagnosis of schizophrenia have smaller or normal pituitary volume compared to controls (Mondelli et al., 2008; Pariante et al., 2004), as also shown by another research group (Tournikioti et al., 2007). These findings are particularly remarkable because a smaller pituitary volume has been described in a variety of chronic mental disorders, including bipolar disorder, eating disorder, obsessive-compulsive disorder, and in prodromal subjects who are not on the trajectory to psychosis (Pariante, 2008). The mechanisms underlying the smaller pituitary volume are yet to be fully understood, and the explanations have ranged from being the consequence of a chronic activation of the HPA axis to being a neurodevelopmental problem (Pariante, 2008).

But the pituitary volume is only an indirect measure of HPA axis activity, and ultimately a study is needed to measure clinical and psychosocial predictors of cortisol levels in psychosis.

Why is the HPA axis hyperactive in psychosis? Robin's "GAP" study

Several factors have been hypothesized to explain the HPA axis hyperactivity at the onset of psychosis: an increased level of stressful life events preceding the onset; an increased sensitivity to stress; an increased rate of childhood trauma; the distress and severity of the psychotic experience; heavy tobacco smoking; and an increased use of cannabis, which in turn increases cortisol levels in humans (D'Souza et al., 2005). Surprisingly, however, these factors had not been yet studied together with HPA axis activity in first-episode psychosis. Therefore, a study was required to investigate HPA axis activity together with all of the putative mechanisms described above, as well as the effects of antipsychotic treatment, in a sample of patients at their first-episode psychosis, and in healthy controls from the same geographical area. This study is the genetic and psychosis (GAP) study—led by Professor Murray and supported by (among others) the South London and Maudsley NHS Foundation Trust (SLAM) and Institute of Psychiatry National Institute for Health Research (NIHR) Biomedical Research Centre for Mental Health.

First-episode psychosis patients have been recruited in London (UK) from the Lambeth, Southwark and Croydon in-patient and out-patient units. The recruitment strategy is based on contacting in-patient and out-patient services regularly, interviewing staff and reviewing clinical notes, and approaching all subjects aged 18–65 who present for the first time to these services for a functional psychotic illness. Controls are recruited from the same catchment areas as the patients through advertisements in local newspapers, hospitals and job centres, as well as from existing volunteer databases.

The first data on this sample have just been published (Aas et al., 2010; Mondelli, Dazzan et al., 2010a; Mondelli, Pariante et al., 2010b). We have found that patients with first-episode psychosis have a trend for higher cortisol levels during the day, but this difference is entirely driven by those with less than two weeks of antipsychotic treatment. These patients also have significantly blunted cortisol awakening response, irrespectively of antipsychotic treatment. Finally, patients have more recent stressful events, higher levels of perceived stress, and higher rates of childhood trauma, but these do not seem to explain the HPA axis abnormalities (Mondelli, Dazzan et al., 2010a).

The increased cortisol levels during the day in patients with less than two weeks of antipsychotic treatment is consistent with previous studies in drug-free patients with first-episode psychosis, including our own work showing an increased pituitary volume. The normalizing effect of antipsychotic treatment on cortisol levels is also in agreement with previous studies in patients with chronic schizophrenia, showing a reduction of cortisol levels following treatment with antipsychotics. Interestingly, we have also shown that those with higher cortisol levels have smaller hippocampus volume, supporting the notion that these stress-related biological mechanisms contribute to the pathogenesis of the brain structural changes described in these patients (Mondelli, Pariante et al., 2010b).

We also find a blunted cortisol awakening response in our patients, which is not influenced by antipsychotic treatment. Awakening acts as a mild stressor, and thus the blunted cortisol awakening response is consistent with previous studies in patients with chronic schizophrenia, also finding a blunted cortisol response to psychological and psychosocial stressors, even in the presence of normal baseline cortisol levels (Jansen, Gispen-de Wied, & Kahn, 2000). It is important to stress that this is the first time that a *blunted* cortisol awakening response has been described in the context of *higher* diurnal cortisol levels. Euthymic or acutely ill patients with major depression, a condition usually characterized by *higher* cortisol levels during the day, show *increased* cortisol awakening response (Bhagwagar, Hafizi, & Cowen, 2005). In contrast, subjects with chronic fatigue syndrome and post-traumatic stress disorder, conditions usually characterized by *lower* cortisol levels during the day (Cleare, 2003; Yehuda, 2001), tend to show *blunted* cortisol awakening response (Roberts, Wessely, Chalder, Papadopoulos, & Cleare, 2004; Wessa, Rohleder, Kirschbaum, & Flor, 2006). This suggests that HPA axis dysfunction in psychosis is not simply a correlate of depression or other general psychopathological symptoms but has a specific profile, perhaps linked to a different genetic background or a different developmental trajectory of the stress abnormalities. Interestingly, the presence of a blunted cortisol awakening response also predicts a worse cognitive function in these patients (Aas et al., 2010).

We have also shown that the patients with first-episode psychosis show more stressful events in the last six months, higher levels of perceived stress, and higher rates of childhood trauma, compared with controls. These results are consistent with a number of previous studies examining these variables in patients with psychosis, as mentioned above. Interestingly, and in contrast with what we hypothesized, diurnal cortisol hypersecretion in our patients is not explained by these stress measures. Indeed, levels of cortisol during the day correlate *negatively* with the number of stressful events, and show non-significant *negative* correlations with perceived stress and childhood trauma. Also of note is that the relationship between cortisol levels during the day and stress measures is different in patients and controls, since cortisol levels in controls (as expected) correlate *positively* with the number of stressful events, and show non-significant *positive* correlations with perceived stress and childhood trauma. A possible hypothesis to explain the *negative* correlations between stress measures and cortisol levels in patients could be the excessive load of stressful events in this sample, with some patients showing as much as fivefold the number of stressful events of controls. Indeed, post-traumatic stress disorder (PTSD), a psychiatric condition caused by highly stressful and life-threatening situations, has also been associated with cortisol hyposecretion (Yehuda, 2001), suggesting that an extreme excess of stressful situations could determine a decrease in the activation of the HPA axis. There are no correlations between psychosocial stress measures and cortisol awakening response.

Also, the HPA axis abnormalities are not explained by tobacco or cannabis smoking, and we also failed to find any correlation between cortisol levels and severity of psychotic symptoms. Therefore, other factors not examined in our paper might play a role in the HPA axis abnormalities found in our patients: for example, the severity of non-psychotic prodromal symptoms *preceding* the onset, the anxiety associated with experiencing psychotic symptoms for the first time, or (as mentioned above) a genetic predisposition to over activate the axis as explained by family history.

Conclusion: Robin's road ahead

This brief review has demonstrated that the role of stress in psychosis has always been a key interest in Professor Murray's research. From social to epidemiological and to biological studies, "Does stress induce psychosis?" is a recurrent question, with a recurrent answer: "Yes, but we do not know how". All the findings described in this review confirm the strong association between stress and psychosis, but also show that the biopsychosocial mechanisms underlying this association are complex and require further studies. What is coming next, Robin?

Acknowledgements

Dr Pariante's research described in this chapter has been supported by a King's College Development Trust (UK) Studentship and a NARSAD Young Investigator Award to Valeria Mondelli; the South London and Maudsley NHS Foundation Trust & Institute of Psychiatry NIHR Biomedical Research Centre for Mental Health; the British Academy; the American Psychiatric Institute for Research and education (APIRE); and the UK Medical Research Council.

References

Aas, M., Mondelli, V., Dazzan, P., Hepgul, N., Di, F. M., Fisher, H., et al. (2010). Abnormal cortisol awakening response predicts worse cognitive function in patients with first-episode psychosis. *Psychological Medicine*, *9*, 1–14.

Axelson, D. A., Doraiswamy, P. M., Boyko, O. B., Rodrigo, E. P., McDonald, W. M., Ritchie, J. C., et al. (1992). In vivo assessment of pituitary volume with magnetic resonance imaging and systematic stereology: Relationship to dexamethasone suppression test results in patients. *Psychiatry Research*, *44*, 63–70.

Bebbington, P., Wilkins, S., Jones, P., Foerster, A., Murray, R., Toone, B., et al. (1993). Life events and psychosis. Initial results from the Camberwell Collaborative Psychosis Study. *British Journal of Psychiatry*, *162*, 72–79.

Bhagwagar, Z., Hafizi, S., & Cowen, P. J. (2005). Increased salivary cortisol after waking in depression. *Psychopharmacology (Berlin)*, *182*, 54–57.

Boydell, J., van Os, J., Lambri, M., Castle, D., Allardyce, J., McCreadie, R. G., et al. (2003). Incidence of schizophrenia in south-east London between 1965 and 1997. *British Journal of Psychiatry*, *182*, 45–49.

Broome, M. R., Woolley, J. B., Tabraham, P., Johns, L. C., Bramon, E., Murray, G. K., et al. (2005). What causes the onset of psychosis? *Schizophrenia Research*, *79*, 23–34.

Ceskova, E., Kasparek, T., Zourkova, A., & Prikryl, R. (2006). Dexamethasone suppression test in first-episode schizophrenia. *Neuroendocrinology Letters*, *27*, 433–437.

Cleare, A. J. (2003). The neuroendocrinology of chronic fatigue syndrome. *Endocrine Reviews*, *24*, 236–252.

D'Souza, D. C., Abi-Saab, W. M., Madonick, S., Forselius-Bielen, K., Doersch, A., Braley, G., et al. (2005). Delta-9-tetrahydrocannabinol effects in schizophrenia: Implications for cognition, psychosis, and addiction. *Biological Psychiatry*, *57*, 594–608.

Fearon, P., Kirkbride, J. B., Morgan, C., Dazzan, P., Morgan, K., Lloyd, T., et al. (2006). Incidence of schizophrenia and other psychoses in ethnic minority groups: Results from the MRC AESOP study. *Psychological Medicine*, *36*(11), 1541–1550.

Fisher, H., Morgan, C., Dazzan, P., Craig, T. K., Morgan, K., Hutchinson, G., et al. (2009). Gender differences in the association between childhood abuse and psychosis. *British Journal of Psychiatry*, *194*, 319–325.

Garner, B., Pariante, C. M., Wood, S. J., Velakoulis, D., Phillips, L., Soulsby, B., et al. (2005). Pituitary volume predicts future transition to psychosis in individuals at ultra-high risk of developing psychosis. *Biological Psychiatry*, *58*, 417–423.

Ismail, K., Murray, R. M., Wheeler, M. J., & O'Keane, V. (1998). The dexamethasone suppression test in schizophrenia. *Psychological Medicine*, *28*, 311–317.

Jansen, L. M., Gispen-de Wied, C. C., & Kahn, R. S. (2000). Selective impairments in the stress response in schizophrenic patients. *Psychopharmacology (Berlin)*, *149*, 319–325.

Kirkbride, J. B., Fearon, P., Morgan, C., Dazzan, P., Morgan, K., Tarrant, J., et al. (2006). Heterogeneity in incidence rates of schizophrenia and other psychotic syndromes: Findings from the 3-center AESOP study. *Archives of General Psychiatry*, *63*, 250–258.

Mineura, K., Goto, T., Yoneya, M., Kowada, M., Tamakawa, Y., & Kagaya, H. (1987). Pituitary enlargement associated with Addison's disease. *Clinical Radiology*, *38*, 435–437.

Mondelli, V., Dazzan, P., Gabilondo, A., Tournikioti, K., Walshe, M., Marshall, N., et al. (2008). Pituitary volume in unaffected relatives of patients with schizophrenia and bipolar disorder. *Psychoneuroendocrinology*, *33*, 1004–1012.

Mondelli, V., Dazzan, P., Hepgul, N., Di, F. M., Aas, M., D'Albenzio, A., et al. (2010a). Abnormal cortisol levels during the day and cortisol awakening response in first-episode psychosis: The role of stress and of antipsychotic treatment. *Schizophrenia Research, 116*, 234–242.

Mondelli, V., Pariante, C. M., Navari, S., Aas, M., D'Albenzio, A., Di, F. M., et al. (2010b). Higher cortisol levels are associated with smaller left hippocampal volume in first-episode psychosis. *Schizophrenia Research, 119*, 75–78.

Myin-Germeys, I., Delespaul, P., & van Os, J. (2005). Behavioural sensitization to daily life stress in psychosis. *Psychological Medicine, 35*, 733–741.

Pariante, C. M. (2008). Pituitary volume in psychosis: The first review of the evidence. *Journal of Psychopharmacology, 22*, 76–81.

Pariante, C. M., Dazzan, P., Danese, A., Morgan, K. D., Brudaglio, F., Morgan, C., et al. (2005). Increased pituitary volume in antipsychotic-free and antipsychotic-treated patients of the AESOP first-onset psychosis study. *Neuropsychopharmacology, 30*, 1923–1931.

Pariante, C. M., & Lightman, S. L. (2008). The HPA axis in major depression: Classical theories and new developments. *Trends in Neurosciences, 31*, 464–468.

Pariante, C. M., Vassilopoulou, K., Velakoulis, D., Phillips, L., Soulsby, B., Wood, S. J., et al. (2004). Pituitary volume in psychosis. *British Journal of Psychiatry, 185*, 5–10.

Read, J., van Os, J., Morrison, A. P., & Ross, C. A. (2005). Childhood trauma, psychosis and schizophrenia: A literature review with theoretical and clinical implications. *Acta Psychiatrica Scandinavica, 112*, 330–350.

Roberts, A. D., Wessely, S., Chalder, T., Papadopoulos, A., & Cleare, A. J. (2004). Salivary cortisol response to awakening in chronic fatigue syndrome. *British Journal of Psychiatry, 184*, 136–141.

Ryan, M. C., Collins, P., & Thakore, J. H. (2003). Impaired fasting glucose tolerance in first-episode, drug-naive patients with schizophrenia. *American Journal of Psychiatry, 160*, 284–289.

Ryan, M. C., Sharifi, N., Condren, R., & Thakore, J. H. (2004). Evidence of basal pituitary–adrenal overactivity in first episode, drug naive patients with schizophrenia. *Psychoneuroendocrinology, 29*, 1065–1070.

Tandon, R., Mazzara, C., DeQuardo, J., Craig, K. A., Meador-Woodruff, J. H., Goldman, R., et al. (1991). Dexamethasone suppression test in schizophrenia: Relationship to symptomatology, ventricular enlargement, and outcome. *Biological Psychiatry, 29*, 953–964.

Tournikioti, K., Tansella, M., Perlini, C., Rambaldelli, G., Cerini, R., Versace, A., et al. (2007). Normal pituitary volumes in chronic schizophrenia. *Psychiatry Research, 154*, 41–48.

Upadhyaya, A. R., El-Sheikh, R., MacMaster, F. P., Diwadkar, V. A., & Keshavan, M. S. (2007). Pituitary volume in neuroleptic-naive schizophrenia: A structural MRI study. *Schizophrenia Research, 90*, 266–273.

Walker, E., Mittal, V., & Tessner, K. (2008). Stress and the hypothalamic–pituitary–adrenal axis in the developmental course of schizophrenia. *Annual Revue of Clinical Psychology, 4*, 189–216.

Walker, E. F., & Diforio, D. (1997). Schizophrenia: A neural diathesis–stress model. *Psychological Review, 104*, 667–685.

Wessa, M., Rohleder, N., Kirschbaum, C., & Flor, H. (2006). Altered cortisol awakening response in posttraumatic stress disorder. *Psychoneuroendocrinology, 31*, 209–215.

Yehuda, R. (2001). Biology of posttraumatic stress disorder. *Journal of Clinical Psychiatry, 62*(Suppl. 17), 41–46.

24 Chasing gene–environment interactions across the psychiatric universe

Jim van Os, Bart P. F. Rutten, Ruud van Winkel and Marieke Wichers

Introduction

Rates of psychiatric disorder vary across regions and demographic groups, suggesting widespread environmental influences (Dean & Murray, 2005). However, reported "environmental" effects are misleading as in reality they represent the effect of the environmental exposure *and* all the genetic influences that render an individual more sensitive to it. Genetic control of sensitivity to the environment is known as gene–environment interaction (G×E; Kendler & Eaves, 1986; Khoury, Beaty, & Cohen, 1993; Moffitt, Caspi, & Rutter, 2005). As study populations always contain a mix of genetically susceptible and non-susceptible individuals, associations between environmental exposures and psychiatric outcomes will be shifted towards the null if there is underlying G×E. For example, in a recent article by Clarke and colleagues, no association was detected between prenatal exposure to infection and schizophrenia. However, stratification of the population into those with and without evidence of genetic susceptibility revealed that prenatal exposure was associated with a large effect size only in the group with evidence of genetic susceptibility, suggestive of gene–environment interaction (Clarke, Tanskanen, Huttunen, Whittaker, & Cannon, 2009).

Gene–environment interaction (genetic control of sensitivity to the environment) must be distinguished from gene–environment correlation (genetic control of exposure to the environment; Kendler & Eaves, 1986; Kendler & Prescott, 1998). G×E includes both genetic control of sensitivity to the environment and environmental impact on gene structure/expression through epigenetic mechanisms (Figure 24.1). Gene–environment correlation may be with or without causal relevance of the environmental exposure for the phenotype in question (Figure 24.2).

G×E approaches in psychiatry

Quantitative genetic epidemiology (QGE)

Traditional epidemiological designs examining environmental exposures can be enriched by modelling genetic variation as a traditional risk factor in hypothesis-based epidemiological analyses. Genetic risk can be indexed by proxy variables

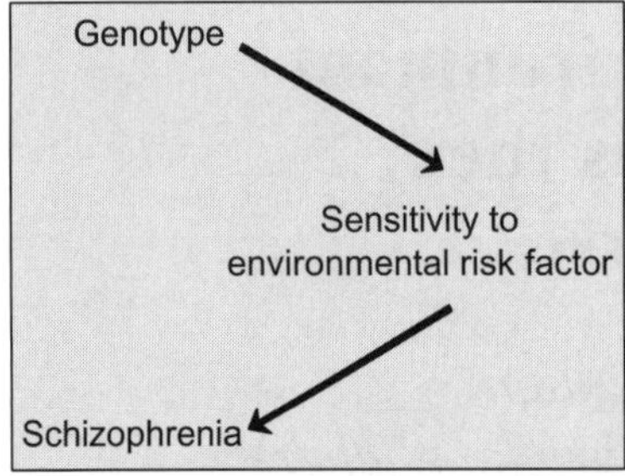

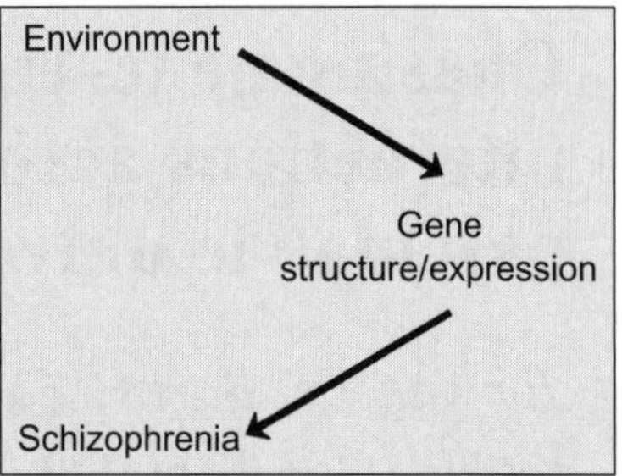

Figure 24.1 Gene–environment interaction, including both genetic control of sensitivity to the environment (left) and environmental impact on gene structure/expression through epigenetic mechanisms (right).

such as a positive family history, intermediary phenotypes (Weiser et al., 2007), sibling correlations on a behavioural trait (Wichers et al., 2007) or the quantification of genetic contribution to a trait using structural equation modelling in twin or extended family data (Purcell, 2002; Wichers et al., 2002). Even though measures such as family history induce a high rate of false-negative misclassification and direct molecular genetic information can now be easily incorporated in epidemiological analyses (see below) there is still considerable scope for QGE analyses using indirect measures of genetic risk. This is because QGE in theory provides the possibility of modelling the net total genetic contribution to a trait, including all unspecified gene–gene interactions as well as unmeasured gene–environment interactions that might contribute to differential susceptibility to the exposure of interest. This clearly represents an advantage over molecular genetic

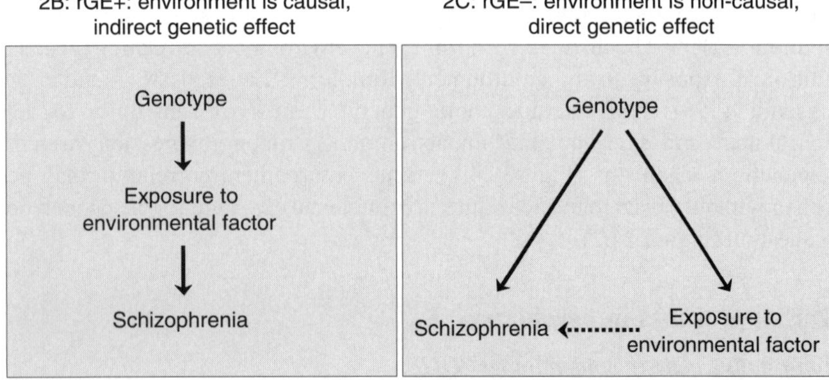

Figure 24.2 Gene–environment correlation, with (left) and without (right) causal relevance of the environmental exposure for the phenotype.

measures of genetic variation contributing to a trait, as even genome-wide association studies with the most densely positioned marker information in the largest of samples currently are able to explain only a fraction of the total heritability of the trait under examination (Maher, 2008).

Hypothesis-based molecular genetic G×E using candidate genes

Traditional epidemiological analyses may also model G×E using direct molecular genetic variation in hypothesis-based candidate genes. One example is the hypothesized interaction between variation in the gene encoding the serotonin transporter and life stress in depression. The initial report generated much interest but the most recent meta-analysis examining the body of work attempting to replicate this finding concluded that there was no evidence to support gene–environment interaction (Risch et al., 2009). One reason for this may be that the prior probability of any G×E hypothesis based on a single measure of molecular genetic variation is so low that only a fraction of the studies reporting a *p*-value of $p < .05$ is likely to have a research hypothesis that is true. Another possible reason, however, may be that behavioural, and therefore "noisy", measures of life events and depression introduce more error than biological measures such as amygdala activation in response to experimental emotional stimuli, where meta-analysis of moderation by the same serotonin transporter polymorphism does suggest gene–environment interaction (Munafo, Brown, & Hariri, 2008), as does experimental animal research (Suomi, 2006).

Another example concerns the observation that acute exposure to tetrahydrocannabinol (THC), the main psychotropic component of *Cannabis sativa*, induces psychotic symptoms (D'Souza et al., 2005; Morrison et al., 2009) in healthy controls. Meta-analysis of epidemiological studies reveals an aetiological signal for psychotic symptoms and psychotic disorder associated with the use of cannabis (Henquet, Murray, Linszen, & van Os, 2005; Moore et al., 2007; Semple, McIntosh, & Lawrie, 2005). Follow-up experimental and observational work has shown that psychosis liability is associated with differential sensitivity to the psychotomimetic effects of THC, the main psychotropic component of cannabis (Arendt, Mortensen, Rosenberg, Pedersen, & Waltoft, 2008; D'Souza et al., 2005; Henquet, Krabbendam et al., 2005; Mason et al., 2009; van Os et al., 2002). The source of the observed differential sensitivity to the psychotomimetic effects of THC has been linked to both familial/genetic factors (Caspi et al., 2005; Henquet et al., 2006; Kuepper et al., 2010) as well as environmental exposures including childhood trauma (Harley et al., 2009; Houston, Murphy, Adamson, Stringer, & Shevlin, 2008; Konings et al., 2010), suggesting that complicated higher order gene–environment interactions may underlie the link between cannabis and psychosis. The findings to date suggest that genes may interact with early environmental exposures associated with psychotic disorder, creating a "sensitized" state (Collip, Myin-Germeys, & van Os, 2008) with regard to later exposure to cannabis and the onset of psychotic symptoms (Cougnard et al., 2007). It has been suggested that the main psychotropic component of cannabis, tetrahydrocannabinol, interacts with dopaminergic neurotransmission (Murray, Morrison, Henquet, & Di Forti, 2007), the net result of which may be increased mesolimbic dopamine signalling (Bossong et al., 2009; Voruganti, Slomka, Zabel, Mattar, & Awad, 2001), which in turn may cause psychotic symptoms (Kapur, 2003). An initial observational study suggested an interaction between cannabis use and the COMT Val^{158}Met polymorphism (Caspi et al., 2005). Although a later study using a case-only design could not replicate this finding (Zammit et al., 2007), an experimental study did provide evidence for the same gene–environment interaction (Henquet et al., 2006).

Agnostic molecular genetic G×E using GWAS: GEWIS

Undoubtedly the greatest challenge in the years to come is to combine the agnostic, previously much berated but very recently re-invigorated, mass-marker approach of genomic interrogation on the one hand with the hypothesis-based approach of epidemiology and neurobiology on the other. Genome-wide association studies (GWAS) have brought about a revolution in the search for molecular genetic variation underlying psychiatric disorders. While it is not likely that every genetic variant relevant for psychiatry will be found through the hypothesis-free genome-wide approach of GWAS, fears of yet more inconclusive "fishing expeditions" have been refuted as GWAS of large samples have detected associations with common single nucleotide polymorphisms (SNPs) and rare copy-number variants (Owen, Williams, & O'Donovan, 2009). This development is important for G×E research for two reasons. The first is that findings from GWAS will yield genetic variation for candidate approach G×E analysis with a much higher prior probability than was hitherto the case. The second is that GWAS identify associations that misleadingly are interpreted as "genetic" but in reality also include all underlying gene–environment interactions. This creates the challenge to enrich GWAS with environmental information so that gene–environment-wide interaction studies (GEWIS; Khoury & Wacholder, 2009) may be conducted. GEWIS obviously pose formidable conceptual and epidemiological challenges. Traditional epidemiological tools and methodologies are not equipped for the mass-marker agnostic approach of GWAS and the scale, cost and precision of environmental measurements differs radically from the ones used in molecular genetics. In addition, new statistical approaches need to be developed beyond interaction as departure of additive or multiplicative joint effects while guarding against non-interpretable flooding of false-positive signals from GEWIS (Murcray, Lewinger, & Gauderman, 2009). An important challenge for GEWIS remains the sheer amount of data for statistical analysis; alternatives for testing each SNP separately are the use of gene-wide hypotheses, as power to detect association might be enhanced by exploiting information from multiple (quasi) independent signals within genes (Moskvina et al., 2009), or the examination of overrepresentation of biological pathways, indexed by gene-ontology terms, in lists of significant SNPs (Holmans et al., 2009).

In order to meet the challenges occasioned by GEWIS, new multidisciplinary collaborations need to be formed (EU-GEI, 2008), ethical implications need to be examined and novel statistical approaches need to be developed. GEWIS, therefore, are poised to produce the first results in the years to come.

Levels of environmental and genetic variation in G×E

While GEWIS may soon become feasible, new sources of DNA variation continue to be discovered at a rapid pace. Apart from common genetic variation in the form of single nucleotide polymorphisms, simple-sequence repeat polymorphisms and copy-number variants there are many non-coding RNA (ncRNA) genes that produce functional RNA molecules rather than encoding proteins. There are many classes of ncRNA molecules that impact on the regulation of protein-coding genes. As ncRNA genes vary in sequence between people just as protein-coding genes do, variations in ncRNA may render individuals differentially sensitive to environmental exposures. Epigenetic variation refers to the regulation of various genomic functions, particularly gene expression, that are not based on DNA sequence but instead are controlled by reversible chemical modifications of DNA and/or the chromatin structure. Epigenetic G×E refers to the mechanism that a wide range of environmental exposures can induce epigenetic alterations that may alter the risk for psychiatric disorders, for example by "silencing" certain genes (Rutten & Mill, 2009). The environment also comprises different levels. Some exposures are conceptualized at the micro-environmental level, for example the continuously changing level of small micro-stressors (social, nutritional, other) occurring in the flow of daily life. Other exposures refer to the macro-environment of shared influences at the level of the neighbourhood, city or even wider social environment.

Momentary assessment technology

G×E research would be greatly facilitated if behavioural phenotypes of environmental sensitivity could be assessed directly in observational or experimental designs. Indeed, the neural mechanisms underlying the majority of epidemiologically identified environmental risk factors remain unknown (Caspi & Moffitt, 2006).

Recently, momentary assessment approaches have been developed that sample repeated measurements of affect, cognition and perception in response to small variations in environmental exposures in the flow of daily life. Research tools allowing for specific within-subject longitudinal data collection include the Experience Sampling Method (ESM; Csikszentmihalyi & Larson, 1987). ESM and related methodologies are now progressively finding their way to research in the area of complex behaviour, allowing for multiple prospective within-subject measurements of behaviour and mood states within the context of daily life and enabling the researcher thereby to capture the film rather than the snapshot of daily life reality (Myin-Germeys et al., 2009). ESM and related methodologies thus represent useful research tools for studying the dynamic relationship between mood states, behaviour and daily life context. This technique was used, for example, to link molecular genetic variation to the ability to experience positive affect in response to natural rewards (Wichers et al., 2008), which was replicated using a neuroimaging phenotype of reward (Dreher, Kohn, Kolachana, Weinberger, & Berman, 2009). Similarly, ESM work showed that the onset of hallucinatory experiences in the flow of daily life following cannabis use was moderated by the COMT $Val^{158}Met$ polymorphism (Henquet et al., 2009), as was the impact of daily life stress on psychotic experiences (van Winkel et al., 2008).

The use of momentary assessment techniques to study G×E brings important advantages. Research findings in the area of behavioural disorders are often inconsistent due to psychometric imprecision, bias, confounding by third variables and a paucity of research designs that may shed light on causality of associations. An important methodological concern, particularly in the context of G×E, is that studies in the field of mental health are largely dependent on between-subject cross-sectional—rather than within-subject longitudinal—research designs (Molenaar & Campbell, 2009). Apart from the fact that it is uncertain to what degree findings obtained by pooling across subjects can be validly applied to the individual subject (Molenaar & Campbell, 2009; Nesselroade, Gerstorf, Hardy, & Ram, 2007), between-subject associations are subject to confounding on a level where within-subject associations are not. For example, the association between smoking during pregnancy and low birth weight may be explained by a range of third variables from alcohol consumption, stress during pregnancy and a range of factors associated with socioeconomic status and group differences in these variables may all confound the observed association. A longitudinal within-subject design, in which smoking and birth weight are assessed over multiple pregnancies in each mother, in contrast, is not affected by the above confounding effects (Rabe-Hesketh & Skrondal, 2008). In addition, analyses using self-reports arguably make sense only in a within-subject design, since all subjects create their own starting set point. Therefore, only within-subject change can reliably reflect true dynamics of the observed behaviour that is the subject of G×E research. Furthermore, within-subject designs with repeated measurements over time will be able to deal better with issues of causality and may reveal dynamic processes that are obscured in cross-sectional, between-subject designs. Future studies of G×E underlying complex behaviour, therefore, should use within-subject methodology in order to uncover dynamic processes in behaviour over time, providing further insights relevant to direction of underlying G×E causality and the possibility of replication within the same research report.

Experimental designs for G×E

Experimental designs are also useful for G×E research, as they allow for the inclusion of special groups, for example individuals with rare genetic variants, who may subsequently be exposed in random order to an (ethically acceptable) environmental exposure in order to measure the behavioural response and molecular genetic moderation thereof. Experimental designs are important, as there are legitimate concerns about how to accurately capture the environmental risk exposure history of participants. This task is particularly challenging when measuring psychosocial risk factors, the negative effects of which may act cumulatively across long periods of the life course. Equally challenging are the inherent difficulties in precisely measuring "unit exposure" for illicit substances such as cannabis, which can be ingested in different forms, with different THC levels, using different methods. Measuring tobacco intake is comparatively straightforward but even this presents problems with accuracy of recall over long periods. Another drawback of observational studies is that most designs cannot reliably tease apart moderation (genetic control of sensitivity to the environment) from mediation (genetic control of exposure to the environment; Kendler & Eaves, 1986; Kendler & Prescott, 1998).

Henquet and colleagues introduced the term "experimental ecogenetics" in human psychosis research (Henquet et al., 2006) to refer to some obvious advantages: (i) randomization precludes confounding by not only known, but, critically, also unknown confounders; (ii) rGE is not an issue if "G" is randomly allocated to "E", and (iii) it is relatively easy to make the sample size match the required power. In Figure 24.3, an example is given of how the association between migration and schizophrenia, and possible genetic moderation thereof, can be examined in the context of an experimental ecogenetic design. This may be accomplished by reducing migration to an experimental exposure of "social hostility" and by reducing the psychosis outcome to an experimental outcome of "abnormal salience attribution", and testing the association between exposure and outcome in a genetically sensitive test design. The advent of controlled experiments with virtual-reality environments may similarly represent an important asset for the study of environmental exposures (Freeman et al., 2003).

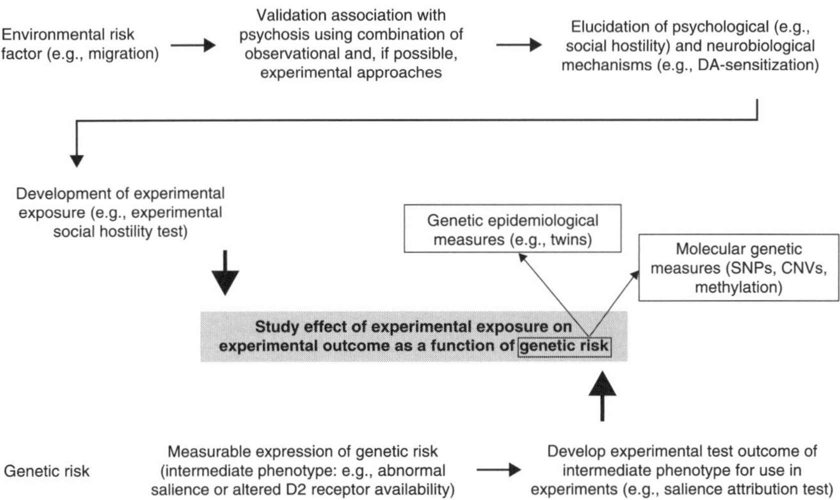

Figure 24.3 Development of experimental G×E approaches.

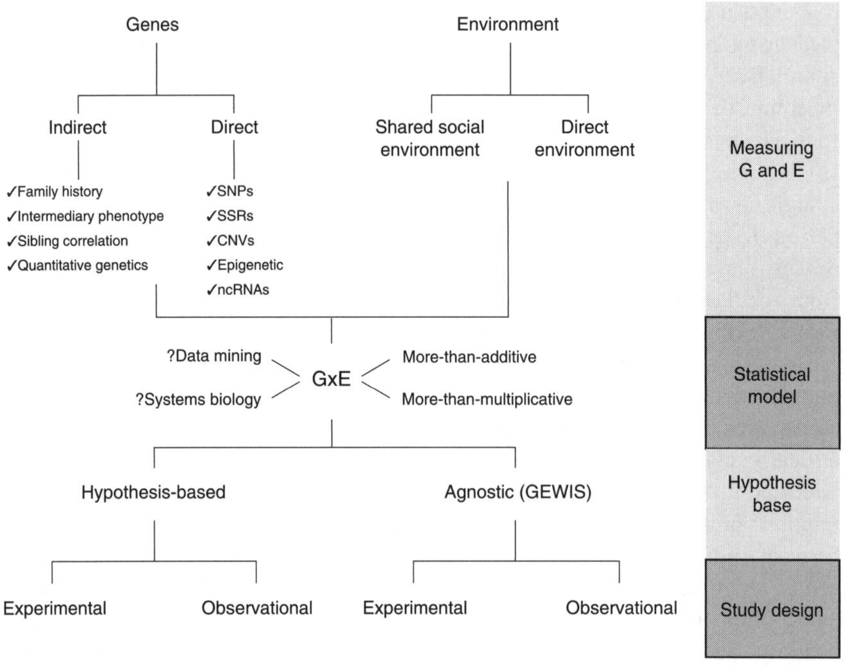

Figure 24.4 The different levels and axes of gene–environment interactions in psychiatry.

Conclusion

The study of G×E takes place along multiple axes and levels as depicted in Figure 24.4. The challenge in the years to come is to combine evidence from all levels and across all axes to build a consistent and replicable picture of the importance of gene–environment interactions in psychiatry. GEWIS are likely to become a main source of information on how gene–environment interplay influences onset and persistence of psychiatric morbidity in populations.

Acknowledgement

The work in our department described in this chapter can be traced to the extremely generous, inspirational—and continuing—direction by Professor Robin Murray.

References

Arendt, M., Mortensen, P. B., Rosenberg, R., Pedersen, C. B., & Waltoft, B. L. (2008). Familial predisposition for psychiatric disorder: Comparison of subjects treated for cannabis-induced psychosis and schizophrenia. *Archives of General Psychiatry*, *65*(11), 1269–1274.

Bossong, M. G., van Berckel, B. N., Boellaard, R., Zuurman, L., Schuit, R. C., Windhorst, A. D., et al. (2009). Delta 9-tetrahydrocannabinol induces dopamine release in the human striatum. *Neuropsychopharmacology*, *34*(3), 759–766.

Caspi, A., & Moffitt, T. E. (2006). Gene–environment interactions in psychiatry: Joining forces with neuroscience. *Nature Review Neuroscience*, *7*(7), 583–590.

Caspi, A., Moffitt, T. E., Cannon, M., McClay, J., Murray, R., Harrington, H., et al. (2005). Moderation of the effect of adolescent-onset cannabis use on adult psychosis by a functional polymorphism in the catechol-O-methyltransferase gene: Longitudinal evidence of a gene environment interaction. *Biological Psychiatry*, *57*(10), 1117–1127.

Clarke, M. C., Tanskanen, A., Huttunen, M., Whittaker, J. C., & Cannon, M. (2009). Evidence for an interaction between familial liability and prenatal exposure to infection in the causation of schizophrenia. *American Journal of Psychiatry*, *166*(9), 1025–1030.

Collip, D., Myin-Germeys, I., & van Os, J. (2008). Does the concept of "sensitization" provide a plausible mechanism for the putative link between the environment and schizophrenia? *Schizophrenia Bulletin*, *34*(2), 220–225.

Cougnard, A., Marcelis, M., Myin-Germeys, I., De Graaf, R., Vollebergh, W., Krabbendam, L., et al. (2007). Does normal developmental expression of psychosis combine with environmental risk to cause persistence of psychosis? A psychosis proneness-persistence model. *Psychological Medicine*, *37*(4), 513–527.

Csikszentmihalyi, M., & Larson, R. (1987). Validity and reliability of the Experience-Sampling Method. *Journal of Nervous and Mental Disease*, *175*(9), 526–536.

D'Souza, D. C., Abi-Saab, W. M., Madonick, S., Forselius-Bielen, K., Doersch, A., Braley, G., et al. (2005). Delta-9-tetrahydrocannabinol effects in schizophrenia: Implications for cognition, psychosis, and addiction. *Biological Psychiatry*, *57*(6), 594–608.

Dean, K., & Murray, R. M. (2005). Environmental risk factors for psychosis. *Dialogues in Clinical Neuroscience*, *7*(1), 69–80.

Dreher, J. C., Kohn, P., Kolachana, B., Weinberger, D. R., & Berman, K. F. (2009). Variation in dopamine genes influences responsivity of the human reward system. *Proceedings of the National Academy of Sciences of the United States of America*, *106*(2), 617–622.

EU-GEI. (2008). European Network of Schizophrenia Networks for the Study of Gene Environment Interactions. Schizophrenia aetiology: Do gene–environment interactions hold the key? *Schizophrenia Research*, *102*(1–3), 21–26.

Freeman, D., Slater, M., Bebbington, P. E., Garety, P. A., Kuipers, E., Fowler, D., et al. (2003). Can virtual reality be used to investigate persecutory ideation? *Journal of Nervous and Mental Disease*, *191*(8), 509–514.

Harley, M., Kelleher, I., Clarke, M., Lynch, F., Arseneault, L., Connor, D., et al. (2009). Cannabis use and childhood trauma interact additively to increase the risk of psychotic symptoms in adolescence. *Psychological Medicine*, 1–8.

Henquet, C., Krabbendam, L., Spauwen, J., Kaplan, C., Lieb, R., Wittchen, H. U., et al. (2005). Prospective cohort study of cannabis use, predisposition for psychosis, and psychotic symptoms in young people. *British Medical Journal*, *330*(7481), 11–15.

Henquet, C., Murray, R., Linszen, D., & van Os, J. (2005). The environment and schizophrenia: The role of cannabis use. *Schizophrenia Bulletin*, *31*(3), 608–612.

Henquet, C., Rosa, A., Delespaul, P., Papiol, S., Fananas, L., van Os, J., et al. (2009). COMT ValMet moderation of cannabis-induced psychosis: A momentary assessment study of "switching on" hallucinations in the flow of daily life. *Acta Psychiatrica Scandinavica*, *119*(2), 156–160.

Henquet, C., Rosa, A., Krabbendam, L., Papiol, S., Fananas, L., Drukker, M., et al. (2006). An experimental study of catechol-O-methyltransferase Val^{158}Met moderation of delta-

9-tetrahydrocannabinol-induced effects on psychosis and cognition. *Neuropsychopharmacology, 31*(12), 2748–2757.

Holmans, P., Green, E. K., Pahwa, J. S., Ferreira, M. A., Purcell, S. M., Sklar, P., et al. (2009). Gene ontology analysis of GWA study data sets provides insights into the biology of bipolar disorder. *American Journal of Human Genetics, 85*(1), 13–24.

Houston, J. E., Murphy, J., Adamson, G., Stringer, M., & Shevlin, M. (2008). Childhood sexual abuse, early cannabis use, and psychosis: Testing an interaction model based on the National Comorbidity Survey. *Schizophrenia Bulletin, 34*(3), 580–585.

Kapur, S. (2003). Psychosis as a state of aberrant salience: A framework linking biology, phenomenology, and pharmacology in schizophrenia. *American Journal of Psychiatry, 160*(1), 13–23.

Kendler, K. S., & Eaves, L. J. (1986). Models for the joint effect of genotype and environment on liability to psychiatric illness. *American Journal of Psychiatry, 143*(3), 279–289.

Kendler, K. S., & Prescott, C. A. (1998). Cannabis use, abuse, and dependence in a population-based sample of female twins. *American Journal of Psychiatry, 155*(8), 1016–1022.

Khoury, M. J., Beaty, T. H., & Cohen, B. H. (1993). *Genetic epidemiology*. Oxford, UK: Oxford University Press.

Khoury, M. J., & Wacholder, S. (2009). Invited commentary: From genome-wide association studies to gene–environment-wide interaction studies≤—Challenges and opportunities. *American Journal of Epidemiology, 169*(2), 227–230; discussion 234–235.

Konings, M. B., Bakoula, C., Henquet, C., De Graaf, R., Ten Have, M., van Os, J., et al. (2010). *Evidence from two prospective population-based studies that cannabis interacts with childhood trauma in causing psychosis*. Ms submitted for publication.

Kuepper, R., Morrison, P. D., van Os, J., Murray, R. M., Kenis, G., & Henquet, C. (2010). Does dopamine mediate the psychosis-inducing effects of cannabis? A review and integration of findings across disciplines. *Schizophrenia Research* [Epub before print] (doi S0920-9964(10)01352-6 [pii]10.1016/j.schres.2010.05.031)

Maher, B. (2008). Personal genomes: The case of the missing heritability. *Nature, 456*(7218), 18–21.

Mason, O., Morgan, C. J., Dhiman, S. K., Patel, A., Parti, N., & Curran, H. V. (2009). Acute cannabis use causes increased psychotomimetic experiences in individuals prone to psychosis. *Psychological Medicine, 39*(6), 951–956.

Moffitt, T. E., Caspi, A., & Rutter, M. (2005). Strategy for investigating interactions between measured genes and measured environments. *Archives of General Psychiatry, 62*(5), 473–481.

Molenaar, P. C. M., & Campbell, C. G. (2009). The new person-specific paradigm in psychology. *Current Directions in Psychological Science, 18*(2), 112–117.

Moore, T. H., Zammit, S., Lingford-Hughes, A., Barnes, T. R., Jones, P. B., Burke, M., et al. (2007). Cannabis use and risk of psychotic or affective mental health outcomes: A systematic review. *Lancet, 370*(9584), 319–328.

Morrison, P. D., Zois, V., McKeown, D. A., Lee, T. D., Holt, D. W., Powell, J. F., et al. (2009). The acute effects of synthetic intravenous Delta9-tetrahydrocannabinol on psychosis, mood and cognitive functioning. *Psychological Medicine, 39*(10), 1607–1616.

Moskvina, V., Craddock, N., Holmans, P., Nikolov, I., Pahwa, J. S., Green, E., et al. (2009). Gene-wide analyses of genome-wide association data sets: Evidence for multiple common risk alleles for schizophrenia and bipolar disorder and for overlap in genetic risk. *Molecular Psychiatry, 14*(3), 252–260.

Munafo, M. R., Brown, S. M., & Hariri, A. R. (2008). Serotonin transporter (5-HTTLPR) genotype and amygdala activation: A meta-analysis. *Biological Psychiatry, 63*(9), 852–857.

Murcray, C. E., Lewinger, J. P., & Gauderman, W. J. (2009). Gene–environment interaction in genome-wide association studies. *American Journal of Epidemiology*, *169*(2), 219–226.

Murray, R. M., Morrison, P. D., Henquet, C., & Di Forti, M. (2007). Cannabis, the mind and society: The hash realities. *Nature Review Neuroscience*, *8*(11), 885–895.

Myin-Germeys, I., Oorschot, M., Collip, D., Lataster, J., Delespaul, P., & van Os, J. (2009). Experience sampling research in psychopathology: Opening the black box of daily life. *Psychological Medicine*, *39*(9), 1533–1547.

Nesselroade, J. R., Gerstorf, D., Hardy, S. A., & Ram, N. (2007). Idiographic filters for psychological constructs. *Measurement*, *5*(4), 217–235.

Owen, M. J., Williams, H. J., & O'Donovan, M. C. (2009). Schizophrenia genetics: Advancing on two fronts. *Current Opinion in Genetics and Development*, *19*(3), 266–270.

Purcell, S. (2002). Variance components models for gene–environment interaction in twin analysis. *Twin Research*, *5*(6), 554–571.

Rabe-Hesketh, S., & Skrondal, A. (2008). *Multilevel and longitudinal modeling using Stata* (2nd ed.). College Station, TX: Stata Press.

Risch, N., Herrell, R., Lehner, T., Liang, K. Y., Eaves, L., Hoh, J., et al. (2009). Interaction between the serotonin transporter gene (5-HTTLPR), stressful life events, and risk of depression: A meta-analysis. *Journal of the American Medical Association*, *301*(23), 2462–2471.

Rutten, B. P., & Mill, J. (2009). Epigenetic mediation of environmental influences in major psychotic disorders. *Schizophrenia Bulletin*, *35*(6), 1045–1056.

Semple, D. M., McIntosh, A. M., & Lawrie, S. M. (2005). Cannabis as a risk factor for psychosis: Systematic review. *Journal of Psychopharmacology*, *19*(2), 187–194.

Suomi, S. J. (2006). Risk, resilience, and gene × environment interactions in rhesus monkeys. *Annals of the New York Academy of Sciences*, *1094*, 52–62.

van Os, J., Bak, M., Hanssen, M., Bijl, R. V., de Graaf, R., & Verdoux, H. (2002). Cannabis use and psychosis: A longitudinal population-based study. *American Journal of Epidemiology*, *156*(4), 319–327.

van Winkel, R., Henquet, C., Rosa, A., Papiol, S., Fananas, L., De Hert, M., et al. (2008). Evidence that the COMT(Val158Met) polymorphism moderates sensitivity to stress in psychosis: An experience-sampling study. *American Journal of Medical Genetics B, Neuropsychiatric Genetics*, *147B*(1), 10–17.

Voruganti, L. N., Slomka, P., Zabel, P., Mattar, A., & Awad, A. G. (2001). Cannabis induced dopamine release: An in-vivo SPECT study. *Psychiatry Research*, *107*(3), 173–177.

Weiser, M., van Os, J., Reichenberg, A., Rabinowitz, J., Nahon, D., Kravitz, E., et al. (2007). Social and cognitive functioning, urbanicity and risk for schizophrenia. *British Journal of Psychiatry*, *191*, 320–324.

Wichers, M., Aguilera, M., Kenis, G., Krabbendam, L., Myin-Germeys, I., Jacobs, N., et al. (2008). The catechol-O-methyl transferase Val^{158}Met polymorphism and experience of reward in the flow of daily life. *Neuropsychopharmacology*, *33*(13), 3030–3036.

Wichers, M., Myin-Germeys, I., Jacobs, N., Peeters, F., Kenis, G., Derom, C., et al. (2007). Genetic risk of depression and stress-induced negative affect in daily life. *British Journal of Psychiatry*, *191*, 218–223.

Wichers, M. C., Purcell, S., Danckaerts, M., Derom, C., Derom, R., Vlietinck, R., et al. (2002). Prenatal life and post-natal psychopathology: Evidence for negative gene–birth weight interaction. *Psychological Medicine*, *32*(7), 1165–1174.

Zammit, S., Spurlock, G., Williams, H., Norton, N., Williams, N., O'Donovan, M. C., et al. (2007). Genotype effects of CHRNA7, CNR1 and COMT in schizophrenia: Interactions with tobacco and cannabis use. *British Journal of Psychiatry*, *191*, 402–407.

Part VII

Treatment

25 How antipsychotics work

Examining trans-synaptic realities

Sridhar Natesan and Shitij Kapur

Introduction

The dopamine hypothesis of schizophrenia, modified since its initial version, has been the most defensible argument put forward in explaining the symptomatology of this chronic mental disorder (Carlsson & Lindqvist, 1963; Davis, Kahn, Ko, & Davidson, 1991; Howes & Kapur, 2009; Snyder, 1976; van, van der, & Hurkmans, 1962). The current hypothesis states that both subcortical hyperdopaminergia and cortical hypodopaminergia co-exist and these lead to the manifestation of both positive and negative symptoms, respectively. Although antipsychotic agents were initially discovered by serendipity, they fit into this hypothesis as they block the dopamine D2 receptors and thus inhibit excessive dopamine transmission in subcortical areas (Seeman, Chau-Wong, Tedesco, & Wong, 1975; Snyder, Creese, & Burt, 1975). However, the use of antipsychotics for over half a century has revealed their limitations: motor side effects, emergence of treatment resistance, lack of effects on negative symptoms and metabolic abnormalities (Kapur & Mamo, 2003). In this chapter, we discuss the history of antipsychotic discovery and how it led to understanding their mechanism of action, the role of dopamine D2 receptors, mismatch of treatment that is currently targeted at the wrong end of the synapse, and steps needed to be taken towards rational treatment.

History of antipsychotics and understanding their mechanism of action

Two key lines of investigation led to the appreciation of the mechanism of action of antipsychotics: understanding the effects of "neuroleptics", nerve calming agents used as adjuncts for anaesthetics, in contrast to the actions of reserpine; and understanding stimulant (amphetamine) induced psychosis. Converging evidence from these two streams formed the basis for the first postulates that were put forward in describing the mechanism of action of antipsychotics. It started when investigations into the tropical herb *Rauvolfia serpentina*, discovered in India, used for its calming effect in maniac symptoms led to the introduction of reserpine by Ciba laboratories in early 1950s for therapeutic use (Chopra, Gupta, & Mukherjee, 1933; Muller, Schlittler, & Bein, 1952). At the same time, the search for an antimalarial drug, which later turned into a search for better antihistamines, led to the discovery of chlorpromazine, which was launched as an antipsychotic by Rhône-Poulenc in 1952 (Baumeister & Francis, 2002). A notable feature of reserpine and chlorpromazine was that they produced a unique sedative action without the loss of consciousness and became the drugs of choice as a psychiatric "tranquillizer", also coined as "neuroleptics". It was the Nobel laureate Arvid Carlsson's seminal work soon after which recognized that "reserpine" depleted catecholamines and that its effects were reversed by L-dopa (Carlsson, Lindqvist, & Magnusson, 1957). Soon after, the discovery of high concentrations of dopamine in the corpus striatum led to the suggestion that dopamine played an important part in the extrapyramidal motor system and that its depletion causes hypoactivity, reversible by L-dopa (Bertler & Rosengren, 1959; Carlsson et al., 1957). At this time it was not clear how neuroleptic drugs were interfering with brain dopamine function, but the dopamine hypothesis for schizophrenia was being conceived based on anecdotal evidence (Van Rossum, 1966). Simultaneously, research on amphetamine was gaining ground and it was observed that schizophrenic patients who were abusing amphetamine presented the most florid symptoms and it was also possible to induce psychosis in normal subjects by administering amphetamine; a symptom that was blocked by haloperidol (Angrist, Lee, & Gershon, 1974; Ellinwood, 1968). At the same time, Randrup and Munkvad demonstrated that behavioural effects of amphetamines were dependent on the integrity of the dopamine system and were blocked by neuroleptic drugs, thus, providing converging evidence that brought together pathophysiology and therapeutics (Randrup & Munkvad, 1965, 1967).

It only became clear that the antipsychotic effects of neuroleptics were due to antagonism of dopamine receptors after their antipsychotic potency correlated with their affinity for dopamine receptors (Creese, Burt, & Snyder, 1976; Seeman et al., 1975). The success of chlorpromazine resulted in the introduction of nearly 40 more antipsychotics, most notably haloperidol, by the 1990s and the last of its class approved by the US Food and Drug Administration (FDA) was loxapine in 1975 (Shen, 1999). The introduction of clozapine to the US market in 1990 led to the advent of atypical (or second-generation) antipsychotics, primarily as clozapine had minimal extrapyramidal symptoms (EPS; Kane, Honigfeld, Singer, & Meltzer, 1988). Within ten years of clozapine's success, most of the currently used atypicals (having affinity to both dopamine D2 as well as serotonin 5-HT_2 receptors like clozapine) were introduced, namely olanzapine, risperidone and ziprasidone (Shen, 1999). Hence, what started as a chance discovery of a new drug by Rhône-Poulenc had led to better understanding of the disease process of schizophrenia. However, the repertoire of drugs available and currently used in the clinic is limited to blocking postsynaptic dopamine neurotransmission and does not meet clinical needs in their entirety; a subject that will be discussed later in the chapter.

It is clear now that there is no single gene or pathway for schizophrenia, and that a combination of multiple genetic and environmental risk factors lead to this illness (van Os & Kapur, 2009). Further, it is also clear that there is no single pathophysiology of this disorder. Schizophrenia is characterized by changes at the cellular-level organization of the brain and is accompanied by gross changes in cortical volume and distribution. At the same time there are neurochemical alterations in several systems with the abnormality in the dopamine system best understood and examined. However, as the history above highlights, it is not that the field knew that there was a dopaminergic dysfunction and devised rational treatments to address it; if anything, it was the opposite. The treatments came first and the rationale later. Now that we do know a lot about what is wrong with the dopamine system the rational approach towards treating schizophrenia is discussed later in the chapter.

What is wrong with dopamine transmission in schizophrenia?

Post-mortem neurochemical findings have been inconclusive as evidence for an increase in dopamine or its metabolites is lacking, however increased D2 receptor levels in the striatum has been a more consistent finding (Carlsson, Hansson, Waters, & Carlsson, 1997; Crow et al., 1979; Kleinman, Casanova, & Jaskiw, 1988; Zakzanis & Hansen, 1998). These observations are confounded with antipsychotic exposure, as we know from animal studies that chronic treatment can alter dopamine neurotransmission in a dynamic fashion (Burt, Creese, & Snyder, 1977; Samaha, Seeman, Stewart, Rajabi, & Kapur, 2007). However, there is considerable evidence from neuroimaging studies that supports the dopamine hypothesis. The studies demonstrating striatal hyperdopaminergia are clustered in three categories: first, baseline receptor density and dopamine levels; second, amphetamine induced dopamine release; and, finally, presynaptic striatal dopaminergic functioning. The trans-synaptic abnormalities are highlighted in Figure 25.1.

A vast majority of studies on striatal postsynaptic dopamine D2 receptor density measured using positron emission tomography (PET) or single photon emission computed tomography (SPECT) tracers [^{11}C]raclopride and [^{123}I]IBZM, respectively, have indicated a modest elevation in people with psychotic illness (Crawley et al., 1986; Farde et al., 1990; Laruelle, 1998; Wong et al., 1986). Their meaning is not exactly clear as these studies are confounded by the fact that most of them have been carried out during different stages of treatment and a very few are in antipsychotic-naïve patients. Baseline dopamine levels have been examined by depleting dopamine using alpha-methyl-para-tyrosine and a greater [^{123}I]IBZM binding indicated increased occupancy of dopamine receptors in first-episode patients as well as in chronic patients, immediately after an acute episode (Abi-Dargham et al., 2000). Studies on the dopamine transporter (using [^{18}F]CFT/[^{99m}Tc]TRODAT) have also indicated increased dopamine in the synapse in patients as well as in antipsychotic-naïve patients (Hsiao, Lin, Liu, Tzen, & Yen, 2003; Laakso et al., 2001). In summary, these studies indicate an increased receptor density or basal dopamine levels as a contributory factor.

Amphetamine induced dopamine release has been a useful tool in studying the responsiveness of the striatal dopaminergic system and it has been consistently found to be elevated during a psychotic episode as well as during antipsychotic

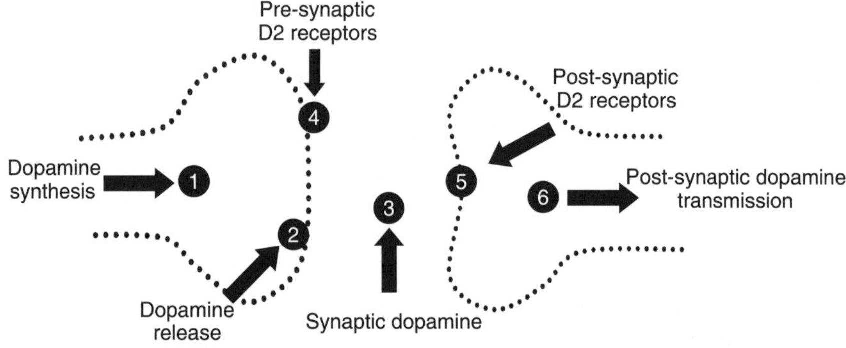

Figure 25.1 Trans-synaptic abnormalities in schizophrenia linked to dopamine transmission: ❶ increased striatal pre-synaptic dopamine synthesis as corroborated by functional imaging studies in which the uptake of labelled L-dopa is increased (observed in patients suffering from psychosis and in patients showing prodromal symptoms); ❷ increased striatal dopamine release due to amphetamine observed in patients; ❸ dopamine concentration in cortical synapses is regulated by COMT the enzyme that breaks down dopamine and polymorphism in its gene is linked with prefrontal cognitive disabilities; ❹ and ❺ striatal D2 receptor density measurements show elevation and could be caused by antipsychotic treatment but elevation of D1 receptor density in the prefrontal cortex is linked to cortical hypodopaminergia. ❻ Post-synaptic transmission mediated by a cascade of signalling molecules is susceptible to genetic polymorphism.

treatment (Abi-Dargham et al., 1998; Breier et al., 1997; Laruelle, Abi-Dargham, Gil, Kegeles, & Innis, 1999; Laruelle et al., 1996). Also, patients in remission have been shown to lack this increased release (Laruelle et al., 1999). It is also being proposed that patients with schizophrenia get sensitized with progressive episodes and show higher elevations of presynaptic striatal dopamine, which contributes to poorer clinical response as the disease progresses (Laruelle, 2000; Lieberman, Sheitman, & Kinon, 1997). Evidence from these studies points to intrinsic changes in the presynaptic terminals leading to altered striatal dopamine levels.

Presynaptic striatal dopaminergic functioning studies, commonly measured by measuring the uptake of [$^{\beta\text{-}11}$C]L-dopa or 6-[^{18}F]fluoro-L-dopa and accumulation of [^{11}C]dopamine or 6-[^{18}F]fluorodopamine after conversion by L-amino acid decarboxylase in vesicles of presynaptic dopamine neurons, have indicated elevated dopamine synthesis in acutely psychotic patients as well as in patients showing prodromal symptoms (Dao-Castellana et al., 1997; Elkashef et al., 2000; Hietala et al., 1995, 1999; Howes et al., 2009; Lindstrom et al., 1999; McGowan, Lawrence, Sales, Quested, & Grasby, 2004; Meyer-Lindenberg et al., 2002; Reith et al., 1994). The presynaptic functioning studies have been quite specific to patients suffering from psychosis and the findings are not observed in patients with other non-psychotic psychiatric illness (Ernst, Zametkin, Matochik, Pascualvaca, & Cohen, 1997; Parsey et al., 2001; Turjanski et al., 1994; Yatham et al., 2002). Thus, these studies prove that more dopamine is present in presynaptic terminals of patients with schizophrenia and is associated with disease morbidity.

The hypodopaminergia in the cortical regions associated with cognitive and negative symptoms, as per the dopamine hypothesis of schizophrenia, initially came from anecdotal evidence like measurements of blood flow while performing a task linked to frontal-lobe function largely because the dopaminergic innervation in this region is diffuse and fluorodopa signal is very weak (Ingvar & Franzen, 1974; McGowan et al., 2004; Weinberger, Berman, & Zec, 1986). The finding of a significant up-regulation of D1 receptor binding by the PET ligand [^{11}C] NNC112 in the prefrontal region in schizophrenic patients, which correlated with poor performance on the *n*-back task, hinted at a deficit of prefrontal dopamine function (Abi-Dargham, 2003). Though a direct biochemical marker has not been identified, poor performance on cognitive tasks linked to prefrontal activation has been correlated to increased presynaptic 6-[^{18}F]fluorodopamine signal in the striatum (McGowan et al., 2004).

The cause for such an abnormal dopamine transmission is not fully understood but a number of risk factors linked to genetic makeup, environment, and their interplay have been hypothesized to be causative of this disorder (van Os & Kapur, 2009). As mentioned earlier, the evidence from most imaging studies indicates that presynaptic functioning of the dopaminergic system is affected. The effect size and specificity of these findings is still very low for routine clinical investigation, however the role of a number of new factors that could contribute or potentiate the illness is increasing. An example of such a case is the polymorphism of the catechol-O-methyltransferase (COMT) genotype, an enzyme that metabolizes dopamine predominantly in the cortex where the dopamine transporter is expressed in low levels. When administered amphetamine, normal subjects who exhibit the Met/Met genotype (amino acid 158) in contrast to the Val/Val form exhibit slower dopamine metabolism and hence perform poorly on mental tasks that involve prefrontal regions (Meyer-Lindenberg et al., 2006); a deficit seen in schizophrenic patients. It is not clear what underlies the increased presynaptic dopamine in patients but it clearly has been linked to the cause of the disease.

Role of dopamine D2 receptors in antipsychotic action

To test the suggestion that antipsychotic drugs act by blocking dopamine receptors in the brain, Seeman et al. (1975) studied the direct effects of such neuroleptic drugs by testing the stereospecific binding of [^{3}H]dopamine and of [^{3}H]haloperidol to rat brain striata and their subfractions. The stereospecific component of binding was defined as that amount of [^{3}H]dopamine or [^{3}H]haloperidol bound in the presence of (–)-butaclamol (an inactive drug) minus that bound in the presence of (+)-butaclamol, a potent neuroleptic drug. Various antipsychotic drugs inhibited this stereospecific component in both the dopamine and haloperidol assays. These inhibitory potencies correlated with the clinical doses used for controlling schizophrenia, and this was the in vitro basis for attributing the role of dopamine receptors to antipsychotic action. Later, this receptor was identified as the D2 receptor subtype (Sibley & Monsma, 1992).

As antipsychotics were discovered serendipitously with the discovery of chlorpromazine, other drugs that followed mimicked chemical structures without knowing how they were acting (Horn & Snyder, 1971). The first in vivo studies in rodents mapped the distribution of these drugs in the brain (Janssen & Allewijn, 1969), these were followed by radiolabelled ligand-binding studies ([^{3}H] spiperone a dopamine antagonist), which identified the distribution of the receptor and also displaced antipsychotics in vivo in rats (Laduron, Janssen, & Leysen, 1978). Very early in the course of evaluating antipsychotics they were found to have a unique ability to suppress conditioned avoidance responses (CAR) selectively in rats without sedation (Cook & Catania, 1964). Even more so, preclinical studies showed that reserpine-induced suppression of CAR was reversed by L-dopa treatment (Seiden & Carlsson, 1963) and that the selective suppression of CAR by haloperidol was reversed by amantadine (Davies, Jackson, & Redfern, 1973); a drug that facilitates dopamine release. Also, the suppression of CAR by neuroleptics correlated well with the daily clinical doses of antipsychotics (Kuribara & Tadokoro, 1981). Given the fact that all clinically available antipsychotics are active in this animal model (Wadenberg & Hicks, 1999), the link between in vitro affinity for D2 receptors, and dose correlation of effectiveness in animal models, which corresponded to clinical doses, established the role of dopamine D2 receptors in antipsychotic action.

These results were further confirmed when PET imaging was used in human schizophrenic patients to identify the ideal percentage occupancy of striatal dopamine D2 receptor for antipsychotic action (Farde, Hall, Ehrin, & Sedvall, 1986; Kapur, Zipursky, Jones, Remington, & Houle, 2000). These studies showed that antipsychotic efficacy was obtained between 60–80% of D2 receptor occupancy and when occupancy exceeded 80% extrapyramidal side effects were observed. These findings were also translatable to rodent models (Kapur, VanderSpek, Brownlee, & Nobrega, 2003; Wadenberg, Soliman, VanderSpek, & Kapur, 2001). Two drugs, clozapine and seroquel, are often criticized for not achieving high levels of occupancy, but in contrast they do achieve high levels of occupancy, albeit for a very short period of time (Suhara et al., 2002; Tauscher-Wisniewski et al., 2002). The recently introduced drug aripiprazole, being a partial agonist, needs higher occupancy levels, indicating that the level of D2 receptor occupancy directly translates to functional antagonism depending on the nature of interaction with the receptor (Mamo et al., 2007; Natesan, Reckless, Nobrega, Fletcher, & Kapur, 2006). Since the introduction of clozapine, the concept of atypicality has evolved and new antipsychotics introduced after it was found to have high affinity for 5-HT_2 receptors (Meltzer, 1991); but with the clinical success of amisulpride (a selective D2 blocker), the role of 5-HT_2 antagonism is not clear (Kapur & Remington, 2001).

The late 1980s and early 1990s also saw the cloning of the dopamine receptor subtypes and led to the classification of D1-like (D1 & D5) versus D2-like

($D2_{short}$, $D2_{long}$, D3 and D4) receptors (Sibley & Monsma, 1992). Most antipsychotics had high affinity for the D2 receptor, but with the cloning of two new dopamine receptor subtypes D3 (Sokoloff, Giros, Martres, Bouthenet, & Schwartz, 1990) and D4 (Van Tol et al., 1991), associations were made about superior efficacy of antipsychotics having affinity to these receptors. However, the role of D4 receptors was ruled out as they lacked efficacy (Bristow et al., 1997) and it has been very difficult to find selective D3 ligands, though their role in the treatment of schizophrenia is being investigated (Sokoloff et al., 2006). It is a matter of curiosity that though all antipsychotics antagonize D2 receptors they vary in their liability for side effects. In preclinical studies, claims of regional specificity are made based on a differential effect of atypical antipsychotics on the "limbic" region (exemplified by the nucleus accumbens) versus motor or striatal regions (dorsolateral striatum). It has been suggested that because atypical antipsychotics have, in general, a lower affinity and faster dissociation from the D2 receptors, they may be more sensitive to endogenous dopamine (Kapur & Seeman, 2000). Also, as the levels of endogenous dopamine within the striatum vary, it is possible that this may account for the differential occupancy in the face of the same receptors and the same drug concentration (Lappin et al., 2009). However, until more definitive assessments of differential regional endogenous dopamine and differential occupancy are possible, the question will remain open as both the CATIE (Lieberman et al., 2005) and CUtLASS (Jones et al., 2006) trials have proven that typical and atypical antipsychotics are equally efficacious over time.

The other question that is commonly asked is whether one needs to treat patients continuously. The typical antipsychotics were associated with tardive dyskinesia (TD) and the acceptance for the newer antipsychotics under the premise that they were less likely to cause TD has led to chronic prescriptions, but, as CATIE and CUtLASS show, a majority of patients drop out after one year of treatment. This was exemplified in a recent rodent study where chronic administration of antipsychotics by osmotic pumps implanted subcutaneously resulted in loss of efficacy (Samaha et al., 2007, 2008). Also, with the emergence of weight gain, metabolic disorders, and lipid dysregulation being more evident with chronic antipsychotic dosing, work needs to be done to investigate whether intermittent dosing regimens could be helpful. A few preliminary studies give hope, especially the demonstration that extending the injection interval for fluphenazine decanoate from every 2 to 6 weeks did not compromise responses (Carpenter et al., 1999) and a pilot study that showed that extended (regular 2- to 3-day interval) dosing with antipsychotics may be sufficient to maintain response (Remington, Seeman, Shammi, Mann, & Kapur, 2005). In summary, there is good evidence that suggests a pivotal role for the dopamine D2 receptor in the action of antipsychotic drugs. However, the recent publication of a study by Patil et al. shows the first non-dopaminergic intervention that has worked since nearly half a century after the discovery of antipsychotic agents (Patil et al., 2007). This finding suggests that there are other pathways modulating the dysfunctional circuitry of the schizophrenic brain.

The grand "mismatch" and the dynamic reality of treatment

In spite of the fact that the first therapeutic agent (reserpine) targeted the presynaptic functioning of the dopaminergic system, schizophrenia treatment currently includes drugs that mainly block postsynaptic dopamine transmission. The consequence of D2 receptor antagonism results in motor side effects and eventually loss of efficacy most likely due to receptor up-regulation. The dynamics of treatment is much more complex. In an acute administration or during the early phase of chronic antipsychotic treatment there is increased presynaptic firing and an increased basal synaptic dopamine concentration, however, due to postsynaptic blockade the net transmission is blockaded (Anden, 1972; Grace & Bunney, 1986; Samaha et al., 2007). Clinically this means the onset of action is immediate and not delayed and recent studies have proved that this indeed occurs (Agid, Kapur, Arenovich, & Zipursky, 2003). However, chronic blockade also results in depolarization block of midbrain dopamine neurons resulting in decreased basal synaptic dopamine and this, coupled with postsynaptic blockade, results in up-regulation of dopamine D2 receptors and loss of efficacy (Chouinard, Jones, & Annable, 1978; Grace & Bunney, 1986; Samaha et al., 2007). In rodents, amphetamine-induced dopamine release is still intact in spite of chronic treatment and it is the tonic depolarization block, coupled with postsynaptic blockade, that results in D2 receptor up-regulation (an increase in the proportion of D2 high state), which essentially negates the drug-induced postsynaptic blockade (Samaha et al., 2007, 2008). An alternative idea that partial agonism, which in theory could decrease presynaptic dopamine synthesis and hence its release and postsynaptically could still maintain subdued neurotransmission, has been tested (Tamminga & Carlsson, 2002). However, success with partial agonists has been less forthcoming, with a lot of them not able to maintain efficacy over a longer period and the only successful partial agonist aripiprazole (which has very little partial agonism) is still in its infancy (Potkin et al., 2003; Tamminga, 2002). Therefore, instead of treating what is effectively a presynaptic dysfunction, blocking postsynaptic neurotransmission is a grand "mismatch" in the dynamics of antipsychotic treatment.

Towards rational treatment

The ideal scenario to treat schizophrenia, which essentially is a presynaptic dysregulation, is to modulate synaptic dopamine levels by presynaptic interventions. The proof of principle demonstrated in animal models as well as in human patients has been the case of reserpine and α-methyl-p-tyrosine (AMPT), both of which reduce catecholamine in presynaptic neurons (Carlsson, 1974). The problem with this class of drugs is that they decrease noradrenaline too, do not have regional specificity, and, hence, lead to other behavioural (e.g., depression) and autonomic function (e.g., blood pressure) disturbances (Carlsson, 1978). A few targets which indirectly affect presynaptic dopamine transmission are under development, notable among them being 5-HT_{2C} agonists (Di Matteo, De Blasi,

Di Giulio, & Esposito, 2001; Siuciak et al., 2007) and the glutamatergic drug $mGlu_{2/3}$ agonist (both class of agents are active in the rodent model of CAR; Patil et al., 2007). The significant findings are that they lack motor side effects and plasma prolactin elevation as seen with D2 receptor antagonists. $mGlu_{2/3}$ receptors are abundantly localized within forebrain regions including limbic structures, and they modulate glutamate transmission as autoreceptors located on glutamatergic terminals (Ohishi, Shigemoto, Nakanishi, & Mizuno, 1993a, 1993b). Microdialysis studies have revealed that they modulate glutamate release in the nucleus accumbens region and local application of selective $mGlu_{2/3}$ receptor agonists decreased extracellular dopamine levels in the nucleus accumbens shell while antagonists increase dopamine levels (Greenslade & Mitchell, 2004; Hu, Duffy, Swanson, Ghasemzadeh, & Kalivas, 1999). Although we have to learn more about its mechanism of action, a recent study by Seeman et al. has revealed that mice lacking $mGlu_{2/3}$ receptors have supersensitivity to dopaminergic agonists, indicating a modulatory role in dopamine neurotransmission. It remains to be seen if this class of drugs is useful for long-term treatments as tolerance to agonists is a common phenomenon and whether they are effective against negative and cognitive symptoms.

Summary

The introduction of antipsychotics in 1952 has not only defined the treatment of schizophrenia but also its theories. While there is no doubt that blocking DA transmission is an effective way to treat schizophrenia, it remains unclear whether we are indeed blocking the optimal end of the synapse. It seems increasingly likely that the primary dopamine dysfunction in schizophrenia may be presynaptic dopaminergic dysregulation, and, if this is the case, the focus needs to be on presynaptic modulation rather than postsynaptic blockade of its transmission. If the field is to make this switch we will need new animal models that replicate this pathophysiology, imaging techniques that can illustrate the defect, and methods to measure the effects of new drugs on the pathophysiology and relevant behaviours. It may turn out that the best way to treat the dopaminergic dysfunction in schizophrenia is not, as we have for the last 50 years, by blocking the postsynaptic receptors but by modulating the presynaptic synthesis and release.

References

Abi-Dargham, A. (2003). Probing cortical dopamine function in schizophrenia: What can D1 receptors tell us? *World Psychiatry*, *2*(3), 166–171.

Abi-Dargham, A., Gil, R., Krystal, J., Baldwin, R. M., Seibyl, J. P., Bowers, M., et al. (1998). Increased striatal dopamine transmission in schizophrenia: Confirmation in a second cohort. *The American Journal of Psychiatry*, *155*(6), 761–767.

Abi-Dargham, A., Rodenhiser, J., Printz, D., Zea-Ponce, Y., Gil, R., Kegeles, L. S., et al. (2000). Increased baseline occupancy of D_2 receptors by dopamine in schizophrenia. *Proceedings of the National Academy of Sciences of the United States of America*, *97*(14), 8104–8109.

Agid, O., Kapur, S., Arenovich, T., & Zipursky, R. B. (2003). Delayed-onset hypothesis of antipsychotic action: A hypothesis tested and rejected. *Archives of General Psychiatry*, *60*(12), 1228–1235.

Anden, N. E. (1972). Dopamine turnover in the corpus striatum and the lumbic system after treatment with neuroleptic and anti-acetylcholine drugs. *Journal of Pharmacy and Pharmacology*, *24*(11), 905–906.

Angrist, B., Lee, H. K., & Gershon, S. (1974). The antagonism of amphetamine-induced symptomatology by a neuroleptic. *The American Journal of Psychiatry*, *131*(7), 817–819.

Baumeister, A. A., & Francis, J. L. (2002). Historical development of the dopamine hypothesis of schizophrenia. *Journal of the History of the Neuroscience*, *11*(3), 265–277.

Bertler, A., & Rosengren, E. (1959). Occurrence and distribution of dopamine in brain and other tissues. *Experientia*, *15*(1), 10–11.

Breier, A., Su, T. P., Saunders, R., Carson, R. E., Kolachana, B. S., de Bartolomeis, A., et al. (1997). Schizophrenia is associated with elevated amphetamine-induced synaptic dopamine concentrations: Evidence from a novel positron emission tomography method. *Proceedings of the National Academy of Sciences of the United States of America*, *94*(6), 2569–2574.

Bristow, L. J., Kramer, M. S., Kulagowski, J., Patel, S., Ragan, C. I., & Seabrook, G. R. (1997). Schizophrenia and L-745,870, a novel dopamine D_4 receptor antagonist. *Trends in Pharmacological Sciences*, *18*(6), 186–188.

Burt, D. R., Creese, I., & Snyder, S. H. (1977). Antischizophrenic drugs: Chronic treatment elevates dopamine receptor binding in brain. *Science*, *196*(4287), 326–328.

Carlsson, A. (1974). Antipsychotic drugs and catecholamine synapses. *Journal of Psychiatry Research*, *11*, 57–64.

Carlsson, A. (1978). Antipsychotic drugs, neurotransmitters, and schizophrenia. *The American Journal of Psychiatry*, *135*(2), 165–173.

Carlsson, A., Hansson, L. O., Waters, N., & Carlsson, M. L. (1997). Neurotransmitter aberrations in schizophrenia: New perspectives and therapeutic implications. *Life Sciences*, *61*(2), 75–94.

Carlsson, A., & Lindqvist, M. (1963). Effect of chlorpromazine or haloperidol on formation of 3methoxytyramine and normetanephrine in mouse brain. *Acta Pharmacologica et Toxicologica (Copenhagen)*, *20*, 140–144.

Carlsson, A., Lindqvist, M., & Magnusson, T. (1957). 3,4-Dihydroxyphenylalanine and 5-hydroxytryptophan as reserpine antagonists. *Nature*, *180*(4596), 1200.

Carpenter, W. T., Jr., Buchanan, R. W., Kirkpatrick, B., Lann, H. D., Breier, A. F., & Summerfelt, A. T. (1999). Comparative effectiveness of fluphenazine decanoate injections every 2 weeks versus every 6 weeks. *The American Journal of Psychiatry*, *156*(3), 412–418.

Chopra, R. N., Gupta, J. C., & Mukherjee, B. (1933). The pharmacological action of an alkaloid obtained from *Rauwolfia serpentina* Benth. *Indian Journal of Medical Research*, *21*, 261–271.

Chouinard, G., Jones, B. D., & Annable, L. (1978). Neuroleptic-induced supersensitivity psychosis. *The American Journal of Psychiatry*, *135*(11), 1409–1410.

Cook, L., & Catania, A. C. (1964). Effects of drugs on avoidance and escape behavior. *Federation Proceedings*, *23*, 818–835.

Crawley, J. C., Owens, D. G., Crow, T. J., Poulter, M., Johnstone, E. C., Smith, T., et al. (1986). Dopamine D2 receptors in schizophrenia studied in vivo. *Lancet*, *2*(8500), 224–225.

Creese, I., Burt, D. R., & Snyder, S. H. (1976). Dopamine receptors and average clinical doses. *Science, 194*(4264), 546.

Crow, T. J., Baker, H. F., Cross, A. J., Joseph, M. H., Lofthouse, R., Longden, A., et al. (1979). Monoamine mechanisms in chronic schizophrenia: Post-mortem neurochemical findings. *British Journal of Psychiatry, 134*, 249–256.

Dao-Castellana, M. H., Paillere-Martinot, M. L., Hantraye, P., Attar-Levy, D., Remy, P., Crouzel, C., et al. (1997). Presynaptic dopaminergic function in the striatum of schizophrenic patients. *Schizophrenia Research, 23*(2), 167–174.

Davies, J. A., Jackson, B., & Redfern, P. H. (1973). The effect of anti-Parkinsonian drugs on haloperidol-induced inhibition of the conditioned-avoidance response in rats. *Neuropharmacology, 12*(8), 735–740.

Davis, K. L., Kahn, R. S., Ko, G., & Davidson, M. (1991). Dopamine in schizophrenia: A review and reconceptualization. *The American Journal of Psychiatry, 148*(11), 1474–1486.

Di Matteo, V., De Blasi, A., Di Giulio, C., & Esposito, E. (2001). Role of 5-HT(2C) receptors in the control of central dopamine function. *Trends in Pharmacological Sciences, 22*(5), 229–232.

Elkashef, A. M., Doudet, D., Bryant, T., Cohen, R. M., Li, S. H., & Wyatt, R. J. (2000). 6-(18)F-DOPA PET study in patients with schizophrenia. Positron emission tomography. *Psychiatry Research, 100*(1), 1–11.

Ellinwood, E. H., Jr. (1968). Amphetamine psychosis. II. Theoretical implications. *The International Journal of Neuropsychiatry, 4*(1), 45–54.

Ernst, M., Zametkin, A. J., Matochik, J. A., Pascualvaca, D., & Cohen, R. M. (1997). Low medial prefrontal dopaminergic activity in autistic children. *Lancet, 350*(9078), 638.

Farde, L., Hall, H., Ehrin, E., & Sedvall, G. (1986). Quantitative analysis of D_2 dopamine receptor binding in the living human brain by PET. *Science, 231*(4735), 258–261.

Farde, L., Wiesel, F. A., Stone-Elander, S., Halldin, C., Nordstrom, A. L., Hall, H., et al. (1990). D_2 dopamine receptors in neuroleptic-naive schizophrenic patients. A positron emission tomography study with [^{11}C]raclopride. *Archives of General Psychiatry, 47*(3), 213–219.

Grace, A. A., & Bunney, B. S. (1986). Induction of depolarization block in midbrain dopamine neurons by repeated administration of haloperidol: Analysis using in vivo intracellular recording. *Journal of Pharmacology and Experimental Therapeutics, 238*(3), 1092–1100.

Greenslade, R. G., & Mitchell, S. N. (2004). Selective action of (–)-2-oxa-4-aminobicyclo[3.1.0]hexane-4,6-dicarboxylate (LY379268), a group II metabotropic glutamate receptor agonist, on basal and phencyclidine-induced dopamine release in the nucleus accumbens shell. *Neuropharmacology, 47*(1), 1–8.

Hietala, J., Syvalahti, E., Vilkman, H., Vuorio, K., Rakkolainen, V., Bergman, J., et al. (1999). Depressive symptoms and presynaptic dopamine function in neuroleptic-naive schizophrenia. *Schizophrenia Research, 35*(1), 41–50.

Hietala, J., Syvalahti, E., Vuorio, K., Rakkolainen, V., Bergman, J., Haaparanta, M., et al. (1995). Presynaptic dopamine function in striatum of neuroleptic-naive schizophrenic patients. *Lancet, 346*(8983), 1130–1131.

Horn, A. S., & Snyder, S. H. (1971). Chlorpromazine and dopamine: Conformational similarities that correlate with the antischizophrenic activity of phenothiazine drugs. *Proceedings of the National Academy of Sciences of the United States of America, 68*(10), 2325–2328.

Howes, O. D., & Kapur, S. (2009). The dopamine hypothesis of schizophrenia: Version III—The final common pathway. *Schizophrenia Bulletin, 35*(3), 549–562.

Howes, O. D., Montgomery, A. J., Asselin, M. C., Murray, R. M., Valli, I., Tabraham, P., et al. (2009). Elevated striatal dopamine function linked to prodromal signs of schizophrenia. *Archives of General Psychiatry*, *66*(1), 13–20.

Hsiao, M. C., Lin, K. J., Liu, C. Y., Tzen, K. Y., & Yen, T. C. (2003). Dopamine transporter change in drug-naive schizophrenia: An imaging study with 99mTc-TRODAT-1. *Schizophrenia Research*, *65*(1), 39–46.

Hu, G., Duffy, P., Swanson, C., Ghasemzadeh, M. B., & Kalivas, P. W. (1999). The regulation of dopamine transmission by metabotropic glutamate receptors. *Journal of Pharmacology and Experimental Therapeutics*, *289*(1), 412–416.

Ingvar, D. H., & Franzen, G. (1974). Distribution of cerebral activity in chronic schizophrenia. *Lancet*, *2*(7895), 1484–1486.

Janssen, P. A., & Allewijn, F. T. (1969). The distribution of the butyrophenones haloperidol, trifluperidol, moperone, and clofluperol in rats, and its relationship with their neuroleptic activity. *Arzneimittelforschung*, *19*(2), 199–208.

Jones, P. B., Barnes, T. R., Davies, L., Dunn, G., Lloyd, H., Hayhurst, K. P., et al. (2006). Randomized controlled trial of the effect on quality of life of second- vs. first-generation antipsychotic drugs in schizophrenia: Cost Utility of the Latest Antipsychotic Drugs in Schizophrenia Study (CUtLASS 1). *Archives of General Psychiatry*, *63*(10), 1079–1087.

Kane, J., Honigfeld, G., Singer, J., & Meltzer, H. (1988). Clozapine for the treatment-resistant schizophrenic. A double-blind comparison with chlorpromazine. *Archives of General Psychiatry*, *45*(9), 789–796.

Kapur, S., & Mamo, D. (2003). Half a century of antipsychotics and still a central role for dopamine D_2 receptors. *Progress in Neuropsychopharmacology and Biological Psychiatry*, *27*(7), 1081–1090.

Kapur, S., & Remington, G. (2001). Dopamine D(2) receptors and their role in atypical antipsychotic action: Still necessary and may even be sufficient. *Biological Psychiatry*, *50*(11), 873–883.

Kapur, S., & Seeman, P. (2000). Antipsychotic agents differ in how fast they come off the dopamine D_2 receptors. Implications for atypical antipsychotic action. *Journal of Psychiatry and Neuroscience*, *25*(2), 161–166.

Kapur, S., VanderSpek, S. C., Brownlee, B. A., & Nobrega, J. N. (2003). Antipsychotic dosing in preclinical models is often unrepresentative of the clinical condition: A suggested solution based on in vivo occupancy. *Journal of Pharmacology and Experimental Therapeutics*, *305*(2), 625–631.

Kapur, S., Zipursky, R., Jones, C., Remington, G., & Houle, S. (2000). Relationship between dopamine D(2) occupancy, clinical response, and side effects: A double-blind PET study of first-episode schizophrenia. *The American Journal of Psychiatry*, *157*(4), 514–520.

Kleinman, J. E., Casanova, M. F., & Jaskiw, G. E. (1988). The neuropathology of schizophrenia. *Schizophrenia Bulletin*, *14*(2), 209–216.

Kuribara, H., & Tadokoro, S. (1981). Correlation between antiavoidance activities of antipsychotic drugs in rats and daily clinical doses. *Pharmacology Biochemistry and Behavior*, *14*(2), 181–192.

Laakso, A., Bergman, J., Haaparanta, M., Vilkman, H., Solin, O., Syvalahti, E., et al. (2001). Decreased striatal dopamine transporter binding in vivo in chronic schizophrenia. *Schizophrenia Research*, *52*(1–2), 115–120.

Laduron, P. M., Janssen, P. F., & Leysen, J. E. (1978). Spiperone: A ligand of choice for neuroleptic receptors. 2. Regional distribution and in vivo displacement of neuroleptic drugs. *Biochemical Pharmacology*, *27*(3), 317–321.

Lappin, J. M., Reeves, S. J., Mehta, M. A., Egerton, A., Coulson, M., & Grasby, P. M. (2009). Dopamine release in the human striatum: Motor and cognitive tasks revisited. *Journal of Cerebral Blood Flow and Metabolism*, *29*(3), 554–564.

Laruelle, M. (1998). Imaging dopamine transmission in schizophrenia. A review and meta-analysis. *Quarterly Journal of Nuclear Medicine*, *42*(3), 211–221.

Laruelle, M. (2000). The role of endogenous sensitization in the pathophysiology of schizophrenia: Implications from recent brain imaging studies. *Brain Research Reviews*, *31*(2–3), 371–384.

Laruelle, M., Abi-Dargham, A., Gil, R., Kegeles, L., & Innis, R. (1999). Increased dopamine transmission in schizophrenia: Relationship to illness phases. *Biological Psychiatry*, *46*(1), 56–72.

Laruelle, M., Abi-Dargham, A., van Dyck, C. H., Gil, R., D'Souza, C. D., Erdos, J., et al. (1996). Single photon emission computerized tomography imaging of amphetamine-induced dopamine release in drug-free schizophrenic subjects. *Proceedings of the National Academy of Sciences of the United States of America*, *93*(17), 9235–9240.

Lieberman, J. A., Sheitman, B. B., & Kinon, B. J. (1997). Neurochemical sensitization in the pathophysiology of schizophrenia: Deficits and dysfunction in neuronal regulation and plasticity. *Neuropsychopharmacology*, *17*(4), 205–229.

Lieberman, J. A., Stroup, T. S., McEvoy, J. P., Swartz, M. S., Rosenheck, R. A., Perkins, D. O., et al. (2005). Effectiveness of antipsychotic drugs in patients with chronic schizophrenia. *New England Journal of Medicine*, *353*(12), 1209–1223.

Lindstrom, L. H., Gefvert, O., Hagberg, G., Lundberg, T., Bergstrom, M., Hartvig, P., et al. (1999). Increased dopamine synthesis rate in medial prefrontal cortex and striatum in schizophrenia indicated by L-(beta-^{11}C) DOPA and PET. *Biological Psychiatry*, *46*(5), 681–688.

Mamo, D., Graff, A., Mizrahi, R., Shammi, C. M., Romeyer, F., & Kapur, S. (2007). Differential effects of aripiprazole on D(2), 5-HT(2), and 5-HT(1A) receptor occupancy in patients with schizophrenia: A triple tracer PET study. *The American Journal of Psychiatry*, *164*(9), 1411–1417.

McGowan, S., Lawrence, A. D., Sales, T., Quested, D., & Grasby, P. (2004). Presynaptic dopaminergic dysfunction in schizophrenia: A positron emission tomographic [^{18}F] fluorodopa study. *Archives of General Psychiatry*, *61*(2), 134–142.

Meltzer, H. Y. (1991). The mechanism of action of novel antipsychotic drugs. *Schizophrenia Bulletin*, *17*(2), 263–287.

Meyer-Lindenberg, A., Miletich, R. S., Kohn, P. D., Esposito, G., Carson, R. E., Quarantelli, M., et al. (2002). Reduced prefrontal activity predicts exaggerated striatal dopaminergic function in schizophrenia. *Nature Neuroscience*, *5*(3), 267–271.

Meyer-Lindenberg, A., Nichols, T., Callicott, J. H., Ding, J., Kolachana, B., Buckholtz, J., et al. (2006). Impact of complex genetic variation in COMT on human brain function. *Molecular Psychiatry*, *11*(9), 867–877.

Muller, J. M., Schlittler, E., & Bein, H. J. (1952). Reserpin, the sedative principle from *Rauwolfia serpentina* B. *Experientia*, *8*(9), 338.

Natesan, S., Reckless, G. E., Nobrega, J. N., Fletcher, P. J., & Kapur, S. (2006). Dissociation between in vivo occupancy and functional antagonism of dopamine D_2 receptors: Comparing aripiprazole to other antipsychotics in animal models. *Neuropsychopharmacology*, *31*(9), 1854–1863.

Ohishi, H., Shigemoto, R., Nakanishi, S., & Mizuno, N. (1993a). Distribution of the messenger RNA for a metabotropic glutamate receptor, $mGluR_2$, in the central nervous system of the rat. *Neuroscience*, *53*(4), 1009–1018.

Ohishi, H., Shigemoto, R., Nakanishi, S., & Mizuno, N. (1993b). Distribution of the mRNA for a metabotropic glutamate receptor ($mGluR_3$) in the rat brain: An in situ hybridization study. *Journal of Comparative Neurology*, *335*(2), 252–266.

Parsey, R. V., Oquendo, M. A., Zea-Ponce, Y., Rodenhiser, J., Kegeles, L. S., Pratap, M., et al. (2001). Dopamine D(2) receptor availability and amphetamine-induced dopamine release in unipolar depression. *Biological Psychiatry*, *50*(5), 313–322.

Patil, S. T., Zhang, L., Martenyi, F., Lowe, S. L., Jackson, K. A., Andreev, B. V., et al. (2007). Activation of mGlu2/3 receptors as a new approach to treat schizophrenia: A randomized Phase 2 clinical trial. *Nature Medicine*, *13*(9), 1102–1107.

Potkin, S. G., Saha, A. R., Kujawa, M. J., Carson, W. H., Ali, M., Stock, E., et al. (2003). Aripiprazole, an antipsychotic with a novel mechanism of action, and risperidone vs. placebo in patients with schizophrenia and schizoaffective disorder. *Archives of General Psychiatry*, *60*(7), 681–690.

Randrup, A., & Munkvad, I. (1965). Special antagonism of amphetamine-induced abnormal behaviour. Inhibition of stereotyped activity with increase of some normal activities. *Psychopharmacologia*, *7*(6), 416–422.

Randrup, A., & Munkvad, I. (1967). Brain dopamine and amphetamine-induced stereotyped behaviour. *Acta Pharmacologica et Toxicologica (Copenhagen)*, *25*(Suppl. 4), 62.

Reith, J., Benkelfat, C., Sherwin, A., Yasuhara, Y., Kuwabara, H., Andermann, F., et al. (1994). Elevated dopa decarboxylase activity in living brain of patients with psychosis. *Proceedings of the National Academy of Sciences of the United States of America*, *91*(24), 11651–11654.

Remington, G., Seeman, P., Shammi, C., Mann, S., & Kapur, S. (2005). "Extended" antipsychotic dosing: Rationale and pilot data. *Journal of Clinical Psychopharmacology*, *25*(6), 611–613.

Samaha, A. N., Reckless, G. E., Seeman, P., Diwan, M., Nobrega, J. N., & Kapur, S. (2008). Less is more: Antipsychotic drug effects are greater with transient rather than continuous delivery. *Biological Psychiatry*, *64*(2), 145–152.

Samaha, A. N., Seeman, P., Stewart, J., Rajabi, H., & Kapur, S. (2007). "Breakthrough" dopamine supersensitivity during ongoing antipsychotic treatment leads to treatment failure over time. *Journal Neuroscience*, *27*(11), 2979–2986.

Seeman, P., Chau-Wong, M., Tedesco, J., & Wong, K. (1975). Brain receptors for antipsychotic drugs and dopamine: Direct binding assays. *Proceedings of the National Academy of Sciences of the United States of America*, *72*(11), 4376–4380.

Seeman, P., Battaglia, G., Corti, M., & Bruno, V. (2009). Glutamate receptor mGlu2 and mGlu3 knockout striata are dopamine supersensitive, with elevated D2 (High) receptors and marked supersensitivity to the dopamine agonist (+) PHNO. *Synapses*, *63* (3), 247–251.

Seiden, L. S., & Carlsson, A. (1963). Temporary and partial antagonism by L-dopa of reserpine-induced suppression of a conditioned avoidance response. *Psychopharmacologia*, *4*, 418–423.

Shen, W. W. (1999). A history of antipsychotic drug development. *Comparative Psychiatry*, *40*(6), 407–414.

Sibley, D. R., & Monsma, F. J., Jr. (1992). Molecular biology of dopamine receptors. *Trends in Pharmacological Sciences*, *13*(2), 61–69.

Siuciak, J. A., Chapin, D. S., McCarthy, S. A., Guanowsky, V., Brown, J., Chiang, P., et al. (2007). CP-809,101, a selective $5\text{-}HT_{2C}$ agonist, shows activity in animal models of antipsychotic activity. *Neuropharmacology*, *52*(2), 279–290.

Snyder, S. H. (1976). The dopamine hypothesis of schizophrenia: Focus on the dopamine receptor. *The American Journal of Psychiatry*, *133*(2), 197–202.

Snyder, S. H., Creese, I., & Burt, D. R. (1975). The brain's dopamine receptor: Labeling with (3H) dopamine and (3H) haloperidol. *Psychopharmacology Communications*, *1*(6), 663–673.

Sokoloff, P., Diaz, J., Le Foll, B., Guillin, O., Leriche, L., Bezard, E., et al. (2006). The dopamine D_3 receptor: A therapeutic target for the treatment of neuropsychiatric disorders. *CNS and Neurological Disorders—Drug Targets*, *5*(1), 25–43.

Sokoloff, P., Giros, B., Martres, M. P., Bouthenet, M. L., & Schwartz, J. C. (1990). Molecular cloning and characterization of a novel dopamine receptor (D3) as a target for neuroleptics. *Nature*, *347*(6289), 146–151.

Suhara, T., Okauchi, T., Sudo, Y., Takano, A., Kawabe, K., Maeda, J., et al. (2002). Clozapine can induce high dopamine D(2) receptor occupancy in vivo. *Psychopharmacology (Berlin)*, *160*(1), 107–112.

Tamminga, C. A. (2002). Partial dopamine agonists in the treatment of psychosis. *Journal of Neural Transmission*, *109*(3), 411–420.

Tamminga, C. A., & Carlsson, A. (2002). Partial dopamine agonists and dopaminergic stabilizers, in the treatment of psychosis. *Current Drug Targets CNS and Neurological Disorders*, *1*(2), 141–147.

Tauscher-Wisniewski, S., Kapur, S., Tauscher, J., Jones, C., Daskalakis, Z. J., Papatheodorou, G., et al. (2002). Quetiapine: An effective antipsychotic in first-episode schizophrenia despite only transiently high dopamine-2 receptor blockade. *Journal of Clinical Psychiatry*, *63*(11), 992–997.

Turjanski, N., Sawle, G. V., Playford, E. D., Weeks, R., Lammerstma, A. A., Lees, A. J., et al. (1994). PET studies of the presynaptic and postsynaptic dopaminergic system in Tourette's syndrome. *Journal of Neurological and Neurosurgical Psychiatry*, *57*(6), 688–692.

van, R. J., van der, S. J., & Hurkmans, J. A. (1962). Mechanism of action of cocaine and amphetamine in the brain. *Experientia*, *18*, 229–231.

van Os, J., & Kapur, S. (2009). Schizophrenia. *Lancet*, *374*(9690), 635–645.

Van Rossum, J. M. (Ed.). (1966). *The significance of dopamine-receptor blockade for the action of neuroleptic drugs*. Amsterdam, The Netherlands: Excerpta Medica Foundation.

Van Tol, H. H., Bunzow, J. R., Guan, H. C., Sunahara, R. K., Seeman, P., Niznik, H. B., et al. (1991). Cloning of the gene for a human dopamine D_4 receptor with high affinity for the antipsychotic clozapine. *Nature*, *350*(6319), 610–614.

Wadenberg, M. L., & Hicks, P. B. (1999). The conditioned avoidance response test re-evaluated: Is it a sensitive test for the detection of potentially atypical antipsychotics? *Neuroscience and Biobehavioral Review*, *23*(6), 851–862.

Wadenberg, M. L., Soliman, A., VanderSpek, S. C., & Kapur, S. (2001). Dopamine D(2) receptor occupancy is a common mechanism underlying animal models of antipsychotics and their clinical effects. *Neuropsychopharmacology*, *25*(5), 633–641.

Weinberger, D. R., Berman, K. F., & Zec, R. F. (1986). Physiologic dysfunction of dorsolateral prefrontal cortex in schizophrenia. I. Regional cerebral blood flow evidence. *Archives of General Psychiatry*, *43*(2), 114–124.

Wong, D. F., Wagner, H. N., Jr., Tune, L. E., Dannals, R. F., Pearlson, G. D., Links, J. M., et al. (1986). Positron emission tomography reveals elevated D2 dopamine receptors in drug-naive schizophrenics. *Science*, *234*(4783), 1558–1563.

Yatham, L. N., Liddle, P. F., Shiah, I. S., Lam, R. W., Ngan, E., Scarrow, G., et al. (2002). PET study of [(18)F]6-fluoro-L-dopa uptake in neuroleptic- and mood-stabilizer-naive first-episode nonpsychotic mania: Effects of treatment with divalproex sodium. *The American Journal of Psychiatry*, *159*(5), 768–774.

Zakzanis, K. K., & Hansen, K. T. (1998). Dopamine D2 densities and the schizophrenic brain. *Schizophrenia Research*, *32*(3), 201–206.

26 Metabolic disturbance and schizophrenia

Emma Nicholson and David J. Castle

Introduction

In comparison to the general population, people with schizophrenia have poorer physical health and increased mortality. Their life expectancy is reduced by some 20%, and around 60% of the excess mortality is due to physical illness, primarily cardiovascular disease (Brown, Birtwistle, Roe, & Thompson, 1999; Newman & Bland, 1991). In fact, more premature deaths result from cardiovascular disease than suicide among patients with schizophrenia. The excess in early death is largely related to increased risk of metabolic disturbance including obesity, dyslipidaemia and diabetes. Lifestyle factors such as physical inactivity, unhealthy diets and high rates of smoking and alcohol use all contribute to the metabolic problems in this group. Iatrogenic factors are also pertinent. In particular, antipsychotic medications are known to cause metabolic disturbance and some of the atypical antipsychotics, now widely used in preference to typical agents, tend to have particularly problematic metabolic side effects. Patients with schizophrenia frequently take other medication including antidepressants and mood stabilizers, some of which are also associated with metabolic problems. Compounding this is the poor standard of medical care patients with schizophrenia receive due to barriers that include under utilization of medical services, therapeutic nihilism, and the separation of medical and mental-health care systems. This chapter reviews the metabolic problems associated with schizophrenia and provides an overview of a concerted service-based programme set up to tackle these problems.

Metabolic syndrome

Metabolic syndrome (MS) refers to a clustering of cardio-metabolic risk factors, which include abdominal obesity, hyperglycaemia, dyslipidaemia and hypertension. It has become the focus of increased attention in recent years. Various definitions exist, the best recognized being those of the 2005 International Diabetes Federation (IDF), which focuses on the importance of central obesity, and uses ethnicity-specific cut off points for waist circumference.

The prevalence of MS has been increasing and it is now estimated to affect 20–25% of the world's adult population. It is even more common in people with schizophrenia, affecting over a third of males and around 50% of females, with higher rates in the United States than in Europe (McEvoy et al., 2005). The significance of MS is that it identifies those at increased risk of developing diabetes and cardiovascular disease in the future. Those with metabolic syndrome are two to three times more likely to have a heart attack or stroke, and five times more likely to develop diabetes, than those without (Stern, Williams, Gomnzalez-Villalpando, Hunt, & Haffner, 2005). It is therefore essential that patients with schizophrenia receive appropriate monitoring and treatment of all components of metabolic syndrome.

Weight gain/obesity

Individuals with schizophrenia have metabolically unfavourable body compositions compared to the general population. They have been shown to have increased obesity and abdominal adiposity, higher proportional fat and lower muscle masses (Saarni et al., 2009). This is attributed to multiple factors including poor diet, sedentary lifestyle and antipsychotic medication, interacting with underlying genetic factors.

Obesity, defined by a body mass index (BMI) greater than 30 is a major health concern and is associated with excess disability and mortality.

$$\text{BMI} = \text{Weight (kg)}/\text{Height (m)}^2$$

Obesity, abdominal obesity in particular, results in insulin resistance, hypertension and dyslipidaemia, and leads to an increased risk of type II diabetes and cardiovascular disease. Obesity is also associated with a number of other illnesses including osteoarthritis, sleep apnoea and certain cancers especially endometrial, breast, and colon cancer (Visscher & Seidell, 2001).

Obesity produces negative psychological consequences for those with schizophrenia. Weight gain has been shown to be associated with poorer quality of life in individuals with schizophrenia; indeed, they appear more affected by their weight than the general population across a range of quality-of-life domains including physical function, self-esteem, public distress, and work function (Tham, Jones, Chamberlain, & Castle, 2007). Furthermore, weight gain is associated with non-adherence with antipsychotic medication among patients with schizophrenia. Obese patients are two and a half times more likely to report stopping their medication than those who are not obese (Weiden, Mackell, & McDonnell, 2004).

Individual antipsychotics vary widely in their potential to cause weight gain, reflecting their diversity of action across different neurotransmitter systems. A meta-analysis (Allison et al., 1999) estimated that over a 10-week period the mean weight change for specific atypical antipsychotics were—clozapine 4.45 kg, olanzapine 4.15 kg, sertindole 2.92 kg, risperidone 2.1 kg, and ziprasidone 0.04 kg. Some typical antipsychotics, notably thioridazine, also produced significant weight gain (3.19 kg). Mood stabilizers such as lithium and sodium valproate, and certain antidepressants (notably mirtazepine) are also associated with weight gain and these are frequently prescribed in addition to antipsychotics for patients with schizophrenia. It is unclear whether combining these medications with antipsychotics has an additive or synergistic effect on weight gain, or if there is a ceiling effect (Faulkner & Cohen, 2006).

Various underlying mechanisms for antipsychotic-induced weight gain have been proposed. Patients frequently describe increased appetite, reduced satiety, and changes in food preferences including carbohydrate craving while taking antipsychotic medication. Fatigue and sedation caused by antipsychotics may also lead to weight gain as a result of reduced energy expenditure. Histamine antagonism stimulates appetite and a number of atypical antipsychotics are H1 blockers. Serotonin (5-HT_{2C} receptor in particular), dopamine and noradrenaline antagonism are also thought to play a role. Prolactin is believed to stimulate feeding centres in the brain, however the atypical antipsychotics that produce the most weight gain (clozapine and olanzapine) tend to only cause mild and transient prolactin elevation in comparison to other atypical antipsychotics (Dickson & Glazer, 1999). The peptide leptin has become a focus of recent research into obesity. It is released by adipose cells and acts on the hypothalamus modulating appetite, metabolism and the neuroendocrine axis. Antipsychotics such as clozapine and olanzapine have been shown to raise leptin levels; however, these rises in leptin may be secondary to weight gain (Stanton, 1995).

Several studies have identified factors that appear to influence antipsychotic-induced weight gain. The risk of weight gain appears to be increased in patients who are younger, and those with baseline "normal weight" (Wetterling & Mubigbrodt, 1999). The relative risk of gender is unclear as studies looking at sex have been contradictory (McIntyre, McCann, & Kennedy, 2001). Interestingly, there appears to be a positive association between weight gain and antipsychotic response for a number of antipsychotics including olanzapine and clozapine (Meltzer, Perry, & Jayathilake, 2003). Some patients appear to be more biologically prone to antipsychotic-induced weight gain and hence the pharmacogenetics of antipsychotic-induced weight gain has recently become an area of interest. For example a 5-HT_{2C} receptor promoter region polymorphism is strongly associated with increased weight gain and metabolic syndrome in patients on antipsychotic medication (Reynolds, Zhang, & Zhang, 2002).

High rates of obesity in the general population indicate that losing weight and maintaining weight loss is extremely difficult. It is particularly challenging for those with schizophrenia who may be impaired by negative symptoms such as amotivation. As a result, strategies to prevent antipsychotic-induced weight gain such as appropriate antipsychotic choice, warning patients about weight gain, and providing dietary and exercise advice are very important. Weight, BMI and waist circumferences should be regularly monitored. In patients with schizophrenia waist circumference has been shown to be a better indicator of cardiovascular risk factors and hence need for weight management than other measures such as BMI (Kato, Currier, & Villaverde, 2005). Figure 26.1 illustrates a form that allows longitudinal collection of such data, with suggested time intervals: these can be adjusted according to individual requirements.

StV

ST VINCENT'S MENTAL HEALTH

METABOLIC MONITORING

INSTRUCTIONS FOR USE:

- *This form should be used for all patients on antipsychotics or mood stabilisers. It is suggested pertinent positive or negative results are documented in the boxes.*
- *Clozapine: This form is to be used only after the first 18 weeks.*
- *An authorised signed entry to be completed in the medical record progress notes for each measure on each occasion.*
- *Filing: this form should be filed in the Mental Health forms section of the record in order of most recent date of entry.*

UR No.:________

Surname:________

Given Name:________

D.O.B.:________

Please fill in if no Patient Label available

Rapid No.		Base Date	3 Months	6 Months	12 Months	18 Months	24 Months	30 Months	36 Months
INSERT RESULT IN EACH CELL		..../..../....	..../..../....	..../..../....	..../..../....	..../..../....	..../..../....	..../..../....	..../..../....
Metabolic (for ***all*** patients on antipsychotics and mood stabilisers)	Height								
	Weight (in kg)								
	BMI = weight in kg by height in m2.								
	Waist								
	Blood Pressure								
	Fasting Blood Glucose								
	Lipids (Chol, LDL, HDL, TG)								
	LFT								
	U&E								
Lithium	TFT								
	Lithium Level								
Sodium Valproate	FBE								
	Valproate Level								
Carbamazepine	FBE								
	Carbamazepine Level								
Clozapine *Note: FBE as per Clozapine protocol*	ECG								
	Echocardiogram								
	Troponin I/CK								
	Clozapine Level								
Prolactin elevating antipsychotics	Prolactin Level								
For patients on QTc prolonging antipsychotics	ECG								
Print name & signature of doctor completing this collection occasion:									

ST. VINCENT'S MENTAL HEALTH – METABOLIC MONITORING FORM

Figure 26.1 St Vincent's Mental Health metabolic monitoring form.

Once weight gain has occurred, switching a patient's antipsychotic to one with a more favourable metabolic profile has been shown to be an effective weight-loss strategy (Weiden, 2007). This strategy risks worsening of psychiatric symptomatology and needs to performed in a carefully controlled manner, with appropriate psychoeducation and risk discussion with the patient. There is evidence that antipsychotic-induced weight gain can be ameliorated by lifestyle changes including dietary modification and increased exercise (Sharpe & Hills, 2003). There are a number of systematic reviews examining behavioural interventions in patients with schizophrenia. One review by Loh and colleagues identified 23 such studies, 19 of which resulted in weight loss, however the effect sizes were generally modest and the authors concluded that many of the studies had flawed methodology (Loh, Meyer, & Leekband, 2006).

While there are a number of pharmacological strategies to treat obesity in the general population, these medications have not been widely assessed in patients with schizophrenia, and most have potential psychiatric side effects. Orlistat, a lipase inhibitor which reduces the absorption of dietary fats, is likely to be beneficial, however the dietary restrictions required are often difficult to adhere to, especially for people with schizophrenia. Topiramate, an anticonvulsant, has been shown to produce weight loss in antipsychotic-associated weight gain in two randomized controlled trials (RCTs; Ko, Joe, Jung, & Kim, 2005; Nickel et al., 2005). Sibutramine, an effective weight-loss medication in the general population, is a serotonin and noradrenaline reuptake inhibitor that acts centrally to reduce appetite. Its safety and efficacy has not been adequately studied in psychiatric populations and its use may be limited in this group as case reports suggest that it may cause psychosis and mania (Cordeiro, & Vallada, 2002; Taflinski & Chojnacka, 2000). Metformin, an oral hypoglycaemic agent, has been shown to be effective in attenuating antipsychotic-induced weight gain in adolescents and children (Klein, Cottingham, Sorter, Barton, & Morrison, 2006), however the few small studies in adults have been less conclusive (Baptista et al., 2006, 2007). Rimonabant, a cannabinoid CB1 receptor antagonist, showed promise as a weight-loss medication in non-psychiatric populations, but its depressogenic side effects resulted in its withdrawal from the market; further studies of cannabinoid receptor blockers in obesity would seem warranted. Bariatric surgical procedures have been little used in patients with schizophrenia and, again, the dietary restrictions could be particularly problematic for this group.

Dyslipidaemia

Patients with schizophrenia appear to have a naturally higher risk of dyslipidaemia (Osby, Correia, & Brandt, 2000) and their antipsychotic medications can also cause lipid abnormalities. Clozapine and olanzapine are strongly implicated and have been shown to raise low density lipoprotein (LDL) and triglycerides, and lower high density lipoprotein (HDL). In one study, after 12 weeks of olanzapine treatment the triglyceride levels of 25 patients with schizophrenia rose by 37%

(Osser, Najarian, & Dufresne, 1999). Other antipsychotics such as aripiprazole, ziprasidone and amisulpride do not appear to cause significant lipid changes (Rettenbacher et al., 2006).

Weight gain is believed to be the main mechanism for the dyslipidaemia that develops in patients commenced on atypical antipsychotics. Abdominal adiposity promotes the release of free fatty acids in the liver, increasing liver triglyceride synthesis and very-low-density lipoprotein secretion. A statistically significant relationship has been found between the increase in cholesterol caused by olanzapine and weight gain (Kinon, Basson, Gilmore, & Tollefson, 2001). However, lipid abnormalities may rise very early in treatment before significant weight gain has occurred, and may reverse before weight loss if the medication is ceased. Furthermore, a number of patients develop lipid abnormalities in the absence of significant weight gain suggesting that some antipsychotics may have direct and immediate effects on lipid levels beyond obesity effects (De Leon et al., 2007). Genetic differences are believed to play an important role in determining individual susceptibility.

The successful treatment of dyslipidaemia is essential, as reducing cholesterol by 10% may result in a 30% reduction in cardiovascular disease risk (Hennekens, Hennekens, Hollar, & Casey, 2005). If dietary modification is not effective, lipid-lowering medication such as statins have been shown to be effective in treating dyslipidaemia in patients with schizophrenia, and should be strongly considered (De Hert et al., 2006).

Hyperglycaemia/diabetes

Type II diabetes is a chronic disease diagnosed by a repeat fasting glucose ≥7 mmol/l or random glucose ≥11.1. It is caused by a combination of insulin resistance and insufficient insulin production to meet the body's requirements. The prevalence of type II diabetes is rapidly increasing in the general population and is two to four times higher in people with schizophrenia (American Diabetes Association, 2004). Diabetes is associated with high morbidity and mortality from macrovascular complications including cardiovascular disease, stroke and peripheral vascular disease, and microvascular disease such as retinopathy and renal impairment.

The nature of the relationship between type II diabetes and schizophrenia is complicated. While the evidence has been largely based on retrospective studies that have not controlled for important confounders, schizophrenia appears to be an independent risk factor for diabetes (Ryan, Collins, & Thakore, 2003). An association between the two conditions was first recognized in the pre-antipsychotic era, and patients with schizophrenia are three times more likely to have a family history of diabetes than the general population (Lambert & Newcomer, 2009). Patients with schizophrenia also have multiple other lifestyle risk factors for diabetes including high rates of obesity, poor diets, and sedentary lifestyles. To add complexity, psychotic stress appears to lead to transient changes in glucose and insulin levels (Shiloah et al., 2003).

Both typical and atypical antipsychotics are associated with an increased risk of diabetes. Atypical antipsychotics (in particular clozapine and olanzapine) appear to confer the greatest risk (Smith et al., 2008), however some of this apparent increase may be due to increased detection, as those taking atypical antipsychotics tend to have more screening. It is not clear whether antipsychotics simply exacerbate pre-existing subthreshold glucose abnormalities, or whether they can disrupt a normal glucose homeostatic system. Most atypical antipsychotics are associated with weight gain, which is itself a significant risk factor for type II diabetes as it leads to insulin resistance. Another postulated mechanism for antipsychotic-induced hyperglycaemia is that blockade of serotonin 5-HT_{1A} receptors reduces the response of pancreatic β-cells.

There are a number of case reports of patients taking atypical antipsychotics where life-threatening diabetic ketoacidosis (DKA) or pancreatitis was the presenting symptom of their diabetes. This presentation usually occurs within the first 3–6 months of treatment and has primarily been associated with olanzapine and clozapine use (Jin, Meyer, & Jeste, 2002).

When commencing antipsychotic medication it is essential to regularly screen for diabetes to ensure early detection and minimize complications. Patients and their families should also be made aware of possible symptoms of diabetes such as lethargy, polyuria and polydipsia. As a minimum, regular fasting blood glucose levels should be monitored. The oral glucose tolerance test, however, has been shown to be more sensitive in detecting early diabetes and impaired glucose tolerance in those taking antipsychotic medication (Subramaniam, Chong, & Pek, 2003). General evidence indicates that people with pre-diabetes can delay or reduce the risk of developing type II diabetes by adopting lifestyle changes. Metformin has been shown to improve insulin sensitivity, glucose, and HbA1C in patients with schizophrenia and could be considered for diabetes prevention in those at very high risk (De Hert et al., 2009).

Hypertension

Hypertension, defined as blood pressure of 140/90 mmHg or above recorded on at least two occasions, is common in patients with schizophrenia due to multiple risk factors including obesity, physical inactivity, and smoking. With the possible exception of clozapine, antipsychotics are not believed to increase blood pressure directly (Henderson et al., 2004). In fact, most antipsychotics cause orthostatic hypotension, especially during initiation, as a result of blockade of α-adrenergic receptors. Over time, however, antipsychotic-induced weight gain may eventually contribute to hypertension.

It is important to monitor and assertively treat hypertension as it is a significant and readily modifiable risk factor in the development of cardiovascular disease. Antihypertensive therapy has been shown to be associated with a 20–25% reduction in the incidence of myocardial infarction and a 35–40% reduction in stroke (Neal, MacMahon, & Chapman, 2000).

Smoking

The prevalence of cigarette smoking among people with schizophrenia is extremely high: up to 70% in some samples (Brown et al., 1999). While smoking rates have been steadily falling in the general community it seems that patients with schizophrenia have not heeded the public health campaign to quit smoking (Polgar, McGartland, & Hales, 1996). Reasons for this are complex, and include social factors, but there is also evidence to suggest they self-medicate with nicotine to improve cognitive deficits and reduce some side effects of antipsychotic medication (Forchuk et al., 2002).

There are a number of strategies to assist with smoking cessation including education/support programmes, and a variety of forms of nicotine replacement therapy (NRT). It is essential that these options are offered to patients with schizophrenia as stopping smoking will dramatically reduce their risk of cancers, in particular lung cancer, and may reduce cardiovascular risk by up to 50% (British Cardiac Society, 1998). However, existing programmes for smoking cessation are often not well suited to people with schizophrenia and need to be tailored to their needs to be effective (Baker et al., 2009). Also, the most commonly used pharmacological agent to assist smoking cessation, NRT, is associated with only modest success in the schizophrenia population (Addington, El-Guebaly, Cambell, Hodgins, & Addington, 1998). Placebo controlled trials of another agent bupropion have demonstrated that while it is initially effective, there is substantial relapse to smoking within 6 months (George et al., 2002). One novel agent is the nicotinic receptor partial agonist–antagonist varenicline, which has been associated with depression and suicidality in the general population (Food and Drug Administration, 2008) and exacerbation of psychosis in a patient with schizophrenia (Freedman, 2007), but which is an effective antismoking agent that deserves formal study in patients with schizophrenia.

Addressing metabolic disturbance in patients with schizophrenia

In recent years there has been increased awareness among clinicians of the elevated metabolic risk among patients with schizophrenia. In a postal survey, 97% of psychiatrists rated cardio-metabolic monitoring as a “very serious” or a “serious” concern when prescribing antipsychotics (Buckley, Miller, Singer, Arena, & Stirewalt, 2005). Unfortunately this has largely not yet translated into a significant improvement in clinical practice. Thus, a survey of US psychiatrists indicated that 65–75% of schizophrenia patients had not had regular glucose and lipid monitoring and 25% were not regularly weighed, while 95% were not having their waist circumference measured despite it being a very good predictive tool for the later development of cardiac disease and diabetes (Buckley et al., 2005).

Rates of treatment of metabolic disturbance also remain low among patients with schizophrenia. The CATIE (Clinical Antipsychotic Trials in Intervention Effectiveness) study showed a lack of appropriate treatment in 30% of those with diabetes, 88% of those with dyslipidaemia, and 62% of those with hypertension (Nasrallah et al., 2006).

New strategies are clearly required to adequately address metabolic problems in patients with schizophrenia. The following approach was undertaken by St Vincent's Mental Health in Victoria, Australia, to improve the physical health of their patients.

1 An evidence-based set of metabolic monitoring guidelines were produced for use within the service. These were incorporated into a form in the patient's file to record the results longitudinally (see Figure 26.1).
2 A staff survey highlighted some of the barriers to metabolic monitoring including limited knowledge, lack of access to equipment, and confusion about individual responsibility. As a result, staff were provided with education, educational materials, additional monitoring equipment, and a letter proforma to facilitate communication with general practitioners. To ensure monitoring was being undertaken, regular audits have been undertaken and results fed back to staff.
3 As part of a multi-site collaboration, a pilot study was undertaken to assess the feasibility of a multi-component intervention to promote smoking cessation and change in BMI among people with psychosis. Forty-three patients were provided with education about diet, exercise and smoking cessation, in conjunction with cognitive-behaviour therapy (CBT; motivational interviewing) and NRT. The intervention resulted in a significant decrease in smoking from 30.8 to 17.2 cigarettes per day, a non-significant decrease in weight from 101 kg to 99 kg and a significant reduction in overall coronary risk percentile (Baker et al., 2009).

Conclusions

Patients with schizophrenia have a significantly elevated risk of metabolic disturbance and cardiovascular disease as a result of their lifestyles and medication. Their increased morbidity and dramatically reduced life expectancy due to physical illness is unacceptable and needs to be urgently addressed. Psychoeducation, including dietary and exercise advice, should be routinely provided to all patients with schizophrenia. It is essential that clinicians consider the metabolic side-effect profile of antipsychotics in conjunction with the patient's past medical history and family medical history when prescribing. Once a patient has developed metabolic disturbance consideration needs to be given to switching antipsychotic medication to a more metabolically benign agent, initiating interventions to increase physical activity, improve diet, and reduce weight, and where necessary commence appropriate medication such as statins.

Fortunately, new antipsychotics are being developed with more favourable metabolic profiles. Increased research in the field of pharmacogenomics is expected to enable clinicians to identify those at high risk of antipsychotic-related metabolic disturbance and therefore better target antipsychotic medication to the individual patient (Basile et al., 2001).

References

Addington, J., El-Guebaly, N., Cambell, W., Hodgins, D., & Addington, D. (1998). Smoking cessation treatment for patients with schizophrenia. *American Journal of Psychiatry*, *155*, 974–976.

Allison, D. B., Mentore, J. L., Heo, M., Chandler, L. P., Cappelleri, J. C., Infante, M. C., et al. (1999). Antipsychotic-induced weight gain: A comprehensive research synthesis. *American Journal of Psychiatry*, *156*(11), 1686–1696.

American Diabetes Association. (2004). Consensus development conference on antipsychotic drugs and obesity and diabetes. *Obesity Research*, *12*, 362–368.

Baker, A., Richmond, R., Castle, D., Kulkarni, J., Kay-Lambkin, F., Sakrouge, R., et al. (2009). Coronary heart disease risk reduction intervention among overweight smokers with a psychotic disorder: Pilot trial. *Australian and New Zealand Journal of Psychiatry*, *43*, 129–135.

Baptista, T., Martinez, J., Lacruz, A., Rangel, N., Beaulieu, S., Serrano, A., et al. (2006). Metformin for prevention of weight gain and insulin resistance with olanzapine: A double-blind placebo-controlled trial. *Canadian Journal of Psychiatry*, *51*, 192–196.

Baptista, T., Rangel, N., Fernandez, V., Carrizo, E., El Fakih, Y., Uzcategui, H., et al. (2007). Metformin as an adjunctive treatment to control body weight and metabolic dysfunction during olanzapine administration: A multicentric, double-blind, placebo-controlled trial. *Schizophrenia Research*, *93*, 99–108.

Basile, V. S., Masellis, M., McIntyre, R. S., Meltzer, H. Y., Lieberman, J. A., & Kennedy, J. L. (2001). Genetic dissection of atypical antipsychotic-induced weight gain: Novel preliminary data on the pharmacogenetic puzzle. *Journal of Clinical Psychiatry*, *62*(Suppl. 23), 45–65.

British Cardiac Society. (1998). Joint British recommendations on prevention of coronary heart disease in clinical practice. *Heart*, *80*(Suppl. 2), 1–29.

Brown, S., Birtwistle, J., Roe, L., & Thompson, C. (1999). The unhealthy lifestyle of people with schizophrenia. *Psychological Medicine*, *29*, 697–701.

Buckley, P. F., Miller, D. D, Singer, B., Arena, J., & Stirewalt, E. (2005). Clinicians' recognition of the metabolic adverse effects of antipsychotic medications. *Schizophrenia Research*, *79*, 281–288.

Cordeiro, Q., & Vallada, H. (2002). Sibutramine induced manic episode in a bipolar patient. *International Journal of Neuropsychopharmacology*, *5*, 283–284.

De Hert, M., Dekker, J., Wood, D., Kahl, K., Holt, R., & Moller, H. (2009). Cardiovascular disease and diabetes in people with severe mental illness: Position statement from the European Psychiatric Association (EPA), supported by the European Association for the Study of Diabetes (EASD) and the European Society of Cardiology (ESC). *European Psychiatry*, *24*, 412–424.

De Hert, M., Kalnicka, D., Van Winkel, R. M., Wampers, M., Hanssens, L., Van Eyck, D., et al. (2006). Treatment with rosuvastatin for severe dyslipidaemia in patients with schizophrenia and schizoaffective disorder. *Journal of Clinical Psychiatry*, *67*, 1889–1896.

De Leon, J., Susce, M. T., Johnson, M., Hardin, M., Pointer, L., Ruano, G., et al. (2007). A clinical study of the association of antipsychotics with hyperlipidaemia. *Schizophrenia Research*, *92*, 95–102.

Dickson, R. A., & Glazer W. M. (1999). Neuroleptic-induced hyperprolactinaemia. *Schizophrenia Research*, *35*(Suppl. 1), S75–S86.

Faulkner, G., & Cohen, T. A. (2006). Pharmacologic and non-pharmacologic strategies for weight gain and metabolic disturbance in patients treated with antipsychotic medications. *Canadian Journal of Psychiatry*, *51*(8), 502–11.

Food and Drug Administration. (2008). *Information for healthcare professionals: Varenicline*. (Available at: http://www.fda.gov/Drugs/DrugSafety/PostmarketDrugSafety InformationforPatientsandProviders/ucm124818.htm)

Forchuk, C., Norman, R., Malla, A., Martin, M., McLean, T., Cheng, S., et al. (2002). Schizophrenia and motivation for smoking. *Perspectives in Psychiatric Care*, *38*(2), 41–48.

Freedman, R. (2007). Exacerbation of schizophrenia by varenicline. *American Journal of Psychiatry*, *164*(8), 1269.

George, T. P., Vessicchio, J. C., Termine, A., Bregartner, T. A., Feingold, A., Rounsaville, B. J., et al. (2002). A placebo controlled trial of buproprion for smoking cessation in schizophrenia. *Biological Psychiatry*, *52*(1), 53–61.

Henderson, D., Daley, T., Kunkel, L., Rodrigues-Scott, M., Koul, P., & Hayden, D. (2004). Clozapine and hypertension: A chart review of 82 patients. *Journal of Clinical Psychiatry*, *65*, 686–689.

Hennekens, C. H., Hennekens, A. R., Hollar, D., & Casey, D. E. (2005). Schizophrenia and increased risks of cardiovascular disease. *American Heart Journal*, *150*, 1115–1121.

Jin, H., Meyer, J. M., & Jeste, D. V. (2002). Phenomenology of and risk factors for new-onset diabetes mellitus and diabetic ketoacidosis associated with atypical antipsychotics: An analysis of 45 published cases. *Annuals of Clinical Psychiatry*, *14*, 59–64.

Kato, M. M., Currier, M. B., & Villaverde, O. (2005). The relationship between body fat distribution and cardiovascular risk factors in patients with schizophrenia: A cross-sectional pilot study. *Primary Care Companion to the Journal of Clinical Psychiatry*, *7*, 115–118.

Kinon, B. J., Basson, B. R., Gilmore, J. A., & Tollefson, G. D. (2001). Long-term olanzapine treatment: Weight change and weight related health factors in schizophrenia. *Journal of Clinical Psychiatry*, *62*, 92–100.

Klein, D. J., Cottingham, E. M., Sorter, M., Barton, B. A., & Morrison, J. A. (2006). A randomized, double-blind, placebo-controlled trial of metformin treatment of weight gain associated with initiation of atypical antipsychotic therapy in children and adolescents. *American Journal of Psychiatry*, *163*, 2072–2079.

Ko, Y. H., Joe, S. H., Jung, I. K., & Kim, S. H. (2005). Topiramate as an adjuvant treatment with atypical antipsychotics in schizophrenic patients experiencing weight gain. *Clinical Neuropharmacology*, *28*, 169–175.

Lambert, T. J., & Newcomer, J. W. (2009). Are the cardiometabolic complications of schizophrenia still neglected? Barriers to care. *Medical Journal of Australia*, *4*(Suppl.), 39–42.

Loh, C., Meyer, J. M., & Leekband, S. G. (2006). A comprehensive review of behavioural interventions for weight management in schizophrenia. *Annuals of Clinical Psychiatry*, *18*, 23–31.

McEvoy, J. P., Meyer, J. M., Goff, D. C., Nasrallah, H. A., Davis, S. M., Sullivan, L., et al. (2005). Prevalence of the metabolic syndrome in patients with schizophrenia: Baseline results from the Clinical Antipsychotic Trials of Intervention Effectiveness (CATIE) schizophrenia trial and comparison with national estimates from NHANES III. *Schizophrenia Research*, *80*(1), 19–32.

McIntyre, R. S., McCann, S. M., & Kennedy, S. H. (2001). Antipsychotic metabolic effects: Weight gain, diabetes mellitus and lipid abnormalities. *Canadian Journal of Psychiatry*, *46*, 273–281.

Meltzer, H. Y., Perry, E., & Jayathilake, K. (2003). Clozapine-induced weight gain predicts improvement in psychopathology. *Schizophrenia Research*, *59*, 19–27.

Nasrallah, H. A., Meyer, J. M., Goff, D. C., McEvoy, J. P., Davis, S. M., Stroup, T. S., et al. (2006). Low rates of treatment for hypertension, dyslipidaemia and diabetes in schizophrenia: Data from the CATIE schizophrenia trial sample at baseline. *Schizophrenia Research*, *86*, 15–22.

Neal, B., MacMahon, S., & Chapman, N. (2000). Effects of ace inhibitors, calcium antagonists and other blood pressure-lowering drugs: Results of prospectively designed overviews of randomised trials. Blood pressure-lowering treatment trialists' collaboration. *Lancet*, *356*, 1955–1964.

Newman, S. C., & Bland, R. C. (1991). Mortality of a cohort of patients with schizophrenia: A record linkage study. *Canadian Journal of Psychiatry*, *36*(2), 39–45.

Nickel, M. K., Nickel, C., Muehlbacher, M., Lieberich, P. K., Kaplan, P. M., Lahmann, C., et al. (2005). Influence of topiramate on olanzapine-related adiposity in women: A random, double blind, placebo-controlled study. *Journal of Clinical Psychopharmacology*, *25*, 211–217.

Osby, U., Correia, N., & Brandt, L. (2000). Mortality and causes of death in schizophrenia in Stockholm County, Sweden. *Schizophrenia Research*, *45*, 21–28.

Osser, D. N., Najarian, D. M., & Dufresne, R. L. (1999). Olanzapine increases weight and serum triglyceride levels. *Journal of Clinical Psychiatry*, *60*, 767–770.

Polgar, S., McGartland, M., & Hales, T. (1996). Cigarette smoking and schizophrenia. A public health issue. *Australian Journal of Public Health*, *2*(2), 21–28.

Rettenbacher, M., Ebenbichler, C., Hofer, A., Kemmler, G., Baumgartner, S., Edlinger, M., et al. (2006). Early changes of plasma lipids during treatment with atypical antipsychotics. *International Clinical Psychopharmacology*, *21*, 369–372.

Reynolds, G. P., Zhang, Z., & Zhang, X. (2002). Association of antipsychotic drug-induced weight gain with a 5-HT_{2C} receptor gene polymorphism. *Lancet*, *359*, 2086–2087.

Ryan, M. C., Collins, P., & Thakore, J. H. (2003). Impaired fasting glucose tolerance in first episode, drug naïve patients with schizophrenia. *American Journal of Psychiatry*, *160*, 284–289.

Saarni, S. E., Saarni, S. I., Fogelholm, M., Heliovaara, J., Perala, J., Suvisaari, J., et al. (2009). Body composition in psychotic disorders: A general population survey. *Psychological Medicine*, *39*, 801–810.

Sharpe, J. K., & Hills, A. P. (2003). Atypical antipsychotic weight gain: A major clinical challenge. *Australian and New Zealand Journal of Psychiatry*, *37*, 705–709.

Shiloah, E., Witz, S., Abramovitch, Y., Cohen, O., Buchs, A., Ramot, Y., et al. (2003). Effect of psychotic stress in non diabetic subjects on beta-cell function and insulin sensitivity. *Diabetes Care*, *26*, 1462–1467.

Smith, M., Hopkins, D., Peveler, C., Holt, G., Woodward, M., & Ismail, K. (2008). First vs. second-generation antipsychotics and risk for diabetes in schizophrenia: Systematic review and meta-analysis. *The British Journal of Psychiatry*, *192*, 406–411.

Stanton, J. M. (1995). Weight gain associated with neuroleptic medication: A review. *Schizophrenia Bulletin*, *21*, 463–472.

Stern, M. P., Williams, K., Gomnzalez-Villalpando, C., Hunt, K., & Haffner, S. (2005). Does the metabolic syndrome improve identification of individuals at risk of type 2 diabetes and/or cardiovascular disease? *Diabetes Care*, *2*, 2676–2681.

Subramaniam, M., Chong, S. A., & Pek, E. (2003). Diabetes mellitus and impaired glucose tolerance in patients with schizophrenia. *Canadian Journal of Psychiatry*, *48*, 345–347.

Taflinski, T., & Chojnacka, J. (2000). Sibutramine-associated psychotic episode. *American Journal of Psychiatry*, *157*, 1793–1794.

Tham, S. P., Jones, S. G., Chamberlain, J. A., & Castle, D. J. (2007). The impact of psychotropic weight gain on people with psychosis—Patient perspectives and attitudes. *Journal of Mental Health*, *16*(6), 771–779.

Visscher, T. L., & Seidell, J. C. (2001). The public health impact of obesity. *Annual Review of Public Health*, *22*, 355–375.

Weiden, P. J. (2007). Switching antipsychotics as a treatment strategy for antipsychotic-induced weight gain and dyslipidaemia. *Journal of Clinical Psychiatry*, *68*, 34–39.

Weiden, P. J., Mackell, J. A., & McDonnell, D. D. (2004). Obesity as a risk factor for antipsychotic noncompliance. *Schizophrenia Research*, *66*, 51–57.

Wetterling, T., & Mubigbrodt, H. E. (1999). Weight gain: Side effect of atypical neuroleptics? *Journal of Clinical Psychopharmacology*, *19*, 316–321.

27 Clinical trials and schizophrenia

Shôn Lewis

The rise of the clinical trial

In trying to treat any disorder, how do we know what works and what doesn't? The familiar hierarchy of expert opinion at the bottom, then up through case studies and case series, case control and cohort studies, ending with the gold standard of randomized controlled trials, is well accepted now (Table 27.1). Most academics would now agree that not only are randomized controlled trials the benchmark level of evidence to demonstrate efficacy, they are the only way. This, of course, is a pity because randomized controlled trials, perhaps particularly in mental health, are difficult to do. They are cumbersome, expensive and long-winded. Because of this, they are easy to do badly, again perhaps particularly in mental health.

Why is the randomized trial the only formal proof that is acceptable as evidence that a treatment works? Random allocation to the experimental or control treatment is the only way truly to eliminate bias, as well as control for known and unknown prognostic factors (Table 27.2). Yet the randomized trial is a relatively recent development, first seriously advocated by the statistician Bradford Hill (inventor of the chi-square test) in the 1950s in the UK, and only generally accepted by the scientific community at large well after that. There were effective treatments before the 1950s, however, so how was it that they became established? One reason is that early treatments tended to have large effect sizes with a plausible if

Table 27.1 The hierarchy of assessing effectiveness

RCTs
Parallel group
Cross over
Controlled observational studies
Historical control designs
Case-control studies (e.g., drug safety)
Before and after studies
Case series
Expert opinion

Table 27.2 The pros and cons of randomized controlled trials

Pros	
	Eliminate bias
	Control for known prognostic factors
	Control for unknown prognostic factors
Cons	
	Null hypothesis has an obscure historical basis (and ignores previous findings)
	Costly
	Generalizability may be low if patients wrongly chosen
	May not be needed if a high (e.g., 10 : 1) signal–noise ratio

not obvious mechanism: limb amputation for gangrene for instance had such a clear and immediate effect that a randomized comparison was not needed. Some later treatments, usually surgical such as corneal transplantation, also fall into this category, where the signal to noise ratio is very high. However, most treatments these days are claiming relatively modest incremental advantages over standard treatments such that randomized trials are mandatory. Before the clinical-trial era, case studies and expert opinion tended to hold sway and this approach was certainly more transparent to the average patient and clinician, even if potentially uninformative or misleading. In a recent biography (Keating, 2009), the great epidemiologist Richard Doll recalls an instance of this from his days as a wartime junior medical officer. In the field, Doll was faced with a limited supply of the new sulphonamide drugs and proposed that he treat 50% of wounded soldiers prophylactically, comparing healing times to the other 50% who would remain untreated. His superior medical officer:

> … berated me soundly. Either it was a good idea to give wounded soldiers sulphonamides prophylactically at the earliest opportunity in which case I should give sulphonamides to all of them, or it was not, in which case I should not waste His Majesty's money. I obviously agreed, but when I asked whether or not it was a good idea I was told that it was my job to decide, not his, and I was sharply dismissed.
>
> (Keating, 2009, p. 31)

Clinical trials in schizophrenia

The first evaluations of chlorpromazine in St Anne's hospital in Paris by Pierre Deniker were not clinical trials, but were convincing because of the huge effect size seen in an essentially untreated population. Jean Thuillier describes the day-to-day revolution brought about by the drug:

> … stretched out on their beds, calm and drowsy, or with a fixed gaze, lost in a limitless distance, these patients had been set free from their strait-waistcoats and hemp straitjackets … I can no longer remember who it was who said that the results obtained with chlorpromazine could be measured in psychiatric hospitals in decibels recorded before and after the introduction of this drug.
>
> (Thuillier, 1999, p. 113)

So, the first, and still most important, milestone was such a therapeutic paradigm shift that controlled trials were not needed, at least initially. In the nearly sixty years since that time, randomized controlled trials have reigned, yet key milestones in the clinical psychopharmacology of schizophrenia have been relatively few, in large part a result of the continuing incomplete understanding of the pathophysiology of the disorder. One would count as genuine milestones the pivotal trials of long-acting injectables in the early 1970s, and the 1988 rediscovery of clozapine by John Kane (Kane, Honigfeld, Singer, Meltzer, & The Clozaril Collaborative Study Group, 1988). Otherwise, psychosocial interventions have seen the most milestones: family intervention in reducing relapse by Vaughn and Leff (1976); the demonstration that cognitive therapy may have benefits by Tarrier and colleagues (1993); and the development of cognitive remediation.

New targets

New treatment targets are emerging in schizophrenia. In the past, the therapeutic focus has been particularly on positive symptoms, in part because these have appeared most directly to relate to the underlying dopaminergic lesion for which there is now direct evidence. Now, attention is increasingly being paid to other domains of symptoms and deficits that may be closer to the core of the syndrome. Such domains include negative symptoms and cognitive deficits, with increasing emphasis on early intervention to avert progressive impairments, possibly through neuroprotection. Part of the rationale for this is that such domains have greater impact on the long-term prognosis. Also, although the precise aetiology of schizophrenia remains obscure, it is becoming clear that different elements of the clinical syndrome may have different risk factors. There is preliminary evidence that individual risk genes may link to different components of the schizophrenia syndrome: neuregulin and preserved affect, COMT and working memory for example. It is possible in future that the genes themselves will be therapeutic targets, but at the moment there is a recognition that direct dopamine blockade has run its course as an avenue for further investigation and lesions further upstream, such as glutamate, are attracting attention.

The conceptual shift to intervening early in the course of the disorder has led to the delineation of the prodromal or high-risk mental state, a collection of subthreshold state plus trait variables that identify individuals who are at several hundredfold increased risk (perhaps 20%) of developing first-episode schizophrenia over the coming twelve months. The headline focus of treatment here is the prevention of this transition and the first antipsychotic drug and psychological treatment studies have been done. However, ethical issues abound, not least that 80% of those exposed to treatment would not have developed the full disorder in any case, and it remains to be proven that this route to psychosis has a sufficiently large population-attributable fraction to encourage this approach at a public-health level.

Design challenges

There are still major methodological issues facing schizophrenia trials. One is the problem of reliable outcome assessment. This is particularly an issue with open trials, where double-blind treatment allocation is not done, either because, as with pragmatic phase 4 drug trials, the design tries to mimic closely the real-life treatment setting, or because it is simply impossible, as with psychological treatment trials. The preferred solution is to have hard outcomes, which are objective and indisputable, such as survival or death in the trial of a cancer medicine. The few such outcomes available to schizophrenia trials, such as admission to hospital, are imperfect because they are open to many factors unrelated to direct treatment effects. Time to all-cause discontinuation of allocated treatment is a perfectly acceptable pragmatic endpoint in double-blind trials, as in the CATIE trial (Lieberman et al., 2005). However, in an open trial, time to all-cause discontinuation is at the mercy of clinician bias, as was seen in the EUFEST trial (Kahn et al., 2008). EUFEST was pan-European open head-to-head randomized trial of different second-generation antipsychotics (SGAs) and haloperidol where the primary endpoint was all-cause discontinuation.

The obvious categorical (yes/no) endpoints in schizophrenia trials are those that mean most to patients. Antipsychotic medicines and other interventions have two important clinical targets, promotion of recovery (remission) and prevention of relapse. Both are well recognized clinically, especially relapse. The first problem is that relapse cannot be defined without first having an agreed definition of prior response, or remission. But, despite many attempted definitions, there is an absence of an agreed criterion for clinical response in schizophrenia. This stands in contrast to the situation with mood disorders, for example, where there are universally adopted Hamilton-score-based criteria for response in trials of major depression. Likewise, there are many definitions for relapse in schizophrenia, such as 20% or 30% increase in Positive and Negative Syndrome Scale (PANSS) positive scores, perhaps accompanied by a management change, but none is widely agreed. The absence of agreed operational definitions of important clinical endpoints such as response, remission and relapse will always hamper summary approaches such as meta-analysis.

Symptom assessments such as the PANSS are widely used as primary outcome measures, particularly in regulatory trials. The PANSS, however, requires training to achieve respectable inter-rater reliability, particularly where assessors are not clinically trained. In multi-site trials, with multiple assessors, this is particularly important. Yet most published trials fail to report intra-class correlation or even straightforward Pearson correlations between raters. Good inter-rater reliability is achievable on the PANSS, in excess of .9, but if this is not attained, there will be a dramatic negative impact on the power of the trial.

Inappropriate statistical analyses can provide another potential source of type 1 error, generating findings erroneously in support of the experimental compound. One example is the widespread practice of dealing with missing data points from drop-outs by using the "last observation carried forward" statistical adjustment. It would be surprising if this crude statistical technique did not generate bias in some studies, however, particularly where there were major disparities early on in drop-out rates between treatment arms. Trials such as CATIE and CUtLASS moved beyond this potentially misleading approach, using instead imputational techniques to deal with missing data.

So, we need a new approach to trial design in schizophrenia. Symptom assessments using the PANSS have problems with inter-rater reliability, as well as being open to recall bias and averaging of responses. Ambulatory monitoring of symptoms in real time must be a better approach, using a PDA or smartphone handset for the patient to record symptoms at intervals during the day, the data uploaded wirelessly in real time. In future, biomarkers may be identified that help predict treatment-response subgroups, allowing patient sample stratification. Just as increasing the intra-class correlation between raters on the PANSS from .7 to .9 will increase power from 50 to 70% for a given sample size, so stratifying the sample to increase the treatment response rate from 20 to 30% will reduce the sample size needed by more than half. Early-phase studies would benefit from the use of intermediate or surrogate phenotypes, such as high schizotypy in healthy volunteers, with proxy endpoints such as signal detection or facial affect recognition.

Lies, damned lies and meta-analyses: The case of SGAs

The reappraisal since 2006 of the status of the non-clozapine second-generation antipsychotic drugs, compared to their first-generation (FGA) predecessors, has been a lesson in how the results of short-term efficacy trials with built in design biases, added to aggressive marketing and a prescribing community eager to embrace change, can lead to mistaken conclusions. The claims that clinicians came to believe in the 1990s were that the SGAs were superior to FGAs in terms of their impact on positive symptoms, negative symptoms, mood symptoms, adverse effects, adherence rates and neurocognitive effects. The higher costs of SGAs were justified in terms of the improved quality of life they produced. In any case, these costs, it was believed, would soon be repaid through savings on in-patient stays. These claims were readily taken up by a community of clinicians in part because the superior efficacy of clozapine showed for the first time that some drugs might be better than others. The SGAs, or new atypicals, were seen as a class because of a common preclinical model of their mechanism of action and adverse effect profile, because they appeared to share a reduced risk of extrapyramidal symptoms (EPS), and because they were marketed as such.

Industry sponsored trials against FGA comparators, usually haloperidol, generally supported the increased efficacy of SGAs and thus the resulting meta-analyses appeared to consolidate the body of evidence purporting to show the clear advantages of the SGAs in terms of efficacy and safety, compared to their predecessors. However, there were some dissenting voices starting in 2000, when John Geddes and colleagues' meta-analysis suggested that a large part of the variance in the difference between SGA and FGA might be explained by the choice of the comparator drug and its dosage: specifically, haloperidol at relatively high dosage. However, it was the advent of large, non-industry-funded pragmatic trials beginning ten years after the introduction of the SGAs that began seriously to challenge what was by then an accepted dogma. First, Robert Rosenheck's trial (Rosenheck et al., 2003) showed no advantages to olanzapine compared to haloperidol when used in modest dosages with anticholinergic cover. The CATIE trial (Lieberman et al., 2005), then CUtLASS (Jones et al., 2006), then EUFEST (Kahn et al., 2008), all pointed to the absence of major effectiveness advantages of the non-clozapine SGAs over carefully prescribed FGAs.

The expert position now is summarized by the UK clinical guidelines body, NICE, which published its 400-page 2009 update of schizophrenia treatment guidelines (the previous edition being in 2002) supported by a range of systematic reviews. One striking feature of the guideline is that at no stage is any distinction between FGAs and SGAs employed, and even for first-line treatment there is no explicit recommendation that SGAs are preferred. In considering relapse prevention for example, the guideline states:

> All the antipsychotics identified for review have established supremacy over placebo in preventing relapse, although the evidence that any individual drug or group of drugs (FGA vs. SGA) has greater efficacy or tolerability is still very uncertain. … Any small advantage (offered by SGAs) of reduced EPS may be offset by other adverse consequences not shown by earlier drugs.
>
> (NICE, 2009, p. 56)

At a policy level, the main distinction between FGAs and SGAs has been their price, or acquisition cost. FGAs are cheap, and SGAs less so by at least an order of magnitude. Of course, there are caveats here. The older SGAs are becoming generic. The overall costs of health and social care for someone with schizophrenia is high, and drug costs, even for the relatively expensive SGAs, turn out to be a small proportion of this. Both CATIE (Rosenheck et al., 2006) and CUtLASS (Davies et al., 2007) involved sophisticated cost-effectiveness analyses because the rationale for both studies included issues of relative cost. The initial letters of the CUtLASS acronym stand for "cost utility". Analyses of both studies found FGAs to be the "dominant choice": that is, no less effective, but cheaper. The importance of this issue is that, in the real world, resources wasted on an unnecessarily expensive treatment means rationing of other treatments.

The future of clinical trials in schizophrenia

Clinical trial methodology has been tested to its limits by the challenges inherent in schizophrenia, including the fuzzy phenotype, the continued ignorance of the pathogenesis with the lack of animal models, and the lack of objective markers of the disease and its outcome. Nevertheless, the monumental public-health challenge it poses and the imperfect treatments available mean that the discovery of new treatments will continue to be high priority. Clinical trials will continue to be the gold standard.

There are developments that hold promise. New disorders, such as the at-risk syndrome, offer new opportunities. It is perhaps naïve to expect that a single agent can produce global improvements and a new focus on specific therapeutic targets within the overall phenotype will be important, such as negative symptoms and neurocognitive deficits. In the same vein, new trial designs combining different treatment approaches will emerge. For example, the potential interaction between psychological and drug treatments remains largely unexplored. Examples exist already of pharmacological treatments enhancing the effect of psychosocial treatments, such as the demonstration that clozapine improves response to psychosocial intervention (Rosenheck et al., 1998). Conversely, so-called compliance therapy (Kemp, Hayward, Applewhaite, Everitt, & David, 1996) potentially represents a specific psychological treatment (motivational interviewing) enhancing the effect of drug treatment through an effect on adherence. There is considerable potential here, such as testing whether cognitive remediation approaches, increasingly computer based, can enhance the learning effect of putative cognitive-enhancing drugs. New approaches to measurement, data capture and analysis may also make clinical trials more efficient and informative. Increased use of real-time self-monitoring of symptoms and stressors, if validated, promise fine-grained phenotyping and delineation of individual treatment response signatures with a greater chance of personalized medicine. Finally, clinical trials in the UK and several European countries have become increasingly embedded in service-based research infrastructures such as mental health research support networks and academic health sciences centres, which may hold the key to establishing large-scale clinical trials as part of our routine healthcare culture.

References

Davies, L. M., Lewis, S. W., Jones, P. B., Barnes, T. R. E., Gaughran, F., Hayhurst, K., et al., on behalf of the CUtLASS team. (2007). Cost effectiveness of first generation versus second generation antipsychotic drugs to treat psychosis: Results from a randomised controlled trial in schizophrenia responding poorly to previous therapy. *British Journal of Psychiatry*, *191*, 14–22.

Geddes, J., Freemantle, N., Harrison, P., & Bebbington, P. (2000). Atypical antipsychotics in the treatment of schizophrenia: Systematic overview and meta-regression analysis. *British Medical Journal*, *321*, 1371–1376.

Jones, P. B., Barnes, T. R. E., Davies, L., Dunn, G., Lloyd, H., Hayhurst, K. P., et al. (2006). Randomized controlled trial of the effect on quality of life of second- vs. first-generation antipsychotic drugs in schizophrenia—Cost Utility of the Latest Antipsychotic drugs in Schizophrenia Study (CUtLASS 1). *Archives of General Psychiatry*, *63*, 1079–1086.

Kahn, R. S., Fleischhacker, W. W., Boter, H., Davidson, M., Vergouwe, Y., Keet, I. P. M., et al. (2008). Effectiveness of antipsychotic drugs in first-episode schizophrenia and schizophreniform disorder: An open randomised clinical trial. *Lancet*, *371*, 1085–1097.

Kane, J. M., Honigfeld, G., Singer, J., Meltzer, H., & The Clozaril Collaborative Study Group. (1988). Clozapine for the treatment-resistant schizophrenic: A double-blind comparison with chlorpromazine. *Archives of General Psychiatry*, *45*, 789–796.

Keating, C. (2009). *Smoking kills. The revolutionary life of Richard Doll*. Oxford, UK: Signal Books.

Kemp, R., Hayward, P., Applewhaite, G., Everitt, B., & David, A. (1996). Compliance therapy in psychotic patients: Randomised controlled trial. *British Medical Journal*, *312*(7027), 345–349.

Lieberman, J. A., Stroup, T. S., McEvoy, J. P., Swartz, M. S., Rosenheck, R. A., Perkins, D. O., et al. (2005). Effectiveness of antipsychotic drugs in patients with chronic schizophrenia. *New England Journal of Medicine*, *353*, 1209–1223.

McEvoy, J. P., Lieberman, J. A., Stroup, T. S., Davis, S. M., Meltzer, H. Y., Rosenheck, R. A., et al. (2006). Effectiveness of clozapine versus olanzapine, quetiapine, and risperidone in patients with chronic schizophrenia who did not respond to prior atypical antipsychotic treatment. *American Journal of Psychiatry*, *163*, 600–610.

NICE. (2009). *Core interventions in the treatment and management of schizophrenia in primary and secondary care* (update CG82). London, UK: National Institute of Health and Clinical Excellence.

Rosenheck, R., Perlick, D., Bingham, S., Liu-Mares, W., Collins, J., Warren, S., et al. (2003). Effectiveness and cost of olanzapine and haloperidol in the treatment of schizophrenia—A randomized controlled trial. *Journal of the American Medical Association*, *290*, 2693–2702.

Rosenheck, R., Tekell, J., Peters, J., Cramer, J., Fontana, A., Xu, W., et al. (1998). Does participation in psychosocial treatment augment the benefit of clozapine? *Archives of General Psychiatry*, *55*(7), 618–625.

Rosenheck, R. A., Leslie, D., Sindelar, J., Miller, E. A., Lin, H., Stroup, S., et al. (2006). Cost-effectiveness of second generation antipsychotics and perphenazine in a randomized trial of treatment for chronic schizophrenia. *American Journal of Psychiatry*, *163*(12), 2080–2089.

Tarrier, N., Beckett, R., Harwood, S., Baker, A., Yusopoff, L., & Ugarteburu, I. (1993). A trial of two cognitive behavioural methods of treating drug-resistant residual psychotic symptoms in schizophrenic patients: 1 Outcome. *British Journal of Psychiatry*, *162*, 524–532.

Thuillier, J. (1999). *Ten years that changed the face of mental illness*. London, UK: Martin Dunitz.

Vaughn, C., & Leff, J. P. (1976). The influence of family life and social factors on the course of schizophrenia. *British Journal of Psychiatry*, *129*, 125–137.

28 What new evidence tells us about dopamine's role in schizophrenia

Oliver D. Howes

Introduction

The pathophysiology of schizophrenia remains incompletely understood but functional imaging techniques, such as positron emission tomography (PET), single photon emission computed tomography (SPECT) and functional magnetic resonance imaging (fMRI) have advanced understanding of the neurobiology of the disease. An advantage of neurochemical imaging techniques such as PET and SPECT over fMRI is that they can directly quantify receptor densities, and other aspects of neurobiology, in vivo. In the past two decades neurochemical imaging has provided important data that have refined understanding of the nature of dopaminergic abnormalities in schizophrenia. The evolution of the dopamine hypothesis of schizophrenia is summarized with reference to these new data, and the latest version of the dopamine hypothesis described, together with its implications and some of the outstanding questions.

Striatal dopamine D2 receptors

There is a close, direct relationship between the clinical potency of licensed antipsychotic drugs and their affinity for dopamine D2 receptors (Seeman, 1987; Snyder, 1976). Partly as a consequence of this, the early dopamine hypothesis of schizophrenia focused on dopamine D2 receptors (Snyder, 1976), and the initial PET and SPECT studies investigated whether D2 receptor density is abnormal in schizophrenia. In the past two decades at least nineteen PET and SPECT studies have examined this issue with inconsistent findings (Laruelle, 1998). Several factors probably underlie the inconsistency, in particular the effects of antipsychotic treatment, which may alter receptor levels, and differences between the radiotracers used. Three meta-analyses (Kestler, Walker, & Vega, 2001; Laruelle, 1998; Zakzanis & Hansen, 1998) have summarized the findings from these studies, concluding that D2 density is heterogeneous in schizophrenia, and that while D2 receptor density may be increased in a subgroup of patients the increase overall is moderate (10–20%) at most. Another critical issue complicating the interpretation of these studies is that baseline concentrations of extracellular dopamine have been found to be increased in schizophrenia, and alterations in synaptic levels of dopamine may affect radiotracer binding (Laruelle, 1998). Finally, the D2 receptor may exist in intraconvertible high and low affinity states and it has been proposed that the balance between these states is altered in schizophrenia (Seeman et al., 2006). A radiotracer that binds specifically to the D2 high-affinity receptor has recently been developed. In contrast to the theory, the first study using this radiotracer to investigate the D2 high-affinity receptor specifically in schizophrenia found no evidence of an alteration in the illness (Graf-Guerrero et al., 2009). In summary the D2 findings indicate that receptor levels are unlikely to be markedly altered in schizophrenia.

Presynaptic striatal dopaminergic function

PET and SPECT techniques have been developed to index dopamine synthesis, release and putative synaptic dopamine levels. Radiolabelled L-dopa is converted to dopamine and trapped in striatal dopamine nerve terminals ready for release (see Moore, Whone, McGowan, & Brooks, 2003, for a review). Ten out of the eleven studies from multiple centres around the world using this technique in schizophrenia have found elevations, although this was not significant in one study, and there was a significant reduction in the other study (Dao-Castellana et al., 1997; Elkashef et al., 2000; Hietala et al., 1995, 1999; Howes et al., 2009; Kumakura et al., 2007; Lindstrom et al., 1999; McGowan, Lawrence, Sales, Quested, & Grasby, 2004; Meyer-Lindenberg et al., 2002; Nozaki et al., 2009; Reith et al., 1994). The effect sizes in these studies showing an elevation ranged from 0.63–1.89 (Howes et al., 2007). All the studies of patients who were acutely psychotic at the time of PET scanning found elevations, with effect sizes from 0.63–1.25 (Howes et al., 2007). Elevated presynaptic dopamine availability, then, is the single most widely replicated in vivo brain dopaminergic abnormality in schizophrenia, and the effect size appears moderate to large.

Dopamine available in presynaptic terminals is released into the synaptic cleft to initiate neurotransmission. Dopamine released into the synaptic cleft can be indexed using PET and SPECT ligands that bind to D2 receptors. Released dopamine competes with the radioligand, resulting in a reduction in radiotracer binding, which is related to the degree of dopamine release (Laruelle, 2000; Laruelle et al., 1997). The studies using this approach have consistently found evidence of roughly doubled radiotracer displacement in patients following a challenge—an elevation that is again equivalent to a moderate to large effect size (Abi-Dargham et al., 1998; Breier et al., 1997; Kestler et al., 2001; Laruelle & Abi-Dargham, 1999; Laruelle et al., 1996). Furthermore, if presynaptic dopamine availability is elevated and more dopamine is released following a challenge, increased levels of endogenous synaptic dopamine would be expected when patients are psychotic. A SPECT study using a dopamine-depletion technique provides evidence of this, finding that baseline occupancy of D2 receptors by dopamine is also increased in schizophrenia (Abi-Dargham et al., 2000), and that these levels are correlated with the level of dopamine release induced by a challenge (Abi-Dargham, Giessen, Slifstein, Kegeles, & Laruelle, 2009).

Dopamine dysregulation prior to the onset of psychosis

The findings reviewed above were all in people who had at least one psychotic episode. Consequently it is not clear from them whether the dopamine dysregulation predates psychosis or is secondary to some other factor that causes the first psychotic episode. Thus a key piece of missing evidence was whether dopamine dysfunction existed prior to the onset of psychosis. Dopaminergic function has recently been studied in subjects with prodromal signs of schizophrenia (Howes et al., 2009). This study found elevated presynaptic dopamine availability in the group with prodromal schizophrenia predating the onset of psychosis and to a degree approaching that in patients with established schizophrenia (Howes et al., 2009). In the prodromal group, those with higher dopamine levels showed more severe prodromal symptoms (see Figure 28.1).

These findings indicate that increased subcortical dopamine activity predates the full expression of schizophrenia, consistent with the putative role of dopamine in the pathophysiology of psychosis (Kapur, Mizrahi, & Li, 2005; Laruelle & Abi-Dargham, 1999).

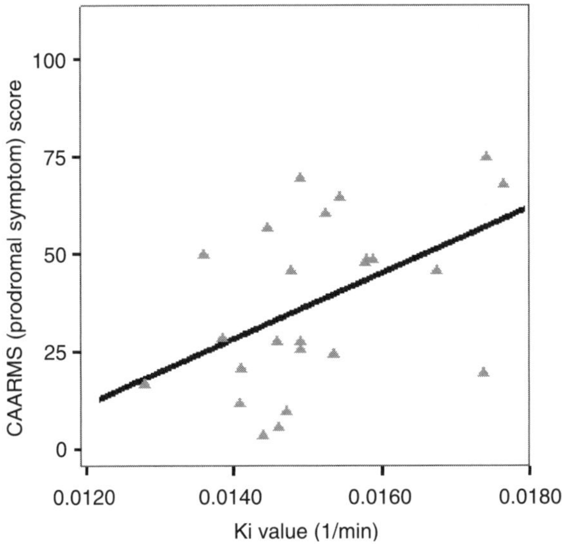

Figure 28.1 Showing a direct relationship between prodromal symptom severity and striatal dopamine availability in people with prodromal signs of schizophrenia. Prodromal symptoms are indexed using the Comprehensive Assessment of At Risk Mental States (CAARMS)—higher scores indicate greater symptom severity (reproduced from Howes et al., 2009, *Archives of General Psychiatry, 66,* 13–20, with permission).

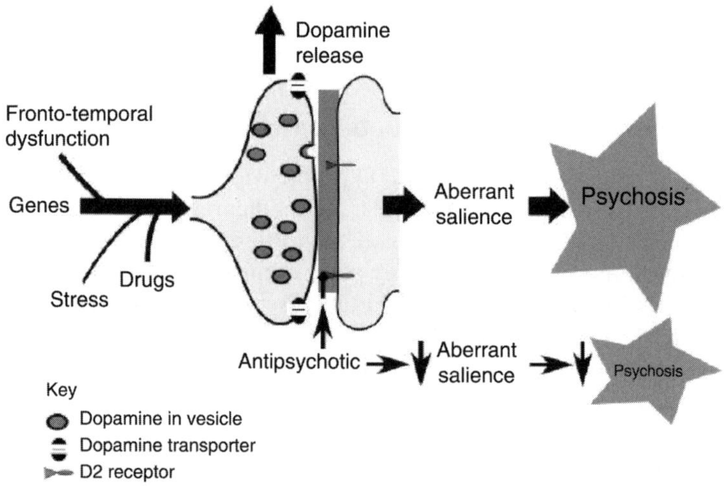

Figure 28.2 Showing how risk factors for schizophrenia may all converge to cause dopamine dysregulation and hence psychosis. Antipsychotic drugs are seen to act downstream of the primary dopaminergic abnormality.

The revised dopamine hypothesis of schizophrenia

A revised version of the dopamine hypothesis has recently been proposed based on the new information from the neurochemical imaging studies, but also drawing on evidence from animal, genetic and other studies (Howes & Kapur, 2009). This proposes that dopamine dysregulation is the final common pathway to psychosis in schizophrenia (illustrated in Figure 28.2). The first component of this hypothesis is that multiple "hits" interact, and lead to dopamine dysregulation. This is analogous to diabetes mellitus, for example, where hyperglycaemia is the final pathophysiology that results in the clinical symptoms, but different paths lead to hyperglycaemia (insulin insensitivity in the case of type II diabetes, or insulin insufficiency in the case of type I diabetes) with an array of risk factors underlying this. The second component of the revised hypothesis is a shift in the localization of dopaminergic dysregulation from the postsynaptic receptor level, to presynaptic dopaminergic regulation. A third component is making a link between dopamine dysregulation and psychosis/"psychosis proneness" rather than schizophrenia per se, with the exact diagnosis reflecting the nature and interacting effects of the upstream hits, as is the case with diabetes mellitus. Finally, dopaminergic dysfunction is linked to symptoms through altered appraisal of stimuli.

Implications of the dopamine hypothesis of schizophrenia: Version III

A major implication of this revised hypothesis is that current antipsychotic drugs are acting downstream of the pathophysiology and not treating the primary abnormality. To extend the analogy, this would be the same as treating diabetes mellitus by blocking glucose rather than treating the cause of hyperglycaemia (e.g., insulin insufficiency). A consequence of this is that antipsychotic drugs may paradoxically worsen the primary abnormality by initiating a compensatory increase in dopamine synthesis. Findings in healthy volunteers indicate that acute antipsychotic treatment does elevate dopamine synthesis (Vernaleken et al., 2006). This compensatory increase in presynaptic dopamine may underlie the rapid relapses observed in patients on stopping their medication, and suggests that, if dopamine dysregulation is increased further, subsequent relapses may be more severe. Future drug development should logically move from further attempts to emulate the existing pharmacology of licensed antipsychotic drugs to focus on the modulation of presynaptic striatal dopamine function.

Since the dopaminergic neurons in the striatum originate in the midbrain—particularly in the substantia nigra (Haber, Fudge, & McFarland, 2000; Joel & Weiner, 2000), a further implication of the revised dopamine hypothesis is that the function and regulation of the dopamine cell bodies in the midbrain is dysregulated in psychosis. Supporting this, post-mortem studies of patients with schizophrenia have found increased dopaminergic markers in the substantia nigra (Mueller, Haroutunian, Davis, & Meador-Woodruff, 2004; Toru et al., 1988). Additionally there is in vivo evidence of abnormal midbrain neural activation during incentive salience processing in schizophrenia (Murray et al., 2008). However, it is unclear whether the abnormalities detected represent dysregulated dopaminergic function or dysfunction in other midbrain neurons as this study used fMRI imaging, which cannot determine if the signal comes from dopamine neurons or not—non-dopaminergic nuclei may contribute substantially to the midbrain signal detected (Cumming & Gjedde, 1998; Duzel et al., 2009). Finally, a recent study has reported increased signal intensity of a new MR-based index of neuromelanin, a by-product of monoamine metabolism, in the substantia nigra of patients with schizophrenia (Shibata et al., 2008).

Conclusions and outstanding questions

In summary, substantial new evidence has accrued in the past 20 years to refine understanding of dopamine's role in the pathophysiology of schizophrenia, resulting in a revised dopamine hypothesis. This evidence has moved the focus from postsynaptic receptors to presynaptic striatal dysfunction, and linked this to the development of symptoms of the illness, particularly psychosis. Furthermore, the large body of evidence on dopamine's function in learning has provided a framework to understand how dopamine dysregulation may translate into symptoms. Additional evidence has shown how the major risk factors for schizophrenia may lead to dopamine dysregulation. The revised dopamine hypothesis draws together these new lines of evidence to propose that presynaptic dopamine dysfunction is the final common pathway to psychosis. This raises a number of questions, such as how the risk factors interact, whether antipsychotic treatment paradoxically worsens the pathophysiology, and whether the primary dopamine dysregulation is at the level of the cell bodies in the nigra or in the striatum. Neurochemical imaging studies currently in progress will address these questions and provide a fuller understanding of dopamine's involvement in the neurobiology of schizophrenia.

References

Abi-Dargham, A., Giessen, E. V., Slifstein, M., Kegeles, L. S., & Laruelle, M. (2009). Baseline and amphetamine-stimulated dopamine activity are related in drug-naive schizophrenic subjects. *Biological Psychiatry*, *15*; 65(12), 1091–1093.

Abi-Dargham, A., Gil, R., Krystal, J., Baldwin, R. M., Seibyl, J. P., Bowers, M., et al. (1998). Increased striatal dopamine transmission in schizophrenia: Confirmation in a second cohort. *American Journal of Psychiatry*, *155*, 761–767.

Abi-Dargham, A., Rodenhiser, J., Printz, D., Zea-Ponce, Y., Gil, R., Kegeles, L. S., et al. (2000). Increased baseline occupancy of D2 receptors by dopamine in schizophrenia. *Proceedings of the National Academy of Sciences of the USA*, *97*, 8104–8109.

Breier, A., Su, T. P., Saunders, R., Carson, R. E., Kolachana, B. S., de Bartolomeis, A., et al. (1997). Schizophrenia is associated with elevated amphetamine-induced synaptic dopamine concentrations: Evidence from a novel positron emission tomography method. *Proceedings of the National Academy of Sciences of the USA*, *94*, 2569–2574.

Cumming, P., & Gjedde, A. (1998). Compartmental analysis of dopa decarboxylation in living brain from dynamic positron emission tomograms. *Synapse*, *29*, 37–61.

Dao-Castellana, M. H., Paillere-Martinot, M. L., Hantraye, P., Attar-Lévy, D., Remy, P., Crouzel, C., et al. (1997). Presynaptic dopaminergic function in the striatum of schizophrenic patients. *Schizophrenia Research*, *23*, 167–174.

Duzel, E., Bunzeck, N., Guitart-Masip, M., Wittmann, B., Schott, B. H., & Tobler, P. N. (2009). Functional imaging of the human dopaminergic midbrain. *Trends in Neuroscience.*, *32*, 321–328.

Elkashef, A. M., Doudet, D., Bryant, T., Cohen, R. M., Li, S. H., & Wyatt, R. J. (2000). 6-(18)F-DOPA PET study in patients with schizophrenia. Positron emission tomography. *Psychiatry Research*, *100*, 1–11.

Graf-Guerrero, A., Mizrahi, R., Agid, O., Marcon, H., Barsoum, P., Rusjan, P., et al. (2009). The dopamine D2 receptors in high-affinity state and D3 receptors in schizophrenia: A clinical [^{11}C]-(+)-PHNO PET study. *Neuropsychopharmacology*, *34*(4), 1078–1086.

Haber, S. N., Fudge, J. L., & McFarland, N. R. (2000). Striatonigrostriatal pathways in primates form an ascending spiral from the shell to the dorsolateral striatum. *Journal of Neuroscience*, *20*, 2369–2382.

Hietala, J., Syvalahti, E., Vilkman, H., Vuorio, K., Rakkolainen, V., Bergman, J., et al. (1999). Depressive symptoms and presynaptic dopamine function in neuroleptic-naive schizophrenia. *Schizophrenia Research*, *35*, 41–50.

Hietala, J., Syvalahti, E., Vuorio, K., Rakkolainen, V., Bergman, J., Haaparanta, M., et al. (1995). Presynaptic dopamine function in striatum of neuroleptic-naive schizophrenic patients. *Lancet*, *346*, 1130–1131.

Howes, O. D., & Kapur, S. (2009). The dopamine hypothesis of schizophrenia: Version III—The final common pathway. *Schizophrenia Bulletin*, *35*, 549–562.

Howes, O. D., Montgomery, A. J., Asselin, M. C., Murray, R. M., Grasby, P. M., & McGuire, P. K. (2007). Molecular imaging studies of the striatal dopaminergic system in psychosis and predictions for the prodromal phase of psychosis. *British Journal of Psychiatry*, *51*(Suppl.), s13–s18.

Howes, O. D., Montgomery, A. J., Asselin, M. C., Murray, R. M., Valli, I., Tabraham, P., et al. (2009). Elevated striatal dopamine function linked to prodromal signs of schizophrenia. *Archives of General Psychiatry*, *66*, 13–20.

Joel, D., & Weiner, I. (2000). The connections of the dopaminergic system with the striatum in rats and primates: An analysis with respect to the functional and compartmental organization of the striatum. *Neuroscience*, *96*, 451–474.

Kapur, S., Mizrahi, R., & Li, M. (2005). From dopamine to salience to psychosis—Linking biology, pharmacology and phenomenology of psychosis. *Schizophrenia Research*, *79*, 59–68.

Kestler, L. P., Walker, E., & Vega, E. M. (2001). Dopamine receptors in the brains of schizophrenia patients: A meta-analysis of the findings. *Behavioral Pharmacology*, *12*, 355–371.

Kumakura, Y., Cumming, P., Vernaleken, I., Buchholz, H. G., Siessmeier, T., Heinz, A., et al. (2007). Elevated [^{18}F]fluorodopamine turnover in brain of patients with schizophrenia: An [^{18}F]fluorodopa/positron emission tomography study. *Journal of Neuroscience*, *27*, 8080–8087.

Laruelle, M. (1998). Imaging dopamine transmission in schizophrenia. A review and meta-analysis. *Quarterly Journal of Nuclear Medicine*, *42*, 211–221.

Laruelle, M. (2000). Imaging synaptic neurotransmission with in vivo binding competition techniques: A critical review. *Journal of Cerebral Blood Flow and Metabolism*, *20*, 423–451.

Laruelle, M., & Abi-Dargham, A. (1999). Dopamine as the wind of the psychotic fire: New evidence from brain imaging studies. *Journal of Psychopharmacology*, *13*, 358–371.

Laruelle, M., Abi-Dargham, A., van Dyck, C. H., Gil, R., D'Souza, C. D., Erdos, J., et al. (1996). Single photon emission computerized tomography imaging of amphetamine-induced dopamine release in drug-free schizophrenic subjects. *Proceedings of the National Academy of Sciences of the USA*, *93*, 9235–9240.

Laruelle, M., Iyer, R. N., al-Tikriti, M. S., Zea-Ponce, Y., Malison, R., Zoghbi, S. S., et al. (1997). Microdialysis and SPECT measurements of amphetamine-induced dopamine release in nonhuman primates. *Synapse*, *25*, 1–14.

Lindstrom, L. H., Gefvert, O., Hagberg, G., Lundberg, T., Bergstrom, M., Hartvig, P., et al. (1999). Increased dopamine synthesis rate in medial prefrontal cortex and striatum in schizophrenia indicated by L-(beta-11C) DOPA and PET. *Biological Psychiatry*, *46*, 681–688.

McGowan, S., Lawrence, A. D., Sales, T., Quested, D., & Grasby, P. (2004). Presynaptic dopaminergic dysfunction in schizophrenia: A positron emission tomographic [^{18}F]fluorodopa study. *Archives of General Psychiatry*, *61*, 134–142.

Meyer-Lindenberg, A., Miletich, R. S., Kohn, P. D., Esposito, G., Carson, R. E., Quarantelli, M., et al. (2002). Reduced prefrontal activity predicts exaggerated striatal dopaminergic function in schizophrenia. *Nature Neuroscience*, *5*, 267–271.

Moore, R. Y., Whone, A. L., McGowan, S., & Brooks, D. J. (2003). Monoamine neuron innervation of the normal human brain: An ^{18}F-DOPA PET study. *Brain Research*, *982*, 137–145.

Mueller, H. T., Haroutunian, V., Davis, K. L., & Meador-Woodruff, J. H. (2004). Expression of the ionotropic glutamate receptor subunits and NMDA receptor-associated intracellular proteins in the substantia nigra in schizophrenia. *Brain Research Molecular Brain Research*, *121*, 60–69.

Murray, G. K., Corlett, P. R., Clark, L., Pessiglione, M., Blackwell, A. D., Honey, G., et al. (2008). Substantia nigra/ventral tegmental reward prediction error disruption in psychosis. *Molecular Psychiatry*, *13*, 267–276.

Nozaki, S., Kato, M., Takano, H., Ito, H., Takahashi, H., Arakawa, R., et al. (2009). Regional dopamine synthesis in patients with schizophrenia using L-[beta-(11)C] DOPA PET. *Schizophrenia Research*, *108*, 78–84.

Reith, J., Benkelfat, C., Sherwin, A., Yasuhara, Y., Kuwabara, H., Andermann, F., et al. (1994). Elevated dopa decarboxylase activity in living brain of patients with psychosis. *Proceedings of the National Academy of Sciences of the USA*, *91*, 11651–11654.

Seeman, P. (1987). Dopamine receptors and the dopamine hypothesis of schizophrenia. *Synapse*, *1*, 133–152.

Seeman, P., Schwarz, J., Chen, J. F., Szechtman, H., Perreault, M., McKnight, G. S., et al. (2006). Psychosis pathways converge via D2 high dopamine receptors. *Synapse*, *60*, 319–346.

Shibata, E., Sasaki, M., Tohyama, K., Otsuka, K., Endoh, J., Terayama, Y., et al. (2008). Use of neuromelanin-sensitive MRI to distinguish schizophrenic and depressive patients and healthy individuals based on signal alterations in the substantia nigra and locus ceruleus. *Biological Psychiatry*, *64*, 401–406.

Snyder, S. H. (1976). The dopamine hypothesis of schizophrenia: Focus on the dopamine receptor. *American Journal of Psychiatry*, *133*, 197–202.

Toru, M., Watanabe, S., Shibuya, H., Nishikawa, T., Noda, K., Mitsushio, H., et al. (1988). Neurotransmitters, receptors and neuropeptides in post-mortem brains of chronic schizophrenic patients. *Acta Psychiatrica Scandinavica*, *78*, 121–137.

Vernaleken, I., Kumakura, Y., Cumming, P., Buchholz, H. G., Siessmeier, T., Stoeter, P., et al. (2006). Modulation of [^{18}F]fluorodopa (FDOPA) kinetics in the brain of healthy volunteers after acute haloperidol challenge. *NeuroImage*, *30*, 1332–1339.

Zakzanis, K. K., & Hansen, K. T. (1998). Dopamine D2 densities and the schizophrenic brain. *Schizophrenia Research*, *32*, 201–206.

Part VIII

Afterword

29 Robin M. Murray

A biographical note

Anthony S. David

Robin Murray was born in Glasgow in January 1944 and his early years were spent in Bearsden, a pleasant residential area on the northern outskirts of the city. His father James Alistair Campbell Murray was a school teacher in a Maryhill Secondary School and his mother Helen MacGregor was also a school teacher. While Robin was still a young boy his father contracted tuberculosis in a severe form and required surgical treatment, there being no effective antibiotics at that time. Murray senior was advised to move to the country so the family moved to a village in Berwickshire in 1951 where he became headmaster of Paxton Primary School. The staff comprised essentially one other teacher, for a while his wife Helen, and the family lived in the school house next door. The couple also taught Sunday school. Robin later remarked that one consequence of having parents for teachers was that you received double punishment for any misdemeanour; first at school and again when you got home.

With the discovery of streptomycin, Robin's father was cured and the family moved to the southwest of Scotland to a village called Boreland near Lockerbie, which according to Robin "lived up to its name", the inhabitants being mostly sheep. This was an isolated hill village 30 miles from the nearest secondary school. His parents therefore decided to send their only child Robin to the Royal High School in Edinburgh where he joined another 40 boarders, from the age of 11 years.

Robin remembers being unhappy at first both because he was isolated from his family and friends and also because this was a single sex school. For solace he reached for a copy of the works of Sigmund Freud and when searching under the letter "S" in the index, he was gratified when he discovered "sublimation". He did well at school and when asked by the housemistress what career choice he intended to follow he said: psychiatry, to which she replied aghast, "But your parents are such normal people!"

Robin Murray chose to study medicine not at Edinburgh but the more down-to-earth Glasgow University and entered in 1962. Following the first two "preclinical" years he too was discovered to have contracted TB and spent 5 months in a sanatorium experiencing personally the boredom of chronic illness and the challenges of adherence to unpleasant medication. He was allowed to resume medical studies at the next start of year but had the summer to fill. He spent this

Figure 29.1 Robin Murray in primary school uniform.

working as a guide in Iona, a tiny island off the West Coast of Scotland, where dressed in the traditional kilt he would meet tourists off the daily ferry and take them round the abbey and the graveyard of many Scottish kings (now also of the late John Smith leader of the Labour Party in the 1990s). Although an agnostic he found himself to be in sympathy with the socialist principles and pacifist beliefs of the Iona Community, at that time a leftish group of Scottish Presbyterians.

He resumed his medical studies in the third of the six-year course no longer sharing lectures with a young Eve Johnstone. Robin was excited by seminars in psychology delivered by Gordon Claridge (who later became a distinguished researcher and theorist on schizophrenia based at Oxford University) who, during one memorable laboratory demonstration, unfortunately electrocuted himself. This perhaps led to a lifelong fascination with human experimental research but an aversion to ECT treatment. More seriously the latter arose from working in the summer vacation in an asylum where ECT was given without muscle relaxant.

In 1966 Robin undertook a student elective in Ohio and travelled across to California eventually arriving in Haight Ashbury at the beginnings of flower power. He strenuously denies that his interest in cannabis and other drugs began there and certainly didn't inhale any.

During his subsequent clinical training, Robin remained enthusiastic about psychiatry and was much impressed by the high calibre personnel at the university department in the Southern General Hospital, Glasgow. He was an avid member of the Glasgow Psychiatric Society and spent many hours haunting the psychiatry department and devouring psychiatric textbooks in the library. During this time

Figure 29.2 Robin Murray graduation photo Glasgow University.

he discovered that he could stay in one of the local asylums, Leverndale Hospital, for free, provided he carried out 150 physical examinations on the patients per year. Satisfying both his twin loves: psychiatry and a good financial arrangement, Robin became an inmate of the asylum for 2 years. He not only got to meet many experienced and encouraging psychiatrists but also a young occupational therapist called Shelagh whom he would later marry.

He graduated in 1968 and worked in general medicine becoming interested in nephrology at the Glasgow Western General Hospital. Robin remembers that the specialty engendered considerable excitement at that time with transplantation and dialysis just becoming established as exciting new treatments. Of this period he once said: "I worked for a very extroverted renal physician who dominated conversation in the pub after work. Status in the pub was determined by two things—one's ability at either golf or in research. Since I wasn't any good at the former, I had to try the latter".

His first experience of research was an exploration into unexpected fatalities in patients with megaloblastic anaemia. He found much to the chagrin of the local professor of medicine that survival rates were far better in small district general hospitals compared to university centres due to the academics insisting on establishing the precise cause of the anaemia rather than treating the patient immediately on a best guess basis. Robin Murray was to learn that, in his words, "research is power" and that facts gleaned from research can be irresistible forces of change for the good. It was during this time that he became interested in a curious culture-bound syndrome namely "analgesic nephropathy". Housewives in the West of Scotland were becoming addicted to "*Askit Powders*" pain-killing sachets, which contained what turned out to be a lethal combination of codeine, caffeine and phenacetin. The codeine provided the addictive potential, the caffeine the "kick" and the phenacetin, irreversible kidney damage. As a young renal physician, Dr Murray studied these patients, and as well as documenting their declining renal function, attempted to establish a psychological profile of dependence on *Askit Powders*. To do so he carried out some "do-it-yourself" epidemiology, knocking on the doors of residents of the Anniesland district of Glasgow who opened their doors to him to explain that taking *Askits* was "good for the nerves". This research led to some good publications and publicity for the young researcher (a spot on BBC's *Panorama* programme) and to a meeting with the managing director of *Askit* in their Yorkhill factory who was proud to be marketing such a popular product and genuinely upset to learn of its ill effects on health. Eventually phenacetin was withdrawn from the powders thanks to a concerted public-health campaign, another important lesson Robin was to learn on how to influence health policy for the better. "By that time I was hooked on research (and sometimes people listened to me in the pub)!"

These experiences helped broaden Robin Murray's view of psychiatry beyond psychoanalysis to its core values in clinical medicine and epidemiology. As well as being encouraged by a wise local psychiatrist, Gerald Timbury, he was told by a contemporary, Colin Douglas, the author of the *Houseman's Tales* books, that someone like him, "had to go to the Maudsley". He applied and was interviewed by Jim Birley and Edward Hare, both distinguished social psychiatrists, who recommended Robin for a position. However, it was under the auspices of D. L. Davies at the Institute of Psychiatry that Robin Murray's research career began to take off. His initial field of enquiry was the science of alcohol dependence, which somewhat to Davies' annoyance included genetic research. However, Robin Murray singles out another figure he met at that time, not yet a consultant or professor, who was to be a charismatic inspiration, the late Anthony Clare, author of *Psychiatry in Dissent*.

Frustrated, perhaps, by the pace of psychiatric research in the UK Robin Murray wrote an editorial in the *Lancet* lamenting the declining standards in psychiatry including at the Maudsley. The article caused a stir and its publication a measure of the young Doctor Murray's courage and self-confidence. It would have been even more courageous had the editorial not been anonymous. However, in a chance meeting in the Underground with the Head of Psychiatry, Professor Denis Hill, he admitted that he was the author of this piece. Denis Hill was stunned. The wily Professor Michael Shepherd advised Robin that the only way he might salvage his career at that point would be to go to the United States for a year by which time Professor Hill would surely have forgotten. This is precisely what Robin Murray did and it seemed to work.

His first major project at the institute had been examining the theory that people with schizophrenia might be walking hallucinogen factories, by collecting gallons of urine from patients to search for a hallucinogen dimethytryptamine (DMT). But then, as Robin said: "I received money from the Medical Research Council to go off to the USA for a year (NIH in Bethesda), where I heard the great neurochemist Seymour Kety say: 'Studying the urine of patients with schizophrenia in order to discern the neurochemical basis of psychosis is like examining the sewers of the Kremlin in an attempt to understand the policies of the Soviet politburo'. So much for DMT". After that he returned to the institute and began research in schizophrenia more generally, first in genetics but also epidemiology and neuroimaging.

The rest of the story may be gleaned from the contributions to this Festschrift.

30 Robin M. Murray

Top 12 publications

Anthony S. David and Robin M. Murray

Introduction

Festschrifts commonly list the honoured persons entire bibliography. In the case of Robin Murray, this would take up a great deal of space and, in the modern era, publication lists are readily available electronically. Furthermore, such a list would rapidly become out of date given the authors continuing productivity. Instead, Professor Murray was asked to nominate what he regarded as his best, or more accurately his favourite, publications with a brief explanation as to why.

1. Murray, R. M., Lawson, D. H., & Linton, A. L. (1971). Analgesic nephropathy: Clinical syndrome and prognosis. *British Medical Journal*, *1*, 479–482

I was fascinated by the strange habit of working-class Glasgow women to consume up to 20 *Askit Headache Powders* a day (often washed down by lemonade or *Iron Bru*). The caffeine gave them a brief lift but codeine withdrawal headaches perpetuated the habit, the repeated aspirin caused peptic ulceration and the years of phenacetin eventually resulted in renal failure. The renal physicians disliked these ladies since many wouldn't stop taking the *Askit*, and so were delighted to find someone who would take an interest in them. *Askit Powders* were very bad for these ladies but very good for me, producing a string of publications and an MD!

2. Reveley, A. M., Reveley, M. A., Clifford, C. A., & Murray, R. M. (1982). Cerebral ventricular size in twins discordant for schizophrenia. *Lancet*, *1*, 540–541

In 1978 Jerry Shields, who had directed the Maudsley Twin Register, died and I volunteered to try and save the register. We assembled a brilliant little group of researchers in the old wooden Genetics Hut who examined alcoholic (Hugh Gurling), bipolar (Peter McGuffin) and schizophrenic (Adrianne and Michael Reveley) twins respectively. The idea for this particular study was very simple—applying standard imaging techniques to twin pairs discordant for schizophrenia—but it provided incontrovertible evidence that there was an environmental contribution to the brain structural abnormalities found in schizophrenia.

3. Murray, R. M., & Lewis, S. W. (1987). Is schizophrenia a neurodevelopmental disorder? *British Medical Journal, 295*, 681–682

In the early 1980s, Shôn Lewis, then my senior house officer, suggested to me over coffee that some of the CT-scan abnormalities found in schizophrenia might be of developmental origin. He went ahead and found data to confirm his suspicions, converting me to a developmental view of schizophrenia in the process. Sometimes I think this little editorial helped to create a monster as many biological researchers now believe that schizophrenia is simply a neurodevelopmental disease; my own view is that this is just one of several routes to schizophrenia.

4. Lee, A. S., & Murray, R. M. (1988). The longterm outcome of Maudsley depressives. *British Journal of Psychiatry, 153*, 741–751

In 1975 I asked Professor Robert Kendell if I could follow up the depressed patients who had formed the subjects in his famous *Maudsley Monograph*. He readily agreed, immediately handing over all his records to me. In 1976 I went to the USA for a year and took them with me but subsequently an airline lost my luggage including all Bob's original data. Five weeks later my suitcase turned up minus my some of my clothes but fortunately not the data! It took a while to get funding but eventually I was able to appoint Alan Lee to chase up the patients, which he did with immense determination and skill. The most memorable finding was that the further a patient lived from the Maudsley Hospital, the better was their outlook!

5. McGuire, P. K., Shah, G. M. S., & Murray, R. M. (1993). Increased blood flow in Brocas area during auditory hallucinations in schizophrenia. *Lancet, 342*, 703–706

This was the first study to attempt to use imaging to catch the physiology underlying active psychotic symptoms. I was sceptical as to whether it would succeed but it was a great idea and Phil McGuire was so keen that I thought it worth a try. The findings and their subsequent elaboration in further research were important in explaining why schizophrenic patients hear voices; relatives found the idea of a miscommunication between the "inner voice" and "inner ear" particularly helpful.

6. Jones, P. B., Rodgers, B., Murray, R. M., & Marmot, M. (1994). Child developmental risk factors for adult schizophrenia in the British 1946 birth cohort. *Lancet, 344*, 1398–1402

In the late 1980s, I had contacted the lady in charge of this cohort to follow it up and see how many would later develop schizophrenia. However, a simple calculation suggested that there might be only 30 or 40 schizophrenics so I gave up. But Peter Jones had gone to the London School and knew that the large number of controls would give sufficient power even with 30 cases. His subsequent findings that many preschizophrenic children show subtle deficits in motor development, cognition, and social behaviour have now been replicated many times.

7. Stewart, A. L., Rifkin, L., Amess, P. N., Kirkbride, V., Townsend, J. P., Miller, D. H., et al. (1999). Brain structure and neurocognitive and behavioural function in adolescents who were born very preterm. *Lancet, 353*, 1653–1657

Anne Stewart was a lovely lady—a paediatrician who was devoted to "her" preterm babies whom she cared for throughout their childhood. She invited us to continue their follow-up into early adult life. This we did, finding that many of these "preterm adolescents" had brains that looked much more abnormal than those of people with schizophrenia though most were performing within the range of normality. There are, however, limits to the plasticity of the infant brain and the increased survival of ever smaller preterm babies is, to my mind, a major public-health issue. I am apprehensive about how such individuals with less brain reserve will fare as they approach middle and old age.

8. Cardno, A. G., Rijsdijk, F. V., Sham, P. C., Murray, R. M., & McGuffin, P. (2002). A twin study of genetic relationships between psychotic symptoms. *American Journal of Psychiatry, 159*, 539–545

For two decades we had been collecting detailed clinical information on all our schizophrenic twins but we hadn't done much with the data. Then Alistair Cardno and Pak Sham with their expertise in statistical genetics produced an impressive series of papers. This one showed that schizophrenia and bipolar disorder had genes in common, an idea that was greeted with considerable antagonism; 8 years later this view is now orthodox.

9. Arseneault, L., Cannon, M., Poulton, R., Murray, R., Caspi, A., & Moffitt, T. (2002). Cannabis use in adolescence and risk for adult psychosis: Longitudinal prospective study. *British Medical Journal, 325*, 1212–1213

For years parents of schizophrenic patients had been asking psychiatrists if they thought heavy use of cannabis had contributed to the development of their children's illnesses, and we had been reassuring them that the *Lancet* said cannabis was a safe recreational drug. However, eventually it seemed we should seriously look at the issue. This paper arose out of the generosity of Avshalom Caspi and Timi Moffit in inviting us to participate in their wonderful Dunedin study and contributed to a revised view of cannabis use as a contributing cause of schizophrenia.

10. Murray, R. M., Sham, P., van Os, J., Zanelli, J., Cannon, M., & McDonald, C. (2004). A developmental model for similarities and dissimilarities between schizophrenia and bipolar disorder. *Schizophrenia Research*, *71*, 405–416

This paper attempted to weld together the Cardno evidence that schizophrenia and bipolar disorder had genes in common and our longstanding view that schizophrenia but not bipolar disorder was subject to neurodevelopmental impairment. Six years on although not yet widely accepted, the evidence increasingly points in the direction that the crucial differences are developmental.

11. Fearon, P., Kirkbride, J., Morgan, C., Dazzan, P., Morgan, K., Lloyd, T., et al. (2006). Incidence of schizophrenia and other psychoses in ethnic minority groups: Results from the MRC AESOP study. *Psychological Medicine*, *36*, 1541–1550

In the early 1990s Julian Leff and I independently tried to get money from the Medical Research Council (MRC) to study the causes of the high rates of psychosis in African Caribbeans living in the UK. The MRC declined but suggested they would be more sympathetic if we collaborated. This we did initially a little reluctantly but eventually going one better by also involving Peter Jones and Glyn Harrison in Nottingham. The large AESOP study which resulted provided a lot of useful evidence demonstrating that the high rates did not result from the actions of "racist" psychiatrists but rather the social pressures on this population in UK society.

12. Stefansson, H., Rujescu, D., Cichon, S., Pietiläinen, O. P., Ingason, A., Steinberg, S., et al. (2008). Large recurrent microdeletions associated with schizophrenia. *Nature*, 455, 232–237

After 15 years of trying, I am finally a co-author of a molecular genetic paper on schizophrenia which has been subsequently confirmed. A total of 1,433 schizophrenic patients were studied as part of a big collaboration, and 66 found to have a de novo copy number variation (CNV). Although I had to share the finding with another 74 co-authors (i.e., more than one author per CNV), nevertheless it was a real replicable finding. Let's hope it won't be the last!

Index

Bold type denotes figure